SAINTS

The Story of
the Church of Jesus Christ
in the Latter Days

PREVIOUSLY PUBLISHED

Volume 1: The Standard of Truth, 1815–1846
Volume 2: No Unhallowed Hand, 1846–1893
Volume 3: Boldly, Nobly, and Independent, 1893–1955

SAINTS

The Story of
the Church of Jesus Christ
in the Latter Days

Volume 4

Sounded in Every Ear

1955–2020

Published by
The Church of Jesus Christ of Latter-day Saints
Salt Lake City, Utah

© 2024 by Intellectual Reserve, Inc.
All rights reserved.
Version: 11/16
Printed in the United States of America
No part of this book may be reproduced in any form or by any means without written permission. For more information, contact permissions@ChurchofJesusChrist.org.

saints.ChurchofJesusChrist.org

Interior art by Greg Newbold
Interior layout by Patric Gerber

Library of Congress Cataloging-in-Publication Data
Names: The Church of Jesus Christ of Latter-day Saints, issuing body.
Title: Saints : the story of the Church of Jesus Christ in the latter days. Volume 4, Sounded in every ear, 1955–2020.
Other titles: Story of the Church of Jesus Christ in the latter days
Description: Salt Lake City : The Church of Jesus Christ of Latter-day Saints, 2024. | Includes bibliographical references and index. | Summary: "The fourth volume in a four-volume series recounting the history of The Church of Jesus Christ of Latter-day Saints"—Provided by publisher.
Identifiers: ISBN 9781639933730 (hardback) | ISBN 9781629726502 (paperback) | ISBN 9781629738130 (ebook)
Subjects: LCSH: The Church of Jesus Christ of Latter-day Saints—History—19th century | Mormon Church—History—19th century | The Church of Jesus Christ of Latter-day Saints—History—20th century | Mormon Church—History—20th century | The Church of Jesus Christ of Latter-day Saints—History—21st century | Mormon Church—History—21st century.
Classification: LCC BX8611 .S235 2024 | DDC 289.309/034—dc23

Printed in Hong Kong
RR Donnelley, Hong Kong, China

10 9 8 7 6 5 4 3 2 1

The standard of truth has been erected.
No unhallowed hand can stop the work from
progressing; persecutions may rage,
mobs may combine, armies may assemble,
calumny may defame, but the truth of God will
go forth boldly, nobly, and independent till it
has penetrated every continent, visited every clime,
swept every country, and sounded in every ear,
till the purposes of God shall be accomplished and
the great Jehovah shall say the work is done.

—*Joseph Smith, 1842*

CONTRIBUTORS

SAINTS
THE STORY OF THE CHURCH OF JESUS CHRIST
IN THE LATTER DAYS

Church Historian and Recorder
Executive Director, Church History Department
Elder Kyle S. McKay

Assistant Executive Director,
Church History Department
Elder Hugo E. Martinez

Managing Director, Church History Department
Matthew J. Grow

Director, Publications Division
Matthew S. McBride

Managing Historian
Jed Woodworth

Editorial Manager
Nathan N. Waite

Product Manager
Benjamin Wood

Project Manager
Petra Javadi-Evans

Artist
Greg Newbold

VOLUME 4
SOUNDED IN EVERY EAR
1955–2020

General Editors
Scott A. Hales
James Perry
Lisa Olsen Tait
Jed Woodworth

Writers
Scott A. Hales
David Bolingbroke
Lisa Christensen
Angela Hallstrom
Dallin Morrow
David Nielsen
James Perry
Tesia Tsai
Jed Woodworth

Editors
Petra Javadi-Evans
Alison Kitchen Gainer
Leslie Sherman Edgington
R. Eric Smith
Nathan N. Waite

CONTENTS

PART 1: *By Degrees*
1955–1966

1	*Where and When*	3
2	*Lead Me, Guide Me*	19
3	*A Good Fight*	34
4	*The Mission of the Church*	49
5	*No Power on Earth*	64
6	*Blessings Everywhere*	83
7	*Children of the Same God*	100
8	*A Matter of Saving Souls*	118
9	*This Marvelous Day*	131

PART 2: *Wait for the Lord*
1966–1978

10	*Time Is Crucial*	149
11	*In Any Other Country*	168
12	*A Complete Way of Life*	185
13	*An Undying Knowledge*	205
14	*Different Now*	222
15	*The Joy of an Eternal Covenant*	243
16	*Just This Day*	257
17	*No Going Back*	277
18	*All the Blessings of the Gospel*	293
19	*United as a Family*	311

PART 3: *His Own Path*
1979–1997

20	*Marvelous and Wonderful Way*	331
21	*A Seed of Love*	348
22	*More Like Our Lord and Master*	363
23	*Every Effort*	382
24	*Our Search for Truth*	399
25	*For the Gospel's Sake*	416
26	*I Want to Serve*	431
27	*The Hand of Friendship*	448
28	*The Lord's Path*	463
29	*One Great Family*	480

PART 4: *Always There*
1997–2020

30	*Precious Blessings*	499
31	*Mysterious Ways*	515
32	*Our Strength Is Our Faith*	530
33	*What Is This Church?*	545
34	*Strength for Any Situation*	562
35	*Hand in Hand*	580
36	*Press Forward*	597
37	*Answers Will Come*	614
38	*Real and Immeasurable*	631
39	*Ever at the Helm*	648

Note on Sources	668
Notes	670
Sources Cited	765
Acknowledgments	805
Index	807

PART 1

By Degrees

1955–1966

"The knowledge of the truth did not
come to me suddenly,
but it had come by degrees,
in such a gentle and natural way
that I had not even realized it had
already been shining upon me."

Hélio da Rocha Camargo

CHAPTER 1

Where and When

"Tell him to send the Church back."

The quiet, urgent voice surprised and confused sixteen-year-old Nora Siu Yuen Koot. "What?" she said.

"Tell him to send the Church back."

Again Nora heard the message clearly. It was as if someone had whispered it in her right ear. But there was no one nearby. She was standing alone outside a hotel in Hong Kong in September 1954. A few visitors from the United States had just boarded a bus to the airport, and she was waving goodbye to them.[1]

The visitors were leaders of The Church of Jesus Christ of Latter-day Saints traveling through East Asia. More than a billion people lived in that part of the world, but only about a thousand of them had embraced the restored gospel of Jesus Christ. The Church had not had an official presence in Hong Kong for several years, not since social unrest in China and a war in nearby Korea had led Church leaders to close the mission in 1951. But now the conflict was over, and the visitors had come to check on Nora and the eighteen other Saints living in the city.[2]

Leading the group was Elder Harold B. Lee, a senior member of the Church's Quorum of the Twelve Apostles. Nora could tell he was important, but she didn't know enough about Church administration to say why. Still, she knew the whispered message was for him.

Without another thought, she stretched out her hand toward the bus, hoping it would not drive away. "Apostle Lee," she said.

Elder Lee reached his hand out an open window, and Nora took it. "Please send the Church back," she cried. "We Saints without the Church are like people without food. We need to be fed spiritually."

The apostle's eyes filled with tears. "It is not for me to decide," he said, "but I will report to the brethren." He told Nora to pray and keep the faith, assuring her that as long as there were faithful Saints like her, the Church *was* in Hong Kong.

The bus then shifted into gear and lumbered away.[3]

Month after month passed, and Nora heard nothing from the Church. She sometimes wondered if she ever would. Latter-day Saint missionaries had always struggled in Hong Kong. Elders had first preached there in the 1850s, but illness, religious and cultural differences, poverty, and a language barrier had led them to abandon the mission after only a few months and no baptisms. The next group of missionaries came in 1949, but that mission had lasted only two years.[4]

During that time, Nora and her two younger sisters became the first Chinese people to join the Church in Hong Kong. Their family was among the hundreds of thousands of refugees who had come to the British colony to escape the unrest in mainland China. The mission headquarters had been located on the street where they lived, and Nora's stepmother sent them there every morning, hoping they would learn English and whatever else the missionaries were teaching.

Nora could still remember the Bible lessons she received from Sister Sai Lang Aki, a Hawaiian missionary of Chinese descent, who helped her learn English. Nora received a witness of the restored gospel at that time. Her testimony helped her stay strong after the mission closed, when it seemed like the sun had set on Hong Kong. Even in the absence of priesthood ordinances, sacrament meetings, meetinghouses, and Church literature in Chinese, she clung fiercely to her faith in Jesus Christ.[5]

In August 1955, nearly a year after Elder Lee's visit, a tall, blond-haired young man approached Nora at the movie theater where she worked. All at once she recognized Grant Heaton, who had served as a missionary in Hong Kong before the mission closed. He and his wife, Luana, had just arrived in Hong Kong to open the newly created Southern Far East Mission.[6]

Nora was overjoyed. As she'd hoped, Elder Lee had spoken with Church leaders about the Saints in Hong Kong. In fact, soon after returning to the United States, he had recommended reopening the mission and even told Nora's story at the Church's general conference. Church president David O. McKay had then called Grant to lead the new mission, which covered Hong Kong, Taiwan, the Philippines, Guam, and other places in the region.

"The sun is rising," Nora thought. "Morning has returned to the Saints in Hong Kong!"[7]

ON SEPTEMBER 22, 1955, NEARLY two months after the opening of the Southern Far East Mission, President David O. McKay returned to Salt Lake City following a five-week visit to the Saints in Europe. Although he and his wife, Emma Ray, had been cooped up in an airplane all day, they cheerfully greeted the Church leaders, family members, and friends who came to the airport to welcome them home.

Stopping on the tarmac to talk to reporters and photographers, President McKay spoke readily about the highlight of his tour: the dedication of the temple near Bern, Switzerland. It was now one of seven operating temples in the world, and the first one to be built in Europe. Its dedication had occurred over ten sessions in seven languages. And hundreds of European Saints had already received their endowment within its walls.

The citizens of Bern were delighted by the sacred building. "They are calling it 'our temple,'" President McKay told one reporter, "and now the Church members there are being looked upon as Christians."[8]

The Swiss Temple was a symbol of the Church's commitment to establishing strong congregations around the world after decades of encouraging the Saints to gather to Utah. Now, with temples under construction in England and New Zealand, the Church was seeking to bring temples closer to its far-flung members and expand the availability of temple ordinances.

President McKay knew these temples were only a start. As Joseph Smith had prophesied, the truth of God would sweep every country and sound in every ear.[9]

That day had not yet come, but the Church was progressing. Although most of the world's population had never heard of the restored gospel of Jesus Christ, regard for the Church had been growing since the end of the Second World War. There were just over a million Latter-day Saints in the world, and many people admired their wholesome lives, Christian values, concern for the poor, and joyful message. The Church's Tabernacle Choir had also become a popular performing group on radio broadcasts around the world. Earlier in the year, when the Church celebrated its 125th anniversary, the *New York Times,* one of the most prominent newspapers in the United States, had nothing but praise for the Saints.[10]

As President McKay and his counselors, Stephen L Richards and J. Reuben Clark, contemplated the destiny of the Church, they were aware of obstacles that lay in the path of even greater growth.

One obstacle was providing good meetinghouses and other facilities for the Saints. In the 1920s, the Church had created a system for supplying congregations with standardized architectural plans and significant funding to help local Saints construct buildings with electricity, indoor plumbing, and, more recently, air conditioning. But in places where the Church was less established, many branches did not have the means or expertise to carry out large-scale projects. As a result, they often had to meet in rented halls.[11]

The problems ran deeper in many parts of the world. Some branches struggled because they had few members, inexperienced local leaders, infrequent contact with Church headquarters, and scant Church literature in local languages. Some places were simply too far from Church stakes or districts to sustain strong congregations.[12]

Also, since over 90 percent of Latter-day Saints lived in the United States, the Church was often associated with America. This perception created problems in communist nations like the Soviet Union, which were deeply suspicious of the United States and of religion in general. In the past decade, many such nations had enacted policies that made it difficult—if not impossible—for the Church to operate within their borders.[13]

The opening of the Southern Far East Mission demonstrated that the First Presidency and Quorum of the

Twelve Apostles were eager to expand missionary work to new regions, particularly in Asia and South America.[14] Africa, though, presented a unique obstacle. Since the early 1850s, the Church had restricted people of Black African descent from holding the priesthood or receiving the endowment and sealing ordinances of the temple, so the Church had undertaken little missionary work on the continent. Still, every now and then Church leaders received letters from people in West Africa expressing interest in the restored gospel.[15]

These challenges and successes were not far from President McKay's mind six months later, when he traveled to California to dedicate the Los Angeles Temple. Plans for the building had begun under the direction of President Heber J. Grant, but the Great Depression and World War II had delayed its completion for nearly twenty years. It was the largest temple the Church had ever built, and its highly publicized open house had given seven hundred thousand people a chance to go inside and learn about its sacred purpose.[16]

At the dedication ceremony, President McKay thanked the Lord as he looked over the congregation in the temple's assembly room.

"We have felt Thy presence and in times of doubt and perplexity have hearkened unto Thy voice," he declared in his dedicatory prayer. "Here in Thy holy house, in humility and deep gratitude we acknowledge Thy divine guidance, Thy protection and inspiration."[17]

AROUND THIS TIME, IN São Paulo, Brazil, an aspiring Methodist pastor named Hélio da Rocha Camargo was beginning his third year at a theological college. One day, an acquaintance from his congregation told him he had met with Latter-day Saint missionaries, and he invited Hélio to attend their follow-up visit.

Hélio was curious about the Saints and their teachings, so he accepted the invitation. The Church had been in Brazil for nearly thirty years, but there were only about thirteen hundred members in the country, and Hélio had never met one. Unfortunately, on the day of the appointment, the missionaries didn't show up.

A short time later, during a class discussion about the nature of God, Hélio asked his professor if Latter-day Saints believed in the Trinity, or the view that God the Father, Jesus Christ, and the Holy Ghost were one being.

"I do not have any information," the professor said. He didn't even know if Latter-day Saints were Christians.

"Well," said Hélio, "I believe that they consider themselves to be Christians because the official name of the church is the Church of Jesus Christ."

"See if it is possible to find one in São Paulo," the professor said. He then suggested that Hélio invite a Latter-day Saint to speak to the student body at their weekly forum.[18]

Hélio went to the Church's headquarters in the city and invited Asael Sorensen, the president of the Brazilian Mission, to speak at the forum. President Sorensen wanted to accept the invitation, but since he had a prior commitment to keep, he offered to send two young missionaries in his place.

"I guarantee that these young men are well prepared," he told Hélio.[19]

On the day of the forum, two missionaries from the United States—Elders David Richardson and Roger Call—arrived at the college. Hélio welcomed the young men and introduced them to a room of around fifty students and a dozen faculty. Elder Richardson, who had more experience speaking Portuguese, walked to the pulpit and began talking about the Church. Elder Call, meanwhile, jotted down important points on a blackboard.

Hélio was impressed by Elder Richardson's courage and calmness. The young man spoke first about the Godhead, testifying that the Father, the Son, and the Holy Ghost were three separate beings. Soon members of the audience began interrupting him, asking question after question. "Let me finish," Elder Richardson finally said, "and then you can ask questions after."

The audience quieted, and the missionary continued his message. He used the Bible often, and every time he quoted a verse, the professors and students flipped open their scriptures to check his accuracy. Hélio could sense that his colleagues did not agree with everything the missionaries were teaching, but they were now listening more respectfully.

Then Elder Richardson raised the topic of priesthood authority and baptism. "If we can prove to you that we have the authority to baptize," he said, "how many of you would submit to baptism?"

One student shouted, "Yes!" and the college director scowled at him in disgust.

When Elder Richardson concluded his presentation, he invited questions from the audience. Immediately, some of the students asked about the Mountain Meadows Massacre and other controversies. Few students, it seemed, wanted to appear interested in the Church.

After the presentation, Hélio and three other students went to lunch with the missionaries. They asked the elders more questions, showing sincere interest in their message. Hélio wanted to learn more about the Church, but his time was precious. He and his wife, Nair, had four young children, with another on the way. Between school and family, he was kept busy.

Before long, he set aside his interest in the Saints and lost contact with the missionaries.[20]

ONE DAY IN MAY 1956, Mosese Muti and his friend and fellow Church member ʻAtonio ʻAmasio were traveling along a road just outside the city of Nukuʻalofa, Tonga, in the Pacific Islands. As they chatted, a car drove past them and stopped abruptly. Both men knew the car belonged to Fred Stone, the president of the Tongan Mission. President Stone was about fifty years old—just a few years older than Mosese. He and his wife, Sylvia, had been serving in the country for about six months.

Mosese and 'Atonio hurried up to the car, and President Stone greeted them. "Do you know anyone who would like to go on a mission?" he asked.[21] Across the South Pacific, the Church was calling dozens of "labor missionaries" to quicken the pace of chapel building in the area. President McKay had recently approved the construction of twenty-one new chapels in Tonga, and President Stone was authorized to call local Saints to carry out the work.[22]

Mosese looked at 'Atonio, and his friend shrugged. There were more than four thousand Church members in Tonga, but no potential missionaries came to mind. Labor missions provided Saints with valuable on-the-job training as bricklayers, electricians, plumbers, and carpenters, which could help them secure employment after the mission. But the work could be grueling.[23]

"You must know someone," President Stone persisted. "How about you, Muti?"

"If it's a call from the Lord, I'll go gladly," Mosese said. He and his wife, Salavia, had been members of the Church for more than twenty years. They had already served several missions, including one to help construct Liahona College, the new Church high school in Tonga. But Mosese was now working as a building supplies manager for the Tongan government and had a large family to support. He did not want to disrupt his life simply because the president needed a willing missionary.[24]

"The Lord wants you," President Stone assured him. "Do you have any money, any savings?"

"That's why I gave you the answer I did," Mosese said. "He knows how poor we are and what He would have to bless us with for us to make it on a mission."[25]

"Why not talk it over with Salavia," President Stone suggested. "Let me know what her feeling is about going on this mission."

"All I want to know is where and when," Mosese said.

The president told him that he would be serving on Niue, a small island nation nearly four hundred miles northeast of Tonga. Four missionaries were already preaching the gospel and preparing to build a chapel there, but progress was slow.[26]

"My wife and family will be happy to go," Mosese said. He told President Stone about a dream he'd recently had in which he and Salavia were walking together on another island. "It was a place where all the villages are located around the island along the seashore," Mosese said. "I had never seen such an island before. It must be Niue!"

"Good," said the president. "You have two and a half weeks to prepare before the boat comes."[27]

Salavia rejoiced when Mosese told her about the mission call, and together they thanked the Lord for it. Since their marriage in 1933, she had never known him to refuse an opportunity to serve in the Church. And she shared his dedication to missionary work, trusting that God would bless them for the sacrifices they made in His behalf.

More than anything, the Mutis longed to receive their temple blessings. The nearest temple was in Hawaii, three thousand miles away, and the cost of travel had always kept them from making the trip. Once the temple in New Zealand was finished, the journey to achieve this goal would be far shorter. But even then, the cost would be more than they could afford, especially now that they were going on another mission.[28]

Still, they had reason to hope that they would someday enter the temple. In 1938, while Mosese was serving a mission, apostle George Albert Smith had visited Tonga and conferred the Melchizedek Priesthood on him. "If you keep up your missionary work," the apostle had promised, "you will go through the temple without a penny spent from your pocket."[29]

On May 29, 1956, Mosese and Salavia boarded a ship to Niue with their four youngest children. The family had just enough money to book the passage. How they would support themselves in the mission field, though, was in the Lord's hands. As Tonga receded from view, replaced by rolling waves and endless horizon, the Mutis were full of faith in God's promises.[30]

A FEW MONTHS AFTER the Muti family set out for Niue, Hélio da Rocha Camargo found himself full of doubts about infant baptism, a common practice among Methodists and other Christian denominations. At first, he simply wanted clarity. Why did these churches baptize infants? How did the baptism benefit the baby? The Bible seemed to say nothing about the practice, so he posed these questions to his professors and fellow students at the theological college. No one could answer them to his satisfaction.

"As a historical custom, it ought to be preserved," one person suggested.

Hélio failed to see the logic. "Why is it beneficial?" he asked. "Are historical traditions necessarily true?"

The more he thought about infant baptism, the more it unsettled him. His wife, Nair, had just given birth to their fifth child, a boy named Josué. Why would an infant like Josué need to be baptized? What sin had he committed?[31]

Other students at the college joined Hélio in questioning the practice. Alarmed, school administrators convened a faculty council and interviewed Hélio and the other students. Hélio was honest with the professors. "I do not find sufficient justification for infant baptism," he told them. "It is a practice that is not supported by doctrine that I can understand or find in the New Testament." As a pastor, he said, he could not in good conscience baptize a baby.[32]

After the interview, Hélio and three of his friends were suspended for a term to seek answers to their questions. When Hélio broke the news to Nair, she was upset. She shared Hélio's devotion to Jesus Christ and Bible study, and she did not like how the college was treating him. If Hélio's studies did not lead him to agree with their views, the faculty council would simply put an end to his studies at the college—if not his career in the ministry.[33]

Hélio tried once more to understand infant baptism. He asked a few of his friends and professors to help him find answers. They refused. "What good would it do?" they said. "You will never change your mind."

"But I want to change my mind," Hélio insisted. "I want to find good reason to change it."

One professor finally agreed to look at the matter with him. They studied every passage about baptism in the New Testament, sometimes consulting commentaries and the original Greek text for more insight. "You are right," the professor said after a few weeks. "There is no scriptural basis for the doctrine."[34]

At the end of his suspension, Hélio met again with the college council and informed them that his position on infant baptism had not changed. Realizing there was nothing more they could do to change his mind, the council terminated his studies at the college.[35]

Hélio began working at a bank, but he continued to read about baptism, seeking to know what other churches taught. Nair supported his search for more truth, but his relatives thought it was odd and a little immature of him to leave the college. Hélio paid them no mind. He prayed often for guidance, not only for his own sake but for the sake of Nair and their family. As a father, he felt an obligation to lead his children toward light and truth.

One day, Hélio remembered the Latter-day Saint missionaries who had come to his school. At the time, he had bought a book about their church called *A Marvelous Work and a Wonder,* but he hadn't read much of it. He found the book on a shelf and opened it. The author, LeGrand Richards, was a Latter-day Saint apostle who had twice served as a mission president. Each chapter outlined a principle of the restored gospel, point by point, relying heavily on the Bible to support each claim.

Hélio soon lost interest in other churches. *A Marvelous Work and a Wonder* had captured his attention completely. "This book," he thought, "has answers that no other one has."

He knew he had to seek out the Church. There was more to learn about the Saints.[36]

CHAPTER 2

Lead Me, Guide Me

As their boat approached Niue, Mosese and Salavia Muti saw a rugged coastline dotted here and there with secluded caves and coves. True to Mosese's dream, the island's thirteen villages were situated along the water's edge. Alofi, Niue's largest village, lay on the western coast and served as a hub for the handful of roads that cut through the tropical forests and coral outcrops that covered the interior of the island. It was an isolated place, home to fewer than five thousand people.[1]

Missionaries had first come to Niue in 1952. Now, four years later, there were around three hundred Saints on the island. The district president was a twenty-three-year-old American missionary named Chuck Woodworth. When he and the other missionaries were not sharing the gospel or tending to the island's six branches, they were working on a new chapel and mission office in Alofi.[2] There was no building supervisor on Niue, so the elders had not yet started digging foundations or putting up walls. Instead, they spent hours crushing the island's hard coral rock into gravel to make concrete for the project.[3]

Chuck was at his wit's end when the Mutis arrived. He was a sincere, hard-working missionary, but he often grew discouraged when the Niuean Saints didn't help the missionaries or live their religion as he thought they should. Salavia and Mosese were more patient and empathetic. The couple understood that every member on the island was new to the faith, still learning and growing.

Don't worry, Mosese would tell Chuck. Everything is going to be fine in the end.[4]

Mosese quickly won the Niuean Saints' friendship and trust with his love of the gospel and knowledge of local culture. He took charge of the Church's Boy Scouts program, taught gospel lessons, and crushed coral alongside the other missionaries. Salavia, meanwhile, looked after the well-being of the missionaries and Church members. She cooked meals, washed and mended clothes, and listened and offered advice when someone needed to talk. She also taught Primary and Sunday School lessons and gave sermons.[5]

In September 1956, Chuck organized the first Relief Society on Niue and called Salavia to be their teacher. At first, some women in the Relief Society did not seem to respect her or show much interest in attending meetings.

Salavia's experience working with women in the Church had taught her to be sensitive to their needs. Knowing many people on Niue did not have modern kitchen appliances, she asked Langi Fakahoa, the Relief Society president, if she could hold an activity to teach the women a simple way of cooking a Tongan pudding without a stove.

Before the meeting, Salavia asked the members of the Relief Society to bring ingredients so they could make a pudding of their own. Of the fifteen women who came, however, only three brought the ingredients. Others simply looked on skeptically.

Undeterred, Salavia demonstrated how to prepare the pudding and boil it in water over an open fire. The women who brought supplies followed her every instruction, step-by-step, until their puddings were cooking as well. Salavia then brought out a pudding she had made before the meeting and offered everyone a few slices.

As the women nibbled at the dessert, their eyes widened. "Wow," they said. No one had ever tasted anything like it. After the meeting, the three women who came with ingredients shared their pudding with the others, who went home determined to come better prepared for the next Relief Society activity.

Word spread about the pudding, and respect for Salavia changed. Women who had shown no interest in Relief Society began attending meetings. Several members invited their friends and relatives to the next cooking activity, and Salavia began calling Relief Society nights *Po Fiafia*—the Night of Fun.

Salavia was finding that teaching cooking and other skills was an excellent missionary tool. When the women gathered as a group, they shared stories, told jokes, and sang songs. The meetings brought the women closer together, creating friendships and strengthening spirits. Church attendance improved, and families seemed happier and more united because of the skills the women were learning in Relief Society.[6]

IN LATE 1956, MEMBERS of the Relief Society throughout the world were looking forward to the dedication of a new building for their organization in Salt Lake City. The Relief Society now had around 110,000 members, and general president Belle Spafford wanted them all, no matter where in the world they lived, to feel part of a united sisterhood.

She herself had not always been an enthusiastic Relief Society member. At the time, women in the Church were not automatically enrolled in Relief Society once they reached adulthood, so she had been thirty years old before she attended any Relief Society meetings regularly. When her bishop called her to serve as a counselor in her ward Relief Society presidency, she balked. "That organization is for my mother," Belle told him, "not for me."

Thirty years later, she was in the eleventh year of her presidency, and establishing a permanent headquarters for the Relief Society was one of her main goals. She wanted the new headquarters to be a beautiful building where the women of the Church could enter and feel at home.[7]

When the Relief Society was first organized in 1842, its members met on the upper floor of Joseph Smith's Nauvoo store. Later, ward Relief Societies in the western United States built Relief Society halls where they could meet, conduct business, minister to those in need, and share their ideas, experiences, and testimonies. Around the turn of the century, the general presidencies of the Relief Society, Young Ladies' Mutual Improvement Association, and Primary raised a sizable amount of money to build a headquarters for their organizations. To their disappointment, however, the plan did not materialize. The First Presidency called for the construction of an office building shared by the three organizations and several others, including the Presiding Bishopric.[8]

The Relief Society had operated out of the second floor of this building ever since. It was a cramped, noisy space with offices, a boardroom, and an area for sewing temple clothes. Soon after receiving her calling in 1945, President Spafford proposed building a new home for the organization. The First Presidency agreed to the plan and asked the Relief Society to raise $500,000, half the cost of the building.

President Spafford and her counselors, Marianne Sharp and Velma Simonsen, then devised a fundraiser, inviting every member of the Relief Society to contribute as much as five dollars toward the building's construction—a considerable amount when a loaf of bread cost twelve cents in the United States. After a few months of fundraising, President Spafford was elated to learn the women of the Church had already donated $20,000. She immediately picked up the telephone and called J. Reuben Clark, the second counselor in the First Presidency, to tell him the good news.

"Don't be discouraged," he said, evidently missing her excitement. "I know $20,000 isn't very much when you have to raise half a million."[9]

President Spafford was not discouraged, and the sisters did not let her down. For decades, the Relief Society had been funding its local organizations by collecting yearly dues and holding regular fundraisers. To make their contributions, the sisters held potluck dinners, sewed and sold quilts, and held dances. Within a year, the building was fully funded.

The Relief Society acquired land across the street from the Salt Lake Temple, and President Spafford and her counselors worked closely with the architect to design the building. It had office space for the Relief Society general presidency, the general board, and staff supporting the organization's many projects, including the *Relief Society Magazine,* welfare and social services, and the manufacture and sale of temple clothing.[10]

Since President Spafford wanted the building to feel like a home rather than an office space, it had a comfortable lounge where women could meet friends, write a letter, or enjoy the wholesome spirit of the place.

On the third floor, it had a large social room with a stage and kitchen, which stake Relief Societies could reserve for special events.[11]

Gifts from Relief Society members around the world, such as a decorative lamp from Australia and an engraved table from Samoa, adorned the building's rooms and halls.[12] In Vienna, Austria, Relief Society president Hermine Cziep and other Saints had pooled their money to purchase a colorful porcelain vase and ship it to Salt Lake City. When they learned the vase had been made in 1830, the year the Church was organized, they felt they had been guided to it by the Lord.[13]

"Just to think," a woman in the Swiss-Austrian Mission said, "we are a part of such a wonderful building, and although we may never see it, we know it will help to make many women happy."[14]

The Relief Society Building, as the new headquarters was called, was ready for dedication in October 1956. Its design was a modern echo of classical architecture, complementing the style of the nearby Church Administration Building, which was completed in 1917 to house the offices of the First Presidency and other general authorities. To honor the Relief Society's long history of storing grain, ornamental stalks of golden wheat adorned the exterior of the new building.

On October 3, President Spafford stood at the pulpit of the Salt Lake Tabernacle, looking out at an audience that represented a fraction of the many women who had sacrificed to bring about the Relief Society Building's completion. She believed the funding and construction efforts had served as a unifying force within the organization.

"It has sealed together as one the sisterhood of Relief Society," she said. "We pray that all that shall go forth from our Relief Society home shall enrich the lives and lead toward the eternal well-being of the daughters of our Heavenly Father."[15]

AFTER BEGINNING HIS STUDY of *A Marvelous Work and a Wonder,* Hélio da Rocha Camargo started attending a nearby branch of The Church of Jesus Christ of Latter-day Saints. Soon his wife, Nair, showed interest in the restored gospel as well. "I no longer want to attend the Methodist church," she said one Sunday. She wanted to go to church with him instead.[16]

Hélio went on to study the Book of Mormon, reading it cover to cover in three days. Then he read the Doctrine and Covenants, the Pearl of Great Price, and every other piece of literature he could find about the Saints. He met often with the missionaries, paid tithing in his local branch, and continued to find answers to his questions about God and His plan.[17]

He also attended enough Church meetings to know the Saints could use his help. Asael Sorensen, the mission president, was eager for the Church to expand in Brazil, and he believed that strong priesthood leaders would become a key part of that growth. Brazil now had roughly two thousand members, but fewer than seventy of them held the Melchizedek Priesthood.[18]

Hélio was not going to join the Church, let alone take on priesthood responsibilities, until he knew God's will for him. President Sorensen had developed a series of seven missionary lessons on such topics as "The Need for a Living Prophet," "The Word of Wisdom," and "The Purpose of Mortality." Hélio practically devoured each of these lessons, but he still had more questions for the missionaries.[19]

He and Nair were particularly shocked to learn about the Saints' former practice of plural marriage. Hélio also questioned why the Church restricted men of Black African descent from holding the priesthood. Like the United States, Brazil had long ago outlawed the practice of enslaving Africans and their descendants. Unlike the United States, however, Brazil had not gone on to sanction laws segregating Black and white people, so there were fewer racial divides among Brazilians.[20]

Hélio, whose own ancestors were Europeans, had never encountered a race restriction in his former church, and the practice troubled him. But his questions were not what was keeping him from joining the Church. As he studied with the missionaries, he longed to have an experience like Paul's in the New Testament—a miraculous conversion, as powerful and sudden as a streak of lightning.

He decided to pray more and reread the Book of Mormon, hoping all the while to receive the confirmation he sought. Nothing extraordinary happened, and the missionaries seemed to be growing impatient with him. "You *know* the Church is true," one of them told Hélio, "and it's time for you now to make a decision."

The missionary was right, Hélio knew. The restored gospel made perfect sense. But knowing that was not yet enough for him.[21]

Early in 1957, in Salt Lake City, forty-eight-year-old Naomi Randall and members of the Primary general board were working hard on a program for Primary leaders worldwide. The committee had chosen "A Child's Plea" as the theme for the program. They believed that many parents and Primary workers did not grasp how vital their role was in teaching the children of the Church. The theme was to serve as a reminder of their sacred call.

Primary general president LaVern W. Parmley wanted to introduce the program at the organization's annual conference in April, so Naomi and her committee had only a few months to finish it. They had fasted and prayed about the program and believed they would have it ready on time. Then President Parmley called Naomi into her office.

"We need a new song to go with the program," she said.

"Where do we get it?" Naomi asked.

"You can do it," the president replied, noting that Naomi was already a well-known poet in the Church.

She gave her the telephone number of Mildred Pettit, a talented musician and composer who had served on the Primary general board. "Get in touch with her," President Parmley said. "The two of you can work out a new song."[22]

Naomi's thoughts churned as she left the meeting. She wanted the adults at the program to remember the theme and recognize that little children needed their help to return to God's presence. But how could she convey that message in a song?[23]

After arriving at home, she spoke with Mildred on the telephone. "Write down any words, phrases, or message you have in mind," Mildred advised her. "It is important to have the message before the music is written."[24]

That night, Naomi asked Heavenly Father to inspire her with the right words for the song. She then went to bed and slept peacefully for some time.

At two o'clock, she awoke. Her room was quiet. "I am a child of God," she thought, "and He has sent me here." The words were the opening lines of a song. She thought of more lines, and soon she had a first and second verse. "It's not bad," she thought. "I believe that's all right."[25]

Before long, she had three verses and a chorus, each in the voice of a child pleading for spiritual guidance from a parent or teacher. Naomi got out of bed and wrote down the lyrics, surprised by how quickly they had come to her. She usually labored over every word she wrote. Dropping to her knees, she thanked her Heavenly Father.

In the morning, she called Arta Hale, a counselor in the Primary general presidency. "I have some words," she said. "See if they have any worth."

"My goodness, girl, they give me goose pimples," Arta said after Naomi had read her the lyrics. "Send them off!"[26]

In less than a week, Naomi received a letter from Mildred. Enclosed she found music for the song and some revisions to the chorus. Since sending the lyrics to Mildred, Naomi had tried to imagine what the song would sound like. When she finally heard the melody, she was thrilled. It was just right.[27]

On April 4, 1957, soloists and a choir of Primary children sang "I Am a Child of God" at the annual Primary conference. Aside from Mildred's help with the words of the chorus, the song was just as Naomi had written it in the middle of the night. The Primary leaders at the conference learned it so they, in turn, could teach it to the children in their own wards and branches.[28]

Some time later, at the invitation of apostle Harold B. Lee, the Primary general board spoke at a dinner for general authorities at the Relief Society Building. Their presentation featured a choir of children from different nations and races dressed in traditional clothes—a reminder of the Church's growing diversity. As the children sang the chorus of "I Am a Child of God," its universal message touched the hearts of the audience:

Lead me, guide me, walk beside me,
Help me find the way.

*Teach me all that I must know
To live with Him someday.*

When the song ended, President David O. McKay approached the children. "We will listen to your plea," he promised. "We will walk beside you." He then turned to the general authorities and said, "We must accept the challenge to teach these children."

Elder Lee was equally moved. "Naomi," he said after the dinner, "this is one song that will last through eternity."[29]

BY MAY 1957, HÉLIO da Rocha Camargo was tired of studying the teachings of the Church to no end or purpose. For all his learning, he lacked a divine witness of its truth. Without that witness, he was standing still.[30]

Finally, he turned to President Asael Sorensen and his wife, Ida, for help. The couple had been an immense support to him and Nair after they left the Methodist church. Sister Sorensen had taken a particular interest in Nair, and she met often with her to make sure she was learning and understanding the gospel. She also perceived Hélio's struggles and wanted to offer what counsel she could.

"Hélio," she said one afternoon, "I think the reason you have not gained a testimony is because you are looking for contradictions in the doctrine."[31]

Sensing the truth of her words, Hélio decided to take an objective look at his religious beliefs. He carefully weighed everything he had learned about the restored gospel and found the doctrine to be both coherent and consistent with the Bible. He still had questions about plural marriage and the priesthood restriction, but now he was willing to accept the limits of his understanding. He had faith that God would lead the Church by revelation.

Hélio also realized that he did not need a flash of lightning to confirm the truth of what he had learned. A testimony had come to him gradually over the last few months—so softly and naturally that he did not even realize that the light of eternal truth already surrounded him. Once he understood this, he fell to his knees and thanked God for revealing the truth to him.[32]

Hélio asked the missionaries to come to his house on a Monday night a short time later. "What do I need to do now to be baptized?" he asked.

Elder Harold Hillam outlined the steps. "You will have to be interviewed and then have your baptism papers signed by the mission president," he said. "We'll have the baptism on Saturday."

Elder Hillam interviewed him immediately and found—to no one's surprise—that Hélio was keeping the commandments and had a solid understanding of the gospel.[33]

On the day of the baptism, June 1, 1957, Hélio went to the mission home, the only place in São Paulo where the Saints had a baptismal font. He and Nair had spoken earlier about her own desire to be baptized, but she wanted to study a little more before she joined the Church. Hélio could understand that desire.

The baptismal font was in the backyard of the mission home. It was a chilly day, and when Hélio stepped into the font, the cold water startled him. But as he came out of the water, newly baptized, a comforting warmth enveloped him. Joy flooded his being, and it lingered with him for the rest of the day.[34]

CHAPTER 3

A Good Fight

At seven o'clock every morning, Monday through Saturday, Mosese Muti and his fellow missionaries met at the chapel construction site on Niue. Elder Archie Cottle, a building supervisor from Ogden, Utah, had come to the island in March 1957 with his family and two more Tongan missionaries to begin construction on the new meetinghouse and mission home. Now, Niue's first permanent Latter-day Saint chapel was finally taking shape beneath a scattering of palm trees.[1]

Mosese enjoyed his work on the island. He and another Tongan missionary were doing the masonry on the exterior walls of the chapel. The missionaries found that getting local men to help with the project could be challenging, especially since the men had other difficult labor to do on the island. But a dedicated group of older women regularly volunteered to help by hauling sand or assisting with other tasks at the construction site.[2]

District president Chuck Woodworth grumbled privately about not making faster progress on the chapel. And Mosese couldn't blame him. Chuck had not been called as a labor missionary, but the lack of volunteer laborers on Niue meant he had to devote more time to construction and less time to the spiritual well-being of the Saints in the district.

Mosese always urged Chuck to be patient. "These are fine people," he once reminded the young man. "They are children of the Lord. I find no fault in them. Let's look for their strengths and concentrate on their strengths."[3]

Besides, building a chapel was no easy feat for unskilled workers. The men had to break coral, dig foundations, pour concrete, and prepare mortar—all by hand. This often caused blisters, cuts, and other injuries. And sometimes people simply needed time to catch the spirit of service.[4]

To illustrate this point, Mosese told Chuck about his experience building Liahona College as a labor missionary. "Five of us had started the Liahona and worked for over a year before anyone helped out," he said. "When we were building it, we did so with our eyes on the future generations."[5]

Mosese was also patient with Chuck. He and Salavia spent many nights talking and counseling with the missionary, and he had become like a son to them.

Chuck had even begun calling them "papá" and "mamá." His own father had walked out on his family, leaving Chuck's mother to raise six children alone. The young man carried around a lot of anger and pain, and he was grateful to have Mosese in his life now.

"He truly knows the meaning of faith and service," Chuck wrote. "He has taught me things that would have taken me years to learn without his help."[6]

Still, from time to time, Chuck longed to serve somewhere else. One day, he learned that Liahona College was starting a boxing team, and he saw an opportunity for change. He had been a professional boxer before his mission. What if he asked the mission president to transfer him to Tonga to finish his mission as a teacher and boxing coach at the school? The college, after all, was occasionally staffed by missionaries.[7]

Mosese was against the idea. Having spent more than a year working and teaching at Chuck's side, he believed that God had sent the young man to Niue for a reason. Whenever a task was particularly difficult, Chuck would double his efforts and carry more than his share of the workload. And when Chuck learned that Mosese and Salavia had fasted so they could feed the missionaries and other laborers, he had quietly eaten as little as possible so there would be enough left over for the couple.[8]

In June 1957, during one of their talks with Chuck, Mosese and Salavia mentioned how much they longed to go to the temple. They knew the temple in New

Zealand was nearing completion, but traveling there was still out of reach for them financially.

Their words moved Chuck, and his desire to end his mission at Liahona College no longer seemed so important. What if, after his mission was over, he went to New Zealand and challenged a champion boxer to a prizefight—an event big enough to make the kind of money the Mutis needed to go to the new temple? It was the least he could do after all they had done for him.

Four days later, he wrote Johnny Peterson, his manager in the United States, and asked him to ship boxing gear to Niue.[9]

AROUND THIS TIME, THE Southern Far East Mission was in dire need of a new missionary. One of the four women serving in Hong Kong had just returned to the United States for health reasons, leaving an unexpected vacancy in the mission. President Grant Heaton knew the remaining sisters needed help immediately, so he called Nora Koot as a local full-time missionary.[10]

During the past two years, Nora had become indispensable to the mission. When the Heatons first arrived in Hong Kong, they enlisted her to contact all the Saints in the area, and the mission headquarters had become like her second home. Sometimes she babysat the Heatons' children. Other times she tutored missionaries in the Cantonese and Mandarin languages.

Together with Luana Heaton, she taught Bible stories in a Sunday school class for children in the city.[11]

Nora readily accepted the mission call. One other local Saint, an elder named Lee Nai Ken, had served a short-term mission in Hong Kong, and President Heaton was enthusiastic about calling more local Saints as missionaries. The North American missionaries often struggled to learn the Chinese language and local culture. Many people in the city were suspicious of foreigners and sometimes confused the elders with agents of the United States government.[12]

Nora and other Chinese Saints, however, already understood the local culture and did not have to worry about the language barrier. Also, they often related better with the people they taught. As a refugee from mainland China, Nora knew what it was like to start life over in a crowded city, where housing and employment were in short supply.[13]

Many Church members and prospective Saints in Hong Kong were refugees, and President Heaton sought ways to provide for their spiritual well-being. In 1952, the Church had introduced seven lessons, or discussions, to help potential converts prepare for Church membership. Adapting to local needs, President Heaton and his missionaries developed seventeen gospel lessons to appeal to the many people in Hong Kong who were not Christian or had only a basic understanding of Christian beliefs. These lessons addressed such topics as the Godhead, the Atonement of Jesus Christ, the first principles and ordinances of the gospel, and the Restoration. Once baptized, converts received an additional twenty lessons for new members.[14]

On the night before she was set apart as a missionary, Nora had a vivid dream. She was standing on a busy street, surrounded by chaos and commotion, when she noticed a beautiful building. She walked inside and immediately felt peace and calm. People inside the building were dressed in white, and Nora recognized some of them as the missionaries currently serving in Hong Kong.

When Nora reported to the mission home the next day, she told the elders about her dream. They were astonished. How did she know what a temple looked like? She had never visited one before.[15]

CHUCK WOODWORTH'S BOXING GEAR arrived on Niue in October 1957, and the whole Muti family rallied behind his training. Salavia made him a punching bag out of potato sacks, and Mosese helped repair it when necessary. With so many mission responsibilities on the island, however, neither Chuck nor the family had much time to spend on training. Some mornings Chuck would wake up as early as five o'clock for a run. Since it was dark outside, the Mutis' sixteen-year-old son, Paula, would ride a motorcycle behind him, illuminating the road with the headlight.

Fortunately, Chuck was in decent shape for boxing. Crushing coral for the past year had kept him physically strong. He had also held a few boxing exhibitions on the island to raise money for the chapel. But would occasional training be enough?[16]

Before his mission, Chuck had spent hours upon hours at the gym, training for prizefights in the western United States and Canada. Most bouts had pitted him against other small-time professional boxers, but he'd also fought world-class boxers like Ezzard Charles and Rex Layne.[17]

The fight against Rex, a famous Latter-day Saint heavyweight, had been the hardest of Chuck's career. Rex was past his prime as a boxer, but he was about twenty-five pounds heavier than Chuck, and his savage, unrelenting attacks kept Chuck on the ropes for ten brutal rounds. Chuck stayed on his feet, but the judges gave the match to Rex.

"Woodworth," the local newspaper reported, "wasn't strong enough."[18]

In December, word arrived on Niue that a boxing association in New Zealand had matched Chuck against Kitione Lave, the "Tongan Torpedo." Like Rex Layne, Kitione was a bull-like fighter who used his size and strength to punish opponents. In a fight against one of the top heavyweight boxers in the world, Kitione won in the second round with a knockout punch.[19]

Chuck was released from his mission in early January 1958, just after he and the other elders put a roof on the new chapel. Salavia wrote him a farewell letter, assuring him of her family's love and unfailing support. "My child, try your hardest," she told him. "Do not be discouraged and you will triumph. When your strength is accompanied with our prayers, there is nothing that will interfere with you. We rely on God to help you."[20]

The fight was scheduled for February 27, 1958. All that day Mosese, Salavia, and their children fasted and prayed for Chuck. When evening came, they gathered at the chapel with dozens of Church members and friends to tune in to the fight on the radio. Since the broadcast was in English, Mosese translated it into Niuean.[21]

A record crowd of almost fifteen thousand people had come out to Carlaw Park in Auckland, New Zealand, to witness the event. The odds were against Chuck as he entered the ring. Kitione had a twenty-pound advantage on him, and in the days leading up to the fight, Chuck heard that Kitione had called him a "sparrow" who wouldn't last a single round against him.

As soon as the bell rang, Kitione rushed at Chuck. "It's going to be a massacre," someone groaned from the crowd.[22]

Chuck dodged the charge and jabbed at Kitione without effect. Kitione fired back with his fists in rapid succession, striking Chuck's head and torso. Then Kitione went for the knockout. He wound up and threw a powerful left-handed hook. Chuck took a step back, and Kitione's glove slammed into his chin. The force of the blow threw Chuck onto the ropes. And for a moment, everything around him seemed to fade.

Acting on instinct, Chuck grabbed hold of Kitione and held on while the world around him spun. The referee tried to break them apart, but the bell rang. The round was over.

Chuck's head cleared as he waited in his corner. When the next round started, he moved to the center of the ring with new momentum. Kitione met him with fists flying, ready to strike a finishing blow, but Chuck stayed light on his feet. He circled his opponent, keeping clear of the corners, and pelted him with jab after jab. The Torpedo couldn't keep up. With each new round, Chuck felt himself getting stronger. He could hear the crowd cheering for him as he racked up points.

The match ended after twelve rounds, and the judges handed the victory to Chuck. Kitione took the loss well. "I enjoyed the fight," he said. "That Woodworth's a good, fast boxer—and a very nice fellow."[23]

Mosese sent Chuck a telegram the next day. "Thank you very much for a good fight—and being victorious," it read. Chuck responded by wiring enough money to feed the family for the rest of their mission and send the couple to the New Zealand Temple.[24]

A FEW MONTHS LATER, on the opposite side of the world, police in the German Democratic Republic arrested twenty-seven-year-old Henry Burkhardt. He was returning to the eastern, communist-controlled sector of Berlin after meeting with Burtis Robbins, the president of the Church's North German Mission, in the city's western sector.²⁵ Although it was not illegal to travel to West Berlin—an area under the authority of the United Kingdom, France, and the United States—doing so as often as Henry did raised suspicions.

It had been nearly a decade since Germany split into the Federal Republic of Germany (BRD), or West Germany, and the German Democratic Republic (GDR), or East Germany. Both countries continued to be key players in the Cold War between the United States, the Soviet Union, and their respective allies. Situated deep in GDR territory, West Berlin had become a symbol of resistance to communism. The GDR, meanwhile, had emerged as one of several Soviet-influenced countries in central and eastern Europe.

As these rival powers vied for global dominance, they raced to develop stronger weapons and more sophisticated technologies. Trust among opposing nations was a scarce commodity. Anyone might be sneaking secrets to the enemy.²⁶

Henry put up no resistance when the police hauled him off to a station in Königs Wusterhausen, a town outside of East Berlin. The Stasi, the GDR's secret police force, had been monitoring him and his family for some time. His calling as first counselor in the mission presidency placed him in regular contact with President Robbins and other American Church leaders. And that, along with his frequent visits to West Berlin, made him a suspected enemy of the state.²⁷

He was nothing of the sort. After being sealed in the Swiss Temple in November 1955, Henry and his wife, Inge, had returned to the GDR and submitted to the government's many restrictions on religious people. There were no foreign missionaries or leaders in the country, and Henry could not communicate directly with Church officials in Salt Lake City. He and the Saints also had to submit their sacrament meeting talks to government officials for screening before they could deliver them.[28]

Being the highest-ranking Church leader in the GDR consumed Henry's life. He only saw Inge and their newborn daughter, Heike, during short visits home. Otherwise, he was traveling throughout the mission, attending to the five thousand Saints spread out in forty-five branches across the country.

Whenever a Church member denounced the government, encouraged someone to emigrate to the United States, or failed to pay a debt, Henry was implicated. Two years earlier, when police had tried to stop local missionaries from visiting another Church member, he submitted a formal complaint to the government, asserting the missionaries' rights and asking for "better cooperation" from the police. He was deliberately polite and diplomatic with government officials, and that usually worked in his favor.[29]

At the police station in Königs Wusterhausen, Henry spent the night under interrogation. In his car were a few gifts from President Robbins and materials for the Church's East German office. When the police saw these items, they accused Henry of violating the GDR's ban on its citizens receiving donations from foreign organizations. He had committed, in their words, a "violation of economic regulations."

Henry had never heard of the ban before. He told his interrogators that he traveled to West Berlin every month. "The only purpose of my meeting with Mr. Robbins," he explained, "was to discuss with him religious activities as well as related financial matters."

The gifts from the mission president were not out of the ordinary either. "I have received presents in this form, or in the form of medicine, at each of our monthly meetings," Henry reported. "We also receive packages in the mail sent to our office in Dresden and from abroad."

The police confiscated the gifts, searched Henry's briefcases, and rifled through some of the mission reports he had brought with him. Finding nothing suspicious, they ordered Henry to read, approve, and sign an official report of his meeting with President Robbins. By that time, it was well past four o'clock in the morning. They finally released him from custody later that day.

Henry's arrest could have turned out much worse. When police caught an East German missionary with a copy of *Der Stern,* the Church's German-language magazine, they had imprisoned him for nine months. Henry and others had tried to help the elder keep his courage up, but there was little they could do. He had confessed to having the magazine, and government officials—at least in this case—were unbending.

Such run-ins with the police were changing Henry. He no longer had any fear when dealing with the authorities, especially when he or the Saints had done nothing wrong. Every day involved taking risks for the gospel, and it was becoming normal.

He'd gotten used to feeling like he was already standing with one foot in jail.[30]

ON THE MORNING OF April 12, 1958, Mosese and Salavia Muti caught their first glimpse of the New Zealand Temple. It stood on the crest of a grassy hill overlooking a sprawling river valley seventy-five miles south of Auckland. Its design was simple and modern, like the Swiss Temple. It had white-painted walls of reinforced concrete and a single spire that rose more than 150 feet in the air.

The Mutis had come to New Zealand just in time to take part in the open house. Thousands upon thousands of people from all over New Zealand, Australia, and the islands of the Pacific were eager to see the temple, so Mosese and Salavia had to wait an hour and a half before they could take the tour.[31]

Once inside, they could admire the beauty of the temple and appreciate the tremendous sacrifice of the local Saints. Like the chapel in Niue, and a growing number of Church buildings throughout Oceania, the temple had been built largely by labor missionaries. These workers had moved there with their families to build not just the temple but also the adjacent campus of the Church College of New Zealand, a new Church-run high school.[32]

The day after their tour of the temple, Mosese was invited to speak at a sacrament meeting of Tongan Saints in the area. As he approached the stand, he thought about the promise George Albert Smith had made him twenty years earlier, when he said that Mosese would attend the temple at no cost of his own. Mosese had not told Chuck Woodworth about this promise. When the young man paid for the Mutis' trip to the temple, he had unknowingly fulfilled prophecy.

"I am a person who testifies of the words the latter-day prophet has spoken," Mosese told the congregation. "I know that George Albert Smith is a true prophet of God, for my wife and I have become testaments of his words." He then spoke of Chuck's sacrifice for the Muti family. "We are here this night because of a man's undying love," he testified. "We will never forget it in our lives, no matter what happens."[33]

One week later, President David O. McKay came to New Zealand and dedicated the temple. The building fulfilled a prophecy he had made almost forty years earlier, when he visited New Zealand on his first apostolic mission around the world. At that time, he told a group of Māori Saints that they would one day have a temple. His interpreter during the talk had been Stuart Meha, who had now just finished translating the endowment into Māori.

As President McKay offered the dedicatory prayer for the temple, he paid tribute to the labor missionaries and other Saints who had consecrated their all to construct the temple and other Church buildings. "May each contributor be comforted in spirit and prospered manyfold," he prayed. "May they be assured that they have the gratitude of thousands, perhaps millions, on the other side for whom the prison doors may now be opened and deliverance proclaimed."[34]

Mosese and Salavia were endowed and sealed for time and eternity a few days later. While in the temple, Mosese felt the glorious presence of God. "How can I not love my Father in Heaven and His Son, Jesus Christ, with everything I have got, when I know They were there for me in the temple?" he said afterward. The experience gave him a new perspective on God's eternal plan.

"All the things I have done and do in the Church are all pointing to the temple," he realized. "It is the only holy place where a family organization can be united and remain intact forever."[35]

CHAPTER 4

The Mission of the Church

On the morning of September 2, 1958, President David O. McKay gazed down at the earth from nineteen thousand feet. Four months had elapsed since he'd dedicated the New Zealand Temple, and already he was on another airplane, flying to the United Kingdom to dedicate the temple in London. Although soaring among the clouds was nothing new for the prophet—since leading the Church, he had flown more than a quarter of a million miles—he was still awed by the ease and speed of air travel. No Church president before him had traveled so far or so fast.

The view from the airplane prompted him to reflect on the rapidly changing world. In the last year, the Soviet Union and United States had launched satellites into orbit around the earth, and now the whole world seemed captivated by the idea of space travel. Yet President McKay believed that even more remarkable changes would unfold over the next several decades, especially for the Church.

"Its great growth of the last twenty-five years can go on to even greater growth and good to the world," he told the Saints flying with him, "if we are truly well qualified for the opportunities which the Lord is opening up."[1]

President McKay was especially optimistic about the British Mission. Apostle Heber C. Kimball had opened the mission in 1837. Since then, some 150,000 people had joined the Church in the British Isles. More than half of them, including President McKay's parents, had emigrated to Utah. President McKay himself had served two missions there—first as a young missionary in the late 1890s and then as the European Mission president in the early 1920s.[2]

But continued emigration, two world wars, economic depression, and lingering public misconceptions had long kept the Church from growing significantly in Britain, and only about eleven thousand Saints now lived there. Still, the new temple had recently sparked immense local interest in the Church.[3]

President McKay arrived in London on September 4, and three days later, Saints from the British Isles and other places in Europe assembled for the dedication. The temple was situated on the grounds of an old English manor in the countryside south of London. The thirty-two-acre site had spacious lawns, ancient oak trees, and an array of shrubs and flowers. A shallow pool nearby reflected the temple's simple stonework and copper steeple.

President McKay wept when he saw the building. "Imagine me living long enough to build a temple in England," he said.

Before offering the dedicatory prayer, the prophet spoke with emotion about the Church in Britain. "This is the opening of a new era," he said, "and we hope and pray for a new era of better understanding on the part of honest people everywhere."

"More spirit of charity, more spirit of love, less contention and strife," he declared. "That is the mission of the Church."[4]

EARLY IN 1959, SISTER Nora Koot and her mission companion, Elaine Thurman, boarded a train with a group of Latter-day Saint youth from Tai Po, a rural district in northeast Hong Kong. There was a Church dance that evening at a rented hall in the city, and the youth were nervous about attending. They were all new members of the Church, and none of them had spent much time in the city. They did not know what to expect.

Nora did not really know what to expect either. The dance was the Church's first Gold and Green Ball in Hong Kong. The Gold and Green Ball, which took its name from the official colors of the Church's Mutual Improvement Associations, had been a popular annual event for Latter-day Saint youth since the 1920s, especially in areas where Young Men's and Young Women's MIAs were well established. The dances provided a good opportunity for young people to meet other Church members, and the American missionaries wanted to introduce the tradition to the Chinese Saints. Over the past year, after all, the Church in Hong Kong had grown by more than nine hundred people.[5]

The train ride to the city took about an hour. When Nora, Elaine, and the Tai Po youth arrived at the dance, they found that the mission's MIA board—composed wholly of American missionaries—had done everything possible to make the dance like a Gold and Green Ball in the United States. Gold and green streamers arched down from the ceiling, and five hundred balloons hung high above the dance floor, ready to be loosed with the pull of a string at the end of the evening. For refreshments, there were cookies and punch.

But once the ball got underway, something seemed off. There was a loudspeaker rigged up to a record player, and the missionaries were playing popular American dance music. The organizers had set up only a few chairs in the room, hoping a lack of seating would coax the young people onto the dance floor. But the ploy wasn't working. Hardly anyone was dancing.

After a while, a few Hong Kong Saints started playing the kind of music they liked, and everything changed. The missionaries, it seemed, had not considered local tastes. They had been playing instrumental tunes when what the Chinese Saints wanted were songs with vocals. The Saints also preferred to dance to slow waltzes, cha-chas, and mambos, which the missionaries weren't playing. Once the music changed, everyone in the room crowded onto the floor and danced.

Despite its rocky start, the Gold and Green Ball was a success. A little before the dance was supposed to end, though, someone released the balloons overhead, sending them tumbling down onto the crowd below. Thinking the ball was over, the Chinese Saints quickly headed for the door. The missionaries tried to call them back so they could at least have a closing prayer, but it was too late. Most everybody was gone.[6]

All evening, Nora had enjoyed watching the Saints from Tai Po mingle with the other young people from the region. Working in Tai Po had been one of the highlights of her mission so far, and the time she spent there had strengthened her testimony.

But a few months after the Gold and Green Ball, she found out it was time to move on. President Heaton was sending her to Taiwan, an island four hundred miles to the east.[7]

THAT SAME YEAR, ELDER Spencer W. Kimball of the Quorum of the Twelve Apostles was enchanted by his first glimpse of Rio de Janeiro, Brazil. Its towering green mountains and beachfront skyscrapers were draped in an early-morning mist. But from the deck of their ocean liner, Elder Kimball and his wife, Camilla, could easily spot the city's most famous attraction: *Cristo Redentor,* a resplendent 125-foot statue of the Savior overlooking the harbor.[8]

Rio de Janeiro was the Kimballs' first stop on a two-month tour of the Church's South American missions. Around eight thousand Saints lived in South America, and branches across the continent were growing steadily. Eager to support these congregations, President McKay and his counselors had recently approved the expansion of the Church's building program into South America, authorizing the construction of twenty-five chapels there.

As Elder Kimball visited with the South American Saints, he wanted to learn their needs and identify ways the Church could help them carry out the work of the Lord.[9] Both he and Sister Kimball had grown up around the Indigenous peoples living on the border between the United States and Mexico. And a few years after being called to the Twelve, Elder Kimball had received a special assignment from President George Albert Smith to minister to Indigenous peoples around the world. He had since taken part in conferences and programs for these Saints in North America, and he hoped to do similar work in South America.[10]

Perhaps more than anything, though, Elder Kimball looked forward to talking with the many Saints he would meet on his tour. A year and a half earlier, doctors had removed cancerous vocal cords from his throat. For a time, he worried he might never be able to speak again. But after many prayers and priesthood blessings, he learned to communicate in a raspy whisper. He was grateful to his Father in Heaven for the miracle.[11]

After staying briefly in Brazil, Elder and Sister Kimball visited Argentina, where the Church had twenty-five branches and about 2,700 members. Since the arrival of missionaries in Argentina in the 1920s, branches of the Church had spread to other Spanish-speaking countries in the region. In the 1940s, missionaries entered Uruguay, Guatemala, Costa Rica, and El Salvador. More recently, in the 1950s, the restored gospel began to be preached in Chile, Honduras, Paraguay, Panama, and Peru.[12]

After several days in Argentina, the Kimballs headed west to Chile, where the Church had seven branches and around three hundred members. Chile had been a part of the Argentine Mission since 1955, and many missionaries believed the country was the most receptive area in the mission.[13]

From the Argentine Mission, the Kimballs traveled to Uruguay to meet with Saints in Montevideo and other cities and towns. They then returned to Brazil for a closer inspection of the mission. Traveling through southern Brazil, they stopped in the city of Joinville, where the Church had first taken root in the country. There Elder Kimball met a Church member who could not hold the priesthood because he had African ancestry. The man was discouraged, sure that the priesthood restriction prevented him from serving in any Church calling.

"I can't even be a doorkeeper, can I?" he said.

Elder Kimball felt his heart sink. "You can serve wherever priesthood is not a requirement," he said, hoping this assurance gave the man some comfort.[14]

At other meetings in Brazil, Elder Kimball did not see many Black Saints, leading him to think the priesthood restriction might not be an immediate obstacle for the Church there. But he recognized that almost 40 percent of Brazil's population had African ancestry, and that raised questions about the future growth of the Church in the country, particularly in its northern states, which had a larger Black population.[15]

The Kimballs' tour eventually brought them to São Paulo, where they met Hélio da Rocha Camargo and his wife, Nair, who had joined the Church not long after her husband. The couple brought their one-year-old son, Milton, to Elder Kimball for a priesthood blessing. Milton had been born healthy, but lately his limbs had lost their strength and coordination. Doctors feared he might have polio, a paralysis-inducing disease that was afflicting many children and adults around the world. Elder Kimball blessed the boy, and the next day the Camargos were overjoyed when Milton gripped the rails of his crib and stood for the first time.[16]

Elder Kimball received many other requests for priesthood blessings in South America, and he was happy to serve people in this way. But he was surprised to discover that, contrary to Church practice, many eligible boys and men were not being regularly advanced in the priesthood. Hélio, for instance, had brought his son to Elder Kimball for a blessing because he did not hold the Melchizedek Priesthood himself, even though he had been an active member of the Church for nearly two years.[17]

Further, Elder Kimball learned that missionaries were often reluctant to delegate branch and district responsibilities to local Saints. Consequently, few Church members in South America had any experience leading and teaching in the Church. And missionaries were so busy doing work local Saints ought to be doing that they had little time to preach the gospel.

By the end of his tour, Elder Kimball believed some changes were in order. Many Saints outside North America attended branches overseen by district and mission leaders, who often came from the United States. Establishing stakes in these areas would give more Saints the freedom to administer the Church locally.[18]

In May 1958, a month after the dedication of the New Zealand Temple, the Church had organized a stake in Auckland. It was the first stake organized outside of North America and Hawaii. Elder Kimball believed a few places in Argentina and Brazil would soon be ready for a stake as well, and he encouraged mission leaders to work toward that goal. He also concluded that the Church was ready to organize a new mission in Chile and Peru and a second mission in Brazil.

"We are but 'scratching the surface' in our work in this land," he informed the First Presidency shortly after his tour. "Certainly the time is ripe to vigorously proselyte the South American countries."[19]

NORA KOOT ARRIVED IN Taiwan in late July 1959, about three years after President Heaton had sent the first group of Latter-day Saint missionaries to the island. With a membership of fewer than three hundred Saints, the Church in Taiwan was neither as large nor as organized as the Church in Hong Kong.[20] Still, the missionaries were finding people to teach among the island's large population of Chinese refugees, who mainly spoke Mandarin, which Nora also spoke.[21]

After settling into her new area, Nora and her companion, Dezzie Clegg, called on Madam Pi Yi-shu, a member of Taiwan's chief lawmaking body. Madam Pi had attended school with Nora's stepmother, who had given Nora a letter of introduction to her old friend. Nora was eager to help Madam Pi see the blessings the Church had to offer the people of Taiwan.

At their meeting, Nora and Dezzie showed Madam Pi the letter of introduction, and she invited them to sit down. A server brought out a beautiful tea set, and Madam Pi offered some Earl Grey tea to her guests.

Although drinking that kind of tea was against the Word of Wisdom, Nora knew it was offensive in her culture to openly refuse tea from her host.[22] But over the years, missionaries and members had devised polite ways to avoid drinking tea when it was offered. For instance, Konyil Chan, a Chinese Saint in Hong Kong who was well versed in social etiquette, had recommended that missionaries simply accept the tea and then discreetly set it aside. "The Chinese people will never force their friends to drink tea," he had assured them.[23]

Nora and Dezzie graciously declined the tea and explained to Madam Pi that they had come to Taiwan to teach people to be obedient and be good members of their community. Madam Pi, though, kept inviting them to have some tea.

"Begging your pardon, Madam," Nora finally said, "we don't drink tea."

Madam Pi seemed shocked. "Why not?" she asked.[24]

"The Church teaches us to follow a principle called the Word of Wisdom to keep our bodies healthy and our minds clear," Nora replied. She then explained that Church members did not drink coffee, tea, or alcohol and did not use tobacco or drugs like opium. Church leaders and publications at this time also cautioned against any other drink that contained habit-forming substances.[25]

Madam Pi pondered this for a moment. "Well, what *can* you drink?" she asked.

"Lots of things," Nora said. "Milk, water, orange juice, 7 Up, soda."

Madam Pi asked her server to remove the tea set and bring the missionaries some cold milk. She then gave them her blessing as they taught the people of Taiwan. "I want our people to be better community citizens, to be healthier and more obedient," she said.[26]

In the days and weeks that followed, Nora shared the restored gospel with many people. Chinese Christians showed the most interest in the Church, but some Buddhists and Taoists were drawn to it as well.[27] Some people in Taiwan were atheists and showed little interest in Christianity or the Church. For others, not having the Book of Mormon or other Church literature in Chinese was an obstacle.[28]

Growth was slow in Taiwan, but the people who joined the Church firmly grasped the importance of the covenants they made at baptism. Before becoming Latter-day Saints, they had to receive all the missionary discussions, attend Sunday School and sacrament meetings regularly, obey the Word of Wisdom and the law of tithing for at least two months, and commit to keeping other commandments. By the time they set a date for baptism, many people meeting with the missionaries in Taiwan were already actively participating in their branches.[29]

One of Nora's primary responsibilities on the island was to strengthen the Relief Society. Until recently, American elders had led all Relief Societies in Taiwan. This changed in early 1959 when President Heaton sent a missionary named Betty Johnson to set up Relief Societies and train female leaders in Taipei and other cities on the island. Now Nora and her fellow sister missionaries carried on Betty's work, traveling from branch to branch to give the Relief Society any support it needed.[30]

Nora's mission ended on October 1, 1959. During her service, she had gained a greater understanding of the gospel and felt her faith increase. For her, the Church's growth in Hong Kong and Taiwan was a fulfillment of the prophet Daniel's dream.

The Church was indeed like a stone cut from a mountain without hands, rolling forth to fill the whole earth.[31]

AT THE TIME NORA Koot was finishing her mission, forty-seven-year-old LaMar Williams worked at the office of the Church's Missionary Department in Salt Lake City. When stake or mission leaders needed Church literature or some kind of visual aid, such as a photograph, he shipped it to them. If someone requested general information about the Church, his office mailed them something to read, along with instructions for how to contact the nearest missionaries.

LaMar did not handle every request personally, but he asked his secretary to notify him whenever something came from an uncommon place.

That was how he learned about Nigeria. One day, his secretary brought him a request from a reverend named Honesty John Ekong in Abak, Nigeria. Honesty John had received a pamphlet about Joseph Smith's story from a Protestant minister, and he filled out a form asking for more information about the Church, a visit from the missionaries, and the location of the nearest Latter-day Saint meetinghouse.

LaMar did not know exactly where Nigeria was, so he and his secretary found it on a map in his office. Since it was in West Africa, they knew right away that the request would be difficult to fulfill. The only congregations in Africa were thousands of miles away on the southern tip of the continent, so he couldn't send missionaries or provide a meetinghouse address. He also knew that if Honesty John were Black, he would be eligible for baptism, but not the priesthood.[32]

"We'll have to kind of tread carefully," LaMar thought. He boxed up some pamphlets and Church books, including six copies of the Book of Mormon, and shipped them to Honesty John's address.

The reverend replied a short time later. "I have to thank you for the generous gifts you sent to me," he wrote. From the letter, LaMar could infer that Honesty John was part of a congregation of believers in the restored gospel.[33]

Over the next few months, letters between LaMar and Honesty John crisscrossed the Atlantic Ocean. Honesty John invited LaMar to come to Nigeria and teach his congregation. LaMar wanted to accept the offer, but he knew it would take time for the First Presidency to approve sending anyone to Nigeria. He kept Church leaders aware of the Nigerians' hunger for more information, though, and went on corresponding with Honesty John and others who contacted him.[34]

In February 1960, LaMar wrote to Honesty John to ask if he had access to a tape recorder. If the Church was not calling missionaries to Nigeria, he could at least send recordings of gospel lessons to the reverend and his congregation. Unfortunately, Honesty John did not have a tape player or the money to buy one. But he did send LaMar his photograph. The image showed a young Black man sitting between his two small children. He wore a suit and tie and had an earnest look on his face.[35]

Honesty John also informed LaMar that his congregation had begun calling themselves The Church of Jesus Christ of Latter-day Saints. They longed to meet LaMar and be members of the Church. "If every soul were with wings," Honesty John told LaMar, "all would like to fly to Salt Lake City to listen to and see you in person."[36]

"I feel honored that you have a desire for me to come to Nigeria," LaMar responded, "but I would have to be assigned by the presidency of this Church for such a responsibility."

"I appreciate the confidence that you have in me, and in your great desire to serve your people," he continued. "I will do all that I can by correspondence."[37]

CHAPTER 5

No Power on Earth

Throughout 1960, Henry Burkhardt struggled to keep the Church from unraveling in the German Democratic Republic. The GDR had barred all foreign missionaries from serving within its borders, so the East German Saints had assumed full responsibility for proselytizing in their country. Since missionaries were restricted from going door to door, however, their reach was limited. In October, the government forbade full-time missionaries from serving in cities where the Church did not already have sizable congregations. It also put an end to almost all Relief Society, MIA, and Primary activities, arguing that the government alone was responsible for providing its citizens with recreation.

One official told the Saints that the government didn't like them for this reason. "You have everything you need in the Church."[1]

Before long, the Church in the GDR was a shadow of what it once was. Rather than endure under these conditions, many East German Saints fled the country in search of greater religious freedom and economic opportunity in West Germany.[2] And the Saints were not the only ones. Droves of people were leaving the GDR, often crossing at the border between East and West Berlin.

This mass migration was an embarrassment to the East German government and its Soviet allies. Many people, including Henry, believed it was only a matter of time before the government closed all access to West Berlin. With mission headquarters on the west side of the city, Henry feared that such a drastic step would cut the East German Saints off from the rest of the Church.[3]

On December 18, Alvin R. Dyer, the president of the European Mission and an Assistant to the Quorum of the Twelve Apostles, came to the GDR to speak with Henry and other local Church leaders about the well-being of the Saints under their care.

The East German leaders presented a bleak picture. The government had placed severe restrictions on importing recently published books or other printed materials. These restrictions made it practically impossible for the Saints to receive new Church magazines, lesson manuals, or hymnbooks without smuggling them in from the West. Branch attendance was in decline. Meetinghouses were functional, but some were in disrepair. And now that youth meetings had stopped, state-sponsored programs were steering many young people away from religion. Henry explained that branches sometimes held youth activities in secret, but everyone in the meeting agreed that doing so was dangerous.[4]

The value of East German currency was also dropping, and the government's welfare programs were woefully inadequate. Many Saints were too poor to afford food and fuel, so they either used funds from the Church's welfare account to purchase coal and potatoes or simply went without.[5]

After the meeting, President Dyer spoke privately with Henry to express concern about the state of missionary work in the GDR. It wasn't just that the East German government had greatly restricted where and how missionaries could serve. The government expected all able-bodied men to be gainfully employed, and full-time missionary service could be seen as harmful to the East German economy. The fact that most missionaries depended on financial support from local branches or from Saints in West Germany was also a problem. To President Dyer, it seemed too much like a paid ministry. For these reasons, he asked Henry to release all full-time missionaries serving in the GDR.

At first, Henry was reluctant to comply with this request. The missionaries were no longer sharing the gospel door-to-door, so the Church was not causing any trouble for the government. And some Church branches still depended on missionaries for priesthood leadership. If the missionaries were released, the branches could fall apart. Yet Henry respected President Dyer and followed the counsel, despite his reservations.[6]

A few months later, young West and East German Saints met in West Berlin for an MIA conference. Everyone knew the border could be closed at any time, and there was anxiety in the air. Yet time and time again, the young Saints expressed a common theme as they bore their testimonies: They did not know what the future held, but even if they never had the opportunity to meet together again, they knew the gospel would be true on both sides of the political divide.

And they would remain firm in their faith.[7]

THE SPREAD OF AUTHORITARIAN governments throughout central and eastern Europe and in other parts of the world greatly alarmed President McKay.[8] For more than a decade now, he had watched such governments gain power, promote atheism, and undermine religious belief in places like eastern Germany and Czechoslovakia, where the Church had once thrived.[9]

The fervent devotion of the Saints gave him hope, however. The United States and western Europe were experiencing great prosperity, and some people feared that society was becoming more concerned with wealth and status than with God. President McKay did not think this was true of Church members. As he met with Saints around the world, he admired their selflessness. "I doubt that there has ever been a time when the membership of the Church have had greater spirituality—more willingness to give and to serve," he told a reporter in January 1961.[10]

He was particularly moved by the Saints' generosity in paying tithes and offerings. In past generations, funding the work of the Lord had often been a challenge for the Church. The contributions of the Saints, combined with a reliance on volunteer service and revenue from various business interests, allowed the Church to continue financing its many endeavors, including educational, welfare, missionary, and building programs.[11]

Although the building program was especially costly, President McKay believed the expense was vital to the growing Church. "The purpose of these buildings," he declared, "is not accomplished when the walls are built, the roof securely placed, the tower completed, and the dedicatory prayer offered. They are built for the edification of the soul."[12]

New chapels around the world served as important gathering places where Saints could worship God and fellowship one another. In Denton, Texas, a small city in the southern United States, two dozen Church members started meeting in 1959 in the home of John and Margaret Porter. When the group outgrew the Porter home, they met in a vacant two-story building with a leaky roof. By 1961, the group had become a branch with enough active members to apply to the Church Building Committee for permission to construct a meetinghouse.

At the time, Church members living in missions were expected to donate 30 percent of the cost of new meetinghouses. In stakes, the expectation was 50 percent. To encourage the Saints in Denton to contribute to the chapel, stake president Ervin Atkerson matched the first $1,000 donated to the fund with his own money. With approval from the Church, John Porter then personally purchased a three-acre lot, sold one acre to a restaurant, and donated the other two acres for the building.

Congregations that built meetinghouses in the early 1960s had several Church-approved architectural plans to choose from. Some plans allowed for meetinghouses to be built over time, in two or three phases, depending on the size and growth of the ward or branch. The first phase of a building consisted of classrooms and a large multipurpose room that could be used as a chapel. The second phase added a large chapel and Primary room, and the third phase included a cultural hall, kitchen, and more rooms. With their branch growing rapidly, the Saints in Denton opted to build a meetinghouse based on a plan that combined the first two phases. While a Church-employed construction supervisor managed the project, the Denton Saints provided most of the labor.

One branch member, Riley Swanson, was a cabinetmaker who did beautiful woodwork for the chapel. Riley was a local convert who had given up smoking to join the Church. When construction began, he started working nights so he could spend his days working on the chapel as a full-time volunteer.[13]

With meetinghouses going up around the world, the Church also planned to construct a large office building in Salt Lake City to provide work space for general Church leaders and Church employees. And plans were underway for a new visitors' center on Temple Square, a vault to store genealogical records deep in the mountains near Salt Lake City, and a new temple in Oakland, California.[14]

President McKay also found hope in the youth of the Church and their desire to share the gospel. In 1959, he had invited every Church member to find, teach, and fellowship new members and potential converts.[15] Since then, missionary work had accelerated, especially in Great Britain, where the new temple had indeed brought about a "new era" of the Church. Convert baptisms in the British Mission began to increase dramatically, particularly among young people, leading the Church to create the North British Mission and the Manchester Stake in March 1960.[16] One year later, President McKay returned once more to England to organize the London Stake and dedicate a beautiful new chapel near Hyde Park in the heart of London.

While in Great Britain, President McKay reiterated his invitation for every member to participate in missionary work. "If every member will carry that responsibility," he reminded missionaries in the North British Mission, "no power on earth can stop this Church from growing."[17]

A few months after President McKay returned from Great Britain, the First Presidency received a memo from LaMar Williams about the dozens of letters he had received from people in Nigeria. "If the gospel is to be preached to this vast number of people, who are certainly the children of God," LaMar wrote, "it seems to me that this is an opportune time to investigate a beginning of the work."[18]

President McKay was already aware of the Nigerians' interest in the restored gospel. The previous year, he had asked Glen Fisher, a mission president returning from South Africa, to visit Nigeria. Glen had made a favorable report of the country's readiness for missionary work, giving President McKay much to consider by the time LaMar's memo arrived.

On July 1, 1961, President McKay addressed the matter at a meeting of the First Presidency and Quorum of the Twelve Apostles. Knowing the Church's priesthood restriction would present serious challenges for missionary work in Nigeria, he likened the situation to the dilemma facing the ancient apostles when questions arose about extending the gospel to the Gentiles. Those apostles had not acted until after Peter received a revelation from God.

President McKay had sought guidance from the Lord on the priesthood restriction, but he had received no clear answer. For now, he did not intend to open a mission in Nigeria until he too knew the will of the Lord.[19]

Still, he believed LaMar was right. The Church needed more information, and he proposed sending Church representatives to Nigeria to observe the faith of the Nigerians. After discussing the matter, the apostles gave their support to the prophet's proposal.[20]

AROUND THIS TIME, SIXTEEN-YEAR-OLD Suzie Towse had a routine. Every day, when she finished her after-school newspaper route, she would go home and ask her father for permission to join The Church of Jesus Christ of Latter-day Saints. She had been interested in the Church for about a year. A friend had invited her to a youth activity at the local branch in Beverley, England, and Suzie soon came to love the restored gospel. But her Catholic and Methodist parents thought her desire to join the Church was only a phase, and they refused to consent to her baptism.[21]

Still, Suzie was determined to be a Latter-day Saint. She was among the thousands of people in the British Isles who were drawn to the Church at that time. Like Suzie, many of them had learned about the Church through a new mission referral program, which encouraged the Saints to invite friends and family to Church meetings and place them in contact with missionaries. In fact, at the time Suzie's friend introduced her to the Church, more than 85 percent of recent baptisms in the British Mission had come from referrals.[22]

Since learning about the Church, Suzie had faced significant opposition. After receiving a copy of the Book of Mormon, she had taken it to her Catholic priest to get his permission to read it. He was normally a kindly man, but when she showed him the book, his whole demeanor had changed. He said the Book of Mormon was of the devil and accused her of contaminating his house with heresy. He then snatched the book out of her hand and pitched it at the fireplace. The book missed the flames, and Suzie managed to retrieve it before the priest forced her out the front door.

"Well, there is no turning back now," she had said afterward.

She soon became a regular presence at Beverley Branch meetings. After worshipping for years in an ornate Catholic chapel, Suzie found it odd at first to worship with a handful of people in a hotel room with bare floorboards and hard, wooden chairs. But after attending her first sacrament meeting, she had felt a warm confirmation that the words she heard there were true. The Spirit bore profound witness to her that she must return.[23]

She felt a similar spirit at MIA meetings, which were far more crowded. Some of the youth, like Suzie, had been referred to the Church by friends. Others were young men who had found the Church by playing baseball with the missionaries.[24] For decades, missionaries had used sports to meet young people and introduce them and their parents to the Church. Lately, baseball had become especially popular in the British missions, and many young men had joined the Church so they could play on missionary-run teams. Since mission leaders at the time often recognized and rewarded missionaries who baptized more than others, some missionaries focused their efforts on young people, who were usually much more willing to be baptized than adults.[25]

Although these young converts generally received some gospel lessons before their baptisms, they were often more interested in being part of a sports team than in attending Church. In most cases, their baptisms had not led to other family members joining the Church, so the Beverley Branch and most other branches in the British Isles had dozens of youth who were Church members in name only.[26]

Week after week, though, Suzie attended Church meetings and talked to her parents about baptism. One day, after arriving home from her newspaper route, she found her father with his feet sticking out from underneath a car he was repairing. "Dad," she said, "can I be baptized?"

"Yes, you can, lass," he said, still under the car. "If it means that much to you, you can."

Suzie was stunned. "Did you really mean that, Dad?" she asked. "Do you want to say that again?"

Yes, he repeated. If she wanted to, she could get baptized.

"Thank you," she cried. "Thank you." She immediately rode her bicycle to the missionaries' apartment and gave them the good news. Neither of them was shocked that her father changed his mind.

"Why aren't you surprised?" she asked. "I was."

"We knew he would," they explained. "We have been fasting for you."[27]

IN THE EARLY MORNING hours of August 13, 1961, the German Democratic Republic set up barricades around the perimeter of West Berlin. Tanks lumbered into position at border crossings, and soldiers installed machine guns in the windows of nearby buildings. At the Brandenburg Gate, a historic monument in the center of the city, large crowds gathered in anger and confusion. The following day, workers jackhammered the streets in front of the monument and began constructing a long makeshift wall of concrete blocks and barbed wire behind a line of armed guards.

After months of rumors, the East German government had finally closed the border between East and West Berlin.[28]

The rapid rise of the wall unsettled Henry Burkhardt. As he feared, the closed borders cut off communication with the West. He could not make a telephone call, send a telegram, or mail a letter to the mission office. If he tried to cross the border, as he had been free to do the day before, guards would stop him—maybe even kill him.

"How can the work continue?" he wondered.[29] Although the districts and branches in the GDR already functioned under local leaders, and member missionaries had largely taken the place of full-time missionaries, Henry had always depended on at least some contact with the Berlin Mission headquarters in West Berlin. What would happen now that the wall created a very real barrier between them?[30]

Henry had his answer at the end of August. While the GDR had prohibited its citizens from traveling outside the country, it allowed West German residents with special permits to travel within its borders. On August 27, Berlin Mission president Percy K. Fetzer and one of his counselors, David Owens, met with Henry and other Saints in East Berlin. Before entering the country, the two men emptied their car and pockets of any unnecessary items. They found a line of police and soldiers at the checkpoint, holding back a mass of thousands of people. Once the soldiers parted the crowd, President Fetzer inched forward, driving through a maze of obstructions until he reached the entrance to the city.[31]

Henry and the Saints were overjoyed to see the mission president. The visit was brief, but President Fetzer and other Church leaders made similar visits in the months that followed. They acted cautiously, aware that their presence in East Berlin could put them and the Saints in danger. Fortunately, the new restrictions did not seem to shake the resolve of the East German Saints. Attendance at sacrament meeting increased, and many people bore firm testimony that the gospel was true.[32]

At a conference of local leaders, Henry acknowledged that the circumstances were not ideal for Saints in the GDR. "The work of the Lord must not suffer as a result of conditions imposed by man," he reminded the leaders. "It will more or less depend on us, and how we carry out our callings, whether the work of God will continue to go forward with success in this country."[33]

A FEW WEEKS BEFORE the October 1961 general conference, President David O. McKay invited Elder Harold B. Lee into his office in Salt Lake City. The prophet had awakened at six thirty that morning with a clear impression that the upcoming priesthood session should introduce a new program designed to unify Church curriculum.[34]

Since the late nineteenth century, each of the Church organizations—Sunday School, Primary, Young Men's and Young Women's MIA, Relief Society, and priesthood quorums—had written its own weekly lessons, independent of one another. Beginning in the early 1900s, Church leaders had sought ways to correlate the weekly lessons and activities of the organizations and quorums of the Church by emphasizing essential doctrine and doing away with any repetitious or overlapping lessons. But these efforts had been sporadic and short-lived.[35]

President McKay, who had taken part in some of the early correlation efforts, believed it was time to try again. More than a third of the Church had become members in the past ten years, and the current curriculum did not always meet the needs of the new

Saints. The prophet was especially concerned about lessons that presented incorrect ideas or strayed too far from basic gospel teachings. He wanted a uniform curriculum grounded in the fundamental principles of the gospel.

"The only program which is valid in our thinking," he declared, "is that which is intended to save souls."[36]

Elder Lee had been studying the matter with a small committee for more than a year. He too wanted teaching in the Church to place more emphasis on saving doctrine. And lately he had been troubled to learn that Church-published training materials had gone out to local congregations before the apostles had seen them. He wanted the new program to ensure that lessons and handbooks received adequate review before they reached the Saints. Better coordination among Church organizations, he believed, would eliminate confusion.[37]

Working together, the committee had proposed to have Church curriculum written under a new organizing principle. Instead of each general organization writing its own lesson material independently, curriculum would be supervised by three committees: one for children, another for youth, and another for adults.

Representatives of the various organizations of the Church, both women and men, would help develop a curriculum focused on a few core, saving principles. The Quorum of the Twelve Apostles would supervise their work, and an All-Church Coordinating Council led by four apostles would oversee the activities of the three committees.

By organizing the curriculum according to age group, the committees could avoid unnecessary duplication in lessons. And developing the lessons with general authorities allowed the curriculum to benefit from their experience visiting members in congregations around the world.

Once the committee drew up its proposal, the First Presidency and Quorum of the Twelve reviewed and approved it, just in time for Elder Lee to introduce the new program to the Saints at the priesthood session of the October general conference.

"In the adoption of such a program," Elder Lee declared, "we may possibly and hopefully look forward to the consolidation and simplification of Church curricula, Church publications, Church buildings, Church meetings, and many other important aspects of the Lord's work."

Elder Lee was certain that President McKay's move to begin correlating the Church's curriculum was inspired. "If we will just keep our eye on the president of this Church," he testified, "we will see him moving to do the thing that will be for the salvation of the children of men in the most effective way possible."[38]

SHORTLY AFTER GENERAL CONFERENCE, LaMar Williams boarded a flight for Nigeria. In his luggage, LaMar had packed a camera and tape recorder so he could later share with the First Presidency the faces and voices of the people he met. His companion for the trip was a twenty-year-old missionary named Marvin Jones, who was on his way to the South African Mission.[39]

Their destination was Port Harcourt, a city on the Nigerian coast, where a crowd—nearly all of the people who had exchanged letters with LaMar—awaited them. Missing from the crowd, though, was Honesty John Ekong, whose letters had first turned LaMar's attention to Africa.[40]

As he greeted his friends, LaMar was surprised to learn that they did not all know each other. He thought they had been working together. Among the group was a man named Matthew Udo-Ete, who had written the most letters to LaMar. He took LaMar and Marvin to his small home, where a crowd of people had gathered to hear them speak. The air was hotter and more humid than anything LaMar was used to, but for the next two hours he taught the people and answered their questions about the Church.

On his first Sunday in Nigeria, LaMar addressed another large crowd in Matthew's chapel. People had come many miles to hear him speak. He taught them about the Godhead, the Apostasy, and the Restoration of the gospel through Joseph Smith. He explained the priesthood restriction and said that he had come to Nigeria to find out if his friends would still be interested in the Church even if they could not hold the priesthood.

When he finished speaking, he turned the time back to Matthew to close the meeting. Suddenly, people in the congregation began speaking in a language LaMar couldn't understand. LaMar looked to Matthew for a translation.

"We have people here who want to bear their testimony," Matthew said.[41]

LaMar was surprised. He expected the people to be tired and perhaps hungry. Instead, for the next three hours people shared their testimonies.

Among them was an old man with graying hair, a white shirt, and rose-colored fabric wrapped around his legs. His feet were bare. "I am sixty-five years of age," he said, "and I am sick. I've walked sixteen miles to be here this morning."

"I haven't seen President McKay, and I haven't seen God," he continued. "But I have seen you, and I'm going to hold you personally accountable to go back to President McKay and tell him that we are sincere."

One woman in the congregation simply asked LaMar, "Will you allow this love we have for the Church to be in vain?"[42]

A little over a week later, in the town of Uyo, LaMar finally met Honesty John Ekong. He learned that his friend had traveled more than one hundred miles to meet him at the airport but had somehow missed him. Honesty John showed LaMar the walls of his home. They were decorated with articles and photographs of general authorities from Church magazines.[43]

Again and again, LaMar was impressed with the faith of the Nigerians. He learned that around five thousand people in nearly one hundred congregations wanted to join the Church. Yet he could see no way forward in Nigeria as long as the priesthood and temple restrictions were in place. He wanted to give his new friends assurances about the future of missionary work in their country, but he knew he was not authorized to do so.

"They insist that if I do my part when I report to the First Presidency, the Church will come to Nigeria," he wrote in his journal. "They do not realize how insignificant I am in the final analysis of such a decision."

But he had hope. "Thank goodness all things are possible with the Lord's help," he wrote.[44]

CHAPTER 6

Blessings Everywhere

In the spring of 1962, Young Women's MIA board member Ruth Funk was drowning in work. The MIA's annual conference was coming up, and she was coproducing a musical play for the event. The conference, which began in the 1890s, drew around twenty-five thousand youth leaders to Salt Lake City to receive counsel and training from general Church leaders. Ruth and the members of her committee wanted to put together a good show for the conference, and they were learning as they went.

As the first performance neared, Ruth was asked to attend a meeting about the focus of the Church. She did not know why she was invited, and she was not keen on going. As it was, she barely had time to see her husband, Marcus, and their four children.[1]

Still, on the appointed night, Ruth hurried over to the meeting. There she found a room full of people, including some general Church leaders, discussing the basic goals of the Church. Reed Bradford, a sociology professor from Brigham Young University, conducted the meeting.

Ruth did not say anything at first. Near the end of the evening, though, Reed said, "Sister Funk, you haven't expressed yourself."[2]

"Well, I have very strong feelings," she replied. Like many people in the United States and elsewhere, Church members were growing more and more worried about divorce, juvenile delinquency, and other social concerns. "I feel that every stop should be pulled to emphasize the strength of the family," she said.[3]

The meeting ended, and Ruth returned to her other responsibilities. Later, after the MIA conference was over and the musical had a successful run, she received a phone call from apostle Marion G. Romney. "Ruth," he said, "we are calling you to serve on the Correlation Committee."

Ruth's heart sank. "What in the world is correlation?" she asked.

She soon found out at an orientation meeting with Elder Harold B. Lee. The committee was chiefly responsible for aligning all Church curriculum with basic gospel principles. But with the Church spreading rapidly throughout the world, the program would also put new emphasis on priesthood, home, and family as central to the restored gospel of Jesus Christ.[4]

Elder Lee described the committees overseeing the programs for adults, youth, and children. To her surprise, Ruth was called to the adult committee despite her years of experience working with youth. Like her, the other committee members—three women, five men—were juggling careers and family responsibilities. The youngest member was thirty-four-year-old Thomas S. Monson, who had just finished serving as president of the Canadian Mission with his wife, Frances.[5]

As months passed, and the committee began researching the Church's past lesson plans, everyone was encouraged to express their opinions freely as they discussed the future of Church curriculum. The committee had years of study and work ahead of it, but Ruth was eager to do whatever she could to help the Church move forward.[6]

Elsewhere at Church headquarters, Henry D. Moyle—an apostle, businessman, and former head of the Church Welfare Program—was serving as President McKay's newly called first counselor.

The prophet had originally called him to serve in the presidency with first counselor J. Reuben Clark after the death of Stephen L Richards in May 1959. Two years later, President Clark's health began to decline, so President McKay had appointed apostle Hugh B. Brown to join them as a third counselor in the presidency. When President Clark passed away in October 1961, President

McKay then designated President Moyle and President Brown to be his first and second counselors.[7]

As first counselor in the First Presidency, President Moyle was involved in all aspects of the Church's missionary program, a duty he relished. Around the world, many people were taking a great interest in Christianity, and President Moyle was responsible for making sure every mission reached them effectively. Under his supervision, baptisms increased over 300 percent worldwide, and the average missionary labored 221 hours a month—44 percent more than in 1960.[8]

With his background in business, President Moyle could appreciate strong numbers and solid percentages. In missionary work, however, numbers alone meant little if conversions were short-lived. President Moyle wanted to ensure that people made enduring changes in their lives.

Like President McKay, he believed in the "Every Member a Missionary" approach to sharing the gospel.[9] But he was troubled by the many problems arising from young people joining the Church simply to play on missionary baseball teams. And he was dismayed when missions emphasized quotas over genuine conversion.[10] As he met with missionaries, he urged them to teach families and help converts feel welcome at Church. He reiterated that youth needed permission from their parents to be baptized.[11]

Not long after the Correlation Committee was organized, President Moyle attended a meeting at which

Elder Harold B. Lee proposed expanding the correlation program to include missionary work. The idea unsettled President Moyle. He had served many years with Elder Lee in the Church Welfare Program and the Quorum of the Twelve Apostles, and he considered him a close friend. Even though he approved of other aspects of correlation, however, he did not agree with him on this point.[12]

For as long as anyone could remember, missionary work had been directed by the First Presidency. They issued mission calls, appointed mission presidents, and corresponded directly with mission offices.[13] Under Elder Lee's proposal, however, a member of the Quorum of the Twelve Apostles, rather than a counselor in the First Presidency, would lead the Church's missionary committee. The presidency would receive written reports from apostles who visited the missions as well as verbal reports from returning mission presidents, but they would be relieved of most of the direct management over the missions.[14]

On September 18, President Moyle discussed Elder Lee's expanded correlation plan with President McKay. The present system was working well, he reasoned. "If this new plan is adopted," he said, "it takes missionary work out of the hands of the First Presidency entirely."

"It has been in our hands since the organization of the Church," President McKay acknowledged. But with the Church growing so rapidly, the First Presidency would soon have to delegate more of its responsibilities. There were sixty-four missions and over ten thousand missionaries to care for—and these numbers would only grow. Already President Moyle and two assistants were spending many hours a week just on mission calls. They were also handling the seemingly endless correspondence with mission presidents over administrative matters like buying land for meetinghouses.

President McKay wanted the First Presidency to continue calling new mission presidents, just as they had always done. But he was open to the changes in Elder Lee's proposal. He wanted to hear more about them.[15]

A FEW MONTHS LATER, on January 11, 1963, the *Deseret News* ran an unexpected headline: "Church to Open Missionary Work in Nigeria."

The announcement came just days after apostle N. Eldon Tanner and his wife, Sara, returned from West Africa. During the two-week trip, Elder Tanner had spoken with several Nigerian officials, met with hundreds of prospective Saints, and dedicated the land for the preaching of the restored gospel.[16] Upon the Tanners' return to Utah, President McKay called LaMar Williams and a few others to serve as missionaries in Nigeria as soon as they obtained travel visas.[17]

Charles Agu, the leader of a group of prospective Saints in Aba, Nigeria, rejoiced at the news. His congregation had more than 150 people, and it was growing fast.

When LaMar visited the country in 1961, Charles had befriended him and joined him on parts of his tour. He and his congregation understood the gospel well and had an abiding faith in the Restoration. Before LaMar returned to the United States, Charles had recorded a message for President McKay. "We believe that this Church has all the revelation and prophecy required by God to guide His people aright," he testified. "We therefore will not refuse this Church because the priesthood is denied us."

Since then, Charles and LaMar had exchanged many letters, and Charles could hardly wait for LaMar to return and officially establish the Church in West Africa. "To all of us here, this is a moment of great expectation," he wrote LaMar in February 1963.

Because he could not hold the priesthood, Charles understood that he would not be able to serve as a branch president once the Church was established in Nigeria. During Elder Tanner's visit, however, the apostle had explained that Charles and other Nigerian leaders would continue to guide their congregations as unordained district or group leaders. Nigerian Saints would also fill all callings that did not require priesthood ordination.[18]

With each passing week, Charles expected to hear that LaMar was on his way to Nigeria. But in nearly every letter he sent, LaMar reported that he was waiting for the Nigerian government to approve his travel visa. No one could explain the delay.[19]

Then, in March, Charles came across an article about the Church in a newspaper called the *Nigerian Outlook*.

It told of a Nigerian college student who had visited a Latter-day Saint meeting in California. At the meeting, the man had been shocked to learn about the priesthood restriction and the justifications used to explain it.

"I do not believe in a God whose adherents preach the superiority of one race over the other," the man wrote in his article. He believed it would damage the reputation of Nigeria to let the Church be established in the country.[20]

Only a few years had passed since Nigeria gained its independence from Great Britain, and the article reflected widespread suspicion of outside influences on the country. Believing the article had something to do with the delayed visa, Charles sent it to LaMar. He thought the presence of an official representative from Church headquarters might help counteract the damage done by the article.[21]

LaMar disagreed. Church leaders had proposed a mission in Nigeria because thousands of Nigerians had patiently and persistently sought out the restored gospel. If anyone was going to speak in defense of the Church in Nigeria, LaMar believed, it should be a Nigerian believer. "I am sure that through your prayers and inspiration you will do and say those things that will convince the government leaders of our sincerity," he wrote.[22]

Charles met with Dick Obot, another prospective Nigerian Saint, and together they placed an advertisement about the Church in the *Nigerian Outlook*. In it, they testified of the Restoration of the gospel of Jesus Christ through the prophet Joseph Smith, the role of modern-day revelation in establishing doctrine, and the Church's concern for the spiritual and temporal well-being of all people.[23]

Charles hoped the advertisement would help change minds and hearts about the Saints. Before he found the Church, he had smoked, drunk alcohol, and lived an undisciplined life. Now he was different.

"I have found joy in my life, progress in my occupation, and blessings everywhere," he told LaMar.[24]

In March 1963, four months after her baptism, thirteen-year-old Delia Rochon wanted to pay tithing. She was a member of a branch of about twenty people in Colonia Suiza, a city in southern Uruguay. She knew tithing was a commandment, and she was willing to do everything the Lord asked of her. Her only problem was that she had no income.

She went to her mother, who was not a member of the Church, for advice. Her mother suggested she find a way to make money.

An elderly neighbor agreed to pay Delia to bring him fresh water. Each day, Delia would take a glass container to a well near her house, fill it with about a gallon of water, and carry it to his house. After a few weeks of saving her earnings, she took a peso to Victor Solari, her branch president, for tithing.[25]

"How much money did you make?" the president asked.

"Three pesos," Delia replied.

"Well," said President Solari, "tithing is 10 percent." One peso—a third of what she made—was too much.

"But I want to give the money," Delia said.

President Solari considered this. "Well," he said, "do a fast offering." He explained what fast offerings were and helped Delia fill out her first donation slip.[26]

A short time later, President Solari asked to meet with Delia. She had never been called into his office before, so she was nervous. It was a small room with a metal desk and a few bookshelves lined with Church manuals. When she took a seat in a chair by the desk, her feet did not quite touch the floor.

President Solari got right to the point. The branch's Primary president had just moved away for a teaching job in another area, and he wanted Delia to take her place.

In times past, missionaries had often led out in branch leadership. But Thomas Fyans, the president of the Uruguayan Mission, was a firm believer in releasing North American missionaries from leadership positions and calling local Saints instead. Doing so had become a priority for South American missions since Elder Kimball's tour of the continent in 1959. Giving more local opportunities to local Saints—even Saints who were only thirteen years old—was seen as a vital step toward establishing stakes in South America.[27]

Delia had never been to Primary as a child. She did not really know what a Primary president did. Still, she accepted the calling, and it felt good.

But she worried about how her parents would react to the news. They were divorced, and neither of them was a member of the Church. Her father's family were devout Protestants and disapproved of her membership in the Church. Her Catholic mother was more accepting of her beliefs, but she would be concerned about the calling interfering with her responsibilities at home and school.

"I will talk with your mother," President Solari said.

It took some convincing, but the branch president and Delia reached an agreement with her mother: Delia would do her chores early on Saturday, the day Primary was held in her branch, and then be allowed to do whatever she needed to fulfill her Church duties.[28]

After being set apart, Delia got to work in her new calling. Since her branch was so small, she alone was responsible for leading and teaching the Primary children. For training, President Solari gave her a thick Primary manual and two typed sheets of instructions.

"If you have questions," he said, "pray!"

Before preparing her first lesson, Delia read the instructions. She then opened the Primary manual, rested her hands on the pages, and bowed her head.

"Heavenly Father," she said, "I need to teach this lesson to the children, and I do not know how. Please, help me."[29]

AROUND THIS SAME TIME, eighteen-year-old Suzie Towse boarded a train bound for London. It had been almost two years since her baptism in the Beverley Branch, and now she was on her way to serve a mission as a secretary in the Church Building Department's office in the United Kingdom.

Her parents were not pleased that she was leaving home. In fact, her mother, who had joined the Church not long after Suzie, had hard feelings against the Church after a missionary offended her. But that did not deter Suzie. Serving a mission had been her goal since joining the Church.

Geoff Dunning, a young man from her branch, saw her off at the station. He had joined the Church about a year earlier, and they had become friends while serving together on the branch's fellowshipping committee. Geoff's strong testimony and work ethic had caught the attention of local Church leaders, and he had already served in a variety of callings.[30]

As she traveled south, Suzie looked forward to serving in the Building Department. The Church had begun its labor missionary program in Europe in July 1960. Mission presidents soon began calling hundreds of local Saints, including some young men who had remained active after joining the Church through mission baseball teams, to serve as "building missionaries." Now the British Saints could look forward to meeting in roomy new chapels instead of cramped rented halls.[31] In fact, Suzie and Geoff had already spent many evenings and Saturdays helping the building missionaries work on a chapel in Beverley.[32]

Suzie received her call to serve from Grant Thorn, the president of the newly organized Northeast British Mission. The minimum age for young women called on proselytizing missions was twenty-one, but building missionaries could be called at a younger age. Since Suzie had worked as a secretary at an accounting firm, she knew how to complete a variety of office tasks. When the Building Department interviewed her about her secretarial work experience, she passed with "flying colours."

In London, Suzie moved into an apartment with two other sister missionaries. They began each morning in the office with a prayer, a hymn, and a scripture. The rest of their time was spent typing letters, taking minutes at meetings, transcribing shorthand notes, and attending and keeping records of chapel dedications.[33]

Among the chapels under construction was a meetinghouse in Merthyr Tydfil, Wales, the birthplace of President McKay's mother. Its groundbreaking happened in March 1961, and the project gained momentum in January 1963, when the prophet decided to dedicate the building personally. Over the next eight months, missionaries and Saints consecrated more than thirty thousand hours to build the chapel, completing it on August 23.[34]

Two days later, Suzie and thirteen hundred other people came to the new meetinghouse for the dedication. As soon as she saw President McKay, a feeling of peace and love filled her soul. She knew at once that she was in the presence of God's prophet.[35]

A few months after the dedication, Suzie received an emotional letter from her mother. "If you do not come home now," her mother wrote, "you need never return."[36]

Suzie did not want to upset her parents, but she also did not want to leave her mission. "Sometimes it is hard to know what to do when your parents advise you one thing and the Church teaches another," she confided in a letter to Geoff. "I feel so mixed up and worried."

Before long, she told President Thorn about her dilemma. "Stay and finish your mission," he advised. "The Lord will prepare a way."

Suzie took his counsel to heart. "My parents will understand someday," she told Geoff. "I know I wouldn't be away from home if it was not the Lord's work."[37]

WHEN ELDER HAROLD B. LEE and his committee presented their final plan for priesthood correlation to the First Presidency and Quorum of the Twelve Apostles in early 1963, President McKay readily approved it. "The whole thing is glorious," he said.[38]

The plan encompassed the entire Church program, a significant expansion of the committee's original mandate to correlate curriculum. Church organizations would no longer be publishing lessons or issuing policies without guidance from general authorities. The new system divided Church governance into four areas—welfare, genealogy and temple, home teaching, and missionary. Each of these areas was to be overseen by a committee of about twenty-five members, led by either an apostle or the presiding bishop.

When Elder Lee had spoken about the correlation program at general conference in April, he explained that the home was the foundation of a righteous life and that the organizations of the Church existed under the authority of the priesthood to aid and support it. "It is upon these fundamentals," he said, "that we have been guided in our correlation studies of the curricula and activities of all the priesthood and the auxiliary organizations."[39]

President Moyle and President Brown had faith in President McKay's calling as God's prophet. Yet, despite his approval of the program, they had reservations about some of its features. After counseling with Elder Lee, President Brown dropped his concerns, and President Moyle accepted most of the plan. But he continued to question whether they should shift oversight of the missions from the First Presidency to the Quorum of the Twelve Apostles.[40]

Elder Lee and President Moyle had been close associates for years. When President Moyle had been called into the First Presidency, Elder Lee could hardly contain his joy. "It seemed to me almost too good to be true," he had written in his journal. Later, when Elder Lee's wife, Fern, died, President Moyle had comforted him and spoken at her funeral. Now, Elder Lee longed to have his friend's wholehearted support for correlation.[41]

As the Church prepared to roll out the new program, Elder Lee began courting Joan Jensen, a schoolteacher who was around his age and had never been married. After deciding to marry, they asked President McKay if he would perform the ceremony, and the prophet gladly consented.

The day before the wedding, Elder Lee asked Marion G. Romney, who was also close friends with President Moyle, to serve as one of the witnesses. As the two men visited, President Moyle walked up and asked if he could attend the ceremony as well. In a moment, the distance between the two men slipped away, and their differences over correlation no longer mattered.

"Would you like to be a witness?" Elder Lee asked.

President Moyle became emotional. "Would you permit me to?"

"If President McKay would perform our marriage and you two would be witnesses," Elder Lee said, "it would be perfect."

The next morning, President McKay sealed Harold and Joan as husband and wife in the Salt Lake Temple. Elder Romney and President Moyle served as witnesses to the sacred ordinance.[42]

A few months later, in September, President Moyle flew to Florida, in the southeastern United States, to inspect a 300,000-acre cattle ranch the Church owned and operated to help fund its program to care for the poor.[43]

Elder Lee, meanwhile, was in Hawaii presiding at a stake conference. Early one morning, a telephone call from Utah jarred him awake. It was President Brown calling to inform him that President Moyle had passed away in his sleep at the Florida ranch. Shocked, Elder Lee boarded a flight home later that morning.

Three days later, at President Moyle's funeral, Elder Lee stood at the pulpit of the Salt Lake Tabernacle and spoke about the friendship he and Marion G. Romney shared with Henry D. Moyle.

"We were strong-willed, stubborn men, the three of us," he said. "But I think no three men ever had greater respect for each other than we had each for the other."[44]

CHAPTER 7

Children of the Same God

In early October 1963, Salt Lake City's local chapter of the National Association for the Advancement of Colored People (NAACP) prepared to stage a peaceful protest outside Temple Square during general conference. As the upcoming protest made headlines across the United States, the organizers hoped the demonstration would persuade Church leaders to clarify their stance on civil rights.[1]

Although the Church-owned *Deseret News* had endorsed gradual racial desegregation in 1956, Utah still lagged behind other nearby states in passing civil rights legislation.[2] The NAACP hoped a strong statement from the Church would influence lawmakers to ensure equal protections and opportunities for all people in the state.[3]

The protest was to be one of many that season in the United States. Earlier in the year, U.S. president John F. Kennedy had proposed a civil rights law to protect African Americans and other people of color against discrimination. A few months later, the NAACP helped organize a massive march in Washington, DC, to protest social and economic inequality in the United States. The march ended with a stirring speech by Dr. Martin Luther King Jr., a prominent civil rights leader, which inspired many people to stand against racial injustice.[4]

After learning about the planned Temple Square protest, Sterling McMurrin, a professor of philosophy at the University of Utah, arranged for leaders of the Salt Lake City NAACP to meet with Hugh B. Brown of the First Presidency.[5]

On the evening of October 3, President Brown welcomed Albert Fritz, the president of the local NAACP chapter, and other protest organizers to the Church Administration Building. N. Eldon Tanner, who had been called earlier that day to replace Henry D. Moyle in the First Presidency, also joined them.

At the meeting, the organizers asked if the Church intended to speak out in support of civil rights.

"As you know," President Brown said, "the Church doesn't get involved in politics." It had a long-standing position of political neutrality.

The organizers then pointed out that the Church often spoke out on moral issues. And civil rights, they reasoned, was a moral issue.

President Brown agreed with them, but neither he nor President Tanner thought a public protest was necessary. They promised to speak with President McKay about the Church issuing a statement on civil rights.[6]

After the meeting, President Brown and President Tanner asked Sterling McMurrin to help them prepare a statement for President McKay's approval. Albert Fritz, meanwhile, urged NAACP members to postpone the demonstration and give the Church time to issue the statement. Some of the protestors had already made picket signs, but they agreed to wait at least another week.[7]

On Saturday, October 5, President Brown notified the NAACP that President McKay had approved a statement, which President Brown then read at general conference the next morning.[8]

"There is in this Church no doctrine, belief, or practice that is intended to deny the enjoyment of full civil rights by any person, regardless of race, color, or creed," it declared. "We believe that all men are the children of the same God, and that it is a moral evil for any person or group of persons to deny any human being the right to gainful employment, to full educational opportunity, and to every privilege of citizenship."

"We call upon all men everywhere, both within and outside the Church, to commit themselves to the establishment of full civil equality for all of God's children," it continued. "Anything less than this defeats our high ideal of the brotherhood of man."[9]

The statement was front-page news in Salt Lake City and elsewhere. At Albert Fritz's request, the NAACP did not stage any demonstrations during the conference. He was hopeful that his organization and the Church could be allies.

"If we work in harmony," he said, "we will have a better state."[10]

THROUGHOUT 1963, HÉLIO DA ROCHA Camargo was frequently on the move in Brazil. He had received the Melchizedek Priesthood not long after Elder Spencer W. Kimball's 1959 South American tour, and now he served as a counselor in the Brazilian Mission presidency. With the Church growing rapidly in many parts of the country, his calling required him to meet with Saints in cities as far away as Rio de Janeiro, Belo Horizonte, Recife, and Brasília, the newly constructed capital of Brazil.[11]

Over the last four years, more than thirty-five thousand people had joined the Church in Latin America. In 1961, the first Spanish-language stake in the Church was organized in Mexico City. At the same time, the number of missions in South America had more than doubled. There were now two missions in Brazil, two in Argentina, one in Uruguay, one in Chile, and one that encompassed Peru and Bolivia.

In each of these missions, the goal was to spread the gospel widely, help the Saints live faithfully, and establish the first stakes in South America. Organizing these stakes would give members more authority to lead and serve in the Church, eliminating the need for leaders from outside their area.[12]

Wayne Beck, the president of the Brazilian Mission, and his predecessor, Grant Bangerter, both believed that the best way to prepare the Saints for the responsibility of stakes was to build up and train local Church leaders.[13] Hélio's experience as a Methodist minister made him an ideal candidate for Church leadership, and President Bangerter had quickly called him into positions of responsibility.

One of his first leadership callings was serving as a counselor in a district presidency with two other Brazilian Saints. His new duties had been unfamiliar at first, and after struggling to understand their purpose, he spoke to President Bangerter. "I'm not doing anything of value here," he said.

"What would you like to do?" the president asked.[14]

"I'd like to go back to my branch and be a teacher," Hélio replied. "I could be a good teacher."

President Bangerter then explained that local Saints were crucial to the development of the Church in their country. As a member of the district presidency, Hélio played a key role in calling and training local Church leaders and teachers.

"Now is the time when the Lord is raising up His servants for the establishment of His work in power in South America," the president said. "Some are to be called to carry the burden, and it has fallen to you."

Hélio suddenly saw Church leadership in a new light. Within a few weeks, he and the other members of the district presidency were working effectively.[15]

After that, Hélio had trained many local leaders—a responsibility that continued after a call to the mission presidency.[16] As a counselor to both President Bangerter and President Beck, he helped his fellow Saints improve the quality of their sacrament meetings, encouraged participation in Church building projects, and worked to strengthen branches. Now, wherever the Church was well established in the mission, branches and districts functioned essentially as wards and stakes. If a baptism or confirmation was needed, a Brazilian priesthood holder performed it.[17]

Hélio's wife, Nair, served as a counselor in the mission's Primary organization, where she did her part to prepare the Saints for stake leadership. Following a Churchwide pattern in the stakes, the presidency held a conference every year for Primary leaders and teachers. In her lessons to the women, Nair offered suggestions for teaching young children, improving Primary attendance, and using available curriculum and visual aids.[18]

"We ask God to bless all the work you have done for the children," she told Primary workers at the conference of 1963, "and that He increase our faith and our desire to live according to the principles of the gospel, dedicating ourselves with enthusiasm and sincerity in the work He has entrusted to us."[19]

In his work in the mission presidency, Hélio magnified his calling with the same fervor he'd had as a minister. He once told President Bangerter that true discipleship required total devotion and dedication to the cause of Christ.

"Any good Methodist knows this," Hélio said. And he believed that Latter-day Saints should understand it as well.[20]

NEAR THE END OF 1963, forty-four-year-old Walt Macey was restless. As the co-owner of three grocery stores in Salt Lake City, he was unsure if he should keep his stores open on Sundays. He had been taught growing up that the Sabbath was a sacred day of rest. But recently, he had noticed that many Latter-day Saints were shopping on the Sabbath just as other people did.

Everywhere he looked, he saw restaurants, gas stations, and shops open on Sunday. And his longtime business partner, Dale Jones, thought their grocery stores should stay open as well. They did a brisk business on Sundays, and Walt accepted the argument that staying open helped families who needed to shop on the weekends. Few households had two cars, and since husbands typically took the car to work on weekdays, Sunday was an important shopping day.[21]

Walt had never felt entirely comfortable operating the stores on the Sabbath. He was distressed by the thought that he was keeping the young people he employed from attending their religious meetings. Some years before, he had told Dale that their business would be blessed if they closed on Sundays. Dale disagreed. "We are not about to close," he said, settling the matter.[22]

Recently, however, a conversation with Joseph Fielding Smith, president of the Quorum of the Twelve Apostles, had troubled Walt. President Smith and his wife, Jessie, were regular customers at their store on the west side of Salt Lake City. One day, President Smith walked over to the meat counter where Walt was working.

"Brother Macey," he said, "I want you to remove that sign from the window." There were many signs on the window, so Walt asked which one he meant.

"The 'Open Sunday' sign," President Smith said. He told Walt that he preferred to shop at stores that honored the Sabbath by closing on Sundays. He then turned and walked out. Walt had not seen him in the store since.[23]

President Smith had been an apostle for over half a century. During that time, he had seen respect for the Sabbath day diminish among Christians around the world. While recognizing that there were understandable reasons for working on the Sabbath, he and other Church leaders worried about Sunday simply becoming another day of recreation and commerce.[24] Time and time again, they had raised their voice against using the Sabbath for sporting events, moviegoing, shopping, and other activities that could be done on other days. More than any other apostle of his time, Joseph Fielding Smith pleaded with the Saints to keep the Lord's day holy.[25]

"We must stop violating the Sabbath day," he had declared at the April 1957 general conference. "I promise you that if you will observe the Sabbath day, you who are opening your stores on the Sabbath day, if you will close them and tend to the duties that the Lord has given to you, and keep His commandments, that you will prosper."

Two years later, the First Presidency taught the same principle, calling on the Saints to cease shopping on Sundays.[26]

After his conversation with President Smith, Walt resolved to change. The impression came to him that he was falling short of what he knew was right.

Once again, he approached Dale about closing the stores on Sunday, and Dale refused to consider it. "Well," Walt said, "because this means so much to me, you better buy me out or I will buy you out."

A month later, Dale agreed to dissolve the partnership. He would take two of the stores and Walt the other. Walt decided to reopen his store under a new name: Macey's.[27]

Not long after, the *Deseret News* announced that Macey's would be closed on Sundays. That night at 11:15, Walt received a call at his home. It was Sister Smith. "The president wishes to speak with you," she said.

President Smith then came on the line. "Brother Macey," he said, "I see by tonight's paper that you have closed your store on the Sabbath. I'll be back."

A short time later, Walt noticed President Smith shopping at the store.[28]

AT THE BEGINNING OF 1964, Belle Spafford was in her nineteenth year as Relief Society general president. The organization had a worldwide membership of 262,002, with women in more more than six thousand ward and branch Relief Societies meeting regularly to learn from one another and provide compassionate service. The Relief Society raised and managed its own funds to run many programs, activities, and initiatives, including the *Relief Society Magazine,* which would soon celebrate fifty years in print.[29]

President Spafford was immensely proud of her Relief Society sisters. "In a day when women engage themselves in many activities and when a high number of them are employed, it is encouraging that average attendance at regular meetings of the society increased," she had recently observed at the organization's annual conference. "We are thankful for your devotion to Relief Society and the righteousness of your lives."[30]

As the new year began, President Spafford and her counselors, Marianne Sharp and Louise Madsen, had several months of travel ahead of them.

Under the new correlation program, the Relief Society general presidency and board were visiting stake conferences during the first half of the year to train local Relief Society leaders and speak to stake presidencies, high councils, bishoprics, and other stake and ward leaders. Attending these conferences gave them new opportunities to educate priesthood leaders about the work of Relief Society.[31]

As the Church organized more and more stakes outside the United States, the presidency also found themselves traveling internationally more often. They had recently trained stakes in Australia, New Zealand, and Samoa, and they visited the Saints in Europe in the spring.[32]

While visiting stake conferences around the world, President Spafford and her board members presented *The Awakening,* a filmstrip highlighting the importance of Relief Society.[33] Filmstrips were becoming a popular educational tool in and out of the Church, largely because they were affordable and simple to use. Through a series of images projected on a screen, *The Awakening* told the fictional story of Mary Smith, a member of the Church whose waning faith was rekindled through Relief Society and personal visits from ward members. In the final images of the filmstrip, Mary and her family had returned to church and were preparing to be sealed in the temple.[34]

For years, President Spafford and her counselors had typically approved Relief Society instructional materials. *The Awakening,* for instance, had been written and produced by Relief Society members of Salt Lake's Butler Stake before it was adopted by the Relief Society general presidency as part of their presentation to stakes.[35]

Recently, though, the responsibility for developing curriculum for Church organizations had been given to Elder Harold B. Lee and the newly created All-Church Coordinating Council. While the Relief Society was not yet using correlated lesson plans, the committee had begun requesting that all Church organizations submit outlines for lessons and other materials for approval.[36] President Spafford supported this change, and as a member of the coordinating council, she participated in the process of correlating Church lessons.[37]

On June 24, 1964, President Spafford's travels took her to the eastern United States for "Relief Society Day" at the New York World's Fair. As with the 1893 Columbian Exposition, the Church saw the fair as an opportunity to share its message on a global stage. It built a massive exhibition hall designed to look like the Salt Lake Temple and provided various presentations about the Savior and His gospel, including a popular fifteen-minute film called *Man's Search for Happiness,* which taught visitors about the plan of salvation.[38]

Relief Society Day was organized to showcase the achievements of Latter-day Saint women. The highlight of the day was a choir of "singing mothers" from stake Relief Societies in New York and other cities. Their performances drew good-sized crowds, and President Spafford thought that each concert improved on the one before it. The fair was a noisy place, but as the women blended their voices together in hymns and other sacred music, all the commotion seemed to fade away. To President Spafford, it was as if angels were singing along.

Afterward, a reporter asked her why there was no choir of "singing fathers."

"Well," she replied, "we are a woman's organization."[39]

AROUND THIS TIME, GIUSEPPA Oliva took a seat in a partially finished meetinghouse in Quilmes, Argentina. It was the first chapel in the country constructed by missionaries in the Church's building program, and the Saints attending district conference that morning were looking forward to its completion. Like so many meetinghouses around the world, it represented years of devoted service and sacrifice by the Saints who met there.[40]

Giuseppa and her husband, Renato, were from the Italian island of Sicily. Like many Italians, they had moved their family to Argentina after World War II to find better work. Although adapting to a new country, culture, and language had been difficult, they had made a home for their five children in South America. Seven years after leaving Sicily, Giuseppa met some Latter-day Saint missionaries, and she and her two daughters soon embraced their message. Since then, both daughters had married young men from the Church.[41]

Yet Giuseppa was troubled as she sat through the conference. An economic crisis was squeezing the nation. The cost of living in Argentina was rising 20 percent a year, and many people were losing their jobs as businesses struggled to pay employees. In the face of so much economic uncertainty, Renato, a basket maker, had moved back to Sicily, and he wanted his family to join him.[42]

Giuseppa was reluctant to go, however. In the five years since Elder Spencer W. Kimball's visit to Argentina, Church membership in the country had risen to more than eight thousand. Its branches were strong, and the tithes of faithful Saints had made the Argentine Mission financially self-sufficient for the first time in its history. The number of convert baptisms was on the rise, strengthening congregations like the one Giuseppa attended.

Italy, on the other hand, did not have a single branch of the Church. If Giuseppa chose to join Renato there, she would have to give up the blessings of regular Church attendance. And since Renato was not a member of the Church, he could not administer the sacrament or other priesthood ordinances to her.[43]

When the morning session of district conference ended, Giuseppa approached Arthur Strong, the president of the Argentine Mission, and told him of her dilemma. She said she wanted to stay with her daughters in Argentina, but she also felt she needed to be with her husband in Europe.

President Strong listened and then recommended that she return to Italy. "That is the place you belong," he said.

"What should I do about the Church?" Giuseppa asked.

"The Church will grow in your own city," he promised. "You will not have to worry about it."

Giuseppa was skeptical. Could such a thing really be possible? But she decided to trust in the Lord and return to Italy. Her faith, after all, had yet to lead her astray.[44]

IN JUNE 1964, EIGHTEEN-YEAR-OLD Darius Gray saw that a new family had moved into his neighborhood. As he walked past their house, he noticed a bunch of kids playing outside.

"We're the Felixes," one of them announced. "We're Mormons!"[45]

Darius, an African American, had grown up attending a variety of churches with his parents, including some predominantly Black churches. His interest in religion had ultimately led him to study Catholicism, Judaism, Islam, and the Baha'i Faith. But even though he lived in Colorado, a state that bordered Utah, he knew very little about the Latter-day Saints. And he was sure he had never met one.

Over the next few months, he got to know the new family. John Felix was a ham radio operator and taught Morse code to Darius. Barbara, John's wife, was more interested in sharing her religion. She and her children gave him a copy of the Book of Mormon. He was hesitant to take it, but he enjoyed books and eventually started reading it.[46]

The words of the Book of Mormon spoke to his soul, and he invited the missionaries to visit him. His father had passed away some years ago, so it was just him and his mother, Elsie, at home. She was a strong Christian who was always open to talking with people of other religions. Darius did not think she would mind if the missionaries came over.

During the visit, however, she stayed in her bedroom. And when the young men left, she called Darius to her.

"I don't want those two young men back here," she said.

"Why not?" Darius asked.

"This is my house," she said, "and I don't want them here."

Darius knew not to question her, but it was hard to let the subject go. When he finally asked her again why she was opposed to the missionaries, she explained that two Latter-day Saint missionaries had once visited her home. They had been inside for only a moment when one of the missionaries asked if she was Black.

"Yes, of course," she had replied.

The two missionaries then left with no explanation, and ever since, she'd had a negative feeling about the Church.

The story bothered Darius. He believed his mother, but he also wondered if her negative experience was somehow unique.[47]

Darius continued to study with the missionaries, and it wasn't long before he decided to join the Church. On the day before his baptism, however, he asked the missionaries about the Church's teachings on race. He wondered how they applied to him.

For a moment, no one spoke. One of the missionaries then stood and walked slowly to the corner of the room, his back turned to Darius. The other missionary said, "Well, Brother Gray, the primary implication is that you won't be able to hold the priesthood."

Darius suddenly felt foolish. "Mom was right," he thought. How could he join the Church now? He knew what it felt like to be treated differently because he was Black, and he refused to see himself as less than anyone else.[48]

That night, Darius climbed into bed and wrapped himself in a quilt. He believed in God and in salvation through Jesus Christ. And, until today, he had believed in everything the missionaries had taught him. Now he did not know what to do. How could he reconcile his faith with what he'd learned about the Church's priesthood restriction?

Sliding open a nearby window, he leaned his head against the sill. The night air filled his lungs, and he offered a prayer. When he finished, he closed the window and tried to sleep. But he tossed and turned until finally he felt he should pray one more time. Once again, he slid open the window and began to pray.

This time, a clear, audible voice spoke to him. "This is the restored gospel," it said, "and you are to join."

All at once, Darius knew what he had to do. The next day, he entered the waters of baptism and became a member of The Church of Jesus Christ of Latter-day Saints.[49]

CHAPTER 8

A Matter of Saving Souls

As the new Primary president in Colonia Suiza, Uruguay, Delia Rochon relied heavily on her lesson manual. The Church had produced the handbook specifically for Primary teachers and leaders living in the missions, and Delia prayed frequently about how best to use it. The manual had been written before the Church's Correlation Committee had begun reviewing and simplifying all Church materials, and it was three hundred pages long. Still, Delia was grateful for the many ideas for activities and crafts it provided. Although the Primary children were sometimes rowdy during her lessons, Delia was patient. If they misbehaved, she could always get their parents to help.[1]

When preparing Primary lessons, Delia felt a duty to follow official Church materials closely. One day, she came across instructions for holding an annual fund drive for the Primary Children's Hospital in Salt Lake City. The drive, which had taken place each year since 1922, encouraged every Primary child to donate pennies to help other children in need. Delia had never seen a penny before, and she knew very little about the hospital. Nor did she have to go looking for children in need—there were plenty in her Primary class. But she and branch president Victor Solari felt she should still hold a penny drive for the hospital.[2]

Instead of pennies, Delia asked the children to donate *vintenes,* the coin with the lowest value in Uruguay. One of the parents made a little wooden collection box, which Delia hung on a wall in the meetinghouse. She told the Primary that the money would help children who were ill, but she was careful not to put pressure on her class. She did not want them donating any *vintenes* they could not afford to give.

Over the next few months, Delia did not look inside the little box or point out who was donating and who was not. Sometimes the children would bring in *vintenes,* and other times a parent would donate a few coins to support the Primary. Occasionally, she would hear the clink of a coin as it was dropped inside, and the children would clap at the sound.

When the mission leaders visited the Colonia Suiza Branch, Delia decided to open the box. It was much fuller than she expected. When she counted the coins, the children had donated nearly two American dollars. In Delia's hands, the coins felt like a fortune.

More than that, she realized, the *vintenes* represented the faith and sacrifice of the Primary children—and the children's families. Each coin was a widow's mite, given with love for others and the Savior.[3]

TWO DAYS BEFORE CHRISTMAS in 1964, Suzie Towse sat nervously on a train. Her mission at the British Area Office of the Church Building Department was over. Now she was on her way back to Beverley. Her parents were glad she was finally coming home, but they were still upset that she had chosen to finish her mission against their will. She had hardly heard a word from them in nine months.

Suzie did not regret her choice. Serving in the Building Department had brought her and hundreds of other young women and men closer to their Heavenly Father, and they returned home with stronger faith and valuable work experience. Their efforts had contributed to the completion of nearly thirty construction projects in the British Isles, including a beautiful chapel in Beverley. And more than forty other projects were still underway. As Suzie reflected on their work, a building missionary motto kept coming to mind: "As we build churches, we build people."[4]

Now, with her mission over, Suzie could look forward to a new chapter in her life. A year ago, mission leaders had let her and other building missionaries return home for the Christmas season. At a New Year's

Eve dance, her friend and fellow branch member Geoff Dunning had approached her and asked her to waltz. Knowing he was a member of the branch's fellowshipping committee, she had teased him. "Geoff," she said, "you don't need to carry your fellowshipping this far."

They had begun writing to each other as boyfriend and girlfriend after that, and they were engaged within a few months. Geoff had even sent her a diamond engagement ring through the mail, and the postman had knelt when he delivered it. They planned to be sealed in the London Temple after Suzie's mission. But since the law required them to be married civilly, they would have a wedding ceremony in the Beverley chapel first.[5]

At Suzie's request, Geoff had visited her parents several times, hoping to soften their feelings toward her and the Church. At first, Suzie's mother had resisted Geoff's efforts, but she soon warmed to him.

When Suzie arrived in Beverley, her parents welcomed her home. But they told her they would not be attending her wedding because it was taking place in the branch meetinghouse. Disappointed, Suzie and Geoff prayed for her parents to have a change of heart.[6]

As she adjusted to life after the mission, Suzie found that her branch had changed in her absence—and not just because of the new chapel. Across Britain, missionaries were now spending more time instructing prospective converts, and they taught whole families when possible. Rapid baptisms, baseball games, and the aggressive mission goals that propelled them were gone. President McKay had continued to oppose such practices and directed local leaders to reach out to the youth affected by them, making every effort to encourage these converts to stay in the Church.

"They are members, and we must keep them," he declared. "It is a matter of saving souls rather than statistics. We must work with these young boys and girls."[7]

Ten days before the wedding, Suzie and Geoff's prayers were answered. Suzie's parents decided to attend the ceremony. Her father wanted to walk her down the aisle, and her mother agreed to organize the wedding reception in the chapel.

On March 6, 1965, many of Suzie's friends from the Church Building Department came to Beverley for the wedding. A week later, Suzie and Geoff traveled to the London Temple to be sealed. While they were at the temple, Suzie's mother cleaned up a small home the couple had purchased for themselves in Beverley.

Thinking about the challenges she had overcome, Suzie remembered what her mission president had told her during those difficult days—"The Lord will prepare a way"—and now she knew He had.[8]

THE FOLLOWING MONTH, IN Salt Lake City, Ruth Funk and the committee over adult curriculum gathered nearly two dozen leaders from various Church organizations to propose a plan for teaching Relief Society, priesthood, and Sunday School classes. The proposal was the result of the committee's three-year study of the Church's past lesson plans. Committee chair Thomas S. Monson, who had been called to the Quorum of the Twelve Apostles a year and a half earlier, conducted the meeting.[9]

The All-Church Coordinating Council, which oversaw the new correlation program, had already introduced several important changes to the Church. Among them was the creation of priesthood executive committees and ward councils to help local leaders serve together more effectively. In response to concerns about the stability of home and family, the coordinating council had also emphasized two programs, home teaching and family home evening, to strengthen gospel learning.[10]

These programs had deep roots in the Church. Since the days of the prophet Joseph Smith, ward or block teachers had regularly visited the homes of Saints to tend to their spiritual and temporal well-being. The home teaching program modified this practice, asking priesthood holders to visit the homes of fellow Saints every month to provide Christlike service and to deliver a correlated message from the Church.[11]

Similarly, the Saints had been holding home evenings since 1915, when President Joseph F. Smith and his counselors had encouraged the Saints to set aside at least one evening a month for gospel lessons and activities in the home. Now, the Saints were to hold family home evening every week and use a manual the Church had recently published.[12]

The Church's correlated curriculum continued to face delays, however. Initially, Elder Harold B. Lee had thought the various correlation committees could produce lesson plans for all age groups by 1963, but they pushed the deadline back to 1966 in order to write lessons for the family home evening program.[13]

As Elder Monson introduced the curriculum proposal to the assembled leaders, he acknowledged the challenge of producing the new lessons, especially when the organizations had generally written their own curriculum in the past.

"Agreement will not come easily," he said. "We should take the instructions of the scriptures in 3 Nephi wherein the Lord said, 'Neither shall there be disputations among you.'"[14]

During the meeting, Ruth presented the committee's plans for the women's curriculum. In drafting their proposal, the committee had consulted women in a variety of circumstances—married, unmarried, divorced, or widowed. The proposal pointed out the many pressures women faced in the modern world and emphasized their purpose in God's eternal plan.

As Ruth described it, the new curriculum for women, like the curriculum for men in the Church, would underscore the importance of priesthood and the role of the home as the center of gospel learning. Its main objectives were to inspire women to live and teach the gospel, provide compassionate service to others, gain practical knowledge of homemaking, and develop a sense of well-being through the teachings of Christ.[15]

In the months following the presentation, Ruth was impressed by Belle Spafford and the other Relief Society leaders who cooperated with the committee. But not everyone was enthusiastic about the coming changes. When Ruth and other committee members suggested adjustments to the curriculum, some members of the Relief Society board resisted their efforts.

Ruth's belief in the need for correlation helped her persist despite these problems. She could see how correlation strengthened the Church and its members. The challenge was finding a way to help skeptics of the program grasp the same vision.[16]

AROUND THIS SAME TIME, LaMar Williams was still trying to secure a permanent visa to Nigeria. He longed to fulfill his duties as the country's presiding elder, but how could he if its government refused to let him in?

Since his first trip to Nigeria in 1961, he had managed to obtain only one other short-term visa, allowing him to return to the country for two weeks in February 1964. At that time, he and his friends Charles Agu and Dick Obot had tried to petition the government to allow missionaries in Nigeria, but the official responsible for deciding their case declined to meet with them.[17]

LaMar returned to Utah deeply frustrated by his lack of success, yet he refused to give up on his friends in

West Africa. With his help, a scholarship fund was created so several Nigerian students could attend Brigham Young University. The students arrived in early 1965, and two of them, Oscar Udo and Atim Ekpenyong, joined the Church.[18]

In Nigeria, meanwhile, Dick Obot learned that his worship group—known locally as "the Church of Jesus Christ of Latter Day Saints"— had received government recognition, suggesting some hearts in Nigeria were softening. LaMar's efforts to provide educational opportunities for Nigerian students, along with the ongoing lobbying of his friends in Nigeria, did not go unnoticed. Although the Nigerian government still refused to grant him a permanent visa, he received another short-term travel visa in August 1965. With President McKay's blessing, LaMar returned to Nigeria in October.[19]

After arriving in Lagos, LaMar met with a lawyer who was optimistic about securing both a permanent visa and Church recognition. Two days later, LaMar spoke with about a dozen communications officials about the Church. He then flew to Enugu, the capital of Nigeria's Eastern Region, and spent time with its minister of state, who declined to drink coffee, tea, or alcohol in LaMar's presence out of respect for his beliefs.

Everywhere LaMar went, strangers asked him if they could become members of the Church. LaMar assured them that if the Church were established in their nation, they could be baptized. One Sunday, over four hundred people gathered to hear him speak.

A Matter of Saving Souls

On November 6, a visit to the premier's office in Enugu resulted in a ninety-day extension to LaMar's visa, and a government official began the paperwork necessary to register the Church in Nigeria. LaMar returned to his hotel room with good reason to be cheerful. After years of roadblocks and runarounds, the permission he needed to begin the work might finally be granted.

Then he heard a knock at the door. The private secretary of the minister of state had a telegram for him from Church headquarters.

"Discontinue negotiations in Nigeria," it read. "Return home immediately." It was signed by the First Presidency, with no further explanation attached.[20]

AT THE TIME LAMAR Williams left Nigeria, Giuseppa Oliva was living in Palermo, Italy, trusting in the promise that the Church would one day come to the city. A century earlier, missionaries had tried to establish the Church in Italy, but their efforts were short-lived. Many of their converts were Waldensian Protestants from northwest Italy who emigrated to Utah before missionaries withdrew from the country in the 1860s. Giuseppa was not one to sit still and wait for missionaries to return, however. Soon after arriving from Argentina, she began sharing the gospel with her relatives, neighbors, and friends.[21]

Some people were put off by her enthusiasm, and they would shut their doors in her face or demand that she leave their homes. But one day one of her brothers, Antonino Giurintano, asked why she was not attending Catholic Mass. When she told him about the Church, Joseph Smith, and the Book of Mormon, he became intrigued. He had spent several years visiting different churches but felt unsatisfied by them.

After that, Giuseppa talked to him about the restored gospel almost every day. Much to her joy, he soon asked to be baptized. But without any missionaries in Sicily, there was no one who could perform the ordinance.

At the time, the Swiss Mission oversaw Italy and several neighboring countries, and the missionary force was spread thin.[22] Although there were some small congregations on American military bases in Italy, the Church had only recently received approval to preach the gospel in the country. The thirty or forty missionaries serving in Italy were mostly in the north, far from Giuseppa and Antonino's island.[23] Still, Antonino wrote to the mission headquarters, and in return, mission president Rendell Mabey sent him some Church literature and a copy of the Book of Mormon.

Then, on the evening of November 22, 1965, Giuseppa was startled by an unexpected visit from her brother. Antonino told her that two men from the Church had finally come. Giuseppa rounded up her husband and son, and they followed Antonino back to his home.

One of the visitors, Giuseppa discovered, was President Mabey. He was a tall, cheerful American who did not speak Italian. The other visitor was Vincenzo di Francesca, an elderly Italian Latter-day Saint who happened to live on the island, some four hours away.[24] In 1910, Vincenzo had found a coverless copy of the Book of Mormon while training to be a Protestant minister in New York City. He read it eagerly and embraced its message of Jesus Christ. Sometimes he even preached from the book, and upon returning to Italy, he learned more about the Church and made contact with it. After years of waiting for someone with priesthood authority to come to Sicily, he was baptized at long last in 1951.[25]

Giuseppa and her family talked with Vincenzo and President Mabey for several hours. Then the mission president concluded that Antonino was ready for baptism.

Early the next morning, Giuseppa, Antonino, President Mabey, and Vincenzo purchased some white clothes and took a taxi to a quiet bay up the coast where they could hold the service. A small cove provided a dressing room, and rocks along the shore offered a place for Vincenzo to sit and act as witness for the baptism.

President Mabey and Antonino hobbled, hand in hand, over the beach's small, sharp rocks. Battling the cold and rough waves, President Mabey spoke the baptismal prayer and lowered Antonino into the water. The men then returned to shore and changed into dry clothes, and Vincenzo confirmed Antonino a member of the Church.

Joy and love filled Giuseppa's heart as she watched the service. Later, she sent an emotional letter to her daughter Maria, who was still living in Argentina. Antonino had joined the Church, she exclaimed. He was the first person baptized since she returned to Palermo.[26]

CHAPTER 9

This Marvelous Day

In late 1965, Hélio da Rocha Camargo answered the telephone in his office in São Paulo, Brazil. Wayne Beck, the president of the Brazilian Mission, was on the other end of the line. He wanted to know if Hélio could leave work early and come to the mission office. Victor L. Brown, a counselor in the Presiding Bishopric of the Church, was visiting São Paulo, and he wanted to speak with Hélio before returning to Utah.

Hélio, who now worked for an automobile company, went immediately to the mission office. He and President Beck had recently discussed various mission-related matters with Bishop Brown, including the state of Church publications in Brazil, and Hélio assumed the bishop wanted to continue the conversation.[1]

When Hélio arrived at the mission office, Bishop Brown told him a major change was coming to the Church in Brazil. There were now over twenty-three thousand Saints in the country, more than ten times as many as when Hélio was baptized eight years earlier. To accommodate this growth, the First Presidency wanted to establish a central editorial office to manage Church publications in Brazil.

Recently, the First Presidency had opened a similar office in Mexico City to oversee Church publications in Spanish-speaking nations. Since the Church was producing several new correlated handbooks and manuals, it made sense to funnel this work through central offices rather than expect the missions to handle the massive publishing task on their own. The new center in Brazil would translate all Church publications into Portuguese and then print and distribute them among the Saints.[2]

"I want to invite you to be in charge of the work, making you a full-time employee of the Church," Bishop Brown told Hélio.

"The only possible response is yes," Hélio replied.[3]

Soon after accepting the new position, Hélio and Nair sold their car so they could visit the United States and attend the Salt Lake Temple. During the month they were in Utah, they met often with the Saints, marveling at the size and strength of their wards and stakes. From what Hélio could tell, Relief Society, Primary, Sunday School, and priesthood quorum classes were full of Church members who were firm in the faith. He knew the Church in Brazil was still growing, and it would take time for it to operate as smoothly as it did in Utah. But he believed the Brazilian Saints were nearly ready for a stake.

"With the leadership we have now," he thought, "we will soon be equaling our brethren of the United States, because our people are also good, and when they want to do something, they do it."[4]

Before leaving Utah, Hélio and Nair were endowed and sealed in the Salt Lake Temple and received their patriarchal blessings from Eldred G. Smith, the patriarch to the Church. Friends from the United States, including former mission presidents Asael Sorensen and Grant Bangerter, attended the sealing. Elder Spencer W. Kimball, who had a special place in the Camargos' hearts after blessing their ill son, performed the ceremony.[5]

Hélio and Nair returned to Brazil in mid-December 1965, and Hélio immediately began setting up the central editorial office while continuing his duties in the mission presidency.[6] As he attended conferences around the mission, he tried to inspire the Saints with a vision of what the Church in Brazil would be once stakes were organized in their part of the world.

At a district conference just outside of São Paulo, he lamented that they had so little time to meet and learn together as Saints. "We must hold on as much as possible to everything we are taught," he said. He urged members to help their branch presidents and be obedient to the principles of the gospel. A branch was like a race car, he explained. "The MIA, Primary, Relief Society, and Sunday School are the four tires," he said. "The priesthood is the motor, and the driver is the branch president." Each individual part had a role in making the car function.

He urged them to keep the commandments enthusiastically. "We must be obedient," he declared, "if we want to be a stake."[7]

AT THE START OF 1966, LaMar Williams still did not understand why the First Presidency had called him home from Nigeria. A few hours after receiving their telegram, he had caught a flight out of the country. His contacts in the Nigerian government did not want him to leave in the middle of their negotiations.[8]

LaMar had hoped to get more clarity once he arrived in Salt Lake City. Shortly after his return, he had met with the First Presidency and expressed his confusion over his sudden call home. He told them about his promising meetings with government officials and the thousands of enthusiastic Nigerians who wanted to join the Church.[9]

But the First Presidency had already voiced misgivings about the future of the mission. While LaMar had been in Nigeria, President McKay had called two additional counselors, apostle Joseph Fielding Smith and Thorpe B. Isaacson, to the First Presidency. President Isaacson, who had been an Assistant to the Twelve before his call, seemed particularly concerned about how Nigerian Saints would respond to the priesthood restriction.

Furthermore, some of the apostles worried that proselytizing among Black populations in Nigeria would prompt civil rights groups in the United States to pressure the Church to rescind the restriction. Others worried that preaching the gospel in Nigeria would offend the segregationist apartheid officials in South Africa and possibly provoke them into restricting missionary work in their country.[10]

LaMar had tried his best to ease the concerns of the presidency. "It might be a good thing for one or more of the general authorities to go to Nigeria and look the situation over before the final decision is made," he suggested. The First Presidency, however, did not think such a course was the right one to take.

LaMar left the meeting discouraged. He believed that the Lord wanted him to establish the Church in Nigeria. The scriptures taught that the gospel message was for all people and that the Lord denied none that came unto Him—"black and white, bond and free, male and female." If that was true, why had the First Presidency called him home?[11]

Then, on January 15, 1966, two months after LaMar had returned to Utah, officers in the Nigerian army staged a military coup, orchestrating the murder of the prime minister and other government officials. Loyalist forces quickly put down the revolt, but the coup aggravated regional tensions and destabilized the country.

News of the conflict unsettled LaMar. Even if he had been able to set up a mission in Nigeria, the coup would have put an end to his work. He now believed the time had not been right to establish the Church there.[12]

Yet he worried about his many friends in Nigeria. "I am sorry that the First Presidency called me home unexpectedly," he told Charles Agu in a letter shortly after the coup. "Please let me know if I can be of any further service or encouragement to you in your desire to serve the Lord and those about you."

"Charles, it would break my heart if you lost faith and courage to continue on the fine work that you have begun," he wrote. "I have never doubted that the Lord's work will eventually be established in your country. I feel it in my heart, and I am sure that the Spirit beareth record. How long it will take I do not know."[13]

Around this time, in Colonia Suiza, Uruguay, Delia Rochon was reading the Book of Mormon at home when she received a spiritual impression: "You need to leave."

It was the most powerful prompting she had ever felt. She was only sixteen, and leaving home would disrupt life as she knew it. But she also knew that staying where she was would keep her from growing and developing as a follower of Christ.

Since Delia's baptism, her mother had supported her and had sometimes even come to Church activities. But the family struggled financially, and there was tension between her stepfather and mother. Her father, meanwhile, lived far away and thought the Church was cutting her off from her family. When she stayed with him, she could not hold Primary or attend her meetings.[14]

Fortunately, several times a year Delia could leave home to go to district conferences and mission activities in Montevideo and other cities. Delia loved attending these faraway meetings, especially MIA conferences where she could make friends with other Latter-day Saint youth—an opportunity she did not have in her own small branch. The testimony meeting at the end of every convention helped her faith grow even more.[15]

Shortly after receiving her impression, Delia spoke to the branch president. President Solari knew Delia's family and did not try to persuade her to stay. He mentioned a couple in town, the Pellegrinis. They were not members of the Church, but their daughter, Miryam, was.

"Let's see if her family could take you in," President Solari said.

The Pellegrinis were always willing to help someone in need, and they gladly invited Delia to live with them. Delia accepted their kind offer and agreed to assist with the house cleaning and to work for a few hours a day in the shop across the street. Although moving away from home was difficult, Delia thrived in her new surroundings. With the Pellegrinis, she found support and stability.[16]

Still, her life was not entirely free of conflict. Uruguay was one of the most prosperous countries in South America, but its economy was in a slump. Some people were deeply suspicious of the United States, and they saw communism as an answer to their country's financial woes. As other countries in South America experienced similar economic setbacks, anti-Americanism swept through the continent.[17] Since the Church's headquarters were in the United States, South American Saints sometimes encountered mistrust and hostility.

Many of Delia's classmates talked about their support of communism. To avoid controversy, Delia revealed her Church membership and beliefs to only a few classmates. If she spoke too openly, she risked being mocked.

One evening, the missionaries stopped by Delia's house. She was just leaving for MIA, so the missionaries joined her. It was pleasant outside, but as they approached the town plaza, Delia knew what was coming. Many of her peers liked to gather at the plaza. If they saw her with the North American missionaries, they would find out she was a Latter-day Saint.

Delia looked at the missionaries, and she decided she couldn't act ashamed of them. "I know I am a Mormon," she told herself, "but how much of a Mormon am I?"

Gathering her courage, she crossed the plaza alongside the missionaries. She knew she would face isolation at school, but she could not turn from her beliefs. Her testimony of the restored gospel was too strong.

Like Joseph Smith, she knew it was true. She could not deny it.[18]

IN FEBRUARY 1966, BRAZILIAN Mission president Wayne Beck submitted a proposal to Church leaders in Salt Lake City recommending the organization of a stake in São Paulo.

The city had three functioning districts, twenty branches, and roughly fifty-five hundred Saints, and President Beck and other local leaders had considered requesting more than one stake. There were no other stakes in South America, however, and they agreed that it would be best to first organize a central stake made up of the strongest units from each of the São Paulo districts. The Church could then create additional stakes in São Paulo and other Brazilian cities over the next few years.[19]

"I think that we have just as fine leadership and as forward-looking people in this area as we have anywhere in the world," President Beck stated in his proposal. "They are prepared, I believe, to accept the responsibilities and to do their part."[20]

The following month, Elder Spencer W. Kimball, the apostle who oversaw the Church's seven South American missions, presented the proposal to the Quorum of the Twelve. Many of the apostles were enthusiastic about the idea. They had traveled throughout the Church and knew how much the Saints benefited from stake responsibilities. Under the prophet's direction, several apostles had already created stakes outside of North America, and they testified of feeling the Spirit while doing this work.[21]

After considering President Beck's proposal, the First Presidency and Quorum of the Twelve Apostles approved the creation of the stake. One week later, President McKay and his counselors sent President Beck a letter announcing the news.

"It was the unanimous sentiment of the council that a stake organization be created in Brazil with headquarters in São Paulo," they informed him. "We are praying that the Lord will continue to bless you in your labors."[22]

In Palermo, Italy, Giuseppa Oliva continued to share the gospel with friends and neighbors. Among the people she taught was an eighteen-year-old named Salvatore Ferrante. He worked at the same factory as her brother Antonino, and he had been fascinated by the teachings of the Book of Mormon.

After giving Salvatore a copy of the book, Giuseppa wrote President Mabey asking for more materials. He agreed to send her another Book of Mormon, as well as a copy of the Doctrine and Covenants, which had recently been translated into Italian. President Mabey also mentioned that he had received a letter from Salvatore expressing interest in baptism.

"He will be baptized," President Mabey promised Giuseppa. "Until then, please continue to teach him and prepare him for baptism."[23]

A few months later, Giuseppa met with President Mabey, Antonino, and Salvatore at Antonino's house to gauge Salvatore's readiness for baptism. They discussed the Word of Wisdom, tithing, and other gospel principles, using the Doctrine and Covenants as a reference. The discussion went well, despite the language barrier, but because Salvatore lived at home, President Mabey said he needed his parents' permission to be baptized.

The group took a bus to Salvatore's home. It was on a narrow street with clotheslines hanging from the buildings. Before long, they saw Salvatore's father, Girolamo, rounding the corner of the street. President Mabey approached him and greeted him in German, the only language he knew other than English. Girolamo responded in German, explaining that he had spent two years as a prisoner of war in Vienna during the Second World War.

The moment Girolamo learned that President Mabey was there to baptize his son, he broke into rapid Italian, his displeasure evident in his tone and waving hands. Giuseppa and her brother shouted back, their overlapping voices echoing through the street.

"I want you to know," President Mabey interjected in German, "that what your son wants to do is right and just."

With those words, the tension dissolved. Girolamo invited the group up to his home, where Giuseppa pressed him to give his permission for the baptism. She bore her testimony and pleaded with him to honor his son's righteous desire.

"Well, if you want to baptize him and if he wants to be baptized," he finally said, "he has my permission on one condition—that I can watch."[24]

Salvatore was baptized later that day at the same beach where Antonino's baptism had taken place six months earlier.

Shortly after Salvatore's confirmation, the Saints gathered at Antonino's house. President Mabey, with the help of Girolamo as translator, taught about priesthood authority and conferred the Aaronic Priesthood on Antonino and Salvatore. He then formally organized the Palermo Branch with Antonino as its leader. After the meeting, Salvatore's father said, "This is a day that I'll never forget."[25]

The following week, the branch met at Giuseppa's home and partook of the sacrament. A short time later, she received word from President Mabey that the Church was organizing an Italian Mission. Soon missionaries would be arriving in Sicily.

"I am just as sure," he wrote, "that your dream of a branch in Palermo as big as the one in Argentina will come true."[26]

ON THE DAY HÉLIO da Rocha Camargo and his staff officially opened the Church's Brazilian central editorial office, they knelt together in prayer. No one there seemed to know exactly what to do, but this did not alarm Hélio. What alarmed him was that everyone there seemed to think that *he* knew what to do.[27]

After returning from Salt Lake City, he had made a detailed inventory of all Church literature at the Brazilian and Brazilian South Mission offices. He rented space in an office building in São Paulo, set up a headquarters, and hired a small team to organize and translate the literature. Among the people he hired was Walter Guedes de Queiroz, who had left the Methodist seminary with him and joined the Church.[28]

By the end of April 1966, after its first month of operation, the editorial office was handling the distribution of all Church literature in Brazil. Individual Saints and Church leaders in the country now ordered materials directly from the office rather than from the mission. Hélio also transferred the production of *A Liahona*, the Church's Portuguese-language magazine for Brazilian Saints, from the mission to the editorial office.[29]

On the afternoon of Tuesday, April 26, Elder Spencer W. Kimball arrived in São Paulo to organize a stake. Since he had a stake presidency to call, along with a stake high council and several bishoprics to fill, he hardly slept over the next few days as he interviewed potential candidates in the city. He did not speak Portuguese, so President Beck usually served as his translator.

In most interviews, Elder Kimball asked, "Are you happy in the Church?" The men responded with a sincerity that brought tears to his eyes. "It is my life," some of them said. "I could never get along without it." Others testified, "It is the greatest thing in the world" and "I never lived until I joined the Church." Some men told Elder Kimball about how the gospel had changed their lives, helping them overcome alcohol, tobacco, or sexual immorality.[30]

Hélio was one of the first people Elder Kimball interviewed, and many people believed he would make a good stake president. In fact, in interview after interview, Elder Kimball listened as people praised Hélio's leadership and recommended him for the position. But after interviewing Hélio one more time, Elder Kimball believed the Lord had another work for him to do.[31]

On Sunday, May 1, Hélio and Nair, their children, and more than fifteen hundred Saints crowded into a large São Paulo meetinghouse to witness the organization of the stake. To make room for more people, the curtains dividing the chapel from the cultural hall were opened. And after every seat was taken, some people set up chairs in the aisles while others sat outside, listening to the conference through a public address system.[32]

President Beck was full of emotion as he opened the meeting. After welcoming the Saints, he turned the time over to Elder Kimball, who said, "It is a great joy for me to be here, on assignment from the First Presidency of the Church, on this marvelous day, to create the first stake of South America in the great land of São Paulo."

He spoke briefly about the beginnings of the Church in South America. Elder Melvin J. Ballard, who dedicated South America for the preaching of the restored gospel in 1925, had prophesied that the Church in South America would grow slowly, like a tiny acorn becoming a mighty oak, and eventually be one of the strongest regions in the Church.

"We see how it is growing throughout South America," Elder Kimball said, "in Argentina, in Uruguay, in Chile, in Peru, in Paraguay, and in great Brazil, with its gentle, sweet people, who accepted Christ's call and have dedicated the best of their lives to the growth of His Church."[33]

Reading from a prepared statement in Portuguese, he then created the São Paulo Stake with seven new wards and one branch. He called Walter Spät, a furniture manufacturer, as stake president. Walter had joined the Church in 1950 and had been a branch and district president before serving as an assistant to the mission presidency.[34]

After Elder Kimball organized the stake presidency and called other stake leaders, all of whom were local Saints, he announced the new bishoprics and branch presidency. Among them was Hélio, who was called to serve as the bishop of the São Paulo Second Ward.[35]

The weight of the calling bore down on Hélio. Although he had a lot of leadership experience in the Church, he had never been a branch or district president, and the responsibility of serving a large congregation seemed enormous.[36] Still, he knew the Lord blessed His servants and helped them succeed.

"Isaiah thought that he could not be a prophet, but he accepted the calling and went forth," he had recently told a group of priesthood leaders. "When we are called to a work, we respond that we are not capable. If we think like that, we will never be capable. We must remember that it is the Lord who is calling us, and we must not deny it."[37]

After the conference, Elder Kimball shook hands with the Saints. Hélio stood nearby, smiling and greeting well-wishers.[38] The following day, he would return to work at the central editorial office, and in the evening, he would hold a bishopric meeting, possibly the first of its kind on the continent.

It marked a new day for Hélio—and a new day for the Church.[39]

PART 2

Wait for the Lord

1966–1978

"I will wait for the Lord.
If it takes me twenty years, I will
wait for the Lord."

Joseph William Billy Johnson

CHAPTER 10

Time Is Crucial

In the spring of 1966, Dr. Aziz Atiya followed an attendant into a storehouse of documents in New York City's Metropolitan Museum of Art. Looking around, he found a file and opened it. What he saw astonished him.

Inside were scraps of ancient Egyptian papyrus. The papyrus was badly damaged, but Aziz could easily make out the image of two men, one of them lying on a lion-shaped couch and the other standing beside him. The portion of the papyrus depicting the arms and torso of the man on the couch, along with the head of the standing figure, was missing. In a crude effort to preserve the document, someone had glued the papyrus to a piece of paper and roughly drawn in the lost parts.[1]

Aziz was not a member of The Church of Jesus Christ of Latter-day Saints, but as a professor of history and languages at the University of Utah, he had lived among the Saints long enough to recognize that he was looking at an image from the Book of Abraham in the Pearl of Great Price.[2]

Nine other papyrus fragments were stored with this image. As Aziz studied them, he found a certificate affirming that they had once been the property of the prophet Joseph Smith. The certificate was dated 1856 and was signed by Joseph Smith III, Emma Smith, and Emma's second husband, Lewis Bidamon.[3]

The fragments came from a set of papyrus scrolls the prophet Joseph and other Saints had obtained when they purchased four mummies from an antiquities exhibitor in 1835. Seven years later, he published images from the papyrus along with a translation called the Book of Abraham. Years after Joseph's death, Emma sold the mummies and papyri, and the new owner divided them up and sold some of them to a nearby museum. For decades, the scrolls had been deemed lost in a fire, but somehow a collection of fragments had found its way east to the Metropolitan Museum.[4]

"These documents don't belong here," Aziz said. He knew how important the fragments were to the Church, and he resolved to help reunite them with the Saints.[5]

That same year, fourteen-year-old Isabel Santana was overwhelmed by her new surroundings. She had just left her home in Ciudad Obregón, a city in northern

Mexico, to attend the Centro Escolar Benemérito de las Américas, a Church-owned school in Mexico City. The capital was a sprawling metropolis of seven million people, and everyone seemed to dress and speak differently than the people she knew back home.

The way they said "please," "thank you," and "excuse me" was so formal. That was not how people spoke in the north.[6]

The restored gospel had taken root in Mexico in the 1800s, and the country now had two strong stakes. Over the past two decades, the number of Latter-day Saints in Mexico had grown from about five thousand to more than thirty-six thousand.

As membership increased, Church leaders wanted to make sure the rising generation of Mexican Saints received every opportunity for schooling and occupational training.[7] In 1957, the First Presidency appointed a committee to investigate education in Mexico and make recommendations for establishing Church schools throughout the country. Finding that urban areas did not have enough schools to accommodate Mexico's booming population, the committee proposed opening at least a dozen primary schools across the country, as well as a secondary school, junior college, and teacher training school in Mexico City.

At the time, the Church operated schools in New Zealand, Western Samoa, American Samoa, Tonga, Tahiti, and Fiji. By the time it opened two primary schools in Chile a few years later, the Church also had education efforts underway in Mexico. When Isabel arrived in Benemérito, some thirty-eight hundred students were enrolled in the Church's twenty-five primary schools and two secondary schools in Mexico.[8]

Benemérito was a three-year secondary school. It opened in 1964 on a 287-acre farm north of Mexico City. Isabel had first learned about the school while attending a Church-run primary school in Obregón. Although she did not like living more than a thousand miles from her home and family, she was eager to attend classes and learn new things.[9]

The school was staffed entirely by Latter-day Saint teachers from Mexico. Students took required classes in Spanish, English, math, geography, world history, Mexican history, biology, chemistry, and physics. They could also enroll in art, physical education, and technology classes. The seminary program, which operated separately from the school, provided students with religious education.

Isabel's father, who was not a member of the Church, supported her desire to attend Benemérito and agreed to allow her and her sister Hilda to enroll together. Hilda was a year younger, but she and Isabel had been in the same grade since primary school because Isabel did not want to go to school alone.[10]

Isabel and Hilda had traveled to Benemérito with their mother. The school was still partly under construction when they arrived, with dirt grounds, few school buildings, and fifteen cottages for students to live in. Even so, Isabel was struck by the size of the campus.[11]

She and her group were directed to house number two. There they were warmly welcomed by a cottage supervisor, who showed them the washing machines, wardrobes for storing their belongings, and bedrooms, each with two bunk beds. The four-bedroom house also had a dining room, kitchen, and living room.

Isabel spent much of her time observing the other students and trying to adapt to an unfamiliar culture. Benemérito had around five hundred students, most of them from southern Mexico. Their life experiences were different from Isabel's, and she found that their food was also more diverse. She was surprised by the spicier flavors and choice of ingredients.[12]

Whatever the cultural differences, every student at Benemérito was expected to abide by the same rules. They followed a strict routine of waking up early, doing chores, and attending classes. They were also encouraged to develop strong spiritual habits, like going to church and praying. Having grown up in a mixed-faith family, Isabel and her sister had never done these things regularly until they came to Benemérito.

Within a few days of her arrival, Isabel noticed some students growing homesick and leaving. But despite the newness of the people, food, and customs, she was determined to stay and succeed.[13]

"IT DOESN'T SEEM POSSIBLE that I am approaching my ninety-fourth year," President David O. McKay recorded in his journal on January 1, 1967. He had passed the day quietly at home, reflecting on his many experiences. "It has been a happy, interesting life!" he thought. "What a long time, and yet how quickly it has passed."

But even as he looked forward to the new year, the prophet was concerned. "The old world is fraught with troubles," he wrote. Every day, newspapers and televisions relayed reports of wars, racial and political unrest, and natural disasters.[14] Tensions between the United States and the Soviet Union remained high. And many people across Asia, Africa, and Central and South America were caught up in fierce regional conflicts that threatened to topple governments and divide communities.[15]

President McKay was especially concerned about a civil war, now more than a decade old, in the southeast Asian nation of Vietnam. In an effort to prevent communism from taking root in the country, the United States had recently deployed 450,000 troops to South Vietnam. Now the guerrilla-style war was escalating rapidly, and countless soldiers and civilians on both sides of the conflict had been killed.[16]

In Saigon, the capital of South Vietnam, the Church had several branches where around three hundred local Saints met with some of the four thousand Church members serving in the American military. Elder Gordon B. Hinckley of the Quorum of the Twelve Apostles and Elder Marion D. Hanks of the First Council of the Seventy had recently visited the war-torn country.[17] During a district conference with the Saints, Elder Hinckley had dedicated the land for the preaching of the gospel and prayed for peace to return to the country. "Hasten the day," he pleaded, "when the noise of battle may cease." Later in the evening, Church leaders bore their testimonies as artillery fire boomed in the distance.[18]

President McKay hoped to see less chaos and strife in 1967, but that was not to be. In June, war erupted between Israel and its neighbors, unsettling the region. The following month, Nigeria's ongoing political instability erupted into civil war. Rising casualties and the unpopularity of the war in Vietnam, meanwhile, helped spark frequent and sometimes violent antiwar protests in the United States. Racial tensions also reached a breaking point across the country, and a wave of violence rocked many major cities.[19]

The prophet worried about the effect of this unrest on youth. Some young people, disheartened by world events, were questioning the values and culture of their parents and grandparents. Many youth experimented with harmful drugs, engaged in sexual promiscuity, and used crude language.

President McKay loved the youth of the Church, and he did not want them to fall prey to these trends. He encouraged Latter-day Saint youth to attend some kind of weekday religious instruction—seminary or institute—where they could develop Christlike character while surrounded by others who shared their values and standards. Recently, the Church had also produced a pamphlet called *For the Strength of Youth* to help young men and young women know, understand, and live the Church's standards for clean living, dating, dancing, dress, and manners. But he believed parents and Church leaders also had a duty to teach and demonstrate to youth that moral living could bring happiness.[20]

At the October 1967 general conference, President McKay's ill health kept him from delivering his talks personally, so he asked his son Robert to read them to the Saints in his place.

"As I think of the future of this Church," the prophet declared at the opening session of the conference, "I feel impressed that there is no more important message to give than 'to be one,' and avoid things that may cause a rift among members."[21]

Over the past few years, the Church's correlation efforts had sought to unify the Saints by coordinating programs and emphasizing the role of priesthood, home, and family. So far that year, Church correlation had standardized the content of its international magazines and introduced a uniform curriculum. In response to worldwide growth, President McKay had also called sixty-nine "regional representatives of the Twelve" to assist in training stake presidencies, thus helping the Church operate efficiently and consistently around the world.[22]

As the Saints confronted social unrest and shifting values in society, President McKay and other general Church leaders hoped that correlated programs would provide a unified message and stable foundation for people throughout the world.

"The challenge is before us," President McKay told the Saints. "Unity of purpose, with all working in harmony within the structure of Church organization as revealed by the Lord, is to be our objective."[23]

THAT SAME YEAR, HWANG Keun Ok was caring for about eighty girls at the Songjuk Orphanage in Seoul, South Korea. When the all-girls' orphanage hired her as superintendent in 1964, she did not tell its Protestant sponsors that she was a Latter-day Saint. The Church was not well understood in South Korea. In fact, when Keun Ok was baptized in 1962, the Christian school where she was teaching fired her.[24]

There were now around thirty-three hundred South Korean Saints. Kim Ho Jik, the first Korean Latter-day Saint, had joined the Church in 1951 while studying in the United States. Before his death in 1959, Ho Jik had returned to South Korea, become a university professor and administrator, and introduced the restored gospel to some of his students. These students, together with American servicemen, helped the Church grow in the country. A Korean translation of the Book of Mormon was published in 1967.[25]

Despite not telling her sponsors about her Church membership, Keun Ok was not ashamed of being a Latter-day Saint. She served as her branch Relief Society president and taught a junior Sunday School class. She also welcomed visits from Church members who wanted to help at the orphanage. One day, an American serviceman named Stanley Bronson called Keun Ok on the telephone. He was a Latter-day Saint stationed in Seoul, and he wanted to visit the orphanage and sing some songs to cheer up the children.[26]

Stan came a few days later. He was nearly six and a half feet tall and towered over everyone. The girls were excited to hear him sing. He had recorded an album of folk songs before being drafted into the army, and he hoped to record another album while in South Korea.

"Before you play your guitar," Keun Ok said to Stan after everyone gathered, "the children have prepared something for you."[27]

She often had the girls sing for guests, and they were well practiced. As they sang a few songs for Stan, his jaw dropped. Their voices blended in perfect harmony.

Stan began visiting the orphanage regularly to sing with the girls. Before long, he suggested they record an album together, with the record sales benefiting the orphanage.[28]

Keun Ok loved the idea. She had vowed as a young woman to devote herself to improving the world. A war refugee from North Korea, she had lost her father at a young age and knew how difficult it was for girls to succeed in Korea without strong family and community support. Many people in the country looked down on orphan girls and did not expect them to amount to much. To get her education, Keun Ok had struggled against poverty and the loss of a parent and a home. She hoped that performing with Stan would help the girls in her care realize their value—and help other Koreans realize it too.[29]

Stan found a recording studio, and for the next few months, Keun Ok helped him and the girls rehearse and record songs. When the army gave Stan a thirty-day leave, he went home to the United States and had the recordings made into vinyl records. He then returned to Korea and arranged to perform with the girls on a popular American television special being filmed there.[30]

The album, *Daddy Big Boots: Stan Bronson and the Song Jook Won Girls,* arrived in Seoul in the early months of 1968. Keun Ok wanted to make the album release a major event in Korea, so she invited the South Korean president, the United States ambassador, and the commander of the United Nations forces in Korea to attend a release party at a local girls' high school. While only the ambassador could attend, the other dignitaries sent representatives in their place, and the release was a success.

Before long, the singers from the Songjuk Orphanage were in high demand.[31]

MEANWHILE, IN THE UNITED States, Truman Madsen, a philosophy professor at Brigham Young University, received a memo from his colleague Richard Bushman, a professor in the history department. Richard was concerned about an academic article he had just read. Its author, Wesley Walters, was a Presbyterian minister in the midwestern United States. He claimed to have disproved Joseph Smith's First Vision.

Over the years, critics had often tried to cast doubt on the Church's sacred history, many times using the same unsupported claims to argue their point. But this article was different. "It is a well-written, well-researched piece," Richard informed Truman. In fact, another colleague believed it posed a serious threat to the faith of the Saints.

Richard sent Truman a copy of the article. Wesley Walters recognized that he could not directly disprove that Joseph Smith had seen the Father and Son in the spring of 1820, so he had investigated the prophet's claims about the historical setting of the First Vision.[32]

For many years, Latter-day Saints had known of only two accounts that the prophet Joseph had written of the vision. The best-known account, begun in 1838, could be found in the Pearl of Great Price. The other account had been published in the *Times and Seasons,* a Church newspaper, in the early 1840s. Recently, however, a graduate student at Brigham Young University and a Church archivist had uncovered two earlier accounts of the First Vision in the Church's collection of Joseph Smith's papers.[33]

Wesley had examined the four accounts carefully to expose any possible historical inconsistencies in them. And when he investigated the prophet's claim that a local religious revival had prompted him to seek the

Lord in prayer, Wesley had found no evidence of any revivals near the Smith home until almost five years after the First Vision occurred. For Wesley, this meant that Joseph Smith fabricated his story.[34]

Truman was sure Wesley's findings were wrong. But because little historical research had been done on the First Vision and the earliest days of the Church, he had no way to prove it. As a former mission president, he knew that many people had embraced the restored gospel because of the prophet's powerful witness of seeing the Father and Son. An attack on the First Vision seemed like an attack on the very foundation of the Restoration.[35]

After reading the article, Truman assembled a small group of historians in Salt Lake City. All of them were respected scholars and committed members of the Church. As they discussed Wesley's article, they realized that they could use their scholarly training to help the Church. They and other believers needed to undertake a fresh study of Church history, beginning with its roots. Until they did, Wesley Walters's claims about the First Vision would go uncontested.[36]

With Truman at the head, the group organized into a committee to encourage Latter-day Saint scholars to study the early history of the Church. To respond to Wesley's article, the committee proposed sending five historians to the eastern United States to research religious revivals and the First Vision. Unfortunately, they lacked funding.

The committee first tried to raise research money from private donors. When this proved only partially successful, Truman reached out to the First Presidency. President McKay and his counselors had supported other efforts to study and preserve Church history. Earlier in the decade, for instance, they contributed funds for purchasing and preserving historical properties in Nauvoo, Illinois, the headquarters of the Church from 1839 to 1846.[37]

The First Presidency had also taken an interest in the Joseph Smith papyrus fragments. Working closely with Aziz Atiya and the Metropolitan Museum of Art, President N. Eldon Tanner had arranged for the papyrus to be returned as a gift to the Church. Newspapers across the United States reported the acquisition, and the Church held a press conference and published images of the fragments in the *Improvement Era*. At the First Presidency's request, the fragments were then loaned to Hugh Nibley, a professor at Brigham Young University, for further study.[38] Hugh, the Church's leading scholar of the ancient world, had found strong historical evidence supporting the Book of Mormon's authenticity and was sure to do the same with the Book of Abraham.[39]

Writing to the First Presidency in the spring of 1968, Truman requested $7,000 to fund the research trips. "The First Vision has come under severe historical attack," he informed them. "Time is crucial."[40]

Initially, the First Presidency decided not to fund the project. In recent years, the Church had gone into debt building more and more chapels worldwide, and since then, Church leaders had been more cautious about spending.[41]

But Truman was persistent. He had recently met Wesley Walters at a conference on Church history, and he sensed the minister's determination to discredit Joseph Smith.

"He will do anything to get at the sources first," Truman told the First Presidency. "We feel we cannot wisely postpone action." This time, he asked for $5,000.

President McKay and his counselors reconsidered the request and agreed to fund the researchers.[42]

ON A WARM SEPTEMBER afternoon later that year, fourteen-year-old Maeta Holiday sat alone on a bus approaching Fullerton, a suburb of Los Angeles, California. She stared out the window at the orange groves spanning both sides of the freeway, a landscape so unlike her home in the sparse desert on the border of Utah and Arizona.[43]

Maeta was Diné, a citizen of the Navajo Nation. She had grown up on a Native American reservation within the four sacred mountains marking the traditional borders of her people's ancestral home. In the nineteenth century, the United States government had created the reservation and others like it from lands they seized from Native American groups like the Navajo to make room for white settlers, including Latter-day Saints. Forced to live on the often-inferior reservation lands, many families struggled.

The Navajo reservation Maeta had lived on was vast, and people lived far apart from one another, making it difficult to transport children to and from school. Government-funded boarding schools, meanwhile, were often overcrowded and underfunded. Under these conditions, many Native American parents sought to improve the lives of their children by sending them to schools off the reservation.[44]

Maeta had come to California as part of the Church's Indian Student Placement Program, and she was on her way to live with a white family she had never met. Maeta's older sisters had participated in the program, and she wished to do the same. But although she had eagerly signed up, she was anxious about her new foster family.[45]

The placement program had been founded in 1954 under the guidance of Elder Spencer W. Kimball. Like many Latter-day Saints at the time, he considered Native Americans to be the direct descendants of Book of Mormon peoples. He believed Church members had a responsibility to help their Lamanite brothers and sisters gain access to educational opportunities and fulfill their divine destiny as a covenant people.

In the placement program, Native American children left their homes on reservations to live with Latter-day Saint families during the school year. The program aimed to give the students access to better schools and experience gospel-centered homes. By 1968, about three thousand students from more than sixty-three tribes had been placed in homes in Canada and seven U.S. states.

While all placement students were Latter-day Saints, some of them had participated very little in the Church before entering the program.[46]

Glen Van Wagenen, who led the program in Southern California, had heard about Maeta while she was living with a family in Kanab, Utah. Maeta loved living with them, and she got along well with their daughter. When Glen invited Maeta to join the placement program in California at the start of her ninth-grade year, she readily accepted the offer.[47]

Maeta was the youngest of six daughters born to Calvin Holiday and Evelyn Crank. Her parents had joined the Church early in their marriage, but they later lost interest in it. Though Maeta was baptized at age eight, she did not attend church regularly, nor did she understand the significance of her baptism. Wanting to improve Maeta's education, her parents put her in Native American boarding schools in Arizona as soon as she was old enough, so she moved around a lot.

Maeta knew of families on the reservation in which the parents loved one another and the children were happy. But her family was not among them. After her parents divorced, her mother remarried twice. Maeta's mother had six more children from these marriages, and her long absences forced Maeta to take care of her younger siblings. More than once, Maeta and her siblings were left alone for days with little food and water. She did her best to feed the children, sometimes with spoiled mutton and a few cans of food.[48]

Once, while Maeta made fry bread over a fire outside, her mother looked at her and said, "The *only* thing you are going to be good for is to make babies." Maeta's heart broke. In that moment, she silently vowed, "I will make something of myself."[49]

Arriving at the bus stop in Southern California, Maeta was relieved to be away from her mother. But she was nervous as she watched a middle-aged couple walk through the door. "They will be my new parents," she thought.[50]

Her foster father, Spencer Black, was quiet and reserved. Maeta greeted him with some wariness, scarred by the abusive men she had known in her life. Her foster mother, Venna, however, had a comforting spirit about her.

They brought Maeta back to their house, where she met their children, fifteen-year-old Lucy and thirteen-year-old Larry. The Blacks also had three older children who had moved out of the house. Maeta became familiar with her new home, with its spacious fireplace and a garden full of flowers. Having shared rooms with siblings all her life, she was especially thrilled to have her own bedroom.[51]

But Maeta was still not entirely comfortable. The city was overwhelming and choked with smog. And while her foster parents were kind, Maeta wondered if they were using kindness to manipulate her into doing chores, as her mother sometimes had.

She did not regret coming to California, but she missed the quiet of the reservation as she lay in bed that night, troubled by the noisy traffic of the freeway.[52]

CHAPTER 11

In Any Other Country

In early October 1968, Isabel Santana was in her second year at Benemérito de las Américas. The Church school now had twelve hundred students—more than twice what it had when Isabel arrived there—and an expanding campus with a new auditorium-gymnasium, a small grocery store, two shop buildings, a reception center, and thirty-five more residential cottages. When President N. Eldon Tanner came to Mexico City earlier in the year to dedicate the new buildings, the Tabernacle Choir had also come to perform at the service.[1]

Isabel and her younger sister Hilda had adapted quickly to life at the school. Isabel was naturally shy, but she refused to let her shyness get in the way of her education. She made a close friend, learned to navigate the cultural differences she encountered, and did her best to talk to people she didn't know.[2]

She also established herself as a diligent student. She regularly sought the advice of teachers and administrators at the school. One of these mentors, Efraín Villalobos, had attended Church schools in Mexico as a young man before studying agronomy at Brigham Young University. He had a good sense of humor, and Isabel and the other students at Benemérito found him to be very relatable. Far from home, they looked to him as a tutor, guide, and father figure.[3]

Another teacher who inspired her was Leonor Esther Garmendia, who taught physics and mathematics at the school. During Isabel's first year, Leonor had asked her students to raise their hands if they liked math. Many hands went up. She asked who did not like the subject. Isabel raised her hand.

"Why don't you like it?" Leonor asked.

"Because I don't understand it," Isabel said.

"You'll understand it here."

The work in Leonor's class was not easy. But sometimes she would give the class an assignment and then ask each student to come to her desk to work out math problems with her. Before long, Isabel was able to figure out the problems in her head—an ability she never thought she would have.[4]

Like many of her classmates, Isabel balanced school with work responsibilities. The Church covered most of the educational costs to keep tuition low. To pay the rest, some students cleaned buildings or worked at the school's on-site dairy. Isabel had found a job as a telephone switchboard operator for the school. Hour after hour, she sat in a narrow phone box and connected calls across campus using a switchboard with pins and numbers. The work was simple, and she often brought a book to help pass the hours.[5]

At the time, university students across the globe were protesting against their governments. In Mexico City, many students took to the streets to demonstrate for more economic and political justice. They also resented the influence of the United States on Mexican leaders. In the students' minds, the Cold War between the United States and Soviet Union was an opportunity for powerful nations to dominate their smaller, more vulnerable neighbors.

Complicating matters, Mexico City was preparing to host the Summer Olympics—the first Olympics ever held in a Latin American country. Tensions reached a peak on October 2, 1968, ten days before the Olympics, when Mexican armed forces fired on demonstrators in Mexico City's Tlatelolco Square, killing nearly fifty people. In the weeks that followed, authorities arrested leaders of the student movement while both the government and the media tried to downplay the brutality of the Tlatelolco massacre.[6]

Benemérito was close to the bloodshed, and Isabel sorrowed when she learned about the killings. But she felt safe at the school, where most students and teachers did not get involved in political protests.

One afternoon, though, a man called the school and threatened to steal its buses. Isabel was scared, but she didn't panic. "Who is speaking?" she asked.

The caller hung up.

Unsure what to do, she inserted a pin into the switchboard and called Kenyon Wagner, the director of the school.

"Isabel," he said, "we are going to take care of it."

The call turned out to be an empty threat, and Isabel was relieved that nothing bad happened.[7] Benemérito had become her oasis, a peaceful place where she could study the gospel and get an education.

While she was there, she knew she would be protected.[8]

On the morning of November 10, 1968, Henry Burkhardt gathered with some 230 Saints for a district conference in Görlitz, a city on the eastern border of the German Democratic Republic. The three-story building where they met was falling apart. Exposed brick could be seen around the windows where the facade had deteriorated.[9]

Suddenly, joy rippled through the meetinghouse. Apostle Thomas S. Monson had shown up at the conference, surprising the Saints. In the seven years since the Berlin Wall went up, they'd had few chances to meet with a general authority.[10]

Elder Monson had recently been assigned to supervise the German-speaking missions, and Henry, as the leader of the Church in the GDR, was eager to work with him. At forty-one, Elder Monson was just a few years his senior. But he was an apostle—and that really set him apart in Henry's eyes. What would he be like? Would they get along?

These questions vanished almost as soon as Elder Monson walked into the meetinghouse. He was down-to-earth and engaging. He couldn't speak German, and Henry couldn't speak English, but they became friends.[11]

The conference began at ten o'clock. The Saints in the congregation were smiling, clearly grateful for Elder Monson's presence. A few of them were sure to be informants—Church members who reported to the government on the words and actions of their fellow Saints. Henry thought he knew who most of them were, but he did not try to stop them. He would much rather have the government get reports from Latter-day Saint informants who told the truth about the Church than from less sympathetic sources.[12]

He resented the many restrictions imposed on him and other East Germans, though. Leading the Church under these conditions continued to keep him away from his family six days a week, and now he and Inge had a second child, a boy named Tobias. Every time he had to deal with government officials—which was often—they tried to convince him of the benefits of communism. He could not see them. When he thought about conditions in the country, and a system that enticed Saints to report on other Saints, he would ask himself, "How is anything like this possible?"[13]

Elder Monson was visibly moved by the conditions in the GDR as well. When he rose to address the Saints at the conference, tears filled his eyes. He tried to speak, but his voice faltered, choked with emotion. Finally he said, "If you will remain true and faithful to the commandments of God, every blessing any member of the Church enjoys in any other country will be yours."[14]

For Henry and the other Saints in the congregation, Elder Monson had just promised everything they longed for as Church members. But so much had to change in the GDR for the words to become reality. When Church leaders had proposed creating a stake in the GDR, Henry had rejected the idea, worried it would attract unwanted attention from the government. And temple blessings had been out of reach since the GDR tightened its borders. Every time Saints sought permission to go to the Swiss Temple, the government denied their requests.[15]

Still, a marvelous spirit filled the room. Elder Monson blessed the Saints, and they closed the meeting with a fervent hymn:

> *God be with you till we meet again;*
> *When life's perils thick confound you,*
> *Put his arms unfailing round you.*
> *God be with you till we meet again.*[16]

AROUND THIS TIME, IN the West African nation of Ghana, Joseph William Billy Johnson was sure he had found the true gospel of Jesus Christ. Four years earlier, his friend Frank Mensah had given him a Book of Mormon and other Latter-day Saint books and pamphlets. Like its neighbor Nigeria, Ghana had no congregation of the Church. Frank had wanted to change that.

"I feel you are the man I should work with," he had told Billy.[17]

Since then, they had organized four unofficial Latter-day Saint congregations in and around Accra, the capital of Ghana. Having contacted Church headquarters, they knew about the Church's reluctance to send missionaries to western Africa. But LaMar Williams and others had encouraged them to study the gospel and gather with like-minded believers. When they learned that Virginia Cutler, a professor from Brigham Young University, was in Accra to start a home economics program at the University of Ghana, they started a weekly Sunday school with her.[18]

Billy loved sharing the gospel. He worked in the import-export industry, but he wanted to quit his job and devote more time to missionary work. His wife did not share his faith. "This church is so new," she said. "I don't want you to resign."

But Billy was anxious to preach more. "There is something burning in me which I cannot hide," he told her.[19]

Religion had long been important to Billy. His mother, Matilda, was a devout Methodist, and she had raised him to have faith in God and to love His word. At school, Billy would often find a private place to sing hymns and pray while the other students played. One of his teachers took notice and told him he would someday become a priest.

As Billy got older, his faith was affirmed by remarkable dreams and visions. Shortly after Frank Mensah introduced him to the restored gospel, Billy was praying when he saw the heavens open and a host of angels appear, blowing trumpets and singing praises to God. "Johnson, Johnson, Johnson," a voice called to him. "If you will take up my work as I will command you, I will bless you and bless your land."[20]

Not everyone had accepted Billy and Frank or their beliefs, though. Some people had said they were following a false church. Others accused them of not believing in Jesus Christ. Their words hurt Billy. Wondering if he had been led astray, he began to fast. After three days, he went to a room in his house where he had hung portraits of the presidents of the Church on the wall. He knelt down and prayed to God for help.

"I would like to see these prophets," he said. "I want them to give me instructions."

That night, as Billy slept, he dreamed that Joseph Smith appeared to him and said, "Very soon missionaries will come. Prophet McKay is thinking of you."

Another man also approached him and introduced himself as Brigham Young. "Johnson, we are with you," he said. "Do not be discouraged." Before the night was over, Billy saw every latter-day prophet down to George Albert Smith.[21]

Billy's desire to devote more time to sharing the gospel soon led him to quit his job and move to Cape Coast, a city southwest of Accra, where he planned to farm and start a new congregation. His wife did not support his decision, so rather than move with the family, she divorced Billy, leaving him to care for their four young children.

Billy was devastated, but he found support in his mother, Matilda. She had her own doubts about Billy quitting his job and moving the family to Cape Coast, wondering if he could be successful in a city that already had many churches. But Billy was her only living child, and she depended on him for her well-being, so she went with him.

Matilda now shared her son's faith. When Billy had first told her of his new beliefs, she had not taken them seriously. But after seeing how those beliefs changed him and the people he taught, she realized that her son had found something special. She knew she and many others would be blessed when the Church came to Ghana, and this knowledge gave her courage.

Once the family settled in Cape Coast, Matilda cared for Billy's children while he established his new congregation. She also gave him moral support and encouragement, lending a hand when she could to strengthen the congregation.

"No matter the circumstances, no matter the future," she affirmed, "I am prepared to fight an honest battle for the Church."[22]

AFTER RELEASING THEIR ALBUM with Stan Bronson, the singers of the Songjuk Orphanage soon found themselves performing regularly at military bases and on American and Korean television shows. Everyone, including the president of South Korea and the U.S. ambassador, seemed to love the choir of little girls.[23]

Hwang Keun Ok enjoyed working with Stan and the singers. The group had a positive effect on the girls. For one thing, participating required that they complete their homework on time. But more than that, Keun Ok was pleased to see the girls gain a sense of self-worth from their singing. As the group's fame increased, she and Stan remained encouraging, gently guiding the singers through each practice, performance, and recording.[24]

They wanted to help the girls at the orphanage both now and in the future. While on leave the previous year, Stan had talked to people in his hometown about buying each girl a new coat or doll for Christmas. He then asked a Korean-speaking friend to dress as Santa Claus to deliver the gifts. Later, he and Keun Ok considered asking people in the United States to provide monthly financial support for the girls.[25]

Once Stan was discharged from the army, he set up a nonprofit organization in Utah. He also spoke at firesides, gave concerts, and sold albums to raise awareness of the girls and their financial needs. Before the organization could operate in South Korea, though, it needed a license from the government. The South Korean government had restricted foreign organizations from doing social work within the country. Fortunately, Keun Ok was able to use the popularity of the singing group and her connections in the government to secure a license for Stan's organization.

While setting up the nonprofit, Stan read an inspiring book titled *Tender Apples* about a Latter-day Saint woman who helped at-risk children. He and Keun Ok liked the title, so he contacted the author, who agreed to let them call their organization the Tender Apples Foundation. Keun Ok converted a room in her two-story home in Seoul into the Korean office for the nonprofit organization, and Stan worked there when he was in Korea. Before long, the singing group took the name Tender Apples as well.[26]

One day, a few of the girls giggled as they brought a dictionary to Stan. Having sung at Latter-day Saint meetings on an American military base, they knew Stan was a member of the Church. But like most Koreans, they still did not know much about the Church or what it taught. When they looked up "Mormon" in the dictionary, it defined the word as a "strange-behaving people."

"Well," Stan asked the girls, "do you think I'm strange?"

"Oh no," they said.

"Do you think Miss Hwang is strange?"

The girls gasped. None of them knew that their superintendent was a "Mormon" too.[27]

Stan told Keun Ok what had happened. She knew it was only a matter of time before the orphanage's Protestant sponsors learned about her Church membership, and she braced herself for their response.[28]

She didn't have to wait long. Once the sponsors found out that Keun Ok was a Latter-day Saint—and that some of the girls at the orphanage had become interested in the Church—they gave her a choice. She could either leave the Church or resign her position. For Keun Ok, that was no choice at all.[29]

She gathered her things and left the orphanage. Several of the older girls who had come to love Keun Ok soon followed after her, carrying their few possessions with them. When they showed up at her door, she knew she would have to find some way to care for them.[30]

IN UTAH, TRUMAN MADSEN had nothing but good news for his committee researching the Church's origins. Throughout the summer of 1968, historians had sent him updates from their research trips to the eastern United States. Thanks to the funding from the First Presidency, they were able to scour libraries and archives, locating historical documents and confirming important dates and facts.

"It has been a great summer!" Truman declared. He was confident that Latter-day Saint historians were now better prepared to respond to Wesley Walters's claims about the First Vision.[31]

One of their most significant discoveries that summer was strong evidence of religious revival near Joseph Smith's home in 1820. Milton Backman, a professor of history and religion at Brigham Young University, observed that Joseph Smith had described the religious excitement in general terms, without identifying any specific locations. This led Milton to believe that Wesley Walters had focused his research too narrowly on Palmyra. After spending weeks combing through historical records in western New York, Milton discovered that a "cyclone" of religious fervor had indeed passed through the region around Palmyra in 1819 and 1820—just as the prophet Joseph described in his 1838 First Vision account.[32]

Over the next few months, Truman and other historians worked on articles about their findings. He wanted to publish all the research together in an issue of *BYU Studies,* an academic journal published by Brigham Young University.[33]

At the same time, Hugh Nibley continued studying the papyrus fragments from the Metropolitan Museum of Art. When the Church acquired the artifacts, many people were eager to learn what they revealed about the Book of Abraham and its translation. For more than a century, after all, some people had cast doubt on

Joseph Smith's interpretation of the three "facsimiles" published alongside the Book of Abraham. Reproduced from illustrations found in the papyri, these facsimiles were almost identical to images on common Egyptian funeral scrolls that seemed to have nothing to do with Abraham or his times.[34]

Early analyses and translations of the fragments confirmed that they were funerary texts from centuries after Abraham's day, and neither the Church nor Hugh disputed this finding. Yet Hugh believed further study could shed more light on the papyrus and the prophet's translation.[35] In more than a dozen articles published in 1968 and 1969, he drew on his knowledge of ancient cultures and languages to advance several theories about the Book of Abraham and its relationship to ancient Egyptian religion and culture. He noted, for instance, that some of the strongest evidence of the Book of Abraham's authenticity was its resemblance to other ancient temple texts and millennia-old traditions about Abraham that Joseph Smith was unlikely to know anything about.[36] Hugh's writing also attested to the book's powerful insights into priesthood, temple ordinances, and the plan of salvation.[37]

In the spring of 1969, the research conducted by Truman's committee appeared in *BYU Studies*. The issue presented the most up-to-date information on the First Vision and provided solid historical support for Joseph Smith's testimony. Leonard Arrington and James Allen, two members of the committee, summarized the existing articles and books published on early Church history. Milton Backman penned an article about his research into religious activities near Palmyra. And Dean Jessee, an archivist for the Church Historian's Office, prepared an article about Joseph Smith's First Vision accounts. Other articles treated similar topics. Aside from their value in defending the faith, Truman believed the essays showed the value of Saints working together to gain a more complete understanding of the history of the Restoration. He noted that many Church members had letters, diaries, and other documents in their possession that could be of immense use to historians.

"There are vital tasks of gathering, researching, and interpreting which are too vast for any one mind, or any one hundred minds," he wrote in his preface to the *BYU Studies* issue. "They must involve us all."[38]

IN THE GERMAN DEMOCRATIC Republic, meanwhile, Henry Burkhardt was overseeing several changes for the Saints under his care. After Elder Monson's visit to Görlitz, the First Presidency had created a mission in Dresden, a major city in the GDR, and called Henry to be its president. A short time later, Elder Monson returned to the country to organize the mission, ordain Henry to the office of high priest, and set him apart in his new calling.[39]

Henry's wife, Inge, was called to serve alongside him. Since meeting the Burkhardts, Elder Monson had been troubled that the couple saw each other for only a few hours a week. "What you are doing is not all right," he had told Henry. Now Inge, as a fellow mission leader, traveled regularly with him around the country and at times attended to duties in the mission office.[40]

Henry preferred to travel alone, however, when he thought he might encounter problems. The government was still monitoring the activities of the Saints, but it had become less suspicious of the Church after Henry, an East German citizen, was called as mission president. As long as the Saints did not hold unscheduled meetings, print or mimeograph any Church materials, or act without caution, the authorities left them alone. They were free to hold sacrament meetings, go home teaching, and gather for Relief Society, Sunday School, priesthood, and Primary meetings.[41]

Henry tried to be cautious. Many Saints in the country were worried about losing contact with the broader Church, and they longed to have more printed Church materials. Sometimes the government allowed the Saints to import large numbers of print materials, like hymnbooks and scriptures. But usually, Church members had to make do with what they had. To accommodate restrictions against printing and mimeographing Church materials, Henry enlisted trusted volunteers who made copies of the manuals with typewriters and carbon paper.

Doing so was not breaking the law, so Henry felt justified in making and distributing the manuals. But the practice still worried him. Laws restricting religious freedom were not always written down or evenly enforced throughout the country. Henry knew all too well that Stasi officers did not need a reason to arrest him. If the wrong officer found him with foreign Church manuals, Henry could easily end up in serious trouble.[42]

Even though conditions in the country were not ideal, the Church carried on. Remarkably, forty-seven people had been baptized in 1968. At the time Elder Monson set up the Dresden Mission, there were 4,641 East German Saints in forty-seven branches and seven districts. The Saints were attending meetings, doing home teaching, and holding Church activities when possible. They even held a "Genealogy Week" and submitted fourteen thousand names for temple work.[43]

As Henry reflected on his new calling, he committed himself and his family to all it required. "It should now be our job to work with all our might to build up the Church," Henry wrote in his journal. "Together with Inge, I hope to master all tasks and overcome my own weaknesses as well."[44]

CHAPTER 12

A Complete Way of Life

"I am very much concerned about my throat," Elder Spencer W. Kimball wrote in his journal on January 8, 1970. "My voice seems to be deteriorating slowly."[1]

In the dozen years since doctors removed a cancerous vocal cord, his voice had been little more than a rough whisper. Yet this setback had hardly slowed his Church service. Since establishing the São Paulo Stake in 1966, Elder Kimball had organized the first stakes in Argentina and Uruguay, dedicated Colombia for missionary work, and ministered to Saints in Ecuador. He had also written an influential book, *The Miracle of Forgiveness,* and begun serving as chair of the Church's budget committee and missionary committee.[2]

But with his voice worsening, he had consulted a doctor, worried that the cancer had come back. The doctor had discovered a red spot on the left side of Elder Kimball's throat and performed two biopsies. This further strained the apostle's voice, compelling him to amplify his speech with a small microphone worn around his neck.

Elder Kimball returned to the hospital on January 12 to learn the prognosis. After studying the results of the biopsies and consulting with other experts, the doctor believed the cancer had returned, and there was little hope that Elder Kimball's voice could be saved.[3]

As Elder Kimball considered how to move forward with treatment, he wondered if he ought to withdraw from the Quorum of the Twelve Apostles to make room for a more capable man.[4]

The next day, Elder Kimball told N. Eldon Tanner what the doctor had said, and President Tanner recommended that the general authorities hold a special fast on his behalf. Two days later, the general authorities gathered in the temple, and Harold B. Lee offered a heartfelt prayer. When he finished, Elder Kimball took a seat in the middle of the room, and Gordon B. Hinckley anointed his head with oil. The other apostles in the room then gathered in a circle around Elder Kimball, and President Tanner sealed the anointing and blessed him.

During the blessing, Elder Kimball felt a nearness to his Heavenly Father and his quorum members. The heavy burden he carried seemed to fall away, and he knew that if God wanted him to continue in his ministry, then He would find a way for him to do so, with or without his voice. After the blessing, Elder Lee wrapped Elder Kimball in an embrace. Other apostles in the circle said they felt blessed to take part in such a powerful and unifying spiritual experience.[5]

On Sunday morning, three days after the blessing, Elder Kimball's neighbor telephoned him unexpectedly. She had heard that President McKay had died, and she wanted to know if it was true.

"I have not heard," Elder Kimball replied. He began making calls, and before long, he learned that the prophet had indeed passed away earlier that morning.[6]

Elder Kimball hurried over to the Church Administration Building. Both Joseph Fielding Smith, the senior apostle, and Harold B. Lee were meeting with the McKay family. Elder Kimball found Joseph Anderson and Arthur Haycock, the secretaries to the First Presidency and the Twelve, and they spent several hours calling general authorities to tell them the news.[7]

President McKay's death saddened the Church. His love for the Saints around the world was legendary. He had led the Church for nearly nineteen years, and two-thirds of its three million members had been baptized while he was president. When he succeeded George Albert Smith in April 1951, the Church had 184 stakes. Now, in 1970, it had 500 stakes, including fourteen stakes in Australia and New Zealand, thirteen stakes in Europe, and the first stakes in Argentina, Brazil, Guatemala, Mexico, Tonga, Uruguay, and Western Samoa.

Almost 90 percent of the new stakes during the McKay administration were formed in the United States and Canada, where Church growth remained high. In North America, the Church's reputation benefited from prominent Latter-day Saints like J. Willard Marriott, founder of a large hotel chain, and George W. Romney, who had been chief executive of American Motors Corporation and governor of the state of Michigan.

President McKay had dedicated five temples in four countries and overseen the translation of temple ordinances into a dozen languages. General conference, likewise, had become even more available as two hundred television stations and dozens of radio stations in North, Central, and South America broadcast the proceedings. As a champion of missionary work and Church education, President McKay had greatly expanded the Church's efforts in both areas. And his implementation of the correlation program, which he considered his most important work as Church president, had made the simple truths of the restored gospel more accessible to a worldwide audience.[8]

Thousands of Saints came to President McKay's funeral to pay their respects. A short time later, the Quorum of the Twelve Apostles met to sustain Joseph Fielding Smith as the new president of the Church. At ninety-three, President Smith was the oldest man ever to lead the Church. He came to the office with nearly sixty years of experience as an apostle, and the Saints respected his considerable knowledge of Church history and the scriptures. As the son of President Joseph F. Smith, he was also the grandson of Hyrum Smith, brother of the prophet Joseph.[9]

President Smith called Harold B. Lee and N. Eldon Tanner to be his counselors in the First Presidency. Since President Lee's new duties prevented him from serving as president of the Quorum of the Twelve Apostles, Elder Kimball was set apart to serve as president of the quorum in his place.

Against the advice of a doctor friend, who urged him to seek cancer treatment in California, Elder Kimball set aside his health concerns after President McKay's death, choosing instead to focus on his apostolic duties. He remained unsure how best to treat the disease, and since his speaking had improved since the blessing, he did not want to undergo any surgery that put his voice at risk.[10]

As President Lee set him apart in his new calling, he spoke of Elder Kimball's health concerns, offering words of comfort and hope.

"We bless particularly your voice," he said, "pleading with the Lord to preserve your ability to communicate by voice as well as by writing instructions, that you may live in the earth as long as life shall be sweet unto you, and until the Lord says it is enough."[11]

SHORTLY AFTER ARRIVING IN California, Maeta Holiday went to a shopping mall with Venna Black, her foster mother in the Indian Student Placement Program. Maeta had never gone to the mall before, so she paid close attention to every turn Venna made in the car.

At the mall, Maeta picked out some clothes she needed, but when it was time to go, Venna wasn't sure how to get back home. "I can't remember where I'm supposed to go," she told Maeta.

"Well, go here," Maeta said, directing Venna down the right street. She then led Venna back to the house, turn by turn.

Venna was impressed. "How do you know how to get home?" she asked.

"I'm always observant," Maeta said. Memorizing landmarks was a habit she had gained while herding sheep as a young girl on the Navajo reservation. If she did not pay attention to landmarks, she might not make it home.[12]

Maeta started attending the local high school soon after this experience. Her first few days there were scary. The school was much bigger than any she had attended before. Its crowded hallways were lined with lockers. Almost all the students were white, and as far as she knew, she was the only student from the placement program there. She did not sense racial prejudice from her peers, though, as some students in the program did at other schools. Her classmates welcomed her, and she quickly made friends.[13]

Like other youth in her ward, Maeta attended early-morning seminary. She and her foster sister Lucy woke up every weekday morning at five o'clock so they could make it to the ward meetinghouse on time for class. On her first day of seminary, Maeta waited in her chair, not really knowing why she was there until class started. Then she figured it out. "Ah," she thought, "we learn about the Church."

Maeta was not too interested in seminary. She was surprised and confused when she found out that she would be given a grade in the class. "How can you be graded for your beliefs?" she wondered. Would God be giving her the grade? Still, she and Lucy rarely missed the class.[14]

During her first year of high school, Maeta joined a school choir. The next year, she played basketball, which she had learned while attending boarding school in Arizona. She excelled at the sport and became point guard for her team. She liked making layups and scoring from the side of the foul line. But she was also good at passing the ball to the other players. At the end of the season, her teammates and coaches voted her most valuable player.[15]

The placement program recommended that students return after each school year to live with their birth families for the summer. Maeta did not like going back home or spending time with her troubled mother, Evelyn. But Venna believed it was important for Maeta to stay connected to her roots and encouraged her to write home every month. Every time summer rolled around, Maeta would catch the bus to Arizona.[16]

In the spring of 1970, as Maeta was finishing her second year in high school, she learned that her mother's home had burned down. No one was hurt, and Maeta was not worried about her family. Venna, however, helped Maeta buy some things to replace what her younger brothers and sisters lost in the fire.

On the day Maeta left for Arizona, Venna dropped her off at the bus stop with cardboard boxes full of food, clothing, and blankets. "This is for your family," she explained. "This is from our ward."

As Maeta watched the boxes being loaded into the bus's luggage compartment, she was overcome with emotion. When she first arrived in California, she had been suspicious of the Blacks' kindness, wondering if they had taken her in just to do their housework. She had since come to know that they cared about her. But until she saw the boxes, she did not know how much her foster family loved her.

And she had not known how much she loved them.[17]

LATER THAT YEAR, SIXTEEN-YEAR-OLD Kazuhiko Yamashita was looking to escape the sun on a hot July morning in Osaka, Japan. He and his older brother, Masahito, had traveled for hours to attend Expo '70, a world's fair featuring hundreds of awe-inspiring displays and pavilions from nations and organizations around the globe. Its theme was "Progress and Harmony for Mankind," and wherever visitors looked, they could see evidence of Japan's impressive recovery from the devastation of World War II.[18]

Kazuhiko and Masahito had already visited a few exhibits together. At the United States Pavilion, they saw one of the expo's most popular exhibits: a moonstone brought back from the historic lunar landing the year before.[19]

But today the brothers had split up, as Masahito looked for engineering exhibits and Kazuhiko wandered the expo grounds with his camera. Kazuhiko wanted to go into the Japan Pavilion to see what kinds of exhibits his home country was showing the world. But by the time he arrived at the pavilion, the line stretched far outside the entrance. A staff member told him the wait was at least two hours.[20]

Rather than stand so long under the hot sun, Kazuhiko moved on, walking for five or ten minutes before seeing a pavilion that looked like a beautiful white building. It had two levels and a tall spire with a golden statue of a man blowing a long trumpet. Kazuhiko did not know what the pavilion was, but it didn't have a line, so he would not have to wait to get inside.

Passing through a Japanese-style garden, he entered a lobby where a guide gathered him and other guests for a tour. The pavilion, Kazuhiko soon learned, provided information about The Church of Jesus Christ of Latter-day Saints and its members. The Church had showcased popular exhibits at other world expositions, but this was the first time it had brought a pavilion to a country where Christianity was not the major religion. The ground floor of the building had a twelve-foot marble replica of the *Christus,* a statue by Danish sculptor Bertel Thorvaldsen. There was also a photographic exhibit about the everyday activities of Church members around Japan.

Kazuhiko's family was Buddhist, and he knew nothing about Jesus Christ or a Heavenly Father. But after he and the other guests moved to the second floor of the pavilion, they entered a series of rooms that taught them about the Savior's ministry and His role in the Creation of the world. They learned about God's plan of happiness and the Restoration of the gospel of Christ through a boy prophet named Joseph Smith.[21]

The tour ended in a small theater with a Japanese version of *Man's Search for Happiness,* the short film the Church had debuted at the New York World's Fair in 1964.[22] At the urging of local mission leaders Ed and Chieko Okazaki, the Japanese film was shot locally with popular Japanese actors, some of whom Kazuhiko recognized. But the questions raised in the film—Where had he come from? Why was he here? Where was he going?—were new to him. He had never given them any thought. And he wasn't sure if he believed the answers the pavilion had given him.

On his way out of the theater, Kazuhiko saw a man standing in the hall.

"Do you believe it?" Kazuhiko asked, referring to the film.

"Yes, I do," the man said without hesitation.

"Are you sure?"

"I am."[23]

Kazuhiko left the pavilion and continued exploring the expo, but he hadn't gone far when he realized he had left his camera behind. He hurried back to the exhibit, where a staff member found the missing camera.

As a show of gratitude, Kazuhiko bought a Japanese copy of the Book of Mormon and left his name and address with the staff member, even though he wasn't especially interested in learning more about the Church.

Three months later, a pair of missionaries showed up at his home outside Tokyo. He had not expected them to actually visit, but he was happy to see them—and willing to hear what they had to say.[24]

IN SEPTEMBER 1970, RELIEF Society general president Belle Spafford stood in the Salt Lake Tabernacle in front of thousands of Latter-day Saint women at the Relief Society's annual conference. The event was usually a time of rejoicing, as women from across the world came together to share experiences and receive instruction from their leaders. This conference, however, was more somber than others.

"We are living in a period of time characterized by crisis after crisis," President Spafford said. In the United States, images of war and civil unrest flashed across television screens every day. Racial strife remained high, and the assassinations of prominent politicians and civil rights leaders shocked the nation. Young people continued to protest against the Vietnam War. Peace and tranquility seemed fleeting.[25]

The Relief Society itself was in a time of transition as the organization adapted to Church correlation. In the past, Relief Society members had raised their own funds and created budgets that were then approved by priesthood leaders. Recently, however, the First Presidency had announced that Relief Societies would be funded by ward or branch budgets.

Under the new system, local priesthood leaders assigned each ward organization a set amount to spend every year. Individual Relief Societies could continue to control how they spent their funds without the added burden of fundraising for their organization. But since Relief Societies were now constrained by a limited budget, they lost some of the financial independence they had enjoyed over the years. Relief Society bazaars, time-honored fundraising events where women displayed and sold their handicrafts, also came to an end.[26]

Other changes affected governance. As part of its social services work, the Relief Society had been in charge of the Indian Student Placement Program, Church adoption and foster care services, and a rehabilitation program for troubled youth.[27] But these programs were largely confined to the western United States, and the desire to extend social services to the global Church membership under a single, correlated organization prompted restructuring.[28]

In 1969, Church leaders created Unified Social Services, which brought all these initiatives together under the leadership of priesthood officers. President Spafford continued as an adviser, but she no longer directed the programs.[29]

As the Relief Society adjusted to the changes, President Spafford and her counselors were candid about the potential problems they saw. When they learned that the Adult Correlation Committee was tasked with writing Relief Society lessons, the presidency spoke up. In the end, the Relief Society wrote its own lessons with input and reviews by the committee.[30]

President Spafford recognized the need for Relief Society to adapt as the restored gospel spread across the globe. The Church's magazine for international readers was now being translated into seventeen languages. Yet the *Relief Society Magazine* was published only in English and Spanish.[31]

To help reach as many readers as possible with correlated messages, leaders had recently proposed changes to Church publications. In June 1970, they announced that most current magazines, including the *Instructor,* the *Improvement Era,* and the *Relief Society Magazine,* would be retired. Longstanding English-language magazines in the missions, such as the *Millennial Star* in the United Kingdom and *Cumorah's Southern Messenger* in South Africa, would also come to an end. In their place, the Church would publish three new magazines, each speaking to a particular age group: the *Ensign* for adults, the *New Era* for youth, and the *Friend* for children.[32]

Standing before her audience in the Tabernacle, President Spafford knew that many women were grappling with the recent changes, just as she had. Her presidency had received letters from women who were grieving over the news about the end of the magazine.[33] And President Spafford could understand their sorrow. When the idea was first proposed, she had objected, feeling that the magazine served an important purpose in the Church and in the lives of the sisters. What could she say now to bring healing and comfort?[34]

She took as her theme a passage from the Book of Mormon: "We lived after the manner of happiness." When faced with trying times, the people of Nephi did not slacken their effort. They kept the commandments of God as best they could. And they were industrious, raising flocks and herds and sowing and harvesting crops.

So it could be with Relief Society. Organizational changes did not alter the things that led to happiness: righteousness, compassionate service, creative expression, and community involvement.

"Relief Society offers limitless opportunities," President Spafford testified, "to nourish the essential elements of a happy life."[35]

IN FEBRUARY 1971, SIX years after his conversion, Darius Gray was living in Salt Lake City. As a member of the Church, he had enjoyed the fellowship of many Saints who befriended him and helped him adapt to his new faith. He had also met a few Church members who mistreated him because he was Black. But he clung to the powerful words he had heard the night before his baptism: "This is the restored gospel, and you are to join."

Darius worked as a reporter for KSL-TV, a local news station. Before getting the job, he'd never considered a career in journalism. Then he met Arch Madsen, the president of the Church-owned communications company that oversaw KSL. Finding Arch to be friendly and direct, Darius took the job. It felt as if God were laying out a path for him.[36]

After Darius was hired, he pursued a degree in journalism from the University of Utah. He also took an active part in his Salt Lake City ward and served as its Sunday School superintendent. Through Arch, he met Monroe Fleming, a Black Latter-day Saint working at the Hotel Utah. Monroe's wife, Frances, was a fourth-generation Saint and a great-granddaughter of Jane Manning James. The Flemings invited him over for dinner, spoke candidly about their experiences in the Church, and introduced him to other members of Salt Lake City's Black Latter-day Saint community.[37]

Among the people Darius met was Lucile Bankhead, the community's beloved matriarch. Like Frances Fleming, she was a descendant of Black Latter-day Saint pioneers and had grown up in the Church. He also met Eugene Orr, who had joined the Church in 1968 and married a woman he met in Utah, Leitha Derricott. Now Eugene and Leitha hosted summer picnics to help fellowship their Black friends in the area.[38]

Darius was particularly impressed by Ruffin Bridgeforth, a Black man who had moved to Utah in 1944 as an employee of the U.S. military. Ruffin and his wife, Helena, joined the Church in 1953 and raised their children in the faith. Darius admired Ruffin's steadfastness, quiet wisdom, and gentle manner. Over the years, Ruffin had become close friends with Elder Thomas S. Monson and other Church leaders. He often spoke to wards, stakes, and missions about Black members in the Church.[39]

One day, Darius received a telephone call from Heber Wolsey, the head of public relations at BYU. He knew Darius's work at KSL and occasionally sought his help when BYU faced a race-related controversy.[40]

Recently, the university had been under intense public scrutiny over the Church's priesthood restriction, and political activists sometimes staged demonstrations and boycotted BYU sporting events. The controversy had spiked in October 1969, when fourteen Black football players at the University of Wyoming asked to wear black armbands during their upcoming game against BYU. Their coach had kicked them off the team, drawing media attention and sparking protests.[41]

Now activists in Wyoming were calling for another protest, this time at a basketball game against

BYU. When BYU president Ernest L. Wilkinson learned of the plan, he issued a written statement in defense of the university and dispatched Heber to speak with the organizers.[42] But the activists wanted to meet a Black member of the Church, so Heber was calling to ask if Darius could catch a plane to Wyoming.

"How soon?" Darius asked.

"Oh," said Heber, "in the next thirty minutes."[43]

Darius rushed to the airport and caught the flight. When he arrived at the university, Heber whisked him off to a packed auditorium. They took their seats at the front, across from the leading activists. Darius maintained a friendly smile, but as he answered their questions, he could tell some of them were unhappy that he was defending the Church. Still, he determined to be true to himself and his beliefs.[44]

During one meeting that weekend, someone accused Darius of disgracing his race by joining the Church. Darius replied, "I was born Black. I am Black now. I will die Black. I am proud of my Black heritage. And I will fight for just Black causes with every power I have."

He then paused. "I am also a Mormon," he added, proudly. "The Mormon church has answers for me I have found nowhere else. There is no conflict between the color of my skin and my religion."[45]

Despite Darius and Heber's efforts, Wyoming students staged a demonstration before and during the game. As Darius observed them, he empathized with their desire for racial equality, yet he did not think they fully understood the Church or its teachings.

"If they were willing to demonstrate universally against prejudice and inequity wherever it may be, but not against the principles of the Mormon faith," he later reflected, "I would have been willing to join them."[46]

ON JANUARY 19, 1971, ANTHONY Obinna, a forty-two-year-old Nigerian schoolteacher, took out a pen and a blue sheet of paper to write a letter to the president of The Church of Jesus Christ of Latter-day Saints. "I have read several books in search of salvation," he wrote, "and at last found the answer."[47]

During the last few years, Anthony, his wife, Fidelia, and their children had been largely confined to their house while the Nigerian civil war raged around them. One day, as Anthony passed the long hours of uncertainty, he had flipped open an old magazine and seen something he was not expecting: a picture of a tall, stately stone building with several large spires.[48]

He had seen the building once before—in a dream he'd had before the civil war broke out. In the dream, the Savior had guided him to the magnificent building. It was full of people, all of them dressed in white.

"What is this?" Anthony had asked.

"These are people who attend the temple," the Savior replied.

"What are they doing?"

"They are praying. They pray here always."

When he woke, Anthony had yearned to know more about the things he had seen. He recounted the dream to Fidelia and his friends, asking what they thought it might mean. No one could help him. He finally asked a reverend for guidance. The reverend could not interpret the dream either, but he told Anthony that if the dream was of God, then his questions would someday be resolved.[49]

As soon as Anthony saw the image in the magazine, he knew he'd found his answer. At the top of the picture was a caption identifying it as the temple in Salt Lake City.

"Mormons—officially the members of the Church of Jesus Christ of Latter-day Saints—are different," the article began. It recounted the Church's history and explained some of its basic doctrine. "It is a complete way of life," the article said. "The religious spark that fires such a community of effort is a belief that everyone on earth is a spiritual son or daughter of God."[50]

The article had set Anthony's mind racing. He lived near his brothers, so he immediately gathered them together and told them about the picture and his dream.

"You're sure about that building?" his brother Francis asked.

Anthony was sure.[51]

Unfortunately, he had not been able to write to Church headquarters at that time because of a wartime blockade. Nor was he aware of any of Nigeria's unofficial

Latter-day Saint congregations. Many of them had scattered during the war, losing contact with each other and the Church. Some believers, like Honesty John Ekong, were never heard from again. But now that the war was over, nothing kept Anthony from contacting the Church.

Continuing his letter to the Church president, Anthony expressed his wish to have a branch of the Church in his town. "Mormonism is indeed unique among religions," he wrote.[52]

A few weeks later, he received a letter. "At the present time we do not have any official representatives from Salt Lake City in your country," it read. "If you wish, I shall be glad to correspond with you concerning the religious teachings of Jesus Christ."

The letter was signed by LaMar Williams, Missionary Department.[53]

CHAPTER 13

An Undying Knowledge

In early May 1971, Darius Gray entered the University of Utah's Marriott Library. His friend Eugene Orr, who worked in the library copy center, had invited him and Ruffin Bridgeforth to meet him there. Lately they had been wanting to talk about the challenges of Black Latter-day Saints. Each of them had been fasting and praying to know what to do.[1]

When Darius met up with his friends, they found an empty study room and started talking. Many of their concerns related to the Church's priesthood and temple restriction. Why had some Black men held the priesthood in the early days of the Church? And when would Black men be able to hold the priesthood again?[2]

As they discussed these questions, more questions arose. They knew Black Saints struggled to understand the restriction and stay active in the Church. What could be done to help them attend their meetings more often? Could the Church organize a branch specifically for its Black members?

And what about the younger generation of Black Saints? As fathers, both Ruffin and Eugene yearned to know how to answer their children's questions about the restriction.[3]

After writing down their questions, the friends knelt and Ruffin offered a prayer, pleading for the Lord's guidance. When they finished, they had the powerful impression to take their questions personally to President Joseph Fielding Smith and other senior Church leaders. But how could they set up such a meeting?

Knowing Eugene was persuasive and full of energy, Darius and Ruffin told him, "Why don't you get in touch with them?" If anyone could speak for the group, it was Eugene.[4]

A few days later, Eugene met with Arthur Haycock, the personal secretary of President Smith, at the Church Administration Building. "Whatever concerns you have," Arthur told Eugene, "I can resolve them for you."

"OK," said Eugene. "My biggest concern right now is that we would like to see the prophet." He showed Arthur the questions he had drawn up with Darius and Ruffin. "Blacks want to hold their heads up and be important and active in the Church," he said. "They don't want to just sit on the back row."

Arthur read the questions and agreed the list was valid. "I'll take it to the brethren and see what they decide," he said.[5]

Eugene heard nothing from Church headquarters after that, so three weeks later he returned to the Church Administration Building. This time Arthur told him that President Smith had appointed apostles Gordon B. Hinckley, Thomas S. Monson, and Boyd K. Packer to speak with them. A meeting was arranged for June 9.[6]

When that day arrived, Darius, Eugene, and Ruffin met with the three apostles in Elder Hinckley's office. The Church leaders had been acquainted with Ruffin for several years, and they knew Darius from his work with KSL. None of the apostles had met Eugene personally.

"We are seriously concerned over the problem in which we, our families, and our people find themselves," Darius and his friends told the apostles. Ruffin spoke of his sons losing interest in the Church after they had grown older and could not hold the Aaronic Priesthood. It pained him that they no longer attended.[7]

During the meeting, Eugene asked most of the questions:

"What do we tell our children when they ask about our baptizing them, when other children in Primary say that they will be baptized by their fathers?"

"Can we attend priesthood meeting?"

"Can missionary work be done among our people?"[8]

Elder Hinckley, Elder Monson, and Elder Packer listened sympathetically, and they agreed to meet again with Ruffin, Darius, and Eugene to discuss these and other questions. As the meeting ended, they acknowledged that the Church needed to do more for its Black members.

"We have faith. We have testimonies," the three friends told the apostles. "We want the blessings of the gospel extended more actively to our people, regardless of the priesthood."[9]

IN TOKYO, JAPAN, MEANWHILE, Kazuhiko Yamashita had basketball games every weekend—and very little time to study with Latter-day Saint missionaries. The elders had started visiting him not long after the world's fair, and he liked meeting with them. They were Americans, and he enjoyed talking with foreigners. But he often made appointments with them only to cancel later.

Religion had simply never been a priority in his life. His Buddhist parents venerated their ancestors by visiting their graves, but the family did not pray, meditate, or study the teachings of their faith. Buddhism was a tradition Kazuhiko had inherited, but it did not greatly influence how he lived his life.

The missionaries, in contrast, represented a church that met several times a week and encouraged its members to study scriptures and keep commandments. Becoming a Latter-day Saint was not just a significant time commitment. It was a major life change.[10]

Kazuhiko was impressed by the missionaries' message, though. When he learned about Joseph Smith's First Vision, he was amazed. He had no questions about it. He immediately believed it. If only he had more time for the Church, maybe he would take its message more seriously.

One day, Kazuhiko stopped by the missionaries' apartment and apologized for being careless with his appointments. "Brother Yamashita, I'm sorry," one of them said. "I'm going home." His mission was coming to an end.

The news surprised and saddened Kazuhiko. He resolved not to waste the elders' time anymore. "I will study harder," he told himself. "I will read the Book of Mormon."[11]

He began meeting regularly with the missionaries, going to church, and learning more about the restored gospel. He enjoyed attending MIA activities on Thursday nights and made friends with the local Saints.[12]

It was an exciting time for the Church in Japan. In the twenty-five years since the end of World War II, membership in Japan had grown from a few hundred to more than twelve thousand. Like Brazil and other countries where the Church was growing quickly, Japan had its own Church translation and distribution office. General authorities visited the country regularly, while day-to-day Church ministry was overseen by local leaders. There were now four missions in Japan and a stake in Tokyo.[13] Soon the Church would also open an institute of religion for university students and enroll younger Saints in the home-study seminary program.[14]

Sounded in Every Ear

Many people in Japan were still unfamiliar with the Latter-day Saints, but the Church's pavilion at Expo '70 had increased its profile in the country. The exhibit had drawn tens of thousands of visitors every day, far surpassing the attendance at the Church pavilion at the New York World's Fair five years earlier. By the end of the expo, more than 650,000 people had filled out comment cards at the pavilion, many requesting visits from the missionaries. And some 50,000 copies of the Book of Mormon had been sold.[15]

As Kazuhiko studied with the missionaries, he did not understand much of what they taught. But their lives and good example were like a message from God, and he wished he could be more like them. While offering his first personal prayer, following instructions given by the missionaries, he felt the presence of the Lord surround him. When the missionaries invited him to be baptized, he accepted.

His baptismal date was July 17, 1971. The branch did not have a baptismal font, so the missionaries had fashioned one in the meetinghouse kitchen from some scrap wood and a large vinyl sheet. The font was not very deep, but there was just enough water to immerse him.

Afterward, as one of the elders confirmed a woman who had also been baptized that day, he stopped midway through the blessing, his voice choked with emotion. Kazuhiko opened his eyes to see what was the matter, and he saw tears streaming down the missionary's face.

At that moment, he could feel the missionary's love—and God's love—for everyone in the room.[16]

AFTER BECOMING ACTING PRESIDENT of the Quorum of the Twelve Apostles, Spencer W. Kimball was busier than he had ever been. He often worked from early in the morning until 10:30 or 11:00 in the evening. And sometimes he awoke in the middle of the night to work. He tried to change his habits in small ways to make his days less hectic, but he struggled to see where he could cut back.

Before long, he began feeling sharp pains on the left side of his throat. At first the pain would come and go, but eventually his neck and throat hurt constantly. He experienced frequent chest pain, and even light physical exertion fatigued him. Exercise did not improve his condition. Soon his wife, Camilla, noticed that his breathing had become more labored.

In September 1971, he spoke privately about his symptoms with Dr. Russell M. Nelson, the newly called general superintendent of the Sunday School and a renowned heart surgeon. Dr. Nelson listened carefully and suggested that Elder Kimball see an expert immediately.[17]

Not long after, Elder Kimball consulted with Dr. Ernest Wilkinson, a heart specialist and son of the former president of Brigham Young University. Dr. Wilkinson reviewed the reports from Elder Kimball's earlier medical exam and conducted more tests. As the doctor studied the results, the apostle could tell he was concerned. "Be frank," he said.[18]

"Aortic stenosis," Dr. Wilkinson replied. He explained that Elder Kimball's aortic valve, which allowed blood to leave the heart, had hardened and narrowed. His heart was wearing out as it strained to pump blood through the diseased valve.[19]

Elder Kimball asked how long he had to live. The doctor said he might have one or two years more, but it was also possible that he would die without warning at any time. Surgery could prolong his life, but at Elder Kimball's age, he had only a 50 percent chance of surviving.

The news was devastating. Elder Kimball had always thought of death as something vague and far away. Now it felt like the end of the world—or the beginning of the end—had come.[20]

The next day, Elder Kimball walked to the Salt Lake Temple for a meeting with the First Presidency and his fellow apostles. During the meeting, he found himself praying for strength to serve well despite the looming possibility of death.

Soon the meeting ended, and the men began leaving the temple. Elder Kimball noticed the others walking in groups of two or three, and a dark thought came to him—perhaps these same men would soon be walking in twos or threes as his pallbearers.

Elder Kimball knew the Lord could heal him. But why would He do that, the apostle wondered, when

An Undying Knowledge

He could call other, more qualified men to serve in the Quorum of the Twelve?

"My leaving would make about as much stir," he mused, "as blowing out one of many candles."[21]

One day, around this time, Ruffin Bridgeforth, Darius Gray, and Eugene Orr were invited to the office of Gordon B. Hinckley.[22]

Since June, the three men had been meeting with Elder Hinckley, Elder Monson, and Elder Packer every few weeks. Difficult questions about the priesthood and temple restriction usually dominated their discussions, yet Ruffin always brought a calming spirit to the room.

In fact, the more the men counseled together, the more they learned to love and respect each other. Darius was impressed that President Smith had thought their concerns important enough to involve three apostles. As they continued to meet, the Lord was with them, and they often cried on one another's shoulders.[23]

Today, Elder Hinckley opened the meeting with good news. "After prayer and consideration," he said, "President Smith and the brethren of the Quorum of the Twelve have been led to establish a support group for Black members of the Church."[24]

Church leaders had been talking about organizing such a group ever since Darius, Eugene, and Ruffin first proposed organizing a branch for Black Saints in their list of questions for the prophet. Elder Hinckley explained that the group would operate as a part of the Liberty Stake in Salt Lake City. Members of the group would continue to attend sacrament meeting and Sunday School in their home wards. But the group would have its own Relief Society, MIA, and Primary. Its purpose was to provide community and outreach for Black Saints, especially young people who struggled to find a place in the Church.

The apostles had already called Ruffin to serve as president of the group, and Ruffin had recommended Darius for his first counselor and Eugene for his second. Elder Hinckley now extended the callings to them, and they accepted.[25]

A short time later, on October 19, 1971, Darius sat on the stand of a Salt Lake City meetinghouse. It was a Tuesday evening, but the chapel was full of people dressed for church. A few of the faces Darius saw were Black, but most of them were white.

Everyone had gathered to witness the start of what Darius, Ruffin, and Eugene had decided to call the Genesis Group, the first official Church organization for Black Latter-day Saints. Elder Hinckley, who conducted the meeting, introduced the group and its purpose. Then Ruffin Bridgeforth, as group president, called for a sustaining vote for its officers, including Lucile Bankhead as Relief Society president. When he finished, he bore his testimony.

"Genesis, as you know, means beginning," he said. "This is a beginning." He spoke of his love for the restored gospel and his gratitude for Church leaders and everyone in the congregation. "The Lord is on our side. We will succeed," he testified. "I will strive more than I have ever strived before to make this succeed."[26]

When President Bridgeforth sat down, Elder Hinckley invited Darius to bear his testimony, catching him off guard. Darius approached the pulpit and said, "I wasn't going to say anything this evening. It feels presumptuous."

Looking into the congregation, he saw members of the Felix family, who had introduced him to the gospel seven years earlier. "They could have easily passed over me, but they didn't," he told the congregation. "It was important for me to have an opportunity to hear the gospel. They were persistent in offering it to me."

He paused for a long time and then said, "I've often heard some men stand in sacrament meeting or fast and testimony meeting, men who bear the priesthood, and they stand and say I believe the gospel is true."

Now he too wanted to bear his testimony. "I know the gospel's true," he declared. "And that's an undying knowledge."[27]

AFTER GRADUATING AT THE top of her class from the secondary school at Benemérito, Isabel Santana returned to her hometown of Ciudad Obregón in northern Mexico. She was not sure what she wanted to do next. She could go back to Benemérito and enroll in the three-year preparatory school, which was designed to ready students for university. But she was seriously considering staying home and attending the local public preparatory school instead.

Isabel's father was content to let her make her own decision about school. Her mother, however, was not keen on her going to school in Obregón, worried she would get caught up in some radical student movement in the area.

"If she stays here," her mother thought, "she's going to become a revolutionary like everybody else."

Still uncertain, Isabel asked Agrícol Lozano, her civics teacher and the director of the preparatory school at Benemérito, for advice. He encouraged her to return and take the entrance exam.

"Come immediately," Agrícol told her. "Here you have a place."

Isabel returned to Mexico City, passed the exam, and was accepted. But she was unsure if she had made the right choice, especially after an aptitude test revealed that she was suited for social work—a career she had no interest in pursuing.

"I'm leaving," she announced to Efraín Villalobos, her trusted mentor, one day. "I don't want to be in the preparatory school."

"No, no, no," Efraín said. "Your place is here." He encouraged her to try Benemérito's teacher training school. Rather than prepare students only for university, the three-year school was also designed to prepare them for teaching at Church-operated schools in Mexico. That meant Isabel would immediately have a job when she completed her coursework.

Efraín's words persuaded her, and she switched schools.

She quickly came to like the courses and her teachers. During the first years, she took general education classes as well as courses on teaching techniques, educational psychology, and the history of education. Her training was in educating children, and during her last year at teacher training school, she spent a week teaching at a Church-run elementary school in Monterrey, a city in northeastern Mexico. Isabel had never felt a strong nurturing instinct, and she worried that she lacked the patience to work with children, but the week went well.[28]

While in teacher training school, Isabel became good friends with Juan Machuca, a young man from Mexico's western coast who had recently served in the North Mexican Mission. Some of their classmates teased them about being a couple. Isabel laughed and said Juan was the last man she would marry. "He is my friend," she insisted. "I'm not going to marry my friend."

After graduation, however, they were both hired to teach seminary and institute at Benemérito. They shared a classroom, and before long, they began going to the movies and spending more time together. In early 1972, as Isabel and Juan chatted in her living room, Juan suddenly asked, "Will you marry me?"

"Yes," she replied, no trace of hesitation in her voice.²⁹

They married civilly in May, during the summer holidays. A few weeks later they traveled fourteen hundred miles with other Church members to the temple in Mesa, Arizona, to receive their temple blessings. The three-day bus ride was stifling as they sat on plastic seats and had no air conditioner.³⁰

But the discomfort was worth it. Mesa was the first temple to offer ordinances in Spanish, and at the time it was the closest temple to Church members in Mexico and Central America. For these Saints, the journey was long and required them to make great sacrifices. They often made the trip to take part in an annual conference of Latin American Church members hosted by the stakes in Mesa. These conferences lasted several days and blessed participants with a sense of belonging and spiritual community.

Once Isabel and Juan arrived at the temple, they received their endowment and then were sealed together for time and eternity. As they worshipped there, they felt the temple enrich their perspective on life and deepen their commitment to the gospel of Jesus Christ.³¹

By early 1972, Billy Johnson's congregations in and around Cape Coast, Ghana, had grown to include hundreds of faithful members. Among the most devoted of them was Billy's mother, Matilda. Jacob and Lily Andoh-Kesson and their children, who joined the group soon after Billy's arrival in Cape Coast, were also committed members and friends.[32]

As his congregations grew, Billy had found an old building that had once been used to store cocoa beans. Now the space was filled with benches, a few small chairs and tables, a pulpit, and a long pew against a wall. Some people around Cape Coast mocked Billy and his followers for meeting in the rundown building, calling them "the cocoa-shed church." But the growing number of believers did not mind meeting there, even when rain leaked through holes in the roof and everyone had to bunch together or use umbrellas to stay dry.[33]

Billy did his best to make the humble building welcoming and comfortable. He hung a sign between the two double-door entrances that read "The Church of Jesus Christ of Latter-day Saints (Mormons)." A mural of Christ on the cross graced one wall, while a mural on another wall showed the Savior with arms uplifted and the words "Come unto Me" above His head. Pictures of Joseph Smith, the Tabernacle Choir, and other Church scenes dotted the walls, which were painted a light blue.[34]

Lily Andoh-Kesson kept the building clean. She arrived there early in the morning to prepare it for meetings. She saw angels there, she told her daughter Charlotte, and she wanted the angels to have a clean place to be.[35]

Billy's congregation met morning and evening three times a week for worship services, which were filled with hymns, dancing, clapping, prayer, shouts of praise, and sermons. Sometimes Billy preached with his young son Brigham sitting on his shoulders.

When he preached, Billy taught the principles he had learned from reading Church materials, like the thirteen Articles of Faith, and shared stories of Latter-day Saint pioneers. But most of all he loved teaching from the Book of Mormon.[36]

Billy believed that missionaries would come someday from Church headquarters, yet he feared that his followers would grow discouraged while waiting for them. Some people had even left the group after critics of the Church told them that Latter-day Saints did not like Black people and would never send missionaries.[37]

Occasionally, Billy's tireless preaching got him in trouble with local authorities. He was accused of spreading falsehoods because he testified that The Church of Jesus Christ of Latter-day Saints was the only true church on the earth.

One time the police arrested him, but before they could take him to the station, he looked around, hoping to see a familiar face—someone who would go with him and the police. At first, he saw no one. But then he spotted a young bystander named James Ewudzie, a family friend.

James was weeping as he approached Billy. He was not a member of Billy's congregation, but he placed a hand on him and called him "Sofo," the Fante word for priest. "Do not worry," he told Billy. "I will go with you."

After being led to the station, Billy quickly engaged James and the police in a religious discussion. Four of the police officers warmed to his message and believed his words. The head of the police also struck up a friendship with Billy, and before long, the officers released him and James. Later, the head of the police invited Billy to teach gospel lessons to the Cape Coast police force every Friday morning.

James, meanwhile, had a dream that he met Billy at the meetinghouse. Billy asked him to kneel, and after he did so, light shone through the roof. James closed his eyes, but the light still illuminated him. Then he heard a voice slowly call his name.

"I want to bring my Church into Ghana," the Lord said. He urged James to join with Billy. "If you help him, I will bless you and I will bless Ghana."

James knew what the Lord told him in the dream was true, and he followed His command.[38]

CHAPTER 14

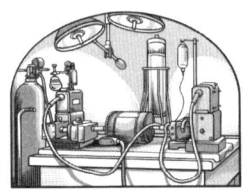

Different Now

In February 1972, Elder Spencer W. Kimball was despairing. Radiation treatments had removed his throat cancer but had ravaged his already-weakened voice, and now he could not speak above a whisper. His failing heart also continued to be a source of anxiety and physical weakness. "I am definitely losing," he wrote in his journal.[1]

Mindful of Elder Kimball's poor health, the First Presidency lightened his travel schedule. He attended the dedications of the Ogden and Provo Temples, issued calls to prospective missionaries, and advised the newly created Church Historical Department and its growing staff of professionals. He was grateful that he could still serve the Lord in these ways, but more and more he worried about being a burden on the Church.[2]

As his condition worsened, he and Camilla met with Presidents Harold B. Lee and N. Eldon Tanner. Dr. Russell M. Nelson joined them to lend medical expertise to the discussion.

"I am a dying man," Elder Kimball explained. "I can feel my life slipping. At the present rate of deterioration, it is my belief that I can live only about two more months."[3]

He was unlikely to recover, he told the group, without a complex surgery. Dr. Nelson, who was familiar with the procedure, explained that it consisted of two distinct surgeries. "First, the defective aortic valve would require removal and replacement with a prosthetic aortic valve," he said. "Second, the left anterior descending coronary artery would have to be revascularized with a bypass graft."

"What would the risks be with such a procedure?" asked President Lee.

Considering Elder Kimball's advanced age, Dr. Nelson did not know. "We have no experience doing both operations on patients in this age group," he said. "All I can say is, it would entail extremely high risk."

"I'm an old man and ready to die," Elder Kimball said wearily. "The Lord could heal me instantly and for as long as He wanted me. But why would He want me when I am getting older and others could do what I am doing and do it better?"[4]

President Lee shot to his feet. "Spencer," he said, pounding his fist on his desk, "you have been called! You are not to die. You are to do everything that you need to do in order to care for yourself and continue to live!"⁵

"All right," Elder Kimball said, "then I will have the operation."⁶

TWO MONTHS LATER, ON the other side of the United States, thousands of screaming girls greeted the Osmond brothers—Alan, Wayne, Merrill, Jay, and Donny—as they stepped onto a coliseum stage in Hampton, Virginia. Ranging in age from fourteen to twenty-two, the brothers wore white bell-bottom jumpsuits with high collars and sparkling rhinestones. When they started to sing and dance, the fans kept on screaming.⁷

Offstage, Olive Osmond thought it was cute the way the girls gawked over her sons. When she and her husband, George Osmond, had married in the Salt Lake Temple during World War II, they could not have imagined that their children would become pop music stars—and some of the most famous Latter-day Saints in the world. Their first two sons, Virl and Tom, were hard of hearing, and a doctor had tried to persuade Olive and George not to have more children. But the couple had seven more, all of them with full hearing.⁸

At a young age, Alan, Wayne, Merrill, Jay, and Donny learned to sing in harmony and became regular performers on a nationally broadcast television show. When they got older, though, they wanted to trade their repertoire of old-fashioned songs for a more contemporary sound.

Many young people liked the driving beat and electric guitars in rock music.⁹ Yet some Church leaders were concerned that it was too provocative. Olive and George shared these concerns, but they and their children believed rock music could promote goodness as well. Olive thought her sons could have a positive influence on the world—if only their music could reach the right audience.

"You have a special mission," she would tell the boys. "God gave you this talent for a reason."¹⁰

In 1970, the brothers recorded a song called "One Bad Apple," with Merrill and Donny on lead vocals. The record was a hit, making the boys celebrities almost overnight. After that, Olive and George worked hard to help their sons keep the commandments. While other rock stars were drinking and using drugs, the Osmonds obeyed the Word of Wisdom. Instead of going to wild parties, the brothers held home evenings with their family, attended church, and gave devotionals while on tour.¹¹

After becoming famous, the brothers met with President Joseph Fielding Smith, who reminded them of their duty to always share the gospel. Later, his counselor Harold B. Lee reminded them that the world was watching them and might judge the Church based on their actions. He encouraged them to avoid morally dangerous situations and to stand up for what they believed.

"There will always be two choices," he taught them. "Always choose that which will bring you closest to the celestial kingdom." He then quoted the Savior's words from the Sermon on the Mount: "Let your light so shine before men, that they may see your good works, and glorify your Father which is in heaven."[12]

Before long, many people in the United States associated the Church with the Osmonds. When speaking with the press, Olive almost always mentioned her religion and its influence on the family's wholesome lifestyle and cheerful music. In their own interactions with reporters, the boys also talked openly about their faith, and fans often sent them mail with questions about the Church. Since the growth of the Church had been especially rapid in the United States, there were usually wards and branches in the cities where the Osmonds performed, making it easier for fans to get in contact with missionaries and meet other Latter-day Saints.

Recently, in fact, the *Church News* had featured excerpts of letters from people who came to know the Church through the Osmonds. One fan had started researching the Latter-day Saints after seeing the happiness and closeness of the Osmond family. "I knew it had something to do with your religion," they wrote.[13]

During the concert in Virginia, the youngest Osmond, eight-year-old Jimmy, joined his brothers onstage for a song. Olive remained backstage with her twelve-year-old daughter, Marie, answering questions from a local reporter.

"I try to make a home away from home," Olive explained. She thought the family was closer now that they were on tour together. In fact, the brothers were collaborating on an ambitious new album—something more profound and personal than anything they'd done so far.

"They are doing what God intended them to," she said. "The kids they attract are looking to them for something."[14]

ONE MONTH LATER, ON the morning of April 12, 1972, Dr. Russell M. Nelson readied himself to perform open-heart surgery. He had performed hundreds of operations in his life, but never on an apostle of the Lord. And although he had prayed about Elder Kimball's procedure and pondered how best to perform it, he was not confident that he or any surgeon could do it successfully.[15]

At his own request, Dr. Nelson had received a blessing from President Lee and President Tanner the day before. Placing their hands on his head, they blessed him that he might perform the surgery without error. They told him he had no reason to fear his inadequacies. The Lord had raised him up to perform this operation.[16]

The procedure began at eight o'clock. In the operating room, an anesthesiologist sedated Elder Kimball, while Dr. Nelson's resident assistant stood ready with several nurses and other members of the surgical team. A heart-lung machine waited nearby, ready to oxygenate and pump Elder Kimball's blood.

Under Dr. Nelson's direction, the team worked skillfully to replace the damaged valve with a prosthesis—a small plastic ball inside a metal cage. The device was about half the circumference of his thumb.

After fitting the valve in place, Dr. Nelson began to stitch. With one precise suture after another, he slowly connected the ring at the base of the valve to the surrounding tissue.

He then turned his attention to bypassing an obstruction blocking blood flow into the heart. Locating an artery running down Elder Kimball's chest, he severed its lower end and placed the artery just below the blocked blood vessel. Once again, the doctor stitched with tiny, intricate sutures until the healthy artery was firmly attached.[17]

As he worked, Dr. Nelson marveled at how smoothly the operation was going. It required thousands of intricate maneuvers, each requiring painstaking technique. Yet not a single error had occurred. When the time finally came to disconnect Elder Kimball from the heart-lung machine, more than four hours after the surgery started, the medical staff jolted his heart with electricity, and it immediately jumped back to life.

After the surgery, Dr. Nelson called President Lee. The First Presidency and the Quorum of the Twelve were gathered in the temple, fasting and praying for Elder Kimball. As Dr. Nelson described the procedure, he told President Lee that he felt like a baseball pitcher who had just pitched a perfect game. The Lord had magnified his skills, allowing him to perform the operation exactly as promised in the priesthood blessing.

President Lee was overjoyed. "Brother Kimball is making good progress and is off the heart machine," he told the apostles. "The Lord has answered our prayers."[18]

THAT SAME MONTH, IN Rio de Janeiro, Brazil, forty-one-year-old Helvécio Martins was driving home from work when a traffic jam forced him to stop. The line of cars in front of him seemed to have no end, and it did not look like the gridlock would clear up anytime soon.

Helvécio took a moment to reflect on the spiritual dissatisfaction he had been feeling for years. Since his youth, he had worked hard to climb his way out of poverty. He dropped out of school at age eleven and became an orange picker. Later, after his family moved to Rio, he worked as a courier. His employers trusted him and appreciated his diligence. Eventually, he met and married Rudá Tourinho de Assis, who encouraged him to attend night school.[19]

After years of persistence, Helvécio obtained a high school diploma and graduated from university with a degree in accounting. He then began working for an oil company, and in time he became head of a department with more than two hundred employees.[20]

Meanwhile he and Rudá and their two children, Marcus and Marisa, enjoyed invitations to social events with prominent people. It was a lifestyle far better than anything Helvécio could have imagined.

But despite his success, Helvécio felt unfulfilled. He and Rudá had tried various religions, participating in Spiritualist practices and later exploring several Christian denominations. No matter where they went, they felt something lacking.[21]

Sitting in traffic, Helvécio's frustration grew. He opened his car door and stepped onto the road. "My God," he prayed, "I know you are there someplace, but I don't know where. Is it possible you don't see the confusion my family and I are experiencing? Is it possible you don't realize we are searching for something and that we don't even know what it is? Why don't you help us?"

When he finished making his plea, the traffic began to clear. Helvécio returned to his car and drove on, soon forgetting the incident.[22]

Two weeks later, the Martinses found a card slipped under their door. On one side it had a picture of the Savior, and on the other was a meeting schedule for The Church of Jesus Christ of Latter-day Saints.

The card intrigued Helvécio, and he took it to work the next day.

"Boss, don't go there," one of his employees said. "That is a church for North Americans. If you don't know a member, I wouldn't even try to go."[23]

Helvécio believed his employee and set aside his interest in the Church. But a short time later, two missionaries, Thomas McIntire and Steve Richards, showed up at the Martinses' door. The moment they entered, Helvécio noticed a calm feeling fill the home.

The missionaries introduced themselves. "We have a blessing for your family if you would like one," they said.

"Yes," Helvécio said. But first he had questions.[24]

They discussed some general information about the Church, and then Helvécio raised a difficult question—one that mattered to him as a descendant of enslaved people from Africa. "Given that your church is headquartered in the United States," he said, "how does your religion treat Blacks? Are they allowed into the church?"

Elder McIntire looked embarrassed. "Sir," he said, "do you really want to know?"

"Yes," said Helvécio.

Elder McIntire explained that Black people could be baptized and participate as members of the Church but were not allowed to hold the priesthood or attend the temple. Helvécio and Rudá accepted his answer and asked more questions about the priesthood and the gospel. The missionaries answered each question calmly and thoroughly.

By the time the missionaries left, four and a half hours had passed. That night, Helvécio and Rudá discussed what the missionaries had taught them. They were impressed by the missionaries' lesson and felt that their questions had been answered fully.[25]

A short time later, the Martinses attended their first sacrament meeting. The service was beautiful, and the congregation welcomed them warmly. Not long after, the branch president stopped by the Martinses' home and introduced them to two men who would be their home teachers.

As the family continued attending church and meeting with the missionaries, their faith grew. One day, they attended an especially powerful meeting of the Rio de Janeiro District, and they knew that they needed to join the Church.

"We are different now," thirteen-year-old Marcus said a week later as the family drove home from Sunday School. "Your faces glow, and I know what is causing it—the gospel of Jesus Christ."

Helvécio pulled the car to a stop at the side of the road, where the family broke down in tears. When the Martinses returned to the chapel that evening for sacrament meeting, they told their branch president they were ready to be baptized.[26]

ONE DAY AROUND THIS time, the Osmonds' manager, Ed Leffler, asked the family if they wanted to perform in England. The brothers' song "Down by the Lazy River" and Donny's solo recording of "Puppy Love" were hits in the United States and Canada. Everyone in North America seemed to know about the Osmond brothers, and now teenagers in Europe were taking notice too.

"Sure," Olive said, "but on one condition—that I can meet the queen."

She was joking, but Ed took her comment seriously. "I'll see if that can be arranged," he said.

A short time later, Ed informed the family that he had lined up a performance for Queen Elizabeth II and her husband, Prince Philip. And Olive was going to get her wish. She and George had an invitation to meet with the royal couple during the intermission.

Olive couldn't believe it. She purchased a formal dress and some white gloves for the occasion. She also bought a brand-new set of scriptures and dared herself to give it as a gift to the queen.[27]

The Osmonds arrived in London in May and spent a few days rehearsing their songs. The performance took place on May 22, 1972, at the London Palladium, a famous theater in the city's West End. It was a televised charity concert featuring singers, actors, and comedians from the United Kingdom and United States.[28]

Olive and George sat in the audience with Marie during the first half of the show. At intermission, Lew Grade, the man who had organized the show, touched George on the arm. "Come quickly," he said.

Olive and George stood up and hurried after Lew. Before she reached the end of the aisle, though, Olive realized that she'd left her gift for the queen beneath her seat. For a split second, she thought about leaving the scriptures there. But she had spent much of the previous night marking and annotating her favorite passages for the queen. And she knew she'd never have the chance again. Turning around, she ran back to her seat and grabbed the book.

Once Lew ushered her and George into the presence of the queen, Olive approached the royal couple, curtsied, exchanged a few words with them, and moved on without delivering her gift. She then looked back and saw that George had stopped to speak with Prince Philip about their mutual interest in hunting and fishing.

Noticing another member of the royal family standing nearby, Olive approached him with her copy of the standard works. "Would you mind giving the queen this little gift after I have left?" she asked.

The man looked at Olive with a twinkle in his eye. "Elizabeth!" he said. "Mrs. Osmond has brought you a present."

"How lovely," said the queen. "Please come here."

Embarrassed, Olive obeyed. "I wanted to bring you a gift," she explained, hardly knowing where she found the words. "It's difficult to know what to give a queen, so I brought you our most valuable possession."

"Can you part with it?" asked the queen.

"Yes," said Olive, "I have another one just like it."

The queen looked at the scriptures. "Thank you, Mrs. Osmond. I'll cherish this," she said. "I'm going to put it on my mantel."

Olive relaxed and chatted briefly about her family with the queen. They then returned to their seats to watch the boys perform.[29]

Later, as the family was getting ready to fly home, Ed Leffler approached Olive. "What do you think?" he asked.

"It was the thrill of a lifetime," Olive said. "I was even able to give her a copy of the Book of Mormon."

"You what?" Ed said, visibly upset. "That's about the worst thing you could have possibly done." He explained that as head of the Church of England, the queen was not in a position to accept the teachings of the Book of Mormon.

Ed's words troubled Olive. She hadn't meant to hurt anyone. She simply believed the queen had a right to hear the restored gospel as much as anyone else. Had she really done something wrong?

Once the family boarded the airplane and everyone was settled, Olive sat down and started reading her scriptures. The pages fell open, and her eyes rested on Doctrine and Covenants 1:23: "That the fulness of my gospel might be proclaimed by the weak and the simple unto the ends of the world, and before kings and rulers."

The words comforted Olive. Her doubts fled, and she knew she had done the right thing.[30]

ON THE EVENING OF June 15, 1972, eighteen-year-old Maeta Holiday smiled as she stood with more than five hundred high school seniors in a gymnasium in Southern California. In a few moments, she and her classmates would receive their high school diplomas and begin the next stage of their lives. They wore matching caps and gowns, with female students in red and male students in black.[31]

For Maeta, the graduation meant that her time in the Indian Student Placement Program was coming to an end. Soon she would be leaving her foster family to start a new life for herself. Like many graduates of the placement program, she planned to attend Brigham Young University. More than five hundred Native Americans, most of whom were Navajo like Maeta, currently attended BYU. The school offered generous scholarships to these students, and Maeta's foster parents, Venna and Spencer Black, had helped her apply for the aid.

Maeta knew the Blacks would continue to support her. When she came to live with them four years earlier, they had immediately treated her like a daughter. They gave her a stable home and helped her feel, for the first time in her life, that she was part of a loving family. And even though she had joined the Church long before she lived with them, they showed her what a family could be when it was centered in the teachings of Jesus Christ.[32]

Not all students in the placement program had such good experiences with their foster families. Some students did not feel welcome in their foster homes or get along with their foster parents or siblings. Others resisted their foster families' efforts to introduce them to non-Native culture. At the same time, some students found ways to value both their heritage and their placement program experience. They returned to the reservations, strengthened their communities, and lived fulfilling lives as Latter-day Saints there.

For her part, Maeta was still haunted by her painful experiences as a child. She did not want the kind of life her parents or grandparents lived.[33] Venna, however, had encouraged her to value her Navajo heritage. "You should be proud of who you are," Venna once told her. "God knows you are special because the Book of Mormon is about your people." Like many Saints at the time, Venna understood Book of Mormon promises to apply to Native Americans. When she looked at Maeta, she saw a descendant of Lehi and Sariah, entitled to covenant blessings.

"Maeta, I want this for you," Venna had said. "I want you to get married in the temple someday. And I want you to keep going to church, and I just want to let you know that you are special, and we love you."

As Maeta received her diploma, she still did not fully understand or accept everything Venna had taught her. And as much as she admired her foster family, she did not know if she could have a successful marriage or family herself. After witnessing her parents' divorce and her mother's struggle to care for her own children, she had no interest in marriage or raising a family.[34]

Following her graduation, Maeta learned that her application to BYU had been accepted. As she boarded the bus to Provo, she thought about her future—and her faith. Attending church and seminary had been an important part of the Indian Student Placement Program. But did she want the restored gospel to be a part of her future?

"Well, if I'm going to BYU, I wonder what I need to do," she thought. "Should I be part of the Church or should I not?"

She began to think about the lessons she learned from Venna and Spencer. Her life had not been easy, but she had been blessed to live with them and become part of their family.

"I do believe in God," she thought. "He has been there all this time."[35]

ON AUGUST 26, 1972, ISABEL Santana and her husband, Juan Machuca, could feel the excitement in the air as they parked their yellow Volkswagen outside the Auditorio Nacional in Mexico City. More than sixteen thousand Saints from Mexico and Central America had converged on the large event center for an area general conference. For many, the conference would be their first time hearing general authorities speak in person.[36]

The Church had begun holding area general conferences under the direction of President Joseph Fielding Smith. Since most Church members could not attend general conference in Salt Lake City, the local conferences gave them an opportunity to gather together and receive instruction from local and general authorities. The first area general conference had been held in Manchester, England, in 1971. With more than eighty thousand Church members, Mexico was home to the largest population of Saints outside the United States, making it an ideal place to hold such a conference.[37]

Isabel and Juan were amazed as they made their way to the event center. There were Church members from all over Mexico and as far away as Guatemala, Honduras, Costa Rica, and Panama. Some of the Saints had traveled three thousand miles to be there. One woman from northwestern Mexico had scrubbed her neighbors' laundry for five months to earn enough money to make the trip. Some Saints had paid their way by selling tacos and tamales, washing cars, or doing yardwork. Others had sold belongings or borrowed money so they could come. A few people were fasting because they did not have money for food. Fortunately, Benemérito provided lodging for many of the Saints from far away.

As the Machucas waited in line to enter the auditorium, a car pulled up nearby, and out stepped Spencer W. Kimball and his wife, Camilla. Four months had passed since Elder Kimball's heart surgery, and he had already recovered enough to resume many of his responsibilities in the Quorum of the Twelve Apostles. In fact, he was scheduled to address the Saints later that afternoon.[38]

Although President Joseph Fielding Smith had helped plan the conference, he had passed away before he could attend. His death marked the end of decades of a long and devoted life of service on behalf of the Church and its members.[39] As an apostle, he had written widely on gospel doctrine and historical topics, promoted genealogical and temple work, and dedicated the Philippines and Korea for the preaching of the gospel. As Church president, he authorized the first stakes in Peru and South Africa, dramatically increased seminaries and institutes around the world, revitalized the Church's public communications, and professionalized Church departments.[40]

"There is no work that any of us can engage in that is as important as preaching the gospel and building up the Church and kingdom of God on earth," he had told the Saints at his final general conference. "And so we invite all our Father's children, everywhere, to believe in Christ, to receive Him as He is revealed by living prophets, and to join The Church of Jesus Christ of Latter-day Saints."[41]

His successor, Harold B. Lee, had since been set apart as president of the Church, making Elder Kimball the new president of the Quorum of the Twelve Apostles.[42]

Once Isabel and Juan gained entrance to the Auditorio Nacional, they found seats among the thousands of Saints. The auditorium had four tiers of seating around a stage area. A choir of Church members from northern Mexico filled the stand. In front of them was a pulpit and a section of high-backed chairs for the general authorities and other speakers.[43]

The conference opened with a talk from President Marion G. Romney, who had been born and raised in the Latter-day Saint colonies in northern Mexico and had recently been made a counselor in the First Presidency. Speaking in Spanish, he told them of his love for the Saints of Mexico and Central America and his appreciation for the Mexican government.[44]

President N. Eldon Tanner then spoke, celebrating the strength of the Church in Mexico and the other Spanish-speaking nations of the Americas. "Growth is taking place, and leadership is being developed throughout the world," he declared through an interpreter. To assist these developing leaders, the Church's *General Handbook of Instructions* had recently been correlated and translated into over a dozen languages, including Spanish. Leaders across the world could administer the Church according to the same pattern.

"It is marvelous to see how people are accepting the gospel and coming into the Church and kingdom of God," President Tanner testified, "all bearing testimony to the blessings that it affords them, realizing that it is the Church of Jesus Christ."[45]

Listening to the speakers made Isabel feel glad to be a Mexican Latter-day Saint. Her education at Benemérito had taught her the value of being a Church member, of making the restored gospel a central part of her life. When she first arrived at the school, she had been a timid girl without a clear sense of her spiritual potential. But her teachers had blessed her in countless ways. She had developed a daily routine of study and prayer, and she walked with confidence and a fervent testimony of truth.

Now, surrounded by so many Saints, she couldn't help but rejoice. "I'm from here," she thought. "I belong to this."⁴⁶

CHAPTER 15

The Joy of an Eternal Covenant

Delayed by Church work in Salt Lake City, President Harold B. Lee arrived late to the area general conference in Mexico City. His plane touched down in the early afternoon of August 26, 1972, and by evening he was being shuttled from venue to venue to speak at individual conference sessions for the Relief Society, Aaronic and Melchizedek Priesthood holders, and young women. The next morning, the Saints at the conference sustained him as the new president of the Church—the first congregation in the world to do so.[1]

The prophet returned to Utah a few days later, only to learn that a member of an apostate group had allegedly made death threats against him.[2]

To ensure President Lee's safety, police began accompanying him wherever he went. He was grateful for their protection, but the presence of the officers bothered him. Recent Church presidents had generally gone without bodyguards. Now every time President Lee went out, his police escort created no small disturbance.

Soon he and his wife, Joan, decided to join Elder Gordon B. Hinckley and his wife, Marjorie, on a trip to visit Saints in Europe and Israel.

The trip would have its own risks, however. They would be traveling without a security detail in a tense region of the world. A Palestinian group had just kidnapped and killed eleven members of the Israeli national Olympic team at the 1972 Summer Games in Munich, West Germany. The attack sent the world reeling, and President Lee worried that an armed conflict might break out in Israel. Still, he and Sister Lee accompanied the Hinckleys as planned.[3]

The group arrived at the airport in Tel Aviv, Israel, on the evening of September 19. David Galbraith, a Church member from Canada who was studying at the Hebrew University of Jerusalem, picked them up and drove them forty miles southeast to Jerusalem. It was dark when they arrived, and they couldn't see much, but there was something wonderful about traveling through the ancient, sacred city.

Over the next three days, the Lees and Hinckleys met with Israeli dignitaries and visited holy sites. Teddy Kollek, the mayor of Jerusalem, told President Lee that he had heard the story of apostle Orson Hyde offering a prayer on the Mount of Olives in 1841. President Lee told him that the Church wanted someday to build a monument or a visitors' center in the city to commemorate the prayer.

"We are trying to acquire property on the Mount of Olives to create a park for meditation," Mayor Kollek said. "It might be possible to have a monument with this inscription in the park."[4]

On the evening of September 20, David and a small group of Saints living in Israel met with the Lees and Hinckleys at a garden tomb some believed might have been the place Jesus was laid after the Crucifixion. A sense of holiness rested over the group. They could imagine seeing the Savior's lifeless body being carried to the tomb, or Mary Magdalene returning to the garden on the third day and beholding the resurrected Lord.

At the tomb, President Lee organized the Saints into a branch, with David as their president. Although there were no more than thirty permanent Church members living in the country, groups of BYU students had recently started coming to study in the Holy Land for a few months at a time, more than doubling the number of Saints at the meetings. President Lee believed the branch would lay the foundation of a great work in the region.

"When people ask you who you are," he counseled, "don't say members of the Mormon Church or of the LDS Church, but say The Church of Jesus Christ of Latter-day Saints."[5]

After the meeting, President Lee returned to his hotel room exhausted. He had been feeling some severe pain in his lower back for several days, and he had developed a painful cough and shortness of breath. Now, with the onset of the fatigue, he worried that something was wrong.

Later that night, at Sister Lee's insistence, Elder Hinckley came to their hotel room and gave President Lee a blessing. The next morning, President Lee coughed up some blood and felt instant relief from his shortness of breath. Soon he was doing well enough to join David and the Hinckleys for a sightseeing tour of Bethany, Jericho, Capernaum, Nazareth, and other sacred sites.

The next day, at breakfast, he told Elder Hinckley he had experienced a miracle. He felt as if he had been on the brink of death, but through Elder Hinckley's blessing, the Lord had restored his health.

"We had to come to the land of miracles to witness a miracle within ourselves," he said gratefully.

They would be leaving Jerusalem that evening, so they spent the time they had left walking where Jesus had walked. They visited Gethsemane, the tomb of Lazarus, Bethlehem, and the remnants of the wall surrounding the temple. David then drove them to the airport, and they caught a plane to Rome, their faith renewed from all they had seen and experienced in the Holy Land.[6]

On November 7, 1972, Ardeth Kapp heard the telephone ring as she entered her apartment in Bountiful, Utah. Francis Gibbons, the secretary to the First

Presidency, was on the other end of the line. "Could you and your husband meet with President Harold B. Lee tomorrow morning in his office at 11:35?" he asked.

Taking a deep breath, Ardeth said, "We'll be there." Right away, she wondered why President Lee wanted to talk with them.[7]

She and her husband, Heber, were teachers by profession. Although they were still relatively young—she was forty-one years old—they had served actively in the Church for many years. She was a member of the education faculty at Brigham Young University and served on the Church's Youth Correlation Committee. He was a former bishop and now a counselor in the stake presidency.[8]

When Heber came home, Ardeth told him about the telephone call. She thought President Lee might ask him to serve as a mission president. Heber did not think so, but he worried that they might have to move. They were in the middle of building a house and would have to abandon the project if called on a mission. Heber was doing most of the construction work himself, and they could not afford to pay anyone to finish it.[9]

Ardeth passed the night sleeplessly, reflecting on her life. The Lord had always helped her with her trials. As a girl living near Cardston, Alberta, Canada, she had failed two grades in school. Few people had expected her to excel at her studies, but with God's help, she had recently earned a master's degree in curriculum development.

But that had not been her greatest struggle. Although she had always wanted a large family, she and Heber had never been able to have children, despite frequent prayers for a miracle. For a while, they had thought about adopting, but every time they sought the Lord's guidance on the matter, they received a "stupor of thought." They felt judged by neighbors, friends, and family who called them selfish for not having children. Only an eternal perspective of God's plan had brought them the peace and acceptance they needed to cope with their pain.[10]

On the morning of their appointment with President Lee, Ardeth and Heber were nervous as they arrived at the Church Administration Building, but they were willing to accept any assignment from the Lord. President Lee greeted them warmly and invited them into his office. "Try to be relaxed," he said. "I'm sure you know this is not just a casual visit."

He then spoke about the need for frequent organizational changes in the Church to keep pace with its rapid growth. The Church's youth program particularly concerned him. He believed the Church needed to do more to strengthen young people and prepare them to serve in the kingdom of God. For this reason, the Mutual Improvement Associations were being restructured to place them under the direct supervision of general Aaronic and Melchizedek Priesthood leaders.[11]

As she listened to President Lee, Ardeth wondered what he was going to ask Heber to do. "Whatever he wants him for," she thought, "I'm sure he can do a good job, and I'll be willing to support him."

President Lee then called Ardeth to serve, catching her by surprise. *She* was the reason he had called them into his office?[12]

President Lee explained that Ruth Funk had recently agreed to serve as general president of the Young Women's Mutual Improvement Association. Having worked with Ardeth on the Correlation Committee, Ruth had recommended her to serve as second counselor. The new presidency would have their offices on the nineteenth floor of the Church Office Building, a recently completed skyscraper in downtown Salt Lake City.[13]

Overwhelmed, Ardeth accepted the call, grateful for the trust it represented. A short time later, the Church officially announced the reorganization of its youth programs. Before this time, the YWMIA had operated under the supervision of the First Presidency. Now, as part of the correlation of Church organizations, the YWMIA and YMMIA would coordinate their efforts under the direction of the Presiding Bishopric and ward and stake priesthood leaders. The new structure also drew distinctions between Melchizedek Priesthood MIA, or single adults older than age eighteen, and the Aaronic Priesthood MIA, or young men and young women between the ages of twelve and eighteen.[14]

While the Aaronic Priesthood MIA would be supervised by priesthood leaders, the program would continue to offer gender- and age-based classes and activities for boys and girls. Paralleling the priesthood offices of deacon, teacher, and priest, the young women classes were called Beehive (ages 12–13), Mia Maid (ages 14–15), and Laurel (ages 16–18)—names the YWMIA had long been using. A few years earlier, Church leaders had asked every ward to start a bishop's youth council, which gave youth new opportunities to lead. Now the First Presidency wanted the new MIA organizations to give the youth even more leadership opportunities.[15]

President Funk supported this vision for the program. As a high school teacher, she had given her students many chances over the years to develop as leaders, and they had done great things. "You don't become anything by hearing about it," she declared. "You become by doing it."[16]

The principle was something Ardeth could take to heart too. Not long after her call, she accepted an assignment to attend several regional conferences in the United Kingdom. She was nervous about the trip because she was new to her calling. But then she remembered the words of Nephi in the Book of Mormon: "The Lord giveth no commandments unto the children of men, save he shall prepare a way for them that they may accomplish the thing which he commandeth them."

"I've known that all my life," she told herself, "but I need to know it now."[17]

The Joy of an Eternal Covenant

AFTER THEIR BAPTISMS, HELVÉCIO and Rudá Martins found that other Brazilian Saints often wanted to discuss the Church's priesthood and temple restriction with them. Some people wondered how the family could stay faithful in the Church when neither Helvécio nor their son, Marcus, could be ordained to the priesthood. A few, upset by the Martinses' devotion, criticized or mocked them.

"If I were in your situation," one man told Helvécio, "I don't believe I would stay in the Church."[18]

Still, many fellow Saints admired the Martinses for their strong testimonies and commitment to their callings. Four months after they joined the Church, Elder Bruce R. McConkie—the newest member of the Quorum of the Twelve Apostles—had come to Rio de Janeiro to organize the fifth stake in Brazil. At the time, Helvécio did not fully understand the difference between a district and stake, but he agreed to serve as a counselor in the stake Sunday School presidency. Rudá, meanwhile, accepted a call to serve in the stake Primary presidency.[19]

The new stake covered an immense area, stretching thousands of square miles. Helvécio's and Rudá's new callings gave them the opportunity to visit the stake's many far-flung wards and branches. Often Helvécio would pick Rudá up at the bus stop late at night as she returned from fulfilling an assignment. Though the new demands on them were difficult, the Martinses were happy to serve.[20]

Their baptism had also changed their relationship with family. Rudá's family members did not like that she joined the Church, and they tried to persuade her and Helvécio to abandon their new faith, predicting that tragedy would befall them otherwise. Some in her family even warned that God might take their son Marcus's life.[21]

But the Martinses felt comfortable among the Saints. The branch members embraced them so warmly that Helvécio had first wondered if his family was receiving special treatment because of his prominent professional status. After he was assigned a menial task at a branch activity, however, he realized that his family was not being treated any differently.[22]

One day, a friend at Church told Helvécio, "Faithful members like you have demonstrated your claim on the priesthood to the Lord. I have no doubt that one day you will receive the priesthood."

Helvécio and Rudá appreciated the support of their friends and fellow Church members. But they preferred not to dwell on the question of when or how Black Saints would receive the blessings of the priesthood. They had faith that God would someday fulfill all His promises. Still, the Martinses kept their expectations low to protect themselves against disappointment and heartache. They believed that the full blessings of the priesthood and temple would come to them in the Millennium. Until then, they simply prayed for more faith and the strength to serve in the Church.[23]

After the Rio de Janeiro Stake was organized, Helvécio and Rudá made appointments to receive their patriarchal blessings. When Walmir Silva, the stake patriarch, blessed Helvécio and Rudá, he promised them that they would live together "on the earth in the joy of an eternal covenant." The promise was beautiful, but the family arrived home feeling confused. Because of the priesthood restriction, Helvécio and Rudá could not enter the temple and did not expect to make temple covenants during their mortal lives. What could the patriarch have meant?

Seven weeks later, fourteen-year-old Marcus visited the patriarch's home to receive his own blessing. As the patriarch blessed him, he promised Marcus that he would have opportunities to preach the gospel and bear his testimony of truth. Helvécio and Rudá interpreted this promise to mean that Marcus would serve a mission. But that too seemed impossible. Marcus could not serve a mission unless he held the priesthood.

The Martins family did not want the patriarch's words to upset the steady, peaceful rhythm of their lives. They decided to continue living just as they had before and not think too much about the experience.

And yet, Helvécio and Rudá did not want to ignore the promises they had been given. Just in case, they quietly opened a new savings account—a missionary fund for Marcus.[24]

CHRISTMAS DAY 1973 PASSED quietly for Spencer W. Kimball. He and Camilla exchanged gifts with each other and with Camilla's sister Mary, who had been born deaf and now lived with them. Camilla put a turkey in the oven, and he helped her set up an extra table for the guests they expected for dinner.

Elder Kimball spent the rest of the morning at his typewriter as he tried to catch up on a stack of unanswered letters. Christmas music played on the phonograph, and he took an occasional break from typing to flip the record over.

As the morning turned to afternoon, some of the Kimballs' children, grandchildren, and great-grandchildren arrived for Christmas dinner. Among the guests were Mangal Dan Dipty, a man whom Elder Kimball had baptized twelve years earlier in Delhi, India, and a young Zuni girl named Arlene, who lived with the Kimballs' daughter, Olive Beth, as part of the Indian Student Placement Program. The group ate and sang, and Elder Kimball went to bed feeling the day had passed pleasantly.[25]

The next evening, sometime after eight o'clock, Elder Kimball answered the telephone at his home. "This is Arthur," the caller said. At once, Elder Kimball knew it was Arthur Haycock, President Lee's secretary.

"Well, Arthur," Elder Kimball said pleasantly, "how are you tonight?"

"Not very good," Arthur said. "I am at the hospital with President Lee, and he is very sick. I think you should come at once."[26]

Elder Kimball hung up the phone and drove straight to the hospital, where he met Arthur in the hallway. Arthur explained that President Lee had come to the hospital for rest and a checkup. He had been sitting on the bed when he suddenly went into cardiac arrest. Arthur called for help, and in a moment the room filled with doctors, nurses, and equipment. The place still bustled with frantic activity.[27]

Joan, President Lee's wife, arrived with his daughter Helen and son-in-law Brent. Arthur told them they should keep clear of President Lee's room, so the small group found an empty room just down the hall where they could wait. They prayed together and asked the Lord to preserve the prophet's life. As they waited, Marion G. Romney, President Lee's second counselor in the First Presidency, arrived.

Unsure what else they could do, President Romney led the group in another prayer. A doctor then entered the room.

"We are doing all we can," he said, "but it doesn't look good."[28]

Elder Kimball was shocked. President Lee, who had supported him constantly through his own illnesses, was seventy-four years old—younger than he himself was. And he had seemed much healthier. Many in the Church had assumed that he would be around long after Elder Kimball was gone. And no one had prayed harder than the Kimballs that President Lee's good health would continue.

Ten minutes passed. Elder Kimball left the room and walked down the hallway toward President Lee's room. As he approached, a doctor stepped out.

"We have given up," he said. President Lee was dead.[29]

CHAPTER 16

Just This Day

After spending a year at Brigham Young University, Maeta Holiday decided to leave school and look for a job. She had loved taking ballroom dance classes and singing and dancing in Lamanite Generation, a popular Native American performance group. But she had found some of her classes, like physics, too challenging. In early 1974, she was living in Salt Lake City and working as a receptionist at KSL, the Church-owned radio and television station.[1]

She was also dating a returned missionary named Dennis Beck. He had introduced himself at a dance in Provo the previous September, and they had danced together all evening. Then he had invited her to go to church with him.

Maeta was taken aback. Since leaving BYU, she had not been as active in the Church as she'd been in

California. Still, she had accepted Dennis's invitation and enjoyed being there with him. She agreed to go again the following week, and before long, they were dating regularly.[2]

As Maeta got to know Dennis better, she admired his goodness and sincerity. He was an active member of the Church who kept the commandments and went to the temple regularly. Born in Utah, he had served in the North Indian Mission in the northern United States, where he grew to love the Native Americans he taught and to value his own Mexican American heritage. Maeta felt comfortable and uplifted whenever she was around him.[3]

One day, about six months after they met, Dennis came by in his old red pickup truck, which he had fixed up and restored. They went for a drive, and then Dennis parked in front of the new Provo Temple and proposed to Maeta.

From the time she was a young teenager, Maeta had vowed that she would never get married. But when Dennis proposed, she did not focus on her parents' divorce or her mother's multiple marriages. Instead, she thought of Venna and Spencer Black and their example of what a happy marriage could be. "I can be happy too," she thought. So she said yes.[4]

Later that summer, on June 27, Maeta knelt across from Dennis in the Salt Lake Temple. She wore a dress she had made herself, with an empire waist and lace overlay. The couple's reflections in the parallel mirrors on the walls seemed to stretch into infinity. In the sealing room with them were her foster parents, Venna and Spencer, and their daughter Lucy.

"I'm proud of you," Venna had said after hearing of Maeta's engagement. "We spent a lot of time on our knees, praying for you that you would make the right choices."[5]

As Maeta knelt at the altar with Dennis, she was grateful that Venna had prayed so diligently. Joy enveloped her. She knew that marrying Dennis was the right decision.

Maeta later drove to Arizona to introduce Dennis to her mother. Evelyn came away from the meeting impressed with Dennis. She liked his sense of humor, honesty, and commitment to the Word of Wisdom.

"He is a good man," she told Maeta. She approved of her daughter's choice.[6]

"MY BODY IS TIRED, very tired, tonight," thought Belle Spafford as she lay in bed on October 5, 1974. Earlier that week, at the Relief Society's annual conference, President Spencer W. Kimball had released her as Relief Society general president. A collective gasp had resounded through the Salt Lake Tabernacle, so shocked and disappointed were the women by the news. But Belle had known the release was coming, and she welcomed it as the Lord's will.

Yet her mind was racing. "Remember this! Remember that!" it seemed to say. She wanted to put her thoughts down on paper, so she got out of bed and started to write. "Why would you sleep," she asked herself, "when there has been so much that has been so glorious for you to review in memory?"

She recalled the feeling of inadequacy that swept through her when the First Presidency called her to replace Amy Brown Lyman as the leader of the Relief Society in April 1945. Now, twenty-nine years later, she had served longer than any other Relief Society general president.[7]

During that time, she had suffered many personal trials, including breast cancer and the deaths of her husband and daughter.[8] Under her guidance, though, the organization had ministered to the victims of World War II, constructed the Relief Society Building, started evening Relief Society meetings for working women, encouraged programs in abuse prevention and child adoption, and provided additional community aid through other social services.[9]

More recently, Belle and her general board had overseen changes to Relief Society enrollment to encourage more women to participate. In years past, women signed up to join the organization and paid yearly membership dues. Now these fees were discontinued, and every woman in the Church was automatically enrolled in Relief Society as soon as she turned eighteen.[10]

"These have been busy, demanding, challenging years, yet rewarding beyond my power to measure," Belle wrote. The Lord had been good to her. "Many,

many times He has put ideas into my mind and even words into my mouth that have enabled me to meet difficult situations or remove resistant obstacles."[11]

Her successor, Barbara B. Smith, would need the same divine help as she guided the Relief Society into an ever-changing future. During Belle's final years as general president, the movement for women's rights had gained momentum in the United States as many women, young and old, questioned traditional gender roles and worked against the unfair and unequal treatment of women.

Following similar legislative efforts in other countries, the United States Congress had passed the Equal Rights Amendment in 1972. The amendment sought to revise the U.S. Constitution to specifically include equal legal rights for women. Now the American public was debating the future of the amendment. If three-fourths of the states approved it, it would become the law of the land.

For some people, the amendment seemed like a good remedy to longstanding gender inequalities in the legal system. Other people, including many Church members, were not so sure.[12]

Belle had recently given her views on the amendment and the rising women's movement in a speech to a group of business professionals in New York City. "There are some things for which women are agitating that merit support," she had said, citing equal pay for equal work and fair hiring practices. But she worried that the women's movement would lead to a weakening of the roles of wife, mother, and homemaker. She believed that change to a woman's legal rights should come through local, state, and federal governments, not by amending the Constitution.[13]

As Belle sat up late reflecting on her long tenure as Relief Society general president, she felt gratitude mixed with a sweet sense of relief and joy that her responsibilities had fallen on new shoulders. "There is within my soul," she wrote, "a feeling of peace and good promise for the future—my personal future and that of my beloved Relief Society."

With this sense of peace, she was at last ready to sleep. "Tonight I will rest," she wrote, "for in my heart is the assurance that all is well."[14]

AROUND THIS TIME, IN Cape Coast, Ghana, Billy Johnson saw the pictures and names of past Church presidents on the front page of a local religious newspaper. Beside the pictures were articles disparaging the Church and its leaders. The newspaper was clearly trying to sow doubt among the members of Billy's growing congregation.

Billy and his fellow believers had been criticized for their faith in the restored gospel many times before. Some people heckled Billy for abandoning the religion of his youth. They said the Saints worshipped Joseph Smith and did not believe in God. Others pointed out that no Black men held the priesthood in the Church and mocked Billy and his followers for wasting their time.[15]

It was hard to stay faithful amid such attacks. A year earlier, members of the congregation had grown frustrated that after so many years, no one had come to baptize them. Billy had immediately asked his followers to join him in fasting and prayer. As they did so, some people felt a powerful impression that missionaries would soon come to Ghana.

Although this impression had reassured the congregation, the persecution had not stopped. Some members worried when they saw the newspaper criticizing the prophets, not knowing what to do. Billy prayed with them and urged them not to pay the newspapers any mind. "Just throw them away," he said.[16]

But Billy too was feeling weak. One night, he went to the meetinghouse to pray. "Father, even though I believe the Church, that this is the true Church on earth today," he said, "I need more strength and more confirmation to testify about the Church."

He pleaded with the Lord to reveal Himself. Then he fell asleep and dreamed that he saw the Salt Lake Temple, full of light, descending from heaven. The building soon surrounded him. "Johnson, don't lose faith in my church," the voice of the Lord said. "Whether you believe it or not, this is my true church on earth today."

When Billy awoke, he was no longer troubled by the persecution. "Father has spoken," he said. "I will not be afraid anymore."

In the days that followed, Billy's faith felt stronger whenever he heard someone criticize the Church, and he worked to fortify his fellow believers. "There will be a time the Church will come up," he testified. "We will see the beauty of the Church."[17]

IN 1974, FIVE YEARS after resigning as superintendent of the Songjuk Orphanage, Hwang Keun Ok had opened a new home for girls in Seoul, South Korea. She now cared for seventeen girls, several of whom were Latter-day Saints, and helped others find adoptive families through the Tender Apples Foundation. The foundation supported other groups of children as well, including a boys' orphanage. Keun Ok also opened a preschool to educate the youngest of Korea's children who were in need.

Though smaller than the singing group had been at the orphanage, the Tender Apples still performed on television and gave concerts. The girls led busy lives, and Keun Ok made sure they felt at home with her. Every Monday night she gathered them for a home evening.[18]

When she wasn't caring for her girls, Keun Ok ministered to the women of her district as Relief Society president. Her calling put her in contact with Eugene Till, the newly called president of the Korea Mission. President Till was concerned that many Koreans still knew nothing about the Church, despite there being a thriving stake and institute of religion in Seoul. In fact, he had learned that fewer than 10 percent of Koreans recognized the full name of the Church. And those who knew of the Church did not often have a good opinion of it. The government, moreover, was limiting the number of American missionaries allowed in the country.[19]

But if President Till could show Korean officials that the Church was centered on families, the government might be willing to loosen its restriction on missionary work.[20]

One day, he reached out to Keun Ok for help. A few elders in the mission were incorporating music into their teaching. Like the Osmonds, they believed popular music could inspire people with messages about the restored gospel. A year earlier, the Osmonds had released *The Plan,* the ambitious rock album they'd been working on for several years. Musically, the album sounded like other recordings by popular bands of the time. But the brothers had made a special effort to write songs about every stage in the plan of salvation, from premortality to exaltation. Although critics dismissed the album because of its Latter-day Saint themes, its gospel-centered message reached many young people in North America, Europe, and Australia.[21]

The musical efforts of the missionaries in South Korea were modest by comparison, but their goals were the same. The group's leader, Elder Randy Davenport, wrote most of the group's original songs, and Elder Mack Wilberg arranged the music. They called themselves New Horizon.[22]

Recognizing the group's potential, President Till asked Keun Ok if the Tender Apples would perform alongside New Horizon at a Christmas concert. Keun Ok saw the value in having the Tender Apples share the restored gospel and, after consulting with Stan Bronson, the group's cofounder, she agreed.

The Christmas concert was a huge success, and everyone agreed that New Horizon and the Tender Apples were a good match. They began touring the country together and found a wide audience on television and radio programs. The Tender Apples were particularly popular at military bases, where many members of the audience were reminded of their own children back in the United States. The elders in New Horizon, on the other hand, were popular among Korean audiences, who loved seeing American performers speaking and singing in Korean. The groups went on to record albums together.[23]

Keun Ok had once had to conceal her faith. Now the Tender Apples and New Horizon included the name of the Church in every performance and interview. At concerts, full-time missionaries were there to tell people more about the Church. Missionaries knocking on doors were more frequently welcomed in, with investigators saying they recognized the Church's name from a concert or album. In some places, missionaries would arrange for a concert to be given in a public venue to increase the number of people who might be willing to listen to them.[24]

As the Tender Apples and New Horizon became more popular, President Till conducted a survey and learned that the number of residents in and around Seoul who had heard of the Church was now eight out of ten. More important, the impression most of them had of the Church was very positive.

Although they had come from very different backgrounds and cultures, New Horizon and the Tender Apples had helped spread the gospel together, one song at a time.[25]

In April 1975, Henry and Inge Burkhardt were thousands of miles away from home. At the First Presidency's invitation, they had journeyed to Utah from the German Democratic Republic to attend general conference. The trip was a rare opportunity for a Latter-day Saint couple living in a country that maintained strict control over its borders and its citizens.

It was not Henry's first time in Salt Lake City. President Joseph Fielding Smith and his counselors had invited him and Inge to attend general conference four years earlier. Knowing that East German officials would read the invitation, the First Presidency had written respectfully of their hopes for world peace, universal brotherhood, and other ideals the GDR professed. The government had approved Henry's travel request, and he had attended general conference in 1972.[26]

At the time, the GDR had not permitted Inge to go with him, fearful that the couple would not return if they were allowed to leave the country together. In the two years that followed, however, both of Henry's counselors in the Dresden Mission presidency had received permission to travel to general conference with their spouses, giving the Burkhardts reason to hope that government officials would approve Inge's next visa application. But when they petitioned to attend the 1975 conference, Inge's request was again denied.

Upon learning of Inge's dilemma, Church leaders in Salt Lake City offered a special prayer for her in the temple. And when Henry and Inge appealed the decision, the government approved the visa without any apparent problem.[27]

Attending conference was an extraordinary experience. Spencer W. Kimball opened the conference for the third time as Church president. His message was for Latter-day Saints across the globe. There were nearly 700 stakes and 150 missions worldwide, and over the past year, he had been able to meet with Saints at area general conferences in South America and Europe. He had also dedicated a temple in Washington, DC, announced a new temple in São Paulo, Brazil, and initiated plans for a temple in Mexico City. Often, while meeting with the Saints, he encouraged them to "lengthen their stride," or increase their efforts, in sharing the gospel.

Now, as he addressed the Saints at general conference, he urged them to live moral lives. He condemned pornography and abortion, a practice recently legalized in the United States. He also encouraged the Saints to plant gardens, share the gospel, and establish the Church in their homelands. "The gathering of Israel," he said, "is effected when the people of the faraway countries accept the gospel and remain in their native lands."[28]

It was a message that spoke deeply to Henry and Inge's experience in the Church. Twenty years earlier, when they had decided to return to the GDR after being sealed in the Swiss Temple, they had sacrificed their chance to practice their religion freely and attend the temple regularly.[29] But their example and leadership had helped to gather the Saints not only in the GDR but also in nearby Hungary, Poland, and Czechoslovakia, where Henry and other East German Church leaders made periodic visits.[30]

Before returning home, Henry spoke with President Kimball about the Church's struggle with the government in the GDR. President Kimball doubted the Church could improve its standing there through political negotiations. "If you want to see a change of things in East Germany, it must begin with you personally," he told Henry. "You must force yourself to befriend the communists. You cannot hold any grudges against them. You must change your whole outlook and attitude."

Henry was surprised by what the prophet was suggesting. "You don't know the communists," he wanted to say. "You cannot develop a good relationship with them. They are against religion." He recalled the many times the authorities had harassed him and tried to throw him into prison.

The thought of making friends with them was repulsive.³¹

ON A BRIGHT SUNDAY in the war-torn country of Vietnam, Nguyen Van The, president of the Saigon Branch, passed through the outer gate of a French-style villa serving as the local meetinghouse. Right away, members of the branch surrounded him, their faces full of frustration and hope. "President The! President The!" they cried out. "What news do you have?"³²

He had news, but he was not sure how the branch would respond to it. He walked to the door of the chapel, and the Saints followed him, shouting more questions. Without answering, The shook hands and patted people on the back. Cong Ton Nu Tuong-Vy, the Relief Society president and lead translator of the Vietnamese Book of Mormon, took him by the arm.

"What counsel do you have, President The?" she asked. "What shall I tell the sisters?"

"Come inside, Sister Vy," The said. "I will tell you everything I know after sacrament meeting." He then urged everyone in the crowd to remain calm. "All of your questions will be answered."³³

For decades, Vietnam had been a divided land. Conflict had erupted shortly after World War II when Vietnamese forces ousted the French colonial rulers who had governed Vietnam since the late nineteenth century. When rival parties in South Vietnam resisted communist rule, the region had descended into fierce guerrilla warfare. American forces had fought alongside the South Vietnamese for nearly a decade, but the high casualties had made the conflict unpopular in the United States, leading to the country's gradual withdrawal from the war. Now the North Vietnamese forces were closing in on the southern capital of Saigon, and all remaining Americans were leaving.[34]

The arrival of the North Vietnamese forces threatened to end the Saigon Branch. Up until a week earlier, when the last Latter-day Saint missionary evacuated the country, the branch had seen new members joining every month. More than two hundred Vietnamese Saints had worshipped regularly with Church members from the United States. Now the Vietnamese Saints feared the North Vietnamese would punish them for this association. Some Church members had already scattered, many of them joining the crowds at the airbase, hoping to escape the country.[35]

As The entered the chapel and took a seat at the front of the room, he could hear the rumble of artillery fire—and some explosions sounded terrifyingly close. The irony of the moment was not lost on him. The war had brought the American soldiers who had introduced him and so many Vietnamese Saints to the restored gospel. Now that same war was tearing the branch apart. He felt as if he were attending a funeral for the small congregation.[36]

There were about 125 branch members at the meeting when The stood up and approached the pulpit. They looked anxious, and many of them were weeping. He was feeling emotional too, but he stayed composed as he opened sacrament meeting. The Saints sang "Come, Come, Ye Saints" and partook of the sacrament. Then The bore his testimony and invited others to do the same. But as the Saints stood and shared their testimonies, he could not concentrate on their words. The Saints were looking to him at this time of crisis, and he felt inadequate.[37]

After the meeting, The informed the Saints that the United States embassy was willing to evacuate Church members and anyone preparing for baptism. But Saints with family who were not Church members had to either leave their loved ones or stay behind. This news caused some Saints to cry out in anguish. "What about my family?" they asked. "I cannot leave without my family!"

With the help of the branch members, The created an evacuation list that identified which Saints would leave first. Despite the embassy's request, the list included dozens of nonmember family and friends of branch members. The's wife, Lien, and their three small children were among the Saints on the list. The branch members insisted that The's family evacuate immediately so he could give his full attention to evacuating everyone else. As branch president, The felt it was his duty to be the last to leave.[38]

Lien and the children, along with her mother and sisters, flew out of Saigon a few hours later.

The following day, the North Vietnamese shelled the airport in Saigon, damaging the runway and preventing military transport aircraft from landing. Then, over the next forty-eight hours, helicopters evacuated the remaining Americans and whatever Vietnamese refugees they could carry. The rushed to the U.S. embassy, hoping to find a way out for him and the other Saints still in the city. When he arrived, the building was on fire and smoke was choking the sky. Firefighters and crowds had gathered outside, but the embassy itself was empty. The Americans had already left the city.

Desperate to help the remaining branch members escape, The and a fellow Saint, Tran Van Nghia, hopped onto a motorbike to seek help from the International Red Cross. But they soon met a mass of people running down a one-way street in a panic. A tank with a large gun was rolling rapidly toward them.

Nghia swerved off the road, and he and The clambered into a ditch to hide. The tank rumbled by them, shaking the ground as it passed.

Saigon was now in North Vietnamese hands.[39]

ONE WEEK LATER, IN May 1975, Le My Lien stepped off a crowded bus at a military camp near San Diego, California, on the West Coast of the United States. In front of her was a sprawling city of tents set up to shelter eighteen thousand refugees from Vietnam. Grass and sand covered the grounds, with trees sparsely dotting the horizon. Children walked around in oversized military jackets, and adults went about their day with unsmiling faces.[40]

Although Lien's mother and sisters were with her, she felt lost. She was nauseated from her journey to the camp. She had no money and spoke little English. And she had her three children to care for while awaiting news of her husband in Vietnam.[41]

On their first day at the camp, Lien and other Saigon Branch members—mostly women—were greeted by volunteers with badges identifying them as members of the local California stake. A neatly dressed woman introduced herself as Dorothy Hurley, the stake Relief Society president. She and the other stake volunteers were there to distribute food, clothing, and medicine to the refugee Saints, organize them into home teaching districts, and set up Primary and Relief Society. To Lien, the Relief Society sisters looked like angels.[42]

The members of the Saigon Branch spent the afternoon on a tour of the camp. Gravel crunched underfoot as Lien and her family were shown the mess hall, Red Cross kiosk, and outhouses. The long walk took all afternoon, leaving Lien fatigued. She weighed less than ninety pounds, and her body was too weak to produce milk for her infant daughter, Linh.

That night, Lien did her best to make her children comfortable. The camp had provided her with no blankets and only one cot. Her sons, Vu and Huy, crammed onto the cot while the baby slept in a hammock Lien fashioned out of a sheet and rubber bands.

There was nowhere for Lien to lie down, so she slept sitting on the edge of the cot, leaning against a tentpole. The nights were cold, and the chilly air did nothing to help her worsening health. Soon she was diagnosed with tuberculosis.[43]

Despite her sickness, Lien woke early each morning to pick up six small bottles of formula for her baby and get the boys fed. At mealtime, the mess hall was crowded with people waiting for their turn. With her daughter in her arms, she helped her sons load and carry their plates. Only when they finished eating would she go back to get her own food.

Lien's heart ached when she saw other children waiting hungrily in line. Since rations in the mess hall ran out quickly, Lien would often pass food along to the children to ensure they ate. Some shared their carrots and broccoli with her in return.[44]

She prayed continually that her husband would remain strong, believing that if she could survive her ordeal, then he could survive his. She had heard nothing from him since her flight out of Saigon. But a few weeks after her arrival, Elder A. Theodore Tuttle of the First Council of the Seventy came to the camp and gave Lien a personal message from President Spencer W. Kimball, who had visited the camp and met with refugees shortly before she got there.

"I testify that your husband will be preserved," the prophet's message declared, "and that you will be reunited as a family in the Lord's own due time."[45]

Now, as Lien rocked her crying baby each morning, she cried too. "Please," she begged the Lord, "let me get through just this day."[46]

CHAPTER 17

No Going Back

On the morning of October 10, 1975, several shiny antique automobiles rumbled to life on the campus of Brigham Young University, signaling the start of the school's Founders Day parade. Thousands of faculty, students, and alumni, representing the university's many colleges and associations, marched briskly behind the cars. In the distance, on a mountainside east of campus, a giant whitewashed "Y" gleamed in the sunlight.

BYU celebrated its founding every fall, but this year marked the university's one hundredth anniversary. To commemorate the occasion, President Spencer W. Kimball and his wife, Camilla, rode in the lead car, a red 1906 Cadillac. In keeping with the nostalgic feel of the parade, President Kimball wore an old-fashioned derby hat and striped suit coat. Sister Kimball, meanwhile, held a black lace parasol above her head.[1]

Although his clothes recalled the past, President Kimball had his eyes fixed on the future. Now that the Church was rapidly becoming a worldwide organization, it did not seem right to provide programs and services for some Saints and not others. Already leaders had done away with Churchwide sports tournaments in Salt Lake City. And in 1974, the First Presidency had announced that the Church would divest itself of the fifteen hospitals it operated in the western United States. Then, the following year, President Kimball had announced that all annual conferences of the general organizations—MIA, Sunday School, Primary, and Relief Society—would be coming to an end because they took place in Salt Lake City and generally benefited only the Saints in and around Utah.

"With the distances growing greater and membership greatly increasing," he explained, "it seems high time to take another long stride in our decentralization."[2]

The prominence of the new area general conferences was evidence of the Church's commitment to its global membership. In 1975 alone, President Kimball had presided at large conferences in Brazil, Argentina, Japan, the Philippines, Taiwan, Hong Kong, and South Korea. And the Church was calling more missionaries than ever before. During his travels as an apostle, President Kimball had passed out silver dollars to children he met, asking them to begin a missionary fund.

Now, as Church president, he asked every young man to serve a mission and encouraged the Saints in every country to supply their own missionary force.[3]

While in Japan, he had announced plans to build a temple in Tokyo, the first in Asia. More recently, at the October general conference, he had called men to serve in a new general priesthood quorum, the First Quorum of the Seventy. According to the Doctrine and Covenants, the Quorum of the Twelve Apostles was to "call upon the Seventy, when they need assistance." The members of the new quorum would support the Twelve, preside at local conferences, and create new stakes across the globe. Although only a few men had been called into the new quorum so far, it could have up to seventy members.[4]

BYU's anniversary had also caused President Kimball to think about the future of the school. With around twenty-five thousand students, BYU was the largest of the Church's four institutions of higher education, which also included Ricks College in Idaho, BYU–Hawaii on Oahu, and LDS Business College in Salt Lake City. It was also the largest private university in the United States. The students there, and at all Church schools, abided by an honor code requiring high standards of morality, honesty, and decency.

In 1971, Dallin Oaks, a young Latter-day Saint law professor from the University of Chicago, replaced BYU president Ernest Wilkinson. Under President Oaks's leadership, the university had provided greater opportunities for female faculty and students, founded the J. Reuben Clark Law School, and expanded other academic programs.

Recently, though, the school had come under scrutiny because some of its honor code policies seemed to violate new federal equal opportunity laws. President Oaks and the board of trustees were concerned about the regulations, noting that they could force BYU to eliminate such things as separate housing for men and women. They were committed to the principle of equal opportunity in education and employment. Yet they objected to any law requiring the university to compromise religious liberty by adopting policies that could undermine the beliefs and practices of the Church.[5]

So far, the issue remained unresolved. Yet President Kimball, as head of the BYU board of trustees, was adamant about upholding Church standards. He believed BYU's commitment to both secular and spiritual learning was key to its future success, even if that approach set the school apart from other universities.

After the Founders Day parade, President Kimball spoke to a large assembly about his vision for BYU's second century. "This university shares with other universities the hope and the labor involved in rolling back the frontiers of knowledge even further," he declared, "but we also know that through the process of revelation there are yet 'many great and important things' to be given to mankind which will have an intellectual and spiritual impact far beyond what mere men can imagine."

He encouraged the faculty and students to be more "bilingual" in their studies. "As LDS scholars you must speak with authority and excellence to your professional colleagues in the language of scholarship," he said, "and you must also be literate in the language of spiritual things."

He urged the university to embrace the future with faith, following the Lord's direction, line upon line. He testified that the university would go forward. "We understand," he said, "that education is a part of being about our Father's business and that the scriptures contain the master concepts for mankind."

"We expect—we do not simply hope—that Brigham Young University will become a leader among the great universities of the world," he continued. "To that expectation I would add: Become a unique university in all of the world!"[6]

AROUND THIS TIME, REPRESENTATIVES from a Protestant church in the United States came to Cape Coast, Ghana, looking for Billy Johnson. They had heard that Billy had performed powerful miracles, and they were hoping to persuade him and his followers to join their church. About four thousand Ghanaians in forty-one congregations called themselves Latter-day Saints. Billy oversaw five of the congregations. The representatives needed someone to take charge of their Ghanaian congregations, and Billy struck them as the right man to lead.

Billy and his followers agreed to worship with the visitors at a community center in the city. The Americans greeted them with gifts of soap and cosmetics. "You kind people must be our brothers," they said, "and we should be together." They urged Billy and the others to stop waiting for the missionaries. "They are not coming."[7]

One of the visitors urged Billy to join them and be a leader in their church. "We'll pay you," he said. "We will pay your ministers." They also offered to help Billy visit the United States and promised to supply his congregation with musical instruments and a new church building.[8]

That night, Billy invited the visitors to stay in his home while he considered their offer. Being as poor as he was, he took the proposal seriously. But he did not want to betray God or his own faith in the restored gospel.

Alone in his bedroom, Billy wept. "Lord, what should I do?" he prayed. "I have waited for so long, and my brothers have not come."[9]

"Johnson, don't ever confuse yourself or your members," a voice told him. "Stay fast to the Church and very soon your brothers will come and assist you."[10]

Billy ended his prayer and left his bedroom. Soon, one of the guests emerged from another room. "Johnson," the man said, "you are not asleep?"

"I'm thinking how to sort out things," Billy admitted.

"Brother Johnson," the man said, "I wanted to come and knock on your door to tell you your church is organized already. I should not confuse you." He said the Lord had revealed this truth to him. "I should only be a brother to you," he said. "Keep up with your church."

"The Lord has spoken to me too," Billy said. "It is the Lord's church. I cannot give the church to anyone."[11]

Representatives from other American churches came later with similar offers. Billy rejected them all. Soon, leaders from his own congregation learned that he was refusing money and gifts from the Americans. Enraged, the leaders burst into his home. "These people have come to help," one of the men said. "They'll pay us."[12]

"I will not sell the church," Billy said. "If it takes me twenty years, I will wait for the Lord."[13]

"You don't have money," one man said. "They want to pay us."

"No," Billy said, "no."

The men seemed ready to beat him, but he refused to change his mind. Finally, they backed down, and as they left, Billy embraced them one by one. The last man broke down in tears when Billy took him in his arms.

"I'm sorry I'm hurting you," the man said. "Please ask God to forgive me my sins."

Billy cried with him. "Father," he prayed, "forgive him."[14]

IN AUGUST 1976, IN another part of West Africa, Anthony Obinna sent a letter to President Kimball. "We here wish you to turn your attention to Nigeria," he wrote, "and have the land dedicated for the teachings of the true gospel of our Lord Jesus Christ."[15]

Two years had passed since Anthony had last heard from his contact in the missionary department, LaMar Williams.[16] In the meantime, Lorry Rytting, a Latter-day Saint professor from the United States, had spent a year teaching at a university in Nigeria. Anthony and other believers had met with Lorry, and they hoped that his visit would result in more direct contact with Church headquarters—and perhaps the beginnings of a mission. Lorry had returned to Utah and given Church leaders a favorable report of the readiness of Nigeria for the gospel, but nothing had yet come of it.[17]

Anthony was unwilling to give up. "Your church's teachings embody such good things that cannot be found in others," he wrote President Kimball. "God calls on us to be saved, and we wish you to hasten the work."[18]

Anthony soon received a reply from Grant Bangerter, the president of the Church's International Mission, a special mission supervising areas where Church members lived but where the Church was not officially recognized. President Bangerter told Anthony he sympathized with his situation but informed him there were still no plans to organize the Church in Nigeria.

"We encourage you with all expressions of brotherly love to pursue the practice of your faith as best as you can until such time in the future as it may be possible for the Church to take more direct action," he wrote.[19]

Around this time, Anthony and his wife, Fidelia, learned that their children were being harassed and humiliated at school because of their religious beliefs. Their eight-year-old daughter told how teachers would call her and her siblings out in front of the student body during school prayers, force them to kneel down with their hands raised, and strike their hands with a stick.

After Anthony and Fidelia found out what was happening, they went to speak with the teachers. "Why are you doing such things?" they asked. "We have freedom of worship in Nigeria."[20]

The beatings stopped, but the family and their fellow believers continued to face opposition from their community. "Lack of visit of any of the authorities from Salt Lake City has made us a laughingstock from some people here," Anthony wrote President Bangerter in October 1976. "We are doing everything we can to establish the truth among so many of our Heavenly Father's children in this part of the world."[21]

Anthony waited for a reply, but none came. Had his letters not reached Salt Lake City? He did not know, so he wrote again.

"We shall not be tired in writing and asking for the Church to be opened here as you have done all over the world," he declared. "We in our group are earnestly following the teachings of our Saviour, Jesus Christ. There is no going back."[22]

When Katherine Warren first learned about the restored gospel, she was working as a nurse's aide in the home of a woman in the northeastern United States. One day, she answered the door and found a pair of Latter-day Saint missionaries there.

"The lady of the house is in bed," Katherine told them.[23]

"Tell her that the elders from The Church of Jesus Christ of Latter-day Saints came by," they replied, offering a pamphlet containing the testimony of the prophet Joseph Smith. Katherine took it, and the missionaries went on their way.

Katherine was impressed by the young men. But when her employer found out about them, she took the pamphlet from Katherine's hand and threw it in the trash can.

Katherine remained intrigued, so she retrieved the pamphlet. As she read about Joseph Smith's First Vision and the Book of Mormon later that day, she believed everything.

Katherine told a friend about the pamphlet a short time later. "I believe I have that Book of Mormon," her friend told her, "and you can have it."

Katherine trusted that the Lord had been leading her to search for something important. Once she started reading the Book of Mormon, she knew it was what the Lord wanted her to find. When some of what it taught about baptism contradicted what she had learned growing up, she heard a voice urging her not to cast it aside. "Believe all things," the voice said.[24]

Not long after that, Katherine moved to New Orleans, a city in the southern state of Louisiana, and got married. Eager to worship with the Latter-day Saints, she looked up the Church in the telephone book and attended the local ward. She felt good at church, and she began attending regularly. Yet, as a Black woman, she was treated differently. Some people seemed uncomfortable with her being there and even refused to speak with her. She eventually met an elderly Black woman in the ward, Freda Beaulieu. Although Freda loved the gospel and had been a member of the Church since childhood, she did not attend the ward regularly.[25]

Several years went by, and Katherine wanted to join the Church, but she did not know how. She wrote to President Kimball about her desire, and he forwarded the letter to Church leaders in Louisiana. Two missionaries, serving under mission president LaMar Williams, went to her house right away.

The elders taught Katherine the standard missionary discussions, and soon she was ready for baptism. But at the time, to avoid introducing conflict in marriages, the Church had a policy that a woman could not get baptized without her husband's permission. And Katherine's husband refused to give his consent.[26]

"Sister Warren, this is your church. You can continue to come here," the elders said when she told them the bad news. "It might be fifty years before you get baptized, but you continue to come to church."[27]

So Katherine continued to go to church. When a new set of missionaries came to the area, they started teaching her again, but she knew all the answers to their questions. "We came to teach you," they told her, "but you're teaching us."

Still hoping to be baptized, Katherine again sought her husband's permission. This time she gave him a form the missionaries had written up for him to sign. "If this is what you want, I will sign it," he told her.

But when President Williams traveled to New Orleans to interview Katherine for baptism, her husband would not let her go to meet with him. Discouraged, Katherine almost gave up. She knew the Spirit had led her to the Church, but trying to join had been one problem after another. Was the effort worth it?

She decided to fast, and while she did, she had a vision. A figure in a gray suit appeared in her home. At first she thought it was a missionary, but she quickly recognized that it was an angel. His face shone, and he spoke no words to her. He simply took her by the hand. She felt impressed to invite the missionaries and

President Williams to interview her at her home. They did not need to worry about her husband interfering.

President Williams came to New Orleans and interviewed Katherine. She was then baptized on Christmas Day 1976.[28]

AT THE TIME KATHERINE Warren embraced the restored gospel, Saigon Branch president Nguyen Van The was imprisoned in Thành Ông Năm, a squalid Vietnamese fortress serving as a prison camp. He was desperate for news of his wife and children, but the camp had largely cut him off from the outside world. All he knew about his family's whereabouts came from a telegram from the president of the Hong Kong Mission: "Lien and family fine. With Church."[29]

The had received the telegram just before entering the camp. In an effort to restore order after capturing Saigon, the North Vietnamese government had required all former members of the South Vietnamese military to submit to a "reeducation" course on the new government's principles and practices. Since The had served as a junior officer and English-language teacher for South Vietnam, he had reluctantly turned himself in, expecting the reeducation process to last about ten days. Now, more than a year later, he wondered when he would be free again.[30]

Life in Thành Ông Năm was degrading. The and his fellow captives were organized into units and housed in rat-infested barracks. They slept on bare floors until their captors had them build beds out of steel slabs. Meager and spoiled food, along with the unsanitary conditions in camp, left the men vulnerable to sicknesses like dysentery and beriberi.[31]

Reeducation also involved backbreaking labor and political indoctrination. When not cutting trees or tending crops to feed the camp, the men were forced to memorize propaganda and confess their crimes against North Vietnam. Anyone who broke camp rules could expect a brutal beating or solitary confinement in a dumpster-like iron box.[32]

The had survived so far by lying low and clinging to his faith. He tried to obey camp rules and practiced his religion privately. He observed fast Sundays, despite being malnourished, and silently recited scriptures from memory to strengthen his faith. When a fellow Christian in camp gave him a smuggled Bible, he read the entire book twice in three months, cherishing the chance to read the word of God again.[33]

The longed to be free. For a time, he contemplated escaping from the camp. He was sure he could use his military training to evade his captors, but as he prayed for help in the escape, he felt the Lord restrain him. "Be patient," the Spirit whispered. "All will be well in the due time of the Lord."[34]

Sometime later, The learned that his sister, Ba, would be allowed to visit him in the camp. If he could slip her a letter to his family, she could send it to President

Wheat in Hong Kong, and he could forward it to Lien and the children.

On the day of Ba's visit, The waited in line as guards conducted full-body searches of the prisoners ahead of him. Knowing the guards would send him straight to solitary confinement if they found his letter to Lien, he had hidden the message behind the cloth band on the inside of his hat. He had then placed a small notebook and pen into the hat and set them on the ground. With any luck, the notebook would distract the guards just enough to keep them from searching the rest of the hat.

When his turn came to be searched, The tried to remain calm. But as the guards inspected him, he began to tremble. He thought of the confinement that awaited if his captors discovered the letter. Several tense moments passed, and the guards shifted their attention to his hat. They examined the pen and notebook, but when they found nothing out of the ordinary, they lost interest in The and let him pass.

Soon, The saw his sister approaching, so he discreetly removed the letter from his hat and pressed it into her hands. He wept as Ba gave him some food and money. She and her husband ran a produce business, and they did not have a lot to spare. The was grateful for all she could offer. When they parted, he trusted that she would get his letter to Lien.[35]

Six months later, Ba returned to the camp with a letter. Inside was a photograph of Lien and the children. The's eyes brimmed with tears as he stared at their faces.

His children had grown so much. He realized that he could wait no longer.

He had to find a way out of the camp and into the arms of his family.[36]

CHAPTER 18

All the Blessings of the Gospel

On the afternoon of March 9, 1977, Helvécio Martins stood with news reporters at the temple construction site in São Paulo, Brazil. President Spencer W. Kimball had come to the country for the temple's cornerstone ceremony, and around three thousand people were there to watch, some carrying umbrellas to protect themselves from the blazing sun. As the public relations director for the Church's Brazil North Region, Helvécio was there to aid the reporters covering the event.[1]

Helvécio had accepted the call to serve in Church public relations three years earlier. He had thought it was an extraordinary amount of trust to place in a new member. But he immersed himself in the calling, using his prominence as a business executive to make important contacts in the media and open doors for the Church.[2]

293

Part of Helvécio's new duties involved spreading the word about the temple. The building was now about one-third complete, its walls already high above the ground. Church architect Emil Fetzer had wanted Italian white marble for the temple's exterior, but when that and other options proved unworkable, he brought in a craftsman to teach local Church members how to make cast stone blocks directly on the temple site.[3]

The Brazilian Saints, along with Saints from other parts of South America and the nation of South Africa, had made many financial sacrifices to help fund the temple construction. In Brazil, Saints paid 15 percent of the total cost. Helvécio's wife, Rudá, had donated jewelry she had received from her parents to the fund.[4]

While Helvécio and Rudá looked forward to the temple's completion, it grieved them that they would not be able to participate in endowments and sealings because they were Black. On one occasion, while walking around the temple's steel frames and unfinished floors, they had stopped on a patch of ground. The Spirit touched their hearts. They were standing on the spot where the celestial room would be.

Embracing, they wept. "Don't worry," Helvécio said, "the Lord knows everything."[5]

As Helvécio waited for the cornerstone ceremony to begin, he glanced at President Kimball, who was sitting on a small stage next to the temple walls. The prophet seemed to be motioning to him, but Helvécio wasn't sure. He saw President Kimball whisper something to

Elder James E. Faust, a newly called member of the First Quorum of the Seventy who had served a mission in Brazil during the 1940s. Elder Faust then looked at Helvécio. "Come here," he mouthed. "He wants to talk to you."

Helvécio quickly excused himself and made his way to the stage. As he approached, President Kimball stood up and embraced him. Then he put his arm around him and looked up at him. "Brother, the watchword for you is faithfulness," he said. "Remain faithful and you will enjoy all the blessings of the gospel."[6]

Helvécio appreciated the gesture, but he was confused. What did President Kimball mean?

Later, after the cornerstone had been laid and the ceremony ended, President Kimball approached Helvécio and held his hand firmly. He then placed his other hand on Helvécio's arm.

"Don't forget, Brother Martins," he said. "Don't forget."[7]

LATER THAT YEAR, IN the German Democratic Republic, Henry Burkhardt saw an East German official sitting on the front row at a special Church meeting in Dresden. Her name was Mrs. Fischer, and she supervised local religious activity in the area. For over two years, Henry had made no effort to make friends in the East German government. He had asked Mrs. Fischer to come as a matter of duty.[8]

The meeting was special because President Kimball himself was there. He was finishing a seven-nation tour of the Church in Europe, and he had just a few hours to meet with the Saints in the GDR. It was taking place on an afternoon in the middle of the week—an inconvenient time for a meeting—but around twelve hundred Saints filled the seats and standing room.[9]

Henry had no idea what President Kimball planned to speak about. The GDR paid attention to the words of Church leaders, and Henry and other East German Saints often worried whenever a general authority publicly condemned communism. Such talks offended the government and put the East German Saints at risk of retaliation.[10]

As President Kimball stood at the pulpit in Dresden, Henry had little to worry about. The prophet spoke about the twelfth article of faith: "We believe in being subject to kings, presidents, rulers, and magistrates, in obeying, honoring, and sustaining the law." He thought the Church acted best when it abided by this precept.[11]

The talk impressed both Henry and Mrs. Fischer. "Mr. Burkhardt," she said after the meeting, "did your president talk about this article for my sake?"

"Not at all," Henry replied. "This is a message that all the Saints needed at this time."[12]

Not long after President Kimball's visit, Erich Honecker, the GDR's top official, spoke publicly of his desire to work with religious groups to improve humankind. Although his words gave many East Germans hope for the future, GDR officials continued to deny visas to

Church members wishing to travel to the Swiss Temple. The government did not understand why Church members needed to go to Switzerland when they could worship in chapels in the GDR. Besides, they were afraid the Saints would use the trip to flee the country.[13]

A short time later, Bishop H. Burke Peterson, first counselor in the Presiding Bishopric, came to the GDR. While discussing the Saints' difficulties in getting visas to visit the Swiss Temple, Bishop Peterson asked Henry, "Why should it not be possible to consecrate a room here where members can receive their endowment?"[14]

The idea intrigued Henry, but he did not think it was possible. Three weeks later, though, he was meeting with some East German officials when the topic of temples and travel visas came up again. The officials still refused to budge on the issue. But they believed an agreement could be reached with the Saints.

"Why don't you build a temple here?" one official asked.[15]

"That is not possible," said Henry. There were only about forty-two hundred members in the GDR—not nearly enough to warrant a temple. "Moreover," he said, "the ordinances in the temple need to be kept sacred." The government could not monitor them the same way it monitored other Church meetings.

"No problem at all," the officials said. "If your members can have the same experience here like they do in Switzerland, you need not travel to Switzerland."[16]

Henry had never expected to hear those words. Nor did he think it was possible for the Church to build a temple in the GDR. But what a change had taken place! He could now see the wisdom in President Kimball's counsel to improve his relationship with the government. "When the prophet gives you an assignment," he concluded, "then you certainly should honor it."

Of course, he did not know if the First Presidency would approve a temple in the GDR. But he would ask.[17]

AT THE START OF 1977, the proposed Equal Rights Amendment to the United States Constitution divided Americans. Only four more states needed to approve the ERA for it to take effect. That summer, at state women's conventions held in anticipation of a national convention in November, the amendment and other related issues were debated and contested.[18]

Relief Society general president Barbara B. Smith and other Church leaders frequently spoke in opposition to the ERA. When they studied the amendment, they were concerned that its broad application of rights did not account for differences between women and men. They worried that the ERA could overturn laws protecting the interests of women in matters of divorce, spouse and child support, military service, and other areas of everyday life.[19]

Church leaders were also alarmed that many ERA advocates championed practices such as abortion, which the Church condemned except in cases of rape or when the health of the mother was in grave danger.[20] Ultimately, they favored legislation that brought about equality by targeting specific cases of injustice or unfairness in society.[21]

In the months leading up to the national convention, Church leaders encouraged the Saints to participate in the political process. While most Latter-day Saints understood that Church leaders supported laws benefiting women, some Saints had questions about the Church's position on the ERA.[22]

On October 25, Ellie Colton, a stake Relief Society president in Washington, DC, received a telephone call from Don Ladd, a regional representative who was Ellie's former stake president. He was calling with a special request from Church headquarters.[23]

A prominent supporter of the ERA was holding a dinner party in Washington, DC, to discuss the amendment, and she intended to bring together women on both sides of the issue, including Latter-day Saint women. Church leaders wanted Ellie to attend.[24]

"If given the opportunity," Elder Ladd told Ellie, "you should explain the Church's stand against the ERA."

"Brother Ladd," Ellie said, "I am not sure I understand that myself."

"Well," he assured her, "you have three days to find out."[25]

After the call ended, Ellie felt stunned by what she had agreed to do. She had always been a peacemaker and someone who avoided confrontation. How could she hold her own against a roomful of well-informed women? It wasn't just that she didn't understand the ERA or the Church's position on it. She also had some hearing loss and worried that her disability would make it hard to understand what was said at the gathering.

Right away, Ellie retreated to the woods behind her house to pray. She told the Lord about her many inadequacies and fears. She then reviewed her life's blessings, pledging to do everything in her power to understand and explain the Church's position on the ERA.

Returning home, she called Marilyn Rolapp, the stake Relief Society social relations leader, and asked her to join her at the party. She also called a friend in Utah and asked her to send more information.[26]

The information arrived the next day. Ellie and Marilyn began studying, and by the time they left for the party, they felt ready to discuss the ERA with anyone. The night before, Ellie had felt insecure and mentally exhausted, but her daughter had cheered her. "Stick to the issues you understand," she had said, "and before you go to bed, read section 100, verse 5 of the Doctrine and Covenants."

The scripture was just what Ellie needed to hear: "Lift up your voices unto this people," it read, "speak the thoughts that I shall put into your hearts, and you shall not be confounded."[27]

When Ellie and Marilyn arrived at the party, though, they learned that its organizers had canceled the event, believing it would not be productive. The chair of the national women's conference had also just held a press event in which she numbered the Church among several "subversive" groups that planned to disrupt the convention.[28]

Troubled by these comments, Ellie decided to publish her views in an editorial for the *Washington Post,* a newspaper with a large national readership. "The Church is *not* against women's rights," she wrote. "It is unworthy of the conference's leaders to suggest that our Church is a threat to the conference simply because its official position differs from theirs."

She explained the Church's concerns about the amendment and its effects on family. And she voiced her own support for such measures as equal pay and professional opportunities for women such as her daughter, who was planning to attend law school soon.

"I am *for* women's rights. I am *for* correcting inequities," she declared in her editorial. "I resent being told I am against women's rights if I'm not for the ERA."[29]

ON A COOL, OVERCAST evening in January 1978, Le My Lien sat nervously in a car headed for the Salt Lake City International Airport. She was on her way to meet her husband, Nguyen Van The, for the first time in nearly three years. She worried what he would think of the life she had built for their family in his absence.[30]

As part of its mission to care for families, LDS Social Services had arranged with Church members in the

United States to care for about 550 Vietnamese refugees, most of whom were not members of the Church. Lien and her family were sponsored by Philip Flammer, a professor at Brigham Young University, and his wife, Mildred. They helped the family relocate to Provo, Utah, where Lien was able to rent and later purchase a mobile home from a local Saint.[31]

At first, Lien had struggled to find work in Utah. Philip took her to a thrift store to apply for a janitorial position. But during the interview, the manager tore her high school diploma in half and told her, "This does not apply here." Lien wept as she picked up the pieces, but she later taped the diploma back together and framed it on the wall to motivate her children to pursue higher education.[32]

She soon found temporary work picking cherries at a nearby orchard. She then found work as a seamstress and added to her income by baking wedding cakes. With help from Philip, she also earned money by typing reports for BYU students.[33]

While Lien struggled to provide for her family, her children struggled to adapt to their new life in America. The youngest, Linh, was underweight and frequently sick. The boys, Vu and Huy, had difficulty making friends in school because of the language barrier and cultural differences. They often complained to Lien about their peers teasing them.[34]

Amid her family's hardships, Lien remained faithful to the Lord. She attended Church meetings regularly and continued to pray for her family and her husband. "Give me strength," she would plead with her Heavenly Father. She taught her children about the power of prayer, knowing it could carry them through their ordeals.[35]

Then, in late 1977, Lien learned that her husband was in a refugee camp in Malaysia. He had managed to leave Vietnam on an old fishing boat after finally being released from the camp at Thành Ông Năm. Now he was ready to reunite with his family. All he needed was a sponsor.[36]

Lien began working even more hours to save enough money to bring The to the United States. The Red Cross gave her a list of everything she needed to do to sponsor him, and she followed the instructions carefully. She also talked to the children about their father's return. Her daughter had no memory of The, and the boys could hardly remember him. They couldn't imagine what it would be like to have a father.

After arriving at the airport, Lien joined other friends and Church members who had come to welcome The. Some of them held balloons that shone in the evening light.[37]

Before long, Lien saw The descending an escalator. He looked pale and had a lost look in his eyes. But at the sight of Lien, he called out to her. They reached for one another at the same time and clasped hands. Emotion welled in Lien's chest.[38]

She pulled The into a hug. "Thank God in heaven," she whispered, "you are home at last!"[39]

IN THE EARLY MONTHS of 1978, President Spencer W. Kimball was so concerned about the Church's priesthood and temple restriction that he often struggled to sleep. The public outcry against the restriction had largely quieted, but he continued to think about the countless worthy Saints and other good people it affected. His recent trip to Brazil had been a reminder of the many challenges it posed for Saints around the world.[40]

All his life, President Kimball had upheld the Church's practice of withholding the priesthood from people of Black African descent, and he was ready to spend the rest of his life upholding that practice. Yet he knew the restored gospel of Jesus Christ was destined to flood the earth, and he had asked the Saints to pray for nations to open their doors to missionary work.[41]

He began spending more and more time in the Salt Lake Temple's Holy of Holies, a special sanctuary adjoining the celestial room. There he would remove his shoes, kneel in prayer, and humbly plead with heaven.[42]

On March 9, he spoke with his counselors and the Quorum of the Twelve Apostles about race and the priesthood. The meeting lasted a long time. They reviewed statements by Church presidents David O. McKay and Harold B. Lee indicating that the priesthood restriction would someday end. But the apostles unanimously agreed that the practice would not change until the Lord revealed His will to the prophet.[43]

Before the meeting ended, President Kimball urged the apostles to fast and pray about the issue. And over the next several weeks, he invited them to study the subject and write down their thoughts. He assigned elders Howard W. Hunter and Boyd K. Packer to compile a history of the priesthood restriction and document everything that had been said about the issue in meetings of the First Presidency and the Twelve. The previous year, he had also asked Elder Bruce R. McConkie to review the scriptural basis for the practice.[44]

President Kimball, meanwhile, continued to pray about the restriction. While concerns still beset him, they became less and less important. He felt a growing spiritual impression, deep and abiding, to move forward. When Elder McConkie submitted a report on his findings, he concluded that no scriptures barred the Church from lifting the restriction.

On Tuesday, May 30, President Kimball shared with his counselors a rough draft of a statement extending the priesthood to all worthy men, regardless of their race.[45]

Two days later, June 1, the First Presidency had their monthly meeting with all general authorities. They had come to the meeting fasting, as usual, and at its conclusion, the presidency dismissed everyone but the apostles.

"I would like you to continue to fast with me," he said. He then told them of the many hours he had spent asking the Lord for answers. A change would bring the restored gospel and temple blessings to countless Saints—men, women, and children—all across the world.

"I have not been determined in advance what the answer should be," he said. "But I want to know. Whatever the Lord's decision is, I will defend it to the limits of my strength."[46]

He asked everyone to share their thoughts, and for the next two hours, the apostles spoke in turn. A feeling of unity and peace rested over them.[47]

"Do you mind if I lead you in prayer?" President Kimball asked.

He knelt at a temple altar, surrounded by the apostles. Humbly and fervently, he asked the Father to cleanse them from sin so they could receive the Lord's word. He prayed to know how to expand the work of the Church and spread the gospel throughout the world. He asked the Lord to manifest His mind and will on extending the priesthood to all worthy men in the Church.[48]

After the prophet finished his prayer, the Holy Spirit flooded the room, touching the hearts of everyone in the circle. The Spirit spoke to their souls, binding them together in total harmony. All doubt fled.[49]

President Kimball sprang from his knees. His fragile heart was pounding. He wrapped his arms around Elder David B. Haight, the junior apostle, and embraced the others one by one. The apostles had tears in their eyes. Some wept openly.

They had received their answer from the Lord.[50]

"We left that meeting subdued and reverent and joyful," Elder Gordon B. Hinckley later recalled. "All of us knew that the time had come for a change and that the decision had come from the heavens. The answer was clear. There was perfect unity among us in our experience and in our understanding."

"It was a quiet and sublime occasion," he declared. "The voice of the Spirit whispered with certainty into our minds and our very souls."[51]

"Following the prayer, we experienced the sweetest spirit of unity and conviction that I have ever experienced," Elder Ezra Taft Benson recorded in his journal. "We took each other in our arms, we were so impressed with the sweet spirit that was in evidence. Our bosoms burned."[52]

"It was the most spiritual event of my entire life," Elder Marvin J. Ashton wrote. "It left me weak."[53]

"From the midst of eternity, the voice of God, conveyed by the power of the Spirit, spoke to His prophet," Elder Bruce R. McConkie also witnessed. "President Kimball's prayer was answered and our prayers were answered. He heard the voice and we heard the same voice. All doubt and uncertainty fled. He knew the answer and we knew the answer. And we are all living witnesses of the truthfulness of the word so graciously sent from heaven."[54]

"The answer came strong to all of us," President N. Eldon Tanner testified. "There was absolutely no question in the mind of any one of us."[55]

Eight days after President Kimball's prayer, Darius Gray was sitting in his office at a paper company in Salt Lake City when a coworker poked her head into the room. She said she'd heard that the Church was now giving the priesthood to Black men.

Darius thought she was making a bad joke. "That's not funny," he told her.

"No, really," she insisted. She had just spoken with a customer at the Church Administration Building. There were rumors that President Kimball had received a revelation extending the blessings of the priesthood and temple to all worthy members of the Church.[56]

Skeptical, Darius picked up the telephone and dialed the number for President Kimball's office. A secretary told him that President Kimball was in the temple, but he confirmed that the rumors were true. The prophet had indeed received a revelation on the priesthood.

Darius was stunned. He could not believe the news. Nothing had prepared him for it. The change seemed to have come out of nowhere.[57]

The *Deseret News* published an announcement from the First Presidency later that day. "As we have witnessed the expansion of the work of the Lord over the earth, we have been grateful that people of many nations have responded to the message of the restored gospel, and have joined the Church in ever-increasing numbers," it read. "This, in turn, has inspired us with a desire to extend to every worthy member of the

Church all of the privileges and blessings which the gospel affords."

"He has heard our prayers, and by revelation has confirmed that the long-promised day has come," the announcement continued. "Every faithful, worthy man in the Church may receive the holy priesthood, with power to exercise its divine authority, and enjoy with his loved ones every blessing that flows therefrom, including the blessings of the temple."[58]

After Darius heard the news, he went to Temple Square. The whole block was buzzing with excitement. Darius spoke to a news reporter about the revelation and then walked across the street to the office of his old friend Heber Wolsey, who was now director of public communications for the Church.

Heber was not in his office, but his secretary asked Darius to stay. "I know he would want to see you," she said.

Darius waited. Heber's office overlooked the east face of the Salt Lake Temple. The sun was high and bright, and through the window, Darius could see the stones of the temple gleaming.[59]

Before long, Heber returned to his office. As soon as he saw Darius, he gathered him in a tearful embrace.

"I never thought . . ." Heber whispered.

Darius looked at his friend and then out the window at the temple. And he knew that the revelation would not affect just the present and future. It would affect the past as well. For the first time in this dispensation, people like him, living and dead, would have a chance to receive every available ordinance of the temple.

Darius looked back at Heber, closed his eyes, and then slowly opened them again.

"God is good," he said.[60]

CHAPTER 19

United as a Family

One evening in June 1978, Billy Johnson returned to his home in Cape Coast, Ghana. He and other members of his congregation had been fasting, as they often did, but the fast had done nothing to lift his spirits. He was tired and discouraged because more believers had stopped worshipping with him and returned to their old churches.[1]

Billy longed to feel spiritually and emotionally strong again. A couple of months earlier, a member of his congregation had told him about a revelation she'd had. "Very soon the missionaries will come," she had said. "I have seen white men coming to our church. They embraced us and joined us in worship." Another woman announced that she had received a similar revelation. Billy himself had dreamed of some white men entering his chapel and saying, "We are your brothers, and we have come to baptize you." Afterward, he'd dreamed of Black people coming from far and wide to join the Church.[2]

Still, Billy could not shake his discouragement.

It was getting late, but he couldn't sleep. A strong impression overtook him to listen to the British Broadcasting Corporation (BBC) on the radio—something he hadn't done in years.[3]

He found the radio, a brown model with four silver knobs near the base. The radio crackled to life as he turned it on. He fiddled with the knobs, and the red pointer glided back and forth across the dial. But he couldn't find the broadcast.

Then, after an hour of searching, Billy finally made out a newscast from the BBC. The reporter announced that the president of The Church of Jesus Christ of Latter-day Saints had received a revelation. All worthy men in the Church, regardless of race, could now hold the priesthood.

Billy collapsed, bursting into tears of joy. Priesthood authority would finally come to Ghana.[4]

LIKE THE VAST MAJORITY of Saints, Ardeth Kapp, second counselor in the Young Women general presidency, celebrated when she heard that all worthy men could now receive the priesthood. "Another new revelation, and this one so beautiful," she reflected. "How blessed we are, how thankful for a prophet to guide us in these latter days."[5]

The announcement of the revelation on priesthood came not long after Young Women general president Ruth Funk informed Ardeth that their presidency would be honorably released. The news had surprised everyone. Most previous presidencies had served for at least a decade. Her presidency would be ending after only five and a half years.[6]

Now Ardeth was struggling to understand the Lord's timing. Serving the young women had given her a new sense of purpose. Now that her calling was coming to an end, what did the future have in store for her?

"At forty-seven years of age, I don't believe it's all over—especially at a time when I'm better prepared than ever before to understand and see the big picture," she wrote in her journal. She knew she had more to offer. "Yet," she wrote, "I don't see an opportunity at this moment to make a difference of much consequence."[7]

The release was particularly difficult because the Young Women presidency still had much more they wanted to do. The first years of their service had been slowed down by organizational adjustments in the Church. The name Aaronic Priesthood MIA had proven cumbersome, and it left people confused about how the young women fit into the program.[8] After President Harold B. Lee's death, the new First Presidency had retired the name "Mutual Improvement Association" and created two separate youth organizations, Young Women and Aaronic Priesthood.[9]

Even after these changes took place, Ardeth and other Young Women leaders continued to be unsure about the place of young women in the Church structure. Initially, the changes created communication channels that did not allow for the general presidency to train or correspond directly with local Young Women leaders. Instead, they had to relay their messages through local priesthood leaders. Although communication with local leaders had since improved, the Young Women general president still had little contact with the First Presidency or Quorum of the Twelve, since most contact with them took place through a member of the Seventy acting as an intermediary.[10]

The Young Women presidency had done their best to move forward. President Funk had decided early in her presidency to develop a program to help young women nurture their spirituality, achieve personal goals, and honor the roles of wife and mother, which she believed were under attack in popular media.[11]

The new program debuted in 1977. Called "My Personal Progress," it encouraged young women to develop skills in six areas: spiritual awareness, service and compassion, homemaking arts, recreation and the natural world, cultural arts and education, and personal and social refinement. It also encouraged young women to keep a journal, something President Kimball invited all Saints to do.[12] That same year, Ardeth published a bestselling book, *Miracles in Pinafores and Bluejeans,* which told stories from her own life and the lives of heroic young women, past and present.[13]

In late June 1978, Ardeth and other Church leaders were in Nauvoo, Illinois, for the dedication of the Monument to Women Memorial Garden. The two-acre garden featured twelve statues of women at different stages of life, with emphasis on motherhood. Along with a general women's satellite broadcast to be held later that year—a first in the Church—the monument was designed to honor the significance of women in the gospel plan, affirm their contributions as wives and mothers, and commemorate the founding of the Relief Society in 1842. The day of the dedication was rainy, but twenty-five hundred women witnessed the ceremony from under a huge tent.[14]

A few weeks after the dedication, the First Presidency honorably released the Young Women general presidency. Ardeth now felt better about it. "At this moment in time," she wrote, "I feel more optimistic, more committed, more confident, and more grateful than I can express."[15]

Ardeth's bishop soon called her to serve as the ward's first-year Laurel adviser. She was eager to draw on her recent experience in the general presidency to teach and train these sixteen-year-old girls. In her journal, she wrote, "I really believe with the Lord's help, I can reach each one."[16]

On September 29, 1978, President Kimball spoke in Salt Lake City at a seminar for the Church's regional representatives. "We have an obligation, a duty, a divine commission," he said, "to preach the gospel in every nation and to every creature."

The Church now had more than four million members, and it was growing by well over one hundred thousand converts a year. But people everywhere still needed the gospel. He felt an urgency to reach them. "We have hardly scratched the surface," he declared.[17]

More than twenty-six thousand missionaries were now serving full-time across the globe, far more than could be trained in existing facilities. To prepare this vast group, Church leaders had recently built the Missionary Training Center in Provo, Utah, where new missionaries would come for four to eight weeks to study one of twenty-five different languages, including sign language for the deaf.[18]

New fields of labor were opening all the time. With President Kimball's encouragement, David Kennedy, the First Presidency's personal representative, had recently helped the Church become officially recognized in Portugal and Poland. Now he was working on doing the same in India, Sri Lanka, Pakistan, Hungary, Romania, and Greece. But there was so much more left to do.[19]

In President Kimball's talk before the regional representatives, he referred to believers in Ghana and Nigeria. "They have waited so long already," he said. "Can we ask them to wait any longer?" He did not think so. "What of Libya, Ethiopia, Ivory Coast, and Sudan, and others?" he asked. "These are names that must become as familiar to us as Japan, Venezuela, New Zealand, and Denmark have become."

China, the Soviet Union, and many other nations also needed the restored gospel, but they had not yet officially recognized the Church and had no local congregations. "There are almost three billion people now living on the earth in nations where the gospel is not now being preached," he said. "If we could only make a small beginning in every nation, soon the converts among each kindred and tongue could step forth as lights to their own people and the gospel would thus be preached in all nations before the coming of the Lord."

He wanted the Saints to pray and prepare. He thought barriers to the Church's growth would remain until the Saints were ready for them to fall. The Church needed its members, young and old, to learn languages and serve missions. "The only lasting peace that can come is the peace of the gospel of Jesus Christ," he told the regional representatives. "We must take it everywhere to everyone."[20]

The next day, the Salt Lake Tabernacle was filled to capacity for general conference. At President Kimball's request, his counselor N. Eldon Tanner approached the pulpit and read the First Presidency's statement announcing that all worthy men could hold the priesthood, regardless of race.

"Recognizing Spencer W. Kimball as a prophet, seer, and revelator," he said, "and president of The Church of Jesus Christ of Latter-day Saints, it is proposed that we as a constituent assembly accept this revelation as the word and will of the Lord."

He asked everyone in favor to raise their right hand, and a sea of hands rose into the air. He asked if anyone opposed. Not a single hand went up.[21]

Shortly after the conference, President Kimball sat at the end of a long table in a boardroom of the Church Administration Building. Joining him were his counselors, several general authorities, and two older couples, Edwin and Janath Cannon and Rendell and Rachel Mabey. The Cannons and the Mabeys had just agreed to serve as the first missionaries in West Africa, though the call meant that Janath would have to be released as first counselor in the Relief Society general presidency.

The group discussed the missionaries' assignment and the challenges they were likely to face as they made contact with believers in Ghana and Nigeria. When the time came to end the meeting, forty minutes later, President Kimball thanked the couples for their faithfulness.

"Are there any more questions?" he asked.

Elder Mabey looked at the other missionaries. "Only one for the moment," he said. "How soon would you like us to leave?"

President Kimball smiled.

"Yesterday."[22]

RUDÁ MARTINS WAS THE first member of her family to learn about the priesthood revelation. When the news broke, the phone lines in their Rio de Janeiro neighborhood were down, so a family friend had traveled forty minutes by bus to tell her. The young woman had knocked on the door, calling out that she had news.

"I heard the Church received a revelation," she said, telling Rudá that all worthy men could now hold the priesthood.

Helvécio was at work, so Rudá had to wait to tell him.[23] "I have news, amazing news!" she said when he finally got home. "Helvécio, you will hold the priesthood."

Helvécio was speechless. He couldn't believe it. Then the phone started ringing and he answered it. On the other end was a colleague in Salt Lake City.

"I have the official declaration in my hands," the colleague said, "and I'm going to read it to you."

After Helvécio hung up the phone, he and Rudá wept as they offered a grateful prayer to their Heavenly Father. The dedication of the São Paulo Temple was only a few months away. And now they would be able to receive their endowment and be sealed together with their four children.[24]

Two weeks later, Helvécio and Marcus received the Aaronic Priesthood. One week after that, Helvécio was ordained an elder, and he immediately conferred the Melchizedek Priesthood on Marcus. Marcus was engaged to marry a returned missionary, Mirian Abelin Barbosa, and they had already sent out invitations to their wedding. Yet they decided to postpone their marriage so Marcus could serve a mission.[25]

In early November 1978, the Martinses attended the temple dedication. Rudá sat with the choir near President Kimball and other general authorities who had come for the ceremony. Helvécio was sitting in the congregation with their children. Missionaries from Brazil's four missions had been given permission to attend the dedication, so Marcus, now a full-time missionary in the São Paulo North Mission, was able to attend as well.[26]

A few days later, on November 6, Rudá, Helvécio, and Marcus received their endowment. They were then ushered to a sealing room, where Marcus served as a witness as Rudá and Helvécio were sealed for time and eternity. The three younger children were brought into the room, dressed in white.

"Mom," the couple's three-year-old daughter asked, "what will we do here?"

"We will kneel at this table," Rudá said, referring to the altar, "and we will be united as a family."

The little girl then said, "I'm glad I will really be your daughter."

"You already are my daughter," Rudá assured her.

The family took their places around the altar, and the sealer performed the ceremony. Of the children, only Marcus was old enough to fully understand the significance of the moment. But each of the children seemed to sense the wonder and happiness in the room. For Rudá and Helvécio, the sight of their family together in the temple was beautiful. Joy overwhelmed them.

"They are mine now," Rudá thought. "They are truly mine."[27]

AFTER HER BAPTISM, KATHERINE Warren often traveled to the city of Baton Rouge, Louisiana, some eighty miles northwest of her home in New Orleans, to study the Bible with her extended family. Many of them had recently begun attending a Pentecostal church in the area. Katherine would bring insights from the restored gospel to her study, but she was careful not to weary her relatives with her enthusiasm for the Church. "I don't want to pile too much on you at once," she told them.[28]

When she learned about the priesthood revelation, however, Katherine could hardly contain herself. Katherine called her niece Betty Baunchand about the news. Betty's family had been studying the Bible with her, but she didn't know much about the Church and didn't understand the significance of the revelation.

But Katherine's bishop did. He called her up right away. "Sister Katherine," he said, "are you familiar with what's happening now?"

"Yes," she replied.

The bishop didn't quite know what to say. "You're a good person," he finally said. "I'm thinking about making you a missionary."[29]

One month after the announcement, Freda Beaulieu, the one other Black woman in the New Orleans Ward, traveled over a thousand miles to the nearest temple, in

Washington, DC, where she received her endowment and was sealed by proxy to her late husband.[30]

Although temple blessings were now available to her and so many others for the first time, Katherine did not go to the temple right away. But she did give thanks to her Heavenly Father.[31]

One day, Betty Baunchand's husband, Severia, saw a coworker reading a Book of Mormon. Having talked with Katherine about the Church, Severia struck up a conversation with him, and he asked Severia if he wanted to meet with the missionaries. "OK," Severia said, "let them come by."[32]

The elders visited that night and taught the first of seven lessons from *The Uniform System for Teaching Families,* the Church's latest series of missionary discussions. Published in 1973, the lessons were available in twenty languages, including English, and opened with an introduction to the First Vision, the Book of Mormon, and the restoration of the priesthood.[33]

The family enjoyed the discussion and scheduled another visit with the missionaries. Both Betty and Severia were eager to learn more, and they invited other family members to attend the discussions. Soon, the Baunchand home was full whenever the missionaries were there.[34]

On a weekend when Katherine was visiting the family, she overheard Betty talking on the telephone. "No," Betty said, "we'll go another time. My aunt is up here from New Orleans."

"Who is that?" Katherine asked.

"Elders from the Latter-day Church." They were inviting the family to attend Sunday meetings.

"Tell them yes."

So that Sunday, everyone in the family attended the meetings in Baker, Louisiana. And during subsequent lessons with the missionaries, everyone made commitments to obey the Word of Wisdom and law of chastity, pay tithing, accept Jesus Christ as their Savior and Redeemer, and endure to the end.

About two weeks after their first visit to the church, the Baunchands called Katherine. "Guess what?" they said. "We're getting baptized, and you've got to come to our baptism!"[35]

On the day of the baptism, the meetinghouse was packed. One hundred and ten Church members came out to welcome Betty and Severia and eleven of Katherine's other relatives into their ward. The cultural hall and baptismal font area were under construction, so the whole service was chilly. But the Spirit was powerful, warming everyone in the room.

Katherine wept as she wrapped dry towels around her newly baptized family members. "This was a moment for which I have waited and prayed for a long time," she said afterward.[36] She loved the Church, and she wanted Black members like her and her family to receive all the blessings it offered.

She knew the Savior had His eyes on the Saints.[37]

On November 18, 1978, Anthony Obinna solemnly approached three Americans—one woman and two men—waiting for him at his congregation's meetinghouse in southeast Nigeria. Anthony had come as soon as he'd heard about their arrival. He had been expecting them for more than a decade.[38]

The Americans were Elder Rendell Mabey, Sister Rachel Mabey, and Elder Edwin Cannon. They asked, "Are you Anthony Obinna?"

"Yes," Anthony replied, and they entered the meetinghouse. The building was about thirty feet long. The letters "LDS" adorned the wall above one door, and the words "Missionary Home" above another. Just under the roof someone had painted the words "Nigerian Latter Day Saints."[39]

"It has been a long, difficult wait," Anthony told the visitors, "but that doesn't matter now. You have come at last."

"A long wait, yes," Elder Cannon said, "but the gospel really is here now in all its fullness."

The missionaries asked Anthony to tell his story, so he told them he was forty-eight years old and the assistant schoolmaster at a nearby school. He recounted how he had dreamed years ago of the Salt Lake Temple and then later happened upon a picture of it in an old magazine. He had never even heard of the Church before. "But there before my eyes," Anthony said, his voice struggling with emotion, "was the very building I had visited in my dream."

He told the missionaries about his careful study of the restored gospel of Jesus Christ, his correspondence with LaMar Williams, and his sorrow over the continued lack of a Church presence in Nigeria. But he also bore witness of his faith and his refusal to give up hope, even when he and his fellow believers had faced persecution because of their devotion to the truth.[40]

After Anthony finished his story, Elder Mabey asked to speak with him privately. They stepped into the neighboring room, and Elder Mabey asked if there were any laws in Nigeria that would restrict baptism because the Church was not yet legally registered. Anthony said there were none.

"Well," Elder Mabey said, "I'm delighted to hear that. We must do a lot of traveling during the next few weeks to visit other groups like your own." He said that visiting these groups might take five to six weeks and that the missionaries could return then to baptize Anthony and his group.

"No, please," Anthony said. "I know that there are many others, but we have been waiting for thirteen years." He looked into Elder Mabey's eyes. "If it is humanly possible," Anthony said, "go ahead with the baptisms now."

"Are most of your people truly ready?" asked Elder Mabey.

"Yes, absolutely, yes!" Anthony replied. "Let us baptize those strongest in the faith now and teach the others further."[41]

Three days later, Anthony met with Elder Mabey to discuss how to lead a branch of the Church. Outside, little children sang a new song they had learned from the missionaries:

I am a child of God,
And he has sent me here,
Has given me an earthly home
With parents kind and dear.[42]

Soon, Anthony, the missionaries, and the other believers gathered on the bank of a secluded pool on the Ekeonumiri River. The pool was about thirty feet across, with dense green bushes and trees all around. Patches of bright sunlight filtered through the trees and danced on the water's surface, while small, colorful fish darted back and forth near the bank.

Elder Mabey waded into the water and took Anthony by the hand. Anthony smiled and followed him in. After steadying himself, Anthony gripped Elder Mabey's wrist, and the missionary raised his right hand.

"Anthony Uzodimma Obinna," he said, "having been commissioned of Jesus Christ, I baptize you in the name of the Father, and of the Son, and of the Holy Ghost."

Anthony felt the water envelop him as Elder Mabey immersed him. And when he came out of the water, the crowd along the bank let out a collective sigh—followed by joyous laughter.[43]

Once Anthony's wife, Fidelia, and seventeen other people were baptized, the group returned to their meetinghouse. Anthony and three of his brothers—Francis, Raymond, and Aloysius—were ordained to the office of priest in the Aaronic Priesthood. Elder Mabey set Anthony apart as president of the Aboh Branch, with Francis and Raymond as his counselors.

By the authority of the priesthood he held, Anthony then set Fidelia apart as the branch Relief Society president.[44]

PART 3

His Own Path
1979–1997

"Despite hardship, great disappointment,
or even personal danger, our Heavenly Father
guides us on His own path."

Olga Kovářová

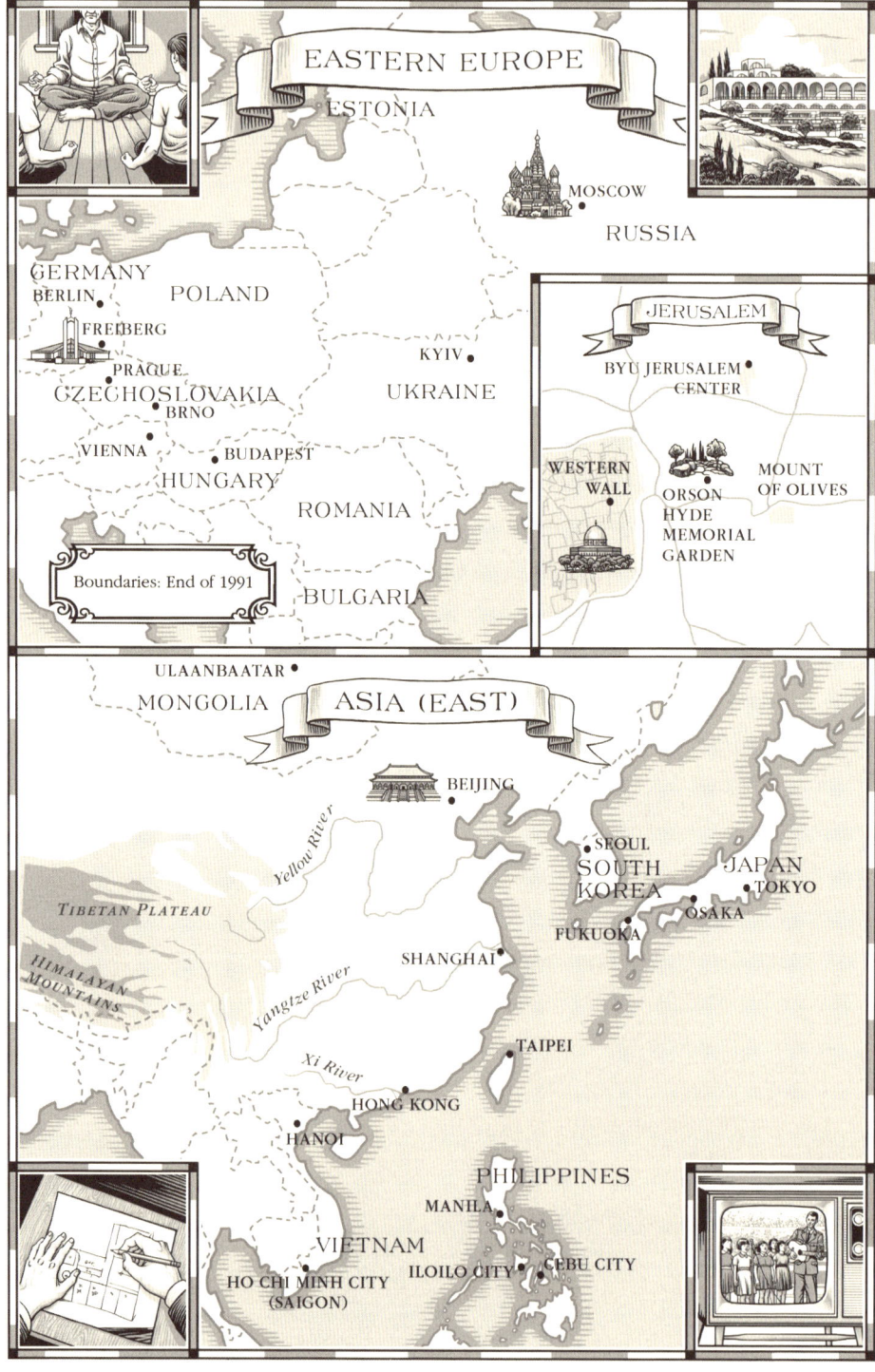

CHAPTER 20

Marvelous and Wonderful Way

Five years into his presidency, Spencer W. Kimball was feeling the effects of his age. He turned eighty-four years old in March 1979. His doctor advised him to get more rest to save his strength, yet he and his wife, Camilla, continued to keep a busy travel schedule. To do everything he wanted to do, he woke up early and went to bed late, with only a short nap after lunch.

"I don't want to be saved in this world," he told his doctor. "I want to be exalted in the world to come."[1]

His age caught up with him in the summer. Doctors found blood pooling beneath his skull, and they immediately sent him to surgery to relieve the pressure on his brain. The operation was a success, and one month later, President and Sister Kimball were traveling again—this time to Jerusalem.[2]

The prophet was visiting the Holy Land to dedicate the Orson Hyde Memorial Garden, a beautiful five-acre park the Church had recently constructed on the Mount of Olives. Created at the invitation of Jerusalem mayor Teddy Kollek and funded by thirty thousand private donors, the park was named for the latter-day apostle who came to the city in 1841 to dedicate the land for the gathering of the people of Judah and as a land of promise for Abraham's descendants.[3] Mayor Kollek wanted to create more green spaces around Jerusalem, and he had worked with Elder Howard W. Hunter to make the park a reality.[4]

The prophet's visit to Jerusalem, like the memorial garden, reflected the Church's desire to add to the light and truth people cherished around the world. President Kimball had immense respect for the religious traditions found in the Holy Land and elsewhere. He taught that salvation and lasting happiness came only through Jesus Christ. Yet he affirmed that God's light had inspired Muhammad, Confucius, the Protestant reformers, and other religious leaders. He also believed that Socrates, Plato, and other great thinkers had been enlightened by God.

"Our message," the First Presidency had recently declared, "is one of special love and concern for the eternal welfare of all men and women, regardless of religious belief, race, or nationality."[5]

On October 24, 1979, the anniversary of Elder Hyde's dedicatory prayer, President Kimball linked arms with Mayor Kollek as they followed a winding path down through the garden. The prophet walked with difficulty, but it felt good to be at the park. From the garden, he could see many sites where the Savior had walked and taught.[6]

At the base of the hill, a platform had been set up for the dedication. Elder Hunter opened the service, and a choir of nearly three hundred Saints, including BYU students studying in the city, sang "The Morning Breaks." Mayor Kollek then rose and spoke of the long history of Jerusalem.

"I wish you to continue as many generations as we have," he told the Saints, "and that this good relationship between you and us should persist during all these coming centuries."[7]

When it was President Kimball's turn to speak, he marveled at the sacred history around him. "Jesus Christ traversed this mount on several occasions," he said. "In a garden called Gethsemane, just below us, He fulfilled that part of His Atonement which enables us to return to our Heavenly Father."

Bowing his head, he offered a prayer dedicating the garden to God and His glory. "Let it be a haven," he declared, "where all who come may meditate upon the glory which Thou hast shed upon Jerusalem in ages past and the greater glory yet to be."[8]

David Galbraith, the Church's district president in Israel, closed the meeting with a benediction. "May this spiritual garden, with its magnificent view, be a source of inspiration and a place of meditation for Muslims, Christians, and Jews alike," he prayed. "May it serve to unite us all in the bonds of brotherhood and peace."[9]

Before the Kimballs left the city, David showed them some property near the memorial garden. For several years, the Church had wanted to build a campus in Jerusalem to house BYU's study abroad students, provide a meetinghouse for the local branch of Saints, and serve as a welcome center for visitors. This site had a striking view of the Temple Mount, but strict zoning laws made it impossible for private organizations to build on the property. Still, President Kimball thought it was the best location he'd seen for the center.[10]

The Kimballs returned to Salt Lake City on October 26, tired but happy. A short time later, as President Kimball prepared to attend area conferences in Australia and New Zealand, he noticed that his left hand was numb. He checked himself into the hospital, and his doctors discovered more blood pooling beneath his skull.

The next morning, the prophet was back in the operating room.[11]

AROUND THIS SAME TIME, thirty-five-year-old Silvia Allred and her family moved from Costa Rica to Guatemala. A convert from El Salvador, Silvia had served a mission in Guatemala some fifteen years earlier, and she was eager to return with her husband, Jeff, and their six young children.

Jeff was the Church's director for temporal affairs in Central America. This position—and others like it around the world—had been created in 1979 to help the Presiding Bishopric's Office with such tasks as distributing Church curriculum, maintaining Church properties, and purchasing sites for new meetinghouses.[12]

The Allreds arrived in Guatemala City at the start of the school year. They enrolled their children in an English-language school with local and international students. On Sundays, the family attended a large Spanish-speaking ward in the city.[13]

When Silvia was a missionary in the 1960s, there were about eleven thousand Church members and no stakes in Central America. She had spent much of her time serving in small, struggling branches where missionaries provided most of the leadership. Although Guatemalans spoke many languages and dialects, she and the other missionaries had taught exclusively in Spanish.[14]

Since then, Church membership had exploded across Latin America. By 1980, Guatemala alone had five stakes, about eighteen thousand Church members, and strong local leadership. The neighboring countries of El Salvador, Costa Rica, Honduras, and Panama also had stakes of their own. And almost a thousand women and men from Central America were now serving full-time missions.[15]

But with this growth had come the need for changes. More and more Indigenous people were joining the Church in Central America, and many of them did not speak Spanish. Other converts also needed help learning and understanding the teachings of the restored gospel.[16]

To meet these needs, the Church had approved the translation of portions of the Book of Mormon into local Indigenous languages—K'iche', Q'eqchi', Kaqchikel, and Mam.[17] New converts could also study *Gospel Principles,* a simple, easy-to-read Sunday School manual the Church had recently produced to teach basic truths to members everywhere.[18]

Greater growth had also required adjustments to how Latter-day Saints around the world met together each week. For half a century, the Church had held Sunday School, priesthood, and sacrament meetings at different times on the Sabbath, with Primary, Relief Society, and youth meetings on weekdays. But Saints who lived far from their meetinghouses and did not have cars or access to public transportation often found this schedule challenging.[19]

Recently, apostle Boyd K. Packer had come to Guatemala and dedicated nine small meetinghouses in the nation's highlands. These meetinghouses greatly reduced the travel time for many Church members, and Jeff recommended building more of them throughout rural Central America. Mission leaders in the Guatemalan highlands had also implemented a meeting schedule that let rural Saints meet only once during the week. Under the new plan, Primary children met together while men and women held their own meetings. Saints of all ages then met together for sacrament meeting.[20]

Silvia and Jeff's ward in Guatemala City followed the traditional meeting schedule. But in 1980, just as the Allreds were settling into their new home, the First Presidency announced a Churchwide meeting schedule much like the one used in rural Guatemala. Instead of holding meetings at different times during the week, all wards and branches would now meet on Sundays for a three-hour block of meetings.

In congregations where this schedule had been tested, Church attendance had improved, and Saints had more time to teach and study the gospel at home. Church leaders hoped the same thing would happen now throughout the world. They encouraged families to spend the Sabbath day together and make their home a place where everyone could find love, encouragement, support, and appreciation. With oil costs rising across the globe, Church leaders also hoped the new schedule would allow the Saints to conserve fuel and save on transportation costs.[21]

Silvia could see the wisdom of having a meeting schedule that worked for Saints anywhere in the world. Her daughters would be able to attend Young Women classes on Sunday when they became teenagers, and Jeff and their sons would not have to get up as early to attend morning priesthood meetings.

Still, the new schedule would take some getting used to.[22]

ON APRIL 6, 1980, APOSTLE Gordon B. Hinckley awoke to a beautiful Easter morning. It was the 150th anniversary of the Church. He and President Spencer W. Kimball had come to Fayette, New York, to broadcast part of general conference from the Peter and Mary Whitmer farm, where the Saints had held their first meeting in 1830.[23]

The Church had much to celebrate on its sesquicentennial. The restored gospel of Jesus Christ had spread to eighty-one countries—nearly half the nations of the world—bringing purpose, hope, and healing to people who had long yearned for its message. The number of temples was on the rise, with new houses of the Lord announced or under construction in Argentina, Australia, Chile, Japan, Mexico, Samoa, Tahiti, Tonga, and the United States.[24] And thanks to the faithful payment of tithes, coupled with wise financial investments, the Church was building hundreds of new meetinghouses each year. Although local Saints continued to pay a small percentage for these buildings, the Church no longer called labor missionaries to do the construction.[25]

Yet Elder Hinckley knew the Church still faced significant opposition. In many places around the world, congregations struggled to retain new members, and Elder Hinckley estimated that half of the Church's

4.5 million members were not practicing their faith. There were also people who viewed the Church's rapid worldwide growth, financial security, and distinctive teachings as threats to mainstream Christianity, leading critics to produce pamphlets, books, and films attacking the Latter-day Saints.[26]

Other people objected when the First Presidency spoke on current political issues, claiming it was inappropriate for the Church to do so publicly. In response to criticism of the Church's opposition to the Equal Rights Amendment, Elder Hinckley had recently drafted a major Church statement on the subject. Published in February 1980, the statement expressed support for the equal rights of women, reiterated the First Presidency's concerns about the ERA, and affirmed the Church's right to speak on moral issues.[27]

Having studied Church history, Elder Hinckley knew the Saints experienced cycles of good times and bad. Through it all, the Church had grown stronger. "So it will be in the future," he had recently reminded his fellow apostles. "The Church shall grow and prosper and enlarge in a marvelous and wonderful way."[28]

The Church had never broadcast general conference from two locations before, so Elder Hinckley arrived at the Whitmer farm two hours early to make sure everything was in order.

Under his direction, the Church had recently built a historic log home and a modern meetinghouse on the Whitmer property. He and President Kimball planned to address the Saints from inside the home. If everything worked as planned, a large satellite dish on the site would transmit the proceedings in real time to the Salt Lake Tabernacle and chapels around the world.[29]

After inspecting the home, Elder Hinckley and President Kimball rehearsed their talks. Knowing the prophet was still recovering from his recent surgeries, Elder Hinckley wondered if he had the strength to deliver his remarks. The day before, President Kimball had looked and sounded tired as he opened the conference in the Tabernacle. Now, as he rehearsed his talk, he continued to speak with difficulty.[30]

It pained Elder Hinckley to see the prophet struggle. Recently, the Church had implemented a new policy whereby older members of the First Quorum of the Seventy retired from active duty. Church presidents and apostles continued to serve to the end of their lives, however, and they sometimes experienced health problems that made it difficult to be out among the Saints. At such times, the counselors in the First Presidency usually did more to assist the president. Sadly, President Kimball's counselors, N. Eldon Tanner and Marion G. Romney, were in poor health as well, and they could not always give the prophet all the support he needed.[31]

The broadcast started at noon. In the Whitmer cabin, Elder Hinckley and President Kimball watched a television feed of President Tanner opening the conference session in the Tabernacle. After a prayer and hymns by the choir, President Kimball stood, and the feed switched to a shot of him in the log home, welcoming the Saints.

"Standing here today," he said, "we review in our minds the mighty faith and works of those who, from this humble beginning, gave so much to help move the Church to its present wondrous stature; and more importantly, we behold through the eye of faith a vision of its sure and glorious future."

As Elder Hinckley watched, he felt like he had seen a miracle. President Kimball was speaking without any difficulty!

When the prophet finished his talk, Elder Hinckley presented a special proclamation from the First Presidency and Quorum of the Twelve Apostles.

"The mission of the Church today, as it has been from the beginning, is to teach the gospel of Christ to all the world," he declared. "It is our obligation, therefore, to teach faith in the Lord Jesus Christ, to plead with the people of the earth for individual repentance, to administer the sacred ordinances of baptism by immersion for the remission of sins and the laying on of hands for the gift of the Holy Ghost."

Elder Hinckley felt the Spirit powerfully as he read the proclamation. "We contemplate humbly and gratefully the sacrifices of those who have gone before us," he said. "We are resolved to build on that heritage for the blessing and benefit of those who follow."[32]

SHORTLY AFTER THE CHURCH adopted the consolidated meeting schedule, Silvia Allred's bishop in Guatemala City asked to meet with her. "The sisters in the Primary are having great difficulty in implementing the new program," he said.

Since Primary was now held at the same time as adult classes, Primary teachers had to miss the Sunday School, Relief Society, and priesthood meetings they had long enjoyed. Primary now lasted twice as long as it did before, and managing energetic children for that long could be exhausting.

"The sisters don't know what to do with two hours of Primary," the bishop explained, "so they are just taking the children to the garden to play." The bishop wanted the Primary leaders to follow the new program precisely. "You can help us do this," he told Silvia.[33]

In Primary, Silvia found the biggest challenge to be "sharing time," when the children all met together to learn more about living the gospel of Jesus Christ. Silvia worked with the Primary leaders to include music, visual aids, and playacting in their lessons. And before long, the children loved to participate. In one gospel-themed activity, they put together a big puzzle. In another, they sang louder or softer whenever a leader raised or lowered the temperature on a make-believe thermometer. The children also acted out scripture stories, like Jesus's parable of the good Samaritan.[34]

Silvia's time in Primary was short-lived, though. While visiting Salt Lake City in April 1980, she and Jeff learned that the First Presidency planned to move the Central American headquarters of the temporal affairs office out of Guatemala. For more than two decades, the country had been enmeshed in civil war, and rebel groups were gaining strength.[35]

Although Silvia and Jeff had been mindful of the conflict since moving to Guatemala, their family had carried out a normal routine, attending church and school, shopping, and going on family outings without much concern.[36]

Still, one month after the Allreds returned from Utah, the Church moved the temporal affairs office to San José, Costa Rica. The relocation would not be ideal for Jeff, whose work projects were mainly in Guatemala and El Salvador. And Silvia had mixed feelings about moving back to Costa Rica. She and her family had lived in Guatemala for less than a year, and Silvia liked being part of the Church's great growth in the country. She had especially enjoyed watching young Guatemalan men and women saving money for missions and growing spiritually in their youth and seminary classes.

In July 1980, just before the family moved away, their ward threw them a small farewell party. Though the people of Guatemala faced ongoing trials, the Allreds knew the Saints there would continue to thrive. The civil war was not interfering with Church meetings, and no mission leaders or missionaries were being removed from the country.

Despite their sadness, the Allreds were willing to go where the Lord directed, and no matter where they were, they were excited to help build His kingdom.[37]

AT THE TIME THE Allreds moved to Costa Rica, twenty-year-old Olga Kovářová was studying physical education at a university in Brno, Czechoslovakia. In one of her classes, she learned about yoga and its benefits on the mind and body. Fascinated, she wanted to learn more.

One day, a classmate told her about a local yoga instructor, Otakar Vojkůvka. Olga agreed to go with her to meet him.

Otakar was a small, elderly man, and he smiled as he answered the door. Olga felt an instant connection to him. During the visit, he asked her and her friend if they were happy.

"We don't know," they replied honestly.

Otakar told them about the trials he'd faced in life. In the 1940s, he had run a profitable factory. But after a Soviet-influenced government gained power in Czechoslovakia, the state seized the factory and sent Otakar to a prison camp, leaving his wife, Terezie Vojkůvková, to raise their two children alone for a time. Terezie had since died, and Otakar now lived with his son, Gád, and his family.

As Olga listened to Otakar's story, she was astonished. Most people she knew in her country were cheerless and cynical. She wondered how Otakar could be so happy after experiencing so many hard things.[38]

Olga soon visited Otakar again. This time Gád was there too. "So," he said, "you are interested in yoga?"

"I don't know anything about yoga," Olga said, "but I would like to learn because you all seem to be so happy. I assume it's because of yoga."

They began discussing spirituality and the purpose of life. "God sent us to earth to sow joy, life, and love into souls," Otakar told her.

Growing up in an atheistic society, Olga had never given God or the purpose of life much thought. Her ancestors had been Protestants, though, and now she found that she had many questions about religion. Unlike her professors and schoolmates, who discouraged interest in religion, Otakar took her questions seriously and lent her books on the subject.[39]

As Olga studied, she longed to find more purpose in life. She continued meeting with Otakar, growing happier as he taught her about his beliefs. He talked more about his Christian faith and his devotion to God. And the more Olga learned, the more she yearned for a spiritual community.

One day, Otakar recommended that she read a book by Elder John A. Widtsoe about The Church of Jesus Christ of Latter-day Saints. After her reading, she told Otakar she was fascinated by the Saints. "Could you give me the address of a Czech Mormon?" she asked.

"You don't need any address," Otakar said. "You are in the home of one of them."[40]

Otakar had been baptized shortly before World War II and was one of the earliest Church members in Czechoslovakia. In 1950, when the Czechoslovak government forced all foreign Latter-day Saint missionaries to leave the country, he and some 245 Church members had continued to practice their faith, worshipping together in private homes in Prague, Plzeň, and Brno.[41]

As Olga learned more, she borrowed a Book of Mormon from Otakar. When she read the words of Lehi, "Men are that they might have joy," she felt as though she had discovered a lost truth. Love and light seemed to flood every cell in her body. She knew, without a doubt, that Heavenly Father and Jesus Christ lived. She felt Their love for her and for all people everywhere.[42]

For the first time in her life, she knelt in prayer and poured out her gratitude to God. And in the morning, she went to Otakar's apartment and asked, "Is there any way I can start my life like a new person?"

"Yes, there is," he said. He opened his Bible and showed her Jesus's teachings about baptism.

"What does it mean to enter the kingdom of God?" she asked.

"To become Christ's disciple," he said. He then explained that she would need to be baptized and keep God's commandments. He told her about some lessons she'd need to receive first and invited her to visit his home the next Sunday for a gathering of Saints. Olga happily accepted.

They met in a room on the upper floor of Otakar's apartment. A few sofas offered seating for the small group, and the blinds were pulled down to prevent neighbors who were wary of religion from seeing inside. Looking around, Olga was surprised to find that the seven members were the age of her parents and grandparents.

"Is this Church meant for old people only?" she wondered. "What am I doing here?"[43]

CHAPTER 21

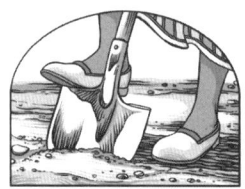

A Seed of Love

At the start of 1981, sixty-three-year-old Julia Mavimbela ran a community garden near her home in Soweto, a Black township of over a million people on the west side of Johannesburg, South Africa. Julia, a former elementary school principal, had started the garden a few years earlier to help the young people of the township as they grew to adulthood under apartheid, South Africa's official policy of racial segregation.

As a Black woman herself, she knew how difficult it was to live under this system. The laws demeaned Black people and treated them as lesser citizens. For decades, the government had forced every Black South African to carry an identification booklet stating where the person could and could not go. If Black individuals were discovered in white neighborhoods at the wrong time of day, they could be beaten, arrested, or even killed.

When Julia was younger, she had been forced to move from her multiracial neighborhood in Johannesburg to a house in segregated Soweto. Now, as she watched young people struggle against these injustices, she worried about the bitterness growing in their hearts. With her garden, she hoped to teach them how to move beyond their anger before it destroyed them and their loved ones.

"Look," she would say, "this soil is solid and hard. But if we push a spade or a fork, we will crack it and come out with lumps. Then, if we break those lumps and throw in a seed, the seed grows."

She wanted the young people to carry the message of the hard earth in their hearts. "Let us dig the soil of bitterness, throw in a seed of love, and see what fruits it can give us," she would tell them. "Love will not come without forgiving others."[1]

This was a lesson Julia was still learning. Decades earlier, her husband, John, had been killed in a head-on collision with a white driver. When Julia went to the police station to claim his belongings, she found that the money he'd had with him at the time had been stolen after the crash. And although she believed John was not at fault in the accident, an all-white court had blamed him for it.

John's death had left Julia to raise their children alone, and she had struggled to support them. Yet when times got difficult, she had felt the presence of Jesus Christ near her, giving her comfort and reassurance.

Now, more than a quarter century after John's death, Julia knew forgiveness was vital to healing her pain. But she still struggled to forgive those who marred John's good name and stole from her and her family.[2]

One day, in June 1981, Julia was invited to help clean out a youth facility and library that had been looted and set on fire in recent riots over apartheid. When she arrived there, Julia was surprised to see two young men clearing out the debris with shovels. The men were white—a shocking sight in Soweto.

With big smiles, the young men told Julia they were American missionaries who had come to help. They knew a little bit about gardening and talked with Julia about her community garden. They also asked if they could visit her. Julia was not eager to meet with them. By inviting two white men to her house, she risked violent retribution against her and her family. Would her neighbors think she was collaborating with the police or the apartheid government?

She started to make an excuse, but then she felt a thump in her chest and knew she had to let them visit. She told them to come in three days.

The men arrived right on schedule, dressed in white shirts and wearing name tags. They introduced themselves as missionaries from The Church of Jesus Christ of Latter-day Saints. She listened politely to their message. But by the second visit she was trying to figure out how she could graciously tell them she wasn't interested.

One of the missionaries then pointed to a picture of Julia and her late husband and asked, "Where is he?"

"He is deceased," she explained.

The missionaries told her about baptism for the dead. She was skeptical. Over the years, she had attended many churches. Never once had she heard anyone say the dead could be baptized.

A missionary opened the New Testament and asked her to read 1 Corinthians 15:29: "Else what shall they do which are baptized for the dead, if the dead rise not at all? Why are they then baptized for the dead?"

The verse captivated her. She started listening to the missionaries with an open heart. As they taught her about eternal families, she learned that baptisms and other ordinances could be performed for the deceased by their loved ones in temples. She could also be reunited with those she had lost—including John—in the next life.

When she began reading the Book of Mormon, her life began to change. For the first time, she realized that all people were one family. The restored gospel of Jesus Christ gave her hope that she could finally forgive those who had hurt her and her children.[3]

Six months after meeting the missionaries, Julia was baptized. A month later, she was invited to speak in stake conference. Under government apartheid, the Church had made no attempt to proselytize among

Black people in South Africa. But apartheid had begun unraveling by the early 1980s, making it easier for Black and white members of the same religion to meet and worship together. A few months before Julia's baptism, a congregation was established for the Saints from Soweto.

Julia was nervous when she stood before the mostly white stake. She worried that her pain over John's death might act as a wedge between her and other Church members. But her heart was full of prayer, and the Lord prompted her to share her story.[4]

She spoke about her husband's death, the cruel treatment she received from the police, and the bitterness she had carried for so long. "I have finally found the church that can teach me to truly forgive," she testified. Like the lumps of soil in a garden, her bitterness was broken.

What remained, she said, was peace and forgiveness.[5]

WHEN GOVERNMENT OFFICIALS PROPOSED constructing a temple in the German Democratic Republic, the First Presidency authorized Henry Burkhardt to secure a permit to build a meetinghouse with a special wing for administering endowments and sealings for the living, but no proxy ordinances for the dead.[6]

After fasting and prayer, Henry and his counselors in the Dresden Mission presidency proposed constructing the building in Karl-Marx-Stadt. The city had a large number of Saints, and they needed a new meetinghouse.

Local officials refused to issue a permit to the Church, however, reasoning that the city did not need more churches. They instead proposed Freiberg, a university town nearby.

"Impossible," Henry told them. "We want to have Karl-Marx-Stadt."[7]

The matter seemed settled in the mission presidency's minds. But as they fasted and prayed, Henry and his counselors began to seriously consider building in Freiberg. The town was home to a small branch of Saints and close to branches in Dresden and other cities and towns in the region.

The more Henry and his counselors pondered the matter, the more convinced they became. "Yes," they said to themselves, "the Freiberg option is in fact not that bad."[8]

Civic leaders in Freiberg seemed eager for the Church to construct a building like the Swiss Temple in their town. Across the GDR, the government was seeking to strengthen relationships with people of faith who respected state authority. The GDR now officially recognized some religions and sought to rebuild historic churches that had been damaged during World War II.

Since the Saints in Freiberg already had a suitable meetinghouse, Henry had a strong impression that the Church should set aside its plan to construct a hybrid building and instead build a standard temple that included a baptismal font and allowed for other proxy ordinance work. He proposed the idea to Church leaders in Salt Lake City and received approval to obtain a site for a fully functioning house of the Lord in Freiberg.[9]

Henry then brought the plan to a Freiberg town meeting alongside Frank Apel, the mission executive secretary and a Freiberg native. The council offered the Church two possible building sites. The first lot was in the center of town, but it was small and below the level of the road, making it hard for passersby to see it. The other site was an undeveloped field on a hill northwest of town. There were no public transportation stops nearby, but the site itself was highly visible to the surrounding area.

Once Henry and Frank saw the second site, they knew they had found the right place for the temple.[10]

On February 27, 1982, Elder Thomas S. Monson visited the GDR to check on the East German Saints and speak with Henry about the new temple site. It had been nearly fourteen years since Henry and his wife, Inge, had first met the apostle, and they shared a cherished friendship. Elder Monson presented Inge with a decorative plate and new skirt from his wife, Frances. He also surprised Tobias, the Burkhardts' fourteen-year-old son, with a pocket calculator—a rare commodity in the GDR.[11]

The next day, Henry took Elder Monson to the site. Although he understood why the Church could not build the temple in Karl-Marx-Stadt, Elder Monson had questions about the Freiberg location.

"Have you thoroughly considered this choice?" he asked Henry. "Is this really the right place? How will the people come here without adequate public transportation?"

Henry answered Elder Monson's questions as best he could. He then affirmed that he and his counselors strongly supported building a temple there. They had fasted and prayed about the site, he said, and they felt it was where the Lord wanted His house in the GDR.[12]

Elder Monson needed no more convincing. The Church purchased the land and submitted revised architectural drawings to the East German government.[13]

ON MARCH 31, 1982, DAVID Galbraith sat quietly in an office in Jerusalem as Amnon Niv, the city's chief engineer, examined a large hand-colored map of the Mount of Olives. A half dozen other city planners stood in the room with them.[14]

David had been anticipating a meeting with Amnon for months. The Church was ready to move forward with its plans to build a Jerusalem Center for BYU study abroad students and local Saints. Once established, the center would give the Church an official presence in the Holy Land. It would be a place of learning, understanding, and peace, where Church members could come to walk where Jesus walked, learn more about the ancient roots of their faith, and gain an appreciation for the cultures and beliefs of the people living in the Middle East.[15]

Church leaders, including David, wanted to build the center on the spot President Kimball had admired during his 1979 visit to the city. But the site was near Mount Scopus, the highest point on the Mount of Olives, and a government-designated "green zone" cut through part of it, making it virtually off-limits for construction. Other developers had attempted to overturn the zoning without success. If the Church hoped to build there, Amnon would need to adjust the green zone's boundary.[16]

Mayor Teddy Kollek supported the Church's desire to build a center in the city. He believed the Church's friendship with Muslims and Jews would help both groups better understand one another and live in peace. Still, he agreed that the Mount Scopus property would be impossible to acquire. At his urging, David had looked at other possible sites. And whenever he found a promising location, he reached out to Church headquarters. Yet none of these sites received approval, and President N. Eldon Tanner had advised him to focus on Mount Scopus.

One day, Mayor Kollek had encouraged Amnon to set up a meeting with David and listen to what he had to say. David Reznik, the local architect the Church had hired to design the BYU Jerusalem Center, was also invited.[17]

Reznik showed Amnon some of his plans for the school and pointed out its proximity to the Hebrew University of Jerusalem, which he and Amnon had helped design years before. Amnon continued to study the map for several minutes, his silence matched by

A Seed of Love

the silence from all in the room. "Bring me a felt pen," he said suddenly. Nobody in the room had a pen, so someone scrambled and found one for him. He then stretched his arm out and began to draw on the map.

With everyone watching, he modified the green zone, drawing a red line around the exact spot where the Church wanted to build the Jerusalem Center.

"This is the building line," he proclaimed. He grabbed an official rubber stamp, pounded it down on the map, and signed his name. "That's it!" he pronounced.

Everyone nodded in agreement. David was dumbfounded. The Church had just received approval for something everyone thought was impossible. He couldn't wait to call Church headquarters and tell them about the miracle.[18]

A FEW MONTHS LATER, in July 1982, Olga Kovářová and a small group of Saints traveled by car to a reservoir near Brno, Czechoslovakia, for her baptism.[19]

Since her first sacrament meeting at Otakar Vojkůvka's home, Olga had grown to admire the faith of the older Czechoslovak Saints. She felt uplifted by their discussions during Sunday School and comfortable sharing her own thoughts.[20]

In the months leading up to her baptism, Olga had received the missionary lessons from Jaromír Holcman, a member of the Brno Branch presidency. The first few lessons had been difficult and uncomfortable because the religious words sounded so foreign to her. The plan of salvation seemed like a fairy tale, and Olga wrestled with questions she had about Heavenly Father.[21]

She also worried about the problems that would come after baptism. The Church had begun growing in central and eastern Europe after 1975, when Henry Burkhardt and his counselors in the Dresden Mission presidency appointed a man named Jiří Šnederfler to preside over the Saints in Czechoslovakia. But the Church was still little known and little understood in the country. Even as her mind was telling her to forget about Christ's gospel, though, her heart told her it was the truth.[22]

Olga fasted the entire day of her baptism. When the time came, she rode to the reservoir with Otakar and Gád Vojkůvka and Jaromír and his wife, Maria. The group gathered by the water and said a prayer. But before they could proceed with the ordinance, they were startled by the sound of several fishermen walking along the bank. The men drew closer and settled near the place where Olga was to be baptized.

"The water's edge is pretty steep at most places here," Otakar said. "This is the only place we know of that has a gradual and safe descent into the water."

With no other choice, Olga and her friends waited. Ten minutes passed, then twenty. Still the fishermen showed no signs of leaving.

Olga leaned her head against a tree trunk. "Maybe I am not prepared enough," she thought, "or my testimony isn't strong enough, or I haven't fully repented."

She was about to kneel in prayer when Jaromír took her by the arm and walked her back to the other Saints.

"I think we need to pray again to make it possible for Olga to be baptized today," he said.

The group knelt together as Jaromír pleaded with God on Olga's behalf. She could hear the emotion in his voice. When the prayer ended, a few minutes passed and then the fishermen stood up suddenly and left.

The water was still and quiet as Jaromír led Olga in by the hand and spoke the baptismal prayer. When she heard her name, Olga felt that a chapter in her life was ending. Everything was about to change now that she had decided to follow Christ and His restored gospel. Complete joy swept over her, and she knew her baptism was being recorded in heaven.

The small group was soon on their way back to Brno in Jaromír's car. As they rode, they listened to a cassette tape of the Tabernacle Choir. Olga felt like she was hearing angels, and she marveled when Jaromír told her that the singers were all members of the Church. She wondered what life must be like for Saints who lived in a country with religious freedom and a living prophet.

After arriving in Brno, the Saints gathered in Jaromír's house. Jaromír, Otakar, and other priesthood holders placed their hands on Olga's head. As they confirmed her a member of the Church, she felt the Holy Ghost envelop her. In that moment, she knew she was a daughter of God.

In the blessing, Jaromír declared that through Olga, many young people would join the Church and be taught the gospel in a way they could understand. The words surprised her. It seemed impossible, for the time being, that she could share the gospel openly.

Even so, she kept those words in her heart and longed for a day when they would come true.[23]

ON NOVEMBER 27, 1982, THE skies over Johannesburg, South Africa, were overcast as 850 people gathered for the groundbreaking of the first house of the Lord on the African continent. Julia Mavimbela had come to the ceremony with ten families from Soweto, the Black township on the west side of the city. From the moment Julia learned about temples, she had wanted to have ordinance work done for her late husband and parents. She was determined to take part in every important event in the temple's construction.[24]

Presiding at the ceremony was Elder Marvin J. Ashton of the Quorum of the Twelve Apostles. In his concluding remarks, he spoke of the spiritual excitement he sensed from the South African Saints. Once the house of the Lord was completed, Saints who had once needed to travel thousands of miles to temples in the United States, Switzerland, the United Kingdom, or Brazil could now look forward to having their own temple nearby.

After Elder Ashton spoke, he and other Church leaders ceremonially broke the ground with spades.

Other Saints then pressed forward, eager to participate. Not wanting to push through the crowd, Julia and the other Saints from Soweto backed away. Some of the leaders saw them and invited them to step forward, pick up a spade, and break the ground as well. Julia was sure the Spirit had a hand in calling them to the front.[25]

Over the next months, Julia found joy in serving in the Relief Society. Many people in her branch were recent converts, and experienced Church members from other wards in the stake mentored them until they were ready to lead the branch themselves. The Relief Society president, a white woman, called Julia as her first counselor.[26]

The branch was one of the first organized from a Black township. It met in a ward building in a neighborhood in Johannesburg. To get there, Julia and other Black Saints from Soweto had to take a taxi into the city and then walk the rest of the way to the chapel. After a while, the branch began meeting in a high school in Soweto, and Julia was pleased that she could attend church closer to home.

But the new meeting place presented challenges of its own. Every Sunday morning, the Saints had to arrive early to sweep the floors and clean the windows and chairs to make the school suitable for sacrament meeting. And sometimes the person who scheduled the building would double-book it to make more money, leaving the Saints without a place to meet.

Soon, the Johannesburg Stake began calling more and more Black Saints as leaders in the township branches. In her branch, Julia was called as the new Relief Society president.

She immediately felt inadequate. Although she was an experienced community leader who knew how to help and motivate people, the Saints in her branch were used to Church leaders being white. She could almost hear her branch members doubting her abilities and thinking, "She is Black like us."

Still, Julia refused to be discouraged. She knew what she was capable of accomplishing. And she knew the Lord would be with her.[27]

CHAPTER 22

More Like Our Lord and Master

On the morning of April 7, 1984, Ardeth Kapp sat on the front row of the Salt Lake Tabernacle. Gordon B. Hinckley, who had been called as an additional counselor in the First Presidency nearly three years earlier, was standing at the pulpit, asking for a sustaining vote of the general authorities and officers of the Church. He announced the calling of two new apostles, Russell M. Nelson and Dallin H. Oaks. He also put forward Ardeth's name as the new Young Women general president.

The Saints in the Tabernacle sustained them unanimously. "A title is given, a call is made," Ardeth later reflected in her journal, "and the members respond in love."[1]

Four months later, Ardeth and her counselors, Patricia Holland and Maurine Turley, and her administrative assistant, Carolyn Rasmus, met at a cabin in the mountains near Provo, Utah. It was the first Sunday of the month, and they came fasting.[2]

The focus of their fast was Personal Progress, the Church's achievement program for young women since the late 1970s. Ardeth had been a member of the Young Women general presidency that had introduced Personal Progress, yet she felt that many young women were not engaging with the program.

She and her counselors believed that each young woman needed a greater sense of divine purpose and identity. They also believed more could be done to help young women feel seen and appreciated as they sought to make and keep covenants with the Lord.[3]

At the cabin, Ardeth, Patricia, Maurine, and Carolyn listed universal principles they thought were vital to a young woman's life and well-being. Each of them then retreated to a spot in the woods to ponder the list and narrow it down to the most important principles. When they returned to the cabin, they found that their lists all looked similar. A warmth enveloped them. They felt the Lord was leading them in the right direction.

In its current form, Personal Progress focused on values shared by all Christian denominations. Ardeth and her counselors thought it should include distinct Latter-day Saint beliefs as well. As the women discussed what to emphasize, they identified five values that could help any young woman, no matter where she lived, grow closer to God and understand her true identity:

faith, divine nature, obedience, knowledge, and choice and accountability.[4]

In the months that followed, Ardeth and her counselors organized a Young Women general board and settled on seven values, replacing obedience with individual worth, good works, and integrity. Ardeth taped long sheets of paper to the walls of the Young Women boardroom, and she and the other board members filled the space with insights they gleaned from research studies and discussions with young women in the Church.

The board believed that each young woman ought to know who she was and how she fit in God's plan. Each young woman needed to have spiritual experiences, make and keep covenants with the Lord, receive recognition for Christlike works, and be supported by her priesthood leaders.[5]

At the start of 1985, Ardeth and her board were preparing to submit their ideas to the Church's Priesthood Executive Council for approval. Under President Kimball's leadership, decision-making through councils had become more frequent in the Church. The Priesthood Executive Council was one of the three main executive councils that made policy recommendations to the First Presidency and the Quorum of the Twelve Apostles. These councils included several apostles and other general authorities. During her presidency's meeting with the Priesthood Executive Council, Ardeth hoped to present the board's vision for Young Women clearly. But she was unsure how to do it.[6]

One morning in January, Ardeth woke up early and grabbed a yellow notepad she kept at her bedside. Everything she and the board had discussed since their call was coming together in her mind like a beautiful mosaic. She began to write until words and inspiration flowed without interruption. When she finally jotted her last word down, she was emotionally drained but spiritually uplifted. She knew what to say to the council.[7]

Six weeks later, Ardeth and her counselors knelt in prayer at the Church Administration Building. In a few minutes, they would be presenting their plan for the future of Young Women to the Priesthood Executive Council. If the plan was right, they prayed, let the ears of the brethren be open to it. But if it was wrong, they asked the Lord to close the council's ears instead.

Before long, they were invited into a nearby boardroom where Ezra Taft Benson, the president of the Quorum of the Twelve Apostles, sat with other members of the council.[8]

Standing at the front of the room, Ardeth began her presentation. "Our focus is not so much on programs," she said, "but on the fundamental principles which can help young women come to know and live the gospel."

She spoke of the many problems young women faced in society: harmful media and advertising, crime, sexual immorality, eating disorders, drug and alcohol abuse, suicide. She provided data showing that young women in the Church had fewer resources, opportunities for recognition, and adult leaders than the young men did. In comparing the Young Women and Young Men programs, Ardeth said, she was not suggesting that they needed to be identical. Rather, they needed to receive all the resources and support necessary to help youth succeed.[9]

Finally, Ardeth and her counselors proposed structuring Young Women around the seven values. "Such structure," Ardeth said, "could provide an identity for young women so that they and others better understand what it means to be a young woman."

After the presentation, President Benson invited the council to stand in recognition of the importance of the presentation. "Not only were our ears opened," he said, "but also our tear ducts."

Later that day, Elder Dean L. Larsen, a member of the council, called Ardeth on the telephone. "How soon can you have a satellite broadcast for young women ready?" he asked.

"By November," Ardeth said.

Elder Larsen was surprised. "That long?"

"We've got to have all the pieces in place," Ardeth replied. "We won't have a second chance."[10]

On December 14, 1984, President Gordon B. Hinckley dedicated a house of the Lord in Guatemala City, Guatemala. As she looked on, Carmen O'Donnal, the matron of the new temple, marveled at the miraculous growth of the Church across Central and South America.

In 1948, when Carmen was baptized in a small swimming pool south of Guatemala City, she had been one of the earliest people to join the Church in Guatemala. Now the country had over 30,000 Latter-day Saints, more than half of them baptized in the last four years. More and more people in the region were making covenants to follow Jesus Christ, and temple building was at the center of this work.

"The Lord has allowed me to live to see this miracle with my own eyes," she said during the dedication.[11]

Prior to her call as temple matron, Carmen and her husband, John, had been working in the Mexico City Temple, which was dedicated in December 1983. It was the first house of the Lord in Mexico, which had over 360,000 members—more than any other Spanish-speaking country in the world. Among those who attended its dedication were Isabel Santana and Juan Machuca, the former teachers at Centro Escolar Benemérito de las Américas, who had married more than a decade earlier. They now lived in Tijuana, Mexico, where Juan worked for the Church Educational System.[12]

Farther south, the Church continued to thrive in Brazil. When the São Paulo Temple was dedicated in 1978, the country had 56,000 Saints in twelve stakes. By early 1985, membership had grown to around 200,000 in forty-seven stakes. And as the Church grew, so did the responsibilities of Hélio da Rocha Camargo. After his service as bishop of the São Paulo Second Ward, he served as a stake president in São Paulo, a mission president in Rio de Janeiro, and a regional representative of the Twelve. Then, on April 6, 1985, he was sustained as a member of the First Quorum of the Seventy, the first general authority from Brazil.

"This is an experience I never wanted to have," he told the Saints in the Salt Lake Tabernacle. But his faith in the restored gospel was firm, like that of so many other leaders around the world. "I know that the Lord lives," he testified. "I know that I am a child of God, and that this gospel is the plan for the happiness of all the children of God in this world."[13]

In Chile, meanwhile, there were now over 130,000 Saints in forty stakes. Shortly before the Mexico City Temple dedication, Chilean Saints had rejoiced at the dedication of the Santiago Chile Temple, the first house of the Lord in a Spanish-speaking country. Thousands of Saints assembled for the occasion, some of them traveling hundreds of miles by bus.[14]

Carlos and Elsa Cifuentes were in the temple for the dedication. Carlos was one of the earliest members in Chile. In 1958, two missionaries approached him in his backyard garage, introduced themselves as representatives of Jesus Christ, and asked if he would like to learn about the Church. He was baptized a short time later. In 1972, when the first stake was formed in Chile, Carlos was called to be its president.

By the time of the Santiago Chile Temple dedication, Carlos's body was weakened by cancer. But he mustered the strength to stand and bear fervent testimony. "I know without a doubt that this is the work of the Lord," he said. "I know that God lives. I know that Jesus Christ, His Son, lives." Carlos passed away a month later.[15]

In neighboring Argentina, construction was proceeding on a house of the Lord in Buenos Aires. Fifty-four-year-old Betty Campi was serving as stake Primary president in a rural town called Mercedes. During her lifetime, she had watched the Church in Argentina grow from a tiny acorn to a mighty oak, just as apostle Melvin J. Ballard had predicted it would. In 1942, the year of her baptism, there were around seven hundred Church members in Argentina. Now the number was almost eighty thousand. Betty faithfully held a current temple recommend, eagerly anticipating the day when she could use it in her home country.[16]

And Argentina was not alone. Elsewhere in South America, plans for temples in Colombia, Peru, and Ecuador were moving forward. Brigham Young and Joseph F. Smith had prophesied that temples would be established across the earth. Now it was coming to pass.[17]

AFTER HER BAPTISM, OLGA Kovářová was eager to share her happiness with her family and friends. But because the government in Czechoslovakia did not recognize the Church, she knew her opportunities would be limited. Also, her generation had grown up in an atheistic society and knew very little about religion. If she tried to tell people about the Church, they probably wouldn't understand what she was saying.

As she thought and prayed about how to share her beliefs, she spoke to Otakar Vojkůvka about her dilemma. "You could become a yoga teacher," he said. The government did not restrict yoga instruction, and Otakar saw it as a good way to meet new people and do God's work.

At first, Olga thought his suggestion was strange. But as she thought more about it, she realized he was onto something.[18]

The next day, Olga signed up for yoga teacher training. And not long after she finished the course, she began teaching classes at a gym in Uherské Hradiště, her hometown in central Czechoslovakia. She was surprised by how popular the courses were. Class sizes ranged from 60 to 120 students. People of all ages registered for her lessons, eager to learn more about physical and mental health.

During each class, Olga taught yoga exercises followed by a simple lesson based on true principles. She used nonreligious language, drawing on uplifting quotes from eastern European poets and philosophers to support what she taught.

Through her teaching, Olga realized how much her students hungered for more positive messages in their lives. Some people seemed to attend her classes just for the lessons.[19]

Before long, she and Otakar introduced some of their students to the Church, and several of them chose to be baptized.

The classes were so well received that Olga and Otakar created yoga camps for their interested students. Groups of fifty people spent weeklong breaks during the summer benefiting from Olga's and Otakar's instruction.

Olga wished her parents, Zdeněk and Danuška, could feel the same happiness her students discovered through the camp, and she prayed for them often. But religion was not an important part of her parents' daily lives, and there was not a branch in their town. Olga would have to approach the conversation carefully.

Knowing her mother struggled with headaches, Olga said one day, "Mom, I want to teach you how to relax and strengthen some muscles in your neck. It might help you."

"You know that I always trust you," her mother replied.

Olga demonstrated some simple exercises and recommended her mother continue doing them on her own. Within months, the headaches went away. She and Olga's father both became interested in yoga and attended one of the yoga camps. Within a few days, her father was fully immersed in the camp and was the happiest she had ever seen him. Her mother also embraced the routines and the ideas being shared in the lessons. Soon Olga began sharing her beliefs with them too.

Her parents immediately loved the Book of Mormon and its teachings. They also gained testimonies of Joseph Smith as a prophet of God. Before long, both her mother and father decided to join the Church.

They were baptized in the same reservoir where Olga had received the ordinance. Afterward, Olga and her parents returned home and sat around the kitchen table, holding hands and weeping with joy. "This calls for a celebration," her mother said.

They made Olga's favorite snack and shared their testimonies with each other. Smiling broadly, her father said, "Great beginnings happen within small walls!"[20]

"I WISH THAT YOU could feel what I feel inside," said Henry Burkhardt. "I also wish that I could tell you how much gratitude I have in my heart at this time."

It was June 29, 1985. Henry was standing at a pulpit in the newly completed Freiberg German Democratic Republic Temple, addressing a roomful of Saints who had come for the temple's dedication. President Gordon B. Hinckley had opened the services earlier that morning, and Elder Thomas S. Monson had also spoken.

Henry was no longer the president of the Dresden Mission. Rather, he had the honor of addressing the Saints as the newly called president of the Freiberg Temple.

"For over thirty years," he said, "it has been my desire to do something to make it possible for the Saints in this country to go to a house of the Lord." He spoke of when he and his wife, Inge, had been sealed in the Swiss Temple in 1955, before the border between East and West Germany had closed. Now he was overjoyed that Saints in the GDR and other countries under the political influence of the Soviet Union had a temple in Freiberg.

"It was the will of the Lord," he said. "The Lord made it possible to build this house, a house in which we can receive blessings that cannot be given in any other place than here in His house."[21]

Henry was still amazed, after so many years of dealing with government opposition to the Church, that the temple had been built with so little trouble. After Henry secured land for the project, Church architect Emil Fetzer had worked with officials, architects, and engineers in the GDR to finalize the design for the temple. Inspired by traditional German architecture, they settled on a simple, modern structure with stained-glass windows and a single tower arching over the entrance.

The groundbreaking had taken place a short time later. To Henry's surprise, most of the government officials who attended the ceremony had bowed their heads during the prayer. The building contractor was a government-owned company, so the project had no problem securing workers or getting permits approved. The government allowed the Church to tap into a nearby natural gas pipeline so the temple did not need to be heated by coal. And Henry and Emil were able to find three crystal chandeliers for the celestial room and sealing rooms, a rarity in the GDR.[22]

Perhaps the greatest surprise, though, was the government's willingness to respect the sacredness of the building. Although officials were legally allowed to monitor any religious meeting at any time in the country, the government had agreed not to do so in the temple. In fact, throughout the building process, the officials had been respectful of the Church, its teachings, and its practices. When it came time for the open house, nearly ninety thousand people came to tour the building.[23]

"My wife and I are grateful, my brothers and sisters, that we can serve you here in this house," Henry told the Saints at the dedication. "We do it gladly."

Following Henry's remarks, Inge stood and bore her testimony as the temple matron. "I want to tell you that I have never felt more joy than I feel when I am in the house of the Lord," she declared. "When I think of our young brothers and sisters who will have the possibility in the near future to begin their joint life here in the temple, sealed together, and that their children will also be born with this spirit inside, my heart is filled again with gratitude."

"I believe that we are all trying to become more like our Lord and Master," she continued, "and I give you my testimony that when we come here to His holy temple and when we are prepared to serve, then we will be able to do so."[24]

ON JULY 18, 1985, THOUSANDS of Orthodox Jews, dressed in traditional black coats and wide-brimmed hats, gathered in protest at Jerusalem's Western Wall. With the encouragement of the city's chief rabbis, the demonstrators bowed down and recited prayers usually set aside for days of mourning. Above them hung a massive red banner with a clear message: "Mormons stop your missionary project now."[25]

Since breaking ground a year earlier, the Church had made steady progress on the BYU Jerusalem Center for Near Eastern Studies.[26] But in that time, the city's Orthodox population had come to view the center as a threat to Judaism. They were most alarmed by the Church's reputation for missionary work. After the Holocaust, when the Nazi regime systematically exterminated millions of Jews, many Orthodox Jews had become particularly sensitive to Christians seeking converts among their people. They feared the Jerusalem Center would become a hub of Latter-day Saint missionary activity in Israel.[27]

Reports of Orthodox opposition to the project troubled the First Presidency, prompting them to send apostles Howard W. Hunter and James E. Faust to Jerusalem. The Church had leased the land for the Jerusalem Center fairly, and there had been no public demonstrations during the early phases of the project. The center also continued to enjoy the support of Jerusalem mayor Teddy Kollek and other Jewish leaders in the city. In fact, construction on the center was already a fourth of the way complete.[28]

The day after the protest at the Western Wall, Elder Hunter and Elder Faust met with Rabbi Menachem Porush, an Orthodox member of the Israeli parliament, at his office in Jerusalem. Several other Orthodox leaders crowded into the room as well.

"We would like to appeal to you as friends to quietly withdraw from the project," Rabbi Porush told the apostles. He was a large, imposing man, but he spoke with a subdued, courteous voice. "I don't know if you fully appreciate the significance of what happened at the Western Wall," he continued. "Rabbis from all over Israel gathered together to give expression to their opposition."[29]

"We feel we have done nothing wrong in establishing our center here," Elder Faust told him. BYU students had been coming to Jerusalem for over fifteen years without any disturbances. Their purpose was to study local history and culture, not to conduct missionary work. Like Mayor Kollek, Church leaders believed the Holy Land could be shared peaceably by different faiths.[30]

"We know about your strong youth missionary programs," said another rabbi in the room. "We cannot tolerate such programs here."

"Let us agree that you will stop construction for a two-week period," Rabbi Porush suggested. "I'll fly to

Salt Lake City to explain to the appropriate leaders the need to halt construction."

"We can't stop construction," Elder Hunter said. "We are under contract."

"I have built many buildings," said Rabbi Porush, "and I know arrangements could be made to stop construction."

"We can't stop construction," Elder Hunter repeated, "but we can continue to discuss matters in order to resolve our differences."

"Please think it over," the rabbi insisted.[31]

The following evening, the apostles called the rabbi to inform him that their minds had not changed. Construction would continue.

Once they returned to Salt Lake City, Elder Hunter and Elder Faust counseled with the First Presidency and the Quorum of the Twelve Apostles about what more they could do to gain the trust of those who opposed the project.

To show that the Church was committed to doing no missionary work through the Jerusalem Center, the First Presidency and the Quorum of the Twelve asked Elder Hunter, Elder Faust, and BYU president Jeffrey R. Holland to write up a formal nonproselytizing agreement to reassure religious and political leaders in Israel.

The committee finished the agreement on August 1. The next day, President Holland left for Jerusalem with the document in hand.[32]

As a Relief Society president in Soweto, South Africa, Julia Mavimbela wanted every woman in her branch to feel respected and accepted. Throughout her life, she had seen women mistreated for lacking money or social status. She yearned for everyone in her care to be treated with dignity.[33]

At this time, women in the Church held monthly "homemaking" lessons where they studied principles of self-reliance, money management, first aid, nutrition, and disease prevention. Knowing that many in Soweto were in financial hardship, Julia taught the Relief Society women how to store up food and conserve water, how to save money, and how to make do with little. She urged them to mend their old clothes rather than buy new.[34]

On one occasion, someone donated clothing and other goods to the branch. Nearly everyone in the Relief Society was in need, and Julia prayed about how to distribute the donations fairly. The Lord prompted her to give each Relief Society member a numbered piece of paper. She then randomly drew numbers so every woman got a fair chance to choose something from the donations.

Although most Relief Society lessons were in English, Julia prepared lessons in Sotho and Zulu for women who were not as fluent in English. When assigning Relief Society sisters to minister to each other as visiting teachers, she relied on inspiration for guidance. "This is who the Lord wants you to visit," she would tell the newly called sisters. "Assess the needs in that home, and then we can discuss together what we can do for them as a family."[35]

As Julia led the Relief Society in Soweto, she followed the progress on the temple being built in Johannesburg. She especially looked forward to seeing the angel Moroni statue hoisted atop the temple's tallest spire. But when that day came, anti-apartheid activists in Soweto staged a "stayaway," a community-wide strike to block working and shopping in the white areas of Johannesburg.[36]

Julia supported the activists' cause, but she was determined to witness this milestone in the temple's construction. Joined by her grandson, she made her way into Johannesburg. No one stopped or questioned them along the road. At the temple site, they were able to witness the placement of the statue.[37]

A year later, on September 14, 1985, Julia received her endowment in the house of the Lord. For the first time, she felt a sense of full belonging—a covenant oneness with her brothers and sisters in the gospel, despite their differences in race and language. And, at long last, she was sealed to both her late husband, John, and to her parents.[38]

"What a wonderful day this has been!" she rejoiced. "So many blessings have been given to me."

"Gladly I will pledge, this day, to so live that I may always be worthy to come to the house of the Lord and serve Him, my Savior and Redeemer," she said. "Oh, how very much I appreciate knowing who I am and why I am here."

"Life is sweet, indeed, and my cup runneth over."[39]

CHAPTER 23

Every Effort

On Wednesday, November 6, 1985, Young Women general president Ardeth Kapp looked out her office window in Salt Lake City. A flag nearby was flying at half-staff to honor President Spencer W. Kimball, who had passed away the night before. The prophet's declining health had kept him largely out of the public eye for several years, so his death was not a surprise. Yet Ardeth felt his loss deeply.[1]

The news came as she and the Young Women general board were preparing to hold the first-ever Young Women satellite broadcast. The broadcast was scheduled for that Sunday, and Church leaders decided to proceed with it, despite the prophet's passing.

Ardeth and her board had been planning the event for months. To help introduce the seven new Young

Women values, Ardeth had asked Janice Kapp Perry, her husband's cousin and a prolific Latter-day Saint composer, to write a song for the broadcast. She also sought permission to create a special issue of the *New Era,* the Church's youth magazine, to further promote the values.[2]

After calculating the cost of the issue—roughly fifty cents per copy—she went to Elder Russell M. Nelson, her presidency's adviser in the Quorum of the Twelve Apostles, to approve the large expense. Knowing he had nine daughters, she tried to put the cost in perspective. "Elder Nelson," she asked, "is a young woman worth fifty cents?"

Elder Nelson smiled. "Ardeth, you rascal," he said. The Priesthood Executive Council soon approved the special issue and had it translated into sixteen languages.[3]

On November 10, the day after President Kimball's funeral, young women filled the Salt Lake Tabernacle. The general presidencies of the Relief Society and Primary, many general authorities, and past Young Women leaders sat on the stand with Ardeth and her board members.[4]

A choir of four hundred young women opened the meeting by singing "As Zion's Youth in Latter Days," a hymn written expressly for the Church's new hymnal, published three months earlier. Elder Nelson then gave the first talk.[5]

"Strive to be rooted in Christ the Lord," he urged the young women. "Bind yourselves together—rooted in truth, reaching to teach and testify, preparing to bless others with fruits of the Spirit."[6]

When he finished, Ardeth took the stand to introduce the new Young Women motto, "Stand for Truth and Righteousness," based on the Lord's promise in Moses 7:62: "Righteousness and truth will I cause to sweep the earth as with a flood."[7]

"We have moved into a period in which the adversary is openly flaunting his power, and many are being deceived," she told the young women. "If they should look to you, would they see anything visibly different from the world that would help them identify the right path, the truth, the refuge they are seeking? Could you stand up and lead out for righteousness?"[8]

The broadcast continued with a video presentation introducing the seven values. Next, a young woman from the Philippines stood up and repeated the values, one by one, as colorful banners representing each principle dropped down from the balcony. Second counselor Maurine Turley then presented the new Young Women theme, and the congregation recited it together:

> *We are daughters of a Heavenly Father*
> *who loves us, and we love Him.*
> *We will "stand as witnesses of God*
> *at all times and in all things, and in all places"*
> *as we strive to live the Young Women values.*

The choir performed Janice Kapp Perry's song "I Walk by Faith," and Elder Gordon B. Hinckley offered

Every Effort

closing remarks. After that, as choir and congregation sang the hymn "Carry On," two hundred young women paraded down the aisle carrying flags in the seven colors representing the new values.[9]

Ardeth was overjoyed. "The Young Women fireside was GLORIOUS!!" she wrote in her journal. A new chapter had begun for the young women of the Church.[10]

THE MORNING AFTER THE Young Women broadcast, eighty-six-year-old President Ezra Taft Benson stood at a lectern in the Church Administration Building. The Quorum of the Twelve Apostles had recently ordained him as president of the Church, and the time had come to announce the news to the press. His counselors in the First Presidency, Gordon B. Hinckley and Thomas S. Monson, sat behind him. Reporters and cameras filled the room.[11]

After learning of President Kimball's death, President Benson had felt weak—weaker than he'd ever felt before. Yet the influence of the Spirit had rested powerfully upon him. At President Kimball's funeral, he had honored the late prophet as a man of great humility, meekness, and faith. "He knew the Lord," President Benson had testified. "He knew how to speak to Him and how to receive answers."[12]

Under President Kimball's leadership, the Church had grown by nearly two million members, many of them in Latin America. Among the hundreds of stakes organized during his presidency were the first stakes in Bolivia, Colombia, Nicaragua, Paraguay, Puerto Rico, and Venezuela. To manage this growth, he had created and expanded the First Quorum of the Seventy and advocated leadership through area, regional, and family councils.[13]

President Kimball had also emphasized the need for temples, missionary work, and gospel study. During his presidency, twenty-one temples were dedicated and the number of full-time missionaries increased from seventeen thousand to over twenty-nine thousand. In 1979, the Church had published an edition of the King James Version of the Bible with maps, a Bible dictionary, excerpts from Joseph Smith's inspired translation of the Bible, and thousands of footnotes and cross-references to Latter-day Saint scriptures. Two years later, in 1981, the Church had released similar editions of the Book of Mormon, Doctrine and Covenants, and Pearl of Great Price. The Doctrine and Covenants included two new sections—137 and 138—featuring revelations by Joseph Smith and Joseph F. Smith about the redemption of the dead and the Savior's ministry in the spirit world. The edition also published the historic announcement of the revelation extending priesthood and temple blessings to all worthy Saints, regardless of race.

At the funeral, President Benson numbered this revelation among the most significant of the dispensation. "That revelation," he declared, "opens the door to exaltation to millions of our Father's children."[14]

Now, as President Benson contemplated the future, he was eager to build upon President Kimball's legacy. Many challenges, old and new, still lay ahead of the Saints. For many years, Latin American nationalist groups had resented the Church for sending missionaries and mission leaders from the United States abroad, and their opposition was beginning to threaten the safety of Church members in the region. President Benson was also concerned about the people of central and eastern Europe, where most countries were still closed to the Church.[15]

In Utah, meanwhile, a Church member named Mark Hofmann had recently come under investigation after three bombs exploded in the Salt Lake City area, killing two people. Mark was a rare documents dealer who had sold several items to the Church. Some of these documents contained information that cast doubt on the Church's traditional account of its history, leading some people to question their faith. While the authenticity of these documents had been called into question, the incident had attracted worldwide attention, and reporting often portrayed the Church unfavorably.[16]

As President Benson stood before the press, he also knew people had questions about his own presidency. Throughout his life, he had been active in government, and some people wondered how his views would influence his decisions as Church president.

"My heart has been filled with an overwhelming love and compassion for all members of the Church and our Heavenly Father's children everywhere," he told the press. "I love all our Father's children of every color, creed, and political persuasion."

He planned to lead the Church just as his predecessors had done. A few years earlier, the First Presidency and Quorum of the Twelve Apostles had announced a threefold mission for the Church: proclaim the gospel, perfect the Saints, and redeem the dead.

"We shall continue every effort to carry out this mission," President Benson declared.[17]

IN EARLY 1986, SIXTEEN-YEAR-OLD Manuel Navarro was a priest in the San Carlos Branch in Nazca, a small city in southern Peru. The San Carlos Branch was considered a "basic unit" of the Church, a designation created in the late 1970s for branches where the Church was new and had few members. In some of these units, including the San Carlos Branch, youth and adults met together in combined classes and quorums on Sundays.[18]

Manuel enjoyed meeting with the Melchizedek Priesthood holders during the third hour of church. There were around twenty young Aaronic Priesthood holders in the branch, but fewer than half of them attended regularly. Meeting with the elders in the branch gave Manuel a chance to learn about the duties of both the Aaronic and Melchizedek Priesthoods.

Manuel had been a member of the Church for two years. He was baptized with his parents and younger sister. Now his father was a branch president, and his commitment to the Savior strengthened Manuel's. "If Dad is in this," he told himself, "it is because this is good."[19]

So far, 1986 was turning out to be an important year for the Church in South America. In January, temples were dedicated in Lima, Peru, and in Buenos Aires, Argentina—the third and fourth temples on the continent. The house of the Lord in Lima served not only Manuel and the 119,000 Latter-day Saints in Peru but also the more than 100,000 Saints living in Colombia, Ecuador, Bolivia, and Venezuela. Immediately after the dedication, two hundred Peruvians and two hundred Bolivians received their endowment.[20]

Manuel soon began his second year of seminary, a program the Church had been expanding throughout the world for more than a decade. Previously, Manuel's branch had offered seminary classes in the evening. But in 1986, the regional coordinator for the Church Educational System in Peru had implemented daily early-morning seminary for most of the country's 298 wards and branches. Church members in Peru approved of the change. They wanted seminary classes to be held close to the homes of the students and their local volunteer teachers.[21]

The first seminary classes Manuel attended were held in his home, but eventually they moved to the branch's rented meetinghouse. Each weekday, Manuel walked about two miles to attend class at six o'clock in the morning. At first, waking up early was not easy, but he came to enjoy going to seminary with the other youth. With the encouragement of his teacher, he developed the habit of praying right after he awoke in the morning, even if it required getting up even earlier.

In seminary, Manuel received a set of "scripture mastery" cards. Printed on these cards were important scriptural passages that seminary students around the world were expected to learn. Since Manuel's class was studying the Book of Mormon that year, the first scripture mastery verse he learned was 1 Nephi 3:7: "I will go and do the things which the Lord hath commanded."

One seminary teacher, Ana Granda, taught Manuel and his classmates about their eternal value and destiny as children of God. Listening to her teach, Manuel felt that he mattered to someone. He gained a testimony that God truly cared for His children.

He also saw how keeping the commandments protected him from many of the problems other youth his age experienced. Although he played soccer with friends who were not Latter-day Saints, he found that his closest friends were the youth at church. On Wednesdays, they would attend "missionary nights," where they played games and socialized with the missionaries serving in the area.

Manuel's friends studied with him, supported him, and helped him stay on the right path. When he and his cousin went to parties on Saturday nights, their friends outside the Church never offered them alcohol. They knew they were Latter-day Saints and respected their beliefs.[22]

Every Effort

LATER THAT YEAR, SEVENTEEN-YEAR-OLD Consuelo Wong Moreno visited her older sister Carmen in Cuernavaca, Mexico. Cuernavaca was about six hundred miles south of Consuelo's home in the city of Monterrey. Her father regularly sent her and her siblings there in the summer.

The temple in Mexico City was far away from Consuelo's hometown, so when she learned that the youth in Cuernavaca were going to do baptisms for the dead, she got Carmen's permission to go. She then had an interview with the bishop. He did not know her well and seemed to hesitate when she expressed interest in going on the trip.

"Look," Consuelo said, retrieving an old tithing receipt from her scriptures, "I pay tithes."

The bishop smiled as she unfolded the slip of paper and handed it to him. He conducted the rest of the interview and found her worthy to attend the temple.

"Don't worry, sister," he said. "You can go and do baptisms."

A short time later, Consuelo took a bus to Mexico City with other youth and adults from the ward. When they arrived, no one was sure where the temple was, so they began searching for it on foot. It was a bright, sunny day, and the group of youth attracted the curiosity of passersby as they wandered the streets.

Finally, one of the young men spotted the temple's spire. "There's the Moroni!" he said. Consuelo and the other youth followed his gaze, and sure enough, there was the spire, towering above them.

Consuelo had never seen a house of the Lord in person before, and its grand size and ancient Mesoamerican–inspired architecture impressed her. They entered the temple, and workers greeted them kindly and instructed them on where to go and what to do. Consuelo felt the Spirit strongly as she was baptized for those who had died. One of them was an Indigenous woman, and her name lingered in Consuelo's mind. She imagined meeting her in the next life and celebrating the work she had done for her.[23]

After Consuelo returned to Monterrey at the end of the summer, she learned about an upcoming Young Women's celebration called The Rising Generation. After introducing the seven values at the satellite broadcast, Young Women general president Ardeth Kapp had invited young women everywhere to write a personal message of hope and faith in Jesus Christ. They would then gather in their respective areas, attach each message to a helium-filled balloon, and release them together into the sky.

"Though you may be geographically isolated from many other young women in the Church," President Kapp explained, "we want you to feel the strength of their sisterhood and numbers as you stand together, committed to gospel values."[24]

Consuelo was eager to share the gospel with others, and she wanted to participate in the event with young women from around the globe. But since the city of Monterrey restricted public religious demonstrations, her

Young Women group could not take part in the celebration unless they received permission from the government.[25]

Still, Consuelo took a sheet of paper and wrote a letter to President Kapp in Spanish. "I am a seventeen-year-old Laurel," she wrote. "It's been a week since I found out about the celebration of faith and hope that the Young Women will have worldwide. So, a special joy has filled me, and I want to participate."

In the letter, she attached the message she wanted to send and asked President Kapp to include her in the activity:

> *I had hope and I did not let it die. I developed my faith, and as I nourished it, I discovered charity, yes, the pure love of Jesus, whose perfect love takes away all fear. Then I discovered peace. I discovered that peace puts us in harmony with others, respecting their beliefs and treating them as brothers and sisters.*

"I would like you to imagine how much I want someone to receive and understand my message," Consuelo wrote to President Kapp. "I hope that someday all those I know and love will feel the same way we feel."

When she finished her letter, she put it in an envelope and sent it off to Salt Lake City.[26]

IN AUGUST 1986, PRESIDENT Ezra Taft Benson stood at the foot of the Hill Cumorah on the outskirts of Palmyra,

New York. It was a Sunday morning, and a crowd of about eight thousand people had come to hear him speak at the place where Joseph Smith had received the gold plates from the angel Moroni.

President Benson and his wife, Flora, had attended the Hill Cumorah Pageant the night before. The pageant—an annual event since the 1930s—ran for a week each summer and attracted thousands of visitors. Performed on the hill itself, the production involved elaborate sets and a huge cast of volunteers who acted out the history of the Book of Mormon, culminating in the dramatic appearance of the resurrected Savior to the Nephites.[27]

Now, as President Benson addressed the large crowd in front of him, he focused his remarks on the sacred text celebrated in the pageant.

"The Book of Mormon was written for us today," he told the crowd. When he was a young man, many Church members did not regularly study or quote from the Book of Mormon. The Saints had been doing better in recent years, but he believed there was still room for improvement.

"We have not been using the Book of Mormon as we should," he said. "Our homes are not as strong unless we are using it to bring our children to Christ."[28]

For decades, President Benson had been pleading with the Saints to come to Christ through a study of the Book of Mormon. As a young missionary in England in the 1920s, he had developed a love for the book. One time, when he and his mission companion were invited to speak to a group of critics, Elder Benson had come prepared to preach about the Apostasy. As he stood to speak, however, he was prompted to set aside his prepared text and speak only of the Book of Mormon.[29]

President Benson fervently believed that the Book of Mormon could lead people to Christ. Over the past few decades, Church leaders had spoken more about the Savior than ever before.[30] In 1982, the Church had added the subtitle "Another Testament of Jesus Christ" to the Book of Mormon. The addition emphasized the Savior as well as the book's vital place alongside the Old and New Testaments. Church leaders believed the new subtitle would bear powerful testimony of the Savior and guard against false claims that Latter-day Saints were not Christians.[31]

As he traveled as Church president and met with the Saints, President Benson often testified of Jesus Christ and of the Book of Mormon as a special witness of His divinity.[32] And in his first general conference talk as president of the Church, he urged the Saints to read it every day.

"The Book of Mormon has not been, nor is it yet, the center of our personal study, family teaching, preaching, and missionary work," he taught. "Of this we must repent."[33]

Six months later, on October 4, 1986, he again spoke about Jesus Christ and the Book of Mormon at general conference. "The Book of Mormon is the keystone in our witness of Jesus Christ, who is Himself the cornerstone of everything we do," President Benson testified.

"There is a power in the book which will begin to flow into your lives the moment you begin a serious study of the book," he promised. "You will find greater power to resist temptation. You will find the power to avoid deception. You will find the power to stay on the strait and narrow path."[34]

ON OCTOBER 11, 1986, YOUNG women throughout the Church took part in the Rising Generation celebration. President Ardeth Kapp led the activity from Ricks College, the Church school in Rexburg, Idaho. As a cold wind howled across campus, President Kapp spoke to the young women in an auditorium before everyone stepped outside to release balloons carrying messages of hope, love, and peace. Elsewhere in the world, young women listened to a recording of the same message before they too sent their balloons off into the sky.

"You are a generation known by your Heavenly Father," President Kapp declared. "Now you are being called to come forward, to exert your influence, and to become a mighty force for righteousness."[35]

Fourteen hundred miles away, in Monterrey, Mexico, the restriction on religious demonstrations prevented Consuelo Wong Moreno from releasing a balloon on October 11. But a short time later, she was surprised to get a personal letter from President Kapp. The letter was in English, so Consuelo tried her best to decipher its meaning. When her older sister Aida came home, she helped translate it.[36]

"Dear Consuelo," President Kapp wrote, "I received your beautiful letter expressing your hope to participate in the 'celebration of faith and hope that the Young Women are to carry out.' I wanted you to know that your message was sent up with a balloon by a young woman here."

President Kapp told Consuelo she had mentioned her letter when speaking to the young women at Ricks College. Consuelo was honored that President Kapp had shared her words with so many people. She felt stronger knowing young women across the world were just as eager as she was to spread the gospel.[37]

Weeks later, after much prayer, the young women in Monterrey received permission from the local government to hold their own Rising Generation celebration. Consuelo and Aida joined a hundred young women and leaders from multiple stakes at a plaza in the heart of the city. They arrived before dawn, the sky gradually brightening as they gathered into groups and helped inflate white balloons. Consuelo attached her handwritten testimony to her balloon with a ribbon and released it into the sky with the others.

As she watched her balloon float away, she hoped it would land somewhere safe so someone could find it and read her message.

A short time later, Consuelo completed her Personal Progress goals. She and the other young women in her ward had begun learning about the new values and the colors associated with them. Each Sunday, her Laurel class recited the new Young Women theme. It reminded them that they were daughters of God with a divine destiny. Consuelo was grateful to know that God had a plan for her and cared about her well-being.[38]

In January 1987, Consuelo received public recognition for completing Personal Progress at New Beginnings, an annual event for young women and their families held in wards and branches throughout the Church. New Beginnings was a chance to welcome girls into the program, celebrate young women's achievements, and encourage their efforts. In Consuelo's ward, the Young Women president invited parents to help their daughters complete Personal Progress goals. Next, several young women, each dressed in one of the new Young Women colors, spoke about the values. The bishop then presented medallions to Consuelo and the other young women who had completed their Personal Progress journey.

Consuelo was proud of herself for finishing, and she wore her medallion like she was carrying a trophy. Whenever it caught the attention of people who were not members of the Church, she would explain what it represented and how she earned it.[39]

CHAPTER 24

Our Search for Truth

The BYU Jerusalem Center for Near Eastern Studies opened its doors to eighty students on March 8, 1987. Early that morning, three moving vans and two buses arrived at Kibbutz Ramat Rahel, the community on the southeast edge of Jerusalem where the university's study abroad students had lived and studied for the last seven years. Eager to move into the new center, the students cheerfully loaded their belongings and all the school's equipment into the vehicles. Once they arrived at their new home, they formed a human chain and began passing books, boxes, and suitcases up the staircases ascending Mount Scopus.[1]

David Galbraith, the director of the study abroad program, grinned as he looked on. The school's staff had worked tirelessly to get the building ready, though parts of it remained unfinished. The staff installed washers and dryers, made room assignments, and purchased supplies. Somehow, they had forgotten to buy towels and toilet paper for the center, but the supplies were now on their way from Tel Aviv.[2]

Two years earlier, when BYU president Jeffrey R. Holland came to Jerusalem with a nonproselytizing agreement, he had made a good impression. Yet Orthodox rabbis were skeptical of the agreement. They continued to stage demonstrations at the construction site, outside the mayor's office, and in front of David's home.[3]

Hoping to generate goodwill, the Church had hired one of Israel's largest public relations firms, which had placed informational ads in newspapers and on television. Several Jewish people who were friendly to the Church also wrote letters to Israeli politicians, vouching for the Saints' honesty.[4]

Until recently, the city's municipal inspector had insisted that no one could occupy the building before it was finished. David and his administrative staff, however, had received permission to move into the completed section of the center—the bottom four levels that made up the living quarters and some classrooms. When the municipal inspector learned that multiple city departments had granted the permission, he was amazed.[5]

Once the students were moved in, David assembled them in a large classroom for a three-hour orientation meeting about how to care for the building. The day passed peacefully, with no protests from those who opposed the center's construction. From the school, the students could enjoy a striking view of Jerusalem's Old City at sunset. It was a beautiful setting for them to learn more about the ancient city and the people of faith who lived there.

"We are finally into our new building," David wrote President Holland later that day.

"All these many months we have labored on a building of cement and stone," he wrote. "The students breathe into it the breath of life, and those cold stone corridors and lifeless rooms now take on an air of happiness."⁶

NOT LONG AFTER EZRA Taft Benson became president of the Church, he gave Elder Russell M. Nelson a new assignment. "You are to be responsible for all of the affairs of the Church in Europe and Africa," he told him, "with a special assignment to open up the nations in eastern Europe."

Elder Nelson was startled. "I'm a heart surgeon," he thought. "What do I know about opening countries?" With few exceptions, the Church had not sent missionaries to central and eastern Europe since the region came under the influence of the Soviet Union after World War II. Shouldn't the assignment go to someone more qualified in diplomacy? he wondered. Why not send a lawyer like Elder Dallin H. Oaks?

Keeping his thoughts to himself, Elder Nelson accepted the assignment.[7]

A short time later, diplomatic relations between the United States and the Soviet Union began to improve. In October 1986, Konstantin Kharchev, chair of the Soviet Union's Council on Religious Affairs, met with Church representatives in Washington, DC. He was anxious for them to understand that religious freedom existed in the Soviet Union. After learning of the meeting, Elder Nelson recommended that the Church send two general authorities to meet with Kharchev and continue the discussion. The First Presidency chose him and Elder Hans B. Ringger of the Seventy to go.[8]

On the morning of June 10, 1987, Elder Nelson and Elder Ringger called at Kharchev's office in Moscow. Kharchev was preparing to leave town on other business and did not have much time to talk.

"We just want to ask you a question," Elder Nelson told him. "What would we need to do to get the church we represent established in Russia?"

Kharchev quickly explained that a church could be registered in a district or city once it had twenty adult members living there.

Elder Nelson asked if the Church could open a visitors' center or reading room in the Soviet Union—a place where people could voluntarily come to learn about the Church's teachings.

"No," the chairman replied.

"We have a chicken and egg problem here," Elder Nelson said. "You say we can't receive recognition until we have members, but it will be difficult to get any members if we can't have a reading room or visitors' center."

"That is *your* problem," Kharchev said. He gave them his telephone number and offered to meet with them again. In the meantime, they could speak with his two deputies. "Good day!" he said.[9]

The deputies provided Elder Nelson and Elder Ringger a little more information. In the Soviet Union, they said, citizens had freedom of conscience and could practice their religion openly. Missionaries were not allowed to proselytize in the country, however, and the government regulated the importation of religious literature. Individuals could hold religious services in their homes, invite others to join them, and share their beliefs with people who expressed interest.

Several places of worship operated around the city, and the deputies arranged for Elder Nelson and Elder Ringger to meet with leaders of local Russian Orthodox, Seventh-day Adventist, evangelical Christian, and Jewish congregations. As they traveled through the city, meeting with fellow people of faith, Elder Nelson and Elder Ringger were surprised by the religious diversity they saw in the officially atheistic country.[10]

Still, as Elder Nelson and Elder Ringger thought about the requirements for establishing a church in the Soviet Union, their task seemed insurmountable. Without missionaries or a reading room, how could they ever reach the twenty people they needed to receive recognition for the Church?[11]

On his final day in Moscow, Elder Nelson could not sleep. He got up and went to Red Square, a large plaza outside the Kremlin, the walled headquarters of the Soviet government. The square was empty, and he thought about the crowds of thousands who would visit the spot later that day. Since coming to the city, he had been moved by the sight of everyday people. He wanted to reach out in love and share the restored gospel of Jesus Christ with each of them.

The questions "Who am I?" and "Why am I here?" kept running through his mind. He knew he was a surgeon, an American, a husband, a father, and a grandfather. But he had come to Moscow as an apostle of the Lord. And while his assignment might seem overwhelming, especially now that he knew how difficult it would be to establish the Church in the Soviet Union, he had hope.

"Apostles know their commission," he thought. The Savior had charged them to go out into the world and teach every kindred, nation, tongue, and people. The gospel message was for all of God's children.

In his report of the trip, Elder Nelson expressed his faith in the Lord's power to open doors to places like central and eastern Europe. "Together we can start—even with small steps—to do the will of our Father in Heaven, who loves all of His children," he wrote. "The fate and salvation of the souls of three quarters of a billion people depend on our action."[12]

ON AUGUST 6, 1987, APOSTLE Dallin H. Oaks was somber as he stood at a podium before a large audience at Brigham Young University. Two years had passed since the bombings in Salt Lake City that killed two Latter-day Saints. In that time, rare document dealer Mark Hofmann had been tried and convicted for the murders. It was also discovered that Mark had forged many of the documents he sold and traded to the Church, including several designed to undermine faith in its sacred history.[13]

During the same two years, scholars at BYU had done much to steady faith. *BYU Studies* and the university's Religious Studies Center had published important new books and articles on Joseph Smith and his translations.[14] The Foundation for Ancient Research and Mormon Studies had also begun publishing the collected works of Hugh Nibley, who had written more scholarship than anyone in support of the Book of Mormon and the Pearl of Great Price. And BYU had arranged with a prominent international press to publish the *Encyclopedia of Mormonism,* containing articles on Church history, doctrine, and practice.[15]

Still, many Saints struggled to make sense of Mark Hofmann's deceptions, prompting BYU to organize an academic conference about Church history and the Hofmann case. Today, Elder Oaks had come to the conference to speak about the Church's role in the events surrounding the tragedy.[16]

As the audience knew, Mark was now serving a life sentence in prison. In January, he had confessed to making three bombs, including one that had accidentally injured him. The story he told investigators was complex and tragic. Although he was a lifelong member of the Church, he had lost his faith in God as a young man. In time, he became a skilled forger, and he used his knowledge of Church history to fabricate documents. His purpose in crafting these forgeries, he later admitted, was not only to make money but also to embarrass and discredit the Church. He had murdered two people in a calculated effort to conceal his deceit.[17]

As Elder Oaks opened his remarks, he noted that the murders had received widespread attention in the media. Some commentators had criticized President Gordon B. Hinckley and other Church leaders for acquiring fraudulent documents from Mark, reasoning that truly inspired leaders would not have been fooled by the forgeries. Other people had accused leaders of being secretive about historical issues, even though the Church had published the most significant Hofmann documents and allowed scholars to study them.

Elder Oaks observed that many people, including scholars and nationally recognized forgery experts, had accepted the documents as genuine. He also described the attitude of trust that prevailed among Church leaders.

"In order to perform their personal ministries, Church leaders cannot be suspicious and questioning of each of the hundreds of people they meet each year," he said. "It is better for a Church leader to be occasionally disappointed than to be constantly suspicious." If they failed to detect a few deceivers, it was the price required to better counsel and comfort the honest in heart.[18]

Even before the organization of the Church, the Lord had warned Joseph Smith that "you cannot always tell the wicked from the righteous." Men like Mark Hofmann showed that God does not always protect Church members and leaders from deceitful people.[19]

As he ended his talk, Elder Oaks expressed hope that everyone could learn from the terrible experience. "When it comes to naivete in the face of malevolence," he acknowledged, "there is blame enough to go around."

"We should all pursue our search for truth with the tools of honest and objective scholarship and sincere and respectful religious faith," he concluded. "We all need to be more cautious."[20]

ON APRIL 30, 1988, ISAAC "Ike" Ferguson stepped off a plane and felt the heat of N'Djamena, Chad. It was an instant reminder that he was far from the cool spring weather of his home in Bountiful, Utah. All around him, he could see people in white tunics and head coverings. Sandy deserts stretched in all directions toward the horizon.[21]

At the request of the First Presidency, Ike had come to the edge of North Africa's deserts to check on Church humanitarian projects.[22] For generations, the Church had used its fast offerings mainly to help struggling Saints.

In the early 1980s, though, a famine had devastated Ethiopia, where the Church had no official presence. Television footage of starving children and overloaded relief camps touched people around the world, including the Saints. On January 27, 1985, the Church had held a special humanitarian fast in the United States and Canada that raised $6 million in fast offerings for African relief.[23]

A few months later, Elder M. Russell Ballard, one of the presidents of the First Quorum of the Seventy, traveled to Ethiopia to identify humanitarian organizations that could help the Church do the most good. Ike, who had a doctorate degree and professional experience in public health, was then hired to manage the humanitarian donations from an office in Utah. On his first day, he was given a computer, a telephone, and authorization to distribute millions of dollars in aid from the fast for Ethiopia.[24]

Building on the work of Elder Ballard, Ike had contacted other international aid organizations to seek advice on how to best use the donations. He then issued large grants to aid organizations working in Ethiopia and neighboring countries experiencing similar problems. Ten months after the initial fast, the Church had held a second fast for hunger relief.[25]

The Saints' contributions in Ethiopia proved so helpful that Church Welfare Services began partnering with relief agencies in other parts of the world. Before long, Ike was helping to set up a health fair in the

Caribbean, send medical equipment to assist children with cerebral palsy in Hungary, and deliver immunizations to Bolivia.[26]

After arriving in N'Djamena, Ike spent several days visiting humanitarian sites in Chad and Niger. He flew to Niger's Majia Valley, where the Church had donated hundreds of thousands of dollars to a reforestation project. From the air, he could see rows of drought-resistant trees forming a "living fence" between the valley's rich farmland and the encroaching desert. The plane landed, and representatives from one of the Church's humanitarian partners drove him through the reforested areas.

Ike learned that the trees stopped the winds from eroding the soil and provided fodder for sheep, goats, and cattle. They also provided a long-term fuel source for people living nearby. Farmers in the area had increased their agricultural production by as much as 30 percent since the project began, preserving many lives from the ravages of the desert.[27]

A few days later, Ike flew to Ghana, where the Church now had a mission and dozens of branches. There he met with a partner organization, Africare, to consult on a forty-acre Church welfare farm in Abomosu, a town some eighty miles northwest of Accra.

The farm was created in 1985 after a severe drought depleted food supplies throughout the country. Like the Church's welfare farms in the United States, it provided food for people in need while also fostering independence and self-reliance. Local Saints managed the farm with some assistance from the Ghana Accra Mission. At first, all laborers had been volunteers, but now the farm paid its workers, most of whom were members of the Church.[28]

After three growing seasons, the farm had been moderately successful in producing corn, cassava, plantain, and other crops for people in need. But the good it was doing did not yet match the high cost of its maintenance.

The Africare consultants told Ike they believed the farm would best serve the local community if the Church allowed people in Abomosu to turn the farm into a cooperative venture. Local farmers, using traditional cultivation techniques, could work together to provide more food for the community. The Church would still provide some financial support for the farm without carrying the full responsibility for its success.[29]

Before leaving Ghana, Ike and the consultants presented this idea to about 150 members of the Abomosu community, including the local tribal leader. The plan was well received, and many farmers were eager to take part in the cooperative.[30]

THAT SAME APRIL, MANUEL Navarro came to his father with some disappointing news. For the past few months, he had been in Lima, Peru, studying hard to enter a prestigious university in the city. Yet despite his best efforts, he had failed to get into the school. If he wanted to try again to be admitted, he would need to study for another six months.

"Manuel," his father said, "do you want to continue preparing for university, or do you want to prepare for a mission?"

Manuel knew the prophet had asked every worthy and able young man in the Church to serve a mission. And his patriarchal blessing spoke of missionary service. Yet he had planned to go on a mission after enrolling in the university. He believed it would be easier for him to return to university after the mission if he could reserve his enrollment before leaving. Now he didn't know what to do. His father told him to take some time to decide.

Right away, Manuel read the Book of Mormon and prayed. As he did, he felt the Spirit guiding his decision. By the very next day, he was ready with his answer. He knew he needed to serve a mission.

"OK," his father said. "Let's help you."

One of the first things Manuel did was find a job. He assumed that he'd work at a nearby bank, since his father knew some of the employees there. But instead, his father drove him downtown to the construction site of the branch's first chapel. He asked the supervisor if there was a position for Manuel on the construction crew. "No problem," the supervisor said. "We'll put him to work."

Manuel joined the crew in June, and each time he got paid, the worker who gave him his check reminded him to use it for his mission. Manuel's mother also helped him set aside most of the check for his mission fund and tithing.[31]

Missions were costly, and Peru's struggling economy made it difficult for many Saints there to fully fund their missions. For years, all full-time missionaries had depended on themselves, their families, their congregations, and even the kindness of strangers to fund their missions. After President Kimball urged all eligible young men to serve, the Church invited its members to contribute to a general missionary fund for those who needed financial help.[32]

Now local funds were expected to cover at least a third of mission costs. If missionaries could not pay for the rest, they could draw upon the general fund. In Peru and other South American countries, Church leaders also set up a system where local members provided missionaries one meal each day, helping them save money. Manuel arranged to pay for half of his mission while his parents paid for the rest.[33]

After working for about six months, Manuel received his mission call. His father said they could either open it right away or wait until Sunday and read it in sacrament meeting. Manuel couldn't wait that long, but he would wait until his mother got off work that evening.

When she finally got home, Manuel opened the envelope, and his eyes first went to President Ezra Taft Benson's signature. He then began reading the rest of the call, his heartbeat racing with every word. When he saw that he would be serving in the Peru Lima North Mission, he was overjoyed.

It had always been his desire to serve a mission in his home country.[34]

DURING THE LAST SESSION of the April 1989 general conference, President Ezra Taft Benson sat near the pulpit in the Salt Lake Tabernacle, enjoying the inspired messages of the speakers. But when the time came to give his own remarks, he did not feel strong enough to deliver them. He asked his second counselor, Thomas S. Monson, to read what he had prepared for the occasion.

Over the past couple of years, the prophet had spoken directly to different groups in the Church: young women and young men, mothers and fathers, single adult women and single adult men. Now he wanted to speak to children.

"How I love you!" his talk began. "How our Heavenly Father loves you!"[35]

At the time, more than 1.2 million children belonged to the Church's Primary organization. In 1988, Primary general president Dwan J. Young and her board had chosen a phrase from the Book of Mormon, "Come unto Christ," as its theme for the year. President Young and her board had also invited the children to learn about the Book of Mormon.

President Benson was thrilled that children everywhere had accepted the invitation. At home evenings and in Primary, they were singing about the Book of Mormon, acting out its stories, and playing games that taught its messages. Some children were even earning money to purchase copies of the Book of Mormon that would be given out around the world.[36]

In his message, President Benson urged the children to pray to Heavenly Father every day. "Thank Him for sending our oldest brother, Jesus Christ, into the world. He made it possible for us to return to our heavenly home."[37]

President Benson had spoken many times during his ministry about the Atonement of Jesus Christ. In recent years, he had also drawn on the Book of Mormon to emphasize aspects of Christ's mission familiar to other Christians. A new Primary songbook, which would soon be available to the Saints, reinforced these messages. The *Children's Songbook* had a new section titled "The Savior" and included many more songs about Jesus than its predecessor, *Sing with Me*.

Again and again, President Benson had invited the Saints to become converted to Christ and draw upon His saving grace. "By His grace," the prophet taught, "we receive the strength to do the works necessary that we otherwise could not do by our own power."[38]

At the same time, he encouraged the Saints to live righteously. In his talk to children, he urged them to have the courage to stand up for their beliefs. He also warned them that Satan would seek to tempt them.

"He has captured the hearts of wicked men and women," he said, "who would have you participate in bad things such as pornography, drugs, profanity, and immorality." He urged children to avoid videos, movies, and television that were not good.

Near the end of his talk, President Benson sought to comfort children who lived in fear. In recent years, Church leaders had spoken out more against child abuse and neglect, and the Church had published guidelines to help local leaders assist victims.

"Even when it seems that no one else cares, your Heavenly Father does," the prophet said. "He wants you to be protected and safe. If you are not, please talk to someone who can help you—a parent, a teacher, your bishop, or a friend."[39]

After President Monson sat down, the audience watched a prerecorded video of President Benson singing to a group of children gathered around his knee. Then the Tabernacle Choir sang "I Am a Child of God," and a benediction closed the conference.[40]

CHAPTER 25

For the Gospel's Sake

On June 14, 1989, mission companions Alice Johnson and Hetty Brimah noticed people staring at them as they walked back to their apartment in Koforidua, Ghana. "Why is everybody looking at us?" Hetty wondered aloud.

"We look beautiful," Alice said. They had just had their hair styled by a hairdresser they were teaching. Why wouldn't people be staring?[1]

When Alice and Hetty arrived at their apartment, however, their landlord told them they needed to report immediately to Alice's father and stepmother, who were also serving as missionaries in Koforidua.

Alice was the daughter of Billy Johnson, whose devotion to preaching the restored gospel had helped establish the Church in Ghana. He had been among the first people baptized when missionaries came in late

1978. He then received the priesthood, became the first branch president in Ghana, and later served as a district president. Now, a decade later, there were some six thousand Ghanaian Latter-day Saints. As missionaries, Billy and his wife were assigned to help Saints who were no longer attending their Church meetings.[2]

Alice and Hetty walked to the mission house in the city and found the Johnsons there. Alice's father calmly explained to them and other missionaries that the Ghanaian government had banned—for reasons unknown—all Church activities in the country. Several other Christian churches were also barred from meeting.[3]

"I need all of you to remove your name tags," Billy said. News of the ban had already been broadcast over the radio, which explained why so many people had been staring at Alice and Hetty. "You have to go to your apartment and pack your stuff quickly," Billy instructed. "Tomorrow morning, we have to report to the mission home in Accra."[4]

Growing up, Alice had always admired her father's prayerfulness, kindness, and enthusiasm for the restored gospel. In fact, his faith and eagerness to serve God had inspired Alice to go on a mission at age eighteen, which was permitted in some parts of the world.

Now, as he spoke of the government ban, he urged Alice and the other missionaries to fast and pray for its end.[5]

The next morning, Alice and Hetty traveled fifty miles south to the mission headquarters in Accra. When they arrived, they found dozens of missionaries gathered there. Most of them were Ghanaians, and every face was streaked with tears. The ban had taken everyone, even the mission president, by surprise. Local militias had seized meetinghouses and other Church buildings. Police officers had turned missionaries out of their apartments and impounded mission cars and bicycles. And armed guards had taken position outside the mission home.[6]

Gilbert Petramalo, the mission president, informed everyone that they would have to be released. Only Alice's parents would remain full-time missionaries, but they would act in an unofficial capacity. They would continue to minister to the Saints, but they would dress in everyday clothes and not use name tags.

Following her release, Alice went to live with a friend in Cape Coast. She felt lost and confused. The abrupt end to her mission left her unsure about her future. It was as if everything important in her life had suddenly come to an end.[7]

AFTER ALL CHURCH ACTIVITIES were banned in Ghana, Church member William Acquah was hungry for news. He read the local papers and listened to the radio constantly, all the while hoping to find out more about the "freeze," as the ban was soon called. Sometimes he and other Saints met to compare what they had learned.

Decades of colonial rule had left some Ghanaians wary of outsiders, and it seemed the Church's American headquarters and evident prosperity concerned government officials. Many people in the country had also watched a film that cast the Church as sinister and immoral, and it stoked fears about the Saints. By restricting the Church, the government apparently believed it was protecting Ghanaian citizens. Officials seemed unwilling to lift the freeze until they conducted a thorough investigation into the Saints and their activities.[8]

William lived in Cape Coast. His wife, Charlotte, was part of the Andoh-Kesson family, who had been early supporters of Billy Johnson's ministry. Charlotte had introduced William to the restored gospel in 1978, but he had waited more than a year to get baptized. He came from a prominent family in the region, and as a younger man his education and life experiences had made him suspicious of God. His heart began to soften when Charlotte introduced him to Reed and Naomi Clegg, a missionary couple in Cape Coast. They were patient as he studied the Book of Mormon and other Church literature, giving him time to gain a testimony and make the decision to be baptized.[9]

When the freeze began, Church leaders had authorized the Ghanaian Saints to administer the sacrament and hold Sunday School in their homes. William and Charlotte did this every Sunday with their children. Afterward, William would often leave home to check in on other Saints and make sure they were well.

On Sunday, September 3, 1989, William came upon a group of Church members clustered around a taxi. They told him that two fellow Latter-day Saints, Ato and Elizabeth Ampiah, had just been arrested for holding Church meetings at home. William hopped into the taxi with the others, and they drove to the police station.

The building was a dreary structure from Ghana's colonial era. Inside, an officer stood at a counter. Behind him, the Ampiahs sat barefoot on a bench in front of the iron bars of the prison cells.

The officer looked at William. "Are you also a member of the Church?" he asked.

"Yes," William said.

He brought William behind the counter. "Remove your shoes," he demanded. "Give me your wristwatch." He gave the same orders to the other men who came with William. One of them asked if he could call a friend, a local government official. The officer was furious.

"Into the cells!" he barked.

A foul stench hit William as soon as he passed through the gate. The small room was crammed with ragged prisoners who looked shocked to be sharing a cell with a group of Saints still dressed in their church clothes.

"What is happening in our country," one prisoner asked, "that harmless priests like you would be brought in here?"

Despite their rough appearance, the prisoners made room for the Saints and treated them with respect. It was fast Sunday, and as William and his companions talked over their situation, they decided to continue fasting.

They were tense and afraid, but word of their arrest had spread, and other Church members were working to get them released.

Sometime that afternoon, William's uncle came to the station. He was a calm, dignified old man who was not a member of the Church. He spoke with the police but could not persuade them to let William go. The officers said the Saints were a threat to national security and could not be bailed out.

Hours passed, and afternoon turned to evening. Friends from church came to the jail and likewise pleaded for the prisoners' release, but the officers only threatened to arrest them as well. Finally, when it became clear that William and the other Saints would be spending the night in prison, they joined hands and offered a prayer.[10]

The next morning, the station's commanding officer told the Saints he was waiting for orders on what to do with them. William passed the time talking with other prisoners. Some had families nearby and wanted to contact them. William memorized their addresses and promised to take messages to them. He was inspired when he thought of the New Testament apostle Paul and his imprisonments for the gospel's sake.

Another day passed, and finally, on Tuesday, William and the Saints were brought to see the commanding officer. "You are free to go," he said without further explanation. He tried to sound friendly, but he warned them not to tell anyone about their arrest.

No one said anything in reply. At the counter, the police returned their belongings and sent them on their way.[11]

ON THE EVENING OF November 18, 1989, Olga Kovářová was waiting at a bus station in Brno, Czechoslovakia, when she noticed dozens of police cars swarming a nearby theater. "It must be on fire," she thought.

The bus soon came. Olga climbed aboard and immediately saw a young neighbor who usually rode with her. She looked excited.

"What do you think?" she asked.

"What do you mean?" Olga said.

Her friend lowered her voice. "Well, about the revolution!"

"Where?"

"In Czechoslovakia, in Prague—here!"

Olga laughed. "What other joke do you want to play on me?" she asked.

"Did you see all those police cars around the theater?" her friend said. "Actors started a strike, and it has been spreading."[12]

Olga was still skeptical. For over a year, a wave of peaceful public protests and other demonstrations had sparked political change in Poland, Hungary, the German Democratic Republic, and other nations allied with the Soviet Union. In Berlin, just a few days earlier, people from both sides of the city had begun demolishing the massive concrete wall that had divided them for nearly thirty years.

In Czechoslovakia, though, the government had made no concessions to its citizens' pleas for greater freedom.[13]

Olga longed to worship freely, and she and her fellow Saints had been fasting and praying for this blessing. Elder Russell M. Nelson, meanwhile, had been working with the Czechoslovak government to get the Church officially recognized in the country.

Olga did her best to practice her faith. Fortunately, the gospel continued to fill her with joy. In 1987, she and her parents had driven to the German Democratic Republic to be endowed and sealed together as a family in the Freiberg Temple. The experience had strengthened her. "This is a really beautiful foundation," she had thought, "like you are touching a ceiling, and the ceiling becomes a new foundation."[14]

Now, two years after that experience, Olga came home to her apartment and turned on the television and radio, listening for news. She heard nothing. Could things actually be changing?

The next morning, Olga arrived at the youth center where she worked and found her colleagues rushing up and down the hallway. Many of her coworkers looked distressed. "Something really serious is going on in Prague," Olga's manager told her. "I have an emergency meeting right away."

Other colleagues soon arrived with news of the revolution. "It's true," Olga thought.[15]

Within days, signs in shop windows announced a general strike against the government. Olga joined thousands of people who marched to the city's main square, her heart pounding as she witnessed history unfold around her. She thought of all the hardships her parents and grandparents had suffered. She felt the Spirit of God in the unity and love of the people around her.[16]

After days of protest, the government resigned its power, and a new government began taking shape. The atmosphere in the country changed. People talked openly in the streets. They smiled and helped one another. At church, the Saints were optimistic about the future and happy to meet publicly for the first time in decades.

One day, around this time, Olga visited Otakar Vojkůvka at his home. She found him in tears. He was overjoyed that young people like her would be able to live and worship freely.

He told her he had been waiting his whole life for this to happen.[17]

DIGNARDINO ESPI, LEAD SECURITY officer at the Manila Philippines Temple, was apprehensive as he arrived for work on the evening of December 1, 1989. Earlier that day, armed men in Manila had staged a revolt, throwing the city into chaos. It was the seventh attempt to overthrow the Philippine government in four years.

Despite the political turmoil, the Church enjoyed a firm foundation in the Philippines. Over the past thirty years, its membership had grown from a small group of Filipino believers to more than two hundred thousand Saints. There were now thirty-eight stakes in the country and nine missions. And since its dedication in September 1984, the Manila Philippines Temple had been a source of great joy and spiritual power.[18]

At the temple guardhouse, Dignardino found his colleagues, Felipe Ramos and Remigio Julian. Although they were finishing their shifts, the two men were reluctant to go home. Across the street from the temple was Camp Aguinaldo, a large military base. Knowing the camp could become a target for the armed men, the guards worried about leaving their posts and being caught in the fighting. They preferred to stay and help preserve the sacredness of the house of the Lord and its grounds.

Around one o'clock in the morning, government troops set up a roadblock at an intersection near the temple. A few hours later, a tank plowed through the roadblock, damaging the wall around the temple.

As violence erupted in the street, Dignardino and the other security officers recruited the temple's two custodians to help them keep the building and its grounds safe. Seeking shelter from government fire, a group of men soon broke open the temple gates. Dignardino tried to compel them to leave, but they refused.

Later that afternoon, Dignardino spoke with temple president Floyd Hogan and area president

George I. Cannon over the phone. President Cannon advised him and the staff to take shelter inside the temple. A short time later, the phone lines went dead.[19]

The next morning was fast Sunday, and the staff began their fasts by asking God to spare the house of the Lord from being desecrated or harmed.

The day passed much like the one before it. Helicopters swooped overhead and sprayed the temple grounds with bullets. A plane dropped several bombs nearby, shattering the windows of the Church distribution store and damaging other buildings. At one point a fighter jet fired two rockets over the temple and caught a neighboring field on fire.

In the early afternoon, Dignardino found ten armed men near the temple entrance. "What you will find inside the temple building is purely religious and sacred in nature," he told them. He was nervous, but he kept speaking. "If you insist on entering the sanctity of the building, its sacred character will be gone," he said. "Would you deprive us of these blessings?" The men were silent, and as they walked away, Dignardino knew his words had touched them.[20]

That evening, Dignardino gathered his staff, and they again took shelter inside the temple. He offered a fervent prayer, putting his trust in the Lord to preserve His holy house.

All night, they waited for the bombs to fall, but the hours ticked away in silence. When dawn broke Monday morning, they cautiously emerged from the temple to survey the situation. The armed men were gone. Nothing remained but abandoned weapons, ammunition, and military uniforms.

Dignardino and the other men inspected the grounds and found some damage to a few of the outside buildings. But the temple itself was unharmed.[21]

LATE IN THE DAY on June 7, 1990, Manuel Navarro and his mission companion, Guillermo Chuquimango, were walking back to their house in Huaraz, Peru. Manuel had begun his mission in March 1989 at the Missionary Training Center in Lima, one of fourteen MTCs around the world. He enjoyed being a missionary—working hard, visiting different regions of the country, and bringing people to Jesus Christ.[22]

His current area could be dangerous at night, though. A revolutionary group called Sendero Luminoso, or the Shining Path, had been warring with the Peruvian government for more than a decade. Lately, their attacks had become more aggressive as rising inflation and economic strife beset the South American nation.[23]

Manuel and Guillermo, another native Peruvian, knew the dangers they faced as they left home each morning.[24] Groups like the Sendero Luminoso sometimes targeted Latter-day Saints because they associated the Church with United States foreign policy. There were now more than a million Church members in Spanish-speaking nations, with around 160,000 in Peru.

In recent years, revolutionaries had assaulted Latter-day Saint missionaries and bombed meetinghouses across Latin America. In May 1989, revolutionaries had shot and killed two missionaries in Bolivia. Since then, the political climate had only grown more intense, and attacks against the Church increased.[25]

The five missions in Peru had responded to the violence by setting curfews and restricting missionary work to the daytime. But this evening, Manuel and Guillermo were feeling happy and talkative. They had just taught a gospel lesson and had about fifteen minutes to get home.

As they walked and chatted, Manuel spotted two young men a block or so ahead of them. They were pushing a small, yellow car and looked like they needed help. Manuel thought about lending a hand, but the men soon started the car and drove off.

A short time later, the missionaries approached a park near their home. The yellow car was parked on the pavement about five feet from where they walked. Nearby was a military base with a detachment of troops.

"It looks like a car bomb," Guillermo said. Manuel saw some people running away, and in that instant, the car exploded.

The blast slammed into Manuel, throwing him into the air as shrapnel whizzed around him. When he hit the ground, he was terrified. He thought of his companion. Where was he? Had he taken the brunt of the explosion?[26]

Just then, he felt Guillermo pick him up off the ground. The park looked like a war zone as soldiers from the detachment—the bomb's apparent target—fired their guns past the smoldering remains of the car. Leaning on his companion, Manuel managed to walk the rest of the way home.

When they arrived, he went into the bathroom and looked in the mirror. His face was bloody, but he could not find a wound on his head. He simply felt faint.

"Give me a blessing," he told his companion. Guillermo, who had received only minor injuries, placed his trembling hands on Manuel's head and blessed him.

A short time later, the police came to the house. Thinking the missionaries were the young men who planted the bomb, the officers apprehended them and took them to the police station. There, one of the officers saw Manuel's condition and said, "This one is going to die. Let's take him to the health center."

At the police health center, the chief officer recognized the elders. Manuel had recently interviewed him for baptism. "They are not terrorists," he told the other officers. "They are missionaries."

Under the chief's care, Manuel washed his face and finally found a deep wound beneath his right eye. Once the chief saw it, he rushed Manuel and Guillermo to the hospital. "I can't do anything here," he explained.

Not long after, Manuel fainted from loss of blood. He urgently needed a transfusion. Saints from Huaraz came to the hospital, hoping to donate blood, but none of them had the right type. Doctors then tested Guillermo's blood and found him to be a perfect match.

For a second time that night, Guillermo saved his companion's life.[27]

CHAPTER 26

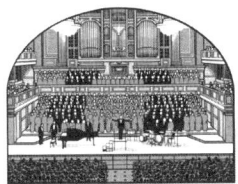

I Want to Serve

The day after the explosion in Huaraz, doctors transferred Manuel Navarro to a clinic in Lima. There he was greeted by his mission president, Enrique Ibarra, and received a blessing from Elder Charles A. Didier, a member of the area presidency. In the blessing, Elder Didier promised that Manuel would soon leave the clinic and return to the mission field.

After attending to Manuel's other injuries, doctors turned their focus to reconstructing his injured face. Shrapnel had cut his cheekbone and severed the optic nerve of his right eye, requiring the eye's removal. His parents, who had come to Lima, broke the news to him. "Son," his mother said, "they're going to operate."

Manuel was shocked. He felt no pain in his eye and, until now, did not know why it was bandaged. His mother comforted him. "We are here," she said. "We are with you."[1]

With full financial support from the Church, Manuel underwent three operations to remove his eye and repair its damaged socket. It would be a long recovery, and members of his extended family thought he should return to his hometown once he was released from the clinic. But Manuel refused to leave the mission field. "My contract with the Lord is for two years, and it's not up yet," he told his father.[2]

While recovering at the clinic, Manuel received visits from Luis Palomino, a friend from his hometown who was attending school in Lima. Although his injuries made it difficult for him to speak with Luis, Manuel began sharing the missionary lessons. Luis was surprised and impressed by Manuel's decision to finish his mission.

"I want to know what is motivating you," Luis told him. "Why is your faith so great?"[3]

Six weeks after the explosion, Manuel left the clinic and started serving at the mission office in Lima. The threat of terrorism still loomed, and he was afraid every time he saw a car like the one that exploded. At night, he struggled to sleep without medication.

Each day, one of the elders in the mission office would change Manuel's bandages. Manuel could not bear to look in the mirror and see his missing eye. Around three weeks after leaving the clinic, he received a prosthetic.

One day, Luis came to the mission office to visit Manuel. "I want to be baptized," he told him. "What do I have to do?" The mission office was not far from where Luis lived, so over the next few weeks, Manuel and his companion taught Luis the rest of the lessons at a nearby chapel. Manuel was excited to teach a friend, and Luis eagerly completed all the goals he set with the missionaries.

On October 14, 1990, Manuel performed Luis's baptism. He was still bothered by his injury, but the ordeal had made it possible for him to baptize a friend from his hometown—something he never expected to do on his mission. After Luis came out of the water, they embraced, and Manuel felt the Spirit strongly. He knew Luis could feel it too.

To commemorate the occasion, Manuel gave Luis a Bible. "When the days get dark," Manuel wrote on the inside cover, "just remember this day, the day you were reborn."[4]

BACK IN UTAH, MEANWHILE, Darius Gray received a telephone call from his friend Margery "Marie" Taylor, a specialist in African American genealogy at the Church's Family History Library in Salt Lake City. She had just found some rolls of microfilm with important African American records on them, and she could hardly contain her excitement. "You need to come here so you can appreciate it," she said.

Intrigued, Darius agreed to meet with her. The Family History Library was the largest genealogical center in the world, and hundreds of thousands of people visited every year. When Darius had first gone to the library, he had known little about his ancestors beyond what he'd gleaned from family stories and photographs. Marie had been the one to help him find more answers. Though not Black herself, she had proved to be an adept guide in introducing Darius to records about his family and the history of Black people in the United States.[5]

When Darius arrived at the Family History Library, Marie showed him the records she found. The Freedman's Savings and Trust Company had been chartered by the U.S. Congress in 1865 to help provide financial security to freeborn and formerly enslaved African Americans. More than a hundred thousand people had set up accounts with the bank, but it failed after nine years, taking its customers' hard-earned savings with it.[6]

Despite the bank's failure, its record books were immensely valuable to genealogists. Descendants of enslaved people often struggled to find details about their ancestors. The records people usually used to identify family names and dates—such as cemetery listings, voter registries, and birth and death certificates—either did not exist for enslaved people or were not widely available. The Freedman's Bank records, however, included a wealth of personal information about account holders, including the names of family members and where they had been enslaved. Some records even contained physical descriptions of clients.⁷

Darius could immediately see the importance of this information for African Americans. But the records themselves posed a major problem for researchers. The clerks who kept the books had recorded the names and details of account holders in the order they had come in to open an account, not alphabetically. This meant that researchers had to comb through the record books line by line until they found the information they were seeking. To be useful, the records needed to be better organized.⁸

Marie asked Darius if members of the Genesis Group could help transcribe and index the records, but not enough people had the time—or a personal computer—to do the work. Darius wrote to one of the apostles to ask if the Church could assist. While the apostle expressed his support, he said the Church could not undertake the project. At the time, Church headquarters did not generally sponsor name-extraction projects. Stakes and wards handled that work.

Running out of options, Marie had another idea. Over the past twenty-five years, the Church had established more than twelve hundred family history centers in forty-five countries. These centers were places where people both in and out of the Church could learn more about their ancestors. Usually, the centers were attached to stakes, but Marie knew a family history center had recently opened at the Utah State Prison. Inmates could use the center an hour a week. What if she and Darius recruited them to help on the Freedman's Bank project?

Marie spoke with the family history director at the prison, and before long, four inmate volunteers were hard at work on the records.[9]

IN SEPTEMBER 1990, ALICE Johnson was taking classes at Holy Child Teacher Training College in Takoradi, Ghana. More than a year had passed since the government had suspended Church operations in the country, abruptly ending her mission. At first, she'd been unsure what to do next. But at her sister's recommendation, she had decided to become a teacher, and she was accepted by the training college for the following academic year.[10]

As the freeze persisted, month after month, Alice and other Church members adapted to home worship. Emmanuel Kissi, the president of the Accra Ghana District, became the acting mission president and presiding Church authority in the country. He traveled extensively throughout Ghana, visiting and strengthening the Saints. The government permitted the Church's "essential services" to remain open temporarily, allowing some Church employees to keep working in welfare, Church education, and distribution. The Saints could not pay tithing or give offerings, but some set aside their earnings, patiently waiting for when they could make donations again.[11]

Unlike William Acquah and the Saints briefly imprisoned in Cape Coast, Alice experienced no harassment during the freeze. She and a few friends would gather on Sundays in a private home to partake of the sacrament, pray, and give talks. Her parents, who continued to serve their mission without wearing a badge or missionary attire, would visit her whenever they were in the area. Yet Alice felt like she was standing still while she waited for regular Church meetings to resume.[12]

Finally, in November 1990, Alice learned that the government had lifted its ban on the Church. From the start of the freeze, President Kissi and other Saints had been lobbying government officials to end restrictions. In response to misinformation about Church teachings, they wrote long letters explaining Church doctrine and history and petitioned government leaders in person. When officials raised concerns about the Church's former priesthood restriction, the Saints explained that Black members enjoyed all the rights of any other people in the Church. Other churches that had been hostile to the Latter-day Saints also defended the Saints' right to worship once they saw that the freeze put their own religious freedom at risk.[13]

A key person in lifting the ban was Isaac Addy, the Church's regional manager for temporal affairs in Ghana. He was the older half-brother of the president of Ghana, Jerry Rawlings. The brothers were estranged, and Isaac had not wanted to speak with Jerry about the freeze. One day, however, Georges

Bonnet, the director for temporal affairs for Africa, prevailed on him to pray until his heart softened toward his brother. Isaac did so, and the Spirit touched his heart. He agreed to meet with Jerry. They spoke that night, and by the end of the discussion, they had resolved their differences. The next day, the government decided to end the freeze.[14]

Alice was emotional when she returned to public Church meetings for the first time in eighteen months. Nearly a hundred Saints attended the Takoradi Branch that day, and the meeting lasted more than two hours because so many people went up to bear their testimonies.

Alice felt both excitement and worry as she thought about the converts from her mission in Koforidua. She wondered if they had stayed true to the gospel over the past year and a half. She knew that some Church members had grown discouraged and left the faith.[15]

Shortly after the freeze ended, the first two stakes in Ghana were organized. In Cape Coast, Alice's father, Billy Johnson, was called to serve as stake patriarch. The government, meanwhile, allowed the Saints to resume missionary work in the country. Grant Gunnell, the newly called president of the Ghana Accra Mission, called Alice in for an interview. He had located sixty of the missionaries who were serving before the freeze and wanted to know if they were willing to return to the mission field.[16]

"Would you like to come back and serve a mission after school?" he asked.

"No," she said without hesitation. "I want to serve right now."

"What?" the president asked, surprised by her quick answer.

"I want to do it right now," she repeated. Her priority had always been to serve God, and she was willing to put her education on hold for Him.[17]

Soon, Alice reported back to the mission field. When she told her father, a man who had devoted so much of his life to preaching the restored gospel, he was not surprised.

"That's my daughter," he said.[18]

When Manuel Navarro completed his mission in March 1991, his parents came to Lima to pick him up. Since he did not live in a stake, the local mission president released him from service. Yet Manuel was not quite ready to return to Nazca, his hometown in southern Peru. He had promised a friend in his last area that he would come to her baptism, so he and his parents stayed in the city for another week.

One morning, Manuel and his father went out to buy bread for breakfast. His father realized he had forgotten to bring money, so he turned around and headed back inside. "Wait for me here," he said.

Manuel froze. After having a mission companion for so long, it felt strange to be alone on the street. After a moment, he decided to stay put. "I'm not a missionary anymore," he thought.

Even after returning to Nazca, Manuel struggled to adapt to life after the mission—especially with his injury. Shaking hands was harder with one eye. He kept putting his hand in the wrong place. Then a brother in his branch began to play ping-pong with him, and tracking the small, white ball with one eye helped him develop better depth perception.

In April, Manuel moved to a larger city, Ica, to begin his university studies in automotive mechanics. It was less than a hundred miles from Nazca, and he had friends and family who lived there. He lived at his aunt's house in a room he had to himself. His mother worried about him and would call him almost every night on the telephone. "Son," she often told him, "always remember prayer." Whenever he felt anguished, he prayed for strength and found refuge in the Lord.[19]

To encourage young, unmarried Saints to meet and socialize, the Ica Stake offered institute classes and had a single-adult group that held activities and devotionals. Manuel found a home at these activities and in his new ward in Ica. While the children at church often stared at his prosthetic eye, adults treated him like any other member.

One day, Manuel was invited to meet with Alexander Nunez, the stake president in Ica. Manuel had known President Nunez since he was a teenager in Nazca, and President Nunez had visited his seminary class as a coordinator for the Church Educational System. Manuel admired him a great deal.

During the interview, President Nunez called Manuel to serve on the stake high council.

"Wow!" Manuel said to himself. Usually, Saints serving in stake callings were older and more experienced than he was. Yet President Nunez expressed confidence in him.

In the weeks that followed, Manuel visited his assigned wards. At first, he was self-conscious as he worked with ward leaders. But he learned to focus on the call, not on himself. As he studied the Church handbooks and reported to the stake, he no longer feared being too young for his position. He found that he enjoyed sharing his testimony with Saints in the stake, attending devotionals, and encouraging young people to serve missions.[20]

The problems caused by Manuel's injuries did not go away. Sometimes, when he was alone, he felt sad and shaken when he thought about the attack he suffered. The scriptures were full of miraculous stories of faithful people being healed of infirmities or preserved from danger. Yet they also told the stories of people like Job and Joseph Smith, who suffered pain and injustice without immediate deliverance. At times, when he thought about his injuries, Manuel wondered, "Why did this have to happen to me?"

Still, he knew he was fortunate to have survived the attack. In the months following his injury, terrorists had targeted and killed Church members and missionaries, spreading sorrow and fear among the Saints in Peru. Yet things were changing. The Peruvian government had begun cracking down on terrorism, leading to fewer attacks. And in the Church, the local Saints embraced an effort called "Trust in the Lord," which invited them to fast, pray, and exercise faith that they would be delivered from the violence in their country.

Manuel found that his schoolwork and service in the Church helped him cope with his hardships. He trusted in the Lord and thought of Him often.[21]

AROUND THE TIME MANUEL returned from his mission, Gordon B. Hinckley, the first counselor in the First Presidency, traveled to Hong Kong to look at potential sites for a house of the Lord. As a young apostle, he had supervised the development of the Church in Asia, and he was overjoyed by its progress. The region now had two hundred thousand Saints and four temples, located in Japan, Taiwan, South Korea, and the Philippines. While countries like Myanmar, Laos, Mongolia, and Nepal had no Church presence yet, new branches were taking root in Singapore, Indonesia, Malaysia, and India.[22]

Hong Kong, home to the Church's Asia Area office, was a British territory. In six years, however, authority over the region would pass from the United Kingdom to the People's Republic of China.

As part of the handover, China promised to honor Hong Kong's economic and political systems and respect the religious practices of its citizens. Even so, with eighteen thousand Saints living in the territory, Church leaders felt compelled to build a house of the Lord there before the transfer of authority.[23]

President Hinckley spent a day looking at various locations, but he did not find any affordable options. In other areas of the world, the Church could avoid purchasing expensive city lots by building temples in suburbs. But Hong Kong was a densely populated region of over five million people, making suitable land almost impossible to acquire.

President Hinckley wondered if the Church should simply build a temple on one of the small lots it already owned in the city. He imagined a high-rise multipurpose building, with lower floors serving as a chapel and mission office.

"The three top floors could become a temple," he thought. "It could be done without any problems."

It was an interesting possibility. But the Church had never built such a building, and he wasn't sure if that was the best option for the Saints in Hong Kong.[24]

ON JUNE 15, 1991, HUNGARY's historic Budapest Opera House thundered with applause as the Tabernacle Choir performed its final encore for an audience of fourteen hundred people. Among the concertgoers were Elder Russell M. Nelson and his wife, Dantzel. They were traveling with the choir on a three-week tour of various European countries.[25]

Elder Nelson had spent five years leading the Church's efforts to improve its relationship with governments in central and eastern Europe. Many of the countries, including Hungary, were transitioning away from communist leadership. Czechoslovakia now enjoyed complete religious freedom, and the government officially recognized the Church. East Germany and West Germany had become one country, bringing the old restrictions in the GDR to an end. Missionaries were now permitted in Poland, Hungary, Bulgaria, Romania, Slovenia, and Croatia as well.

The choir's tour was an opportunity to build bridges. And from the sound of the applause, the concert had done just that.

"I want you to know," one Hungarian man told a choir member after the performance, "my wife and I, we believe in God too. We understand what your music tells us."[26]

The next day, Elder Nelson spoke at a sacrament meeting in a hotel ballroom overlooking the hill where he had dedicated Hungary for gospel preaching four years earlier. He had been with a handful of people then, including the only member of the Church in Budapest. Now the country was home to four hundred Saints.[27]

From Hungary, the choir traveled to Austria, Czechoslovakia, Germany, Poland, and the Soviet Union. Elder Nelson met up with Elder Dallin H. Oaks in the Soviet republic of Armenia, where the Church had given humanitarian aid after a devastating earthquake. Since Elder Nelson's visit to the Soviet Union in 1987, significant political and social changes had taken place in the country. It had become more open to foreigners, and the people of several Soviet republics were now seeking greater control over their local affairs. There was also more religious freedom in the region, and interest in religion was growing.

Although the Church had no official presence in the Soviet Union, nothing prevented Soviet citizens from traveling abroad, finding the restored gospel, and bringing it back with them when they returned home. By 1990, there were enough Saints in Leningrad, Russia, and Tallinn, Estonia, to register the Church in those cities. In the meantime, missionaries and Saints in Finland were assigned to support the new converts.[28]

In Moscow, Elder Nelson was amazed by how tolerant the Russian government had become toward the Church. Over the past few years, he had crossed the Atlantic several times to meet with government officials in eastern Europe. At first, they rarely seemed pleased to see him, and he had often felt that his efforts were fruitless. Then the Lord provided a way forward.[29]

The Saints now had a branch in Leningrad. Church members in the cities of Vyborg and Moscow had also obtained government approval for their small congregations. The progress was remarkable, and Elder Nelson hoped that soon the Church might be publicly recognized throughout Russia, by far the largest republic in the Soviet Union.[30]

After a concert by the Tabernacle Choir at Moscow's Bolshoi Theater, the Nelsons and Elder Oaks crossed the street to the Metropol Hotel, where the Church hosted a postconcert dinner. Elder Nelson had attended many such dinners and receptions on this tour thanks to Beverly Campbell, the director of the Church's International Affairs Office in Washington, DC. In this role, Beverly had arranged meetings and built relationships between Church representatives and government officials around the world.[31]

At the dinner, Elder Nelson stepped up to a microphone and thanked the many dignitaries for coming. He then invited Alexander Rutskoi, the vice president of Russia, to join him in front of the crowd. "We would be grateful," Elder Nelson said, "to have any comment you would care to make."

"My dear guests," Vice President Rutskoi said, "we are pleased this evening to have the opportunity of welcoming these guests here with us tonight. I'd like to read to you this registration form, which is dated May 28, 1991, which registers The Church of Jesus Christ of Latter-day Saints in the Russian Soviet Federative Socialist Republic."[32]

As Vice President Rutskoi read the document, Elder Nelson was overwhelmed. He had hoped the public announcement was coming soon, but he had not expected it that night. Receiving formal recognition meant the Church would be able to send more missionaries to Russia, print and distribute Church literature, and establish more congregations.[33]

The next day, amid visits to government officials with Elder Oaks and a few others, Elder Nelson went to a small park near the Kremlin and offered a prayer of thanksgiving to the Lord.

A week later, the two apostles visited President Benson at his Salt Lake City apartment. They showed him a copy of the document registering the Church in Russia and told him the Church was now established in eastern Europe.

When he heard the news, President Benson's face lit up with joy.[34]

CHAPTER 27

The Hand of Friendship

After President Hinckley left Hong Kong without selecting a temple site, the Asia Area presidency had assigned Tak Chung "Stanley" Wan, the Church's manager of temporal affairs in Asia, to create a new list of potential sites for the building. Stanley and his team soon began their search, and when President Hinckley returned to Hong Kong in late July 1992, they were confident that the location for a house of the Lord was somewhere on their list.[1]

Stanley loved the temple and yearned to have one close to home. His parents were refugees from mainland China. His father had joined the Church soon after missionaries returned to Hong Kong in 1955. His mother, a Buddhist, was baptized a few years later. Although they could not afford the trip to the nearest temple,

The Hand of Friendship

Stanley was able to receive his endowment at the Hawaii Temple in 1975, just prior to his full-time mission. Five years later, he took his parents to Hawaii for their own temple blessings. The trip exhausted his savings, but he believed it was worth the sacrifice.[2]

Six months after taking his parents to the house of the Lord, Stanley had married Ka Wah "Kathleen" Ng, another Hong Kong Saint. In Chinese culture, couples held a nine-course wedding feast for family and friends. Stanley and Kathleen, however, had decided to forgo the custom and spent all their money on a temple trip. They were sealed for time and eternity in the Salt Lake Temple. And since then, the couple had made it a goal to go to the temple at least once a year, despite the high cost.

For Stanley, knowing the Church now wanted to build a temple in Hong Kong was a dream come true. Local Saints would no longer need to travel long distances or empty their savings to take part in the sacred ordinances. First, however, the Church needed a suitable tract of land.[3]

On July 26, 1992, Stanley spent the morning driving President Hinckley to potential sites, but each one was too expensive, too small, or too remote. Stanley and the area presidency were sure the next site—located at Tseung Kwan O—was perfect. It was away from the bustle of the big city and surrounded by beautiful landscape. The Hong Kong government would even sell the site to the Church at a reduced price. Surely President Hinckley would approve of it.[4]

449

It was sunny when the group arrived at Tseung Kwan O. The driver offered to hold an umbrella for President Hinckley to shield him from the sun as he inspected the site. President Hinckley declined. "I want to pray by myself," he said.

Stanley and the others waited beside their cars as President Hinckley walked to the site, looked over the land, and prayed about it. He then returned to the group. "This is not the place," he said.

"If this is not the place," Stanley wondered, "then where?" He felt all their work had been in vain—that a house of the Lord in Hong Kong would continue to be a dream.[5]

Later that morning, Kathleen Wan was at home when the telephone rang. It was Stanley. He was still traveling around Hong Kong with President Hinckley. But he asked Kathleen to meet him at the apartment of Monte J. Brough, the president of the Asia Area. President Hinckley had invited her to join them there for lunch that afternoon.

When Kathleen arrived at the Broughs' apartment, Stanley and the other guests were on their way, so she helped Lanette, Elder Brough's wife, set out a meal of cold cuts, bread, cheese, salad, fruit, ice cream, pumpkin bread, and coconut biscuits. Everything looked delicious.

Before long, Stanley came through the door with President Hinckley, Elder Brough, and a few others. As they took seats at the dining table, President Hinckley sat across from Kathleen. She had seen him several times at public meetings, and she admired his sense of humor and the way he made people feel comfortable, including her. But until now, she had never spoken to him personally. He asked about her three children, and she told him how they were doing.[6]

The temple site, however, was still on everyone's mind. Their search had not gone well, but President Hinckley was not concerned. As they ate, he told them about a sacred experience he'd had around four o'clock that morning.

He had just woken up from a deep sleep, and he found his mind troubled by thoughts of the temple site. He knew he had traveled a long way at great expense to select the site, and he did not have much time—a little more than a day—to make a decision. As he mulled over the problem, he had begun to worry.

But then the voice of the Spirit had spoken to him. "Why are you worried about this?" it had said. "You have a wonderful piece of property where the mission home and the small chapel stand."[7]

Kathleen and Stanley knew the property well. The Church had owned it for nearly forty years. But Stanley had never seriously considered it as a potential site for the house of the Lord. The lot was too small, and besides, it was in a part of town that had become dangerous and disreputable over time.

Yet President Hinckley clearly believed the Church could build a temple there. He said the Spirit had described it to him.

"Build a building of seven to ten stories on this property," the Spirit had said. "It can include a chapel and classrooms on the first two floors and a temple on the top two or three floors, with offices and apartments on the in-between floors." The top floor could be the celestial room, and an angel Moroni could adorn the top of the building.

The design was similar to the inspired thought he'd had a year earlier to place the temple in a high-rise building.[8]

Kathleen was astonished by President Hinckley's idea. As he spoke, he showed her and the other guests a rough sketch of the temple's floor plan, which he had drawn during the night. Kathleen had never thought of placing a temple on top of a building, but she had faith in the Lord's plan. While Kowloon Tong was not the nicest part of Hong Kong, it was convenient to public transportation stops, and the area would continue to develop over time.[9]

When he finished sharing his experience, President Hinckley said, "Will you support this decision?"

"Of course we will!" everyone replied. Their prayers for a house of the Lord in Hong Kong were finally being answered.[10]

The Hand of Friendship

IN AUGUST 1992, TWENTY-THREE-YEAR-OLD Willy Sabwe Binene aspired to a career in electrical engineering. His training at the Institut Supérieur Technique et Commerciale in Lubumbashi, a city in the central African nation of Zaire, was going well. He had just finished his first year at the school and was already looking forward to continuing his formal education.

During the break between terms, Willy returned to his hometown, Kolwezi, some two hundred miles northwest of Lubumbashi. He and other members of his family belonged to the Kolwezi Branch of the Church.[11] After the priesthood revelation of 1978, the restored gospel had spread beyond Nigeria, Ghana, South Africa, and Zimbabwe to more than a dozen other countries in Africa: Liberia, Sierra Leone, Côte d'Ivoire, Cameroon, the Republic of the Congo, Uganda, Kenya, Namibia, Botswana, Swaziland, Lesotho, Madagascar, and Mauritius.[12] The first Latter-day Saint missionaries in Zaire arrived in 1986, and there were now about four thousand Saints in the country.[13]

Shortly after Willy arrived in Kolwezi, his branch president called him in for an interview. "We need to prepare you to go on a full-time mission," he said.

"I should continue with my studies," Willy said, taken aback. He explained that he had three more years in his electrical engineering program.

"You should go on a mission first," the branch president said. He pointed out that Willy was the first young man from the branch to be eligible for a full-time mission.

"No," Willy said, "it won't work. I'm going to finish up first."[14]

Willy's parents were not happy when they found out he had turned down the branch president's invitation. His mother, who was reserved by nature, asked him directly, "Why are you delaying?"[15]

One day, the Spirit prompted Willy to visit his uncle Simon Mukadi. As he walked into his uncle's living room, he noticed a book on a table. Something about it seemed to call to him. He moved closer and read the title: *Le miracle du pardon,* the French translation of Spencer W. Kimball's *The Miracle of Forgiveness*. Intrigued, Willy picked the book up, let its pages fall open, and started to read.

The passage was about idolatry, and Willy quickly became engrossed. Elder Kimball wrote that people not only bowed down to gods of wood and stone and clay but also worshipped their own possessions. And some idols had no tangible form.[16]

The words made Willy tremble like a leaf. He felt that the Lord was speaking directly to him. In an instant, all desire to finish school before his mission left him. He sought out his branch president and told him that he'd changed his mind.

"What kind of a fly bit you?" his branch president asked.

After Willy told him the story, the branch president took out a missionary application. "OK," he said. "We start here, at the beginning."[17]

The Hand of Friendship

As Willy prepared for his mission, violence erupted in the region where he lived. Zaire was in Africa's Congo River Basin, where various ethnic and regional groups had struggled against each other for generations. Recently, in Willy's province, the governor had urged the Katangan majority to oust the minority Kasaians.[18]

In March 1993, the violence spread to Kolwezi. Katangan militants prowled the streets, brandishing machetes, sticks, whips, and other weapons. They terrorized Kasaian families and burned their homes, caring little what people or goods were inside. Fearing for their lives, many Kasaians hid from the marauders or fled the city.[19]

As a Kasaian, Willy knew it was only a matter of time before the militants hunted down his family. To avoid harm, he set aside his mission preparation to help his family flee to Luputa, a Kasaian town some 350 miles away, where some of his relatives lived.[20]

Since trains out of Katanga were infrequent, hundreds of Kasaian refugees had set up a sprawling camp outside Kolwezi's railway station. When Willy and his family arrived at the camp, they had no choice but to bed down beneath the stars until they could find shelter. The Church, the Red Cross, and other humanitarian organizations were at the camp to provide food, tents, and medical care for the refugees. Still, without proper sanitation, the camp reeked of human waste and burning garbage.[21]

After a few weeks in the camp, the Binenes received word that a train could transport some of the camp's women and children out of the area. Willy's mother and four sisters decided to leave on the train with other family members. Willy, meanwhile, helped his father and older brother fix up a broken-down open freight car. When it was ready to travel, they hitched it to an outbound train and left the camp.

When he arrived at Luputa several weeks later, Willy could not help but contrast it to Kolwezi. The town was small and had no electricity, which meant he could not use his electrical engineering training for employment. And there was no branch of the Church.

"What are we going to do here?" he asked himself.[22]

AROUND THIS TIME, SILVIA and Jeff Allred often drove along bumpy roads somewhere in the Chaco, a sparsely settled region in western Paraguay. Thirteen years had passed since the Allreds lived in Guatemala, and it had been an eventful time for their family. After they moved to Costa Rica, Jeff's Church employment had transferred him to South America, so they moved again, first to Chile and then to Argentina. The Allreds were now serving as mission leaders in Paraguay and had been in the country for about a year.

In the Chaco was a small community of Saints from the Indigenous Nivaclé people. They lived in two villages, Mistolar and Abundancia, some distance from the main road. Silvia and Jeff were on their way to Mistolar, the more remote village, to deliver some provisions. The route to the village was notoriously rough, with thorns so large they could pierce a vehicle's tires. As a precaution, the Allreds always traveled there with an additional vehicle loaded with extra tires to replace flats.[23]

The road to Mistolar was only one of many challenges the Allreds faced in Paraguay. When they arrived in Asunción, they knew from Jeff's work in temporal affairs that the Church was growing at a slower rate there than in other South American countries. But why?

As they began meeting with the missionaries, they noticed that the elders and sisters were focusing much of their work on distributing Spanish copies of the Book of Mormon. Yet many Paraguayans, especially in more rural communities, were more comfortable using Guarani, a language with Indigenous roots.

Wherever possible, the Church's missionaries tried to teach people in their preferred tongue. By 1993, complete translations of the Book of Mormon were available in thirty-eight languages. Selected portions of the book had been translated into another forty-six languages, including Guarani.

After recognizing the local Saints' preference for Guarani, the Allreds had felt prompted to direct missionaries to use the language in their work, when appropriate. They also encouraged the elders and sisters to teach people more about the Book of Mormon before challenging them to read it. And they emphasized the importance of teaching the basic principles of the restored gospel, setting realistic goals, and having faith to invite people to follow the teachings of the Savior.[24]

Ministering to the Nivaclé required additional adaptations. Several hundred Nivaclé had been baptized in the early 1980s after Walter Flores, a Nivaclé Latter-day Saint who had joined the Church in Asunción, introduced the missionaries to his people. Living largely in isolation, the Nivaclé had their own language and way of life. They grew squash, corn, and beans and raised goats for milk. The women wove baskets and the men carved wooden figurines to sell to tourists.[25]

In recent years, the tithes of faithful Saints around the world had allowed the Church to cover the entire cost of building and maintaining its meetinghouses. Ward and branch budgets, dispensed from headquarters in Salt Lake City, also paid for Church programs and activities.[26] As an isolated community, the Nivaclé rarely needed money for the kinds of activities taking place in typical wards and branches. Instead, their budget money often went toward rice, beans, flour, oil, batteries, and other provisions. The Church also provided the two communities with clothing and other resources, much as it did for other rural Indigenous peoples in Central and South America.[27]

The deeply rooted faith of the Nivaclé could be seen in the branch president in Mistolar, Julio Yegros, and his wife, Margarita. In 1989, they had been sealed together with their two young children in the Buenos Aires Temple. During the long journey home, their children had become sick and died. To endure the tragedy, the Yegroses had relied on their faith in God's eternal plan and their temple covenants.

"Our children were sealed to us in the house of the Lord," they once told the Allreds. "We know we will have them back with us for all eternity. This knowledge has given us peace and comfort."[28]

ON MAY 30, 1994, PRESIDENT Ezra Taft Benson passed away at home in Salt Lake City. As the Saints reflected on his life and ministry, they remembered him for bringing the Book of Mormon and its Christ-centered message to the attention of the Church—and the world—as never before. They also remembered his counsel about avoiding the dangers of pride and selfishness of any kind, including contention, anger, and unrighteous dominion.[29]

During his presidency, the Church sought new ways to ease the suffering of people across the globe. In 1988, the First Presidency had issued a statement on the AIDS epidemic, expressing and urging love and sympathy for those suffering from the effects of the disease. Under President Benson's leadership, the Church had also dramatically expanded humanitarian aid, and missionaries now spent more time providing service in the communities where they labored.[30]

During this same time, the Church had grown by over 40 percent, to nine million members. Missionary work had expanded in many areas of the globe, especially in

Africa. And, after the recent collapse of the Soviet Union and other political changes in Europe, the Church was officially established in over a dozen countries in central and eastern Europe.

Unfortunately, old age and illness had kept President Benson from speaking in public for almost five years. During that time, he had been unable to say more than a few words at a time. His counselors, Gordon B. Hinckley and Thomas S. Monson, along with the Quorum of the Twelve Apostles, had prayerfully directed the day-to-day business of the Church. When possible, President Benson had given them his support for decisions with a simple "yes" or an approving smile.[31]

The senior apostle at the time of President Benson's death was Howard W. Hunter. At eighty-six years old, he himself was not in good health. He used a wheelchair or walker to get around, and his voice often sounded strained and weary. Yet during his service as an apostle, the Saints had come to admire his humility, compassion, gentleness, and immense courage.[32]

Shortly after his ordination as Church president on June 5, 1994, President Hunter held a press conference and announced Gordon B. Hinckley and Thomas S. Monson as his counselors in the First Presidency. He then invited all Church members to follow the Savior's example of love, hope, and compassion. He urged Saints who were struggling or who had left the fold to return. "Let us stand with you and dry your tears," he said. "Come back. Stand with us. Carry on. Be believing."

The Hand of Friendship

"In that same spirit," he continued, "I also invite the members of the Church to establish the temple of the Lord as the great symbol of their membership and the supernal setting for their most sacred covenants." He urged the Saints to carry current temple recommends and be a "temple-attending and a temple-loving people."

"Let us hasten to the temple as frequently as time and means and personal circumstances allow," he said.[33]

Later that month, President Hunter sat beneath a canopy in front of a large audience at the former site of the temple in Nauvoo, Illinois. The sky was clear and bright, offering an expansive view of the Mississippi River and the Church's historic sites in the area. The humid air was heavy, but everyone seemed eager to hear President Hunter speak. He had come to Nauvoo with President Hinckley and Elder M. Russell Ballard to mark the 150th anniversary of the martyrdom of Joseph and Hyrum Smith.[34]

President Hunter was reflective as he sat at the old temple site. Aside from some gray foundation stones, little evidence remained that a magnificent house of the Lord had once stood on the grassy plot. He thought of the prophet Joseph Smith and felt responsible to do all he could for the Lord's work in the time he had left on earth.

Taking his place at the pulpit, President Hunter again encouraged the Saints to make the temple part of their lives. "As in Joseph's day, having worthy and endowed members is the key to building the kingdom in all the world," he told the Saints. "Temple worthiness ensures that our lives are in harmony with the will of the Lord, and we are attuned to receive His guidance in our lives."[35]

After the service, President Hinckley and Elder Ballard spoke to reporters at the Carthage jail, where the prophet Joseph had been killed. One reporter asked them to contrast the Church in 1844 with the modern Church.

"Their problem 150 years ago was a mob with painted faces," President Hinckley replied. "Our problem is accommodating growth of this Church." He spoke of the challenge of providing meetinghouses and leadership for so many people. The Church continued to spread rapidly in many parts of the world. In Africa, for example, the Church had recently extended into Tanzania, Ethiopia, Malawi, and the Central African Republic.

"What a wonderful, wonderful problem it is," he said.[36]

At the jail, President Hunter spoke again. "The world needs the gospel of Jesus Christ as restored through the prophet Joseph Smith," he told an audience of three thousand people. "We need to be slower to anger and more prompt to help. We need to extend the hand of friendship and resist the hand of retribution."

When the service ended, evening was settling over Carthage. As President Hunter left the grounds of the jail, a large crowd of Saints greeted him enthusiastically. He was tired, but he stopped and shook their hands, each in turn.[37]

CHAPTER 28

The Lord's Path

"He's gone."

President Gordon B. Hinckley felt numb as he spoke the words into the telephone. On the other end of the line was his wife, Marjorie. He could hear her crying. They had prayed this day would never come.

It was March 3, 1995. Earlier that morning, President Hinckley had learned that President Howard W. Hunter had passed away at home. President Hunter had been receiving treatment for cancer, and his health had been declining rapidly. But President Hinckley was still shocked by the news. He and President Thomas S. Monson had gone at once to the prophet's apartment and offered comfort and consolation to Sister Inis Hunter. Then they had stepped into another room and begun making the necessary phone calls.

As he finished his call with Marjorie, President Hinckley felt a deep sadness. He had served the Lord alongside President Hunter for more than thirty years, and now he had lost a good, kind, and wise friend. The prophet's death also made him the senior apostle, which meant the leadership of the Church rested on his shoulders. He felt unexpectedly lonely.

"I can only pray and plead for help," he thought.[1]

Five days later, President Hinckley presided at President Hunter's funeral in the Salt Lake Tabernacle. "Mortal life for President Hunter has been more of a mission than a career," he told mourners. "His has been a leading and powerful voice in declaring the teachings of the gospel of Jesus Christ and in moving forward the work of the Church."[2]

Even though President Hunter's nine-month presidency had been the shortest of any Church president's, he had accomplished much while in office. The First Presidency had sent humanitarian relief to victims of food shortages in Laos in southeast Asia, civil war in Rwanda in east Africa, and flooding and fires in the southern United States. Although his poor health limited his ability to travel, he had dedicated temples in two U.S. cities—Orlando, Florida, and Bountiful, Utah. On December 11, 1994, he traveled to Mexico City to organize the two thousandth stake of the Church.[3]

One of his greatest legacies as an apostle, however, was his love for all people, regardless of religion. He'd had a deep spiritual connection to the Holy Land. Just before his death, he had planned to return to Jerusalem with Elder Jeffrey R. Holland, who was now a member of the Quorum of the Twelve Apostles, for one final visit. He was sad when his failing health prevented him from going.[4]

On March 9, the day after President Hunter's funeral, President Hinckley woke up early and could not fall back asleep. The weight of his new responsibilities—and the decisions he had to make—bore down on him.

He decided to fast and spend some time alone in the Salt Lake Temple. He secured a key to the room on the fourth floor where the First Presidency and Quorum of the Twelve Apostles met every week. There he removed his shoes, put on white temple slippers, and read from the scriptures.

Eventually, his eyes drifted to three pictures of the Savior on the wall. One of them depicted the Crucifixion, and President Hinckley thought deeply about the price the Savior had paid to redeem him. He again thought of his enormous responsibilities as the Lord's prophet, and he wept as feelings of inadequacy enveloped him.

He turned his attention to a painting of Joseph Smith on the north wall. To his right, along the east wall, were portraits of every Church president from Brigham Young to Howard W. Hunter. President Hinckley looked at each portrait in turn. He had personally known each Church president since Heber J. Grant. They had put immense trust in him, and he loved them. Now, as he looked at the portraits, they seemed almost to come alive. He felt their eyes on him, silently encouraging him and pledging their support. He had no need to fear.

Kneeling, President Hinckley brought questions to the Lord and, by the power of the Spirit, received His word concerning them. President Hinckley's heart and mind filled with peace and assurance, and he knew he had the will to move forward with the work.

He had already decided to call Thomas S. Monson as his first counselor. Now he felt impressed to call Elder James E. Faust as his second counselor. While still on his knees, he prayed for confirmation of this choice, and a warmth flooded his heart.

Later, as he reflected on his day, President Hinckley felt better about his new calling. "I hope the Lord has trained me to do what He expects of me," he wrote in his journal. "I will give Him total loyalty, and I will certainly seek His direction."[5]

AROUND THIS SAME TIME, Darius Gray and Marie Taylor were regularly visiting the Utah State Prison to meet with the hundreds of inmates who were extracting genealogical information from the Freedman's Bank records.

The volunteers worked in a family history center adjacent to the prison chapel. To get there, Darius and Marie had to pass through a network of heavy metal gates, locked doors, and guarded hallways. Darius had been a little nervous the first time Marie had brought him, especially in areas where they were surrounded by prisoners. But he now came to the prison every few weeks, and he was used to it.[6]

When the extraction project began, genealogical research was undergoing major changes. Computers were rapidly replacing filing cabinets and printed indexes, making the work of collecting and accessing data more efficient. During the 1970s and '80s, the Church had begun adapting the new technology to temple and family history work. And by the early 1990s, the Church had developed TempleReady, a computer program that allowed patrons at local family history centers, including the one at the prison, to submit names for temple ordinances more easily.[7]

The family history center where the inmates worked had several microfilm readers along the walls. Marie had worked with the Family History Library to get a copy of the Freedman's Bank microfilm to keep at the prison. After the volunteers extracted the information onto a form specifically designed for the project, they would bring the form to an adjoining room and enter the information into a computer database. Under Marie's direction, the volunteers checked each record multiple times. Two volunteers independently extracted the same information, and then a third volunteer compared the extractions with the original document, making sure the information was transcribed correctly.

The man in charge of the prison's family history center was serving a life sentence. He kept the work moving and well organized. Darius was impressed by the enthusiasm of the volunteers and their attention to detail. Prison officials were delighted to report that the inmates working on the bank records typically caused no problems among the other prisoners.[8]

The project was open to all eligible inmates, regardless of their religious beliefs. As Darius and Marie served with the volunteers, they emphasized the spiritual nature of the project. Prisoners who had been raised in the Church understood the role of genealogy in uniting families for eternity. Some of these men had no chance of getting out of prison themselves, but they found joy in working to free others from spirit prison. Darius and Marie always began their prison meetings with a prayer, and they encouraged the volunteers to pray in their own way as they worked on the project.

Sometimes an inmate would approach Darius and ask for a priesthood blessing. He always agreed. As he ministered to the men, who had committed all manner of crimes and offenses, he was struck by a sure knowledge that they were children of God.[9]

At this time, the Church encouraged its members to submit family names to the temple, yet members could also submit the names of people who were not relatives. The inmates regularly used TempleReady to clear names from the Freedman's Bank project for temple ordinances. To help in this work, Marie created a temple "family file" named after Elijah Able, one of the earliest Black Latter-day Saints. The file was available to temple patrons in the United States and South Africa. If patrons wanted to perform ordinances for someone from the Freedman's Bank records, they could simply go to the temple and request a name from the family file.

One evening, Darius and Marie went to the Jordan River Temple in South Jordan, Utah, with several friends to perform sealings for families from the Freedman's Bank records. Although the group numbered around twenty people, they still needed the help of others in the temple. All evening, they sealed together families that had been cruelly separated in life through enslavement.[10]

Before going to the temple, Darius and Marie had told the inmates about the trip. Darius had chosen the Jordan River Temple because it was the one closest to his home, but it also happened to be the closest to the prison.

That evening, several inmates working on the project gathered at a window in a corner of the prison. The window was narrow, but it offered a view of the Salt Lake Valley—including the Jordan River Temple.

Although the volunteers could not be there in person, they quietly supported Darius and Marie in the sacred work.[11]

DURING HIS FIRST YEAR as Church president, Gordon B. Hinckley followed the Church in Asia from afar. Construction on the Hong Kong Temple had begun in January 1994, and President Hinckley received regular updates on its progress. He also counseled with

Asia Area leaders to help plan the events surrounding the temple's dedication.[12]

He was overjoyed with the Church's progress in the region. Since 1955, the Church in Asia had grown from a thousand members to almost six hundred thousand. Japan, South Korea, Taiwan, and the Philippines were now centers of strength with temples of their own. The Church was starting to grow in places like Thailand, Mongolia, Cambodia, India, and, once again, Vietnam. Across Asia, a rising generation of young, faithful Latter-day Saints was making a difference.[13]

In Taiwan, Kuan-ling "Anne" Liu had recently finished her final year at Taipei First Girls High School, where she was the only Latter-day Saint in a student body of over four thousand. Like many students in Taiwan, Anne kept a demanding schedule. She awoke a little before 6:00 a.m., got on a bus at 6:30, and spent the next nine hours at school. After dinner, she studied in a classroom for a few more hours before catching the bus home at 8:00 in the evening.

Still, every night before going to sleep, Anne set aside time to read her scriptures. More and more Church leaders emphasized daily scripture study as an essential component of Latter-day Saint worship. Anne felt that prayer and scripture study helped her avoid discouragement and learn better at school. On Sundays, when many of her classmates were studying for school, she attended a seminary class before her regular Church meetings in Taipei. She also served as the ward pianist.

"If I go to sacrament meeting and listen to the talks," she realized, "my life is always more positive and happy."[14]

In Mongolia, meanwhile, twenty-one-year-old Soyolmaa Urtnasan was teaching the young women in her branch in the capital city of Ulaanbaatar. Of the several hundred branch members, most were in their teens or twenties and had been members for less than a year. Soyolmaa herself had been baptized only a few months earlier, and she was brimming with enthusiasm. When she was a teen, her parents died within a year of each other, leaving Soyolmaa angry with God.

"I was a 'two-faced' person," she recalled, "happy and outgoing on the outside, miserable and shy on the inside." To dull her pain, she went to parties and resorted to drinking.

Things began to change when a friend who was investigating the Church invited her to a sacrament meeting. That first Sunday, Soyolmaa felt peace and belonging she had never experienced before. She soon learned that she could become a new person through Jesus Christ. When she heard the plan of salvation, she melted into tears.

"I knew that I was in the right place," she recalled. Before long, she became one of the first missionaries from Mongolia.[15]

Meanwhile, in Thailand, the Saints understood the importance of temples and made sacrifices to get there. In 1990, about two hundred Thai Saints flew to the Philippines to attend the house of the Lord in Manila. The trip was expensive, so many Saints saved for more than a year to have enough money for airfare.

As president of the Khon Kaen District in central Thailand, Kriangkrai Phithakphong saw such everyday sacrifices firsthand. Many members of the district were poor. Some without steady work or a regular income had barely enough money to survive. Yet they served actively in the Church, attending their meetings even when they had to travel long distances on foot or by bicycle or bus.

"When we flew to Manila, it was a milestone in the history of the Church in Thailand," Kriangkrai remembered. "Everyone worked hard to raise the money to go." Even his ten-year-old daughter sold cooking charcoal to help the family pay for the trip. In the end, Kriangkrai, his wife, Mukdahan, and their children made it to the temple—and their experience there made the struggle and sacrifice all worth it.

"Being sealed together in the temple brought a special spirit into our family," Kriangkrai testified. "Now, not only does our sixteen-year-old son want to go on a mission, but his two younger sisters want to go too."[16]

ON THE EVENING OF August 9, 1995, fifty-nine-year-old Celia Ayala de Cruz decided to walk to her Relief Society activity. She liked to be on time for meetings, and the person who had promised to give her a ride to the church had not shown up. Fortunately, the meetinghouse was only an eight-minute walk from her home. If she left right away, she could arrive at the church with a few minutes to spare. The activity was a quilting class, and she was teaching it.[17]

Celia lived in Ponce, a city on the southern coast of Puerto Rico, in the Caribbean Sea. Missionaries had been serving in the Caribbean since the 1960s, especially in Puerto Rico and later in the Dominican Republic, both of which now had tens of thousands of Saints. The restored gospel had also taken root in other island nations and territories, reaching people of diverse cultures, religions, languages, and ethnicities. Saints could now be found in cities, towns, and villages across the Caribbean.[18]

As she set out for her meeting, Celia carried a handbag containing a five-dollar bill and a gift-wrapped copy of the Book of Mormon. Ever since President Ezra Taft Benson had challenged the Saints to renew their focus on the Book of Mormon, she and other Church members had looked for opportunities to share the book with others. The Church's Family-to-Family Book of Mormon Program had encouraged Saints to write their testimonies on the inside of the book before giving it away.[19] At first, Latter-day Saints had to buy their own copies of the Book of Mormon, but in 1990, the Church set up a donation fund to provide the book free of charge to anyone in the world.[20]

Since joining the Church sixteen years earlier, Celia herself had read the Book of Mormon multiple times. Now, a coworker was having a difficult time in her marriage, and

Celia believed the book could help her. She had placed a copy in a gift box, wrapped it up in nice paper, and tied a ribbon around it. In the box, she had also included a postcard with her address and her written testimony of the Book of Mormon. She was bringing the book to church that evening to show her Relief Society sisters how they could share the Book of Mormon with others.[21]

When she neared the meetinghouse, Celia decided to take a shortcut behind a park. As she was passing through a gate, a tall young man with a knife jumped out at her. He shoved her, and she fell backward onto a patch of damp weeds.

"You are assaulting a servant of the Lord," Celia told him.

The young man said nothing. At first, Celia thought he was going to kill her. But then he snatched her bag and rummaged through it until he found the five-dollar bill and gift-wrapped Book of Mormon. A calm feeling rested over her. She knew the young man was not going to hurt her.

"Lord," she silently prayed, "if that's the way you have chosen for that boy to convert to the gospel, he's not going to kill me."

Clutching his knife, the young man took the money and Book of Mormon and ran off into the night.[22]

ACROSS THE ATLANTIC OCEAN, meanwhile, Willy Binene was still living with his family in Luputa, Zaire.

It wasn't the life he'd imagined as an electrical engineering student in Lubumbashi. Luputa was a farming community, and as long as ethnic strife remained near their home in Kolwezi, he and his family would stay in Luputa and work the land.[23]

Fortunately, Willy's father had taught him how to farm when he was a boy, so he already knew the basics of raising beans, corn, cassava, and peanuts. Until the first bean crop came in, however, the family had very little food to eat. They farmed for sustenance, and what little they could spare from their crops they sold to purchase salt, oil, soap, and some meat.[24]

Of the Saints who fled Kolwezi for safety, around fifty of them had settled in Luputa. There was no branch in the village, but they met together every week in a large house to worship. Although several men in the group held the priesthood, including the former Kolwezi District president, they did not feel authorized to hold sacrament meeting. Instead, they held a Sunday School class, with each elder taking a turn leading the meeting.

During this time, Willy and his fellow Saints made several efforts to contact the mission headquarters in Kinshasa, but without success. Still, whenever the Saints earned money, they set aside their tithing, waiting for a time when they could deliver it to an authorized Church leader.[25]

One day in 1995, Willy's family decided to send him back to Kolwezi to try to sell their old house. Knowing he would see the district president there, the

Saints in Luputa saw this as their best chance to pay tithing. They placed their money in envelopes, gave them to Willy and another Church member traveling with him, and sent them on their way.

Throughout the four-day train ride to Kolwezi, Willy hid the bag with the tithing envelopes under his clothing. He and his traveling companion were nervous and afraid during the journey. They slept on the train and only disembarked at stations to buy fufu and other food. They also worried about traveling into Kolwezi, which was still hostile to Kasaians. But they took comfort in the story of Nephi retrieving the plates of brass. They trusted that the Lord would protect them and their tithing.

When they finally arrived in Kolwezi, they found the home of the district president, and he invited them to stay with him. Several days later, the new leaders of the Zaire Kinshasa Mission, Roberto and Jeanine Tavella, came to the city, and the district president introduced them to Willy and his traveling companion.[26]

"They were members in the Kolwezi Branch," the district president explained. "Because of what happened, they moved to Luputa. And now they've come. They wanted to meet you."

"Tell me more," President Tavella said. "You're from Luputa?"

Willy told the president about their journey and how far they'd traveled. He then took out the tithing envelopes. "This is the tithing of the members in Luputa," he said. "They set aside their tithing because they did not know where to take it."

Without saying a word, President and Sister Tavella began to weep. "What faith you have," the mission president finally said, his voice trembling.

Joy and peace flooded Willy. He believed that God would bless the Saints in Luputa for paying tithing. President Tavella counseled them to be patient. "When you get back, tell everyone in Luputa that I love them," he said. "They are blessed by the Eternal Father, because I've never seen such faith."

He promised to send one of his counselors to Luputa as soon as possible. "I don't know how long it will take," he said, "but the counselor will come."[27]

NOT LONG AFTER BEING robbed, Celia Ayala de Cruz checked her mailbox. Inside she found a one-page letter with no name attached. "Forgive me, forgive me," it read. "You will never know how sorry I am for attacking you."

Celia kept reading. The young man described how the Book of Mormon he stole had changed his life. When he first saw the gift-wrapped book, he thought it was something he could sell. But then he opened it and read the testimony Celia had written for her coworker. "The message you wrote in that book brought tears to my eyes," he told Celia. "Since Wednesday night, I have not been able to stop reading it."

The young man had been particularly moved by the story of Lehi. "The dream of that man of God has shaken me," he wrote, "and I thank God that I found you." He did not know if God would forgive him for stealing, but he hoped Celia could. "I am returning your five dollars," he added, "for I can't spend them." The money was with his letter.

He also wrote of his desire to learn more about the Church. "I want you to know that you will see me again, but when you do, you won't recognize me, for I will be your brother," he wrote. "I am not from your city, but here where I live, I have to find the Lord and go to the church you belong to."[28]

Celia sat down. Ever since the attack, she had been praying for the young man. "If God is willing," she said, "may that boy be converted."[29]

A few months later, the new year started. Sunday Schools throughout the Church began a yearlong study of the Book of Mormon. To assist the Saints in their studies, the *Church News* devoted its first issue of the year to the book. The issue included an overview of the Book of Mormon's teachings about Jesus Christ, various charts and articles to help readers better understand its peoples and events, and information about a new videocassette containing nine short Book of Mormon films to supplement Sunday School lessons. With Celia's permission, the final page of the newspaper featured a short account of her experience with the young man, including the full text of his letter.[30]

In February 1996, Celia received another letter from the young man. He was still too embarrassed about the robbery to tell Celia his name, but he had seen the story in the *Church News,* and he wanted her to know that he was doing well and trying to change his life. He thought often about her and the Book of Mormon. "I know that it is true," he wrote. In fact, he had recently joined the Church and received the priesthood. "I am working for the Lord," he told her.

He let her know that he now lived near a temple, which he had recently visited. Although he did not go inside the building, he had felt the Spirit powerfully there, and he knew it was the Lord's house.

The young man signed the letter as Celia's "brother of faith." He expressed his love for her and her family. He knew the Lord had a purpose for him.

"I don't want to leave the Lord's path," he told her. "I feel very happy."[31]

CHAPTER 29

One Great Family

In early 1996, in the Philippines, Iloilo Stake Relief Society president Maridan Nava Sollesta received good news from her stake president, Virgilio Garcia. A few months earlier, she had written to the Relief Society general presidency to request a visit from Chieko Okazaki, the first counselor to President Elaine L. Jack. Sister Okazaki's faith-promoting conference talks inspired Maridan, and she believed the women in her stake would benefit from hearing her speak in person. And now, President Garcia told her, Sister Okazaki had received an assignment to visit their stake.[1]

Recently, the Church had reached a significant milestone: there were more Saints outside the United States than within. Maridan and her husband, Seb, had both joined the Church more than a decade earlier. They were sealed in the Manila Temple in 1984, and they had since had three sons, who were now ages seven, nine, and ten. In the five years since Maridan's call as Relief Society president, the Church in the Philippines had grown by more than 80,000 members. The total membership in the country was 360,000 members, making it the fifth-largest population of Latter-day Saints in the world, surpassed only by the United States, Mexico, Brazil, and Chile.[2]

The number of general authorities from outside the United States was also increasing steadily. Already the First and Second Quorums of the Seventy had included such members as Angel Abrea from Argentina, Hélio da Rocha Camargo and Helvécio Martins from Brazil, Eduardo Ayala from Chile, Carlos H. Amado from Guatemala, Horacio A. Tenorio from Mexico, Yoshihiko Kikuchi from Japan, Han In Sang from South Korea, and Augusto A. Lim from the Philippines. In 1995, the First Presidency created the role of area authority to replace the position of regional representative, adding to the number of priesthood leaders around the world supporting local units. Sister Okazaki, who was born and raised in Hawaii, was the first person of Asian descent to serve in a general Church presidency.[3]

In Iloilo City, Maridan was witnessing the growth of the Church firsthand. There were now eight wards and six branches in her stake, and visiting every congregation was becoming more difficult for her and other stake leaders. Maridan owned and operated a pharmaceutical company, which kept her busy. But she did her best to minister to the women in her care. Although many new converts had grown into strong members, there were also many Saints in the Philippines who had stopped attending their Church meetings. Sometimes, when Maridan visited them, they would not talk to her. Others accepted her visits and appreciated the interest she took in them.[4]

As Maridan talked with these women, she learned that some were upset with fellow Church members. Others had lost their faith or returned to former ways of life. Some women had been unable to enjoy or get much from meetings because they did not know English or Tagalog, the two main languages the Church used in the Philippines. Although the Church had been working to make materials available in more of the country's nearly two hundred languages and dialects, communication was a major problem among Church members.[5]

Sister Okazaki arrived in Iloilo City on the morning of February 24, 1996. Maridan and President Garcia were part of a welcoming committee that met her, Elder Augusto A. Lim, and Sister Myrna Lim at the airport.

For the rest of the day, Maridan and the members of her stake were taught by Sister Okazaki and Elder Lim. In her first lesson, Sister Okazaki used Doctrine and Covenants 107 to emphasize the importance of learning and fulfilling one's duties in the Church. Later in the evening, she spoke to the entire stake about seeking blessings from Heavenly Father.

"My dear sisters and brothers," she said, "we can ask for the desires of our heart. We can ask with faith and with confidence. We know that a loving Father listens to us. He will willingly give us what we want when He can."[6]

The following day was Sunday, and Sister Okazaki attended meetings of the Iloilo City Ward. During that time, she instructed and encouraged Maridan to counsel with Relief Society sisters in their native language so they could understand her instruction. Before leaving that afternoon, Sister Okazaki gave Maridan a book about leadership.[7]

A few months later, Maridan and the other Filipino Saints had the chance to see another Church leader: President Gordon B. Hinckley. Since becoming Church president, he had traveled throughout the world visiting with Saints. In the Philippines, he visited Manila and Cebu City.

While in Manila, he answered questions about the Church for local television stations. One question referred to "The Family: A Proclamation to the World," a recent declaration by the First Presidency and Quorum of the Twelve Apostles. For many years, Church leaders had been concerned that traditional teachings about marriage and family were changing throughout the world. The proclamation affirmed that marriage between a man and woman was ordained of God and that the family was essential to His plan of salvation. It upheld the sanctity of life, declaring that all people were beloved sons and daughters of heavenly parents, created in the image of God, with a divine nature and destiny. It also urged parents to love their children and raise them in righteousness, working together as equal partners as they established a home based on "faith, prayer, repentance, forgiveness, respect, love, compassion, work, and wholesome recreational activities."

"The family is the organization ordained of God," President Hinckley explained to the interviewer in the Philippines. "God is our Eternal Father, and we are His children, regardless of race, color, or whatever. We are all His children. We are part of His family."[8]

Later, while speaking to a coliseum full of thirty-five thousand Saints, he noted that people sometimes asked him why the Church was growing so rapidly in the Philippines.

"The answer is simply this," he said. "This Church stands as an anchor, a solid anchor of truth in a world of shifting values."

"Every man and every woman who joins this Church and clings to its teachings," he continued, "will live a better life, will be a happier man or woman, will carry in his or her heart a great love for the Lord and His ways."[9]

ONE EVENING IN MARCH 1996, Veronica Contreras stood with her husband, Felicindo, outside their ward building in Santiago, Chile. They had just moved to the capital from Panguipulli, a much smaller city in southern Chile, hoping to find better educational opportunities for their five children. They would also be closer to the Santiago Chile Temple and belong to a stake, which could provide established seminary classes and youth activities. Although it was not Sunday, the couple thought they might find some other Church members at the meetinghouse. But when they got there, they found the doors locked. No one was around.

Later in the week, the couple stopped a pair of missionaries on bicycles and asked them to help their family contact the bishop. Soon after, the bishop came to the Contrerases' house and welcomed them to the ward, but his visit did not prepare them for what awaited them on their first Sunday at church.

In Panguipulli, the Saints had treated their meetinghouse like their home, keeping it clean and well maintained. But when Veronica stepped into the meetinghouse in Santiago, she was surprised to find that the floors and walls were scuffed with shoe marks and tire skids from children riding their bicycles through the halls. During sacrament meeting, most of the pews sat empty, even though the ward had more than seven hundred members on the records.[10]

Sadly, the problems the Contrerases found in their new ward were not unique to Chile. The number of convert baptisms throughout South America had increased rapidly during the 1980s and early 1990s, leading to the creation of dozens of stakes. Yet many new members across the world struggled to maintain their commitment to the restored gospel after their baptisms.[11]

Church leaders had been concerned about retaining recent converts for years and had tried to address the issue in various ways. In 1986, the local priesthood office of seventy was dissolved, adding strength to local elders quorums.[12] Missionaries had also been encouraged to spend more time fellowshipping new members, and the Church created a series of six new-member lessons to help recent converts adapt. Yet many people never received these lessons. And wards like the one in Santiago were often overwhelmed by the enormity of the work. There were just so few members attending meetings compared to the total number of Saints in the ward.[13]

The Contrerases' new bishop was a good and faithful man, but he did not have any counselors to help share his workload. He also had to put in long hours at work and often couldn't meet with members on weekdays. When Veronica and Felicindo met with him, they offered to help by serving wherever they were needed. Soon, their oldest daughter was playing the organ in the ward, and their sons were serving with the other young men. Felicindo began assisting with family history and temple work and serving on the stake high council. Veronica, meanwhile, was called as the ward Relief Society president.

Others joined them in their service. But there was still much to do to help the ward function better.[14]

When the Hong Kong Temple was announced in October 1992, Nora Koot Jue was overjoyed. More than thirty years had passed since her service in the Southern Far East Mission. In that time, she had emigrated to the United States, married a Chinese American named Raymond Jue, and raised four children. But her experiences as an early Chinese convert to the Church in Hong Kong had never left her. They were the stories she had told her children at bedtime.

Raymond thought the entire family should go to the temple dedication.

"No," Nora said. "That's a lot of money."

Raymond insisted. "We have to go," he said.[15]

The family began saving money. The children were now adults, and they knew how important the house of the Lord was to their mother. When she emigrated to the United States in 1963, she had stopped first in Hawaii to receive her endowment in the temple in Laie. Later, she and Raymond were sealed in the Los Angeles Temple, and a short time after that, the Oakland Temple was dedicated near their home in California's San Francisco Bay Area. Nora and Raymond had eventually become temple workers there, giving Nora the opportunity to administer temple ordinances in Mandarin, Cantonese, Hmong, and other languages.[16]

After the Hong Kong Temple was finished in May 1996, the Church held a two-week open house. Nora and her family arrived in the city on the evening of May 23, three days before the temple dedication. When they stepped out of the airport, Nora felt the warm, humid air surround her.

"Welcome to Hong Kong," she told her family with a smile.[17]

Over the next few days, Nora took her family on a tour of the city. Her oldest daughter, Lorine, had also served a mission in Hong Kong, and they enjoyed revisiting the area together. As Nora showed her children the streets and buildings she once knew, the stories they had heard as children came alive. One of the first places she took them was the temple, built on the site of the old mission home where she had spent so much time as a young woman. Nora could not be happier to see the location put to such a sacred purpose.[18]

On the morning of Sunday, May 26, the family attended a special sacrament meeting with Nora's mission president, Grant Heaton, and other former missionaries from the Southern Far East Mission. During the meeting, President Heaton and the missionaries bore testimony. When Nora's turn came, she stood up. "The Spirit is burning within me," she testified. "I am a product of this land and of this mission. And I am grateful."[19]

The next morning, Nora and her family sat together in the celestial room of the Hong Kong Temple. Nora's face was bright and smiling as President Thomas S. Monson opened the meeting and Elder Neal A. Maxwell of the Quorum of the Twelve Apostles spoke. She felt as if her life had come full circle. Forty-two years earlier, she had pleaded with Elder Harold B. Lee to send the Church back to Hong Kong. There were only a handful of Saints in the city at that time. Now Hong Kong had a house of the Lord, and she was there with her husband and children.[20]

At the close of the meeting, President Thomas S. Monson read the dedicatory prayer. "Thy Church has grown and blessed the lives of many of Thy sons and daughters in this place," he prayed. "We thank Thee for all who have accepted the gospel and who have remained true and faithful to covenants made with Thee. Thy Church in this area now comes to full maturity with the dedication of this sacred temple."[21]

Tears streamed down Nora's face as everyone sang "The Spirit of God." When the benediction was over, she gathered her husband and children in her arms and embraced them. Her heart was full.[22]

That evening, the family attended a mission reunion. They arrived a little late and found everyone already chatting together in a room. The crowd quieted when Nora entered, and her family watched in awe as person after person greeted her with honor and respect.

While Nora chatted with old friends, an old man tapped her on the shoulder. "Do you remember me?" he asked.

Nora looked at him, and a flash of recognition crossed her face. It was Harold Smith, one of the first missionaries she had met as a young girl. She introduced him to her children.

"I didn't think I made a difference," he told her. He couldn't believe she remembered him.

"You don't forget people who save you," Nora said.[23]

IN MAY 1997, THE government of Zaire collapsed after years of warfare and political turmoil. President Mobutu Sese Seko, who had controlled the nation for more than three decades, was dying, and he was now powerless to stop the demise of his regime. Armed forces from Rwanda, Zaire's neighbor to the east, had entered the country in search of exiled rebels from its own civil war. Other eastern African nations had soon followed, ultimately joining forces with other groups to oust the weakened president, replace him with a new leader, and rename the country the Democratic Republic of the Congo, or DRC.[24]

The Church continued to function in the region as the conflict raged. Around six thousand Saints lived in the DRC. The Kinshasa Mission covered five countries with seventeen full-time missionaries. In July 1996, several couples from the region had traveled over seventeen hundred miles to receive their temple blessings in the Johannesburg South Africa Temple. A few months later, on November 3, Church leaders organized the Kinshasa Stake, the first stake in the DRC and the first French-speaking stake in Africa. There were also five districts and twenty-six branches spread throughout the mission.[25]

In Luputa, Willy Binene, now twenty-seven years old, still hoped to serve a full-time mission, despite the unrest in his country. But when he shared his hope to Ntambwe Kabwika, a counselor in the mission presidency, he received disappointing news.[26]

"My brother," President Kabwika told him, "the age limit is twenty-five years. There is no way to call you on a mission." Then, trying to console him, he added, "You are still young. You can go to school, get married."

But Willy did not feel consoled. Disappointment welled up inside of him. It seemed unfair that his age prevented him from serving a mission. Why couldn't an exception be made, especially after all that had happened to him? He wondered why the Lord had inspired him to serve a mission in the first place. He had postponed his education and career to follow that prompting—and for what?

"You can't be troubled by this," he eventually told himself. "You can't very well condemn God." He resolved to stay right where he was and do all the Lord asked of him.[27]

Later, in July 1997, the Saints in Luputa were formally organized into a branch. After Willy was called as a financial clerk and branch missionary, he came to realize the Lord had been preparing him to establish the Church where he lived. "OK," he said, "my mission is here."[28]

A few other Saints in the Luputa Branch were also called as branch missionaries. Three days a week,

Willy tended his crops. The other days he would go door-to-door telling people about the gospel. Afterward, Willy would wash his only pair of trousers so they would be clean the next day. He wasn't quite sure what drove him to preach the gospel so diligently, especially at times when he had to go out on an empty stomach. But he knew that he loved the gospel, and he wanted his people—and someday his ancestors—to have the blessings he had.[29]

The work could be challenging. Some people threatened the branch missionaries or warned others to avoid them. A few people in the village even gathered together to destroy copies of the Book of Mormon. "Burn the Book of Mormon," they'd say, "and the Church will disappear."[30]

Yet Willy saw the Lord work miracles through his efforts. Once, when he and his companion knocked on a door, it opened into a foul-smelling house. From inside, they heard a quiet voice calling out to them. "Come in," it said. "I'm sick."

Willy and his companion were afraid to enter the house, but they stepped inside and found a man who seemed to be wasting away. "Can we pray?" they asked.

The man agreed, so they offered a prayer, blessing him that his disease would go away. "We'll be back tomorrow," they told him.

The next day, they found the man outside his house. "You are men of God," he said. Since their prayer, he had been feeling better. He wanted to jump for joy.

The man was not yet ready to join the Church, but others were. Every week, Willy and the other missionaries met people—sometimes whole families—who wanted to worship with the Saints. On some Saturdays, they baptized up to thirty people.

The Church in Luputa was beginning to grow.[31]

ON JUNE 5, 1997, PRESIDENT Gordon B. Hinckley stood at a pulpit beneath a large canopy in Colonia Juárez, Mexico. Around six thousand people were seated in front of him. "Some people in the Church feel a little sorry for you," he joked with the audience. "You seem to be so far away from everybody."[32]

Church members from the United States had settled Colonia Juárez and other towns in northern Mexico during the U.S. government's raids against plural marriage in the 1880s. These towns were situated in the arid Chihuahuan Desert, about two hundred miles from any major city. Their local Church-run school, the Juárez Academy, was turning one hundred years old, and President Hinckley had come to commemorate the occasion.[33]

President Hinckley knew the history of the Colonia Juárez Saints, and he admired their determination to keep the faith. "You have helped one another in times of trouble and distress. You had to because you were alone," he told them. "You have become as one great family."[34]

The next day, President Hinckley spoke at the school's graduation ceremony and rededicated the newly remodeled academy building. Meredith Romney, the president of the Colonia Juárez Stake, then drove him two hundred miles north to the airport in El Paso, Texas.[35]

The road to El Paso was rough and bumpy. At first, President Hinckley passed the time talking with President Romney. But after a while the conversation lulled, and President Hinckley quietly reflected on the Colonia Juárez Saints and the great distance they had to travel to attend the house of the Lord. "What can we do to help these people?" he wondered.[36]

The question was relevant to Saints all around the world. With more than a dozen temples currently planned or under construction, 85 percent of Church members would soon be within three hundred miles of a temple.[37] In northern Brazil, for example, Saints who had formerly traveled thousands of miles to attend the temple in São Paulo would be much closer to the new temple in Recife, a city on Brazil's northeastern coast. A newly announced temple in Campinas, a city some sixty miles north of São Paulo, would likewise make the blessings of the temple more available to Brazil's six hundred thousand Saints. Soon, temples would also be needed in cities like Porto Alegre, Manaus, Curitiba, Brasília, Belo Horizonte, and Rio de Janeiro.[38]

But President Hinckley wanted to bring temples even closer to more Saints. He believed the house of the Lord played a vital role in helping Church members stay committed to the restored gospel of Christ. Recently, the prophet had learned that only 20 percent of new converts were still attending and participating in the Church after one year. The startling percentage troubled him and his counselors, and in May they had sent a letter to all Church members.[39]

"We are deeply concerned about many of our brothers and sisters of all ages who have received a testimony of the gospel of Jesus Christ but have not felt the sustaining warmth of fellowship among the Saints," the letter read. "Too many are not receiving the blessings of the priesthood and the covenant promises of the temple."

"Every new member needs three things," the letter continued, "a friend, a responsibility, and spiritual nourishment through gospel study."[40]

In Colonia Juárez, President Hinckley realized, the Church had nearly everything it needed to provide this kind of support for local Saints. The only thing it lacked was a house of the Lord. The same was true for stakes in other remote places across the globe. But it was hard to justify building temples in places where there were not enough Saints to use and maintain them.

He thought about the high cost of laundry and cafeteria facilities in temples. Both features provided a convenient service for temple patrons. But what if the patrons brought their own temple clothes and found food elsewhere?[41]

For years, President Hinckley had thought about modifying the design of some temples in order to build more of them around the world. Already, the Church had adapted temple designs to meet the needs of local Saints in places like Laie, São Paulo, Freiberg, and Hong Kong. Why not build a temple with just the essentials: a baptistry and rooms for confirmations, initiatories, endowments, and sealings? If the Church did so, the Lord's house could be established in lands far and wide, bringing sacred covenants and ordinances closer to many more Saints.[42]

Later, President Hinckley sketched out a simple floor plan for the kind of temple he envisioned. The inspiration came clear and strong. When he arrived in Salt Lake City, he showed it to President Monson and President Faust, and they approved the concept. The Quorum of the Twelve Apostles also supported the idea.

Finally, President Hinckley brought the sketch to a Church architect. The architect examined the drawing. "Beautiful," he said. "It's a very workable concept."[43]

PART 4

Always There
1997–2020

"I know this work is the Lord's work, because I have felt His hand constantly in every detail of what we do. In ways that I cannot even describe or tell, His hand was always there."

Silvia Allred

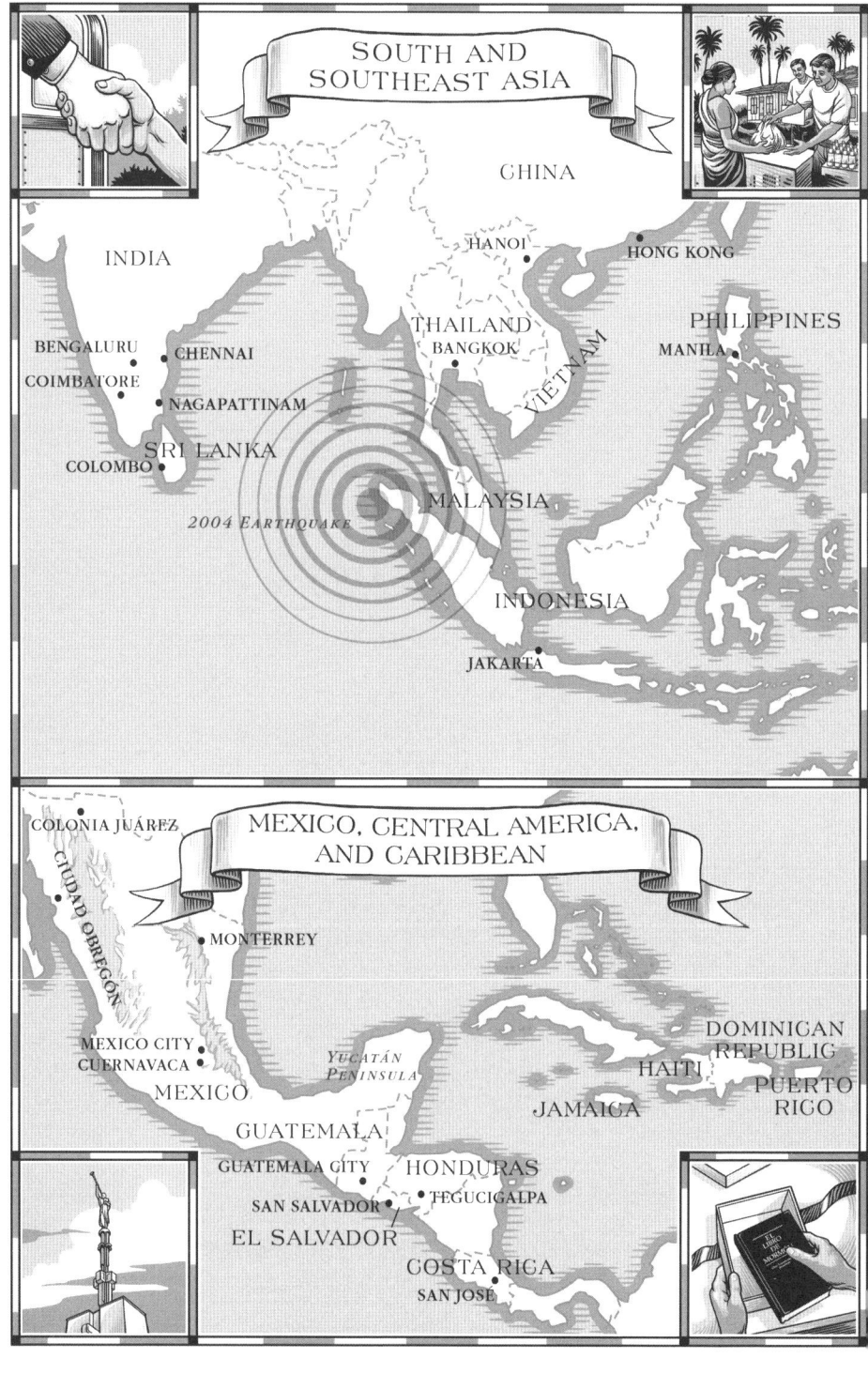

CHAPTER 30

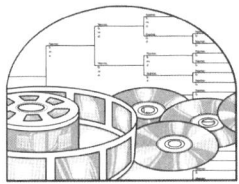

Precious Blessings

On the evening of October 4, 1997, during the priesthood session of general conference, President Gordon B. Hinckley announced the new temple design and spoke of the Church's plan to use the pattern for several new temples around the world.

"We are determined," he declared, "to take the temples to the people and afford them every opportunity for the very precious blessings that come of temple worship."[1]

Richard "Rick" Turley, managing director of the Church's Family History Department, understood that these new temples would bless the Church and help Saints around the world come to Christ. But the department could barely supply all fifty-one operating temples with enough names for vicarious ordinance work. With temple construction now on the rise, the Church had to change how it did family history.[2]

Part of the problem, Rick and other Church leaders knew, was that preparing names for temple work was time-consuming and costly. In some countries, Church members had to travel great distances to find their ancestors' names in archival records. Other members had to search long and hard for the information they needed. If the right microfilm wasn't at their local family history center, they would have to pay to have it shipped, wait several weeks for it to arrive, and then return to the center to view it. A typical roll held about a thousand images, so cranking through each one could be laborious. Few people had time for all this—and not everyone lived near a family history center.[3]

Personal computers sped up some of this work in the 1980s. Early in the decade, Church software developers created Personal Ancestral File, a computer program that allowed people to record, store, and share information about their ancestors and build family trees. The program also made it easier for hundreds of thousands of users to submit names to the temple through TempleReady.[4]

Yet the submission process could still be complicated, especially for people who weren't used to personal computers. Users of PAF created their own personal database, often resulting in duplicate records when someone submitted family names to the Church. Since these files did not automatically update after someone did temple work for an ancestor, different Church members often performed ordinances for the same person without knowing it.[5]

Such problems troubled President Hinckley as well. Two years earlier, when Rick joined the Family History Department, the prophet had called him into a meeting. He wanted to know whether the Church was doing all it could to fulfill its mission to redeem the dead.

"Rick," the prophet said, "can you assure me that all of the resources that we're putting into family history are freeing spirits from spirit prison?"

"I'd like to think that we are," Rick replied. But he believed the system could be improved.

President Hinckley agreed and asked him to fix it.[6]

With this mandate, the Family History Department needed to develop a simpler way of submitting names for temple work—a process simple enough that more people would get involved. Computers could speed up the process of extracting family information from records and organizing it in a searchable database. But to prevent duplication, the computers had to communicate with each other—something the current system could not do. The database needed to be on the internet.

At the time, the World Wide Web was less than a decade old, and the Church had only a small online presence. It had launched a website without much fanfare in 1996, and some Church leaders remained skeptical of the new technology and had little experience with it. The Family History Department lacked the technical expertise to build the kind of online platform required to host the database. They needed help—and they needed time.[7]

And already the clock was ticking. At the April 1998 general conference, President Hinckley announced that the Church would build thirty temples following the new pattern, in addition to the seventeen temples already under construction.

"This will make a total of forty-seven new temples in addition to the fifty-one now in operation," the prophet said. "I think we had better add two more to make it an even hundred by the end of this century, being two thousand years 'since the coming of our Lord and Savior Jesus Christ in the flesh.'"

"We are moving on a scale the like of which we have never seen," he said.[8]

The announcement inspired Rick. But now there was an even greater urgency to speed up the Church's family history work.

The year 2000 was not far away.[9]

IN EARLY APRIL 1998, Felicindo and Veronica Contreras went to the Santiago Chile Temple. Felicindo had just been called to serve as the bishop of their ward, and he was concerned about the Saints under his care. Attendance in the ward was still low. He wanted to ask for the Lord's help in bringing his ward members back to church.

As Felicindo prayed, he yearned especially to help the youth. Few of them attended church regularly, and although fourteen of them were old enough to go on missions, no one was preparing to serve. They were part of a larger trend in Chile, where less than 10 percent of eligible young men were on missions, the lowest percentage in any area worldwide. In his heart, Felicindo longed for the youth to return to church and prepare themselves for the mission field.[10]

A short time later, an eighteen-year-old named Juan came to Sunday meetings for the first time in a while. Juan was a member of the priests quorum, but he usually skipped church so he could play soccer. He was a talented player—good enough that some people thought he could play professionally—and the sport meant everything to him. But lately, he'd felt lonely, restless, and confused. The Spirit was prompting him to return to church and serve a mission. But he felt like he needed a guide to help him make changes in his life.

At church, he asked to speak with Felicindo. "I have decided to get active," he said.

"I was waiting for you," Felicindo said. He invited Juan to his office for an interview. They talked about Juan's desire to prepare for a mission. Knowing that missionary work required young men and women to meet certain spiritual, moral, emotional, and physical standards, Felicindo helped him draw up a plan.

"First, we're going to prepare for you to receive your patriarchal blessing," he told Juan, "so that you know what the Lord has to tell you." After that, they would work on his missionary application. Felicindo also invited him to read the Book of Mormon and pay his tithing. Juan accepted the challenge, and from that moment on, he and Felicindo spoke regularly about mission preparation.[11]

Felicindo worked with other ward members as well. He was impressed by the First Presidency's counsel that every member have a friend, a responsibility, and nurturing with the "good word of God." Following new guidelines from Church headquarters, he and the full-time missionaries made sure that people attended sacrament meeting before they joined the Church. He and other ward members also ensured that everyone who came to church felt welcome and returned home spiritually fed.

When he invited people to come back to church, Felicindo encouraged them to prepare to take the sacrament and renew their baptismal covenants. He asked returning members to attend the Gospel Essentials Sunday School class to help them remember basic teachings about the Creation, the Atonement of Jesus Christ, repentance, and other principles of the gospel. And he found ways for them to serve in the ward.[12]

He also arranged for the meetinghouse to be open during the week. He received permission to light the court behind the building so youth could play soccer and other games in the evening. Ward members began using the meetinghouse for home evenings and other activities, like plays and Chilean cultural programs. Felicindo helped organize a ward choir, and their music added to the Spirit in sacrament meeting.

As members of the ward spent more time at the meetinghouse, they started taking better care of it, and their love for the building grew. Soon, Felicindo saw improvement in sacrament meeting attendance. He believed these changes were answers to his prayer in the temple.[13]

A FEW MONTHS LATER, in the middle of 1998, Mary McKenna, a returned missionary from Brisbane, Australia, traveled to Provo, Utah, to learn more about Especially for Youth, a five-day conference for young Latter-day Saints in the United States. Mary had heard a lot about EFY a year earlier while attending Education Week—a series of classes, devotionals, and other activities for adults and teenagers held each year on the campus of Brigham Young University.

During her earlier visit, she had attended a class taught by Brad Wilcox, a popular speaker and author among English-speaking Latter-day Saint youth. After class, she had stopped to talk with him about Education Week.

"This probably sounds really crazy," she had said, "but I'm a youth leader in Australia, and we need what you've got."[14]

In the century and a half since the first branch was organized in Australia, the Church there had grown to nearly one hundred thousand members. There were stakes in almost every major Australian city and a temple in Sydney. But many youth were struggling, and some were not going on to serve missions, get married in the temple, or stay active in the Church. They felt disconnected from each other and needed role models who could show them how to stay close to God and live His commandments.[15]

As Brad had listened to Mary talk about the challenges of youth in Australia, tears had welled up in his eyes, and he told her more about EFY. Like typical stake youth conferences, EFY was designed to strengthen the faith of young people. But rather than being run by local stakes, it was sponsored by BYU and supervised by young single adult counselors. Hearing Brad describe how joyful it was for the youth, Mary had felt that an experience like EFY could help young women and men in Australia.

She had spent the next several months working to make the idea a reality. Church leaders in and around Brisbane had been supportive, forming a committee of Saints from local stakes to organize an event like EFY in their area.

Now, one year later, Mary was back in Provo meeting with Susan Overstreet, the director of EFY, on BYU's campus. The university was unable to sponsor EFY sessions outside North America, but Susan had been helping Mary and the Brisbane committee. She took Mary to a counselor training event and introduced her to other EFY leaders. Meanwhile, Brad Wilcox and another EFY speaker, Matt Richardson, agreed to come to Australia and speak at the event.[16]

Mary returned to Australia, and over the next few months, the committee met regularly to plan the event, with each participating stake taking the lead in planning the food, housing, devotionals, music, and other responsibilities. Stake presidents recommended additional speakers, and Mary found young adults to serve as counselors. Some were returned missionaries, some were preparing for missions, and others had no plans to serve a mission at all. Mary arranged training courses for everyone.

The committee hoped to make EFY welcoming for all youth in the Brisbane area, not just Latter-day Saints. Unlike the program in the United States, which cost hundreds of dollars to attend, the Australian EFY would be subsidized by local stakes so people could attend at a low cost. And while everyone in attendance was expected to uphold Church standards at the conference, the committee encouraged stakes to invite youth who were not members.[17]

In April 1999, Mary and her committee launched the first Especially for Youth event outside of North America at a stake center in Brisbane. Nearly a thousand teenagers from the city and the surrounding area came. When Brad and Matt got in front of the crowd, the first thing they did was lead them in some cheers. The youth were a bit taken aback, but they joined in enthusiastically. It was immediately clear that EFY was not a typical Church conference.

Over the next few days, the youth learned from speakers, sang songs, enjoyed dances and talent shows, and shared their testimonies. Photographers, meanwhile, snapped pictures for a slideshow on the last day.[18]

Mary was thrilled by how much the youth and their counselors enjoyed EFY. Everyone who took part in the event, it seemed, went home with stronger faith in Jesus Christ. Counselors who hadn't planned on serving missions changed their minds and submitted their missionary applications. Some of the youth who weren't members of the Church when they attended went on to meet with missionaries and accept baptism. And young single adult counselors returned to their wards wanting to serve in Young Women and Young Men.

Especially for Youth had gone incredibly well in Brisbane—and Mary and the committee were ready to do it again.[19]

ON THE PACIFIC ISLAND of Fiji, meanwhile, Juliet Toro and her husband, Iliesa, had never had much interest in the Church. That changed when their older children, prodded by Juliet's Latter-day Saint mother, began attending Sunday meetings and weekday seminary classes. Juliet decided it was time to invite the missionaries over to teach her. And when they did, she liked what she heard.

The Toro children joined the Church in March 1999, and Juliet followed two weeks later. Iliesa, however, continued to show little interest. Fearing her husband would be the only one in the family to not embrace the restored gospel of Jesus Christ, Juliet began praying earnestly that he too would join the Church.[20]

At the time of Juliet's baptism, the Church in Fiji had four stakes and around twelve thousand members. The Fijian Saints were eagerly awaiting the construction of a temple in Suva, the capital city where Juliet and her family lived. After the Church came to Fiji in the mid-1950s, members often made immense financial sacrifices to attend the house of the Lord in Hawaii or New Zealand. This burden was reduced in 1983, when the Church dedicated temples in Samoa, Tonga, and Tahiti. Still, traveling to the Nukuʻalofa Tonga Temple, the nearest of the three, remained expensive.

When President Gordon B. Hinckley had named Fiji as the site for one of the thirty new temples, the Fijian Saints rejoiced. Having a house of the Lord in Suva would allow them and the Saints in the island nations of Vanuatu, New Caledonia, Kiribati, Nauru, and Tuvalu to attend the temple more regularly—and with much lower travel costs.[21]

Temple construction began in May 1999, two months after Juliet's baptism. Around that time, she learned that Brigham Young University was trying out a distance learning program at the Fiji LDS Technical College, a Church-owned secondary school in Suva.

BYU's slogan was "The World Is Our Campus," and the school's administrators were looking for affordable ways to bring educational opportunities to more Church members around the globe. The internet enabled professors in Provo to communicate with students in Fiji almost instantaneously.

The program enrolled secondary school graduates in several university-level classes. Knowledgeable student facilitators from BYU would administer the classes in person, while the BYU professors who created the courses would provide online support from six thousand miles away. For a small application fee, students could earn credit toward a university degree.[22]

The program interested Juliet. She and Iliesa had been university students when they first met, but they had left school to work and eventually started a family. For over a decade, Juliet had been raising her children at home. She wanted to further her education, so she spoke with Iliesa about it. He agreed that she should enroll.[23]

On the first day of class, Juliet and the other students introduced themselves. Many were young Church members, just out of secondary school or newly returned from full-time missions. Only a handful of students were in their early thirties, like Juliet.[24]

As classes began, Juliet was worried that she was too old to go back to school. The classes focused primarily on developing practical business skills. Over the course of two semesters, she and her fifty-five classmates would take courses in accounting, business management, economics, English, organizational behavior, and the Doctrine and Covenants. Juliet didn't think she knew as much as the younger students, and she was nervous that someone might find out how little she knew. The last thing she wanted was to look foolish in class.[25]

On a Thursday evening, not long after school started, James Jacob, the director of the program, told Juliet that she needed to attend a meeting that night at a nearby Church building.

Confused, she followed James to the building. When they got there, she found half her ward waiting for her in the chapel. She then saw Iliesa, dressed in white baptismal clothes. He had been receiving the missionary discussions in secret. And now he was ready to join her and their children in the Church.

Tears of joy flooded Juliet's eyes. She knew God had heard her prayers. Her family was finally united in faith. And one day, she hoped, they would be sealed in the house of the Lord.[26]

As the Church began its rapid construction of temples, leaders authorized the Family History Department to create a searchable online family history database. The department hired a technology company to develop an online platform and interface, and the Family History staff readied the data for the new website. By September, the tech company had produced a working prototype, giving Rick Turley and his team hope that they could have the database ready for testing in a matter of months.[27]

In the meantime, the team considered names like Ancestors, RootSearch, and KindredQuest for the database. Ultimately, the Family History Department settled on a name they were already using for their collection of databases distributed on CD-ROM: FamilySearch.[28]

As anticipated, the database was ready for testing in early 1999. The new website provided access to the records of four hundred million deceased people and allowed users to share information with others. No one was sure how well Church members would adapt to using an online database for their family history work. But the team built the site to handle five million visitors at a time.[29]

During testing, someone leaked the web address, and FamilySearch.org got more than three million page hits. A few days later, it had eleven million. Stunned, Rick and his team increased the website's capacity to make sure it was ready for public use on its launch date.[30]

In May, Rick flew to Washington, DC, for one of two simultaneous launch events. While Elder D. Todd Christofferson of the presidency of the Seventy conducted the event at the Family History Library in Salt Lake City, Rick and Elder Russell M. Nelson conducted an event at the National Press Club in Washington. Rick was pleased with the attention already surrounding the website. By the morning of the launch, it was receiving some thirty million hits a day, all without being publicized. People from every continent—even Antarctica—were visiting it.³¹

"Thank you for making it available through the internet!" wrote one user. "A big time-saver for me. I can work at home and still cook dinner and do the laundry—all at the same time!"

"I cannot praise your website enough," wrote another. "Starting here, while at home, will save me a lot of time in the family history center."³²

The following day, Rick represented the Church on the *Today* show, a popular morning television program in the United States. He sat in a director's chair in front of cameras with host Katie Couric. Between them was a computer displaying the new FamilySearch website.

"Tracing our family roots has become a very popular hobby," Katie said as she introduced Rick to the audience. "Now the world's largest collection of genealogical records has gone online."

Katie's first question was about the Church. "Why do Mormons have such extensive genealogical records?" she asked.

"We believe that families can be eternal," Rick said. "To allow our members to do research, we collect records from around the world."

Using the names of one of his ancestors and one of Katie's, he then showed the television audience how to access the site's databases and find information about their ancestors. Katie was impressed by how easy the website made it for people to do family history work.

"Do you get charged for using this?" she asked.

"There's no charge at all," said Rick.[33]

Within a few days, FamilySearch.org was overwhelmed with about one hundred million hits. The website was off to a remarkable start.[34]

CHAPTER 31

Mysterious Ways

On October 26, 1999, Georges A. Bonnet was waiting for President Gordon B. Hinckley to stand up. A budget appropriations meeting with the First Presidency, Presiding Bishopric, and various general authorities and Church administrators had just ended at the Church Administration Building in Salt Lake City. Georges did not usually attend the meeting—he was there in place of the managing director of the Physical Facilities Department—but he knew the meeting wasn't really over until President Hinckley was on his feet and heading for the door.

And the prophet did not appear to be going anywhere. Instead, he looked right at Georges and asked, "What are we going to do about the Ghana Temple?" His eyes were pleading for an answer.[1]

Georges didn't know what to say. The question took him completely by surprise. Nearly a decade earlier, while serving as the director for temporal affairs in Africa, he had helped end the Ghanaian government's freeze on all Church activities by encouraging Isaac Addy, a Church member in Accra, to reconcile with his estranged half-brother, Ghanaian president Jerry Rawlings.

Georges had earned the respect of Church leaders for his work in Ghana. But he now had a new job in the Church, and it wasn't related to Africa. The only thing he knew about the Ghana Temple was that President Hinckley had announced it back in February 1998.

"I'm sorry," Georges finally said, "but I'm not involved with the project."[2]

President Hinckley remained seated, the pleading look still in his eyes. He told Georges that progress on the temple was at a standstill. At first, the Ghanaian government had seemed supportive of the project, and the Church had purchased property on a main thoroughfare in Accra. But then, just before the planned groundbreaking in April 1999, the government had refused to issue a building permit to the Church. No one knew why.[3]

After the meeting, Georges walked back to the Church Office Building with Presiding Bishop H. David Burton and his second counselor, Keith B. McMullin. They were eager to know what Georges thought the Church had to do to get permission to build the temple in Accra.

"Would you mind going to Ghana?" one of them asked.

"Not at all," Georges said. "I'd be glad to go."[4]

A few weeks later, Georges arrived in Ghana and found the Church thriving there. At the time of the freeze, there were nearly nine thousand Church members and no stakes in Ghana. Now, ten years later, the country had five stakes with more than seventeen thousand members. And those members were praying earnestly for progress to resume on the house of the Lord. When President Hinckley visited Ghana in 1998, the Saints had stood and cheered when he announced the temple. No one could have anticipated the delays.[5]

In Accra, Georges met with the temple architect, Church attorneys, and government officials. He also met with Elder Glenn L. Pace, the Africa West Area president, who was grateful for Georges's help. Georges could tell Elder Pace was deeply frustrated by the situation. But he still had hope. Recently, the Saints in West Africa had held a special fast for the temple, and Elder Pace believed change was on the horizon.

After a week of meetings, Georges extended his trip another week to piece together his findings. According to people he spoke to, representatives of the Church had unwittingly offended the Accra Metropolitan Assembly, the government organization that approved building projects in the city. The AMA believed the representatives had been too insistent and arrogant during the permit approval process. There also seemed to be some resistance from President Rawlings, who was no longer on speaking terms with his brother, despite their reconciliation during the freeze.

Georges shared what he learned with Elder Pace, and together they prepared a report for the Presiding Bishopric. Georges then returned to Utah with report in hand, satisfied that he had done his part in Ghana.[6]

BACK IN FIJI, JULIET Toro was enjoying BYU's distance learning program. Her classes were unlike anything she'd ever experienced. Growing up, she'd always been afraid to ask questions in school, worried her teachers would ridicule her for saying the wrong thing. But she soon found that the classroom facilitators encouraged questions and never made her feel foolish. She also felt the Lord's Spirit in the classroom, guiding her learning.[7]

Juliet's first term was extremely challenging. Her hardest class was business management. Although she was already familiar with some basic business principles, Juliet was often overwhelmed by the many new terms and definitions she learned in class. At the end of the term, she felt like there was too much to review for the exam. But she scored well on the test and earned the highest final grade in the class.[8]

Her religion and accounting classes posed other challenges. As a new Latter-day Saint, she was unfamiliar with the Doctrine and Covenants, so she got help from her fellow student Sera Balenagasau, a lifelong Church member who had served a full-time mission. For accounting, she turned to her husband, Iliesa. Until recently, he had worked at a bank, so he understood the subject well and could help her work out problems. At the end of the term, she had top marks in these classes as well.[9]

Since Juliet's house was across the street from the school, it became a place for the students to gather and study. Her classmates often helped prepare meals and tidy up the home. Juliet enjoyed having them as friends and was cheered by their willingness to serve her and her family. Watching them was like seeing the gospel in action.[10]

The second term began on September 1, 1999. Some of the students who had not done well wanted to retake their exams to improve their grades, so summary courses were created for them. And since Juliet had done so well in the first term, she was brought on as a facilitator for the business management students.

For the next three months, Juliet juggled her studies with her other responsibilities as a facilitator and a mother. She treated the five young men in her business management summary course like they were her sons. As the term progressed, she could tell they were more comfortable around her than around their facilitators from BYU. They spoke freely in class and seemed less reluctant to ask her questions. At the end of the term, they all passed the exam.

One day, the program directors called Juliet and told her that she was the valedictorian.

"What's that?" she asked.

To her surprise, it meant that she'd had the best academic performance of all her classmates that year. Her confidence swelled. "Yes," she told herself. "I can do this."

A short time later, the program held a graduation ceremony for the students and around four hundred family members and friends. The graduates, wearing blue caps and gowns from the Fiji LDS Technical College, received recognition for completing the program. Juliet and several others also received introductory business certificates from BYU–Hawaii. Juliet offered the valedictory speech.[11]

Afterward, Iliesa expressed his and Juliet's gratitude in a letter to Elder Henry B. Eyring, the commissioner of Church education. "My wife and I always wondered whether we would be able to further our education," he wrote. "It seemed like our silent prayers have been answered. The Lord does work in mysterious ways."[12]

ON JANUARY 1, 2000, THE First Presidency and Quorum of the Twelve Apostles issued "The Living Christ: The Testimony of the Apostles," a signed declaration honoring the Savior two millennia after His birth. "We encourage you to use this written testimony in helping to build the faith of our Heavenly Father's children," the First Presidency counseled.

The declaration bore collective witness of Jesus's divine mission throughout time and eternity. "We offer our testimony of the reality of His matchless life and the infinite virtue of His great atoning sacrifice," the apostles declared. "None other has had so profound an influence upon all who have lived and will yet live upon the earth."[13]

Three months later, during the April 2000 general conference, the Church released *Special Witnesses of Christ,* an hour-long film featuring each member of the First Presidency and Quorum of the Twelve Apostles bearing personal testimony of the Savior.

The film opened with President Hinckley walking the sunlit halls of the BYU Jerusalem Center. "This great and ancient city," he said, stopping at a balcony, "has always been an inspiration to me. It is so because this place bears the imprint of the Son of God."

He then recounted the story of Jesus, from His birth in Bethlehem to His Resurrection from the tomb. "None can fully comprehend the splendor of His life, the majesty of His death, the universality of His gift to mankind," the prophet testified. "We declare with the centurion, who said at His death, 'Truly this man was the Son of God.'"[14]

Following this introduction, the film moved from one apostle's testimony to another. Each sequence took place in a different location. Some apostles spoke in front of temples while others spoke at historic places like Palmyra, Kirtland, and Nauvoo.

Standing beneath a powerful telescope at an observatory, Elder Neal A. Maxwell testified of the Savior's universal influence. "Long before He was born at Bethlehem and became known as Jesus of Nazareth, our Savior was Jehovah," he testified. "Way back then, under the direction of the Father, Christ was the Lord of the universe, who created worlds without number—of which ours is only one."

"Yet in the vastness of His creations," Elder Maxwell continued, "the Lord of the universe, who notices the fall of every sparrow, is our personal Savior."

Elder Henry B. Eyring, the newest member of the Quorum of the Twelve Apostles, spoke from the east steps of the Salt Lake Temple. "Dedicated temples are sacred places where the risen Savior may come," he declared. "Every part of these buildings and all that goes on inside them reflect the love of the Savior for us and our love for Him."

Walking reverently across the foundation of the old Nauvoo Temple, President James E. Faust bore witness of the Savior and His sacrifice. "I know that through the unspeakable agony of the Atonement, men and women, if they repent, can be forgiven of their sins," he said. "Because of the miracle of the Resurrection, all will rise from the dead. I feel His love and marvel at the price He paid for each of us."

The film closed with a final testimony from President Hinckley as he and his fellow apostles stood in front of the *Christus* statue on Temple Square.

"It is He, Jesus Christ, who stands at the head of this Church which bears His sacred name," the prophet declared. "Unitedly, as His apostles, authorized and commissioned by Him to do so, we bear our witness that He lives and that He will come again to claim His kingdom and rule as King of kings and Lord of lords."[15]

ON MAY 19, 2000, SIX months after Juliet Toro's graduation, armed militants forced their way into the Parliament of Fiji and took the nation's prime minister and dozens of other government officials hostage. The crisis quickly developed into a full-scale coup d'état. Violence and lawlessness enveloped the country for several days.[16]

Juliet was in tears as she watched reports of the coup on television. At first, everyone was put on lockdown. Businesses closed, schools shut down, and churches stopped meeting. Then the restrictions eased up, and Juliet's two oldest children went to a movie with their cousins and a friend from church. But soon after they left, violence again erupted in Suva, throwing the city into chaos. Juliet was frantic when she heard the news. Three hours passed. When her children finally made it home, she held them tight.[17]

The coup began after construction on the Suva Fiji Temple had finished, and the Saints were preparing for an open house and dedication in June. Now many Church members wondered if these events would be postponed until the upheaval was over.[18]

On May 29, the president of Fiji resigned, and the military seized control of the government. Two days later, President Hinckley called Roy Bauer, the president of the Suva Fiji Mission, to ask about conditions there. President Bauer informed him that the country was relatively stable under the military, despite the ongoing hostage situation. The airport in Suva had reopened, and it was again possible to travel around the city.

President Hinckley was satisfied. "I will see you next month," he said.[19]

The Saints in Fiji held a small temple open house in early June, attracting more than sixteen thousand visitors.

One Saturday, three buses arrived at the open house with people from other faiths. As one woman stepped off her bus, she had a wonderful feeling that only grew more powerful as she approached the temple. In the past, she had spoken against the Church. Now she regretted her words, and she prayed for forgiveness before entering the temple.

"Today I know this is the Lord's true church," she told one of the Saints she met during the tour. "Please send the missionaries."

Because of the coup, the First Presidency decided to hold only one dedicatory session instead of four, limiting the number of people who could attend the ceremony. Still, on June 18, the day of the dedication, Juliet and other Fijian Saints stood outside the temple along the main road.

The temple was situated at the top of a hill overlooking the Pacific Ocean. When the car carrying

President Hinckley and his wife, Marjorie, drove slowly by, the Saints waved white handkerchiefs in the air and shouted hosanna. The prophet smiled and waved back at them. Seeing him lifted everyone's spirits. The skies were sunny, and Juliet could feel excitement and emotion in the air.[20]

In his remarks at the dedication, President Hinckley spoke about the significance of the new, modified temples. Already he had dedicated more than two dozen of them around the world. "It's the house of the Lord," he declared at a pulpit in the celestial room. "You can get the washings and the anointings and the endowments and come into this room, beautifully furnished, here having passed through the veil in symbolism of our passage from life into a new life."

"Here are two sealing rooms with beautiful altars where you can look in the mirrors and sense the feeling of eternity," he continued. "There's nothing like it on all the face of the earth."[21]

The temple soon opened for ordinance work. And after preparing to enter the house of the Lord, the Toro family was sealed together for time and eternity.[22]

On August 10, 2000, Georges Bonnet felt very much alone. Nine months after his trip to Ghana, he was returning to the country—this time to serve as the Church's director for temporal affairs in the Africa West Area. His wife, Carolyn, and three of their children would soon join him in Accra. But for now, he was on his own.

Progress on the Accra Temple remained at a standstill, and Church leaders hoped that Georges, with his reputation for informed and sensitive leadership in Africa, could help move the project forward. Feeling the weight of his assignment, Georges yearned to be equal to the challenges ahead of him. He searched his soul and thought about Jesus Christ and His atoning sacrifice.

"Although I firmly believe in the powers of the Atonement to bring peace to the soul," he wrote in his journal, "there are, no doubt, other powers and blessings from the Atonement I have yet to experience."[23]

Once he arrived in Accra, Georges quickly learned that obtaining a building permit for the temple was just one of many serious matters demanding his attention in West Africa.

At first, he was confident he could handle the load, which included other major building projects and a temple in Aba, Nigeria. "I've worked here before," he told himself. "I can do it." And when his family joined him, he felt less alone.

But after a month, he was not so sure of himself. His many other responsibilities left him little time to attend to the Accra Temple's building permit. While Saints throughout Ghana were faithfully preparing to enter the house of the Lord, no one—in or out of the Church—seemed to know how to end the impasse. The one thing people agreed on was that Jerry Rawlings, the president of Ghana, was behind the delay.

Feeling helpless, Georges prayed. "There are too many problems, too many complications," he said. "How do you, Lord, want me to do this? I'll do whatever you say. I'll be your instrument, but I cannot do it by myself."[24]

A short time later, Georges began collaborating with the office of Ghana's First Lady to organize humanitarian aid projects. He hoped doing so would help the Rawlings family get to know the Church and its mission better. He also began fasting every Sunday.

By the middle of November 2000, Georges was optimistic. More and more, he believed Isaac Addy, the president's brother, was vital to resolving the impasse, just as he had been during the freeze. But he hesitated to ask Isaac to approach the president on behalf of the Church.

Although the brothers had reconciled during the freeze, the reconciliation had been short-lived. It pained Isaac, the older brother, to ask another favor. Yet Isaac's wife, June, had encouraged him to trust in Jesus Christ to help mend his relationship with his brother. So, despite his pain, Isaac assured Georges that he was willing to speak with Jerry about the temple.[25]

On December 3, Isaac called the Bonnet house with good news. An aide to the president had contacted him with questions about the temple, and the president was open to supporting the project if the Church could make some minor modifications to the layout of the site. It was fast Sunday, and Georges and Isaac hadn't eaten all day. But rather than break their fast that evening, they went to the temple site together to determine if the president's requests were reasonable.

As they walked the grounds, they felt like they could accommodate the requests. "Isaac, this is where the temple will be," Georges said. "Let's ask Heavenly Father to intervene."

Kneeling, they offered a prayer, asking the Lord to bless their efforts. They felt the Spirit powerfully, and they immediately called the president's aide to say they were willing to negotiate. Both Georges and Isaac felt good about the conversation.

Two days later, Isaac met privately with his brother at Osu Castle, Ghana's presidential residence. Just before the meeting, Georges called Isaac to remind him to tell his brother that he loved him. Georges then went home and prayed and paced the floor, waiting to hear from Isaac. When no call came, Georges went to the temple site to wait. The phone finally rang half an hour later.

"It is over," Isaac said, his voice jubilant. He and Jerry had spoken about the temple for all of ten minutes. They had then spent the rest of the time talking and reminiscing about their family. By the end of their discussion, they were smiling, laughing, and weeping together. Jerry said the Church could begin work on the temple immediately.

Isaac had asked if they needed to consult the city's planning committee first.

"Don't worry about it," the president had said. "I'll handle it."[26]

CHAPTER 32

Our Strength Is Our Faith

On October 1, 2000, President Hinckley—now ninety years old—dedicated the Boston Massachusetts Temple in the eastern United States, achieving his goal of having one hundred operating temples by the end of the year. Two months later, as Christians around the world prepared to celebrate the birth of the Savior and the beginning of a new millennium, he dedicated two more temples, in Recife and Porto Alegre, Brazil. Another nineteen temples were either under construction or in the planning stages. It was a fitting conclusion to a year that saw more temples dedicated than any before in the history of the Church.[1]

During his lifetime, President Hinckley had watched the Church grow from an institution with four hundred thousand members, most of whom lived in Utah, to one with over eleven million members in 148 countries. In 1910, the year of the prophet's birth, the Church had just four temples, and the endowment was available only in English. Now the Church's temples were found all over the globe, and the endowment was available in dozens of languages. The inspired change to temple design had helped make this possible.[2]

But temples were not the only buildings President Hinckley had on his mind. For some time, he had expressed concern that the Salt Lake Tabernacle was not large enough to accommodate everyone who wanted to attend general conference in person. So he commissioned a new assembly hall with three times the seating capacity of the Tabernacle. The Conference Center, built on the block north of Temple Square and dedicated in October 2000, was an engineering marvel, and it delighted the prophet.[3]

Under President Hinckley's leadership, the Church had also continued to embrace new technology. Shortly after becoming Church president, he had approved the creation of a website where internet users could find the scriptures, the testimony of Joseph Smith, and general conference addresses. By the end of 2000, www.lds.org included digital copies of the scriptures, thirty years of Church magazines, "The Family: A Proclamation to the World," and "The Living Christ: The Testimony of the Apostles."[4]

As much as President Hinckley saw great potential in the internet as a force for good, he observed evil in it too. Pornography was a grave concern. "Leave it alone!" he pleaded. "Avoid it like the plague because it is just as deadly." He also condemned physical and sexual abuse and urged Church leaders to help bring perpetrators to justice.[5]

The prophet was still concerned about the number of Saints who fell away from the Church. Under his direction, missionaries were placing greater emphasis on conversion prior to baptism, and mission and stake leaders were meeting together in new coordinating councils to discuss how to better minister to new members.[6] While President Hinckley worried that sacrament meeting attendance was not improving, he was encouraged by the retention efforts of Saints worldwide.[7]

At the dawn of the new millennium, he placed hope in the rising generation. More and more, they were going on missions and getting married in the house of the Lord. He also noted that they were better educated than past generations.

As Church president, he yearned for ways to help young Saints gain the education and career training they needed. Earlier that year, during a meeting of the Church Board of Education, he had felt the Spirit telling him that Ricks College, a two-year institution, should become a four-year university called BYU–Idaho. Such a change would give many more young Latter-day Saints an opportunity to attend a Church university.

The following day, President Hinckley presented the idea to the apostles, and they unanimously approved it. He then counseled with David A. Bednar, the president of Ricks College, and they decided the new university should focus on teaching and the use of online classes to expand the numbers of students enrolled at the school.

The prophet wasted no time in announcing the change. "It will become a great institution," he declared.[8]

Recently, he had also thought much about young women and men in developing nations, especially returned missionaries. Faced with poverty and a lack of education and job prospects, they sometimes grew discouraged and drifted away from the Church. At his encouragement, the Presiding Bishopric had begun developing a new program to provide small loans to Saints worldwide to help them pay for trade school or university. Likening it to the Perpetual Emigrating Fund, the Church's program for helping thousands of European Saints gather to Utah in the 1800s, President Hinckley planned to call it the Perpetual Education Fund.

"I feel that this program is inspired and can bless the lives of so very many young men and women," he wrote. "Their sights can be lifted and their ambitions stirred."[9]

In November, President Hinckley held a special broadcast devotional for the youth of the Church. To help them become better disciples of Jesus Christ, he invited them to learn and practice six B's:

1. Be grateful.
2. Be smart.
3. Be clean.
4. Be true.
5. Be humble.
6. Be prayerful.[10]

A little over a month later, as the year came to an end, he reflected on his life and the goodness of God. Although the prophet's body was weary, his spirit was aglow with peace and contentment. "My feeling is one of profound gratitude to my Father in Heaven and His Beloved Son," he recorded in his journal on December 31, 2000. "We now look forward to a new year."[11]

TWO MONTHS LATER, ON February 26, 2001, Darius Gray and Marie Taylor sat in a crowded auditorium in the Family History Library in Salt Lake City. At the front of the room, apostle Henry B. Eyring was speaking to more than a hundred reporters and special guests about the Freedman's Bank project.

After eleven years of work, Darius, Marie, and more than 550 volunteers at the Utah State Prison had finished extracting the information about all 484,083 African Americans named in the records.[12] Recently, the Church had begun providing technical and financial support to the project, and the information was now searchable and available to researchers on CD-ROM and at any of the Church's family history centers.

"To African Americans, the Freedman's Bank records represent the largest repository of lineage-linked documents known to exist," Elder Eyring announced. "In the near future, it is also our hope to provide the database free of charge on the Church's genealogical website, FamilySearch.org."[13]

In the days leading up to this announcement, Darius had met with leaders in the Family History Department to plan the release of the database. "We're really going to do this," he thought. "It's going to happen."[14]

The project's fate had not always been certain. Early on, extracting names for temple work had become a motivating aspect of the project. But in the mid-1990s, the Church began actively discouraging people from submitting names of nonrelatives to the temple. The change was an important and necessary measure to respect the families of the deceased, but it caused the project to stall. As a result, Darius and Marie shifted their focus to creating a research tool to help African Americans find their ancestors.[15]

The inmates finished extracting names in October 1999. After that, they carefully verified their transcriptions and—despite a three-week prison lockdown—completed the work in mid-July 2000.

One inmate who helped coordinate the project got emotional when they finished. He never expected the work to affect him as much as it did. He had read heartbreaking records of enslaved fathers and mothers being taken away from their families. Other records mentioned people being shot to death. One record he extracted told of a nameless enslaved baby being traded away for farm equipment.

Many inmates had similar life-changing experiences. Once, the coordinator came upon a weeping volunteer. "I cannot believe the way these people have been treated," the inmate said. Placing a hand on the volunteer's shoulder, the coordinator noticed the man was tattooed with the initials of a white supremacist group.[16]

Now that the data was extracted, Darius and Marie had to find a way to make it widely available to researchers—something they did not have the resources to do. A popular genealogy website offered to purchase the data for tens of thousands of dollars, but Darius and Marie declined, feeling it would be wrong to profit from the inmates' work. Instead, they donated it to the Church in exchange for making it available to everyone who wanted to use it.[17]

At the release event for the CD-ROM, which was broadcast to Washington, DC, and eleven other cities in the United States, both Darius and Marie spoke about the project. Darius acknowledged that the records told many painful and uncomfortable stories. "I think oftentimes we have been afraid to talk about race," he told reporters, "but race is a reality. We ought to share in the history together."[18]

He believed family was at the heart of the project. "It lets you know how important family was," he said. "Even in the hostile environment of slavery, people struggled to keep track of each other. They worked at it, they kept track of one another."[19]

Marie agreed. "When I discovered the Freedman's Bank records," she said, "I envisioned African Americans breaking the chains of slavery and forging the bonds of families." Now she hoped the records would continue to bring families together.

"That is what it is all about," she said.[20]

WHEN FELICINDO CONTRERAS WAS called to serve as a bishop in Santiago, Chile, his wife, Veronica, was released as the ward Relief Society president. But she soon received a new calling: stake seminary and institute teacher.[21]

For many years, the Church's institutes of religion had generally operated near university campuses in the United States. But in the early 1970s, leaders in the Church Educational System began adapting institute to operate in stakes across the globe. The change allowed all young adults in the Church, not just university students, to benefit from the program. Regional CES administrators supervised the classes, and the stakes provided teachers.

In Chile, weekday religious education operated for a time alongside more than a dozen Church-run primary and secondary schools. But it was expensive for the Church to operate schools in every country where there were members, and Church policy dictated that as soon as the Saints had access to adequate secular schools, Church schools would close. In 1981, the Church closed its last school in Chile and began relying solely on seminary and institute to provide the Saints with religious education.[22]

Studies had shown that institute students were much more likely to stay active in the Church than those who did not attend. Yet in Chile, only about one in five of all active young adult Saints was enrolled. At the time of Veronica's call, only three or four students in the stake regularly attended institute.

Veronica believed institute classes played a vital role in helping young people progress closer to God. She began mentioning institute to every young adult—and parent of a young adult—she met at church. She also visited the bishops of each ward, urging them to invite young people to attend classes. Many of the bishops were supportive, especially when she shared her convictions of institute's importance. Before long, more than fifty students were taking part in institute.

Since many of her students came straight from work or school, they often did not have time to eat before class started. Worried they would not be able to focus on her lessons if they were hungry, Veronica made sure the students had something to eat when they arrived. She usually provided them with cake or a small snack. Other times she prepared something bigger, like a barbecue or some other meal. But she would never tell the students what food to expect, hoping the mystery of it would encourage them to come to class.[23]

At the start of the year, she would ask her students what they wanted to learn. Based on their feedback, she taught classes on the standard works, temple and mission preparation, and eternal marriage.

Using the institute manuals as a starting point, Veronica prepared her lessons prayerfully, looking for ways to address the everyday struggles of her students. She liked to break the scriptures down verse by verse to encourage her students to think deeply about the lives and teachings of the people and prophets they studied. She also encouraged the young people to ask questions.

"If I don't know the answer to your question or a concern that you have," she would say, "I'm going to look it up and I'm going to give you the answer—or we are going to look it up together."[24]

As the institute class grew, the students became a tight-knit group. They enjoyed spending time with her and with each other. Sometimes, when they were dealing with personal problems, the students would come to her for advice. She always urged them to resolve their concerns with the right people.

"Look," she would tell them, "talk to your bishop or to your dad or mom, because if there is a problem at home, you must solve it at home. And if there is no solution, go and talk with your bishop. That's the best thing to do."

Veronica understood that her students faced challenges. At the time, Chile's economy was struggling, and many young people wondered how they could afford to attend school, get married, and raise a family. On Veronica's wall hung a sign that read "Faith in Every Footstep," and she believed that acting in faith and applying the teachings of Jesus Christ to everyday life would produce good results.

"We are always going to have stumbles," she'd tell her students. "But we are always going to have the hand of the Lord helping us."[25]

In May 2001, Seb Sollesta left his home in Iloilo City, Philippines, to live and work in the United States—a dream he'd had since college. He had friends and relatives from the Philippines who had already moved to the U.S., and they lived happy and successful lives. "Maybe I can have that dream also," he thought.

His wife, Maridan, had not liked the idea of him leaving home to move to the other side of the world. "Your dream is just your dream," she had told him. "That's not my dream." They had three teenage sons to raise, a pharmaceutical business to run, and Church callings to fulfill. She did not understand why he wanted to go away.

"You need to think it over very wisely," she had counseled. "As a husband and wife, we need to live under one roof in one house."

Unwilling to stand in the way of Seb's dream, though, Maridan ultimately agreed to the move. Both of them knew that many Filipino couples lived apart, with one partner staying in the Philippines while the other worked abroad. Why couldn't they do the same?

In the United States, Seb moved in with his uncle in Long Beach, California, a city on the west coast of the country. He found a job working the graveyard shift at a nearby hospital. The nighttime hours were difficult, and the job was challenging, but it paid well, and Seb enjoyed the work.

On weekends, he attended his local ward and then visited relatives with his uncle. He liked making new friends and becoming better acquainted with his relatives. But he also felt lonely and missed his wife and children. He and Maridan tried to talk on the telephone every day, but doing so was expensive. To make a long-distance call to the Philippines, he had to use phone cards at a cost of ten dollars an hour.[26]

After working five months in California, Seb started thinking seriously about returning to the Philippines. His visa would expire soon, and if he wanted to continue working in the United States, he needed to extend it. For a time, he had thought about having Maridan and their sons join him, perhaps permanently, once he had enough money. But Maridan wasn't interested in living in the United States, and he did not want to stay there without his family.

On the morning of September 11, 2001, violent extremists hijacked three commercial airliners in the eastern United States and crashed them into buildings in New York City and the Washington, DC, area. A fourth airliner went down in a field after passengers resisted hijackers. The attacks killed nearly three thousand people and triggered widespread outrage and fear. While people around the world mourned, the United States and its allies vowed a "war on terror" against the militant group behind the attacks.

As Seb watched television news coverage of the tragedy, he no longer felt safe where he was. He wanted to be with his wife and children. His sons were at a vulnerable age. They needed someone to guide and strengthen them as they got older. He needed to be at home with them and their mother.

A few days after the hijackings, Seb boarded a flight for the Philippines. He was returning earlier than planned, but he had no regrets. True happiness, he now realized, did not come from worldly success. It came from family.[27]

LESS THAN A MONTH after the September 11 attacks, President Hinckley spoke to the Saints at general conference about the rising conflict. "We live in a season when fierce men do terrible and despicable things," he declared. "Our strength is our faith in the Almighty. No cause under the heavens can stop the work of God. Adversity may raise its ugly head. The world may be troubled with wars and rumors of wars, but this cause will go forward."

"And as we go forward," he continued, "may we bless humanity with an outreach to all, lifting those who are downtrodden and oppressed, feeding and clothing the hungry and the needy, extending love and neighborliness to those about us who may not be part of this Church."[28]

A few months later, Salt Lake City hosted the 2002 Winter Olympic Games, an event President Hinckley had been anticipating for several years. Despite the recent terrorist attacks, the games brought an unprecedented number of international visitors to Utah, including thousands of journalists eager to ask questions about the city's religious heritage and culture. President Hinckley set the tone for the Church's community support by announcing publicly that missionaries would not preach to Olympic tourists. Still, the Church took steps to help reporters and other visitors learn about the Saints.[29]

In October 2001, Church leaders had launched a new website designed to answer basic questions about Church beliefs and practices. During the games, the Church also set up a media center in the Joseph Smith Memorial Building for reporters. Anyone curious about the Church and its teachings could attend *Light of the World,* a Christ-centered pageant about the history of the Church and the message of the restored gospel, held four days a week in the Conference Center.[30]

After the events of September 11, safety was a major concern at the games. Extensive security measures protected each Olympic venue, yet organizers worked hard to preserve the community spirit of an Olympic host city. To help the games run smoothly, the Church provided resources to the Salt Lake Olympic Committee, parking lots for the crowds, and a range of services. The Tabernacle Choir performed in front of a worldwide audience of three billion people during the opening ceremonies. And many Saints, including returned missionaries who served as translators, contributed by volunteering their time.[31]

After the games were over, the prophet reflected on the experience in his journal. "The Church has been greatly blessed by these Olympics," he wrote. "We have not done any direct proselytizing, but we have made friends and admirers across the world. People who scarcely ever heard of us are now somewhat familiar."

He thought about the many dignitaries, heads of state, and industry leaders who came to the city to enjoy the games. They brought to mind a prophecy by Brigham Young that Salt Lake City would become a "great highway of the nations," a place where kings and emperors would visit.

"The prophecy has been fulfilled in what we have observed during the past two weeks," President Hinckley wrote. "Now we settle down and go back to work."[32]

CHAPTER 33

What Is This Church?

The Saints in northeast Mexico rejoiced on April 28, 2002, when President Hinckley dedicated a house of the Lord in Monterrey, Nuevo León, Mexico. It was the Church's 110th operating temple—and the eleventh temple dedicated in Mexico in three years. As President Hinckley had envisioned, the fifty-eight temples dedicated since the Church began using the new temple design in 1998 had spread blessings and miracles far and wide. Saints who had once traveled several days to attend the temple could now reach one in a matter of hours or even minutes.[1]

Among the first Saints to benefit from the temple-building boom were those in the Church's Mexican colonies, whose isolation had inspired the new temple design. Dedicated in March 1999, the Colonia Juárez

Chihuahua Temple was 6,800 square feet—the smallest in the Church—but it quickly became a beacon in the community.

Bertha Chavez, who attended church in nearby Nuevo Casas Grandes, was delighted when a counselor in the temple presidency invited her to be an ordinance worker in the new temple. It had been Bertha's dream to serve in the house of the Lord since receiving her endowment in the Mesa Arizona Temple in 1987. Now her dream had come true.

"It was a great and beautiful surprise," she recalled. "I jumped up, crying for joy, with gratitude to the Lord for giving me this tremendous opportunity to serve in His house."[2]

Across the Atlantic, Marilena Kretly Pretel Busto traveled from her home in Portugal to the recently dedicated Madrid Spain Temple. A year earlier, her 101-year-old grandmother had passed away. Now Marilena was eager to receive ordinances on her grandmother's behalf.

In the house of the Lord, Marilena expected to feel something special when she was baptized for her grandmother, but she didn't. Nor did she feel anything during the confirmation and endowment ordinances. At first, this absence of feeling left Marilena anxious. But by the time she knelt at the altar in the sealing room, ready to have her grandmother sealed to her parents, she was simply happy that she'd done the temple work.

Then the sealer began to speak, and Marilena felt a shock course through her body. She could not describe exactly what she felt, but she was sure that her grandmother was rejoicing in the spirit world.[3]

In Bolivia, meanwhile, many of the nation's one hundred thousand Saints had prepared themselves to attend the Cochabamba Temple after its dedication in April 2000. Believing that strong families prepared Church members to attend the temple, María Mercau de Aquino, a stake Relief Society president in Cochabamba, organized a meeting designed to strengthen marriages and give women a greater sense of their value.

In the same stake, Antonio and Gloria Ayaviri could see how the new temple strengthened their family. "Raising children is much easier now that we have the gospel and temple blessings in our lives," Antonio testified. "In our home we have a piece of heaven."[4]

A house of the Lord in Fukuoka, Japan, was also changing lives. More than thirty years had passed since Kazuhiko Yamashita, the president of the Fukuoka Stake, had joined the Church after watching *Man's Search for Happiness* at the world's fair in Osaka, Japan. His faith in the plan of salvation continued to give him direction. He and his wife, Tazuko, had been sealed in the Tokyo Temple in 1980, and they had six children together.

The Fukuoka Temple was now the centerpiece of the Church in southern Japan. During the open house, Kazuhiko was pleased to see that many Saints had enthusiastically invited their family and friends to see the house of the Lord. Several Saints who had drifted from the fold had also returned, their faith rekindled by the undeniable influence of the temple. Sitting in the celestial room during the dedication, Kazuhiko felt perfectly at peace. He had a strong sense that the Lord was there and that He loved the Saints in Japan. When he glanced at President Hinckley, Kazuhiko saw tears in the prophet's eyes.[5]

The new temple in Monterrey, Mexico, soon brought blessings of its own. Román and Norma Rodríguez had joined the Church after attending the temple open house. At the time, they had been thinking about renewing their fifteen-year marriage in a lavish ceremony. But something about that plan had never felt right, prompting Norma to pray to God for direction.

The next year, she and Román returned to the Monterrey Temple with their three children. They no longer desired an extravagant wedding. In the beautiful, eternal promises of the sealing power, they found the marriage ceremony they had always wanted.[6]

WHEN ANNE PINGREE WAS called as second counselor in the Relief Society general presidency in April 2002, she was concerned about literacy among Latter-day Saint women. From 1995 to 1998, she and her husband, George, were mission leaders in the Nigeria Port Harcourt Mission. Many of the women she met during that time could not read, making it hard for them to serve in the Church.[7]

As the Church grew in developing nations during the 1970s and '80s, teaching people to read had become part of its mission. In 1992, Relief Society general president Elaine L. Jack had made literacy a major focus of her presidency, leading to the creation of the Gospel Literacy Effort to teach reading and encourage Church members to study the scriptures, instruct their families, and improve themselves.[8]

Anne had served on President Jack's board before her mission, and when she arrived in Nigeria, she had worked with missionaries and local Saints to promote gospel literacy. The Relief Society general board and an artist in Utah had also helped her create some simple training posters and booklets to assist women in the mission who had difficulty reading. As she used these materials, she saw more and more women fulfilling their callings with confidence and understanding.[9]

During her first year in the Relief Society general presidency, Anne was assigned to lead the organization's literacy projects. Studies showed that women in the developing world had less access to education than men, resulting in lower literacy rates. Evidence also suggested that Saints were more likely to stay in the Church and attend meetings regularly when they knew how to read. Along with Anne, Relief Society general president Bonnie D. Parkin and first counselor Kathleen Hughes believed that helping Relief Society members learn to read would empower them to serve effectively in the Church, strengthen their families, find better employment, and gain firmer testimonies of Jesus Christ.[10]

Under President Parkin, the Relief Society board continued to emphasize the Gospel Literacy Effort. They also encouraged the Saints to use *Ye Shall Have My Words,* a literacy manual first developed by the Church Educational System. Like Anne, they understood that many Church members, through no fault of their own, struggled in their callings because they could not read or understand the Church's many handbooks and lesson manuals.[11]

As the presidency discussed these problems, Anne spoke about how simplified training booklets like the ones she used in Nigeria could be used around the world. President Parkin thought the Relief Society general board should develop similar booklets to help members in areas with low literacy rates.

To help with this work, the general board recommended Florence Chukwurah, a Latter-day Saint Anne met in Nigeria, to serve with them. Florence was visiting Salt Lake City while her husband, area authority seventy Christopher N. Chukwurah, received training at Church headquarters. A nurse by profession, Florence had grown up in poverty and understood what it was like to live in a place where the Church was still new.

The First Presidency approved the recommendation, and President Parkin assigned Florence to work with the literacy committee. Before long, she was working with other members of the board to develop simplified training booklets.

Anne was overjoyed to see the work of literacy moving forward. "This is all happening so fast," she thought. "I scarce can take it in."[12]

BACK IN THE PHILIPPINES, Seb Sollesta was grateful to be home again. His absence had unduly burdened his wife, Maridan, and their three sons. Now the family spent every day together, and Seb felt blessed. He could talk with his sons face to face, encourage them to be active in the Church, and help them prepare for missions.[13]

When Seb returned, Maridan was serving as the Church's public affairs coordinator for the stakes in Iloilo City. In this calling, she helped community and government leaders learn about the Church. She also paired the Church with religious and service groups to assist with eye screenings, blood drives, and other projects. Seb, meanwhile, became a high councilor in the Iloilo North Stake.

At the time, the First Presidency remained concerned about the Saints in areas with low Church attendance. The Philippines had nearly five hundred thousand Saints, but only around 20 percent attended meetings regularly. In response to this concern, President Hinckley called Elder Dallin H. Oaks to serve as president of the Philippines Area and Elder Jeffrey R. Holland to serve as president of the Chile Area, which was facing similar challenges. Both apostles began their service in August 2002 with a plan to occupy these positions for one year.[14]

In the Philippines, Elder Oaks and his counselors met regularly with stake, mission, and area leaders. During a special training meeting in Manila, Elder Oaks spoke about the importance of embracing a "gospel culture" based on the plan of salvation, God's commandments, and the teachings of modern prophets. He observed that elements of gospel culture were found in local cultures everywhere. Yet there were also aspects of these cultures that were out of harmony with the teachings of Jesus Christ.

"The covenants we make at baptism commit us to live changed lives," he taught. "We must change all elements of our existing cultural practices or behaviors that are in conflict with gospel commandments, covenants, and culture."

Elder Oaks emphasized that gospel culture strengthened families and individuals by promoting chastity, temple marriage, honesty, self-reliance, and equal partnership in marriage. He urged the leaders to make teaching the Savior's doctrine and building faith in Him their top priority among the Saints. He also counseled them to fortify their wards by balancing missionary work with greater reactivation efforts and holding regular youth activities.[15]

Following the training, Seb and other leaders in the Iloilo North Stake asked ward bishoprics to identify families to bring back into the fold. They believed that if a father and mother returned to church, they would likely bring their children with them. The children would then become future missionaries and leaders in the Church.[16]

As a father of teenagers, Seb was especially concerned about the youth. Low activity in Aaronic Priesthood quorums and Young Women classes was a major issue in their area. Less than 10 percent of wards and branches in the Philippines had all three quorums of the Aaronic Priesthood functioning. And most units did not have midweek activities for youth.

The Iloilo North Stake addressed this problem by encouraging wards to hold regular youth classes even if they had only one or two members. With functioning classes and quorums, no matter how small, young women and men could invite their friends to Sunday meetings and weekday activities.[17]

Seb believed the youth needed to participate in Church activities where they could form friendships and find good role models. When local leaders expressed concerns that they did not have enough budget to pay for the cost of activities, Seb and other stake leaders told them to go ahead and plan the activities. If they needed extra funds, the stake could provide them.[18]

As Seb served the Saints in his stake, applying what he learned from Elder Oaks, he reflected on his own responsibilities at church and at home. When speaking about gospel culture, Elder Oaks had counseled the Filipino Saints against leaving their families for an extended time to work, as Seb had done. Some people in the Philippines had little choice but to work abroad, but Seb knew that he and his family could live happily and provide for themselves in Iloilo City.

And for him, no amount of material gain could make up for being away from his family for so long.[19]

IN APRIL 2003, FOURTEEN-YEAR-OLD Blake McKeown arrived at a stake center in Baulkham Hills, a suburb of Sydney, Australia, with his seventeen-year-old brother, Wade. Typically, the stake center was a calm, quiet place. But today, a large canopy tent had been set up in the parking lot, and the grounds were teeming with youth from stakes across New South Wales. They had come to take part in an Especially for Youth conference—now known in Australia as Time for Youth, or TFY.[20]

After the success of EFY in Brisbane, the area presidency encouraged stakes in Australia and New Zealand to organize events of their own. In 2002, Mary McKenna and her committee organized a TFY in Brisbane and one in New Zealand in 2003. The TFY in Baulkham Hills was the first one held in Australia outside of Brisbane.[21]

Although Blake had grown up in the Church, he had never seen so many Latter-day Saint youth in one place before. He and Wade were from Penrith, about a forty-five-minute drive from the Baulkham Hills stake center. They had a strong youth group in their ward, but Latter-day Saints made up only half of 1 percent of Australia's population, so youth activities—even at the stake level—rarely had more than a few dozen people attending. In Blake's high school, there were only two members of the Church besides him and his brother.[22]

Once TFY got underway, he and Wade rarely saw each other. Following the EFY model, everyone at the event joined a small group led by a young single adult counselor. In these groups, the youth rotated through activities. They also took part in service projects, listened to devotionals and talks, learned songs, studied the scriptures, cheered each other on in a talent show, and attended a dance.

The theme of the conference was "We Believe," with a focus on that year's seminary course of study, the Doctrine and Covenants. The speakers and counselors drew on the theme as they shared spiritual experiences and encouraged participants to come unto Christ, pray, keep journals, and live the other fundamentals of the gospel. Testimony meetings also gave the youth an opportunity to share their witness of the Savior and His restored gospel with their peers.[23]

In church, Blake was often restless in meetings, but he came to TFY with a good foundation of faith from his parents. He and Wade were third-generation Latter-day Saints, and their parents and grandparents had always been great examples of faith and service.

The Young Men program had also strengthened him. As a deacon, Blake had been called as the quorum president. His bishop asked him to select two counselors and a secretary from the eleven other boys in his quorum. After praying for guidance, Blake came back to the bishop the next week with three names. The bishop showed Blake his own list, which had the same three boys. He had arranged the names in a different order, but he adjusted his list to match Blake's. The experience had given Blake confidence in prayer and in his ability to lead.[24]

Blake wasn't very outgoing, but he enjoyed making new friends from other wards and stakes at TFY. At the end of each day, he and Wade would return home to rest up before heading back early the next morning.

Neither of them noticed how three days at TFY affected them, but their mother saw changes. Amid the fun and games, TFY provided youth with opportunities to feel the Spirit in a new environment. When Blake and Wade returned, they were more focused on the scriptures and a little more confident in their testimonies.[25]

ON THE AFTERNOON OF January 10, 2004, Georges A. Bonnet gathered with President Hinckley, Elder Russell M. Nelson, and thousands of West African Saints in a sports stadium in Accra, Ghana. The prophet had come to the city to dedicate its new temple. But before the dedication, he had asked the children and youth of Ghana's stakes and districts to commemorate the occasion with a cultural event featuring joyful music and dancing. He believed holding such celebrations at temple dedications would help young people make unforgettable memories and get excited about the Church.

After an opening prayer, groups dressed in colorful costumes performed on a large stage adorned with beautiful murals. Some of the performers sang songs. Others performed Ghanaian dances, like the Adowa and Kpanlogo, or played traditional music on drums and bamboo flutes.

A highlight of the afternoon came when missionaries stepped onto the stage and sang the missionary anthem "Called to Serve." Eight hundred and fifty Primary children, all dressed in white, also climbed onto the platform and sang "I Am a Child of God" with the missionaries.[26]

The next morning, Georges awoke feeling gratitude. Dedication day had finally arrived. At nine o'clock, he joined President Hinckley and Elder Nelson in the celestial room for the first dedicatory session. It opened with a cornerstone ceremony conducted by President Hinckley. Afterward, the temple matron and president spoke, followed by Elder Nelson and Elder Emmanuel Kissi, now an area authority seventy, who had led the Ghanaian Saints during the freeze.

In his talk, Elder Kissi paid tribute to Joseph William Billy Johnson, who was in the congregation. He also spoke of other early Saints who had made it possible for the Church to grow rapidly in Ghana.

"Our dreams have come true," he said.[27]

Near the end of the session, President Hinckley spoke humbly of the Lord's help in building the temple. "The Lord heard our prayers," he testified. "He heard your prayers. He heard the prayers of many people, and the temple now stands completed."

The prophet then dedicated the building. "We thank Thee for the brotherhood that exists among us, that neither color of skin nor land of birth can separate us as Thy sons and daughters who have taken upon us sacred and binding covenants," he prayed. "May Thy work spread in this land and in adjoining nations."[28]

Later that day, during the third dedicatory session, President Hinckley called on Georges to speak. Surprised, Georges approached the pulpit. "I want you to know that our God is a God of miracles," he testified. "Miracles happen because of faith, and many, many have exercised their faith through prayer and other forms of worship to make this great day happen."

"I believe that having a dedicated temple in West Africa might be one of the most important events since the Atonement of Jesus Christ and the restoration of all things," he continued. "There are millions of Africans who have passed on who are rejoicing with us today."[29]

After the dedication, Georges joined President Hinckley, Elder Nelson, Elder Kissi, and others to visit John Kufuor, Jerry Rawlings's successor as president of Ghana. Since taking office in early 2001, President Kufuor and his administration had been helpful and supportive during the temple's construction. In 2002, he visited the First Presidency in Salt Lake City to learn more about the Church and thank the Latter-day Saints for their humanitarian and religious contributions to Ghana. He had also attended the recent temple open house in Accra and received a tour of the building. What he saw impressed him.

"Your church," he now told President Hinckley, "has gained citizenship in Ghana."[30]

IN JUNE 2004, ANGELA Peterson waited in her car for a safety and emissions inspection near Washington, DC. Several cars stretched ahead of her, the line snaking around the parking lot. This was going to take a while, she realized.

Instead of letting her car idle, she turned off the engine and rolled down the windows to enjoy the summer afternoon breeze. As she waited, she picked up a copy of "The Family: A Proclamation to the World," which she had brought along with her. A few weeks earlier, her stake president had invited the members of her young single adult ward to memorize the proclamation, promising that doing so would bring them blessings. Angela believed that promise, so she had been trying diligently to memorize the document.[31]

In the nine years since the family proclamation was announced at the September 1995 general Relief Society meeting, it had become central to the Church's message about families. Parents organized their homes around its principles, Church members framed it and hung it on their walls, and Brigham Young University offered an entire course on its one page of text. Angela had been a teenager when President Hinckley introduced the proclamation, and she wasn't sure if she had read it before her stake president's invitation.[32]

After finishing high school, Angela had moved from her tiny hometown of Stirling, Alberta, Canada, to attend university in Logan, Utah. After graduation, she took an internship in the Church's Public Affairs Office in Salt Lake City before securing a full-time position in its International and Government Affairs Office in Washington, DC. The capital city streets, lined with museums and monuments and government offices, were very different from the dusty roads of her youth.

When Angela reached the front of the line, she went to a waiting room while a mechanic checked her car. The inspection took longer than she expected, and she began to worry as she watched other customers come and go while she continued to wait. Was something wrong with her car? How much would it cost to get it fixed?

Finally, after what seemed like hours, the mechanic came in and told her that her car had passed its inspection.

Relieved, Angela paid and left the building, still unsure why it had taken so long. At her car, she found the mechanic waiting for her.

"Miss," he said, "I want to apologize for taking so long with your car inspection."

He told Angela he had been drawn to the copy of the family proclamation on her passenger seat. He had read it over and over, moved by its message about families.

"What is this church? What is this document on the family? Can I have a copy of it?" he asked her. "It says it was written by apostles. Do you mean to tell me that there are apostles on the earth today just like in Jesus's time? Please, I need to know."

Stunned, Angela collected her thoughts. "There are apostles and prophets on the earth, just as in the time of Jesus Christ," she told him, explaining briefly about Joseph Smith and the Restoration of the gospel. She gave him her copy of the family proclamation and a Book of Mormon.

He then gave her his name and phone number to share with the missionaries. As Angela drove home from the garage, she blinked back tears, grateful that she'd left the proclamation on her passenger seat.[33]

CHAPTER 34

Strength for Any Situation

On the morning of October 15, 2004, Anne Pingree stepped off a plane in Santiago, Chile. As second counselor in the Relief Society general presidency, she had come to meet with the local Saints and train Relief Society and priesthood leaders.

In her meetings, Anne planned to use the simplified training booklets developed by the Relief Society board's literacy committee. Each booklet had about two dozen pages featuring color photographs and simple principles from the *Church Handbook of Instructions*. She hoped to use the booklet on Church welfare to help Relief Society and priesthood leaders learn to value each other and work together.[1]

Before leaving the United States, Anne had received an email from Elder Carl B. Pratt of the Chile

Area presidency. The Church had recently opened two welfare resource centers in Chile, each one housing a bishops' storehouse, an employment center, and a counseling office. When dispensing welfare resources, bishops were supposed to work with Relief Society presidents. But the bishops in Chile were not doing this.[2]

In Santiago, Anne learned more about the problem during an initial meeting with Elder Pratt and Elder Francisco J. Viñas, the Chile Area president. Elder Viñas explained that many Chilean Saints had a difficult time reading, so they led by tradition instead of consulting the handbook. As in many areas of the world, sexism was strong in Chile, and some stake presidents and bishops did not counsel with their Relief Society leaders.

"What I want you to do is teach the how-tos," Elder Viñas said. "Teach that we lead by learning the principles in the handbook."[3]

Over the next week, Anne talked to hundreds of Saints. Many spoke of their appreciation for Elder Jeffrey R. Holland's recent service as Chile Area president. Although he and Elder Oaks had been called to serve in their respective areas for one year, the First Presidency had extended both assignments another year, giving them more time to support local leaders and strengthen the Saints.[4]

Focusing his attention on Chile's low membership retention and meeting attendance, Elder Holland had worked closely with missionaries and everyday Saints to bring people back to church. To relieve the burden of priesthood leaders in areas where wards and branches were weak, he had reorganized many Church units, reducing the number of stakes in Chile from 115 to 75.

He had also shortened Sunday meetings in the area from three hours to two hours and fifteen minutes, giving Saints more time to study the gospel of Christ, be with family, visit struggling members, and fulfill callings. While the Church in Chile still faced difficulties retaining members, many Saints were optimistic about its future.[5]

In meetings with Relief Society and priesthood leaders, Anne reminded them that they were colaborers in the Lord's work. "Brethren, please follow the example of the First Presidency and the Twelve," she urged. "Listen to women's voices—to their wise understanding as they share helpful information in welfare committee meetings, ward council meetings, and monthly stewardship meetings."[6]

She also urged the Relief Society leaders to be ready to counsel with priesthood leaders. "Come prepared to council meetings to make a meaningful difference," she said. "That means coming with solutions and ideas, and not just identifying challenges or problems."

When speaking about welfare, Anne used an overhead projector and the simplified welfare booklet to teach the leaders how to conduct ward welfare committee meetings and home needs visits. She emphasized that Relief Society presidents were responsible for making the home visits at the request of bishops.

"The president visits the sister in her home. She can evaluate the needs of the sister. When she carefully listens, the Spirit will help her suggest ways to meet those needs," the booklet taught. "After the home visit, the president returns to the bishop or branch president and reports on what she learned."

Anne felt that most of the priesthood leaders came to these meetings with open minds, eager for clarification on how to work with the Relief Society on welfare. And the Relief Society presidents seemed especially grateful for the training. After one meeting, a woman approached her and said, "I was troubled. Now I know what to do."[7]

Later, Anne reflected on the people she met. The goodness of their lives and their dedication to the work of the Lord inspired her.

"I'm grateful for all that I learned and especially for all that I saw in this nation," she reported to the Relief Society general board. "They are trying hard to do what they can do to build the Church."[8]

ON THE OTHER SIDE of the world, meanwhile, Allwyn Kilbert and his fellow missionaries in the India Bangalore Mission welcomed new mission leaders Brent and Robin Bonham to their field of service.

The Bonhams had just come from Utah, where they received training in a new missionary guide called *Preach My Gospel*. The guide was designed to give missionaries the flexibility they needed to teach the Savior's gospel as guided by the Spirit to address the needs of the people they met.[9]

As Allwyn learned more about *Preach My Gospel,* he was excited to implement it. He had joined the Church in his hometown of Coimbatore, India, in March 2001, and he felt indebted to the missionary program. When his grandmother died a few months after his baptism, he found comfort in what the missionaries had taught about the plan of salvation. And after reading articles about missionary work in the *Liahona,* the Church's international magazine, he decided to serve a mission himself.[10]

Latter-day Saint missionaries had first come to India in the 1850s, and since that time a handful of Saints had always lived in the country. Yet the Church did not begin to grow there until the last few decades of the twentieth century. In the 1980s, Church leaders sent senior missionaries from the Singapore Mission to areas in India. Through these missionaries and the efforts of the local Saints, the Church took root. Among the more than one billion people in the country, just over fifty-four hundred were Latter-day Saints.[11]

This growth remained slow for many years. In 1996, three years after the India Bangalore Mission was established, the government restricted the number of foreign missionaries laboring in the country. Most people in India were Hindu or Muslim, while a small minority were Christian, Sikh, Buddhist, Jain, Baha'i, or Parsi. When

Allwyn and other missionaries taught about the Savior and His Church, many people were unfamiliar with basic principles in the lessons.[12]

Allwyn believed *Preach My Gospel* could help the missionaries tailor the gospel message to all people, regardless of their backgrounds or beliefs. For over forty years, the missionary lessons had been made up of six scripted lessons. In contrast, *Preach My Gospel* asked missionaries to focus on learning gospel principles so they could better adapt their lessons to the people they taught.

The new curriculum provided missionaries five lessons on the Restoration, the plan of salvation, the gospel of Jesus Christ, the commandments, and the laws and ordinances of the gospel. Other chapters in the book taught the missionaries more about the role of the Book of Mormon, recognizing the Spirit, developing Christlike attributes, and other important principles.

"Central to our Father's plan is Jesus Christ's Atonement," read one key passage from the first lesson. "Through the Atonement we can be freed from the burden of our sins and develop faith and strength to face our trials."[13]

Over the next few months, President and Sister Bonham prepared the mission to switch to *Preach My Gospel*. At a zone conference in August 2004, they spoke to the missionaries about using time wisely, one of the principles from the new curriculum. The next day, Allwyn wrote home to his family about the changes. "The system that has been introduced is not only for India but all throughout the world," he told them. "Missionaries are given more freedom and also accountability."[14]

In September, President Bonham called Allwyn to be a zone leader in Chennai, a city on India's southeastern coast. At zone meetings, Allwyn used *Preach My Gospel* to train the other missionaries and help them adjust to the new method for sharing the gospel.[15]

Before long, missionary work accelerated in Chennai. Allwyn and his companions met a woman named Mary and her grandson Yuvaraj. The family had become interested in the restored gospel when Yuvaraj enrolled in a school run by a local Latter-day Saint. As the missionaries taught the lessons from *Preach My Gospel,* Mary showed a special interest in being sealed to her late husband, who had died years earlier. The missionaries could tell that family was important to Mary, so they adapted their messages to focus on its eternal nature. When Allwyn and his companions invited her and Yuvaraj to be baptized, they accepted.

On the day of their baptism, five other people were baptized as well.[16]

On Sunday, December 26, 2004, Stanley Wan stepped out of his Church meetings in Hong Kong to take a telephone call. More than ten years had passed since he'd helped President Hinckley select the Hong Kong Temple site. He was now an area authority seventy in Asia and worked as the Church's welfare manager in the area.

The phone call was from Garry Flake, the Church's director of humanitarian response. His voice sounded urgent. He wanted to know about a tsunami in Indonesia.

Stanley didn't know what Garry was talking about. He hung up and called the Church's office in Indonesia. No one there knew much about the tsunami, but news reports were surfacing.[17]

Earlier that morning, a massive earthquake had struck in the Indian Ocean, off the west coast of the Indonesian island of Sumatra. The force of the quake had radiated out across the ocean, propelling towering walls of seawater toward land. In Indonesia, India, Sri Lanka, Malaysia, and Thailand, mountainous waves had crashed into towns and villages, flooding streets and leveling homes and buildings. An unknown number of people were missing or dead.[18]

Once they understood the scope and seriousness of what happened, Stanley and Garry decided to meet in Colombo, Sri Lanka, to assess the situation. The Church had several missionaries and about 850 members on the island. But unlike Indonesia and India, Sri Lanka did not have a Church administrative office or local Church staff.

Right away, Stanley left for the airport. He arrived in Sri Lanka around midnight and found the island teeming with reporters, charity organizations, and people looking for friends and family. At his hotel, his room had been given to a higher-paying guest, so he tracked down the local missionaries and slept on their floor.

The next day, Garry Flake arrived from the United States, and he and Stanley spent the morning meeting with branch leaders and members. They then traveled around the island to assess the damage.

Sri Lanka's eastern coast was the hardest hit. Everywhere they looked, houses and buildings had collapsed. The roads were crammed with cars and people trying to escape the chaos. Trains and buses had stopped running. Thousands upon thousands of people sat homeless beside piles of rubble, while soldiers searched for survivors.[19]

In recent years, the Church had provided disaster relief around the world, helping refugees in war-torn Kosovo, Sierra Leone, and Afghanistan; flood victims in Venezuela and Mozambique; and earthquake survivors in El Salvador, Turkey, Colombia, and Taiwan. Now, in southeast Asia, the Church had several pallets of medical supplies ready for use in the areas affected by the tsunami. With Church humanitarian funds, Stanley and Garry purchased additional emergency medical supplies, food, and other resources for local leaders to distribute to victims. They also directed Church members to use a local meetinghouse to assemble hygiene kits and other relief supplies.[20]

After spending a few days in Sri Lanka, Stanley and Garry traveled to Indonesia. There they met with the country's Coordinating Minister for People's Welfare, with whom Garry had worked before.

"What is your greatest need?" Garry asked him.

"We need body bags for the dead," the minister replied.

Stanley and Garry reached out to contacts in Beijing, and they found a company that could ship ten thousand body bags a day. Stanley and Garry then arranged the transport to Indonesia.

With the body bags on their way, the Church provided tents, tarps, medical kits, and used clothing for the tsunami victims. It also joined with a Muslim relief organization to deliver more than seventy tons of additional supplies.[21]

But there was so much more to do. Everywhere Stanley and Garry turned, they could see people in need. Thousands had been reported dead in Sri Lanka and Indonesia. Thousands more were dead in India and Thailand.

And the death toll was rapidly rising.[22]

ALLWYN KILBERT WAS LYING on his bed, waiting for his turn to use the shower, when the earthquake struck Chennai, India. The night before, he and his fellow missionaries had been exhausted after attending a Christmas activity with their branch. When his bed started to shake, he thought his companion was trying to be funny.

"Why are you shaking my bed?" he called out. "I'm already awake."

His companion, Revanth Nelaballe, entered the room. "It was a tremor," he said. "An earthquake."[23]

Earthquakes were uncommon in southern India, but the missionaries didn't think much about it. Still, when they arrived at church later that morning, Allwyn sensed that something was wrong. After sacrament meeting began, branch president Seong Yang unexpectedly excused himself from the stand and left the chapel. His cell phone had been buzzing almost nonstop with calls about a tsunami flooding the coast. He left the building to check on his home, which was near the beach, and assess the needs of the Saints affected by the disaster.[24]

Later that day, Allwyn and his companions headed to the beach to see what had happened. Police officers had set up barricades to keep onlookers back and were patrolling the area on horseback. Along the beach, people were pulling bodies out of the water, which had reached more than half a mile inland. All along the coast, low-lying fishing communities were ravaged, and many fishermen had lost their boats and equipment. In the town of Nagapattinam, 185 miles south of Chennai, there was widespread destruction.[25]

The next morning Allwyn and his companions went to the Chennai First Branch meetinghouse to help with a service project organized by the two branches in the city. Overnight, the Church had sent truckloads of supplies from a town nearly four hundred miles away. For the next two days, the missionaries and members assembled and sorted relief kits containing clothing, bedding, hygiene items, and eating utensils.[26]

On Tuesday, December 28, Allwyn and his companions met with President Bonham, their mission president. Since the tsunami hit, Latter-day Saints in India had gone to work distributing Church-provided goods among the victims. After loading trucks with hundreds of hygiene kits and other supplies, the missionaries traveled with President Bonham to deliver them to an Indian Red Cross station.

At the station, the man who greeted them recognized their name tags. "Oh, you're from the Church," he said. "What did you bring?"

They replied that they had lanterns, hygiene kits, and several tons of clothes. The official was thrilled with the donations and told them to drive the trucks into the facility.

Inside they found people crowding around huge piles of clothing. Workers wearing masks and gloves sorted through the piles, making sure the clothes were clean and in good condition. People from different religions and organizations were also dropping off supplies, and Allwyn and the other missionaries spent several hours unloading the trucks and moving the supplies to where they were needed.

As he looked at the people from different groups, Allwyn was struck by how they all worked together out of love for their neighbor.

"There are good people everywhere," he thought.[27]

IN MAY 2005, EMMA Acosta and her boyfriend, Hector David Hernandez, had been dating for six months. She was nineteen years old, and he had recently returned from a mission to Guatemala City. They were deeply in love and had begun talking about marriage. But in Tegucigalpa, Honduras, where they lived, young men and women usually did not marry until after they had dated for a few years and completed their university studies.

Emma had recently enrolled at a public university, and she was determined to earn her degree. One year earlier, at the Church's general Young Women meeting, President Hinckley had urged young women to take their studies seriously. "Get all of the education that you possibly can," he'd said. "Training is the key to opportunity."

Hector David also planned to attend university. He and Emma knew that many married students dropped out of school because of the financial responsibilities that came with marriage and raising families. Still, they felt prompted by the Spirit not to put off marriage.[28]

One day, Emma told Hector David about a ward temple trip to the Guatemala City Temple. She had never been to the temple before and wanted to go.

"Why don't we go together and ask the Lord what He wants from this relationship?" Hector David suggested. Over the years, Church leaders had urged young people to seek the Lord's guidance on questions of courtship and marriage. Emma and Hector David did not need to go to the house of the Lord to receive personal revelation, but it was a holy place where they could feel close to Him and His Spirit as they sought guidance.[29]

Guatemala City was a fourteen-hour journey from Tegucigalpa. On their first morning at the temple, Emma and Hector David performed baptisms for the dead. When Emma stepped out of the dressing room, she found Hector David waiting for her by the baptismal font, dressed in white. As he baptized her, she received a personal witness that she should marry him.[30]

Later, after Hector David finished an endowment session, he joined Emma in a garden on the temple grounds. He took her hand and hugged her. He too had received an answer. "I feel that the Lord is going to be with us," he said. "He is going to give us the strength for any situation that comes from here on."[31]

A few weeks later, Emma was working at her family's grocery store when she received a call from Hector David. He told her that he had just spoken to her father about marrying her. The conversation had not gone well. Her father was a Latter-day Saint, but he had not been to church in a while. He did not understand why Emma wanted to get married already.

After the phone call, Emma saw her father enter the store, his face serious. He congratulated her on her engagement, but it was clear he was disappointed. He was worried that she would not finish her degree.

"If you plan to get married, you'd better look for a job," he said. "I don't want you to come to work here anymore."[32]

Unsure where to go for work, Emma went to the Church's employment resource center in Tegucigalpa. Opened in 2002, it was one of hundreds set up around the world to help Saints find better employment. The instructors at the center were local returned missionaries. They talked to her about the Perpetual Education Fund, which President Hinckley had unveiled in 2001, but for the time being she was not interested in taking out a loan for school. They also gave her tips on how to interview for a job and helped her create a résumé. Equipped with these skills, she soon found work at a bank.[33]

As her wedding day approached, Emma felt discouraged. Although her father had agreed to help pay for the wedding, he and other relatives were vocal about their opposition to the marriage.

Their disapproval weighed heavily on Emma. One day, she knelt alone in her living room to pray. "This is what you asked us to do," she told Heavenly Father. "I'm trying to be obedient."

Suddenly, the story of the Savior walking on water came into her mind. She remembered how Peter tried to go to Jesus, only to sink when he became afraid. Like Peter, Emma also felt like she was drowning.

But then a feeling of peace came over her. "Daughter, you are concentrating on the storm," the voice of the

Lord told her. "I just need you to see me. Focus on me, on what I have already put in your heart."

She felt as if the Lord was taking her hand, just as He had taken Peter's.[34]

In late September 2005, Angela Peterson had been hard at work all month getting ready for a visit from a high-ranking public official from the Middle East. As part of her new job at an international and government relations firm in Washington, DC, she was sometimes asked to plan walking tours, dinners, and cultural events for important visitors.

When the official arrived, he and Angela talked, and they found they had several things in common. They had both been raised in rural areas, and both prized family and faith. The official did not drink alcohol because of his Muslim beliefs, and he was impressed that Angela did not drink either.

Angela had planned plenty of events for the official's stay, but after several days, he said, "I think I've seen all of Washington now! Is there something else you could show me, perhaps something different?"

An image flashed through Angela's mind: the Washington DC Temple. She hesitated, wondering if it would be appropriate to take him to a place that was sacred to her. Still, the image of the temple wouldn't leave her mind.

"There is actually one place that I haven't shown you," she told him. "It's the most important place to me in Washington, DC."[35]

The official enthusiastically agreed to go, and Angela started making arrangements. She called the director of the temple visitors' center, Elder Jess L. Christensen, who offered to close the building for a few hours to give the official a private tour.

The next day, Angela picked up the official and drove him along a beautiful, winding parkway to the temple. During the nearly hour-long drive, he asked her question after question about the Church, and she felt thoughts and words coming to her with complete clarity. He listened closely and seemed interested in the First Vision, the Book of Mormon, modern-day prophets, the Church's global humanitarian work, and the law of tithing.

By the time Angela rounded the final bend of the parkway, it was evening, and the house of the Lord shone brightly in the setting sun. As they crossed the temple grounds, the *Christus* statue in the visitors' center was plainly visible. Elder Christensen conducted the tour, which featured a display of the Book of Mormon in many translations, including the official's native Arabic.[36]

At the end of the tour, Elder Christensen played a video of President Hinckley testifying about the importance of families. Beside the television screen was a framed copy of "The Family: A Proclamation to the World." The official read it silently and nodded.

"This is what I believe," he said. "This is what my people believe."

On the drive back to the city, the official told Angela he was impressed with the Church's emphasis on family, and he was happy to know of another faith that valued families as his own did. On the final day of his visit to Washington, Angela gave him a copy of the proclamation.

"I wanted to give you something that I think would be meaningful to the people of your country," she explained.

Accepting the gift, he said, "This will help my people."[37]

CHAPTER 35

Hand in Hand

In early 2006, Willy Binene was eager to move to Kinshasa, the capital city of the Democratic Republic of the Congo, to continue his training in electrical engineering. For thirteen years, he'd been working as a farmer in the village of Luputa, some nine hundred miles from the city.

He was now married to a young woman named Lilly, whom he had baptized during his service as a branch missionary. They had two children together, but for the past two years, Lilly and the children had been living in Kinshasa while Willy earned enough money to join them and return to school.[1]

On March 26, mission president William Maycock organized the first district in Luputa and called Willy to serve as its president. Willy felt unsure of himself, but he abandoned his plans to move and accepted the call. A short time later, Lilly and the children returned to Luputa, and Willy began his new responsibilities with them at his side.[2]

He was only one of many Saints accepting calls to lead the Church in Africa. Nearly thirty years after the first full-time missionaries came to Ghana and Nigeria, the Church had swelled to more than two hundred thousand members across the continent. There were now stakes in the Democratic Republic of the Congo, Kenya, the Republic of the Congo, Ghana, Côte d'Ivoire, Liberia, Madagascar, Nigeria, South Africa, and Zimbabwe. Strong local leaders, firmly grounded in the teachings of the Savior and His restored Church, were a constant need.[3]

An Ivorian named Norbert Ounleu joined the Church as a university student in 1995. Two years later, he became a bishop when the first stake in Côte d'Ivoire was organized. Three years after that, he became a stake president when his stake was divided. Five years later, he and his wife, Valerie, were called as mission leaders in the newly created Ivory Coast Abidjan Mission.[4]

At this same time, Abigail Ituma, a former broadcast journalist and radio DJ, served as a Relief Society president in her ward in Lagos, Nigeria. Outgoing and funny, Abigail enjoyed bringing smiles to the faces of everyone around her. Many of the women in her ward had stopped coming to church, so she made it her mission to bring them back. She called one of these women to be her second counselor, and before long, they were spending hours together, meeting with sisters and inviting them to church.

Abigail believed in the power of connecting with people. On Sundays, she and her counselors taught lesson after lesson about visiting teaching. At first, no one seemed eager to embrace the program. But Abigail was persistent, and after a while, more and more sisters began ministering to each other. Attendance at Relief Society meetings began to improve.[5]

In Kenya, meanwhile, Joseph and Gladys Sitati were well known for their service in the Church and devotion to Jesus Christ. Before their baptism in March 1986, the Sitatis were not a religious family. They sometimes attended local Christian churches, but they never felt spiritually nourished. Joseph often spent his Sundays working or playing golf.

Embracing the restored gospel changed everything. The Sitatis felt good in the Church, and as it became a central part of their lives, they began spending more time together as a family. Joseph served as branch and district president for many years and helped the Church become officially recognized in Kenya in 1991. When the Nairobi Kenya Stake was organized in 2001, he was called as its president. Three years later, in April 2004, he became an area authority seventy. Gladys, meanwhile, served as a branch Relief Society president as well as a teacher in Sunday School, Primary, Young Women, Relief Society, and seminary.[6]

In 1991, the Sitatis traveled to the Johannesburg South Africa Temple and became the first Kenyan family to be sealed for time and eternity.

"As we reflected upon what we had gone through," Joseph later recalled, "it was abundantly clear to all of us that one could not start understanding the true meaning of the gospel of Jesus Christ until one had been sealed in the temple."[7]

BACK IN SYDNEY, AUSTRALIA, eighteen-year-old Blake McKeown was about to graduate from high school—and he needed a plan. If he started university, he wouldn't be allowed to pause his studies for longer than a year. And since he intended to serve a two-year mission when he turned nineteen, he decided to get a seasonal job after graduation rather than follow many of his peers to university.

Blake had been a lifeguard at a pool near his home, and he liked the work. Recently, *Bondi Rescue,* a new reality television show about lifeguards at Sydney's popular Bondi Beach, got him thinking about ocean lifeguarding. Although Bondi Beach was around forty miles from his home, he decided to take part in a one-week "work experience" program there, which introduced him to the day-to-day duties of the job. He also took a fitness test required for anyone who wanted to be a beach lifeguard.[8]

The test was challenging, but Blake was ready for it. As a deacon, he had gotten interested in athletics after going mountain biking with the young men in his stake. Although the Church had adopted Scouting as part of its Young Men program in the early twentieth century, it was seldom used in most countries outside the United States and Canada. In Australia, about a third of local units participated in Scouting. Blake's stake was not one of them. In such instances, leaders used a special guide prepared by the Church for planning Young Men activities.

The leader who took the young men mountain biking, Matt Green, went on to introduce Blake to the triathlon, a sport that combines swimming, bicycling, and running. Under Matt's coaching and mentorship, Blake had developed discipline and focus. When he took the fitness test at Bondi Beach, Blake's years of training and competing paid off. He performed well and was hired as a trainee lifeguard.[9]

After his high school graduation, Blake began working every weekday at the beach. The job did not guarantee him time on *Bondi Rescue*, but the show's producers soon had camera crews recording him as he learned how to use lifeguard equipment, help beachgoers, and enforce beach rules. They also caught the moment when he rescued a person from the ocean for the first time.[10]

Blake enjoyed the work. As the only Church member on staff, he felt a little intimidated by the other lifeguards, whose lives and values were very different from his own. But he never felt pressured to drop his standards around them.[11]

In early 2007, Blake and other lifeguards responded when a man was spotted struggling in a treacherous part of the water. They searched for forty-five minutes, but there was no sign of a drowned or struggling swimmer, and none of the twenty-five thousand beachgoers had reported a missing friend or family member. Ultimately, the lifeguards gave up the search, hoping whoever they saw had found his way back to shore.[12]

Two hours later, a young man approached Blake at the lifeguard tower. He said he couldn't find his father. "Just stay there for a second," Blake told the young man. He then went and informed the other lifeguards.

The crew rushed back into the water on boards and a Jet Ski. They also called in a police helicopter to patrol the ocean from above. Blake, meanwhile, stayed with the young man and his mother, asking questions about the missing man. But even as Blake calmly spoke to them, he worried that their husband and father was dead.

With daylight fading, one of the rescuers spotted someone under the waves. A lifeguard dove in and carried the man back to shore. They tried to resuscitate him, but it was too late.

Blake reeled at the news. How had he and the other lifeguards lost track of the man, especially when the beach had been so well patrolled? Blake had never thought much about death, and no one close to him had ever died. Now death felt very real to him.

It was late when Blake finished work that night. As he thought about the senselessness of the tragedy he'd just witnessed, he reflected on the plan of salvation. All his life, he had been taught that death was not the end of existence, that Jesus Christ had made it possible for everyone to rise in the Resurrection.

In the weeks that followed, faith in these principles gave him comfort.[13]

On March 31, 2007, the Saints sustained Julie B. Beck, Silvia H. Allred, and Barbara Thompson as the new Relief Society general presidency. At the time, Silvia was serving alongside her husband, Jeff, the president of the Missionary Training Center in the Dominican Republic. Although she had enjoyed being among the missionaries in the Caribbean, she looked forward to working with the women of the Church. This new call made her the first Latin American to serve in the Relief Society general presidency.[14]

A short time later, Boyd K. Packer, the acting president of the Quorum of the Twelve Apostles, invited the new presidency to meet with him in his office. When they arrived, he showed them a row of binders on a shelf. "I've had these for about fifteen years," he explained.

Inside the binders were more than a thousand pages of Relief Society history. Decades earlier, as a young apostle, he had been a general authority adviser to the Relief Society and had gained an immense admiration for the organization and its then-president, Belle Spafford. Later, he'd asked writers Lucile Tate and Elaine

Harris to compile a history of the Relief Society for his own use. Their work was contained in the binders.

"These are my personal copies," he now told the new presidency. "I'm giving them to you."[15]

Under President Bonnie D. Parkin, the Relief Society general board had studied *Women of Covenant: The Story of Relief Society,* a lengthy history published for the organization's sesquicentennial in 1992. Now President Beck and her counselors felt impressed to read the history in the binders, so they divided them up and studied each volume in turn. As they read, they gained a clear sense of the vision and purpose of their organization.[16]

Relief Society, they understood, was originally established by priesthood authority. Its activities and endeavors had changed over the years, with some presidencies establishing hospitals or focusing on social work, literacy, or some other kind of service. Yet giving women opportunities to expound the gospel of Jesus Christ and provide relief to those in need had always been central to the organization's work.

Still, the presidency worried that Relief Society had become just another class to attend on Sunday. Weekday Relief Society meetings and activities, especially where the Church and its members were well established, were often social events that had little to do with giving service or teaching the gospel. Many members did not know the organization's inspired beginnings or its rich history. Younger women especially showed little enthusiasm for it. The presidency believed the women in the Church needed to find strength and value in their identity as Relief Society sisters.[17]

As the presidency discussed the past and present Relief Society, they thought about the organization's core message and purpose for the Church's global sisterhood. Each member of the presidency had lived outside the United States, and each knew they needed to craft a clear, simple message that could unite and inspire Relief Society members despite differences in language, culture, and experience.

Together, the presidency identified three purposes of Relief Society: first, increase personal righteousness and faith; second, strengthen families and homes; and third, search out and provide relief for those who are in need. Moving forward, they decided to promote "faith, family, and relief" at every opportunity.[18]

One of their first assignments was to revise the Relief Society section of the *Church Handbook of Instructions*. As the previous Relief Society general presidency had known, the complex language of the handbook could be hard for some members to read and understand. President Beck's presidency thought that some of its guidelines were better suited for Church members in Utah than for Saints worldwide. Like other Church leaders at the time, they wanted an easier-to-read handbook that gave Church members the flexibility to adapt to local needs and circumstances.[19]

The current handbook devoted more than twenty pages to the Relief Society. President Beck hoped to produce something much shorter and simpler. Using faith, family, and relief as their foundation, the presidency drafted a four-page document and submitted it to Elder Dallin H. Oaks, the apostle supervising the revision. Although he liked what they did, he recommended adding more instructions. They expanded it to twelve pages, and it was approved.[20]

The handbook was only one of the Relief Society's many projects. While helping with the revision, Silvia worked on committees devoted to training, visiting teaching, and integrating new sisters into Relief Society. She also traveled to many countries around the world to meet with Relief Society sisters and tend to their needs.

She and the other members of the presidency were determined to help everyone catch the vision of Relief Society.[21]

IN MAY 2007, SILVINA Mouhsen, a Latter-day Saint living in Buenos Aires, Argentina, was troubled. For the last couple of years, she had been supporting her sister, who had been diagnosed with depression and severe psychosis. During that time, Silvina had also experienced the death of a close relative, given birth to her third child, and served as a ward Relief Society president. Her husband, David, meanwhile, was seeking a promotion at work, furthering his education, and serving in the Church. Because of their conflicting schedules, she hardly saw him during the week.[22]

Now, Silvina struggled to get out of bed in the morning, and she found herself making disconcerting mistakes. First, she had been driving to the supermarket and suddenly couldn't remember where she was. On another day, she had gone to pick up her son, Nicolás, from school and accidentally grabbed another child's hand. More recently, she had dropped her daughter off at a party on the wrong day.[23]

When Silvina spoke to her doctor about these incidents, he told her that she was experiencing symptoms of depression. He recommended that she go to therapy, take a leave of absence from her teaching job, and get medication.

Silvina had a hard time accepting this advice. She knew from caring for her sister that mental illnesses were complex, sometimes stemming from genetic factors that were beyond anyone's control. Yet she had always considered herself a strong person—someone who took care of others during hardships, not one who experienced hardships herself. For a while, she told few people about her diagnosis.[24]

As Silvina thought more about mental health—her sister's and her own—she noticed others who struggled with similar symptoms. Yet no one talked about them. One woman at church had mental health problems that prevented her from attending Church meetings. Whenever she asked her local leaders for help, they usually suggested that she draw closer to God and trust in Him to solve her problems.

From her own experience, Silvina knew that this was only a partial solution to the woman's problems, and she encouraged her to seek professional help. Months later, Silvina learned that the woman had taken her advice and was improving.[25]

The Church had been talking more openly about mental illness in recent years, urging the Saints to respond compassionately to those who struggled. It also provided various mental health resources. The Relief Society Social Services Department, now called LDS Family Services, had long offered counseling and other mental health assistance to Saints.[26] Although Family Services only operated agencies in the United States, Canada, Australia, New Zealand, Great Britain, and Japan, it was in the process of expanding into still more countries, including Argentina. Some Welfare Services Centers in South America, such as those in Chile, offered counseling with trained therapists. The Church also provided mental health support during natural disasters. After the tsunami in the Indian Ocean, for instance, LDS Family Services had conducted training in the affected region to help people cope with loss and trauma.[27]

As Silvina followed her doctor's advice, her health improved. In addition to therapy, rest, and medication, she found comfort in exercise and music. She also looked for ways to find balance in her life. At home, she and David spent more time with each other. Sometimes they met at the temple after work so they could do an endowment session. Other times, they simply went to the grocery store together.

Silvina found additional strength in the family proclamation. It taught that spirit daughters and sons of God had accepted His plan in the premortal life, making it possible for them to progress toward a divine destiny as "heirs of eternal life." Knowing this truth gave her purpose, direction, and perspective as she faced her challenges.[28]

At church, she relied more on her counselors in the Relief Society presidency to help fulfill her duties. She leaned on the Savior, and her faith in Him began to have new meaning to her. She listened more to the sacrament prayers each Sunday, which became an opportunity to reflect more deeply on the ordinance. One evening, David gave her a priesthood blessing, promising that her mind would function in the way she needed. Her friends also prayed for her, and her brother put her name on the temple's prayer roll.

Through these experiences, Silvina grew in spirit. She realized the Savior knew her hardships perfectly. She did not have to deal with her struggles alone.

Friends, family, and the Lord were there to support her as she healed.[29]

IN JUNE 2007, HECTOR David Hernandez returned home from school exhausted. Shadows hung beneath his eyes as he sat down with his wife, Emma, and told her he had fallen asleep in class.[30]

A year and a half had passed since Emma and Hector David were sealed in the Guatemala City Temple. Now they were both taking classes at a public university near their home in Honduras. And along with balancing work, school, and marriage, they were caring for their infant son, Oscar David.

The university they attended offered a limited course selection each semester, which meant it would take longer for Emma and Hector David to graduate. And being new parents came with a lot of sleepless nights, causing their schoolwork to suffer.[31]

As they sat together, Hector David also told Emma that he had just received his grades.

"I didn't do very well," he said, frustrated.

Emma realized that something needed to change. As they discussed their options, she thought about the Perpetual Education Fund. The Church's loan program had remained on her mind over the years, but she and Hector David had wanted to be self-sufficient. Now they felt prompted to change their plans.[32]

"What if you go to a private university and we use the Perpetual Education Fund?" Emma suggested.

Hector David had dreamed of graduating from the accounting program at the university they attended. But the private university Emma mentioned offered a similar finance major. It also had three terms a year, meaning he could take more classes and graduate sooner. The Perpetual Education Fund, meanwhile, could help pay the high cost of the university.

"OK," Hector David agreed. But he wanted Emma to use the PEF to reach her academic goals as well. "We're going to study," he said. "I'm going to study. You're going to study."

"OK," Emma said, excited by the plan.

From there, they jointly applied for a PEF loan and enrolled in the private university. Emma took a leap of faith and quit her bank job, giving her more time to spend at home with Oscar David.[33]

People who used the Perpetual Education Fund were required to take a course to prepare them for future employment. The class offered resources to help participants discover their ideal career and how to prepare for it.

One of Emma's assignments was to write down her talents and interests. She noted that she was creative and that she was interested in the advertising aspect of business. She then spoke to people who worked in marketing and graphic design. After those interviews, Emma decided to change her major from business administration to marketing and advertising.

She did not know much about these subjects, but when she sat down in her first marketing class at the private university, she realized she was in the right place.

"This is what I was born to do," she thought.[34]

Even with financial help from the PEF, being a student and parent was not easy. She and Hector David continued to face sleepless nights and difficulty juggling their responsibilities. Some days, Emma wondered if she should set school aside and finish her education later.

But during hard moments she and Hector David repeated a motto to each other: "This is the time."[35]

ON JANUARY 12, 2008, PRESIDENT Gordon B. Hinckley stood at the grave of his wife, Marjorie, in the Salt Lake City Cemetery. It had been nearly four years since her death. She had taken ill on the flight home from the Accra Ghana Temple dedication and passed away a few months later, on April 6, 2004.

Together, President and Sister Hinckley had crisscrossed the globe, ministering to the Saints and enjoying one another's companionship. He missed her immensely. Only his Church service and family kept him from being overcome with loneliness.[36]

President Hinckley tried to visit her grave every week to leave her flowers and meditate on their sixty-six years of marriage. He worried that some people might think he visited the grave too often. But he went anyway.

"She was my everything, the one whom I held most dear," he'd once reflected. "The least I can do is to leave an expression of beauty each week."[37]

On this visit, there were still wreaths on the grave from previous weeks, and President Hinckley decided to leave them there a little while longer.

A short time later, the prophet sat down to dictate his wishes for his funeral. At ninety-seven, he was the oldest living Church president in history. He had survived a cancer operation a few years before, but now the cancer had spread. He knew his time on earth was ending.[38]

"I desire that I be buried in a cherrywood casket, the same as my wife," he dictated. He hoped his funeral would be held in the Conference Center, even if it meant that there would be empty seats in the massive auditorium.

"I broke ground for it, dedicated it," he explained, "and think it appropriate that my funeral service be held there."[39]

President Hinckley did not want a long funeral. It should be no more than ninety minutes, he said, just as the *Church Handbook of Instructions* advised. He asked that his longtime first counselor, President Thomas S. Monson, conduct. He also requested that the Tabernacle Choir sing "My Redeemer Lives," a hymn he had written years before:

> *I know that my Redeemer lives,*
> *Triumphant Savior, Son of God,*
> *Victorious over pain and death,*
> *My King, my Leader, and my Lord.*

At the end of his funeral dictation, the prophet mentioned Sister Hinckley. He had every assurance that their marriage covenants would endure in the life to come. It was his final wish to be buried next to her.

"I thus place myself in the hands of the Lord," he concluded, "and join my beloved eternal companion to walk hand in hand on the road of immortality and eternal life."[40]

CHAPTER 36

Press Forward

President Gordon B. Hinckley passed peacefully away on the evening of January 27, 2008. During the prophet's brief final illness, family and friends sat at his bedside in Salt Lake City. President Thomas S. Monson, who had served with him in the First Presidency for over two decades, visited him a few hours before his death and gave him a blessing.[1]

Six days later, sixteen thousand mourners gathered in the Conference Center for the prophet's funeral. Countless others watched the proceedings on BYU TV, on the Church's website, and in meetinghouses across the world.

During the service, President Monson spoke of how he and President Hinckley had shared much happiness, laughter, and sorrow over the years. "He was an island of calm in a sea of storm," President Monson recalled. "He comforted and calmed us when conditions in the world were frightening. He guided us undeviatingly on the path which will lead us back to our Heavenly Father."[2]

The Saints remembered President Hinckley as a world-traveling and temple-building prophet. He had journeyed over a million miles to visit the Saints around the world—more than any Church president. He had also expanded the use of satellite and digital technologies to reach the Saints wherever they lived. The Church now broadcast general conference in eighty languages. In 2003, he had initiated worldwide leadership broadcasts, allowing Church leaders to train many Saints from a single location. The same technology had since made large regional and national conferences possible, some involving over eighty stakes at a time.[3]

During his presidency, the number of operating temples had more than doubled, from 47 to 124. Among the temples he had dedicated was a reconstruction of the Nauvoo Temple, which had been destroyed a few years after its dedication in 1846.[4]

These new temples brought sacred ordinances and covenants closer to more people than ever before. In August 2005, for instance, forty-two Saints from the central African nation of Cameroon had traveled five hundred miles to attend a newly dedicated temple in Aba, Nigeria. Recent rains had turned the unpaved roads to mud, but the Saints kept going, even when they had to push their rented passenger vans through the deep mire. While the slow journey was often difficult, it was shorter and more affordable than a trip to the temples in Ghana and South Africa. And the Cameroonian Saints rejoiced as they received their endowment and sealing blessings.[5]

President Hinckley had been grateful to play a part in spreading the blessings of the house of the Lord to so many people. He believed temples served a unique purpose. "At their altars we kneel before God our Creator and are given promise of His everlasting blessings," he taught. "We commune with Him and reflect on His Son, our Savior and Redeemer, the Lord Jesus Christ, who served as proxy for each of us in a vicarious sacrifice in our behalf."[6]

Since his mission to England in the 1930s, President Hinckley had enjoyed a great love for the European Saints. And it had pained him in recent decades to see Europeans drift away from churchgoing. To provide support, he encouraged the creation of "outreach centers" where young single adults could come together to socialize and share their faith in Jesus Christ. Between 2003 and 2007, over seventy such centers were opened across Europe, resulting in many new converts, reactivations, and temple marriages.[7]

President Hinckley had transformed Church public relations as well. Under his watch, the Church started its own website, filled it with Christ-centered messages and training materials, and provided an online newsroom where reporters and others could go for accurate information about the faith.

He had also made himself a visible presence in the wider media, accepting televised interviews with prominent journalists and writing books for major publishing houses. In 2001, he launched the Joseph Smith Papers Project, which aimed to publish all of the prophet's papers online and in scholarly volumes that could be found in libraries around the world.[8]

Of all President Hinckley's many innovations, President Monson felt the Perpetual Education Fund would bless more lives than any other. Already it had benefited nearly thirty thousand students in forty countries.

"What a miracle this is in lifting young people from poverty and helping them enter the workforce," President Monson reflected in his journal. "It is successful beyond our fondest dreams and is a very worthy contribution source for those who wish to advance education in many parts of the world where education does not come to the poor."[9]

THE DAY AFTER THE funeral, Boyd K. Packer, the next most senior apostle, ordained and set apart President Monson as the new Church president. President Monson called Henry B. Eyring, previously a second counselor under President Hinckley, to serve as his first counselor, and Dieter F. Uchtdorf, an apostle from Germany, to serve as his second counselor.[10]

The new presidency took over the construction projects still ongoing at the time of President Hinckley's death, including a dozen temples and about three hundred meetinghouses. The Church was also developing housing for temple missionaries in Nauvoo, constructing a new Church History Library and a large building to help manage philanthropic donations, and building up residential and commercial properties across the street from Temple Square.[11]

But as President Monson began his administration, serious troubles arose. Many homeowners in the United States had begun to default on their mortgages, and the banks holding the unpaid mortgages buckled under the heavy debt. Before long, the United States lapsed into the worst economic crisis since the Great Depression, triggering financial panic and rising unemployment around the world.[12]

"The financial markets are in jeopardy," President Monson reflected in his journal. "Our people, along with others in our nation and in the world, are extended in their debt."[13]

As the crisis worsened, the First Presidency had to consider suspending the Church's various building projects. Having lived through the Great Depression, President Monson understood the dangers of exceeding one's limits. But he also saw that if construction were suspended, it meant unemployment for hundreds of workers such as carpenters and electricians. The construction industry was grinding to a halt, and jobs were hard to come by.

The Presiding Bishopric, who had stewardship over the Church's building and humanitarian efforts, met with the First Presidency every Friday to review the status of projects. One Friday in early 2008, the bishopric asked President Monson what should be done.

"We've got all these construction projects going, in one state or another," the bishopric said. "What is your desire?"

President Monson was firm. "Press forward," he said.[14]

Around this time, Blake McKeown was back on Sydney's Bondi Beach for another summer of lifeguard training in front of the TV camera. His appearance on the second season of *Bondi Rescue* had made him a local celebrity in Australia. Every now and then, while shopping in his hometown or riding a train to work, he'd notice people glancing his way and discreetly pointing. The attention was a little annoying, but he couldn't complain. He liked getting paid to hang out on the beach day after day with his friends. "How could life get any better?" he wondered.[15]

His parents were concerned, though. Had the fame of being on television changed his priorities? Blake had gotten the lifeguarding job a year earlier to make money while waiting to serve a full-time mission. Now his nineteenth birthday had long since come and gone.

"What do I do?" his mother asked their bishop one day. "How's this going to turn out?"

"I don't know," the bishop replied, also concerned. "He was doing so well."

Blake tried to reassure his parents. He told them that he was praying to know the right time to serve. He just didn't feel like the time had come yet. "It's important that I go, not when I go," he told them, echoing something his father had always told him.[16]

Then his brother Wade returned from his mission to Japan. Wade saw his parents' concern and talked to Blake. Blake took Wade's words to heart and began thinking more seriously about leaving on a mission. "If the Church is true," he told himself, "then I have to go on a mission."

He thought about his testimony and the Church. Growing up, he had attended TFY, the multiday youth conference in Australia, which had spread to countries in South America and Europe in 2006 under the Especially for Youth name. He had also faithfully attended early-morning seminary and other Church activities. He may not have always been excited to go, but he had tried to keep the commandments and do what was right. And he had faith in Jesus Christ and in the truth of the restored gospel. That was reason enough to serve.[17]

Blake soon submitted his missionary application. It was a moment of unprecedented opportunities for missionary work. In recent years, Church leaders had "raised the bar" for missionary service, emphasizing the need for committed elders and sisters with high moral standards who knew how to hear and respond to the Holy Spirit. The Church had also introduced service missions for young people with certain health conditions or for whom traditional proselytizing missions weren't a good fit.

When Blake's call came, he received an assignment to serve a full-time proselytizing mission in the Philippines Baguio Mission, one of fifteen missions in the country. All he had left to do was tell his fellow lifeguards.[18]

A short time later, during a filming of *Bondi Rescue*, Blake spoke to the cameras about his faith. "Growing up, I've always been a member of The Church of Jesus Christ of Latter-day Saints," he said. "I go to church every Sunday. I guess I have a bit stricter standards that I live by, but other than that, I'm just a normal person."

After Blake's shift ended, the show's producers had him put on a suit and tie. He then walked to the main lifeguard tower and knocked on the door. "I guess my hands are gonna have to get used to that," he said, looking at the camera.

The lifeguards greeted him with good-natured laughs. "Do you like it?" he asked, showing them his suit. "It's me for the next two years."

"Where are you going?" one of the lifeguards asked.

"To the Philippines," Blake said. "I'm serving my mission, for my church."

"You're Mormon?" said another lifeguard.

"Yeah," Blake said. "I think I've got the best thing in my life, so why shouldn't I share it with other people?"

Blake explained that he would soon be leaving for the United States to receive missionary training and learn Tagalog. He would then go to his assigned field of service. "We'll be actively knocking on doors," he said, "and just trying to teach people about Jesus Christ."

"Well, man, all the best," a lifeguard said, shaking Blake's hand and pulling him into a warm embrace. Blake was sad to leave the beach, and he knew he was going to miss his friends. But he was eager to begin his mission and do good in the world.[19]

Back home, Blake told Wade about the experience. "My challenge as a missionary was to speak to ten people a day in Japan," Wade said. "You've just done that to ten million people in one go."[20]

IN JUNE 2008, WILLY and Lilly Binene caught a bus with their three children to the airport in Mbuji-Mayi, about a hundred miles north of their home in Luputa, Democratic Republic of the Congo. From there, they flew to Kinshasa, spent the night in the city, and then boarded a flight to South Africa. The trip was long, but the children were happy, enjoying their travels. The family was heading to the Johannesburg Temple to be sealed together for eternity.

Two years had passed since Willy's call as president of the Luputa District had reunited them as a family. After moving back to Luputa, Lilly had opened a nursery school. It was an immediate success, and before long, she expanded it to a primary school. Willy had set aside his dream of becoming an electrical engineer to begin training as a nurse at the local hospital. He balanced this work with the demands of his calling, and he relied on the support of his counselors in the district presidency as they learned their new responsibilities, trained local leaders, and visited the Saints.[21]

Recently, the presidency had taken on additional duties to help with a three-year, Church-funded project to pipe clean water into Luputa. The residents of the city had long depended on various pools, springs, and drainage ditches for water. Twice a day, women and children would walk a mile or more to one of these spots, collect water in whatever container they had on hand, and then carry it home. These water sources were teeming with dangerous parasites, and nearly everyone knew someone—often a small child—who had died from the contaminated water. And sometimes women were assaulted as they walked to and from the water source.

For many years, ADIR, a humanitarian organization in the DRC, had wanted to bring clean water to the 260,000 people in and around Luputa. But the best source for the water was a group of hillside springs twenty-one miles away, and ADIR did not have $2.6 million to build the pipeline. Then the organization's managing director heard about Latter-day Saint Charities and contacted local humanitarian missionaries about collaborating on the project.[22]

Created in 1996 under the direction of the First Presidency, Latter-day Saint Charities supported hundreds of Church humanitarian projects across the globe every year. Although its services varied according to need, its recent core initiatives were immunization, wheelchairs, vision care, infant care, and clean water.[23] When word came about the need for a water pipeline to Luputa, Latter-day Saint Charities donated the necessary funds, and volunteers from Luputa and other nearby communities agreed to help provide the labor.

As a district presidency, Willy and his counselors worked with ADIR and Daniel Kazadi, a local Latter-day Saint hired as the site monitor. They also volunteered as laborers themselves.[24]

Now, as the Binenes landed in Johannesburg, they could set aside their busy lives and focus on the house of the Lord. At the airport, they were greeted by a family and driven to the temple's onsite patron housing. Later, Willy and Lilly entered the temple, dropped their children off at the Church-sponsored day care, and changed into white clothes.

Before leaving Luputa, the Binenes had studied the Church's temple preparation manual, *Endowed from on High,* and read apostle James E. Talmage's *The House of the Lord.* Still, when they got to the temple, they were a little disoriented because everything was new and no one spoke French. But by using gestures, they figured out where to go and what to do.

Later, in the sealing room, they were overjoyed to reunite with their three children. Dressed in white, they looked like angels as they came into the room. Willy felt goosebumps on his arms. He and his family no longer seemed to be on the earth. It was like they were in God's presence.[25]

"Wow," he said.

Lilly too felt like they were in heaven. Knowing they were bound together for eternity seemed to multiply the family's love for one another. They were inseparable now. Not even death could part them.[26]

IN EARLY 2009, ANGELA Peterson was living in Utah with her husband, John Fallentine. She and John had met in a single adult ward in Salt Lake City shortly after Angela had left her demanding job in Washington, DC. John was from the western United States, and he had also lived and worked for a time in Washington. He was older than Angela and a little shy, but they had quickly become the best of friends. In November 2007, they were sealed in the Bountiful Utah Temple.

Now the Fallentines were ready for a new adventure. After John received permission from his employer to work remotely, the couple packed up their belongings and moved to New Zealand's North Island. They had both been there before, and they thought it was the most beautiful place on earth.[27]

The New Zealand Saints had recently celebrated the 150th anniversary of the arrival of the Church in their country, and fifty years had passed since the dedication of the New Zealand Temple. At that time, the Church had about seventeen thousand members in the country and no wards or stakes. Now, there were nearly one hundred thousand Saints spread throughout 25 stakes, 150 wards, and 54 branches.[28]

The Fallentines settled in Thames, a coastal town on the Coromandel Peninsula, and soon began serving in their small branch. Most of the members of their branch and stake were Māori, and Angela loved getting to know them. She served in Young Women while John, a Sunday School teacher, volunteered to help the branch president with the young men. Angela and John also served as branch missionaries and ordinance workers in the temple in Hamilton, an almost two-hour drive away.[29]

At home, however, the couple was growing concerned. All her life, Angela had wanted to be a mother. But so far, she and John had not been able to have children. They consulted a doctor in Auckland and underwent various tests to see what, if anything, could be done. When the results came back, both Angela and John learned that they had significant fertility issues. Even with the help of doctors and specialists, Angela's chances of becoming pregnant were slim.

The news was devastating. Every day, Angela walked past a framed copy of the family proclamation in their home. Its message raised a troubling question in her mind. If the family was ordained of God, why couldn't she and John have children?

She felt confused and adrift—yet still hopeful that God would answer her and John's prayers.[30]

On August 9, 2009, President Thomas S. Monson met with Roman Catholic friends at the Cathedral of the Madeleine in Salt Lake City. The magnificent house of worship was one hundred years old, and President Monson had come with other religious and civic officials to celebrate.

President Monson took the occasion to speak about how Catholics and Latter-day Saints had set aside their religious differences to care for people in need. The cathedral's "Good Samaritan" program provided a daily lunch to the hungry, with bread and other food supplied by Church Welfare Services. Similarly, the Catholics operated a local substance abuse facility, which the Church stocked with food. The two churches had also partnered to help refugees arriving in Salt Lake City get adequate hygiene supplies and home furnishings.

This partnership extended far beyond Salt Lake City. In recent years, Catholic charitable agencies had helped the Church distribute over $11 million in humanitarian aid across the world, ensuring that aid was given to those who needed it the most.

"When we have eyes that see, ears that hear, and hearts that know and feel," President Monson told his audience, "we will recognize current needs of our fellow beings among us who cry out for help."³¹

During the past year and a half, President Monson had paid close attention to the Church's many building and humanitarian projects. Even as the United States economy remained stagnant and unemployment high, he had seen unexpected benefits to pressing forward with these efforts. Demand for construction work was down, yet the Church was able to provide jobs for plenty of skilled laborers on its projects.

President Monson had also urged local leaders to cut costs where possible. He asked mission leaders to teach missionaries to be thrifty. He endorsed a plan recently proposed by the Presiding Bishopric to reduce the size of new stake centers by a fourth. Instead of constructing larger, more expensive buildings that accommodated all stake members, stakes could meet in multiple ward buildings and connect to stake conferences through broadcast technology. This allowed Saints to cut down on travel expenses as well.³²

During the recession, President Monson was mindful of people in need—especially widows. Fast offering requests had increased, and he wanted no one to be forgotten. As a young man, President Monson had served as bishop of a Salt Lake City ward with more than a thousand people. Eighty-five of them were widows. Long after his five years as bishop were over, President

Monson had continued to visit these widows, bearing gifts and bringing cheer. As Church president, he regularly visited the lonely and forgotten.

"That service to which all of us have been called is the service of the Lord Jesus Christ," he taught the Saints. "As He enlists us to His cause, He invites us to draw close to Him. He speaks to you and to me."[33]

In 2003, the Church had launched a new website, www.providentliving.org, which taught basic welfare principles. Prior to the recession, the site was receiving over a million page views every month. Now, to help reemphasize these time-honored truths, the Presiding Bishopric prepared a new pamphlet and DVD, *Basic Principles of Welfare and Self-Reliance.* The Saints were urged to pay their tithes and offerings, live within a budget, avoid debt, eat out less often, and keep a reserve of food on hand.

"I declare that the welfare plan of The Church of Jesus Christ of Latter-day Saints is inspired of Almighty God," President Monson testified. "Indeed, the Lord Jesus Christ is its architect."[34]

For decades, Church leaders had defined the mission of the Church as including three elements: perfecting the Saints, proclaiming the gospel, and redeeming the dead. Now President Monson felt that welfare should be the "fourth leg of the stool." In September 2009, he approved editing the *Church Handbook of Instructions* to include "caring for the poor and needy" as part of the Church's mission.[35]

"We are surrounded by those in need of our attention, our encouragement, our support, our comfort, our kindness," he said a few weeks later at general conference. "We are the Lord's hands here upon the earth, with the mandate to serve and to lift His children. He is dependent upon each of us."[36]

CHAPTER 37

Answers Will Come

"What do you think?"

The question hung in the air as Marco Villavicencio waited for his wife, Claudia, to respond. His employer, a telecommunications company in Machala, Ecuador, had just offered him a chance to open a new office in Puerto Francisco de Orellana, a small city in the Amazon rainforest of eastern Ecuador.

Marco was interested in the position, which included a promotion, but he did not want to decide without Claudia. The job would require the Villavicencios and their four-year-old son, Sair, to move more than four hundred miles away.

Claudia, like Marco, had grown up in a big city, so moving to a rainforest would be a major change. But she supported Marco and wanted him to advance in his career. She also liked the idea of moving to a rural area. She thought it would bring their family closer together.

Still, she and Marco had the same question about Puerto Francisco de Orellana: "Is the Church there?" They were both returned missionaries, and the Church was important to them. They wanted their son to grow up in a place where he could attend Primary, learn the gospel, and have spiritual experiences. Ecuador had nearly two hundred thousand Latter-day Saints, but most of them lived near major cities like Quito, the nation's capital, and Guayaquil, where a house of the Lord was dedicated in 1999.[1]

Puerto Francisco de Orellana, known locally as El Coca, was small by comparison, though it had grown rapidly after oil was discovered there some years earlier. Using the Meetinghouse Locator on the Church's website, Claudia searched for a ward or branch near the city. The search produced no results, but a short time later, friends of Marco and Claudia told them about a few other Church members who had moved there for work.

Hearing this comforted Marco and Claudia. After praying about the offer, they decided to accept the job.

The Villavicencios arrived in El Coca in February 2009. The city was in the middle of dense jungle, but to the Villavicencios' surprise, it didn't feel disconnected from the rest of the world. Everywhere they looked, people were coming and going on business.[2]

When their landlord learned they were members of the Church, he told them he knew where a group of members met to read the scriptures together. "I lent them the house," he said.

The group had been getting together every Sunday morning at nine o'clock to sing hymns, read from the *Liahona,* and study the scriptures. They had also contacted Timothy Sloan, president of the Ecuador Quito Mission, who sent two missionaries to visit them. But the missionaries lived four hours away and could not come to El Coca very often.[3]

Marco, Claudia, and Sair began attending Sunday meetings every week. At first, Sair missed Primary and wondered where the other children were. Marco and Claudia missed their old life too, but immersing themselves in the Lord's service made them less homesick.

When the missionaries came to town, Marco enlisted their help to find more members. "Elders," he said, "you must walk around the city." He thought that if people recognized the missionaries, they would ask them where they could gather with other local members.[4]

Little by little, Church members in the city found out about the meeting and joined the group. As the group grew, Marco became its leader. The missionaries began coming every week to teach people and find more Church members. Before long, the Saints in El Coca received permission to follow the Church's basic unit program.

And with this permission came authority to administer the sacrament.[5]

WHEN ANGELA PETERSON FALLENTINE learned that it would be extremely difficult for her and her husband to have biological children, she called her mother on the telephone. "I don't know how to do this," she said. "I don't know anyone who has gone through this." She was terrified.

Her mother listened and then asked if she remembered Ardeth Kapp, the former Young Women general president. "She and her husband were never blessed with children," she reminded Angela, "but she has always been such an example of navigating infertility without letting it define her."

"Don't let this be a stumbling block for you," her mother continued. "I get the sense that you're going to need to sort out the doctrine of motherhood and family, because otherwise, it will be something that you'll keep bumping up against for the rest of your life."

She then said, "I don't know why you and John have to go through this or how long it will last, but if you can hang on and try to understand what the Lord needs you to learn from it, answers will come."[6]

Angela could feel her mother's love and support, and she kept these words close to her heart as she and John encountered more trials while exploring other paths to parenthood, like adoption and in vitro fertilization. When they looked into adoption through LDS Family Services and New Zealand's national program, they learned that their chances of adopting were extremely low.[7]

As Angela faced disappointment after disappointment, she leaned on prayer, fasting, and temple worship for support. She thought often about the Savior, confident He was helping her endure her trials. Yet she also found herself wishing He would simply take them away. At these times, John comforted her. He had faith that all would be well.

Angela's eyes were still drawn to the family proclamation hanging on the wall. She had always loved its teachings. But after finding out about her infertility, she often felt a pang when she read its affirmation of "God's commandment for His children to multiply and replenish the earth." She understood that she and John were not breaking any commandments, since they could not have children naturally. But even as they began treatments for their infertility, Angela wondered if they were doing enough.[8]

Around this time, they moved to Tauranga, a large city on New Zealand's Bay of Plenty, and Angela was called as the stake Young Women president. The new calling intimidated her. She was in her early thirties and felt too young to tell other leaders what to do. At the same time, she also worried about being too old to relate to the young women. She prayed to know how to guide them.

She soon found that she could relate to the girls in ways she hadn't expected. She was younger than their parents, and many of the young women looked up to her and took her counsel to heart. She in turn could encourage and befriend them in a way their mothers couldn't. Without children of her own, she found that she could give them the extra time and counsel they needed from a trusted adult.

The Fallentines also found joy in supporting other families in their ward and stake. They often hosted barbeques, outdoor movie nights, and home evenings. During general conferences, they would invite the young women over to eat crepes before going to the stake center for the general Young Women broadcast. Since it was hard to be so far from family at Christmastime, they held a party on Christmas Eve for some immigrants they knew from South Africa and the island of Niue. These activities always filled their home with children, and Angela and John loved spending time with them and their parents.[9]

One day, while passing the framed family proclamation on her wall, Angela caught sight of its opening words: "We, the First Presidency and the Council of the Twelve Apostles of The Church of Jesus Christ of Latter-day Saints, solemnly proclaim . . ."

"Do I really believe this?" she asked herself. "Do I really believe that these are prophets and apostles saying these words?" Her experiences had changed how she read and understood the family proclamation. Yet she knew that prophets and apostles bore special witness of Jesus Christ, and she believed their words.

She was beginning to see that there were many ways to mother, and she had faith that she and John would have the opportunity to become parents in the eternities. This knowledge helped her understand the importance of marriage and family in the plan of salvation.

She remembered how the family proclamation had inspired and impressed the mechanic and the Middle Eastern official she'd met in Washington, DC. The truths it taught were powerful and relevant to her life, and she trusted in them.[10]

BACK IN EL COCA, Ecuador, Marco Villavicencio had made quick work of opening a telecommunications office in the city, but managing it was a daily challenge. His employees were new to the industry and needed training before they could adequately meet clients' needs. Then there was the matter of finding clients. Since the office was brand new, Marco and his team spent much of their time meeting people and promoting their business. They worked hard, though, and the office was growing.[11]

As busy as Marco was, he made time for his family and the Church. With each passing month, more and more people came to sacrament meeting on Sunday mornings. The Spirit of the Lord had prepared many people for the restored gospel of Christ. They yearned to know about God and His love.

Missionaries now came to the city multiple times a week to teach people and invite them to church. Marco and Claudia wondered how long it would take before their group became a branch.

Seven months after the Villavicencios arrived in El Coca, mission president Timothy Sloan visited the city. Since Marco led the local Church group, President Sloan asked him to introduce him to the Saints while they toured El Coca.

For the rest of the morning and well into the afternoon, Marco took the mission president around the city. President Sloan was especially interested in meeting Melchizedek Priesthood holders, and he interviewed several of them. While traveling from place to place, he also asked Marco about his family, career, and experience in the Church.[12]

At the end of the day, President Sloan told Marco that he wanted to talk. They went to the house where the Saints held their meetings and found an empty room. President Sloan then confided that he'd been praying to find a branch president in the city. "I had the feeling that you are that person," he said. "Do you accept this call of the Lord?"

"Yes," said Marco.

The next day, September 6, 2009, President Sloan organized the Orellana Branch and set Marco apart as its president. A week later, the Church's area office in Quito sent chairs, blackboards, desks, and other items for the branch's meeting place.[13]

The branch had many new leaders, including Claudia, who served as the Young Women president.

Most of the leaders had little experience in the Church, so Marco made training a top priority. He wanted branch leaders to be examples of Christlike love and service. He used every resource he had on hand—every Church manual and video—to help the new leaders learn their responsibilities. Since mobile phones were becoming more common in the city, he would call branch members or send text messages during the week to conduct branch business, plan activities, and meet the needs of his fellow Saints.[14]

Among the items the branch received from the Church was a desktop computer with internet access. The Church had developed a computer program called Member and Leader Services to help local leaders and clerks record and report tithing, attendance, and other data accurately and securely. Marco was familiar with computers from his experience in the tech industry, and he quickly learned how to use the software. Computers were rare in El Coca, though, so he also had to show some of the new leaders how to use them. Fortunately, the Spirit guided them, and they were eager learners who readily adapted to the technology.[15]

In branch council meetings, Marco and the other leaders freely shared their thoughts on how to help the people under their care. The council understood that everyone in the branch needed to develop a testimony of Jesus Christ. At branch meetings and activities, Marco and the other leaders spoke of Christ frequently, creating an environment where visitors and new members could feel His love and come unto Him.

One month after the organization of the branch, the Church broadcast its semiannual general conference over radio, television, satellite, and the internet. Although these channels reached most areas of the world, the branch in El Coca did not yet have access to satellite television or a strong enough internet connection to stream conference. Shortly after, though, the Church's office in Quito sent the branch a Spanish-language recording of the conference on DVD.[16]

Hoping to replicate the experience of watching conference live, Marco and other branch leaders decided to show the recording over the course of a weekend, dividing it up by session. They set up chairs, a television, and loudspeakers at the meetinghouse and sent out special invitations to each of the members. Claudia was in charge of welcoming people when they arrived.

The day of the first session, the Saints came dressed in Sunday clothes. Some were familiar with general conference, while others had no idea what to expect. The Spirit filled the room as everyone listened carefully to the speakers and enjoyed the music of the Tabernacle Choir.

Many of the newer members had assumed the Church was small and local. As they watched conference, though, they saw that they were part of a worldwide organization. Like them, millions of other Saints were working together to further the Lord's work.[17]

AT THE START OF 2010, more than 170,000 Church members lived on the islands of the Caribbean. In the Dominican Republic, home to two-thirds of these Saints, there were eighteen stakes and three missions. In 1998, the Church established a Missionary Training Center in Santo Domingo, the capital of the Dominican Republic, to prepare Caribbean missionaries for service. Two years later, in September 2000, President Hinckley came to the city to dedicate the Santo Domingo Temple, the first house of the Lord in the region.[18]

When Latter-day Saint missionaries arrived in the Dominican Republic in 1978, around a dozen Church members—the only Saints in the country—met them at the airport. Among them were Rodolfo and Noemí Bodden. The Boddens and several of their children had joined the Church three months earlier through their friends John and Nancy Rappleye and Eddie and Mercedes Amparo. In the years that followed, Rodolfo and Noemí served faithfully in the Church.[19]

The restored gospel spread to other Caribbean nations in similar ways. In Jamaica, an island west of the Dominican Republic, Latter-day Saint missionaries had preached the gospel as early as the 1850s. But the Church did not become established there until Jamaican-born converts Victor and Verna Nugent took an interest in the 1970s. One day, Victor and Verna received a Book of Mormon from an American coworker, Paul Schmeil. He also introduced them to the Church film *Man's Search for Happiness,* and its message, together with Paul's Christlike example, inspired Victor.

On January 20, 1974, the Nugent family was baptized. Four years later, after President Spencer W. Kimball's revelation opened the doors for the Nugents and other people of Black African descent to receive the full blessings of the priesthood, the family was sealed in the Salt Lake Temple.[20]

That same year, 1978, another American Latter-day Saint, Greg Young, baptized his friends John and June Naime in Barbados. A little over a year later, the first branch in Barbados was organized with John as branch president and June as Relief Society president. Later, Barbados served as the headquarters of the West Indies Mission, and the gospel spread from there to Grenada, Guadeloupe, Saint Lucia, Martinique, Saint Vincent, French Guiana, Sint Maarten, and other neighboring countries.[21]

In Haiti, meanwhile, Chilean-born Haitian Alexandre Mourra learned about the Church from a relative who had obtained a copy of the Book of Mormon and other Church literature from missionaries in Florida. After reading the testimony of the prophet Joseph Smith, Alexandre sent for a Book of Mormon of his own and received a witness of its truth. Since the Church was not yet in Haiti, he flew to Florida, met with the mission president there, and was baptized in July 1977. He then returned to his home in Port-au-Prince and taught others the gospel. One year later, the mission president visited Haiti and officiated at the baptism of twenty-two of Alexandre's friends.[22]

The Church in Haiti continued to grow in the years that followed, despite the social and political unrest that often beset the country. By the end of 2009, there were some sixteen thousand Saints spread throughout two stakes and two districts. Their resilience was tested on January 12, 2010, when a devastating earthquake struck Haiti, leveling homes and killing more than two hundred thousand people, including forty-two Latter-day Saints.[23]

When the earthquake struck, Soline Saintelus was meeting with her bishop at their Port-au-Prince meetinghouse. Her husband, Olghen, was working at a local hotel. They rushed home to their apartment building, where a babysitter was watching their three small children. The building was a heap of rubble.

"Heavenly Father," Olghen prayed, "if it be Thy will, if there could be just one of my children alive, please, please help us."

For ten hours, rescuers dug through the wreckage. At one point, they heard the oldest child, five-year-old Gancci, singing "I Am a Child of God," his favorite song. His voice led the workers to rescue him, his siblings, and their babysitter.[24]

Over the next few weeks, the Church assisted local leaders and humanitarian organizations in providing doctors, tents, food, wheelchairs, medical supplies, and other necessities. It also opened meetinghouses to provide shelter and refuge for many of the people left homeless by the disaster. Later, the Church helped people find employment and start new businesses.[25]

After being rescued, Gancci Saintelus was taken to Florida for treatment of serious injuries. There, local Church members came to the Saintelus family's aid, bringing them toys, food, diapers, and other supplies. Their kindness brought tears to Olghen's eyes.

"I'm so grateful to my church," he said.[26]

IN SEPTEMBER 2010, THE residents of Luputa, Democratic Republic of the Congo, were nearly finished laying pipe for their Church-sponsored clean water pipeline. Speaking with a journalist, district president Willy Binene stressed the pipeline's importance.

"Man can live without power," he said. "But the lack of clean water is a burden almost too difficult to bear."[27]

Whether the reporter realized it or not, Willy was speaking from a lifetime of experience. As an electrical engineering student, he had never aspired to live in Luputa, a city without electricity. His plans had changed, and he'd managed fine—even thrived—without power. But he and his family, and every family in the area, had suffered the painful effects of waterborne diseases. To protect themselves at church, they had even sacrificed to purchase clean bottled water for the sacrament.[28]

Now, with a little more work, life in Luputa was about to change. From the start of the project, every neighborhood in and around the city had been assigned days to work on the pipeline. On those days, trucks from ADIR, the organization managing the project, arrived in the neighborhood early to pick up volunteers and transport them to the worksite.

As the district president, Willy wanted to be a model leader. On the days his neighborhood was assigned to labor, he had set his nursing work aside and started digging. Between Luputa and the clean water source were miles of hills and valleys. Since the pipeline was powered by gravity, the volunteers had to dig the trench and bury pipe just right to make sure the water flowed properly.

Willy and the volunteers dug everything by hand. The trench had to be eighteen inches across and three feet deep. In some places, the ground was sandy, and the work went quickly. In other places, it was a snarl of tree roots and rocks, making for backbreaking work. Volunteers could only pray that brushfires and nests of biting insects did not slow their progress. On a good day, they could dig nearly five hundred feet of trench.

The Saints in the Luputa District worked special shifts in addition to their normal neighborhood assignments. On those days, the men of the Church joined the regular volunteers in digging the trench while women from the Relief Society prepared meals for the workers.

The Saints' commitment to the project helped others learn more about their faith. People in the area saw the Church as an institution that looked out not only for its own members but also for the broader community.[29]

When construction on the pipeline ended in November 2010, many people came to Luputa to witness the water's arrival. Massive cisterns, perched atop high stilts, had been built in the city to store the water from the pipes. Yet some people wondered if the pipeline could really bring enough water to fill the tanks. Willy himself had his doubts.

Then the floodgates opened, and everyone could hear the roar of water pouring into the cisterns. Immense joy swept through the crowd. Dozens of small concrete water stations, each equipped with multiple spigots, could now dispense clean water throughout Luputa.[30]

To mark the occasion, the city held a celebration. The festivities drew fifteen thousand people from Luputa and its neighboring villages. Among the honored guests were government and tribal dignitaries, ADIR officials, and a member of the Church's Africa Southeast Area presidency. On one of the water tanks hung a large banner with bright blue letters:

> THANK YOU TO THE CHURCH
> THANK YOU TO ADIR
> FOR POTABLE WATER

As the guests arrived and took seats beneath specially constructed gazebos, a choir of young Latter-day Saints sang hymns.

Once everyone was in place, and the buzz of the crowd quieted down, Willy raised a microphone to his mouth and addressed the audience as a local representative of the Church. "Just as Jesus performed many miracles," he said, "today it is a miracle that the water came to Luputa." He told the crowd that the Church had sponsored the pipeline for the whole community, and he urged everyone to make good use of it.

And to anyone who wondered why the Church had taken such an interest in a place like Luputa, he gave a simple reply.

"We are all children of our Heavenly Father," he said. "We must do good to everyone."[31]

CHAPTER 38

Real and Immeasurable

In February 2011, Marco and Claudia Villavicencio were surprised to receive an email from Joshua Perkey, an editor for Church magazines in Salt Lake City. The previous year, Joshua had come to El Coca, Ecuador, as part of an effort to publish more magazine articles about Saints worldwide. For several days, Joshua had visited with the Villavicencios and other branch members, attended Church meetings and seminary classes, and taken photographs of the city and its residents.[1]

At the time of Joshua's visit, the branch in El Coca was only a year old. But it had grown from twenty-eight members to eighty-three. Marco credited the growth to the branch's efforts to help everyone feel needed and loved. "We try to put in practice President Gordon B. Hinckley's admonition that every new convert needs to be nurtured by the good word of God, have a friend, and have a responsibility," Marco had told Joshua. Claudia, who still served as the branch Young Women president, agreed. "When people arrive at church for the first time," she said, "what makes an impression on them is how they are received. So we teach the young women how important each soul is to the Lord."

Many of the members had shared heartfelt stories and testimonies with Joshua. Lourdes Chenche, the branch Relief Society president, spoke of the joy she and her presidency experienced serving the women in the branch. "We draw close to them when they have problems," she said. "We let them know they are not alone, that we have the help of Jesus Christ and the branch."[2]

Now, in his email to the Villavicencios, Joshua explained that he was putting together a short video for the Church magazines. The video was part of a new online series for Primary children. Called "One in a Million," it featured children from around the world telling stories about their lives and bearing testimony. In one, a boy in Ukraine talked about President Thomas S. Monson inviting him to place some mortar for the cornerstone of the new temple in Kyiv. In another, a girl in Jamaica talked about trying to be a good example at her school.

Each video was about a minute and a half long, and Joshua wanted to know if Marco and Claudia would allow their six-year-old son, Sair, to be featured in a video. Moving away from his relatives and Primary class had been hard for Sair. But over the last year, as more children came to church, he had been able to attend Primary again. Claudia thought the video would be a good opportunity to help him remember his divine identity.

Joshua sent Sair questions about his favorite hobbies, foods, and Church hymns, and Claudia and Marco helped him prepare his answers. Sair was eager to make the recording with Claudia, and she treasured the time they spent on it.[3]

They sent the audio file to Joshua, and it was combined with some photographs he had taken during his visit to El Coca. A while later, after the video was finished and posted online, the Villavicencios sat at a computer in their living room to watch it. Sair was very excited to see how it turned out.

The video began with a picture of the family. Sair's tiny voice then said in Spanish, "My name is Sair, and I'm from Ecuador." Pictures of El Coca appeared on the screen, and Sair described the city's colorful birds and animals as well as his favorite foods and sports. He also spoke about moving to El Coca before the branch was established. "There wasn't a church for us to go to," he said. "Soon other families moved here, and more people were baptized."

"We are all missionaries!" he said. "Now I have a lot of friends in Primary. We sing about Jesus and Heavenly Father just like other children all over the world. I like singing 'I Am a Child of God.'"

As Claudia sat with her son, she could hardly believe that people everywhere could now see how happy the gospel made her family. The video reminded her that God watched over places like El Coca—and worked through people like her, Marco, Sair, and the other Saints in the branch.

She hoped the video would remind Sair that he was part of a big and important organization like the Primary—and that even as a child, he was able to serve the Lord.[4]

IN LATE FEBRUARY 2011, Emma Hernandez personally delivered a graduation invitation to her father. Six years earlier, he had opposed her marriage to her husband, Hector David, because he thought it would get in the way of her education. But through the financial support of the Perpetual Education Fund, Emma had earned a degree in marketing from a prestigious Honduran university.

Her father was happy for her, and she was proud of him. He had long since changed his mind about her marriage. Leading up to the wedding, Emma had prayed for his heart to be softened. And her mother had helped him see that Hector David was a good match for their daughter. More recently, the ministering efforts of a diligent elders quorum president, combined with a fervent desire to come unto Christ and make covenants with Him, had brought her father back to church after many years away.

Emma had rejoiced in her father's return to the Church. She and her mother had prayed for years that his heart would change so their family could go to the house of the Lord together. These prayers were answered on the morning of April 1, 2010, when Emma and most of her family arrived at the Guatemala City Temple to be sealed to each other for eternity. The sky was clear, and newly planted flowers adorned the temple garden as she entered the temple with her father, mother, and sister.[5]

Emma felt the Spirit when she walked into the sealing room and saw her parents kneeling at the altar. Peace and love settled over them as they held hands and looked into each other's eyes. After the ceremony, in the celestial room, they hugged one another and wept tears of happiness. Emma's father was not an expressive man, but she could sense his emotions in his embrace.[6]

Now, a year after the sealing, she and Hector David both had achieved their educational goals while building a family and always serving in the Church. Emma had discovered her passion for marketing, and now she had the knowledge and tools to qualify for her profession. With Hector David's degree in finance, they both had a better income to take care of their family. Most important, Emma had matured during her studies, learning how to overcome challenges and rely on the Lord.

In the beginning, she had been overwhelmed by school. There had been a time when she didn't think their family had enough money to finish her degree. But the Perpetual Education Fund had eliminated that concern, and the support of her family empowered her to pursue her dreams and kept her motivated. Her gratitude to the Lord grew, and she and Hector David saw their service in the Church as an opportunity to give thanks and show love to the Savior. Now, Emma was eager to use her education and pay back her PEF loan. And she believed she was capable of even greater successes in the future.[7]

On March 4, 2011, the day of Emma's graduation, her family gathered again, this time in her university gymnasium for her graduation ceremony. She arrived early with her fellow graduates to rehearse the ceremony, dressed in a matching black cap and gown. When her family arrived, Emma was delighted to see not only Hector David and Oscar David but also her mother, father, and other relatives.

As she walked through the line of university officials, shaking their hands and finally receiving her diploma, Emma thanked the Lord for her blessings. Her father was the first to hug her when the ceremony ended. "Congratulations, daughter," he said, looking as if a weight had been removed from his shoulders. Emma was happy to see him so at peace.

She then hugged and kissed Hector David, grateful for the support he had given her throughout her studies.

"Thank you," she told him as they embraced. "I couldn't have done it without you."[8]

ON THE MORNING OF April 2, 2011, President Thomas S. Monson stood at the pulpit of the Conference Center and looked at the thousands of Saints gathered for the Church's annual general conference. "When this building was planned, we thought we'd never fill it," he said, smiling broadly. "Just look at it now."

The conference marked his third year as president of the Church, a calling that kept him busier than most people could imagine. He was deeply grateful to the Saints around the world, who now numbered more than fourteen million. "I thank you for your faith and devotion to the gospel, for the love and care you show to one another, and for the service you provide in your wards and branches and stakes and districts," he said.[9]

It was an exciting time to be a Latter-day Saint. Half a century earlier, President David O. McKay had rejoiced in the Church's good reputation, especially in the United States. But even then, the Church had been relatively unknown to most people. That was no longer the case. Decades of widespread missionary work, effective public relations initiatives, large- and small-scale humanitarian aid projects, and the humble, everyday actions of individual Saints had made the Church a familiar presence in many parts of the world.

Lately, too, the Church had become the focus of significant media attention. Coverage of the Church during the 2002 Winter Olympics turned out to be a prelude to a flood of publicity that came when Mitt Romney, the head of the 2002 Olympic organizing committee and a prominent Latter-day Saint politician, announced he was running for president of the United States. Although he did not win his political party's nomination in 2008, many people expected him to run again in 2012.

And public interest in the Church remained high. Latter-day Saints made news as lawmakers and business leaders. Some competed on reality television shows and in professional sports arenas. Others gained fame as rock stars and concert hall musicians. Still others wrote bestselling novels, some adapted into blockbuster films.[10]

The growing interest in the Church and its members did not mean that everyone was eager to embrace the restored gospel. Many people misunderstood the Church or disagreed with its teachings. In fact, President Monson and other leaders worried that society was drifting away from long-standing Christian values and the teachings and practices of the Church. Nowhere did the drift seem more evident than in beliefs about marriage.[11]

In recent years, advocates for lesbian, gay, bisexual, transgender, and queer (LGBTQ) individuals had lobbied for the right to same-sex marriage. The Church and other faith-based organizations had opposed these measures, affirming that marriage between a man and woman was ordained of God.

The most prominent instance had come in November 2008, when residents in California were given a chance to vote on a state constitutional amendment that would legally define marriage as between one man and one woman. The Church joined other faith-based groups in fundraising in support of the proposition.

Church leaders in Salt Lake City also encouraged members in California to actively support and promote it.[12]

Although the proposition narrowly passed, the Church received considerable criticism for its role in the vote, leading some people to stage protests outside temples.[13]

President Monson and other Church leaders remained committed to upholding the doctrine of marriage and the standards of the Church. They spoke of religious liberty and the freedom to define and teach marriage as a sacred union between a man and a woman. They also sought to build bridges with other groups, like the Roman Catholic Church, that believed the same.

Yet more and more, they worked to find common ground with the LGBTQ community. As debates over marriage and gay rights continued, Church leaders encouraged Latter-day Saints to be loving and respectful when disagreements arose and to condemn the bullying of LGBTQ people. In November 2009, the Church joined Salt Lake City lawmakers in supporting fair housing rights for all, regardless of sexual orientation.[14] Church leaders also sought to provide better resources and promote more empathy for LGBTQ Church members, who often felt caught in the middle of the debates. Among these resources in development was a new Church website with articles and videos of Saints and their families sharing their experiences and testimonies.[15]

One of the videos told the story of Suzanne Bowser, a Latter-day Saint who struggled for years to come to terms with her attraction to women. She kept going to church, but at times her heart felt torn in two. Over time, with the help of friends and family who walked with her on her journey, she arrived at a more peaceful place. "This is part of me, it is going to be a part of me, and I'm OK," she realized. "I can still be happy. I can still have my Savior in my life." His love for her filled the emptiness she sometimes felt.

She also had Church leaders who were willing to listen to her, and that made a big difference. "I have had priesthood leaders," she recalled, "who have absolutely just wanted to learn."[16]

As President Monson closed general conference in April 2011, he urged the Saints to let their lights shine, as the Savior taught. "May we be good citizens of the nations in which we live and good neighbors in our communities, reaching out to those of other faiths as well as to those of our own," he said. "May we be examples of honesty and integrity wherever we go and in whatever we do."[17]

He and other Church leaders understood and emphasized the importance of being followers of Christ in word and deed. If nothing else, the recent media attention had shown that while many people had heard of the Church, perceptions of the faith and its core message varied widely. For many people, the Church was still a mystery.

Church leaders knew that this must change. There should never be any doubt that Latter-day Saints followed Jesus Christ.[18]

ON AUGUST 17, 2011, SILVIA and Jeff Allred flew into San Salvador, El Salvador, the city where Silvia was born and raised and where, in four days, a house of the Lord would be dedicated. The temple had been announced not long after her call to the Relief Society general presidency, and her new responsibilities had prevented her from attending the groundbreaking. But now, at the invitation of the First Presidency, she had the opportunity to take part in its dedication. She and Jeff were thrilled.[19]

Silvia had been serving in the Relief Society general presidency for four years. During that time, the themes of faith, family, and relief had guided every effort of the organization. The presidency traveled extensively, using the revised *Church Handbook of Instructions* to train local Relief Society leaders in receiving revelation, working in Church councils, ministering to those in need, and fulfilling other responsibilities. Silvia herself had visited with Relief Society sisters in twenty countries on five continents.

The presidency also worked with their board members to create videos that provided immediate training for newly called leaders worldwide. These videos could be accessed from the Relief Society's web page and were included in the Leadership Training Library, a new collection of online instructional resources found on the Church's website.[20]

Strengthening visiting teaching was another major focus of their work. For years, Church magazines had published simple visiting teaching lessons. Now the lessons were printed alongside additional tips and resources to enhance the sisters' teaching. Under Silvia's supervision, board members also sought ways to support the transition from Young Women to Relief Society. While traveling, Silvia would often talk with local Relief Society and Young Women leaders about bridging the gap between the organizations by encouraging them to interact more. She also encouraged Relief Society sisters to reach out to their newest members and seek ways to mentor young women.[21]

Inspired by the history they had received from President Boyd K. Packer and at the assignment of the First Presidency, the Relief Society was preparing to publish a book, *Daughters in My Kingdom: The History and Work of Relief Society*. The book was fully illustrated and written in a simple style appropriate for readers of all abilities. It would also be translated into twenty-three languages and distributed to the women of the Church. The presidency hoped it would help the sisters learn from the past, better understand their spiritual heritage as disciples of Christ, and embrace the Relief Society's divinely appointed mission.[22]

On the day before the San Salvador Temple dedication, Silvia and Jeff toured the building and marveled at its ornate details—the beautifully carved wood and the decorative glass and brass fixtures etched with the yucca flower, the national flower of El Salvador. Near the entrance, behind the recommend desk, Silvia saw an original painting of the Savior. He had His arms around two children, about eight or nine years old, who looked like they could have been from Central America. The background was lush and green, like the vegetation throughout El Salvador. Overcome with the Savior's love for all His children, Silvia wept.

At the dedication the following day, Silvia could not help thinking about the past. She had been one of the earliest members of the Church in El Salvador, and although her travels had taken her around the world, it was powerful to see the Church flourish in her homeland.

Sitting in the celestial room, she looked around at the local members who filled the seats. Many of them were older and had, like her, been baptized when the Church was new in El Salvador. They had remained faithful to their covenants, often amid poverty and adversity. Some of them would be ordinance workers when the temple opened its doors. She knew they had prayed for this temple for many years.[23]

When Silvia had joined the Church as a teenager in 1959, the closest temple had been in Mesa, Arizona—four days of travel away. Now there were one hundred thousand Saints in El Salvador. The Church had thrived there in ways Silvia could not have imagined when she was younger.[24]

When it was her turn to speak, Silvia stood. Although she spoke English fluently, Spanish continued to be the language she thought in, prayed in, and sought the Holy Ghost in. At this dedication, she would deliver her remarks in her native tongue, which made it far easier for her to convey her deepest feelings. She was speaking not only to the people in the house of the Lord but also to the thousands of Saints in the temple district watching a broadcast of the dedication at their meetinghouses.

"My heart is full of happiness and gratitude today," she said. "I testify to you that the blessings that are promised us in the temple are real and immeasurable. The temple is the house of the Lord. He Himself has sanctified it. His eyes and His heart will be here perpetually."[25]

SIX WEEKS LATER, ON October 2, 2011, a gasoline-powered generator coughed to life at the Luputa meetinghouse in the Democratic Republic of the Congo. Inside, around two hundred Saints—including Willy and Lilly Binene—were finding seats in front of a television set in the chapel. In a few moments, a Sunday night broadcast of the Church's 181st Semiannual General Conference would begin, translated into French—one of fifty-one languages in which conference was available to Saints around the world. It was the first general conference the Church members in Luputa would enjoy as members of a stake in Zion.[26]

The organization of the Luputa Stake three months earlier had come as no surprise to anyone familiar with the Church's rapid growth in the city. In 2008, the same year the Binene family was sealed in the temple, over twelve hundred Latter-day Saints lived in Luputa. At that time, there were no full-time missionaries serving there. Yet over the next three years, Willy and other Church leaders had worked with faithful branch missionaries to more than double the number of Saints in their district—an effort doubtless aided by the Church's role in bringing clean water to the city. The district had even sent out thirty-four full-time missionaries to serve in other parts of the DRC, Africa, and the world.

Still, Willy had been surprised when Elder Paul E. Koelliker and Elder Alfred Kyungu of the Seventy called him to be president of the new stake. The Church in Luputa had several experienced priesthood leaders, each of whom could serve capably as a stake president. Wasn't it someone else's turn to lead?

On June 26, the day the stake was organized, Willy helped Elder Koelliker and Elder Kyungu distribute full-time mission calls to fifteen young women and men in the stake. Afterward, Willy smiled as he posed for a photograph with the group. Two decades earlier, ethnic strife and bloodshed had driven him from his home, robbing him of a chance to serve his own full-time mission for the Lord. Yet his years of devoted Church service in Luputa had helped give the rising generation of Saints opportunities he did not have.[27]

As the conference broadcast began, Willy settled back to listen to the speakers. Normally President Monson was the first speaker at the opening session of conference, but a health problem had delayed his coming to the Conference Center. After the intermediate hymn, however, he approached the pulpit and welcomed the Saints to conference with a cheerful "hello."

"When we're busy, time seems to pass far too quickly," he said, "and the past six months have been no exception for me."

President Monson spoke of the dedication of the temple in El Salvador as well as the rededication of the temple in Atlanta in the southern United States. "The building of temples continues uninterrupted, brothers and sisters," he said. "Today it is my privilege to announce several new temples."

Willy listened carefully. Lately, temples had been on the minds of Church leaders in Luputa. In fact, at the first stake conference in the city, many of the talks had centered on preparing the Saints to attend the house of the Lord. Aside from the Binenes, only a few Saints in Luputa had been able to go to the Johannesburg Temple. While passports were relatively easy to acquire in the DRC, travel visas to South Africa were not. This meant that many Saints in the DRC were stuck waiting, worrying that their passports would expire before they could receive a visa and attend the temple.[28]

The first temple President Monson announced was the second for the city of Provo, Utah. Recently, the city's historic tabernacle had accidentally caught fire, and flames had consumed almost everything except its exterior walls. Now the Church planned to rebuild and repurpose it as a house of the Lord.[29]

"I am also pleased to announce new temples in the following locations," President Monson continued. "Barranquilla, Colombia; Durban, South Africa; Kinshasa in the Democratic Republic of the Congo; and—"

As soon as they heard "Kinshasa," Willy and everyone around him stood and cheered. The news had taken them completely by surprise. Soon, Congolese Saints would not have to worry about travel visas or expiring passports. The prophet's simple announcement had changed everything.

There had been no rumors, no hints that the Church had plans to build a temple in the DRC. There had only been hope—hope that one day the Lord would establish His house in their land.

Now it was happening! It was finally happening![30]

CHAPTER 39

Ever at the Helm

As 2013 dawned, President Thomas S. Monson looked forward to a momentous year. It marked not only his fifth as president of The Church of Jesus Christ of Latter-day Saints but also his fiftieth as an apostle of the Lord. The time seemed right to reflect on his presidency and the state of the Church.[1]

Some years earlier, President Monson had received a letter from a struggling Church member. "The gospel has never left my heart, even though it has left my life," the man wrote. "Please don't forget those of us who are out here—the lost Latter-day Saints."

The man's moving words had reminded President Monson of a painting he once saw of a lifeboat plunging into roiling, white-capped waters to save a stranded ship. The painting had a long, unremarkable name, which

President Monson had shortened to three simple words: *To the Rescue.* The phrase had turned into something of a theme for his presidency. Since becoming prophet, he had felt a greater urgency to follow the Savior in reaching out with understanding and love to those who felt unhappy, afraid, lost, or alone.[2]

On February 3, President Monson commemorated his presidency's five-year anniversary with a message to the Saints. "Our opportunities to serve one another are limitless," he declared. "We're surrounded by those in need of our attention, our encouragement, our comfort, our support, our kindness."

He urged the Saints to remember the Savior's words: "Inasmuch as ye have done it unto one of the least of these my brethren, ye have done it unto me."[3]

In his message, the prophet also spoke of missionary work, one of the many ways Church members could come to the rescue of others. A few months earlier, he had announced a change to the minimum age for missionary service, lowering it to nineteen for young women and eighteen for young men.

Thousands of missionary applications, more than half of them from young women, soon poured into Church headquarters. The change had given more youth new opportunities to strengthen their testimonies of the Savior and renew their commitment to the Church through missionary service. It also created fewer conflicts for Church members in countries where university policies or military service made serving difficult.[4]

Continuing his message, President Monson noted that thirty-one new temples had been announced and sixteen had been dedicated during the past five years. "These numbers will continue to increase," he promised, "as we move forward in making temples accessible to all of our members, wherever they may live."

Finally, he remarked on his advancing age. "Last August I celebrated my eighty-fifth birthday," he said. "Age eventually takes its toll on all of us." Yet he assured the Saints that the Church was in good hands.

"Our Savior, Jesus Christ, whom we follow, whom we worship, and whom we serve, is ever at the helm," he testified. "As we now go forward, may we follow His example."[5]

ON MAY 28, 2017, WILLY Binene stood to bear his testimony at his ward meetinghouse in Luputa. It was his family's last Sunday there—at least for a while. He and Lilly had recently received a call from the First Presidency to serve as the leaders of the Côte d'Ivoire Abidjan Mission, on the western coast of Africa. Having missed his chance to serve a full-time mission as a young man, Willy had always hoped to one day serve a mission alongside Lilly. But neither of them had expected the call to come so soon.[6]

A year earlier, Elder Neil L. Andersen of the Quorum of the Twelve Apostles had come to the DRC to break ground for the temple in Kinshasa. During the trip, he and his wife, Kathy, traveled to Mbuji-Mayi, a city some ninety miles north of Luputa, to meet with the Saints in the area. Willy met Elder Andersen and shared his story with him.[7]

Several months after Elder Andersen's visit, the apostle surprised Willy and Lilly with a video call. He told them the Lord had another assignment for them and asked some questions about their life and work responsibilities. He then asked Lilly, "Would you agree to leave your country to go and serve the Lord elsewhere?"

"Yes," Lilly told him. "We are willing."

About a week later, President Dieter F. Uchtdorf extended the call to serve as mission leaders. They received it with a mix of joy and fear. Both felt unsure if they could measure up to their new responsibilities. But it was not the first time the Lord had asked them to do something hard, and they were willing to commit themselves wholly to His service.

"If it is God who called us," Lilly thought, "He alone will manifest Himself and qualify us for the work."

Their four children—aged five to sixteen—took the news well. The Saints in Luputa, however, could not hide the sadness on their faces when Willy and Lilly's call was announced. For over two decades, Willy had helped the Church blossom in Luputa, growing from a small group of displaced believers to a thriving stake of Zion. The Saints did not simply think of him as their former district and stake president. The restored gospel had taught them to see each other as brothers and sisters, so Willy, Lilly, and the Binene children were *their* family.[8]

As Willy bore his testimony to ward members, he felt immense love for them. Yet his eyes remained dry—even as Lilly, the choir members, and everyone else around him wept. Few things in his life had gone as expected. It seemed every time he had made a plan—for school, for a full-time mission, for work—something happened, sending him off in another direction. But looking back on his life, he could see the Lord had always had a plan for him.

After the meeting, Willy's emotions finally overwhelmed him, and tears poured from his eyes. He did not think that he had ever done anything special. In fact, he felt a bit inconsequential, like a drop in the ocean. But he knew the Lord was guiding him, urging him along as the plan became clearer and more defined.

At their house, he, Lilly, and the children said goodbye to their friends. The family then climbed into a car waiting to take them to their next field of service.

"You can never be in a hurry," Willy realized. "Leave time up to God."[9]

PRESIDENT MONSON PASSED AWAY on January 2, 2018. Although his health had been declining for several years, his testimony had always remained vibrant. One day, shortly before his death, his counselors in the First Presidency visited him at his home. Just as they were leaving, he had stopped them and said, "I love the Savior Jesus Christ. And I know that He loves me."[10]

During his ten years in office, President Monson had guided the Saints through an era of rapid social change and astonishing technological advancements. Social media platforms had provided Church members with new ways to share the gospel, foster understanding with people outside the faith, and connect with general authorities. The development of smartphones and other mobile devices had aided this work and given rise to the Gospel Library app in 2010, giving Saints across the world easier access to the scriptures, Church magazines, and other resources.[11]

President Monson had also overseen the expansion of missionary work, a greater emphasis on interfaith outreach, and an increase in humanitarian efforts. Under his leadership, the Church had partnered with several organizations to assist refugees from war-torn areas, aid the victims of natural disasters, and ease the suffering of the sick and hungry.[12]

The Church had also built on the work of the Perpetual Education Fund and other efforts to provide educational opportunities to people around the globe. In 2009, BYU–Idaho and three other locations had piloted a program that blended in-person classes and online instruction to make higher education more available and affordable to students. In 2017, this program became BYU–Pathway Worldwide, which had gone on to serve tens of thousands of students in over fifty countries.[13]

But above all, President Monson's greatest legacy was his compassionate, Christlike ministry. The day after his death, newspapers ran story after story about a life lived quietly visiting hospitals and funerals, sitting at the bedsides of sick friends, and encouraging young people and adults to come unto Jesus Christ.[14]

On January 14, 2018, the Quorum of the Twelve Apostles ordained and set apart Russell M. Nelson as the seventeenth president of The Church of Jesus Christ of Latter-day Saints. The new prophet spoke to Church members two days later with President Dallin H. Oaks and President Henry B. Eyring, his counselors in the First Presidency.

"Our divine mandate," he said, "is to go to every nation, kindred, tongue, and people, helping to prepare the world for the Second Coming of the Lord." As a presidency, they wanted each member to "keep on the covenant path" and "begin with the end in mind."

"The end for which each of us strives is to be endowed with power in a house of the Lord, sealed as families, faithful to covenants made in a temple," he declared. "Your commitment to follow the Savior by making covenants with Him and then keeping those covenants will open the door to every spiritual blessing and privilege available to men, women, and children everywhere."[15]

President Nelson soon introduced several adjustments within the Church to aid this important work. At the April 2018 general conference, he announced that high priests would begin attending quorum meetings with elders. With the assistance of Elder Jeffrey R. Holland and Relief Society general president Jean B. Bingham, he also introduced a new way of caring for others, called "ministering," to replace home and visiting teaching.

In a talk about ministering, Elder Holland urged the Saints to embrace "heartfelt discipleship," reminding them of the Savior's great commandment to His apostles: "Love one another." Sister Bingham likewise encouraged the Saints to follow Christ's example. "As you have the privilege to represent the Savior in your ministering efforts," she said, "ask yourself, 'How can I share the light of the gospel with this individual or family? What is the Spirit inspiring me to do?'"[16]

Less than three months after being set apart, President Nelson embarked on the first of many global ministry tours. Traveling with Sister Wendy Nelson, whom he married in 2006 after the death of his first wife, Dantzel, the prophet visited Saints in eight cities on four continents in eleven days.

"Whenever I'm comfortably situated in my home, I'm in the wrong place," he said. "I need to be where the people are. We need to bring them the message of the Savior."[17]

Later, at the October 2018 general conference, President Nelson announced a change to Sunday meeting schedules to make gospel living more home centered and Church supported. The change reduced the length of weekly Church meetings by one hour, giving

Saints more time to study the gospel at home. *Come, Follow Me*—a new curriculum for adult Sunday School, youth and Primary classes, and individual and family study—began playing a key role in bringing Saints to Christ through gospel learning.[18]

At the conference, President Nelson also spoke about using the correct name of the Church, instead of nicknames. "I realize with profound regret that we have unwittingly acquiesced in the Lord's restored Church being called by other names, each of which expunges the sacred name of Jesus Christ!" he declared. "When we omit His name from His Church, we are inadvertently removing *Him* as the central focus of our lives."[19]

Under President Nelson's direction, the Church instituted a new children and youth program to replace Scouting, Personal Progress, and other activities for young Saints. As part of this change, the Church extended For the Strength of Youth conferences to all Latter-day Saint teenagers between the ages of fourteen and eighteen. Like EFY and TFY, FSY gave youth a chance to spend a week attending gospel-centered classes and talks, making new friends, and strengthening their testimonies.[20]

Following these adjustments, the Church released a new handbook of instructions, *General Handbook: Serving in The Church of Jesus Christ of Latter-day Saints*. Designed to help all people come unto Christ, the guidebook provided clear direction to help the Saints assist in God's work. Unlike its predecessors, the *General*

Handbook was a single volume available through the Church's website and mobile app. To support consistent, inspired leadership in the global work of the Church, it was available in fifty-one languages.[21]

Early in his administration, President Nelson began working closely with the National Association for the Advancement of Colored People, or NAACP, to promote respect, civility, and racial and ethnic harmony throughout the world. He condemned racism and urged the Saints to uplift and respect all of God's children.[22]

Throughout the 2010s, questions about the status of women in the Church also led to important changes in Church practice. As a member of the Quorum of the Twelve Apostles, Russell M. Nelson had taught that women were "full partners in the work of salvation" and that their perspective in Church councils was essential. Elder Dallin H. Oaks had also clarified that women have priesthood authority in fulfilling their callings. "We are not accustomed to speaking of women having the authority of the priesthood in their Church callings," he had said, "but what other authority can it be?"

Beginning in 2015, women who served as general officers began sitting on key general administrative councils at Church headquarters. Relief Society general president Linda K. Burton became a member of the Priesthood and Family Executive Council, Young Women general president Bonnie L. Oscarson joined the Missionary Executive Council, and Primary general president Rosemary M. Wixom joined the Temple and Family History Executive

Council. And in 2019, President Nelson and his counselors authorized women to serve as official witnesses at baptisms and in temple sealings.[23]

Like President Monson, President Nelson sought understanding as the Church addressed issues affecting LGBTQ individuals. In 2015, the United States had become the nineteenth country to legalize same-sex marriage. Since then, the First Presidency had reiterated the Church's respect for the law of the land while also affirming its commitment to marriage between a man and a woman.[24]

As the Church strove to understand and provide for the needs of LGBTQ members and their families, it added more videos and resources to its website. During a Brigham Young University devotional, Elder M. Russell Ballard urged Church members to be more sensitive to the feelings and experiences of LGBTQ Saints. "Certainly we must do better than we have done in the past," he declared, "so that all members feel they have a spiritual home where their brothers and sisters love them and where they have a place to worship and serve the Lord."[25]

From the start of his administration, President Nelson had testified of the importance of temples in keeping God's children on the "covenant path" and gathering Israel on both sides of the veil. During his first two years, he announced thirty-five new temples in places as diverse as Bengaluru, India; Port Moresby, Papua New Guinea; and Budapest, Hungary. During that time, eight new temples were also dedicated, including a house of the Lord in Rome, Italy.[26]

The prophet believed the Rome Temple marked a turning point in the history of the Church. "Things are going to move forward at an accelerated pace," he declared after the dedication. "The Church is going to have an unprecedented future, unparalleled. We're just building up to what's ahead now."[27]

At the October 2019 general conference, President Nelson announced that 2020 would be a bicentennial celebration, a time for the Saints to remember the two hundredth anniversary of Joseph Smith's First Vision of Heavenly Father and Jesus Christ.

He invited the Saints to immerse themselves in the light of the Restoration. "In the next six months, I hope that every member and every family will prepare for a unique conference that will commemorate the very foundations of the restored gospel," he said. "As you do, general conference next April will be not only memorable; it will be unforgettable."[28]

SHORTLY AFTER THE OCTOBER 2019 general conference, seventeen-year-old Laudy Kaouk felt alone as she drove down the street. "Heavenly Father," she prayed, "I just need to feel that you are there."

Laudy was in her final year of high school in Provo, Utah. When she wasn't in class or applying to universities, she was involved in extracurricular school groups or going to her job at a local restaurant. She was also the president of her Young Women class and a dancer in Luz de las Naciones, the Church's annual Latin American cultural celebration at the Conference Center. Life could hardly get busier or more hectic.[29]

Things were changing at home, too. She loved being part of a large, close-knit family. Her father was from Syria and her mother was from Venezuela. They were longtime converts to the Church who had immigrated to Provo before Laudy, the youngest in the family, was born. The whole family came home on Sundays, married siblings bringing their spouses and children with them. Laudy always looked forward to these gatherings.

But recently, her house felt a lot emptier. Her older sister had left on a mission to Japan, so Laudy was the only child at home. She had always had siblings living with her, and now she felt lonely. So she poured out her soul to God.

Two weeks later, Laudy received a call from her stake president. He told her that Bonnie H. Cordon, the Young Women general president, wanted to visit with her. Laudy was surprised, but she agreed to the visit. A short time later, President Cordon attended Laudy's Spanish-speaking ward and sat down to talk with her. "I go and minister to a lot of people around the world and wanted to come and minister to you," she told Laudy.

As soon as President Cordon said these words, Laudy knew that Heavenly Father had heard her prayer. This visit was His answer.[30]

One month later, Laudy came home from work to find her parents waiting anxiously for her. "You have a letter!" they said. It was from the First Presidency.

Confused, Laudy sat down with her parents and opened the letter. It was an invitation for her to speak at the April 2020 general conference.

"How am I going to do this?" she thought.

The Spirit then whispered Nephi's words to her: "I will go and do the things which the Lord hath commanded." All at once, she felt excited and humbled. She knew that God would help her.[31]

On January 30, 2020, the World Health Organization declared a "public health emergency." An aggressive coronavirus had surfaced in Asia, infecting hundreds of people in China. The virus first manifested in pneumonia-like symptoms, but standard medical treatment had little effect on it. It spread rapidly and unpredictably.[32]

By early February, the disease had a name: COVID-19. Responding quickly to the crisis, Church leaders sent more than two hundred thousand respiratory masks to China. They also began canceling meetings, closing temples for proxy ordinances, and putting missionaries in affected areas under quarantine.[33]

On March 11, WHO declared COVID-19 a pandemic. By then, the disease had spread to 114 countries, infecting more than a hundred thousand people and resulting in thousands of deaths. As with the global influenza pandemic of 1918–19, the First Presidency suspended all in-person Church meetings. The Church stopped admitting new missionaries to some MTCs and devised a system for training missionaries at home through video conferencing. The First Presidency also announced plans for a virtual general conference in April and directed the Saints to hold worship services in their homes, granting priesthood holders temporary authorization to administer the sacrament to their own families.[34]

On March 14, President Nelson addressed the Saints in an online video. "We as a global Church are facing a unique challenge," he said. "We pray for those who are suffering and for those who have lost loved ones."

He urged the Saints to take care of themselves and others. "Heavenly Father and His Son, Jesus Christ, know us, love us, and are watching over us," he said. "Of that we can be certain."[35]

On April 4, 2020, Laudy Kaouk sat in the nearly empty auditorium of the Church Office Building, nervously doodling in her notebook. The Saturday evening session of the Church's 190th Annual General Conference was underway, and soon it would be her turn to speak.[36]

Earlier that day, President Nelson had opened the conference in the small auditorium. The spread of COVID-19 had led the Church to cease in-person events at its schools, reassign or release missionaries, and close all temples indefinitely. As he stood before the Saints, the prophet had no choir behind him, and no familiar rows of general authorities and officers. Instead, his counselors and a handful of speakers sat nearby, each of them spaced several feet apart as a precaution against the spread of COVID-19.

As he addressed the Saints, President Nelson reminded them of the promise he'd made at the end of the last conference—that this bicentennial commemoration of Joseph Smith's First Vision would be "unforgettable" to those who prepared themselves for it.

"Little did I know," he said, "that speaking to a visible congregation of fewer than ten people would make this conference so memorable and unforgettable *for me!*"[37]

Laudy had done her best to prepare for the conference, as President Nelson had asked the Saints to do. She had read some of Joseph Smith—History in the Pearl of Great Price and marveled at the young prophet's determination to do the Lord's work, despite his lack of education. "Wow," she'd thought, "he probably felt really inadequate."

It was a feeling she herself knew. She wasn't someone who dreaded public speaking, but the thought of being in front of millions of people was intimidating. Sometimes she doubted herself, but she also had experiences that boosted her confidence. As she worked on her talk, she had felt the Lord guiding her, as He had guided Joseph Smith. Her talk did not take shape all at once. Rather, it had come little by little, one prompting at a time, as she prayed, pondered, and went to the temple.[38]

Now Elder Gerrit W. Gong was finishing his talk, and Laudy put her notebook away. She approached the pulpit, and as soon as she took her place behind it, her nervousness vanished. "I am grateful to be here," she said. "I have spent a lot of time thinking about what I could share, and I hope the Spirit speaks to you directly through my message."[39]

When the pandemic struck, Laudy's school had shifted to remote learning, and her daily routines changed dramatically. As conference approached, she and her parents had carefully followed lockdown procedures to make sure she stayed healthy and did not put anyone else at the conference at risk. She was sad that her parents and other family members were not in the room with her now. But she knew they were nearby, watching on television, and she could sense that her ancestors were also listening to and supporting her.[40]

Laudy's talk lasted about six minutes. She spoke of the power of priesthood blessings and the love and peace she felt when she received them from her dad. "Don't hesitate to ask for a blessing when you need extra guidance," she said. "Some of us might suffer with anxiety, depression, addiction, or feelings that we are not enough. Priesthood blessings can help us overcome these challenges and receive peace as we move forward into the future."

She testified—from experience—that God knew His children personally. "He is always aware of us and blesses us even when we feel we don't deserve it," she said. "He knows what we need and when we need it."[41]

When Laudy finished, another youth speaker, Enzo Petelo, stood and gave a talk. And as she listened to him, Laudy could hardly remember what had happened during her own talk. Did she do all right?

As soon as the session was over, she ran outside the auditorium to meet her parents. "Did I say it too fast?" she asked.

"No, *hija*," her mother said. "You did such a good job."[42]

THE NEXT MORNING, PRESIDENT Nelson thanked the Saints for choosing to hear the word of the Lord, despite global upheaval. "The increasing darkness that accompanies tribulation makes the light of Jesus Christ shine ever brighter," he testified. "Just think of the good each of us can do during this time."

He invoked the Father's words to Joseph Smith in the Sacred Grove: "This is My Beloved Son. Hear Him!"

"In those two words—'Hear Him'—God gives us the pattern for success, happiness, and joy in this life," he said, urging the Saints to hear, hearken, and heed the word of the Lord. "I promise that you will be blessed with additional power to deal with temptation, struggles, and weakness," he said. "I promise miracles in your marriage, family relationships, and daily work. And I promise that your capacity to feel joy will increase even if turbulence increases in your life."[43]

Following these remarks, President Nelson announced a new proclamation from the First Presidency and Quorum of the Twelve Apostles on the Restoration of the gospel of Jesus Christ. The broadcast then cut to a video of him reading the proclamation as he stood in the Sacred Grove.

"Two hundred years have now elapsed since this Restoration was initiated by God the Father and His Beloved Son, Jesus Christ," the proclamation declared. "We affirm that God is making known His will for His beloved sons and daughters. We testify that those who prayerfully study the message of the Restoration and act in faith will be blessed to gain their own witness of its divinity and of its purpose to prepare the world for the promised Second Coming of our Lord and Savior, Jesus Christ."[44]

AT THE CLOSE OF President Nelson's message, Saints in countries around the world stood up, wherever they were gathered, and raised white handkerchiefs in the air. Since the dedication of the Kirtland Temple in 1836, Church members had praised the Father and Son with a sacred Hosanna Shout. And today was no different.

Following the prophet's lead, the Saints waved their handkerchiefs in the air as their voices rejoiced together across the globe:

> *Hosanna, Hosanna, Hosanna to God and the Lamb.*
>
> *Hosanna, Hosanna, Hosanna to God and the Lamb.*
>
> *Hosanna, Hosanna, Hosanna to God and the Lamb.*
>
> *Amen, Amen, and Amen.*[45]

NOTE ON SOURCES

This volume is a work of narrative nonfiction based on hundreds of historical sources. Utmost care has been taken to ensure its accuracy. Readers should not assume, however, that the narrative presented here is perfect or complete. The records of the past, and our ability to interpret them in the present, are limited.

All sources of historical knowledge contain gaps, ambiguities, and biases. They often convey their creator's point of view, and witnesses of the same events experience, remember, interpret, and record them differently. The challenge of the historian is to assemble known points of view and piece together an accurate understanding of the past.

Saints is a true account of the history of The Church of Jesus Christ of Latter-day Saints, based on what we know and understand at the present time from existing historical records. It is not a comprehensive history, nor is it the only possible telling of the Church's sacred history. But the scholars who researched, wrote, and edited this volume know the historical sources well, used them thoughtfully, and documented them in the endnotes and list of sources cited. Readers are invited to evaluate the sources themselves, many of which have been digitized and linked to the endnotes. It is probable that the discovery of more sources, or new readings of existing sources, will in time yield other meanings, interpretations, and possible points of view.

The narrative in *Saints* draws on historical sources of two kinds: primary and secondary. Primary sources contain information about events from those who witnessed them firsthand. Some primary sources, like letters, journals, and reports or recordings of discourses, were produced at the time of the events they describe. These contemporaneous sources reflect what people thought, felt, and did in the moment, revealing how the past was interpreted when it was the present. Other primary sources, like autobiographies and oral history interviews, were written after the fact. These reminiscent sources reveal what the past came to mean to the writer over time, often making them better than contemporary sources at recognizing the significance of past events. Since they rely on memory, however, reminiscent sources can include inaccuracies and be influenced by the author's later understandings and beliefs.

Secondary historical sources contain information from people who did not witness the events described firsthand. Such sources include later family histories and academic publications. This volume is indebted to many such sources, which proved valuable for the broader contextual and interpretive work they provided. Nevertheless, the Church does not endorse all the opinions of authors whose voices are found in the endnotes of *Saints*.

Every source in *Saints* was evaluated for credibility, and each sentence was repeatedly checked for consistency with the sources. Lines of dialogue and other quotations come directly from historical sources. Spelling, capitalization, and punctuation in direct quotations have been silently modernized for clarity. In some instances, more significant modifications, like shifting from the past tense to present tense or standardizing grammar, have been made to quotations to improve

Note on Sources

readability. In these cases, endnotes describe the changes made. Choices about which sources to use and how to use them were made by a team of historians, writers, and editors who based decisions on both historical integrity and literary quality.

As the story of the Church becomes more global, *Saints* increasingly relies on sources created in languages other than English. At times, the writers of this volume relied on volunteer or machine translation to craft the narrative. All quotations from translated sources come from professional translators.

Some antagonistic sources were used to write this volume and are cited in the notes. Though hostile to the Church, these documents sometimes contain details that were not recorded elsewhere. Some of these details were used when other records confirmed their general accuracy. Facts from these antagonistic records were used without adopting their hostile interpretations, and citing a source in the endnotes does not signal Church endorsement.

As a narrative history written for a general audience, this volume presents a history of the Church in a coherent, accessible format. While drawing on the techniques of popular storytelling, it does not go beyond information found in historical sources. When the text includes even minor details, such as facial expressions or weather conditions, it is because these details are found in or reasonably deduced from the historical record.

To maintain the readability of the narrative, the volume rarely addresses challenges in or to the historical record in the text itself. Instead, such source-based discussions are found in topical essays on saints.ChurchofJesusChrist.org and are referenced in endnotes under the bolded heading "Topic." Readers are encouraged to consult these essays as they read *Saints*.

NOTES

Some sources are referred to with a shortened citation. The "Sources Cited" section provides full citation information for all sources. Many sources are available digitally and are linked from the electronic version of the book, available at saints.churchofJesusChrist.org and in Gospel Library.

Text in bold in the notes points to topical articles with additional information online at saints.ChurchofJesusChrist.org and in Gospel Library under "Church History Topics."

CHAPTER 1: WHERE AND WHEN

1. Jue, Reminiscence, 4; Harold B. Lee, in *One Hundred Twenty-Fifth Semi-annual Conference*, 131.
2. Jue, Reminiscence, 3–4; Britsch, *From the East*, 234–35; Lee, Diary, Sept. 25, 1954; Harold B. Lee to "Dear Brethren," Oct. 13, 1954, First Presidency, Mission Correspondence, 1950–59, CHL; Harold B. Lee, in *One Hundred Twenty-Fifth Semi-annual Conference*, 125–26. **Topic: Hong Kong**
3. Jue, Reminiscence, 4; Harold B. Lee, in *One Hundred Twenty-Fifth Semi-annual Conference*, 131. **Topic: Harold B. Lee**
4. Jue, Reminiscence, 5; Britsch, *From the East*, 33–39, 231–35; Stout, Diary, June 9, 1853; Xi, "History of Mormon-Chinese Relations," 24–25.
5. Jue, Reminiscence, 1–4; Britsch, *From the East*, 231–33.
6. Jue, Reminiscence, 5; Southern Far East Asian Mission Report, May 9, 1955; Britsch, *From the East*, 235–37.
7. Harold B. Lee, in *One Hundred Twenty-Fifth Semi-annual Conference*, 131; Jue, Reminiscence, 5; Heaton, Personal History, volume 2, 19; Britsch, *From the East*, 98, 236; Harold B. Lee to "Dear Brethren," Oct. 13, 1954, First Presidency, Mission Correspondence, 1950–59, CHL. Quotation edited for readability; "was" and "had" in original changed to "is" and "has." **Topics: Guam; Philippines; Taiwan**
8. Lee, Diary, Sept. 22, 1955; S. Perry Lee, "Third European Temple Site Chosen," *Deseret News*, Sept. 23, 1955, 1; S. Perry Lee, "Pres. McKay Home, Pleased with Bern Temple, Choir," *Church News*, Sept. 24, 1955, 2; "Pres. McKay Tells Plans for Third Europe Temple," *Salt Lake Tribune*, Sept. 23, 1955, section 2, 1; *Saints*, volume 3, chapter 39. **Topics: David O. McKay; Switzerland**
9. *Saints*, volume 3, chapter 39; Rebecca Franklin, "A Mighty People in the Rockies," *New York Times*, Apr. 3, 1955, 17; David O. McKay, in *One Hundredth Annual Conference*, 82–83; David O. McKay, "The Church—A World-Wide Institution," *Deseret News*, Dec. 20, 1947, Church News section, 4; Joseph Smith, "Church History," Mar. 1, 1842, in *JSP*, H1:499–500. **Topics: Globalization; Temple Building**
10. *Deseret News 1989–90 Church Almanac*, 205; Rebecca Franklin, "A Mighty People in the Rockies," *New York Times*, Apr. 3, 1955, 17; David A. Smith, in *One Hundred Fourth Semi-annual Conference*, 73; Wallace F. Toronto to J. Spencer Cornwall, Nov. 24, 1946; Kenneth Lyman and others to Mormon Tabernacle Choir, Feb. 10, 1949, Mormon Tabernacle Choir Fan Mail, CHL; "Listening Post," *Tab* (Salt Lake City), Oct. 2, 1949, 1, 3–4; Cornwall, *Century of Singing*, 278–94; O'Dea, *Mormons*, 2, 146–47, 255; Lythgoe, "Changing Image of Mormonism in Periodical Literature," 147, 182–83, 186–87, 193–94; Shipps, *Sojourner*, 68–72. **Topic: Tabernacle Choir**
11. Paul L. Anderson and Richard W. Jackson, "Building Program," in Ludlow, *Encyclopedia of Mormonism*, 1:236–38; Allen and Leonard, *Story of the Latter-day Saints*, 551, 571–72; Gordon T. Allred, "The Great Labor of Love," *Improvement Era*, Apr. 1958, 226–29, 268–71; see also, for example, Jackson, *Places of Worship*, 175–89, 222–25, 239–52; and "Chicken Dinner Helps Pay for Boise Air Conditioning," *Deseret News*, Aug. 22, 1951, Church section, 12.

670

12. See, for example, John Csarnecki to "Dear Brothers," Jan. 1, 1954; Aug. 12, 1954; Dr. N. K. Panchal to Joseph Anderson, Jan. 9, 1954; Joseph Anderson to "Dear Bishop Panchal," Jan. 25, 1954; John Beturas and Mary Beturas to David O. McKay, Oct. 25, 1954; Joseph Anderson to John Beturas and Mary Beturas, Nov. 10, 1954, First Presidency, General Correspondence Files, CHL. **Topic: Church Growth**
13. McKay, Diary, Oct. 25, 1955; David O. McKay, in *One Hundred Twenty-Third Semi-annual Conference,* 11–12; Plewe, *Mapping Mormonism,* 156; Kuehne, *Mormons as Citizens of a Communist State,* 40–44, 55–61; Mehr, "Enduring Believers," 140–44; Van Orden, *Building Zion,* 193–215; see also *Saints,* volume 3, chapters 33, 35, and 36.
14. McKay, Diary, Jan. 22–Feb. 14, 1954; Sept. 28, 1955; June 13, 1956; Quorum of the Twelve Apostles, Missionary Committee Minutes, Apr. 14, 1955; Albert L. Zobell Jr., "President McKay Visits Missions in Latin America," *Improvement Era,* Apr. 1954, 228–29; Ilma Lewis, "Pres. McKay Lays Chapel Cornerstone," *Church News,* Feb. 13, 1954, 3; Joseph Fielding Smith, in *One Hundred Twenty-Sixth Semi-annual Conference,* 42–44.
15. Allen, "West Africa before the 1978 Priesthood Revelation," 210–18; *Saints,* volume 2, chapters 12 and 39; *Saints,* volume 3, chapter 16; First Presidency to Bryan Bunker, June 10, 1952, First Presidency, General Correspondence Files, CHL; E. O. Dick to "Brother in Christ," June 6, 1953; First Presidency to Harvey Taylor, Feb. 27, 1959, First Presidency, Mission Correspondence, 1946–69, CHL; C. E. Otu to "Dear Brethren," Sept. 24, 1955, First Presidency, General Administration Files, 1923, 1932, 1937–67, CHL. **Topic: Priesthood and Temple Restriction**
16. McKay, Diary, Mar. 10, 1956; *Saints,* volume 3, chapter 24; Cowan, *Beacon on a Hill,* 16–38, 120–46.
17. McKay, Diary, Mar. 11, 1956; David O. McKay, "Dedicatory Prayer," *Improvement Era,* Apr. 1956, 226.
18. Hélio da Rocha Camargo, "Meu testemunho," *Liahona* (São Paulo, Brazil), Mar. 1959, 75; Camargo, Oral History Interview, 9; *Saints,* volume 3, chapter 18; Missionary Department, Full-Time Mission Monthly Progress Reports, June 1956. Quotation edited for readability; "he did," "believed," and "considered" in English translation of original changed to "I do," "believe," and "consider." **Topic: Brazil**
19. Sorensen, "Personal History," 172; Camargo, Oral History Interview, 9–10; Hélio da Rocha Camargo, "Meu testemunho," *Liahona* (São Paulo, Brazil), Mar. 1959, 75–76; Chipman and Richardson, Oral History Interview, 19. Quotation edited for readability; original source has "he guaranteed that those young men were well prepared."
20. Sorensen, "Personal History," 173; Camargo, Oral History Interview, 10; Hélio da Rocha Camargo, "Meu testemunho," *Liahona* (São Paulo, Brazil), Mar. 1959, 76; Chipman and Richardson, Oral History Interview, 19–20; Camargo, Reminiscences, 43–44; "Onward March," *Church News,* Oct. 5, 1957, 15. **Topic: Mountain Meadows Massacre**
21. Muti, Book of Remembrance, [55], [71]; Muti, "Mosese Lui Muti," 169; Muti, Oral History Interview, 16; Muti and Muti, *Man of Service,* 145–46; Britsch, *Unto the Islands of the Sea,* 475.
22. Allen and Leonard, *Story of the Latter-day Saints,* 571–72; First Presidency to D'Monte Coombs, Dec. 14, 1954, First Presidency, Mission Correspondence, 1950–59, CHL; Moffat, Woods, and Anderson, *Saints of Tonga,* 200–204, 222; Britsch, *Unto the Islands of the Sea,* 474–75. **Topics: Building Program; Tonga**
23. Muti and Muti, *Man of Service,* 146; Missionary Department, Full-Time Mission Monthly Progress Reports, Apr. 1956; Allen and Leonard, *Story of the Latter-day Saints,* 571–72; Feinga, "Labor Missions in Tonga and Hawai'i," 46–48; Gordon T. Allred, "The Great Labor of Love," *Improvement Era,* Apr. 1958, 270–71.
24. Muti, "Mosese Lui Muti," 170; Muti and Muti, *Man of Service,* 16, 27, 30, 36, 145, 336–37; Charles Woodworth to Marsha Davis, June 10, 1956, Charles J. Woodworth Papers, CHL; Moffat, Woods, and Anderson, *Saints of Tonga,* 188–95, 207–9.

25. Muti, Oral History Interview, 17; Muti, "Mosese Lui Muti," 170.
26. Muti and Muti, *Man of Service,* 146–47; Woodworth, Mission Journal, Feb. 16 and May 23, 1956; Charles Woodworth to Marsha Davis, May 25, 1956, Charles J. Woodworth Papers, CHL; Mortensen, "Serving in Paradise," 18–19, 37–39. Quotation edited for readability; original source has "let me know what her feeling about going on this mission."
27. Muti, "Mosese Lui Muti," 170. Quotation edited for readability; original source has "two and one half weeks."
28. Muti, "Mosese Lui Muti," 170; Muti and Muti, *Man of Service,* 148; Muti, Book of Remembrance, [71], [84]; Muti, Oral History Interview, 9–10; Charles Woodworth to Marsha Davis, June 10, 1956; Feb. 18, 1957; June 18, 1957, Charles J. Woodworth Papers, CHL.
29. Muti, Book of Remembrance, [92]–[93]; Muti, Oral History Interview, 15–16; Muti, "Mosese Lui Muti," 172.
30. Muti, Book of Remembrance, [71]–[72]; Woodworth, Mission Journal, May 29, 1956; Woodworth, "District News," 2; Muti, "Mosese Lui Muti," 170–71; Muti and Muti, *Man of Service,* 48–51, 150–51.
31. Camargo, Oral History Interview, 10; Camargo, Reminiscences, 42; Rodriguez, *From Every Nation,* 131. Quotation edited for readability; "Why beneficial" in English translation of original changed to "Why is it beneficial."
32. Camargo, Oral History Interview, 10–11; Camargo, Reminiscences, 42; de Queiroz, Oral History Interview [2011], 6. Quotation edited for readability; "did not" in English translation of original changed to "do not," two instances of "was" changed to "is," and "could" changed to "can."
33. Camargo, Oral History Interview, 10–13; Camargo, Reminiscences, 42, 45; de Queiroz, Oral History Interview [2011], 6; de Oliveira, Oral History Interview, 2–3; John L. Hart, "Skills Gained in Military, Business and Ministry Prepared Him for New Calling," *Church News,* June 16, 1985, 4.
34. Rodriguez, *From Every Nation,* 132; Camargo, Reminiscences, 43.
35. Rodriguez, *From Every Nation,* 132; Camargo, Oral History Interview, 11.
36. Camargo, Oral History Interview, 10, 12–13; Camargo, Reminiscences, 43, 44; Rodriguez, *From Every Nation,* 132–33; Hélio da Rocha Camargo, "Meu testemunho," *Liahona* (São Paulo, Brazil), Mar. 1959, 76; LeGrand Richards, *A Marvelous Work and a Wonder* (Salt Lake City: Deseret Book, 1950); "4 Churchmen Elevated after Long Service," *Deseret News,* Apr. 7, 1952, A1. Quotation edited for readability; two instances of "had" in English translation of original changed to "has."

CHAPTER 2: LEAD ME, GUIDE ME

1. Charles Woodworth to Marsha Davis, July 15, 1957, Charles J. Woodworth Papers, CHL; *New Zealand Official Year-Book,* 57:925; Mortensen, "Serving in Paradise," 19–22; see also Smith, *Niue,* 1–10; and Woodworth, Mission Journal, May 29, 1956.
2. Mortensen, "Serving in Paradise," 21, 24–26, 28, 47–48; Goodman, *Niue of Polynesia,* chapter 2; Woodworth, Mission Journal, Dec. 21, 1955; May 17–18 and 29, 1956; June 26, 1956; Mar. 2, 13, and 16, 1957; "Comparative Report," 3.
3. Mortensen, Mission Journal, Aug. 27, 1955; June 6, 9, and 24–30, 1956; July 1–24, 1956; Mar. 28, 1957; Woodworth, Mission Journal, Oct. 10, 1956; Jan. 29, 1957; Feb. 11, 1957; Mar. 2 and 5, 1957; May 27–June 10, 1957; Muti and Muti, *Man of Service,* 154–55; Muti, "Mosese Lui Muti," 172.
4. Woodworth, Mission Journal, Jan. 14, 29, and 31, 1956; May 23–29, 1956; July 10, 1956; Jan. 21, 1957; Woodworth, Oral History Interview, 55–56; Price, "History of the Church of Jesus Christ of Latter Day Saints on Niue Island," 1–2; Muti and Muti, *Man of Service,* 164.

5. Muti and Muti, *Man of Service*, 154–55, 164–69, 171–72, 175–76, 179–80; Woodworth, Mission Journal, May 30, 1956; June 3 and 26, 1956; Aug. 28, 1956; Sept. 30, 1956; Dec. 9, 1956; Feb. 17, 1957; July 7, 1957; Mortensen, Mission Journal, May 30, 1956; June 3, 1956; Aug. 22, 1956; May 5, 1957; Mortensen, "Serving in Paradise," 28; Muti, Interview Notes [2012]; Niue District, Tongan Mission, Minutes, Sept. 29–30 and Nov. 24, 1956, 3:36–37, 40.
6. Woodworth, Mission Journal, June 27, 1956; Sept. 30, 1956; Mar. 17, 1957; Charles Woodworth to Marsha Davis, Oct. 9, 1956; June 15, 1957, Charles J. Woodworth Papers, CHL; "District News," 3; Muti and Muti, *Man of Service*, 163–64, 167. **Topics: Church Callings; Relief Society**
7. Peterson and Gaunt, *Elect Ladies*, 151; Spafford, Oral History Interview, 107–8, 115, 122; Derr, Cannon, and Beecher, *Women of Covenant*, 309, 345–46. **Topic: Belle S. Spafford**
8. Derr and others, *First Fifty Years*, 24–25; Reeder, "To Do Something Extraordinary," 150–75; *Saints*, volume 2, chapter 24; Derr, Cannon, and Beecher, *Women of Covenant*, 174–76; "Rooms Are Assigned in Bishop's Building," *Deseret Evening News*, Oct. 30, 1909, 5; "Physical Needs Met by Vast Construction," *Deseret News*, Apr. 6, 1951, C2.
9. Relief Society General Presidency to First Presidency, Aug. 6, 1945, Relief Society Building Files, CHL; First Presidency to Belle S. Spafford and Counselors, Sept. 16, 1947, First Presidency, Letterpress Copybooks, volume 139; Belle S. Spafford, Marianne Sharp, and Velma Simonsen to Relief Society Presidents, Oct. 21, 1947, in Relief Society, General Board Minutes, volume 26, Oct. 22, 1947, 354A–54B; Spafford, Oral History Interview, 108–11, 115; *Retail Food Prices by Cities*, 10.
10. Coral Webb to Belle S. Spafford, Dec. 10, 1947; Genevieve C. Hickison to Relief Society General Board, Feb. 19, 1948; Marena Grigsby to Hilda Richards, May 31, 1948; Holly Fisher to Marianne Sharp, Nov. 5, 1948, Relief Society Building Fund Files, CHL; Spafford, Oral History Interview, 112–17, 119; Derr, Cannon, and Beecher, *Women of Covenant*, 309, 319; "Relief Society Building One-Sixth Completed," *Church News*, July 3, 1954, 1; "Builders Complete Relief Society's Center," *Salt Lake Tribune*, Aug. 11, 1956, 8.
11. Spafford, Oral History Interview, 115, 122; Belle S. Spafford, "A Relief Society Building to Be Erected," *Relief Society Magazine*, Dec. 1945, 752; "Builders Complete Relief Society's Center," *Salt Lake Tribune*, Aug. 11, 1956, 8; "A Home of Our Own," Church History website, history.ChurchofJesusChrist.org.
12. Spafford, Oral History Interview, 123; "Relief Society Building Gifts," 1:19, 24; Photographs of Artifacts Donated to the Relief Society Building Fund, CHL; Relief Society Building Inventory, circa 1956, CHL; "Relief Society General Presidency with Gifts for the Relief Society Building," *Relief Society Magazine*, Aug. 1956, 511.
13. Heidi S. Swinton and LaRene Gaunt, "The Relief Society Building: A Symbol of Service and Sacrifice," *Ensign*, Sept. 2006, 56–57; Lenora Bringhurst to Marianne Sharp, June 14, 1949; Marianne Sharp to Lenora Bringhurst, June 22, 1949, Relief Society Building Fund Files, CHL; Collette, *Hermine Weber*, [40]; Hatch, *Cziep Family History*, 201. **Topic: Austria**
14. Lenora Bringhurst to Marianne Sharp, May 6, 1949, Relief Society Building Fund Files, CHL.
15. Smith, Journal, Oct. 3, 1956; "Handsome Church Office Building Near Completion," *Deseret Evening News*, Mar. 24, 1917, section 2, 3; "Grain Saving in the Relief Society," *Relief Society Magazine*, Feb. 1915, 50–58; Young, Oral History Interview, 33; Spafford, Oral History Interview, 122–23; Belle S. Spafford, "We Built as One," *Relief Society Magazine*, Dec. 1956, 801. **Topic: Church Headquarters**
16. Camargo, Oral History Interview, 13–15; Camargo, Reminiscences, 44–45; Rodriguez, *From Every Nation*, 132–33.
17. Hélio da Rocha Camargo, "Meu testemunho," *Liahona* (São Paulo, Brazil), Mar. 1959, 76; Camargo, Oral History Interview, 14; Sorensen, "Personal History," 173; de Queiroz, Oral History Interview [2011], 13.

18. Sorensen, "Personal History," 139; "Estatistica da area brasileira," 1955–56, Brazil South Area, Statistical Reports, CHL; Missionary Department, Full-Time Mission Monthly Progress Reports, Jan.–May 1957.
19. Hélio da Rocha Camargo, "Meu testemunho," *Liahona* (São Paulo, Brazil), Mar. 1959, 76; Camargo, Oral History Interview, 14; de Queiroz, Oral History Interview [1982], 4–6; Sorensen, "Personal History," 139, 363.
20. Camargo, Oral History Interview, 16–18; de Queiroz, Oral History Interview [2011], 13–14; de Queiroz, Oral History Interview [1982], 12–14; Grover, "Mormon Priesthood Revelation and the São Paulo, Brazil Temple," 40–41; Lovell, "Development and the Persistence of Racial Inequality in Brazil," 397–400. **Topics: Priesthood and Temple Restriction; Racial Segregation**
21. De Queiroz, Oral History Interview [1982], 12–14; Spencer W. Kimball, Journal, May 1, 1966; Hélio da Rocha Camargo, "Meu testemunho," *Liahona* (São Paulo, Brazil), Mar. 1959, 75–76; Hillam, Oral History Interview, 6–7, emphasis in original.
22. Oakes, "Life Sketch of Naomi W. Randall," 11; Randall, "Heavenly Truth in Words and Music," 2–3; Randall, Interview [1989], [00:02:36]–[00:04:40]; Naomi Randall to Mildred Pettit, Jan. 29, 1957, Collection of Materials pertaining to the Song "I Am a Child of God," CHL; *Fifty-First Annual Conference of the Primary Association,* 27, [62]–[64]. **Topics: Hymns; Primary**
23. Oakes, "Life Sketch of Naomi W. Randall," 11; Randall, "Heavenly Truth in Words and Music," 2–3; Randall, Interview [1989], [00:03:30]–[00:03:45]; Naomi Randall to Mildred Pettit, Jan. 29, 1957, Collection of Materials pertaining to the Song "I Am a Child of God," CHL.
24. Oakes, "Life Sketch of Naomi W. Randall," 11; Randall, "Heavenly Truth in Words and Music," 3.
25. Oakes, "Life Sketch of Naomi W. Randall," 11–12; Randall, "Heavenly Truth in Words and Music," 3; Randall, Interview [1976], 1.
26. Oakes, "Life Sketch of Naomi W. Randall," 11–12; Randall, "Heavenly Truth in Words and Music," 4; Randall, Interview [1976], 1; Primary Association, General Board Minutes, Jan. 31, 1957.
27. Naomi Randall to Mildred Pettit, Jan. 29, 1957; Feb. 5, 1957, Collection of Materials pertaining to the Song "I Am a Child of God," CHL.
28. *Fifty-First Annual Conference of the Primary Association,* 27; Randall, "Heavenly Truth in Words and Music," 2, 4–5; Naomi Randall to Mildred Pettit, Jan. 29, 1957; Feb. 5, 1957, Collection of Materials pertaining to the Song "I Am a Child of God," CHL.
29. Randall, "Heavenly Truth in Words and Music," 5–6; Lee, Diary, Apr. 7, 1959; Spencer W. Kimball, Journal, Apr. 7, 1959; Lucile Reading to Robert D. Hales, Sept. 14, 1976, Collection of Materials pertaining to the Song "I Am a Child of God," CHL. Later, the line "Teach me all that I must know" was changed to "Teach me all that I must do" at the recommendation of Spencer W. Kimball. (Davidson, *Our Latter-day Hymns,* 303–4.)
30. Hélio da Rocha Camargo, "Meu testemunho," *Liahona* (São Paulo, Brazil), Mar. 1959, 76; Hillam, Oral History Interview, 5–7.
31. Sorensen, "Personal History," 173.
32. Hélio da Rocha Camargo, "Meu testemunho," *Liahona* (São Paulo, Brazil), Mar. 1959, 76; Camargo, Oral History Interview, 16–18.
33. Hillam, Oral History Interview, 6; Hillam, Missionary Journal, May 27, 1957. Quotation edited for readability; "he would" in original changed to "You will," "his baptism papers" changed to "your baptism papers," and "president" changed to "mission president."
34. Camargo, Reminiscences, 45; Hillam, Oral History Interview, 6; Camargo, Oral History Interview, 14–15; Helio da Rocha Camargo entry, Vila Mariana Branch, São Paulo District, Brazilian Mission, Record of Members, 1957, 330, in Brazil (Country), part 3, Record of Members Collection, CHL.

Chapter 3: A Good Fight

1. Muti and Muti, *Man of Service*, 154; "J. Archie Cottle and Family Called to Tongan Mission," *Church News*, Feb. 4, 1956, 10; Woodworth, Mission Journal, Mar. 2–June 1, 1957; Niue District, Tongan Mission, Minutes, June 27, 1956, 3:27–28; "Mission Home," "West Side of the Chapel," "Concrete Wall and Part of the Tower; One Classroom and Office," and Partially Finished Mission Home, Photographs, Charles J. Woodworth Papers, CHL. **Topic: Building Program**
2. Muti and Muti, *Man of Service*, 168; Muti, Book of Remembrance, [33], [73]; Woodworth, Mission Journal, Dec. 29, 1956; Mar. 2, 1957; Apr. 1–3, 9, 13, 15, and 17, 1957; Charles Woodworth to Marsha Davis, Jan. 8, 1957, Charles J. Woodworth Papers, CHL; Mortensen, Mission Journal, Mar. 30 and Apr. 11, 1957; Mortensen, "Serving in Paradise," 20–22.
3. Muti and Muti, *Man of Service*, 155; Woodworth, Mission Journal, July 1, 4, 9–10, 14, 22, and 30, 1956; Aug. 17, 1956; Sept. 10, 1956; Nov. 9, 1956; Dec. 9 and 13, 1956; Jan. 21, 1957; June 8–9, 1957; Charles Woodworth to Marsha Davis, June 25, 1956; Feb. 26, 1957, Charles J. Woodworth Papers, CHL; First Presidency to Mission Presidents, Dec. 2, 1949, First Presidency, Circular Letters, CHL; Muti, Interview Notes [2012].
4. Muti and Muti, *Man of Service*, 154–55; Mortensen, "Serving in Paradise," 37; Woodworth, Mission Journal, Sept. 17, 1955; Oct. 22, 1955; June 7 and 13, 1956; Mar. 5–7, 9, 15, 18–19, 21, and 30, 1957; July 30, 1957; Mortensen, Mission Journal, Sept. 3, 1956.
5. Muti and Muti, *Man of Service*, 126–27, 336–37; Woodworth, Mission Journal, Dec. 26, 1956; Harold Lundstrom, "Unification Affects Many Campuses," *Church News*, July 18, 1953, 9. Quotation edited for readability; "them," "they," and "their" in original changed to "us," "we," and "our."
6. Woodworth, Mission Journal, Aug. 16, 1955; Sept. 21, 1955; Aug. 4–5, 10, 24, and 26, 1956; Nov. 7 and 19, 1956; Dec. 8, 13, and 29, 1956; Feb. 17–18, 1956; Mar. 31, 1957; July 22, 1957; Muti, Interview Notes [2021], 2; Woodworth, Oral History Interview, 42, 47, 56; Muti and Muti, *Man of Service*, 181–82; Macke, "Oral History of Lois Maurine Lambert Woodworth Macke," 13; Charles Woodworth to Marsha Davis, Aug. 16 and 25, 1956; Jan. 8, 1957, Charles J. Woodworth Papers, CHL. Quotation edited for readability; "know" in original changed to "knows."
7. Woodworth, Mission Journal, Jan. 22, 1956; Nov. 19, 1956; Jan. 2 and 18, 1957; Feb. 3, 1957; Apr. 25, 1957; May 5–6, 1957; Charles Woodworth to Marsha Davis, Jan. 8, 1957; Charles Woodworth to Ralph Olson, Feb. 17, 1957; Charles Woodworth to Fred Stone, Feb. 26, 1957, Charles J. Woodworth Papers, CHL; Dalton, Autobiography, 1, 4–5, 14–15.
8. Muti and Muti, *Man of Service*, 155, 165–66, 182.
9. Woodworth, Mission Journal, Apr. 24, 1957; June 15, 19, and 22, 1957; Woodworth, Autobiography, 3; Woodworth, Oral History Interview, 56; Charles Woodworth to Marsha Davis, Feb. 18, 1957; June 18, 1957, Charles J. Woodworth Papers, CHL.
10. Heaton, Personal History, volume 2, 116; Jue, Reminiscence, 5; China Hong Kong Mission, Manuscript History and Historical Reports, May 26, 1957; "Local Sister Called to Be a Missionary," [18].
11. Heaton, Personal History, volume 2, 19; Hardy, "Personal History," volume 2, 87; Heaton and Heaton, *Documentary History*, 175; "Local Sister Called to Be a Missionary," [18].
12. Jue, Reminiscence, 5; Southern Far East Asian Mission Report, 16, 19–21.
13. Jue, Mission Reminiscences, 1; Heaton and Heaton, *Documentary History*, 175; Jue, Reminiscence, 1–2; Southern Far East Asian Mission Report, 16–19; Peterson, "Crisis and Opportunity," 141; Britsch, *From the East*, 232–33.
14. Heaton and Heaton, *Documentary History*, 25, 32, 35–36, 54–55; Heaton, Personal History, volume 2, 70; Britsch, *From the East*, 242–43, 251; Allen and Leonard, *Story of the Latter-day Saints*, 568; *A Systematic Program for Teaching the Gospel* ([Salt Lake City]: The Church of Jesus Christ of Latter-day Saints, 1952); Heaton, Oral History Interview [Interview 3], 72. **Topic: Hong Kong**

15. Britsch, *From the East,* 244; Jue Family, Oral History Interview [2019], 56–61; Hardy, "Personal History," volume 2, 83.
16. Woodworth, Mission Journal, Aug. 15–16, 1957; Sept. 2, 1957; Oct. 17, 1957; Nov. 1, 16, and 29, 1957; Dec. 21, 1957; Muti and Muti, *Man of Service,* 201; Muti, Interview Notes [2021], 1; Woodworth, Oral History Interview, 57; Charles Woodworth to Marsha Davis, Nov. 2, 1957, Charles J. Woodworth Papers, CHL.
17. "Chuck Woodworth Quits Ring to Perform Service for Church," *Joplin (MO) Globe,* July 31, 1955, C2; "Charles Pleases in Ring Exhibitions Here," *Rocky Mountain News* (Denver), Apr. 30, 1954, 52; "Ezzard Charles," in Odd, *Encyclopedia of Boxing,* 26; Al Warden, "The Tragedy of Rex Layne," *Ogden (UT) Standard-Examiner,* May 25, 1954, A8; "Woodworth Set for Ring Return," *Joplin Globe,* Jan. 9, 1958, B2.
18. Art Grace, "U-M Boxer Started Layne's Ring Career," *Miami Daily News,* Apr. 1, 1953, B2; Woodworth, Oral History Interview, 63; "Layne, Chuck Tangle in Bout Tonight," *Salt Lake Tribune,* Aug. 30, 1954, 25; Al Warden, "The Tragedy of Rex Layne," *Ogden (UT) Standard-Examiner,* May 25, 1954, A8; "Tale of Tape for Monday's Woodworth-Layne Scrap," *Salt Lake Tribune,* Aug. 29, 1954, B10; "Layne Continues Comeback with Win over Woodworth," *Daily Herald* (Provo, UT), Aug. 31, 1954, 6.
19. Woodworth, Mission Journal, Nov. 13 and Dec. 6, 1957; "Kitione Lave—The Tongan Torpedo," *New Zealand Ring,* Feb. 25, 1958, 5; "Island Boxers Are Doing Well," *Pacific Islands Monthly,* Apr. 1955, 143; "Boxing Youth Prevails," *Times* (London), Apr. 25, 1956, 15; "Grand Slam," *Daily News* (New York City), Apr. 27, 1956, 72.
20. Woodworth, Mission Journal, Dec. 26 and 30–31, 1957; Jan. 3 and 14, 1958; Salavia Muti to Charles Woodworth, Feb. 2, 1958, Charles J. Woodworth Papers, CHL.
21. Woodworth, Mission Journal, Feb. 29, 1958; Muti, Interview Notes [2021], 2; Woodworth, Oral History Interview, 64.
22. "Ringwise American Too Good," *Auckland (New Zealand) Star,* Feb. 28, 1958, 7; "Return Fight Here Soon for Woodworth and Kitione Lave?," and "Noel Holmes' Sports Talk," *Auckland Star,* Feb. 28, 1958, 24; Auckland Boxing Association, "Announcer's Card," [Feb. 27, 1958], Charles J. Woodworth Papers, CHL; Woodworth, Oral History Interview, 60–61; see also Britsch, "Charles ('Chuck') J. Woodworth," 175–76.
23. "Ringwise American Too Good," *Auckland (New Zealand) Star,* Feb. 28, 1958, 7; Woodworth, Oral History Interview, 61–63; "Return Fight Here Soon for Woodworth and Kitione Lave?," *Auckland Star,* Feb. 28, 1958, 24; Woodworth, Mission Journal, Feb. 29, 1958; see also Britsch, "Charles ('Chuck') J. Woodworth," 175–77.
24. Mosese Muti to Charles Woodworth, Telegram, Feb. 28, 1958, Charles J. Woodworth Papers, CHL; Woodworth, Oral History Interview, 63; Woodworth, Mission Journal, Feb. 29, 1958.
25. Kuehne, *Henry Burkhardt,* 33–34. The East German Mission was renamed the North German Mission in 1957. (Kuehne, *Mormons as Citizens of a Communist State,* 436.)
26. Wilke, *Path to the Berlin Wall,* 65–66, 122; Trachtenberg, *Constructed Peace,* 96–103, 146–47, 195, 204–5.
27. Kuehne, *Henry Burkhardt,* 13–37; Hall, "The Church of Jesus Christ of Latter-day Saints in the Former East Germany," 489–95; Alvin R. Dyer to First Presidency, Oct. 25, 1960, First Presidency, Mission Correspondence, 1946–69, CHL. **Topics: Cold War; Germany**
28. Burkhardt, Journal, Nov. 11, 1955; Spencer W. Kimball, Journal, Jan. 14, 1962; Burkhardt, Oral History Interview [1991], 4–8; Kuehne, *Henry Burkhardt,* 42; see also Kuehne, *Mormons as Citizens of a Communist State,* 437–39.
29. Kuehne, *Henry Burkhardt,* 20–31, 34; Spencer W. Kimball, Journal, Jan. 14, 1962.
30. Kuehne, *Henry Burkhardt,* 30–35. Quotation edited for readability; "Herr Robbins" in original changed to "Mr. Robbins."
31. Muti, Book of Remembrance, [70]; Gordon B. Hinckley, "Temple in the Pacific," *Improvement Era,* July 1958, 506–8; Theodore L. Cannon, "The President in New Zealand," *Church News,* Apr. 26, 1958, 8–9; Theodore L. Cannon, "Inside the New Zealand Temple," *Church News,* Apr. 19, 1958, 8–9; *Saints,* volume 3, chapter 39.

32. Wendell Mendenhall, "Story of New Zealand Temple," 1–7, in First Session, Apr. 20, 1958, New Zealand Temple Dedication Services, CHL; Newton, *Tiki and Temple*, 226, 232, 242–44, 249–50, 255–56; Cummings, *Mighty Missionary of the Pacific*, 30, 38–39, 57–68; see also Gordon T. Allred, "The Great Labor of Love," *Improvement Era*, Apr. 1958, 229, 269–71. **Topics: Building Program; Church Academies; New Zealand; Temple Building**
33. Muti, Book of Remembrance, [70], [84]; Woodworth, Oral History Interview, 64.
34. Gordon B. Hinckley, "Temple in the Pacific," *Improvement Era*, July 1958, 508–9; *Saints*, volume 3, chapter 14; McKay, Diary, May 16, 1957; June 18, 1957; Nov. 4, 7, and 15, 1957; Newton, *Tiki and Temple*, 257; "Dedicatory Prayer by Pres. McKay," *Church News*, May 10, 1958, 6. **Topics: David O. McKay; Temple Dedications and Dedicatory Prayers**
35. Hamilton New Zealand Temple, Temple Records for the Living, 1955–91, Apr. 23, 1958, microfilm 458,071, FSL; Muti, Book of Remembrance, [82]; Muti and Muti, *Man of Service*, 199. **Topic: Sealing**

Chapter 4: The Mission of the Church

1. McKay, Diary, Apr. 20–22 and Sept. 2, 1958; Reiser, Diary, Sept. 2, 1958; "President McKay Leaves S.L. for London Temple Dedication," *Deseret News*, Sept. 2, 1958, A1; McDougall, "Technocracy and Statecraft," 1010–40; Harvey, *Europe's Space Programme*, 23–25, 34–35, 61. **Topic: David O. McKay**
2. Doyle L. Green, "The Improvement Era Takes You to the London Temple Dedication," *Improvement Era*, Oct. 1958, 781, 783–84; *Saints*, volume 1, chapter 24; *Saints*, volume 3, chapter 39; Missionary Department, Missionary Registers, book C, 51; book E, 81. **Topic: England**
3. Rasmussen, *Mormonism and the Making of a British Zion*, 129–50; Cardon, "First World War and the Great Depression," 335–60; Cardon, "War and Recovery," 361–93; Moss, "Great Awakening," 394–406; Cuthbert, *Latter-day Saints in Great Britain*, 30–33; Doyle L. Green, "The Improvement Era Takes You to the London Temple Dedication," *Improvement Era*, Oct. 1958, 781. **Topic: Temple Building**
4. McKay, Diary, Sept. 4, 1958; Boyer, Oral History Interview, 37; Cowan, "Tale of Two Temples," 219–22; Doyle L. Green, "The Improvement Era Takes You to the London Temple Dedication," *Improvement Era*, Oct. 1958, 782, 784. Quotation edited for readability; "pray a new era" in original changed to "pray for a new era."
5. Jue, Mission Reminiscences, 3; Cameron, Mission Journal, Mar. 28, 1959; China Hong Kong Mission, Manuscript History and Historical Reports, Mar. 31, 1959, 5–6; Josephson, *History of the YWMIA*, 211–13, 293; Britsch, *From the East*, 245.
6. Jue, Mission Reminiscences, 3; Cameron, Mission Journal, Mar. 28, 1959; China Hong Kong Mission, Manuscript History and Historical Reports, Mar. 31, 1959, 5–6.
7. Jue, Mission Reminiscences, 3–4.
8. Spencer W. Kimball, Journal, Jan. 26, 1959; Spencer W. Kimball to Children and Grandchildren, Jan. 29, 1959, in Spencer W. Kimball, Journal, [Jan. 29, 1959].
9. Spencer W. Kimball to First Presidency and Quorum of the Twelve, May 6, 1959, in Spencer W. Kimball, Journal, 1959; Missionary Department, Full-Time Mission Monthly Progress Reports, Dec. 1958; McKay, Diary, Oct. 6, 1958. **Topic: Spencer W. Kimball**
10. Kimball and Kimball, *Spencer W. Kimball*, 236–37; Spencer W. Kimball, Journal, Sept. 13, 1946; May 1 and 10, 1947; Spencer W. Kimball to First Presidency and Quorum of the Twelve, May 6, 1959, in Spencer W. Kimball, Journal, 1959.
11. Spencer W. Kimball to First Presidency, Dec. 5, 1957, First Presidency, General Administration Files, 1923, 1932, 1937–67, CHL; Spencer W. Kimball, Journal, Feb. 8 and 12, 1958; Apr. 4, 1958; Spencer W. Kimball to Lorene Threepersons, Mar. 4,

1958, in Spencer W. Kimball, Journal, Feb. 25, 1958; Kimball and Kimball, *Spencer W. Kimball*, 301–12.

12. Bangerter, Diary, Jan. 26–28, 1959; Spencer W. Kimball, Journal, Jan. 26–27 and 31, 1959; "LDS Leader Sees Growth in South," *Stockton (CA) Record,* Feb. 7, 1959, in Argentina Buenos Aires North Mission, Manuscript History and Historical Reports, Feb. 7, 1959; *Saints,* volume 3, chapter 16; Plewe, *Mapping Mormonism,* 220, 222–23; *Deseret News 1997–1998 Church Almanac,* 372. **Topics: Costa Rica; El Salvador; Guatemala; Honduras; Panama; Paraguay; Peru; Uruguay**

13. Spencer W. Kimball, Journal, Feb. 4, 1959; Spencer W. Kimball to First Presidency and Quorum of the Twelve, May 6, 1959, in Spencer W. Kimball, Journal, 1959; Mark E. Petersen to First Presidency, [Jan. 1955], Missionary Department, Executive Secretary General Files, CHL; First Presidency to Lee Valentine, May 18, 1955, First Presidency, Mission Correspondence, 1950–59, CHL. **Topic: Chile**

14. Spencer W. Kimball, Journal, Feb. 19–Mar. 7 and Mar. 10, 1959; *Saints,* volume 3, chapter 18. **Topic: Priesthood and Temple Restriction**

15. Spencer W. Kimball to First Presidency and Quorum of the Twelve, May 6, 1959, in Spencer W. Kimball, Journal, 1959.

16. Spencer W. Kimball, Journal, Mar. 11 and 15, 1959; Nair Belmira da Rocha Camargo entry, Vila Mariana Branch, São Paulo District, Brazilian Mission, Record of Members, 1957, 330, in Brazil (Country), part 3, Record of Members Collection, CHL; Bangerter, Diary, Mar. 15, 1959; Rodriguez, *From Every Nation,* 138; "Elder Helio R. Camargo of the First Quorum of the Seventy," *Ensign,* May 1985, 93. **Topic: Healing**

17. Spencer W. Kimball, Journal, Feb. 8, 1959; Spencer W. Kimball to First Presidency and Quorum of the Twelve, May 6, 1959, in Spencer W. Kimball, Journal, 1959; Camargo, Reminiscences, 45; "Elder Helio R. Camargo of the First Quorum of the Seventy," *Ensign,* May 1985, 93; Hélio Camargo entry, Vila Mariana Branch, São Paulo District, Brazilian Mission, Record of Members, 1958, 336, in Brazil (Country), part 3, Record of Members Collection, CHL.

18. Spencer W. Kimball to First Presidency and Quorum of the Twelve, May 6, 1959, in Spencer W. Kimball, Journal, 1959; First Presidency to Mission Presidents, May 23, 1960, First Presidency, Circular Letters, CHL; Tobler, "Church in Europe," 39; Busche, "Church in Germany, Switzerland, and Austria," 49; Tullis, "Church Development Issues among Latin Americans," 97–98; Cowan, *Church in the Twentieth Century,* 263, 266. **Topic: Wards and Stakes**

19. Spencer W. Kimball to First Presidency and Quorum of the Twelve, May 6, 1959, in Spencer W. Kimball, Journal, 1959; McKay, Diary, May 18, 1958; "Ex-Salt Laker Heads New Auckland Stake," *Deseret News and Salt Lake Telegram,* May 19, 1958, A1; Newton, *Tiki and Temple,* 263–64; *Deseret News 1989–90 Church Almanac,* 210–21. **Topics: Growth of Missionary Work; New Zealand**

20. Crossley, Mission Journal, July 17, 1959; "Report of Elder Mark E. Petersen's Visit to the Southern Far East Mission," 1, Missionary Department, Executive Secretary General Files, CHL; "A Look at Taiwan," [8], China Hong Kong Mission Publications, CHL; "Four-Day Conference Conducted in Formosa," *Church News,* Dec. 27, 1958, 8.

21. China Hong Kong Mission, Manuscript History and Historical Reports, June 30, 1959, [17]; Heaton and Heaton, *Documentary History,* 107; "Report of Elder Mark E. Petersen's Visit to the Southern Far East Mission," 1, Missionary Department, Executive Secretary General Files, CHL; Jue, Reminiscence, 2. **Topic: Taiwan**

22. Lorine Jue to Scott Hales and Jed Woodworth, Email, Oct. 11, 2021, copy in editors' possession.

23. Heaton and Heaton, *Documentary History,* 408–9.

24. Lorine Jue to Scott Hales and Jed Woodworth, Email, Oct. 11, 2021, copy in editors' possession.

25. Asael Sorensen to First Presidency, Dec. 14, 1960; First Presidency to Asael Sorensen, Feb. 15, 1961, First Presidency, Mission Correspondence, 1946–69, CHL; Joseph Anderson to Richard Magleby, June 11, 1956, First Presidency, General

Correspondence Files, CHL; Peterson, "Historical Analysis of the Word of Wisdom," 98–103; Richard E. Ostler, "A Pharmacist Looks at the Word of Wisdom," *Millennial Star,* Oct. 1952, 224–25, 240; Richards, *Marvelous Work and a Wonder,* 310–13. **Topic: Word of Wisdom (D&C 89)**

26. Lorine Jue to Scott Hales and Jed Woodworth, Email, Oct. 11, 2021, copy in editors' possession, emphasis in original.
27. Lorine Jue to Scott Hales and Jed Woodworth, Email, Oct. 11, 2021, copy in editors' possession; Heaton and Heaton, *Documentary History,* 25, 54–55; Heaton, Personal History, volume 2, 70; Britsch, *From the East,* 242–43, 251; Heaton, Oral History Interview, Interview 3, 72; Chou and Chou, *Voice of the Saints in Taiwan,* 29.
28. Michael Walker, Journal, Apr. 4, 1957, in Hilton, "LDS Church in Taiwan," 58; Hilton, "LDS Church in Taiwan," 56, 66, 78.
29. "Taiwan Firsts," [20]; China Hong Kong Mission, Manuscript History and Historical Reports, Mar. 31, 1959, 8.
30. China Hong Kong Mission, Manuscript History and Historical Reports, Dec. 31, 1959, 5; Heaton and Heaton, *Documentary History,* 175, 497, 527; Hilton, "LDS Church in Taiwan," 77–78.
31. China Hong Kong Mission, Manuscript History and Historical Reports, Dec. 31, 1959, 5; Jue, Mission Reminiscences, 4–5; see also Daniel 2:31–45.
32. Williams and Williams, Oral History Interview, 1–2; Williams, Journal, [1]; Allen, LaMar Williams Interview Notes [July 6, 1988], [2]; Allen, "West Africa before the 1978 Priesthood Revelation," 213; Missionary Department, Full-Time Mission Monthly Progress Reports, Oct. 1959; see also Honesty John Ekong to [LaMar Williams], Oct. 12, 1959, LaMar S. Williams Papers, CHL. **Topic: Nigeria**
33. Williams and Williams, Oral History Interview, 2; LaMar Williams to Honesty John Ekong, Nov. 3, 1959, Missionary Department, Africa and India Correspondence, CHL; Honesty John Ekong to [LaMar Williams], Oct. 12, 1959, LaMar S. Williams Papers, CHL; see also LaMar Williams, Memorandum, May 3, 1961, LaMar S. Williams Papers, CHL.
34. Honesty John Ekong to LaMar Williams, Feb. 29, 1960; LaMar Williams to Honesty John Ekong, Mar. 18, 1960, LaMar S. Williams Papers, CHL; Allen, "West Africa before the 1978 Priesthood Revelation," 213; Allen, LaMar Williams Interview Notes [July 6, 1988], [2]–[3]; Williams and Williams, Oral History Interview, 2; McKay, Diary, June 22, 1961.
35. Honesty John Ekong to LaMar Williams, Feb. 5, 1960; Mar. 8, 1960; LaMar Williams to Honesty John Ekong, Mar. 18, 1960, LaMar S. Williams Papers, CHL; Honesty John Ekong with His Children, Photograph, International Mission Files, CHL.
36. Honesty John Ekong to LaMar Williams, Feb. 29, 1960; Mar. 8, 1960; Mar. 25, 1960, LaMar S. Williams Papers, CHL; Hurlbut, "LDS Church and the Problem of Race," 6.
37. LaMar Williams to Honesty John Ekong, Mar. 18, 1960, LaMar S. Williams Papers, CHL.

Chapter 5: No Power on Earth

1. *Saints,* volume 3, chapter 36; Albrecht, Nikol, and Nikol, "Book Burning," 164; ElRay Christiansen to First Presidency and Quorum of the Twelve Apostles, Jan. 14, 1959, Missionary Department, Executive Secretary General Files, CHL; Fetzer, Mission President Journal, Oct. 13, 1960; Germany Hamburg Mission, Manuscript History and Historical Reports, Oct. 13, 1960; European Mission, Historical Reports, Dec. 31, 1960, 341, 343.
2. Germany Hamburg Mission, Manuscript History and Historical Reports, Oct. 13, 1960, and Mar. 26, 1961; Albrecht, Nikol, and Nikol, "Book Burning," 164–69; Burtis Robbins and Edith Robbins, North German Mission Report, Feb. 23, 1960, 2, First Presidency, Mission Correspondence, 1964–2010, CHL; Kuehne, *Mormons as Citizens of a Communist State,* 84–86, 97–98; Dennis, *Rise and Fall of the German Democratic Republic,* 90. **Topics: Cold War; Germany**

3. Sheffer, *Burned Bridge*, 142–46; Germany Hamburg Mission, Manuscript History and Historical Reports, Dec. 31, 1958; see also Kuehne, *Henry Burkhardt*, 49.
4. Germany Hamburg Mission, Manuscript History and Historical Reports, Dec. 18, 1960; European Mission, Historical Reports, Dec. 31, 1960, 340–42, 344; Kuehne, *Mormons as Citizens of a Communist State*, 98; Burtis Robbins and Edith Robbins, North German Mission Report, Feb. 23, 1960, 1, 5–6, First Presidency, Mission Correspondence, 1964–2010, CHL.
5. Dennis, *Rise and Fall of the German Democratic Republic*, 88–89; European Mission, Historical Reports, Dec. 31, 1960, 343.
6. Kuehne, *Henry Burkhardt*, 36–37; European Mission, Historical Reports, Sept. 30 and Dec. 31, 1960, 247–49, 344; Alvin R. Dyer to First Presidency, May 23, 1960; Oct. 25, 1960; Dec. 21, 1960, First Presidency, Mission Correspondence, 1946–69, CHL.
7. Germany Hamburg Mission, Manuscript History and Historical Reports, Apr. 2, 1961.
8. Dunbabin, *Cold War*, 19–21, 149–54, 264–66.
9. McKay, *Statements on Communism and the Constitution*, 1–30; David O. McKay, in *One Hundred Eighteenth Annual Conference*, 70; Henry A. Smith, "Pres. McKay Hits Atheism Rise in World," *Deseret News*, Mar. 17, 1952, A1; "Church President Dedicates New Chapel in Detroit Stake," *Church News*, May 2, 1959, 5; David O. McKay, in *One Hundred Twentieth Annual Conference*, 175; McKay, Diary, Nov. 12, 1957, and May 13, 1959; *Saints*, volume 3, chapters 33 and 35.
10. McKay, Diary, Apr. 7, 1960, and Jan. 5, 1961; Patterson, *Grand Expectations*, 311–15; Eichengreen, *European Economy*, 3–47.
11. McKay, Diary, Jan. 5, 1961; "Change Comes to Zion's Empire," *Business Week*, Nov. 23, 1957, 108–10, 112, 114, 116; Leonard J. Arrington, "Economic History of the Church," and Richard C. Edgley and Wilford G. Edling, "Finances of the Church," in Ludlow, *Encyclopedia of Mormonism*, 2:435–41, 507–9. **Topic: Church Finances**
12. David O. McKay to Stephen L Richards, Jan. 30, 1954; David O. McKay, Address, Uruguayan Mission, Montevideo, Uruguay, Jan. 30, 1954, volume 138, David O. McKay Scrapbooks, CHL. **Topic: Building Program; David O. McKay**
13. Hubbard, *When the Saints Came Marching In*, 3, 28–32, 35, 58–65; Jackson, *Places of Worship*, 237, 266, 270–73; Relief Society Annual Report, 1961, Denton Ward, Relief Society Minutes and Records, CHL; McKay, Diary, Feb. 24, 1961.
14. McKay, Diary, Mar. 18, 1960; June 28, 1960; Aug. 17, 1960; Jan. 18 and 23, 1961; "Skyscraper Included in Program," *Deseret News and Salt Lake Telegram*, Oct. 7, 1960, A1, A10; Henry A. Smith, "Pres. McKay Tells of Decision to Build New Oakland Temple," *Church News*, Jan. 28, 1961, 3.
15. McKay, Diary, Jan. 5, 1961; David O. McKay, in *One Hundred Twenty-Ninth Annual Conference*, 122.
16. "Missionary Activity Boosts Baptisms to New High in 1960," *Church News*, Dec. 31, 1960, 10; McKay, Diary, Mar. 1 and 29, 1960; Sept. 8, 1960; Rasmussen, *Mormonism and the Making of a British Zion*, 150–52; Romney, Journal, Jan. 12, 19, and 21, 1960; Cuthbert, *Latter-day Saints in Great Britain*, 51–52, 197; Harold B. Lee, "A Stake Is Born," *Millennial Star*, May 1960, 188–94. **Topics: Church Growth; England**
17. Henry A. Smith, "Pres. McKay Dedicates Hyde Park Chapel at London Session," *Church News*, Mar. 4, 1961, 3, 15; "Text of the Dedicatory Prayer," *Millennial Star*, Apr. 1961, 180–83; David O. McKay, Address, North British Mission, Mar. 1, 1961, 1, Percy K. Fetzer Papers, CHL.
18. LaMar Williams, Memorandum, May 3, 1961, LaMar S. Williams Papers, CHL.
19. Fisher, Report, Sept. 16, 1960, 2, 5–7, 12; McKay, Diary, June 30–July 1, 1961; Acts 10–11; 15:7–9; Arrington, *Adventures of a Church Historian*, 180; see also Hunter, Journal, Mar. 1, 1962. **Topic: Priesthood and Temple Restriction**
20. McKay, Diary, July 1, 1961; Hunter, Journal, July 1, 1961; Allen, LaMar Williams Interview Notes [July 6, 1988], [3].
21. Dunning, Oral History Interview, 10, 12; Dunning, "My Life and Legacy," 1–4.

22. British Mission, Manuscript History, part 1, Dec. 31, 1960, 6; part 2, June 30, 1961, 3; North British Mission, Manuscript History, Sept. 30, 1961, [1]; Dunning and Dunning, Email Interview [Sept. 12, 2021]; Franklin D. Richards, in *One Hundred Thirty-First Annual Conference,* 83–87; "Mission Meet Focuses on Referral Plan," *Deseret News and Salt Lake Telegram,* June 27, 1961, A1.
23. Dunning, "My Life and Legacy," 2–3; Dunning, Email Interview [Sept. 23, 2021]; Dunning, Email Interview [July 21, 2021]; Transcript of Record of Members, 1961, Beverley Branch, Hull District, North British Mission, 49, in England (Country), part 50, Record of Members Collection, CHL. **Topic: Sacrament Meetings**
24. Dunning, "My Life and Legacy," 2; Dunning, Email Interview [Sept. 23, 2021]; Dunning and Dunning, Email Interview [Sept. 12, 2021]; Dunning, Oral History Interview, 2; Hawkins, Oral History Interview, [00:01:05]–[00:03:02]; Fletcher, Oral History Interview, 2–4.
25. Spencer W. Kimball, Journal, Feb. 17, 1963; Troy Thornton and Rosaland Thornton to Joseph Bentley, Feb. 10, 1961, Missionary Department, Executive Secretary General Files, CHL; Rasmussen, *Mormonism and the Making of a British Zion,* 150–52; Cuthbert, *Latter-day Saints in Great Britain,* 52–53; Embry and Brambaugh, "Sports and Recreation in Missionary Work," 53–84.
26. Mark E. Petersen to First Presidency, Apr. 5, 1963, First Presidency, Mission Correspondence, 1946–69, CHL; Dunning, Oral History Interview, 2; Dunning, "My Life and Legacy," 1–2; Rasmussen, *Mormonism and the Making of a British Zion,* 151; Embry and Brambaugh, "Sports and Recreation in Missionary Work," 82–83; Cuthbert, *Latter-day Saints in Great Britain,* 52–53; Transcript of Record of Members, 1961, Beverley Branch, Hull District, North British Mission, 50–52, in England (Country), part 50, Record of Members Collection, CHL.
27. Dunning, Oral History Interview, 10–11; Dunning, "My Life and Legacy," 3–4. **Topic: Fasting**
28. Large, *Berlin,* 446–52; Taylor, *Berlin Wall,* 161–62, 177–78; Hilton, *The Wall,* 52–53, 83–85; Fetzer, Mission President Journal, Aug. 13–14, 1961; Christensen, Mission Journal, Aug. 13, 1961. **Topic: Cold War**
29. Fetzer, Mission President Journal, Aug. 14, 1961; Kuehne, *Henry Burkhardt,* 48.
30. European Mission, Historical Reports, Sept. 30, 1961, 580; Kuehne, *Henry Burkhardt,* 48; Kuehne, *Mormons as Citizens of a Communist State,* 98–100; Germany Hamburg Mission, Manuscript History and Historical Reports, Apr. 25, 1961; Scharffs, *Mormonism in Germany,* 196–201.
31. Hilton, *The Wall,* 132–35; Fetzer, Mission President Journal, Aug. 27, 1961.
32. Fetzer, Mission President Journal, Aug. 27, 1961; Oct. 8 and 19, 1961; Nov. 19, 1961; Owens, "Future Prophets, the Berlin Wall and Missionaries," 5–6; Albrecht, Nikol, and Nikol, "Book Burning," 169–71; Kuehne, *Mormons as Citizens of a Communist State,* 98.
33. North German Mission, Auxiliary Training Minutes, Dec. 9, 1961; Kuehne, *Henry Burkhardt,* 50.
34. Lee, Diary, Sept. 16, 1961; McKay, Diary, Sept. 15, 1961.
35. Curriculum Department, Priesthood Correlation Executive Committee Minutes, June 21, 1962, 47; Bowman, "Progressive Roots of Mormon Correlation," 15–34; Goodman, "Correlation," 319–38.
36. Goodman, "Correlation," 324–25, 329–30; First Presidency to General Priesthood Committee, Mar. 24, 1960, Curriculum Department, Priesthood Correlation Executive Committee Minutes, CHL; *Deseret News 1989–90 Church Almanac,* 205; Romney, "History of the Correlation of L.D.S. Church Auxiliaries," [F1]–[F2]; Curriculum Department, Priesthood Correlation Executive Committee Minutes, May 23, 1962, 35; see also Harold B. Lee, in *One Hundred Thirty-First Semi-annual Conference,* 79. **Topic: Correlation**
37. Lee, Diary, Jan. 20, 1955; Feb. 14, 1957; circa May 18–19, 1960; Romney, Journal, Apr. 20, 1960; May 11 and 24, 1960; June 28, 1960; Oct. 17 and 20, 1960; Jan. 24, 1961; Mar. 15, 1961; Aug. 22, 1961; Priesthood Committee, Minutes, Apr. 20, 1960, 697;

681

Harold B. Lee, in *One Hundred Thirty-First Semi-annual Conference,* 79; Harold B. Lee, in *One Hundred Nineteenth Annual Conference,* 47; Lee, *Ye Are the Light of the World,* 109. **Topic: Harold B. Lee**

38. Council Minutes, Sept. 7, 1961, First Presidency, General Administration Files, 1923, 1932, 1937–67, CHL; Harold B. Lee, in *One Hundred Thirty-First Semi-annual Conference,* 77–82; Romney, Journal, Sept. 5, 7, and 14, 1961; Lee, Diary, circa Sept. 6–7, 1961 [Sept. 5, 1961].
39. Williams, Journal, Oct. 16, 1961, [11]; McKay, Diary, Oct. 13, 1961; Williams and Williams, Oral History Interview, 5–6, 10, 18.
40. Williams, Journal, Oct. [20] and 31, 1961, [13], [28]; Williams and Williams, Oral History Interview, 6.
41. Williams and Williams, Oral History Interview, 6–10; Williams, Journal, Oct. 22, 1961, [22]–[23]; Jones, Diary, Oct. 18 and 20–22, 1961; LaMar Williams, "Report to the First Presidency regarding Missionary Work in Nigeria," 1, First Presidency, Mission Correspondence, 1946–69, CHL; see also Allen, "West Africa before the 1978 Priesthood Revelation," 219–23.
42. Williams and Williams, Oral History Interview, 9; Allen, "West Africa before the 1978 Priesthood Revelation," 223; Jones, Diary, Oct. 22, 1961.
43. Williams, Journal, Oct. 31, 1961, [28]; Williams and Williams, Oral History Interview, 13.
44. LaMar Williams, "Report to the First Presidency regarding Missionary Work in Nigeria," 1–2; First Presidency, Minutes, Dec. 18, 1961; LaMar Williams to David O. McKay, Nov. 14, 1961, First Presidency, Mission Correspondence, 1946–69, CHL; Williams, Journal, Oct. 29, 1961, [26]. Quotation edited for readability; original source has "(and I can't tell them because they know I was sent here)" after "They do not realize."

Chapter 6: Blessings Everywhere

1. Funk, Oral History Interview, 126–27, 129; Peterson and Gaunt, *Keepers of the Flame,* 106–9; *Saints,* volume 3, chapter 4; "General Boards Guide Mutual Aides through Days of Play, Study, Work," *Church News,* June 23, 1962, 3–4.
2. Funk, Oral History Interview, 126–27; "Outlines Assist Parents to Teach Gospel," *Church News,* Jan. 13, 1962, 14.
3. Funk, Oral History Interview, 126–27; Spencer W. Kimball, in *One Hundred Thirty-First Semi-annual Conference,* 33; Mintz and Kellogg, *Domestic Revolutions,* 179, 194–205; Holt, *Cold War Kids,* chapter 3; Patterson, *Grand Expectations,* 369–71; Relief Society, General Board Minutes, volume 34, Feb. 21, 1962, 39–40.
4. Funk, Oral History Interview, 127; Funk, "Ruth, Come Walk with Me," 119–20; "General Boards Guide Mutual Aides through Days of Play, Study, Work," *Church News,* June 23, 1962, 3. **Topics: Church Growth; Correlation; Harold B. Lee**
5. Curriculum Department, Priesthood Correlation Executive Committee Minutes, June 12, 1962, 40; Funk, "Ruth, Come Walk with Me," 119–20; "Pres. Monson Reports Canada Mission Labors," *Church News,* Feb. 3, 1962, 6. **Topic: Thomas S. Monson**
6. Curriculum Department, Priesthood Correlation Executive Committee Minutes, Nov. 1, 1962, 58; Funk, "Ruth, Come Walk with Me," 120–21; Pulsipher, *Ruth Hardy Funk,* 113–15; Norman R. Bowen, "Announcement Made of First Application of Church Correlation Program," *Church News,* Dec. 29, 1962, 14.
7. Poll, *Working the Divine Miracle,* chapters 9 and 10; Anderson, *Prophets I Have Known,* 146–53; McKay, Diary, May 19, 1959; June 12, 14, and 18, 1959; June 21–22, 1961; Oct. 6 and 12, 1961; Romney, Journal, Oct. 27, 1960; Nov. 3, 1960; Dec. 7, 1960; Brown, *Abundant Life,* 131–32. **Topic: First Presidency**
8. McKay, Diary, June 12 and 26, 1959; Poll, *Working the Divine Miracle,* 199–205; Anderson, *Prophets I Have Known,* 147–48; First Presidency, Minutes, Sept. 18, 1962,

First Presidency, General Administration Files, 1923, 1932, 1937–67, CHL; Mullin, *Short World History of Christianity,* 275, 280, 290. **Topic: Growth of Missionary Work**

9. Henry D. Moyle, Address, Berlin Mission Missionary Conference, Oct. 18, 1961, 185–87, Henry D. Moyle Papers, CHL; First Presidency to Mission Presidents, Nov. 30, 1962, David O. McKay Papers, CHL; Henry D. Moyle, Address, Mission Presidents' Seminar, June 26, 1961, 7–8, Missionary Department, Seminar for Mission Leaders, CHL; Tanner, Journal, July 17, 1961; June 6, 1962; July 17, 1962.
10. Poll, *Working the Divine Miracle,* 211; Quorum of the Twelve Apostles, Missionary Committee Minutes, Nov. 20, 1962; Henry D. Moyle, Address, French East Mission Supervising Elders' Conference, Feb. 12, 1963, 131, Henry D. Moyle Papers, CHL; Marion D. Hanks to First Presidency, Apr. 17, 1962; First Presidency to Marion D. Hanks, May 11, 1962; Mark E. Petersen to First Presidency, Feb. 8, 1961, First Presidency, Mission Correspondence, 1964–2010, CHL.
11. Quorum of the Twelve Apostles, Missionary Committee Minutes, Nov. 20, 1962; First Presidency to Mission Presidents, Nov. 30, 1962, David O. McKay Papers, CHL; Henry D. Moyle, "Jurisdictions and Procedures for Missions," Mar. 18, 1961, 13–14, 16, Henry D. Moyle Papers, CHL; Tanner, Journal, Feb. 2 and June 6, 1962; British Mission, Manuscript History and Historical Reports, July 11, 1962.
12. Council Minutes, Aug. 30, 1962, First Presidency, General Administration Files, 1923, 1932, 1937–67, CHL; Romney, Journal, Aug. 30, 1962, and Feb. 1, 1963; First Presidency, Minutes, Sept. 18, 1962, First Presidency, General Administration Files, 1923, 1932, 1937–67, CHL; Anderson, *Prophets I Have Known,* 148–49; Henry D. Moyle, Address, New England Mission Missionary Conference, May 21, 1962, Henry D. Moyle Papers, CHL; Poll, *Working the Divine Miracle,* 85, 183–84.
13. First Presidency, Minutes, Sept. 18, 1962, First Presidency, General Administration Files, 1923, 1932, 1937–67, CHL; see also Tanner, Journal, July 28, 1962; "Church Officials Visit 21 Missions in Europe," *Church News,* Aug. 11, 1962, 3; and McKay, Diary, Aug. 9, 1962.
14. First Presidency, Minutes, Sept. 18, 1962, First Presidency, General Administration Files, 1923, 1932, 1937–67, CHL; Quorum of the Twelve Apostles, Missionary Committee Minutes, Oct. 4, 1960, and Jan. 7, 1964; Spencer W. Kimball, Journal, Nov. 21, 1963; see also, for example, Spencer W. Kimball to First Presidency, May 29, 1964; and J. Vernon Sharp and Fawn Hansen Sharp, Andes Mission Report, Oct. 30, 1963, First Presidency, Mission Correspondence, 1964–2010, CHL. **Topics: First Presidency; Quorum of the Twelve**
15. First Presidency, Minutes, Sept. 18, 1962, First Presidency, General Administration Files, 1923, 1932, 1937–67, CHL; "Spirit of Conversion Places 75,500 on Mission Records," *Church News,* Dec. 30, 1961, 4.
16. "Church to Open Missionary Work in Nigeria," *Deseret News and Salt Lake Telegram,* Jan. 11, 1963, B1; "Elder Tanner Arrives Home after Two-Year Assignment in Europe," *Church News,* Jan. 12, 1963, 3; Tanner, Journal, Dec. 24 and 28–30, 1962; Jan. 2, 1963; McKay, Diary, Jan. 10, 1963; see also "Envoys to Go to Nigeria LDS Mission," *Salt Lake Tribune,* Jan. 12, 1963, B9.
17. First Presidency, Minutes, Oct. 11, 1962; Missionary Setting Apart Blessing for LaMar Williams, Nov. 21, 1962, First Presidency, Mission Correspondence, 1964–2010, CHL; David O. McKay to N. Eldon Tanner, Sept. 4, 1962, David O. McKay Papers, CHL; McKay, Diary, Jan. 10, 1963; LaMar Williams, Memorandum, Jan. 16, 1963, David O. McKay Papers, CHL; "Five Missionaries Sent to Nigeria," *Church News,* Jan. 19, 1963, 7. **Topic: Nigeria**
18. McKay, Diary, Jan. 10, 1963; Charles Agu to LaMar Williams, Feb. 14, 1963; Feb. 18, 1963, Missionary Department, Africa and India Correspondence, CHL; Williams, Journal, Oct. 23 and 28–31, 1961; Nov. 1–2, 5, and 12, 1961, [24]–[26], [29]–[30], [32]; Charles Agu and LaMar Williams to David O. McKay, Nov. 3, 1961, LaMar S. Williams Papers, CHL; LaMar Williams to Charles Agu, Dec. 20, 1961; June 5, 1962; Dec. 17,

1962, Missionary Department, Africa and India Correspondence, CHL. **Topic: Priesthood and Temple Restriction**
19. See, for example, LaMar Williams to Charles Agu, Jan. 17, 1963; Mar. 12, 1963, Missionary Department, Africa and India Correspondence, CHL.
20. Charles Agu to LaMar Williams, Mar. 16, 1963, Missionary Department, Africa and India Correspondence, CHL; "Evil Saints," and Ambrose Chukwu, "They're Importing Ungodliness," *Nigerian Outlook* (Enugu), Mar. 5, 1963, 3, in Williams, Journal, Mar. 5, 1963, [55]–[63]; "Race and the Priesthood," Gospel Topics Essays, ChurchofJesusChrist.org/study/manual/gospel-topics-essays.
21. Allen, "West Africa before the 1978 Priesthood Revelation," 210–11; Charles Agu to LaMar Williams, Mar. 16, 1963; Apr. 30, 1963, Missionary Department, Africa and India Correspondence, CHL; see also LaMar Williams to Charles Agu, Apr. 17, 1963, Missionary Department, Africa and India Correspondence, CHL; and Stevenson, "Latter-day Saint Experience in West Africa," 591.
22. LaMar Williams to Charles Agu, May 28, 1963, Missionary Department, Africa and India Correspondence, CHL.
23. Charles Agu to LaMar Williams, June 8, 1963, Missionary Department, Africa and India Correspondence, CHL; Charles Agu and Dick Obot, "What You Ought to Know about The Church of Jesus Christ of Latter-day Saints," *Nigerian Outlook* (Enugu), June 26, 1963, 5, in Williams, Journal, [79].
24. Charles Agu to LaMar Williams, June 8, 1963, Missionary Department, Africa and India Correspondence, CHL; see also Charles Agu to LaMar Williams, July 11, 1963, Missionary Department, Africa and India Correspondence, CHL.
25. Rochon, Interview, 1–2, 12–13, 47–49; Colonia Suiza Branch, Minutes, Nov. 18, 1962, and Feb. 24, 1963, 231, 247; Delia Rochon to James Perry, Email, Dec. 2, 2021, Delia Rochon Interviews, CHL; Solari, Oral History Interview, [3]; Rochon, *Come and See,* 1–2, 12.
26. Rochon, Interview, 12–13, 47–49; Delia Rochon, Tithing Slip, Apr. 14, 1963, Delia Rochon Interviews, CHL. Quotation edited for accuracy; original source, later corrected by the interviewee, has "three dollars." **Topic: Tithing**
27. Rochon, *Come and See,* 8–9; Rochon, Interview, 21–22; Colonia Suiza Branch, Minutes, Apr. 28, 1963, 256; A. Theodore Tuttle to First Presidency, Mar. 27, 1962, First Presidency, Mission Correspondence, 1964–2010, CHL; Grover, *Land of Promise and Prophecy,* 162–66. **Topics: Church Callings; Uruguay**
28. Rochon, *Come and See,* 8–9; Rochon, Interview, 2, 6, 16–18, 21–22; Delia Rochon to James Perry, Email, Jan. 4, 2022, Delia Rochon Interviews, CHL.
29. Colonia Suiza Branch, Minutes, Apr. 28, 1963, 256; Rochon, Interview, 21–22; Rochon, *Come and See,* 9–11. **Topic: Primary**
30. Dunning, "My Life and Legacy," 4–6, 13; Dunning and Dunning, "Conversion Story at Beverley," [2], [3]; Dunning and Dunning, Email Interview [Sept. 12, 2021]; Beverley Branch, Manuscript History and Historical Reports, Mar. 3, 1963; Suzette Dunning and Geoff Dunning to James Perry, Email, Mar. 17, 2022, Suzette Towse Dunning and Geoffrey Dunning Papers, CHL.
31. McKay, Diary, July 6, 1960; "Labor-Missionary Program Adopted for European Chapels," *Church News,* July 9, 1960, 7–8; European Mission, Historical Report, Dec. 31, 1960, 312–17; "237 Attend British Labor Mission Conference," *Church News,* Mar. 10, 1962, 14; "The Building Programme," *Millennial Star,* July 1960, 283; Wendell Mendenhall, "Buildings for Britain," *Millennial Star,* July 1960, 284–92; Fletcher, Oral History Interview, 8.
32. Dunning and Dunning, "Conversion Story at Beverley," [3], [6]–[9]; Dunning and Dunning, Email Interview [Sept. 12, 2021]. **Topic: Building Program**
33. Dunning, "My Life and Legacy," 6–8; N. Eldon Tanner, "Elder Tanner Notes Progress in West European Mission Area," *Church News,* Dec. 29, 1962, 7; Quorum of the Twelve Apostles, Missionary Committee Minutes, Feb. 6, 1962; Boyd K. Packer to Donald Fry, July 26, 1962, Missionary Department, Executive Secretary General Files, CHL; Perry, Brown, and Blease, "If the Walls Had Ears," 125, 136, 139, 183.

34. McKay, Diary, Aug. 25, 1963; Mahoney, "Merthyr Tydfil Chapel." **Topic: Wales**
35. McKay, Diary, Aug. 25, 1963; George L. Scott, "Merthyr Tydfil: New Church Era in Wales," *Church News*, Sept. 7, 1963, [6]–[7]; Dunning, Oral History Interview, 5–6; Dunning, "My Life and Legacy," 8–9; Dunning, Email Interview [July 21, 2021].
36. Dunning, Oral History Interview, 5–6; Dunning, "My Life and Legacy," 16.
37. Suzette Towse to Geoffrey Dunning, Apr. 1, 1964, in Dunning, "My Life and Legacy," 17; Dunning, "My Life and Legacy," 16–17; Suzette Towse to Geoffrey Dunning, Mar. 30, 1964, in Dunning, Excerpts from Letters and Journals, [6]. Quotation edited for readability; original source has "I feel so unsure about things and feel so mixed up and worried."
38. Council Minutes, Feb. 7, 1963, First Presidency, General Administration Files, 1923, 1932, 1937–67, CHL; Romney, Journal, Feb. 7, 1963; Hunter, Journal, Feb. 7, 1963; Harold B. Lee, in *One Hundred Thirty-Third Annual Conference*, 88; Lee, Diary, Aug. 30, 1962, and circa Feb. 7–9, 1963.
39. Council Minutes, Feb. 7, 1963, First Presidency, General Administration Files, 1923, 1932, 1937–67, CHL; Harold B. Lee, in *One Hundred Thirty-Third Annual Conference*, 82, 85–86; "Chairmen Announced for Four Priesthood-Centered Committees," *Church News*, Apr. 13, 1963, 9.
40. Lee, Diary, Feb. 2 and 22, 1963; Apr. 2–4 and 11, 1963; Tanner, Journal, Apr. 1–8, 1963; Romney, Journal, Feb. 1 and Apr. 2, 1963; Hugh B. Brown, in *One Hundred Thirty-Seventh Semi-annual Conference*, 113–14; McKay, Diary, Apr. 3, 1963.
41. Poll, *Working the Divine Miracle*, 183–84, 213–14; Lee, Diary, June 12, 1959; Henry D. Moyle, Funeral Remarks for Fern Tanner Lee, Sept. 26, 1962, 438–41, Henry D. Moyle Papers, CHL.
42. Goates, *Harold B. Lee*, 358; Lee, Diary, Jan. 11 and June 16, 1963; Romney, Journal, June 16–17, 1963; McKay, Diary, June 17, 1963. Quotations edited for readability; original source has "I asked if he would like to be a witness" and "they two would be witnesses."
43. "He Invests Mormons' Money," *Fortune*, Dec. 1957, 65; Poll, *Working the Divine Miracle*, chapter 12.
44. Lee, Diary, Sept. 6–19, 1963; Harold B. Lee, Funeral Remarks for Henry D. Moyle, Sept. 21, 1963, 5, First Presidency, General Administration Files, 1923, 1932, 1937–67, CHL.

CHAPTER 7: CHILDREN OF THE SAME GOD

1. "Negroes May Picket Mormon Conference," *Newport (RI) Daily News*, Oct. 4, 1963, 4; "Negro Threat to Picket Mormon Session in Utah," *Kansas City (MO) Times*, Oct. 5, 1963, 19; "Mormon Temple May Be Picketed in NAACP Move," *Arizona Daily Star* (Tucson), Oct. 5, 1963, B1.
2. "Extremism Is Never the Answer," *Deseret News*, Apr. 3, 1956, A22; McKay, Diary, Apr. 2, 1956.
3. McMurrin, "Note on the 1963 Civil Rights Statement," 60; Fritz, Oral History Interview [1984], 26–30; "NAACP Calls S.L. Protest over Rights," *Salt Lake Tribune*, Oct. 5, 1963, 32; "Negro Group Lauds LDS Rights View," *Salt Lake Tribune*, Oct. 7, 1963, 6; Mason, "Prohibition of Interracial Marriage in Utah," 129–30; Harris and Harris, "Last State to Honor MLK," 6.
4. McMurrin, "Note on the 1963 Civil Rights Statement," 60; Meier and Rudwick, *CORE*, 239, 250; Reed, *Chicago NAACP*, 198–99; Honey, *To the Promised Land*, 75–80; Jackson, *From Civil Rights to Human Rights*, 155–56, 166–69, 171–84; Branch, *Parting the Waters*, 846–50, 872–87; Arsenault, *Freedom Riders*, 8–10. **Topic: Civil Rights Movement**

5. See, for example, Hugh B. Brown to Kelorah Franklin, Sept. 1, 1961; Hugh B. Brown to William Wangeman, Nov. 6, 1961; Hugh B. Brown to Deana Astle, Nov. 26, 1963, David O. McKay Papers, CHL.
6. Mueller, "Pageantry of Protest," 133; Tanner, Journal, Oct. 3, 1963; McKay, Diary, Oct. 4, 1963; Holbrook, Oral History Interview, 7; McMurrin, "Note on the 1963 Civil Rights Statement," 61. **Topic: Political Neutrality**
7. McMurrin and Newell, *Matters of Conscience*, 201; "NAACP Calls S.L. Protest over Rights," *Salt Lake Tribune*, Oct. 5, 1963, 32; Fritz, Oral History Interview [1984], 28–29.
8. Holbrook, Oral History Interview, 7.
9. Hugh B. Brown, in *One Hundred Thirty-Third Semi-annual Conference*, 91.
10. "Give Full Civil Equality to All, LDS Counselor Brown Asks," *Salt Lake Tribune*, Oct. 7, 1963, 1; "Negro Group Lauds LDS Rights View," *Salt Lake Tribune*, Oct. 7, 1963, 6; "Mormon Church Calls for Full Civil Equality for All," *Herald Bulletin* (Burley, ID), Oct. 7, 1963, 1; "Digest of the News," *Arizona Republic* (Phoenix), Oct. 7, 1963, 1; "Mormon Leader Appeals for Civil Equality for All," *Fort Myers (FL) News-Press*, Oct. 7, 1963, 1.
11. Camargo, Oral History Interview, 19, 20, 22; Hélio Camargo entry, Vila Mariana Branch, São Paulo District, Brazilian Mission, Transcript of Record of Members, 1959, 316, in Brazil (Country), part 3, Record of Members Collection, CHL; William Bangerter to First Presidency, Apr. 18, 1960, First Presidency, Mission Correspondence, 1946–69, CHL; A. Theodore Tuttle to First Presidency, Sept. 2, 1963, First Presidency, Mission Correspondence, 1964–2010, CHL; Reid, *Brazil*, 91–92.
12. A. Theodore Tuttle to First Presidency, Sept. 2, 1963, First Presidency, Mission Correspondence, 1964–2010, CHL; Missionary Department, Full-Time Mission Monthly Progress Reports, Dec. 1958; Jan. 1959; Jan. 1963; "Elder Romney Creates New Mexico City Stake," *Church News*, Dec. 9, 1961, 3. **Topics: Church Growth; Wards and Stakes; Bolivia; Peru**
13. Missionary Department, Full-Time Mission Monthly Progress Reports, Jan. 1963; "Brief Report to the First Presidency on the Brazilian Mission from President and Sister Wayne M. Beck," Aug. 9, 1966, [6], First Presidency, Mission Correspondence, 1964–2010, CHL; Bangerter, Oral History Interview, 86–88, 103–4; Bangerter, Reminiscence, 12.
14. Rodriguez, *From Every Nation*, 135–37; Bangerter, Oral History Interview, 87–88; Bangerter, Diary, Oct. 28–29, 1959; Nov. 8, 1959; Feb. 22, 1961. Quotation edited for readability; original source has "I asked him why and what he'd like to do."
15. Bangerter, Oral History Interview, 87–88; Bangerter, Diary, Feb. 22, 1961. Quotation edited for readability; two instances of "was" in original changed to "is," "were" changed to "are," "had" changed to "has," and "them" changed to "you."
16. Brazil São Paulo North Mission, Manuscript History, Aug. 4, 1963. **Topic: Church Callings**
17. Bangerter, Diary, Mar. 1 and 27, 1962; May 6, 1962; Sept. 14, 1962; Nov. 1, 1962; Brazil São Paulo North Mission, Manuscript History, June 20 and July 28, 1963; Camargo, Oral History Interview, 20, 22; Wayne Beck and Evelyn Beck, Oral History Interview, 76–78, 88–89; Spät, Oral History Interview, 9; "Programa Dinamismo," 2.
18. Brazilian Mission, *Congresso da Associação da Primária* [1962], [11]–[13], [16], [20], [32]; *Guide for Primary Stake Boards*, 55.
19. Brazilian Mission, *Congresso da Associação da Primária* [1963], 27.
20. Bangerter, Oral History Interview, 74.
21. "Sava-Nickel Acquires S.L. Market," *Salt Lake Tribune*, Jan. 24, 1964, D4; Macey, Biographical Sketch, [31]–[33], [35]–[36], [38], [40]; "Macey Takes Over Grocery Store," *Deseret News and Salt Lake Telegram*, Mar. 23, 1964, B9.
22. Macey, Biographical Sketch, [32]–[36]. Quotation edited for readability; original source has "they were not about to close."
23. Macey, Biographical Sketch, [38]; Smith, Journal, June 17 and Aug. 19, 1963; Joseph Fielding Smith, in *One Hundred Thirty-Third Annual Conference*, 21.

24. Joseph Fielding Smith to First Presidency, June 12, 1939, First Presidency, Miscellaneous Correspondence, CHL; "Return to Religion Held Big Need," *Deseret News*, Apr. 5, 1943, 6; Miller, *Peculiar Life of Sundays*, 168–70, 263–65; Harline, *Sunday*, 215–99, 351–67; Mrs. Richard Harston to Heber J. Grant, May 22, 1934; Heber J. Grant to Mrs. [Richard] Harston, May 26, 1934, First Presidency, Miscellaneous Correspondence, CHL.
25. Joseph Fielding Smith, in *Eighty-Seventh Semi-annual Conference*, 70; Joseph Fielding Smith, in *One-Hundred and First Semi-annual Conference*, 25–26; Joseph Fielding Smith, "A Warning Cry for Repentance," *Deseret News*, May 4, 1935, Church section, 6, 8; Woodger, "Restoration of the Perpetual Covenant to Hallow the Sabbath Day," 289–310; Thomsen, "History of the Sabbath in Mormonism," 102–5; Merrill and Cannon, "Legal and Cultural War over Utah's Sunday Closing Laws," 167–76. **Topic: Joseph Fielding Smith**
26. Joseph Fielding Smith, in *One Hundred Twenty-Seventh Annual Conference*, 62; "The Sabbath," *Church News*, July 11, 1959, 3.
27. Macey, Biographical Sketch, [35]–[37]; "Sava-Nickel Acquires S.L. Market," *Salt Lake Tribune*, Jan. 24, 1964, D4; "Macey Takes Over Grocery Store," *Deseret News and Salt Lake Telegram*, Mar. 23, 1964, B9; "Grand Opening," *Deseret News and Salt Lake Telegram*, May 14, 1964, E5.
28. Macey, Biographical Sketch, [38]–[39]; "Grand Opening," *Deseret News and Salt Lake Telegram*, May 14, 1964, E5; Smith, Journal, July 17, 1964.
29. Derr, Cannon, and Beecher, *Women of Covenant*, 304, 324; Belle S. Spafford, "Report and Official Instructions," *Relief Society Magazine*, Nov. 1964, 816, 820–22; Belle S. Spafford, "Report and Official Instructions," *Relief Society Magazine*, Nov. 1963, 821–22. The *Relief Society Bulletin* was first published in 1914. Its name was changed to the *Relief Society Magazine* in January 1915. **Topics: Belle S. Spafford; Relief Society**
30. Belle S. Spafford, "Report and Official Instructions," *Relief Society Magazine*, Nov. 1963, 818, 822.
31. Relief Society, General Board Minutes, volume 34, Sept. 19, 1962, 145; Oct. 17, 1962, 156; Jan. 9 and 23, 1963, 244, 254; Mar. 27, 1963, 286; May 29, 1963, 345, 351; Oct. 30, 1963, 402–3; Nov. 6, 1963, 405–6.
32. Relief Society, General Board Minutes, volume 34, Jan. 31, 1962, 23–24; Mar. 6, 1963, 275, 277; May 15, 1963, 334; volume 35, May 20 and 27, 1964, 89–90, 100; Belle S. Spafford, "Talk Given by Sister Belle S. Spafford," Apr. 25, 1964, Relief Society, Belle S. Spafford Files, CHL. **Topics: Australia; New Zealand; Samoa**
33. Relief Society, General Board Minutes, volume 34, Oct. 23, 1963, 392, 396; volume 35, Jan. 2, 1964, 7; Jan. 22, 1964, 24; Mar. 11, 1964, 52; Relief Society General Board, "The Awakening," 1964, Relief Society, Belle S. Spafford Files, CHL. **Topic: Globalization**
34. Saettler, *History of Instructional Technology*, 178–87; Whitaker, *Pioneering with Film*, 3–4, 90; *"The Awakening": A Sound-Filmstrip Presentation of the General Board of Relief Society*, Filmstrip Script, CHL.
35. "'Mary Smith' Story . . . Told World Wide," *Church News*, Aug. 15, 1964, [8]–[9].
36. Relief Society, General Board Minutes, volume 35, Feb. 19 and Mar. 11, 1964, 44, 52.
37. Relief Society, General Board Minutes, volume 34, Sept. 19, 1962, 144–47; J. Reuben Clark to Belle S. Spafford, Sept. 14, 1961, First Presidency, General Administration Files, 1923, 1932, 1937–67, CHL. **Topic: Correlation**
38. "Visitors Welcomed to Mormon Pavilion at N. Y. Fair," *Church News*, Apr. 25, 1964, 3; Kogan, "Mormon Pavilion," 37–38; McKay, Diary, Mar. 21, 1963; Whitaker, *Looking Back*, 61–62; Whitaker, *Pioneering with Film*, 57–62. **Topic: Columbian Exposition of 1893**
39. "Mormon Mothers Chorus to Sing at Fair," *Church News*, Feb. 29, 1964, 3; Gay Pauley, "Utah's Singing Mothers Perform at N.Y. Fair," *Los Angeles Times*, July 12, 1964, E12; Belle S. Spafford and Counselors to First Presidency, June 29, 1964, First Presidency, General Administration Files, 1921–72, CHL; see also Derr, Cannon, and Beecher, *Women of Covenant*, 273–74, 338–40.

40. Argentina Buenos Aires North Mission, Manuscript History and Historical Reports, Feb. 23, 1964; "Construction Program," 6; Strong, Autobiography Excerpt, 35. **Topics: Argentina; Building Program**
41. [Maria Oliva] to Omar Esper, Email, July 15, 2021, Maria Oliva Family Papers, CHL; Lewis, *Argentina*, 101; Jack E. Jarrard, "She Remembers Well the Day the Elders Called," *Church News*, Oct. 5, 1968, 11; Giuseppa Oliva, María Oliva, and Rosa Oliva entries, Baptisms and Confirmations, 1957, Quilmes Branch, Argentine Mission, 66–67; Rosa Oliva entry, Marriages, 1958, Quilmes Branch, Argentine Mission, 72; María Oliva entry, Marriages, 1960, Córdoba Branch, Argentine Mission, 148, in Argentina (Country), part 4, Record of Members Collection, CHL; Strong, Autobiography Excerpt, 35.
42. John Bausman, "World of '64: Foreign Correspondents Survey Trouble Spots around Globe," *Gazette* (Montreal), Jan. 25, 1964, 13; Edward C. Burks, "Argentina Faces Growing Deficits," *New York Times*, Jan. 17, 1964, 70; Lewis, *Argentina*, 132–33; "Argentine Costs Up," *Miami Herald*, Mar. 19, 1965, Palm Beach edition, A2; Strong, Autobiography Excerpt, 36; [Maria Oliva] to Omar Esper, Email, July 15, 2021, Maria Oliva Family Papers, CHL.
43. *Saints*, volume 3, chapter 16; Missionary Department, Full-Time Mission Monthly Progress Reports, Nov. 1963 and Jan. 1964; "Argentine Mission Is Now Self-Supporting," *Church News*, Nov. 9, 1963, 6; Toronto, Dursteler, and Homer, *Mormons in the Piazza*, 259–77; Jack E. Jarrard, "She Remembers Well the Day the Elders Called," *Church News*, Oct. 5, 1968, 11; Strong, Autobiography Excerpt, 35.
44. Strong, Autobiography Excerpt, 35–36; Jack E. Jarrard, "She Remembers Well the Day the Elders Called," *Church News*, Oct. 5, 1968, 11. Quotations edited for readability; original sources have "that was the place I belonged," "what she should do about the Church," and "I promised her that the Church would grow in her own city and she would not have to worry about it."
45. Gray, Oral History Interview, 21–23.
46. Gray, Oral History Interview, 5, 15–19, 21, 23.
47. Gray, Oral History Interview, 1, 4, 15–16, 18, 24–25; Darius Gray to Jed Woodworth, Email, Jan. 3, 2023, copy in editors' possession.
48. Gray, Oral History Interview, 8–10, 25–26, 55–56. **Topic: Priesthood and Temple Restriction**
49. Gray, Oral History Interview, 26–27, 198–99; Darius Gray entry, Baptisms and Confirmations, Colorado Springs Second Ward, Pikes Peak Stake, 388, in Colorado Springs 2nd Ward, Record of Members Collection, CHL.

Chapter 8: A Matter of Saving Souls

1. Rochon, *Come and See*, 9–11; Rochon, Interview, 6–8, 21; *Primarias de las misiones: Manual de lecciones. Para los grupos menores, niños de 4, 5 y 6 años de edad*, translated by Eduardo Balderas ([Salt Lake City]: La Iglesia de Jesucristo de los Santos de los Últimos Días, [1962]); Solari, Oral History Interview, [3]–[4].
2. Rochon, Interview, 32–34; Rochon, *Come and See*, 13–15; Primary Children's Hospital, Circular, Primary Association, Primary Children's Hospital Files, CHL; LaVern Parmley, Address, Primary Conference, Apr. 7, 1966, Primary Association, General Board Minutes, CHL.
3. Rochon, *Come and See*, 14–15; Rochon, Interview, 32–35; Mark 12:41–44. **Topic: Primary**
4. Dunning, Email Interview [July 21, 2021]; Dunning, "My Life and Legacy," 6, 16, 23; Dunning, Oral History Interview, 7, 19–20; "News Notes at Home and Abroad," *Church News*, Mar. 28, 1964, 2; John Butcher, "A Closing Thought," *Millennial Star*, Oct. 1964, [365]; *Construction Era*, July 1970, 10; Dunning and Dunning, "Conversion Story at Beverley," [6], [13]. **Topic: Building Program**

5. Dunning, "My Life and Legacy," 18, 22; Dunning, Email Interview [July 21, 2021]; Dunning, Oral History Interview, 6–7; Suzette Dunning and Geoff Dunning to James Perry, Email, Mar. 16, 2022, Suzette Towse Dunning and Geoffrey Dunning Papers, CHL.
6. Dunning, Oral History Interview, 7; Beverley Branch, Manuscript History and Historical Reports, Mar. 1965; Dunning, Email Interview [Sept. 23, 2021]; Dunning, "My Life and Legacy," 23.
7. Marion D. Hanks to First Presidency, Dec. 31, 1962; Alva D. Greene, "Report on the North British Mission," June 10, 1964; A. Ray Curtis and Elaine Curtis, Report, Feb. 23, 1965, First Presidency, Mission Correspondence, 1964–2010, CHL; Hanks, Recollections, 149, 154; First Presidency to Stake and Mission Presidents, Feb. 19, 1964, First Presidency, Circular Letters, CHL; McKay, Diary, July 25, 1963, and Dec. 15, 1965.
8. Dunning, "My Life and Legacy," 23–24.
9. Adult Correlation Committee, Minutes, Apr. 23, 1965; Curriculum Department, Priesthood Correlation Executive Committee Minutes, Mar. 11, 1965, 277; Monson, Journal, Mar. 25, 1965; Henry A. Smith, "Thomas S. Monson Chosen New Apostle," *Deseret News and Salt Lake Telegram,* Oct. 4, 1963, A1.
10. Curriculum Department, Priesthood Correlation Executive Committee Minutes, Mar. 11, 1965, 277–79; Ludlow, "Church History Events Concerned with Correlation Development," [2]–[3].
11. Hartley, "LDS Aaronic Priesthood Offices," 85–86, 90–91, 97, 115–17, 128; *Home Teaching,* A1–A11.
12. Smith, Lund, and Penrose, *To the Presidents of Stakes, Bishops and Parents in Zion,* [2]–[3]; Harold B. Lee, in *One Hundred Thirty-Fourth Semi-annual Conference,* 83–85; Curriculum Department, Priesthood Correlation Executive Committee Minutes, Jan. 9, 1964, 152; Feb. 13, 1964, 161; Apr. 9, 1964, 170–72; May 6, 1964, 178–79; June 3 and 11, 1964, 191, 199; Sept. 10, 1964, 216; Oct. 8, 1964, 225–26; Nov. 4, 1964, 230–31; *Family Home Evening Manual,* iii–xiv; "Home Teachers Distribute Family Manuals," *Church News,* Dec. 19, 1964, 4. **Topic: Family Home Evening**
13. Curriculum Department, Priesthood Correlation Executive Committee Minutes, Feb. 13, 1964, and Mar. 11, 1965, 156–57, 278–79; Blumell, "Priesthood Correlation," 23–24. **Topics: Correlation; Thomas S. Monson**
14. Adult Correlation Committee, Minutes, Apr. 23, 1965; 3 Nephi 11:28. Quotation edited for readability; "would" in original changed to "will."
15. Adult Correlation Committee, Minutes, Apr. 23, 1965; Adult Correlation Committee, "Review of Present and Proposed Programs for the Adults of the Church," 19–20.
16. Adult Correlation Committee, Minutes, June 9, 23, and 30, 1965; Aug. 4, 1965; Smith, Oral History Interview, 113–15, 148–49; Curriculum Department, Priesthood Correlation Executive Committee Minutes, Nov. 10, 1966, 134.
17. Allen, "West Africa before the 1978 Priesthood Revelation," 236; Williams, Journal, Jan. 20, 1964; Feb. 4 and 11–14, 1964, [92]–[95]; McKay, Diary, Jan. 11, 1963.
18. Williams, Journal, Feb. 14, 1964; Jan. 20, 1965; Feb. 19, 1965; Mar. 7, 1965, [95], [119]–[20]; Allen, "West Africa before the 1978 Priesthood Revelation," 233–35; Brigham Young University, Board of Trustees Executive Committee Minutes, Mar. 25, 1965; John Chase to LaMar Williams, June 15, 1965, Missionary Department, Africa and India Correspondence, CHL.
19. Allen, "West Africa before the 1978 Priesthood Revelation," 234; Certificate of Incorporation, Lagos, Nigeria, Sept. 29, 1964, copy, Edwin Q. Cannon Papers, CHL; Dick Obot and others to LaMar Williams, Oct. 29, 1964, Missionary Department, Africa and India Correspondence, CHL; Williams, Journal, Jan. 20 and Oct. 18, 1965, [119], [153]; McKay, Diary, Aug. 25 and Oct. 14, 1965; see also Palmer, *Mormons in West Africa,* 8. **Topic: Nigeria**
20. Williams, Journal, Oct. 20, 22–24, and 30–31, 1965; Nov. 4 and 6, 1965, [153]–[55]; "Report on Nigeria," in McKay, Diary, Nov. 10, 1965; First Presidency to LaMar

Williams, Telegram, Nov. 4, 1965, First Presidency, Mission Correspondence, 1964–2010, CHL.
21. Toronto, Dursteler, and Homer, *Mormons in the Piazza,* 1–44, 132–77; Simoncini, Interview, [3]. **Topic: Italy**
22. Simoncini, Interview, [3]; Abner, Italian Mission Reminiscences, 30–31; Simoncini, "La storia dei primi pionieri del ramo di Palermo," [1]; Arthur Strong to Giuseppa Oliva, Sept. 16, 1965, copy in editors' possession; "Italian Zone," [1]; Mabey, "Amazing Swiss Mission," [1].
23. Toronto, Dursteler, and Homer, *Mormons in the Piazza,* 232–40, 277; Ezra Taft Benson to First Presidency, Dec. 7, 1964; First Presidency to Ezra Taft Benson, Dec. 17, 1964, First Presidency, Mission Correspondence, 1964–2010, CHL; Quorum of the Twelve Apostles, Missionary Executive Committee Minutes, Jan. 14, 1965; "Missionary Work Resumed in Italy after Lapse of Century," *Church News,* Mar. 20, 1965, 12; Ezra Taft Benson to First Presidency, Oct. 11, 1965, First Presidency, Mission Correspondence, 1964–2010, CHL.
24. Arthur Strong to Giuseppa Oliva, Dec. 17, 1965, copy in editors' possession; Mabey, Journal, Nov. 22, 1965; Mabey, "Sicilian Baptism," [1]; Giurintano, Interview, [2].
25. Vincenzo di Francesca, "Burn the Book," *Improvement Era,* May 1968, 4–7; Vincenzo di Francesca to Franklin Harris, May 8, 1930; Vincenzo di Francesca to Heber J. Grant, June 26, 1930; Heber J. Grant to Vincenzo di Francesca, Apr. 29, 1931, First Presidency, Miscellaneous Correspondence, CHL; Toronto, Dursteler, and Homer, *Mormons in the Piazza,* 226–29; see also "Berne: Work in Italy Progressing," *Church News,* Feb. 19, 1966, 4.
26. Mabey, Journal, Nov. 22–23, 1965; Mabey, "Sicilian Baptism," [1]–[2]; Strong, Autobiography Excerpt, 35; [Maria Oliva] to Omar Esper, Email, July 15, 2021, Maria Oliva Family Papers, CHL; "Berne: Work in Italy Progressing," *Church News,* Feb. 19, 1966, 4.

Chapter 9: This Marvelous Day

1. Camargo, Oral History Interview, 26; Camargo, Reminiscences, 51–52.
2. Camargo, Oral History Interview, 26; Camargo, Reminiscences, 52; Grover, "Mormonism in Brazil," 299–300; Missionary Department, Full-Time Mission Monthly Progress Reports, May 1957 and Oct. 1965; First Presidency and Presiding Bishopric, Minutes, Sept. 5, 1964, and Jan. 29, 1965, First Presidency, General Administration Files, 1921–72, CHL; "Fyans to Head Translation Unit," *Church News,* May 1, 1965, 13. **Topics: Mexico; Brazil**
3. Camargo, Reminiscences, 52; Camargo, Oral History Interview, 26; Wayne Beck and Evelyn Beck, Oral History Interview, 80–81. Quotations edited for readability; "he" in English translation of original changed to "I," "wanted" changed to "want," two instances of "me" changed to "you," and "would be" changed to "is."
4. Camargo, Reminiscences, 53; Spencer W. Kimball, Journal, May 1, 1966; "Reunião da presidencia com as juntas das organizações auxiliares da missão brasileira," Dec. 16, 1965, Brazil São Paulo North Mission, Manuscript History, CHL; Grover, "Mormonism in Brazil," 186–87; "New Brazilian Post," *Church News,* Dec. 4, 1965, 10.
5. "Reunião da presidencia com as juntas das organizações auxiliares da missão brasileira," Dec. 16, 1965, Brazil São Paulo North Mission, Manuscript History, CHL; Camargo, Reminiscences, 57; "Elder Helio R. Camargo of the First Quorum of the Seventy," *Ensign,* May 1985, 93; Helio da Rocha Cam[a]rgo and Nair Belmira de Gouvea Camargo, Sealing Record, Nov. 24, 1965, Temple Records for the Living, 1955–91, microfilm 470,944, FSL; Spencer W. Kimball, Journal, Nov. 24, 1965. **Topics: Patriarchal Blessings; Sealing**
6. Camargo, Oral History Interview, 27.

7. "Conferencia do distrito de Tietê," Jan. 30, 1966, Brazil São Paulo North Mission, Manuscript History, CHL.
8. Williams and Williams, Oral History Interview, 20; Williams, Journal, Nov. 6–7, 1965, [155]; McKay, Diary, Nov. 10, 1965.
9. Williams, Journal, Nov. 7, 1965, [155]; Williams and Williams, Oral History Interview, 20; McKay, Diary, Nov. 10, 1965; Allen, LaMar Williams Interview Notes [July 11, 1988], [2].
10. Williams and Williams, Oral History Interview, 20; Tanner, Journal, Nov. 8, 1965; McKay, Diary, Oct. 18, 21, and 28, 1965; Nov. 4 and 10, 1965; Henry A. Smith, "Pres. McKay Appoints Two More Counselors: Church Growth Is Cited," *Deseret News*, Oct. 29, 1965, A1, A3; Saunders, "1968 and Apartheid," 133–35.
11. McKay, Diary, Nov. 10, 1965; Allen, LaMar Williams Interview Notes [July 11, 1988], [2]; Williams and Williams, Oral History Interview, 20; 2 Nephi 26:33.
12. Falola and Heaton, *History of Nigeria*, 172–73; Gould, *Struggle for Modern Nigeria*, 26–32; "Military Chief Rules Nigeria Government," *Deseret News*, Jan. 17, 1966, A4; Williams and Williams, Oral History Interview, 20–21; see also Allen, "West Africa before the 1978 Priesthood Revelation," 236–37.
13. LaMar Williams to Charles Agu, Feb. 18, 1966, Missionary Department, Africa and India Correspondence, CHL.
14. Delia Rochon to James Perry, Email, Jan. 18, 2022, Delia Rochon Interviews, CHL; Rochon, Interview, 3–6, 18–19, 22–24, 28–29, 54–55, 57; Colonia Suiza Branch, Minutes, Dec. 11, 1966, 37–38.
15. Rochon, Interview, 8–9, 30, 42–44. **Topics: Young Men Organizations; Young Women Organizations**
16. Rochon, Interview, 4–5, 53–55, 57. Quotation edited for readability; "the family" in original changed to "her family."
17. Paul and others, *Paths to Victory*, 266; "Reds of Every Shade Moving In on Uruguay," *Daily News* (New York City), Oct. 4, 1964, home edition, 121; McDonald, "Struggle for Normalcy in Uruguay," 72; George Natanson, "Chaos Reigns in Latin Nations," *Boston Globe*, Aug. 15, 1965, 51.
18. Rochon, *Come and See*, 19–21; Rochon, Interview, 9–10, 62, 64–65, 67–68; Theodore Tuttle to First Presidency, June 22, 1965, First Presidency, Mission Correspondence, 1964–2010, CHL; Joseph Smith—History 1:25.
19. Brazil São Paulo North Mission, Manuscript History, Feb. 17, 1966; Wayne Beck to A. Theodore Tuttle, Feb. 11, 1966, A. Theodore Tuttle Files, CHL; Proposal to Joseph Fielding Smith and Council of the Twelve, Mar. 23, 1966, First Presidency, Mission Correspondence, 1964–2010, CHL; Wayne Beck and Evelyn Beck, Oral History Interview, 93–95; "1st Latin Stake in Church," *Deseret News*, May 3, 1966, B1.
20. Proposal to Joseph Fielding Smith and Council of the Twelve, Mar. 23, 1966, First Presidency, Mission Correspondence, 1964–2010, CHL.
21. Spencer W. Kimball, Journal, Mar. 17 and 24, 1966; "Foreign Stakes: Shall We Organize Stakes Other Than in America?," in Spencer W. Kimball, Journal, Mar. 20, 1966; First Presidency to Spencer W. Kimball, May 18, 1965, First Presidency, General Administration Files, 1921–72, CHL; Spencer W. Kimball to First Presidency, June 9, 1966, First Presidency, Mission Correspondence, 1964–2010, CHL; Cowan, *Church in the Twentieth Century*, 263, 266. **Topics: Globalization; Quorum of the Twelve**
22. First Presidency to Wayne Beck, Apr. 1, 1966, First Presidency, Mission Correspondence, 1964–2010, CHL; Spencer W. Kimball, Journal, Mar. 24, 1966. Quotation edited for readability; "We are" added.
23. Rendell Mabey to Giuseppa Oliva, Feb. 25, 1966, copy in editors' possession; Salvatore Ferrante entry, Baptisms and Confirmations, 1966, Palermo Branch, Palermo District, Italian Mission, 31, in Italy (Country), part 2, Record of Members Collection, CHL; Giurintano, Interview, [2]; Simoncini, "La storia dei primi pionieri del ramo di Palermo," [1].
24. Mabey, Journal, May 10, 1966; "Day I'll Never Forget," [1]–[2]; Salvatore Ferrante entry, Baptisms and Confirmations, 1966, Palermo Branch, Palermo District, Italian Mission,

31, in Italy (Country), part 2, Record of Members Collection, CHL. Quotation edited for readability; "that being that I can watch" in original changed to "that I can watch."
25. Mabey, Journal, May 10, 1966; "Day I'll Never Forget," [2]; Toronto, Dursteler, and Homer, *Mormons in the Piazza,* 275–76.
26. Toronto, Dursteler, and Homer, *Mormons in the Piazza,* 276; Rendell Mabey to Giuseppa Oliva, June 16, 1966, Giuseppa Oliva Papers, CHL; Abner, Italian Mission Reminiscences, 26–28.
27. Camargo, Reminiscences, 63.
28. Camargo, Oral History Interview, 14, 27; Camargo, Reminiscences, 63; de Queiroz, Oral History Interview [2011], 6.
29. "Reunião da presidencia da missão com presidentes dos distritos e membros do sacerdócio da missão distritos," Jan. 30, 1966, Brazil São Paulo North Mission, Manuscript History, CHL; Brazil São Paulo North Mission, Manuscript History, Apr. 16, 1966; *Liahona* (São Paulo, Brazil), Apr. 1966, 3; May 1966, 3.
30. Spencer W. Kimball, Journal, Apr. 25–May 2, 1966; Brazil São Paulo North Mission, Manuscript History, Apr. 26–30, 1966.
31. Spencer W. Kimball, Journal, May 1, 1966; Brazil São Paulo North Mission, Manuscript History, Apr. 26 and 28, 1966.
32. Spencer W. Kimball, Journal, May 1, 1966; Camargo and others, Oral History Interview, 13–14.
33. *Saints,* volume 3, chapter 16; "São Paulo: A primeira estaca da América do Sul," *Liahona* (São Paulo, Brazil), June 1966, 10; Sharp, Autobiography, 48.
34. Evelyn Beck, Letter, May 6, 1966, copy in editors' possession; "São Paulo: A primeira estaca da América do Sul," *Liahona* (São Paulo, Brazil), June 1966, 11; Spencer W. Kimball, Journal, May 1, 1966; Camargo, Oral History Interview, 23. **Topic: Wards and Stakes**
35. "São Paulo: A primeira estaca da América do Sul," *Liahona* (São Paulo, Brazil), June 1966, 11; Spencer W. Kimball, Journal, May 1, 1966; Camargo, Reminiscences, 64. **Topic: Bishop**
36. Camargo, Oral History Interview, 23–24.
37. "Reunião do sacerdócio da missão brasileira," Apr. 30, 1966, Brazil São Paulo North Mission, Manuscript History, CHL.
38. Spencer W. Kimball, Journal, May 1, 1966.
39. Camargo, Reminiscences, 64. **Topic: Brazil**

Chapter 10: Time Is Crucial

1. Jay M. Todd, "Egyptian Papyri Rediscovered," *Improvement Era,* Jan. 1968, 13–14; Fragment of Book of Breathing for Horos–A, between 238 and circa 153 BC, in *JSP,* R4:8–9; Nibley, *Message of the Joseph Smith Papyri,* 183–84; Muhlestein, "Papyri and Presumptions," 40, 44–45.
2. McKay, Diary, Nov. 27, 1967; "Arabic Documents to U," *Deseret News,* Dec. 15, 1966, C1; "U. Professor to Speak on Mideast," *Salt Lake Tribune,* Oct. 4, 1959, A17; Jay M. Todd, "Egyptian Papyri Rediscovered," *Improvement Era,* Jan. 1968, 13–14; "A Facsimile from the Book of Abraham, No. 2."
3. Jay M. Todd, "Egyptian Papyri Rediscovered," *Improvement Era,* Jan. 1968, 12–14, 16; Lewis Bidamon, Emma Smith Bidamon, and Joseph Smith III to Abel Combs, Certificate of Sale, May 26, 1856, CHL.
4. *Saints,* volume 1, chapter 20; "Book of Abraham and Related Manuscripts," in *JSP,* R4:xix–xx, xxiii–xxix; Peterson, *Story of the Book of Abraham,* 203–16, 242–47; Gee, "Stranger in a Strange Land," 501–3. **Topic: Book of Abraham Translation**
5. Jay M. Todd, "Egyptian Papyri Rediscovered," *Improvement Era,* Jan. 1968, 14.

6. Isabel Santana entry, Births and Blessings, 1958, Obregon Branch, Northern Mexican Mission, 158–59, in Mexico (Country), part 6, Record of Members Collection, CHL; Isabel Santana, Oral History Interview [Jan. 5, 2022], 1–2, 22–23; Santana and Machuca, Oral History Interview, 32–33; Morgan, "Benemérito de las Américas," 108, 110.
7. *Saints*, volume 2, chapter 31; *Saints*, volume 3, chapter 31; *Deseret News 1991–1992 Church Almanac*, 178, 190; Morgan, "Century of LDS Church Schools in Mexico," 364; Missionary Department, Full-Time Mission Monthly Progress Reports, Jan. 1966; Daniel Taylor to Ernest L. Wilkinson, Sept. 26, 1962, Church Educational System, Harvey L. Taylor Administrative Files, CHL; Morgan, "Benemérito de las Américas," 94, 96–97.
8. Romney, Journal, Nov. 19, 1957; Feb. 6, 1958; Apr. 5, 1958; Nov. 5, 1959; Dec. 9, 1959; Bentley, *Life and Family of Joseph T. Bentley*, 98–99; Daniel Taylor to Ernest L. Wilkinson, Sept. 26, 1962; Harvey Taylor to M. James Penton, Sept. 7, 1966, Church Educational System, Harvey L. Taylor Administrative Files, CHL; Taylor, *Story of L.D.S. Church Schools*, 1:34–45, 62–71; 2:6–11; Griffiths, "Globalization of Latter-day Saint Education," 82, 97–125. **Topics: Church Academies; American Samoa; Chile; Fiji; Mexico; New Zealand; Samoa; Tonga**
9. Joseph Bentley, "El Arbolillo (The Little Tree)," in Joseph Bentley to N. Eldon Tanner, Apr. 29, 1968, Church Educational System, Harvey L. Taylor Administrative Files, CHL; Morgan, "Benemérito de las Américas," 99–104; Taylor, *Story of L.D.S. Church Schools*, 2:6–15, 18–19, 21, 24; Santana and Machuca, Oral History Interview, 34–35.
10. Santana and Machuca, Oral History Interview, 2–3, 10; Isabel Santana, Oral History Interview [Jan. 5, 2022], 16; Isabel Santana, Oral History Interview [Feb. 2, 2022], 16; Taylor, *Story of L.D.S. Church Schools*, 2:4, 5, 20; Harvey Taylor to Marion D. Hanks, Apr. 19, 1966, Church Educational System, Harvey L. Taylor Administrative Files, CHL; Morgan, "Impact of Centro Escolar Benemérito," 156.
11. Santana and Machuca, Oral History Interview, 32; Isabel Santana, Oral History Interview [Feb. 2, 2022], 1; Wagner and Wagner, *Historia*, 39; Church Board of Education, Executive Committee Minutes, Aug. 26, 1965; Romney, Journal, Oct. 26, 1966.
12. Isabel Santana, Oral History Interview [Feb. 2, 2022], 1–4; Santana and Machuca, Oral History Interview, 32–34; Isabel Santana, Oral History Interview [Jan. 5, 2022], 1–2, 23; Wagner and Wagner, *Historia*, 39.
13. Isabel Santana, Oral History Interview [Feb. 2, 2022], 2, 10; Santana and Machuca, Oral History Interview, 2–4; Isabel Santana, Oral History Interview [Apr. 19, 2022], 25.
14. McKay, Diary, May 24, 1960; Mar. 28, 1964; Aug. 19, 1965; Aug. 22, 1966; Nov. 7, 1966; Jan. 1, 1967; Henry D. Taylor, in *One Hundred Thirty-Sixth Annual Conference*, 83; Garrow, *Protest at Selma*, 161–66; Patterson, *Grand Expectations*, 580–81, 598, 620–21.
15. Powaski, *Cold War*, 135–60; Hartlyn and Valenzuela, "Democracy in Latin America since 1930," 139–43; Falola and Heaton, *History of Nigeria*, 158–75.
16. McKay, Diary, Jan. 1, 1967; Patterson, *Grand Expectations*, 512–17, 594–99; Boot, *Invisible Armies*, chapter 52.
17. Gordon B. Hinckley, "Asian Diary," *Instructor*, Sept. 1967, 346–47; Marion D. Hanks to First Presidency, Jan. 18, 1967, First Presidency, Mission Correspondence, 1964–2010, CHL; "1967 Membership Population Report," 2; McKay, Diary, Jan. 20, 1966; Apr. 15, 1966; Sept. 15; Nov. 17, 1966.
18. Gordon B. Hinckley, "Asian Diary," *Instructor*, Sept. 1967, 346–47; Marion D. Hanks to First Presidency, Jan. 18, 1967, First Presidency, Mission Correspondence, 1964–2010, CHL; Allen Rozsa, Memorandum, Oct. 31, 1966, Gordon B. Hinckley Files, circa 1935–70, CHL; Hinckley, Journal, Oct. 30, 1966; Palmer, *Church Encounters Asia*, 143.
19. McKay, Diary, Jan. 1, 1967; Steininger, *Germany and the Middle East*, 108–19; Gould, *Struggle for Modern Nigeria*, 8–9, 63, 211; Patterson, *Grand Expectations*, 448–49, 579–81, 588–89, 598–600, 620–30; Lytle, *America's Uncivil Wars*, chapter 8.
20. David O. McKay, in *One Hundred Thirty-Seventh Annual Conference*, 5–7; Lytle, *America's Uncivil Wars*, chapters 8 and 9; "Early Registrations Show Banner Year for Seminaries," *Church News*, Sept. 7, 1957, 12; *For the Strength of Youth*, 3–16; see also Patterson, *Grand Expectations*, 669–72.

21. David O. McKay, Hugh B. Brown, in *One Hundred Thirty-Seventh Semi-annual Conference,* 4–5, 94, 149.
22. Hugh B. Brown, Harold B. Lee, in *One Hundred Thirty-Seventh Semi-annual Conference,* 25–26, 98–108; Henry A. Smith, "Top Church News of '67," *Church News,* Dec. 30, 1967, 5; Correlation Executive Committee, "Church Curriculum Programs: Time Changes," *Instructor,* Sept. 1967, 361. **Topic: Church Growth**
23. David O. McKay, Harold B. Lee, in *One Hundred Thirty-Seventh Semi-annual Conference,* 5–10, 98–108.
24. "LDS Teacher Helps Korean Orphans," *Church News,* Feb. 6, 1971, 7; Hwang, "Hwang Keun Ok," 293; Shirleen Meek Saunders, "Whang Keun-Ok: Caring for Korea's Children," *Ensign,* Oct. 1993, 46; Roby, Oral History Interview, 1, 4–5; Bronson, Oral History Interview, 2. Sources variously spell her name "Hwang" and "Whang."
25. "1967 Membership Population Report," 2; Palmer, *Church Encounters Asia,* 94–98, 108; "Korean Student at U. of U. Called to Far East Mission," *Church News,* Nov. 17, 1956, 10; Joseph Lundstrom, "President McKay Given New Korean Translation," *Church News,* Aug. 31, 1968, 3. **Topics: Servicemember Branches; South Korea**
26. Hwang, "Hwang Keun Ok," 293; Bronson, Oral History Interview, 2, 91; Shirleen Meek Saunders, "Whang Keun-Ok: Caring for Korea's Children," *Ensign,* Oct. 1993, 46–47; "LDS Teacher Helps Korean Orphans," *Church News,* Feb. 6, 1971, 7.
27. Bronson, Oral History Interview, 2–4, 27–28; Roby, Oral History Interview, 1; Shirleen Meek Saunders, "Whang Keun-Ok: Caring for Korea's Children," *Ensign,* Oct. 1993, 46.
28. Roby, Oral History Interview, 1; Shirleen Meek Saunders, "Whang Keun-Ok: Caring for Korea's Children," *Ensign,* Oct. 1993, 46–47; Hwang, "Hwang Keun Ok," 293; Bronson, Oral History Interview, 2–3, 27–28; "Shoes Big, Heart Bigger," *Church News,* May 25, 1968, 10.
29. Bronson, Oral History Interview, 2–3; Sarah Jane Weaver, "Orphanage Founder's Life Spent Serving," *Church News,* Aug. 19, 2000, 4, 7; Shirleen Meek Saunders, "Whang Keun-Ok: Caring for Korea's Children," *Ensign,* Oct. 1993, 46; Hwang, "Hwang Keun Ok," 291–92; Roby, Oral History Interview, 1–3.
30. Bronson, Oral History Interview, 9–10, 13, 28–31, 74, 81–82; Roby, Oral History Interview, 1, 4, 9; "Shoes Big, Heart Bigger," *Church News,* May 25, 1968, 10.
31. Bronson, Oral History Interview, 15–16, 52, 74–75; Roby, Oral History Interview, 1–4.
32. Richard Bushman to Truman Madsen, Memorandum, Oct. 17, 1967, Truman G. Madsen Correspondence, CHL; Walters, "New Light on Mormon Origins," 59–61; Godfrey, "Kenneth W. Godfrey," 254; Harper, *First Vision,* 211–14.
33. Harper, *First Vision,* 204–6, 214–15; "First Vision Accounts," Gospel Topics Essays, ChurchofJesusChrist.org/study/manual/gospel-topics-essays; Allen, "Significance of Joseph Smith's 'First Vision,'" 29–46. **Topic: Joseph Smith's First Vision Accounts**
34. Harper, *First Vision,* 214–16; Walters, "New Light on Mormon Origins," 60–73.
35. Harper, *First Vision,* 219; Bushman, "First Vision Story Revived," 82–83; Truman Madsen to First Presidency, Apr. 17, 1968, First Presidency, General Administration Files, 1921–72, CHL.
36. Harper, *First Vision,* 219–20; Allen and Arrington, "Mormon Origins in New York," 241–42.
37. [Truman Madsen] to Harold Snow, Nov. 9, 1967; Truman Madsen to "Dear Brethren," Jan. 18, 1968, Truman G. Madsen Correspondence, CHL; Allen and Arrington, "Mormon Origins in New York," 241–42; Truman Madsen to First Presidency, Apr. 17, 1968, First Presidency, General Administration Files, 1921–72, CHL; Pykles, *Excavating Nauvoo,* 18–19, 53–128.
38. Jay M. Todd, "Egyptian Papyri Rediscovered," *Improvement Era,* Jan. 1968, 13–14; Tanner, Journal, Nov. 26–27 and Dec. 5, 1967; "Mormons Get 'Lost' Egyptian Papyrus Texts," *Los Angeles Times,* Nov. 28, 1967, section 1, 4; "Old Papyri Find Linked to Mormons," *Sun* (Baltimore), Nov. 8, 1967, A3; George W. Cornell, "Missing Documents Found," *Austin (TX) Statesman,* Nov. 30, 1967, A5; "LDS Orders Papyri to Y. for Study," *Salt Lake Tribune,* Nov. 29, 1967, B2.

39. Nibley, *Lehi in the Desert and the World of the Jaredites*, 20–95; Nibley, *Approach to the Book of Mormon*, 164–89, 256–69; Nibley, *Since Cumorah*, 251–58, 297–327.
40. Truman Madsen to First Presidency, Apr. 17, 1968, First Presidency, General Administration Files, 1921–72, CHL.
41. First Presidency to Truman Madsen, May 8, 1968, First Presidency, General Administration Files, 1921–72, CHL; Spencer W. Kimball, Journal, Dec. 14, 1961; Lee, Diary, Dec. 7, 1961, and Dec. 17, 1963; Tanner, Journal, July 17, 1964, and Dec. 2, 1965; Quinn, *Mormon Hierarchy*, 120–23; Durham, *N. Eldon Tanner*, 208–9. **Topic: Church Finances**
42. Truman Madsen to Hugh B. Brown and N. Eldon Tanner, May 15, 1968, First Presidency, General Administration Files, 1921–72, CHL; Harper, *First Vision*, 221; McKay, Diary, May 24, 1968; First Presidency to Truman Madsen, June 4, 1968, First Presidency, General Administration Files, 1921–72, CHL.
43. Shumway and Shumway, *Blossoming*, 96–97; Maeta Beck and Dennis Beck, Oral History Interview, 4, 6–7, 29–30, 51, 69–70.
44. Shumway and Shumway, *Blossoming*, 89; Berlo, "Navajo Cosmoscapes," 11; Prucha, *Great Father*, 1:562–81; 2:631–58, 814–40; *Saints*, volume 2, chapters 5 and 8; Garrett, *Making Lamanites*, 43–57; White, *Roots of Dependency*, 290–315; Bailey and Bailey, *History of the Navajos*, 26–28, 295–96.
45. Maeta Beck and Dennis Beck, Oral History Interview, 5, 49–50, 67–68; Shumway and Shumway, *Blossoming*, 92, 96.
46. Allen, "Rise and Decline of the LDS Indian Student Placement Program," 88–96, 100–101; First Presidency to Spencer W. Kimball, Sept. 6, 1968, First Presidency, General Administration Files, 1921–72, CHL; Dorothy O. Rea, "Indian Student Plan," *Deseret News*, Aug. 22, 1968, E8. **Topics: Indian Student Placement Program; Lamanite Identity; Spencer W. Kimball**
47. Shumway and Shumway, *Blossoming*, 96–97; Maeta Beck and Dennis Beck, Oral History Interview, 2–3, 6.
48. Shumway and Shumway, *Blossoming*, 90–91, 94–96; Maeta Beck and Dennis Beck, Oral History Interview, 2, 55, 71, 137.
49. Shumway and Shumway, *Blossoming*, 96, emphasis added; Maeta Beck and Dennis Beck, Oral History Interview, 16–17.
50. Maeta Beck and Dennis Beck, Oral History Interview, 5, 48–49; Black and Black, *Life Stories*, [4].
51. Maeta Beck and Dennis Beck, Oral History Interview, 3–4, 10, 25–26, 48, 68; Shumway and Shumway, *Blossoming*, 92; Black and Black, *Life Stories*, [158]; Pierce, Oral History Interview, 2–4.
52. Maeta Beck and Dennis Beck, Oral History Interview, 6–7, 9–10, 50–51.

Chapter 11: In Any Other Country

1. "School Complex Dedicated," *Church News*, Aug. 3, 1968, 3–4; Joseph Bentley to N. Eldon Tanner, Apr. 29, 1968; Joseph Bentley to Harvey Taylor, June 25, 1969, Church Educational System, Harvey L. Taylor Administrative Files, CHL.
2. Isabel Santana, Oral History Interview [Feb. 2, 2022], 2; Santana and Machuca, Oral History Interview, 32–33; Isabel Santana, Oral History Interview [Jan. 5, 2022], 3.
3. Isabel Santana, Oral History Interview [Jan. 5, 2022], 6–7; Santana and Machuca, Oral History Interview, 2, 28, 34; Isabel Santana, Oral History Interview [Feb. 2, 2022], 5, 8; Hilda Santana, Oral History Interview, 14; Morgan, "Century of LDS Church Schools in Mexico," 372; Morgan, "Impact of Centro Escolar Benemérito," 151.
4. Isabel Santana, Oral History Interview [Jan. 5, 2022], 13; Isabel Santana, Oral History Interview [Feb. 2, 2022], 14; Isabel Santana, Oral History Interview [Apr. 19, 2022], 2.

5. Joseph Bentley to Harvey Taylor, June 25, 1969, Church Educational System, Harvey L. Taylor Administrative Files, CHL; Morgan, "Benemérito de las Américas," 100–101; Isabel Santana, Oral History Interview [Jan. 5, 2022], 3; Isabel Santana, Oral History Interview [Feb. 2, 2022], 24–25; *Eleven Year Report of the President,* 394.
6. Suri, *Power and Protest,* 1–6, 164–212; Carey, *Plaza of Sacrifices,* 11–34, 139; Kriza, "Student Massacre on Tlatelolco Square," 82–86; Sloan, "Carnivalizing the Cold War"; Zimelis, "Let the Games Begin," 266–67.
7. Isabel Santana, Oral History Interview [Jan. 5, 2022], 21; Santana and Machuca, Oral History Interview, 5–7, 31; Isabel Santana, Oral History Interview [Feb. 2, 2022], 25.
8. Isabel Santana, Oral History Interview [Jan. 5, 2022], 24; Santana and Machuca, Oral History Interview, 7; Isabel Santana, Oral History Interview [Feb. 2, 2022], 10.
9. Monson, Journal, Nov. 10, 1968; Görlitz Branch, Minutes, Nov. 9–10, 1968; Germany Hamburg Mission, Manuscript History and Historical Reports, Nov. 10, 1968; Monson, *Faith Rewarded,* 3; Peterson, Journal, May 9, 1978.
10. "Distriktskonferenz in Görlitz," *Der Stern,* Mar. 1969, 94; Stanley Rees to Thomas S. Monson, May 29, 1968, Germany North Mission, President's Files, CHL; Kuehne, *Henry Burkhardt,* 62; Kuehne, *Mormons as Citizens of a Communist State,* 110. **Topics: Germany; Thomas S. Monson**
11. "Authorities Assigned to New Areas," *Church News,* May 25, 1968, 8; Monson, Journal, June 13 and July 12, 1968; Kuehne, *Mormons as Citizens of a Communist State,* 110; Kuehne, *Henry Burkhardt,* 67; Burkhardt, Oral History Interview [2018], 4, 12.
12. Dresden District, Quarterly Reports, Nov. 9–10, 1968; Monson, Journal, Nov. 10, 1968; Burkhardt, Oral History Interview [1991], 16–17; *Saints,* volume 3, chapter 36.
13. Burkhardt, Oral History Interview [1991], 8, 14–17; Burkhardt, Oral History Interview [2018], 3–4. Quotation edited for readability; "was" in original changed to "is."
14. Monson, Journal, Nov. 10, 1968.
15. Kuehne, *Henry Burkhardt,* 61, 88–89; Burkhardt, Oral History Interview [1991], 8–9, 12.
16. Görlitz Branch, Minutes, Nov. 10, 1968; "Gott sei mit euch," *Gesangbuch,* no. 179; "God Be with You Till We Meet Again," *Hymns,* no. 152.
17. Joseph Johnson, Oral History Interview [1988], 12–14; Joseph Johnson, Oral History Interview [1998], 2; Joseph Johnson, Oral History Interview [2005], 3–4; Johnson, "History of The Church of Jesus Christ of Latter-day Saints in Ghana," [1]–[2].
18. E. Dale LeBaron, "Steadfast African Pioneer," *Ensign,* Dec. 1999, 46–47; Joseph Johnson, Oral History Interview [1988], 18; Lamar Williams to Clement Osekre, June 6, 1968; July 17, 1968, Correspondence regarding the Establishment of LDS Church in Ghana, CHL; Cutler, Oral History Interview [1983], 112, 115–21; Cutler, Oral History Interview [1986], 7; Kissi, *Walking in the Sand,* 11–20. **Topic: Ghana**
19. Joseph Johnson, Oral History Interview [1988], 1; Joseph Johnson, Oral History Interview [2005], 4; Brigham Johnson, Oral History Interview, [00:01:35].
20. Joseph Johnson, Oral History Interview [1988], 1–6, 13–15, 26, 87–90; Joseph Johnson, Oral History Interview [1998], 1–2; Joseph Johnson to First Presidency, Sept. 9, 1978, International Mission Files, CHL; Johnson, "We Felt the Spirit of the Pioneers," 14.
21. Joseph Johnson, Oral History Interview [1988], 19; Joseph Johnson, Oral History Interview [1998], 3.
22. Joseph Johnson, Oral History Interview [1988], 7, 32, 87–88, 101, 106–7.
23. Bronson, Oral History Interview, 3–4, 15, 74–75; Shirleen Meek Saunders, "Whang Keun-Ok: Caring for Korea's Children," *Ensign,* Oct. 1993, 48.
24. Hwang, "Hwang Keun Ok," 293; Roby, Oral History Interview, 1–4; Bronson, Oral History Interview, 3–5; Till, Till, and Munoa, Oral History Interview, 16–17.
25. Bronson, Oral History Interview, 10, 22.
26. Bronson, Oral History Interview, 5, 12, 22, 36–38, 74–78; Stewart, *Tender Apples,* ix, 281–82.
27. Bronson, Oral History Interview, 11–12, 44–45, 80–81; Sarah Jane Weaver, "Orphanage Founder's Life Spent Serving," *Church News,* Aug. 19, 2000, 7; Shirleen

Meek Saunders, "Whang Keun-Ok: Caring for Korea's Children," *Ensign*, Oct. 1993, 48. Quotation edited for readability; original source has "Do you think Miss Hwang, Sister Hwang, is strange person?"
28. Bronson, Oral History Interview, 84–85.
29. Bronson, Oral History Interview, 11–12, 80–85; "LDS Teacher Helps Korean Orphans," *Church News*, Feb. 6, 1971, 7; Sarah Jane Weaver, "Orphanage Founder's Life Spent Serving," *Church News*, Aug. 19, 2000, 7; Roby, Oral History Interview, 3, 7–8; Shirleen Meek Saunders, "Whang Keun-Ok: Caring for Korea's Children," *Ensign*, Oct. 1993, 48.
30. Sarah Jane Weaver, "Orphanage Founder's Life Spent Serving," *Church News*, Aug. 19, 2000, 7; Bronson, Oral History Interview, 10–13, 83.
31. Truman Madsen to Leonard Arrington and others, Sept. 23, 1968, Richard L. Bushman and Claudia L. Bushman Papers, BYU; Paul Richards to Truman Madsen, July 24, 1968; Larry Porter to Truman Madsen, Aug. 7, 1968, Truman G. Madsen Correspondence, CHL.
32. Milton Backman to Victor Purdy, Sept. 2, 1968, Truman G. Madsen Correspondence, CHL; Truman Madsen to Leonard Arrington and others, Sept. 23, 1968, Richard L. Bushman and Claudia L. Bushman Papers, BYU; Backman, "Awakenings in the Burned-Over District," 301–20; Backman, *Joseph Smith's First Vision*, 71–89; Joseph Smith—History 1:5–9. **Topic: Joseph Smith's First Vision Accounts**
33. Truman Madsen to Leonard Arrington and others, Sept. 23, 1968, Richard L. Bushman and Claudia L. Bushman Papers, BYU; Truman Madsen to Dean Jessee, Nov. 4, 1968, Truman G. Madsen Correspondence, CHL.
34. Barney, "Facsimiles and Semitic Adaptation of Existing Sources," 107–15; Hugh Nibley, "A New Look at the Pearl of Great Price," *Improvement Era*, Apr. 1968, 64–69; Givens, *Pearl of Greatest Price*, 140–46; Abraham, Facsimiles 1, 2, and 3.
35. "New Light on Joseph Smith's Egyptian Papyri," *Improvement Era*, Feb. 1968, 40–41; Wilson, "Summary Report," 67–85; Nibley, "Phase One," 99–105; Hugh Nibley, "A New Look at the Pearl of Great Price," *Improvement Era*, Aug. 1968, 57.
36. Midgley, "Hugh Winder Nibley," xlv–xlvii; Nibley, "As Things Stand at the Moment," 69–102; Hugh Nibley, "The Unknown Abraham," *Improvement Era*, Jan. 1969, 26–31; Nibley, "Phase One," 99–105; Givens, *Pearl of Greatest Price*, 160.
37. Givens, *Pearl of Greatest Price*, 162–63; Nibley, *Approach to the Book of Abraham*, 9–10, 176–77; Nibley, *Message of the Joseph Smith Papyri*, 6–14. **Topic: Book of Abraham Translation**
38. Madsen, "Guest Editor's Prologue," 236–37; see also Allen and Arrington, "Mormon Origins in New York," 241–74; Backman, "Awakenings in the Burned-Over District," 301–20; Jessee, "Early Accounts of Joseph Smith's First Vision," 275–94; and Harper, *First Vision*, 219–21. The following year, an article about the different accounts of the First Vision was published in the official Church magazine *Improvement Era*. (James B. Allen, "Eight Contemporary Accounts of Joseph Smith's First Vision: What Do We Learn from Them?," *Improvement Era*, Apr. 1970, 4–13.) **Topic: Church History and Record Keeping**
39. Thomas S. Monson to First Presidency, Memorandum, June 30, 1969, First Presidency, Mission Correspondence, 1964–2010, CHL; Monson, Journal, June 13–15, 1969.
40. Burkhardt, Oral History Interview [2018], 3; "Geschichte der Dresdener Mission," Aug. 24, 1969, 10.
41. Thomas S. Monson to First Presidency, Memorandum, June 30, 1969, First Presidency, Mission Correspondence, 1964–2010, CHL; Kuehne, *Mormons as Citizens of a Communist State*, 100–103.
42. Kuehne, *Henry Burkhardt*, 56–59, 61; Mission History, 13, in German Democratic Republic Dresden Mission, Historical Record, CHL; Thomas S. Monson to First Presidency, Memorandum, June 30, 1969, First Presidency, Mission Correspondence, 1964–2010, CHL; Burkhardt, Oral History Interview [1991], 15; Monson, Journal, June 14, 1969; Zwirner and Zwirner, "Church or School?," 210–11, 228.

43. Monson, Journal, June 14–15, 1969; Thomas S. Monson to First Presidency, Memorandum, June 30, 1969, First Presidency, Mission Correspondence, 1964–2010, CHL; "Bericht über die Genealogische Arbeitswoche in Dresden," June 9–14, 1969; Kuehne, *Henry Burkhardt,* 66.
44. Burkhardt, Journal, June 19, 1969.

Chapter 12: A Complete Way of Life

1. Spencer W. Kimball, Journal, Jan. 8, 1970.
2. Spencer W. Kimball, Journal, July 29, 1957; May 1 and 11, 1966; Nov. 20, 1966; May 29–30, 1967; Nov. 12, 1967; Oct. 2, 1969; "Committee & Advisor Assignments," Dec. 31, 1969, 1–2, First Presidency, General Administration Files, 1921–72, CHL. **Topics: Spencer W. Kimball; Argentina; Colombia; Ecuador; Uruguay**
3. Spencer W. Kimball, Journal, June 23, 1969; July 14, 1969; Oct. 30, 1969; Dec. 4, 1969; Jan. 8 and 12, 1970.
4. Spencer W. Kimball, Journal, Jan. 12, 1970; Spencer W. Kimball to Leland Cowan, [1957], in Spencer W. Kimball, Journal, Jan. 28, 1957; Homer S. Ellsworth to Spencer W. Kimball, Jan. 10, 1970; Spencer W. Kimball to Andrew Kimball, Jan. 16, 1970, in Spencer W. Kimball, Journal, Jan. 15, 1970.
5. Spencer W. Kimball, Journal, Jan. 13 and 15, 1970; Spencer W. Kimball to Andrew Kimball, Jan. 16, 1970, in Spencer W. Kimball, Journal, Jan. 15, 1970; Lee, Diary, Jan. 15, 1970; Romney, Journal, Jan. 15, 1970.
6. Spencer W. Kimball, Journal, Jan. 18 and 19, 1970. Quotation edited for readability; "had" in original changed to "have."
7. Spencer W. Kimball, Journal, Jan. 18, 1970; Lee, Diary, Jan. 17–18, 1970.
8. Spencer W. Kimball, Journal, Jan. 18, 1970; "Funeral Services Thursday in S.L.," "President Assisted Expansion," and "New Temples Rise," *Deseret News,* Jan. 19, 1970, M1, M3, M5; *Deseret News 1989–90 Church Almanac,* 221–30; "Church Creates Stake in Apia, West Samoa," *Deseret News,* Mar. 19, 1962, B1; Curriculum Department, Priesthood Correlation Executive Committee, Minutes, Mar. 11, 1965, 277–79; *Saints,* volume 3, chapter 38; Gordon B. Hinckley, "Temple in the Pacific," *Improvement Era,* July 1958, 509; First Presidency to Howard McDonald, Feb. 26, 1968, First Presidency, Temple Correspondence, CHL; Rinne, *Kristuksen Kirkko Suomessa,* 157. **Topics: David O. McKay; Broadcast Media; Correlation; United States**
9. "President McKay Laid to Rest," *Church News,* Jan. 24, 1970, 4; J M. Heslop, "Study Scriptures, Pres. Smith Urges," *Church News,* Jan. 31, 1970, 4–5; Neilson and Marianno, "True and Faithful," 6–64. **Topic: Joseph Fielding Smith**
10. Spencer W. Kimball, Journal, Jan. 19–22, 1970; "President Smith Leads Church," *Deseret News,* Jan. 23, 1970, A1; Kimball and Kimball, *Spencer W. Kimball,* 390–91.
11. Spencer W. Kimball, Journal, Jan. 23, 1970.
12. Maeta Beck and Dennis Beck, Oral History Interview, 7.
13. Maeta Beck and Dennis Beck, Oral History Interview, 18–20, 28, 71–72; Garrett, *Making Lamanites,* 119. **Topic: Indian Student Placement Program**
14. Maeta Beck and Dennis Beck, Oral History Interview, 13–14. Quotation edited for readability; "could" in original changed to "can." **Topic: Seminaries and Institutes**
15. Maeta Beck and Dennis Beck, Oral History Interview, 126–32.
16. Maeta Beck and Dennis Beck, Oral History Interview, 5–6, 15–16, 25–26, 52–53, 66; Allen, "Rise and Decline of the LDS Indian Student Placement Program," 102; Shumway and Shumway, *Blossoming,* 97.
17. Maeta Beck and Dennis Beck, Oral History Interview, 15–16, 51–53, 116–17, 137; Shumway and Shumway, *Blossoming,* 97.
18. Yamashita, Interview, 1–5, 9–10, 21; Xue, Jing, and Hui, "Study of Roofed Space in the Osaka, Hannover, and Shanghai Expos," 111–14; Stalker, *Japan,* 331–32,

344–45; "The Mormon Pavilion at the 1970 World's Exposition," Global Histories, ChurchofJesusChrist.org/study/history/global-histories; Peterson, "History of Mormon Exhibits in World Expositions," 143.

19. Yamashita, Interview, 3, 9, 48–49; Massidda, "Cold War, a Cool Medium, and the Postmodern Death of World Expos," 189.
20. Yamashita, Interview, 5, 9–10, 18, 48.
21. Yamashita, Interview, 2, 5–6, 12, 14, 49; Palmer, *Church Encounters Asia,* 8–9; Peterson, "History of Mormon Exhibits in World Expositions," 25, 29–32, 36–39, 47–53, 59–61, 115–28, 143–45; William B. Smart, "Expo '70 Impressive, and So Are Crowds," *Deseret News,* Apr. 9, 1970, A17.
22. Peterson, "History of Mormon Exhibits in World Expositions," 145; Yamashita, Interview, 6–8; Palmer, *Church Encounters Asia,* 9; Astle, "Mormons and Cinema," 21.
23. Okazaki, *What a Friend We Have in Jesus,* 27–29; Yamashita, Interview, 7–8, 10, 15; Palmer, *Church Encounters Asia,* 9–15; Whitaker, *Looking Back,* 69–71; Britsch, *From the East,* 135.
24. Yamashita, Interview, 7, 11, 13; Palmer, *Church Encounters Asia,* 9. **Topic: Japan**
25. "Fulfill Divine Destiny, Relief Society Meet Told," *Deseret News,* Oct. 1, 1970, A1, A5; Belle S. Spafford, "We Lived after the Manner of Happiness," *Relief Society Magazine,* Nov. 1970, 803; Patterson, *Grand Expectations,* 550–51, 685–86, 691–93, 753–56.
26. First Presidency to Stake Presidents and others, June 10, 1970, First Presidency, Circular Letters, CHL; First Presidency to Relief Society General Presidency, May 12, 1970, in Relief Society, General Board Minutes, volume 38, June 3, 1970, 227B; First Presidency to Stake Presidents and others, July 17, 1970, First Presidency, Circular Letters, CHL; Derr, Cannon, and Beecher, *Women of Covenant,* 326–27, 340–41. **Topics: Correlation; Relief Society**
27. Derr, "Period of Transition," 1–3, 10–11; "Church Unifies Social Programs," *Deseret News,* Sept. 27, 1969, B1, B3; Alvin R. Dyer and others to Harold B. Lee, Mar. 27, 1969, First Presidency, General Administration Files, 1921–72, CHL; Relief Society, General Board Minutes, volume 36, Feb. 16, 1966, 28–29.
28. Monson, Journal, Jan. 14, 1969; July 1, 1969; Aug. 14, 1969; Alvin R. Dyer and others to Harold B. Lee, Mar. 27, 1969, First Presidency, General Administration Files, 1921–72, CHL; Spencer W. Kimball to Regional Representatives, Stake Presidents, and Bishops, Nov. 30, 1970, First Presidency, General Correspondence, CHL; Relief Society, General Board Minutes, volume 37, Jan. 31, 1968, 53–55; Derr, "Period of Transition," 1–11.
29. Alvin R. Dyer and others to Harold B. Lee, Mar. 27, 1969, First Presidency, General Administration Files, 1921–72, CHL; Romney, Journal, Oct. 22, 1969; "Church Unifies Social Programs," *Deseret News,* Sept. 27, 1969, B1. **Topic: Social Services**
30. Smith, Oral History Interview, 113–15, 148–49; Curriculum Department, Priesthood Correlation Executive Committee Minutes, June 3 and 11, 1964, 190, 195; Dec. 9, 1965, 329; Relief Society, General Board Minutes, volume 35, Sept. 8, 1965, 302–5.
31. Relief Society, General Board Minutes, volume 34, Sept. 19, 1962, 144–45; volume 35, Oct. 6, 1965, 317; volume 36, Feb. 16, 1966, 25; Spafford, Oral History Interview, 184, 227–32; "Church Launches Unified Magazine for Missions," *Church News,* Mar. 25, 1967, 3; "Copies of Book of Mormon Exceed 4 Million in '60s," *Church News,* Jan. 3, 1970, 11; Relief Society General Presidency to Spencer W. Kimball, Howard W. Hunter, and Doyle Green, Dec. 19, 1969, Relief Society, Belle S. Spafford Files, CHL.
32. "Church Magazines to Be Combined into 3 Publications," *Church News,* June 6, 1970, 3; "Names of New Church Magazines Announced," *Church News,* Oct. 3, 1970, 5; First Presidency to Superintendencies and Presidencies of the Sunday School and others, Apr. 24, 1970, in Relief Society, General Board Minutes, volume 38, May 13, 1970, 217A; Editorial, *Millennial Star,* Dec. 1970, 3; "Yesterday and Today," *Cumorah's Southern Messenger,* Dec. 1970, 313–14. **Topics: Church Periodicals; Globalization**
33. Relief Society, General Board Minutes, volume 38, Aug. 5, 1970, 218; Belle S. Spafford to Ethel Sessions, Sept. 14, 1970, Belle S. Spafford Letters, BYU; Relief Society General

Presidency to Spencer W. Kimball, Delbert Stapley, and John Vandenberg, Apr. 21, 1967, Marion I. Spafford Papers, CHL; Sharon Meikle to Relief Society General Board, July 23, 1970; Marnie Erickson to "Editors of R.S. Magazine," Aug. 14, 1970, Relief Society, Magazine Department, CHL.

34. Spencer W. Kimball, Journal, Dec. 17, 1969; Relief Society General Presidency to Spencer W. Kimball, Howard W. Hunter, and Doyle Green, Dec. 19, 1969, Relief Society, Belle S. Spafford Files, CHL; Spafford, Interview [circa 1980], audiocassette 7.

35. Belle S. Spafford, "We Lived after the Manner of Happiness," *Relief Society Magazine*, Nov. 1970, 803–6; 2 Nephi 5:27.

36. Gray, Interview, [1]–[2]; Gray, Oral History Interview, 27–28, 60–63, 68–71, 78, 81, 97–98, 100–101; Godfrey, Limburg, and Wolsey, "KSL, Salt Lake City," 338–52.

37. Gray, Oral History Interview, 100–103, 105; *University of Utah Annual Commencement, 1974,* 52; Gray, Interview, [2]; "Fleming, Frances Leggroan," Biographical Entry, Century of Black Mormons website, exhibits.lib.utah.edu/s/century-of-black-mormons. **Topic: Jane Elizabeth Manning James**

38. Gray, Oral History Interview, 136–38, 155; Embry, *Black Saints in a White Church,* 42; Williams and Williams, Oral History Interview, 30; Orr, Oral History Interview, 2–5, 11.

39. Gray, Oral History Interview, 136–39; Shawn Foster, "Black Leader in LDS Church Who Waited in Faith to Receive Priesthood Dies at 74," *Salt Lake Tribune,* Mar. 23, 1997, C1, C7; Lee, *Ruffin Bridgeforth,* 11–15, 36–37, 43, 46, 58; Monson, Journal, Apr. 3, 1976, and Mar. 26, 1997.

40. Gray, Oral History Interview, 160, 250–51, 254; Wolsey, "Funny Thing Happened to Me on the Road to the Millennium," 211. **Topic: Public Relations**

41. Bergera, "Race-Based Anti-BYU Athletic Protests of 1968–1971," 204–29; Haws, *Mormon Image in the American Mind,* 50–57, 66–67; Willie Black to William Carlson, Oct. 14, 1969, copy, First Presidency, General Administration Files, 1921–72, CHL; Parker Owens and Jerry Garrett, "Will BYU Be Eliminated from the WAC?," *Daily Universe* (Provo, UT), Nov. 11, 1969, 3. **Topic: Priesthood and Temple Restriction**

42. "No Arm Bands Friday for Wyoming Basketball Crew," *Laramie (WY) Daily Boomerang,* Feb. 18, 1971, 16; Pat McKenna, "BSA Plans Protest Tonight against LDS Doctrines," *Branding Iron* (Laramie, WY), Feb. 19, 1971, 1; "Spectators 'Boo' and Police Stop Marchers," *Branding Iron,* Feb. 26, 1971, 1; "BYU President in Laramie Praises University Here," *Laramie Daily Boomerang,* Feb. 19, 1971, 1; Wolsey, "Funny Thing Happened to Me on the Road to the Millennium," 211.

43. Wolsey, "Funny Thing Happened to Me on the Road to the Millennium," 211; Haws, *Mormon Image in the American Mind,* 64.

44. Wolsey, "Funny Thing Happened to Me on the Road to the Millennium," 211; Gray, Oral History Interview, 254–56, 260; Haws, *Mormon Image in the American Mind,* 64.

45. Wolsey, "Funny Thing Happened to Me on the Road to the Millennium," 212; Gray, Oral History Interview, 258.

46. "Spectators 'Boo' and Police Stop Marchers," *Branding Iron* (Laramie, WY), Feb. 26, 1971, 1; Harold Sohn, "Cowboys Keep Cool, Cage Cougars," *Laramie (WY) Daily Boomerang,* Feb. 20, 1971, 8. **Topic: Civil Rights Movement**

47. Anthony Obinna to "the Mormons' President," Jan. 19, 1971, Missionary Department, Africa and India Correspondence, CHL; Anthony Uzodimma Obinna, "Voice from Nigeria," *Ensign,* Dec. 1980, 29–30.

48. Obinna, Autobiography, 2, 3; Nwachukwu and Nwachukwu, Oral History Interview, 3; Hartzell Spence, "The March of the Mormons," *Reader's Digest,* 1958, 1, copy at CHL; Hartzell Spence, "The Mormon Church: A Complete Way of Life," *Reader's Digest,* Apr. 1958, 184–90.

49. Anthony Obinna, Oral History Interview, 5–6, 15–17; Obinna, Autobiography, 2; Fidelia Obinna, Oral History Interview, 1.

50. Obinna, Autobiography, 3; Francis Obinna, Oral History Interview, 6; Raymond Obinna and others, Oral History Interview, 4; Hartzell Spence, "The March of the

Mormons," *Reader's Digest,* 1958, 1–4, copy at CHL; Hartzell Spence, "The Mormon Church: A Complete Way of Life," *Reader's Digest,* Apr. 1958, 184–90; Anthony Obinna, Oral History Interview, 5.

51. Obinna, Autobiography, 3; Anthony Uzodimma Obinna, "Voice from Nigeria," *Ensign,* Dec. 1980, 30; Francis Obinna, Oral History Interview, 5–6.
52. Obinna, Autobiography, 3; Anthony Obinna, Oral History Interview, 19; Anthony Uzodimma Obinna, "Voice from Nigeria," *Ensign,* Dec. 1980, 30; Anthony Obinna to "the Mormons' President," Jan. 19, 1971, Missionary Department, Africa and India Correspondence, CHL; Allen, "West Africa before the 1978 Priesthood Revelation," 237–38; Charles Agu to LaMar Williams, no date, Missionary Department, Africa and India Correspondence, CHL.
53. LaMar Williams to Anthony Obinna, Feb. 3, 1971, Missionary Department, Africa and India Correspondence, CHL. Quotation edited for readability; "glad to also correspond" in original changed to "glad to correspond."

Chapter 13: An Undying Knowledge

1. Orr, "Eugene Orr's Life History," [7], [9]; Gray, Oral History Interview, 137; Orr, Oral History Interview, 12.
2. Orr, Oral History Interview, 12; Gray, Oral History Interview, 137, 139; Orr, "Eugene Orr's Life History," [7], [9]; Leitha Orr and Eugene Orr, Letter, circa Dec. 1971, Gordon B. Hinckley Files, circa 1971–77, CHL; "Race and the Priesthood," Gospel Topics Essays, ChurchofJesusChrist.org/study/manual/gospel-topics-essays; *Saints,* volume 2, chapter 12. **Topics: Priesthood and Temple Restriction; Elijah Able**
3. Arthur Haycock to First Presidency, Memorandum, May 11, 1971, First Presidency, General Administration Files, 1921–72, CHL; Leitha Orr and Eugene Orr, Letter, circa Dec. 1971, Gordon B. Hinckley Files, circa 1971–77, CHL; Orr, "Eugene Orr's Life History," [7]; Gray, Oral History Interview, 139.
4. Orr, Oral History Interview, 12; Orr, "Eugene Orr's Life History," [7], [9]; Gray, Oral History Interview, 137; R. Scott Lloyd, "Ruffin Bridgeforth, First Black High Priest, Eulogized as a Pioneer," *Church News,* Apr. 5, 1997, 7; see also Lee, *Ruffin Bridgeforth,* 31.
5. Orr, "Eugene Orr's Life History," [7], [9]; Orr, Oral History Interview, 12, 14; Arthur Haycock to First Presidency, Memorandum, May 11, 1971, First Presidency, General Administration Files, 1921–72, CHL. Quotations edited for readability; "resolve that" in original changed to "resolve them," and square brackets around "is" removed.
6. Orr, "Eugene Orr's Life History," [9]; Orr, Oral History Interview, 14; Arthur Haycock to Gordon B. Hinckley, Memorandum, June 4, 1971, Gordon B. Hinckley Files, circa 1971–77, CHL; Hinckley, Journal, June 9, 1971.
7. Monson, Journal, June 9, 1971; Hinckley, Journal, June 9, 1971; Gray, Oral History Interview, 137–39; Orr, "Eugene Orr's Life History," [9]; Genesis Group, First Meeting, Oct. 19, 1971, [00:12:55]–[00:13:27]; Lee, *Ruffin Bridgeforth,* 43, 58.
8. Hinckley, Journal, June 9, 1971; Gray, Oral History Interview, 138–39; Orr, Interview, [1]–[2].
9. Hinckley, Journal, June 9, 1971; Monson, Journal, June 9, 1971; Orr, "Eugene Orr's Life History," [9]; Council Minutes, May 20, 1971, First Presidency, General Administration Files, 1921–72, CHL.
10. Yamashita, Interview, 2, 12–14, 16, 24, 26.
11. Yamashita, Interview, 12, 16–17, 29.
12. Yamashita, Interview, 26–27.
13. Palmer, *Church Encounters Asia,* 3–6, 177; Britsch, *From the East,* 92, 127–31, 134–37; Peterson, "History of Mormon Exhibits in World Expositions," 155; "Translations Director Named," *Church News,* Feb. 22, 1969, 4; Missionary Department, Full-Time Mission Monthly Progress Reports, June 1971.

14. "Brief History of the Church Education in Japan and Okinawa," 1–3; Griffiths, "Globalization of Latter-day Saint Education," 171–81; *By Study and Also by Faith*, 256–57. **Topics: Japan; Seminaries and Institutes**
15. Palmer, *Church Encounters Asia*, 7–15; Britsch, *From the East*, 131–34; Peterson, "History of Mormon Exhibits in World Expositions," 148–55; Edward Okazaki and Chieko Okazaki, Japan Central Mission Report, Oct. 26, 1971, First Presidency, Mission Correspondence, 1964–2010, CHL; "Expo Exhibit 'Great Success,'" *Church News*, Sept. 26, 1970, 3.
16. Yamashita, Interview, 14, 17, 28–31, 50–51; Sarah Jane Weaver, "Missionaries Changed His Life," *Church News*, May 28, 2011, 11; Rupp, Journal, July 17, 1971.
17. Spencer W. Kimball, Journal, Aug. 28, 1971; Sept. 15, 1971; Oct. 15, 1971, supplement; Kimball, *Autobiography of Camilla Eyring Kimball*, 83–84; Kimball and Kimball, *Spencer W. Kimball*, 390–93; Nelson, *From Heart to Heart*, 162.
18. Spencer W. Kimball, Journal, Sept. 15, 1971, and Oct. 15, 1971, supplement.
19. Spencer W. Kimball, Journal, Sept. 15–16, 1971, supplement; Nelson, *From Heart to Heart*, 162. **Topic: Spencer W. Kimball**
20. Spencer W. Kimball, Journal, Sept. 15–16, 1971, supplement, and Oct. 15, 1971, supplement.
21. Spencer W. Kimball, Journal, Sept. 16, 1971, supplement. Quotation edited for readability; "as" added before "blowing."
22. Gray, Oral History Interview, 140.
23. Orr, "Eugene Orr's Life History," [9]; Gray, Oral History Interview, 138–40; Orr, Oral History Interview, 17–19.
24. Gray, Oral History Interview, 140–41; see also Hinckley, Journal, June 27, 1971. Quotation edited for readability; "had" in original changed to "have," and "support group for Negro members or Black members" changed to "support group for Black members."
25. Council Minutes, May 20, 1971, First Presidency, General Administration Files, 1921–72, CHL; Hinckley, Journal, June 9 and 27, 1971; Oct. 19, 1971; Joseph Fielding Smith to First Presidency, Mar. 30, 1955, First Presidency, General Administration Files, 1923, 1932, 1937–67, CHL; Gray, Oral History Interview, 141; Monson, Journal, Oct. 19, 1971; Ruffin Bridgeforth to Catheryn Smith, Dec. 20, 1971; Gordon B. Hinckley Files, circa 1971–77, CHL; Orr, "Eugene Orr's Life History," [9].
26. Gray, Oral History Interview, 141–42; Hinckley, Journal, Oct. 19, 1971; Monson, Journal, Oct. 19, 1971; Genesis Group, First Meeting, Oct. 19, 1971, [00:05:30]–[00:18:40]. Quotation edited for readability; "meaning" in original changed to "means." **Topic: Genesis Group**
27. Genesis Group, First Meeting, Oct. 19, 1971, [00:18:40]–[00:20:14]; [Gordon B. Hinckley], Notes from the First Meeting of the Genesis Group, [Oct. 19, 1971], Gordon B. Hinckley Files, circa 1971–77, CHL. Quotation edited for readability; "Darius wasn't going to" in original changed to "I wasn't going to."
28. Santana and Machuca, Oral History Interview, 27–29; Isabel Santana, Oral History Interview [Feb. 2, 2022], 5, 7–8, 10–11; Isabel Santana, Oral History Interview [Apr. 19, 2022], 2–4, 6, 13; Taylor, *Story of L.D.S. Church Schools*, 2:15, 22–23; *Antorcha de Chiquihuite*, 17; Isabel Santana, Oral History Interview [Jan. 5, 2022], 25. **Topic: Church Academies**
29. Santana and Machuca, Oral History Interview, 8, 11–14, 29; Isabel Santana, Oral History Interview [Feb. 2, 2022], 16–17, 22–23; Isabel Santana, Oral History Interview [Jan. 5, 2022], 17–18. Quotation edited for readability; "was" in English translation of original changed to "is."
30. Isabel Santana, Oral History Interview [Jan. 5, 2022], 19–20; Santana and Machuca, Oral History Interview, 15–16; Isabel Santana, Oral History Interview [Feb. 2, 2022], 18.
31. *Saints*, volume 3, chapters 31 and 36; *Deseret News 1989–90 Church Almanac*, 191; Mecham, Oral History Interview, 57–69; "Mesa: Spanish Temple Sessions Told," *Church News*, May 7, 1966, 4; Isabel Santana, Oral History Interview [Jan. 5, 2022], 19–20; Juan Antonio Machuca Caras and Isabel Santana Guirado, Sealing Record,

May 24, 1972, Temple Records for the Living, 1955–91, microfilm 820,337, FSL. **Topics: Sealing; Temple Endowment**
32. Joseph Johnson, Oral History Interview [2005], 4, 48; Acquah and Acquah, Oral History Interview [1999], 14–16.
33. Cannon and Bateman, "Report of a Visit to Ghana and Nigeria," 14–15; Acquah and Acquah, Oral History Interview [2018], 10–12; E. Dale LeBaron, "Steadfast African Pioneer," *Ensign,* Dec. 1999, 47; Joseph Johnson, Oral History Interview [1988], 101.
34. Cannon and Bateman, "Report of a Visit to Ghana and Nigeria," 14–15; Acquah and Acquah, Oral History Interview [2018], 10–12; E. Dale LeBaron, "Steadfast African Pioneer," *Ensign,* Dec. 1999, 47.
35. Acquah and Acquah, Oral History Interview [2018], 7–8.
36. Joseph Johnson, Oral History Interview [1988], 37, 46–47, 52; Joseph Johnson, Oral History Interview [2005], 4–5; Acquah and Acquah, Oral History Interview [1999], 14–15; Imbrah, Oral History Interview, 8–11; Cannon and Bateman, "Report of a Visit to Ghana and Nigeria," 14–15.
37. Joseph Johnson, Oral History Interview [1988], 26; Johnson, "History of The Church of Jesus Christ of Latter-day Saints in Ghana," [2]–[3].
38. Johnson, "History of The Church of Jesus Christ of Latter-day Saints in Ghana," [2]; Ewudzie, Oral History Interview, [00:02:13], [00:05:30]–[00:10:00].

CHAPTER 14: DIFFERENT NOW

1. Spencer W. Kimball, Journal, Nov. 8–9, 22, and 29, 1971; Dec. 31, 1971; Jan. 20, 1972; July 2, 1972; Russell M. Nelson to Spencer W. Kimball, Sept. 21, 1972, in Spencer W. Kimball, Journal, Apr. 11, 1972. **Topic: Spencer W. Kimball**
2. Benson, Journal, Nov. 18, 1971; Jan. 21, 1972; Feb. 8, 10, 15, and 22, 1972; Spencer W. Kimball, Journal, Dec. 31, 1971, and Jan.–Feb. 1972; Hunter, Journal, Jan. 13–14, 1972; Condie, *Russell M. Nelson,* 156–57.
3. Spencer W. Kimball, Journal, Mar. 13, 1972; Kimball, *Autobiography of Camilla Eyring Kimball,* 90; Nelson, *From Heart to Heart,* 163–64; Lee, Diary, Mar. 13, 1972. **Topic: Russell M. Nelson**
4. Dew, *Insights from a Prophet's Life,* 103–4; Nelson, *From Heart to Heart,* 163–64; Spencer W. Kimball, Journal, Mar. 13, 1972. Quotation edited for readability; original source has "I expressed my sureness that the Lord could heal me instantly and for as long as he wanted me, but that my concern and question was why would He want me."
5. Spencer W. Kimball, Journal, Mar. 13, 1972; Dew, *Insights from a Prophet's Life,* 104; Kimball, Oral History Interview, 90.
6. Spencer W. Kimball, Journal, Mar. 13, 1972; Dew, *Insights from a Prophet's Life,* 104.
7. Dave Noeche, "Music," *Richmond (VA) Times-Dispatch,* Apr. 5, 1972, B5; Nina Banner, "Osmonds for Real and Talented," *Daily Press* (Newport News, VA), Apr. 4, 1972, 25.
8. Kathy Wells, "Osmond Brothers Treat Mom 'like a Queen,'" *Daily Press* (Newport News, VA), Apr. 5, 1972, 6; Nina Banner, "Osmonds for Real and Talented," *Daily Press,* Apr. 4, 1972, 25; Osmond, *Untold Story of Olive Osmond,* 118, 189–94, 233–34, 240–42; Hicks, "Mormons and the Music Industry," 190; Olive Osmond, "The Osmond Story," *Osmonds' World,* May 1974, 4–5.
9. Osmond, *Untold Story of Olive Osmond,* 233–34, 254–68; Dunn, *Osmonds,* 12–31; Osmond and Romanowski, *Life Is Just What You Make It,* chapter 2; Hyatt, *Emmy Award Winning Nighttime Television Shows,* 166–71; Osmond, *Stages,* 71; Curtis, *Rock Eras,* 236, 286–91.
10. Ezra Taft Benson, in *One Hundred Fortieth Semi-annual Conference,* 23–24; Ezra Taft Benson, "Satan's Thrust—Youth," *Ensign,* Dec. 1971, 53–56; Boyd K. Packer, "Inspiring Music—Worthy Thoughts," *Ensign,* Jan. 1974, 25–28; Osmond and Romanowski, *Life*

Notes to pages 225–234

Is Just What You Make It, 64, 81–82; Dunn, *Osmonds,* 192–95; Osmond, *Untold Story of Olive Osmond,* 1.

11. Osmond and Romanowski, *Life Is Just What You Make It,* 80–90; Osmond and Graham, *Let the Reason Be Love,* 70; Osmond, *Stages,* 68–69, 84–85; Dunn, *Osmonds,* 192–95; Barbara Lewis, "Osmonds at Home," *Chillicothe (OH) Gazette,* Dec. 24, 1971, Showcase section, 3; Kathy Wells, "Osmond Brothers Treat Mom 'like a Queen,'" *Daily Press* (Newport News, VA), Apr. 5, 1972, 6; "Osmond Tale 'Paradoxical,'" *New Mexican* (Santa Fe, NM), Mar. 13, 1973, A8; see also Osmond and Osmond, Oral History Interview, 5–7, 23–24.

12. Howard Pearson, "Living Principles of Gospel Not Difficult, Osmonds Say," *Church News,* Mar. 20, 1971, 5; Osmond, *Stages,* 83–84; Osmond, Oral History Interview, 3–4; Osmond, Journal, Feb. 11, 1972; Osmond and Osmond, Oral History Interview, 7; Matthew 5:16.

13. J M. Heslop, "Osmond Fan Mail Heavy," *Church News,* Mar. 11, 1972, 8–9, 12; Kathy Wells, "Osmond Brothers Treat Mom 'like a Queen,'" *Daily Press* (Newport News, VA), Apr. 5, 1972, 6; *Deseret News 1989–90 Church Almanac,* 218–30; see also "Magazine Story Prompts Teen to Study Church," *Church News,* Mar. 4, 1972, 12; and Osmond and Osmond, Oral History Interview, 7, 17. **Topic: United States**

14. Kathy Wells, "Osmond Brothers Treat Mom 'like a Queen,'" *Daily Press* (Newport News, VA), Apr. 5, 1972, 6; Dave Noeche, "Music," *Richmond (VA) Times-Dispatch,* Apr. 5, 1972, B5; Alan Osmond, "Alan Gets Serious about 'The Plan,'" *Spotlight,* Sept.–Oct. 1973, 44.

15. Spencer W. Kimball, Journal, July 2, 1972; Russell M. Nelson to Spencer W. Kimball, Sept. 21, 1972, in Spencer W. Kimball, Journal, Apr. 11, 1972; Kimball, *Autobiography of Camilla Eyring Kimball,* 93; Dew, *Insights from a Prophet's Life,* 73, 105.

16. Spencer W. Kimball, Journal, July 2, 1972; Dew, *Insights from a Prophet's Life,* 106; Nelson, *From Heart to Heart,* 164.

17. Spencer W. Kimball, Journal, May 9 and 12, 1972; Dew, *Insights from a Prophet's Life,* 106; Russell M. Nelson to Spencer W. Kimball, Sept. 21, 1972, in Spencer W. Kimball, Journal, Apr. 11, 1972; Netter, *CIBA Collection of Medical Illustrations,* 194–95, 243–44.

18. Dew, *Insights from a Prophet's Life,* 106–7; Lee, Diary, Apr. 12, 1972; Monson, Journal, Apr. 12, 1972. **Topic: Healing**

19. Martins, *Autobiography of Elder Helvécio Martins,* 4, 9–12, 15–16, 19–22, 38–41.

20. Martins, *Autobiography of Elder Helvécio Martins,* 29–38; Helvécio Martins, Interview, *Friend,* Jan. 1992, 6.

21. Martins, *Autobiography of Elder Helvécio Martins,* 26, 38–40.

22. Martins and Martins, Oral History Interview, 12; Martins, *Autobiography of Elder Helvécio Martins,* 40–41.

23. Martins, *Autobiography of Elder Helvécio Martins,* 41–42; Helvécio Martins, Interview, *Friend,* Jan. 1992, 6; Martins and Martins, Oral History Interview, 12.

24. Martins, *Autobiography of Elder Helvécio Martins,* 42–44; Martins and Martins, Oral History Interview, 12–13. Quotation edited for readability; original source has "they had a blessing for our family if we would like one."

25. Martins, *Autobiography of Elder Helvécio Martins,* 4, 43–44; Martins and Martins, Oral History Interview, 13–14. **Topic: Priesthood and Temple Restriction**

26. Martins, *Autobiography of Elder Helvécio Martins,* 44–47. **Topic: Sacrament Meetings**

27. Osmond, Journal, May 1972; Osmond and Romanowski, *Life Is Just What You Make It,* 113–14.

28. John Barber, "Olympics Setting for Liza Minnelli," *Daily Telegraph* (London), May 23, 1972, 12; Osmond and Romanowski, *Life Is Just What You Make It,* 114–15; "Royal Gala Variety Performance," Through the Years, Donny (website), https://donny.com/timeline_item/royal-gala-variety-performance/.

29. Osmond, Journal, May 1972; George Osmond, "Father Remembers," and Olive Osmond, "The Osmond Story," *Osmonds' World,* Mar. 1974, 5, 13; Osmond and Osmond, Oral History Interview, 22; see also Osmond, Oral History Interview, 9.

30. Osmond, Journal, May 1972; Osmond and Osmond, Oral History Interview, 22; Osmond and Romanowski, *Life Is Just What You Make It*, 114. Quotation edited for readability; "a thrill" in original changed to "the thrill."
31. Commencement Announcement for Troy High School, Fullerton, CA, 1972; Photographs at Troy High School Graduation, June 15, 1972, in Beck, Scrapbook; "Troy High to Graduate 515 June 15," *Fullerton (CA) Daily News Tribune,* June 5, 1972, B5; Maeta Beck and Dennis Beck, Oral History Interview, 111–13.
32. Osborne, "Appraisal of the Education Program," 39–41, 51–52; Priesthood Department, Melchizedek Priesthood General Committee Minutes, May 27, 1975, 82; Metcalf, "Which Side of the Line?," 232; Maeta Beck and Dennis Beck, Oral History Interview, 12–13, 16–19, 25–29.
33. Allen, "Rise and Decline of the LDS Indian Student Placement Program," 96–97; "Indian Unity Caravan Leaves West Jordan for Arizona," *Salt Lake Tribune,* Aug. 19, 1972, B12; Garrett, *Making Lamanites,* 109–10, 114, 118–23, 130, 134–35, 156–58, 192–203, 238–41; Maeta Beck and Dennis Beck, Oral History Interview, 123.
34. Shumway and Shumway, *Blossoming,* 91–92, 94–98; Maeta Beck and Dennis Beck, Oral History Interview, 15–18, 45–46, 54–55, 62–63. Quotation edited for readability; "and just want to let you know that you're special" in original changed to "and I just want to let you know that you are special." **Topic: Lamanite Identity**
35. Maeta Beck and Dennis Beck, Oral History Interview, 18, 29, 61, 113; Shumway and Shumway, *Blossoming,* 98.
36. J M. Heslop, "Spirituality Themes Conference," *Church News,* Sept. 2, 1972, 3; Isabel Santana, Oral History Interview [Feb. 2, 2022], 20; Holzapfel and Lambert, "Photographs of the First Mexico and Central America Area Conference," 69; Santana and Machuca, Oral History Interview, 16–17.
37. Holzapfel and Lambert, "Photographs of the First Mexico and Central America Area Conference," 65–66, 68–69; "Details Announced for First Area Meet," *Church News,* Jan. 16, 1971, 3; J M. Heslop, "Area Conference in Mexico," *Church News,* Aug. 26, 1972, 3. **Topics: General Conference; Mexico**
38. Isabel Santana, Oral History Interview [Feb. 2, 2022], 20–21; Santana and Machuca, Oral History Interview, 16; Jay M. Todd, "The Remarkable Mexico City Area Conference," *Ensign,* Nov. 1972, 89–90; J M. Heslop, "Spirituality Themes Conference," *Church News,* Sept. 2, 1972, 3; Holzapfel and Lambert, "Photographs of the First Mexico and Central America Area Conference," 69; Kimball and Kimball, *Spencer W. Kimball,* 398–403.
39. Monson, Journal, Apr. 11, 1972; Lee, Diary, July 2, 1972; Tanner, Journal, July 2, 1972.
40. "Pres. Joseph Fielding Smith: Church Leader Dies at 95," "A Helping Hand to Missionaries," and "A Lifetime Devoted to Work in Temples," *Deseret News,* July 3, 1972, S1–S2, S5, S6; Neilson and Marianno, "True and Faithful," 6–64; "Peru Stake Created; Idaho Stake Reorganized," *Church News,* Mar. 14, 1970, 6; "4 New Stakes Are Organized," *Church News,* Apr. 4, 1970, 15; Griffiths, "Globalization of Latter-day Saint Education," 208–9, 214–29, 305–6; Allen and Leonard, *Story of the Latter-day Saints,* 603–6. **Topic: Joseph Fielding Smith**
41. Joseph Fielding Smith, "Counsel to the Saints and to the World," *Ensign,* July 1972, 27.
42. "President Harold B. Lee Ordained LDS Leader," *Deseret News,* July 7, 1972, A1.
43. Romney, Journal, Aug. 26, 1972; J M. Heslop, "Spirituality Themes Conference," *Church News,* Sept. 2, 1972, 3; *First Mexico and Central America Area General Conference,* 4; Santana and Machuca, Oral History Interview, 16–17; Holzapfel and Lambert, "Photographs of the First Mexico and Central America Area Conference," 70–71.
44. Marion G. Romney, in *First Mexico and Central America Area General Conference,* 3–4; Harold B. Lee, "Marion G. Romney of the Quorum of the Twelve," *Improvement Era,* Oct. 1962, [714]–[15]; "President Harold B. Lee Ordained LDS Leader," *Deseret News,* July 7, 1972, A1; Lozano, Oral History Interview, 96. **Topic: Colonies in Mexico**
45. N. Eldon Tanner, in *First Mexico and Central America Area General Conference,* 6; J M. Heslop, "Spirituality Themes Conference," *Church News,* Sept. 2, 1972, 3; Curriculum Department, Priesthood Correlation Executive Committee Minutes, May 5,

1965, 284; June 2 and 10, 1965, 294–96, 300–301; Feb. 1, 1967, 148–49; June 7, 1967, 171–72; Dec. 6, 1967, 222; Jan. 3, 1968, 226–27; "New Handbook for Church Officers Out," *Church News,* Apr. 27, 1968, 3; *La Iglesia de Jesucristo de los Santos de los Últimos Días: Manual General de Instrucciones, Número 20, 1968* (Salt Lake City: First Presidency of The Church of Jesus Christ of Latter-day Saints, 1968).

46. Santana and Machuca, Oral History Interview, 1–4, 17–18; Isabel Santana, Oral History Interview [Feb. 2, 2022], 19, 21. Quotation edited for readability; "there" in English translation of original changed to "here."

Chapter 15: The Joy of an Eternal Covenant

1. Lee, Diary, Aug. 26–27, 1972; *First Mexico and Central America Area General Conference,* 110–15; Holzapfel and Lambert, "Photographs of the First Mexico and Central America Area Conference," 70; J M. Heslop, "Spirituality Themes Conference," *Church News,* Sept. 2, 1972, 3. **Topics: Common Consent; Harold B. Lee**
2. Lee, Diary, Aug. 29, 1972; Goates, *Harold B. Lee,* 475–77; Tanner, Journal, Sept. 12, 1972; "7 Sought in Slaying of Cult Leader in Mexico," *Los Angeles Times,* Sept. 2, 1972, section 3, 8.
3. Lee, Diary, Aug. 29, 1972; Sept. 5, 7, 9–10, and 13, 1972; Goates, *Harold B. Lee,* 476–79; Dew, *Go Forward with Faith,* 319; "Olympic Day of Terror Ends with 16 Dead in Gun Battles," *Salt Lake Tribune,* Sept. 6, 1972, 1; Hack Miller, "Terror—And Now the World Weeps," *Deseret News,* Sept. 6, 1972, A1.
4. Gordon B. Hinckley, "Holy Land Tour Thrills Pres. Lee, Elder Hinckley," *Church News,* Dec. 16, 1972, 5; Hinckley, Journal, Sept. 19–22, 1972; Lee, Diary, Sept. 20–22, 1972; Galbraith, Oral History Interview [Oct. 11, 2021], 12–13; *Saints,* volume 1, chapters 35 and 36. Quotation edited for readability; "they" in original changed to "we." **Topic: Dedication of the Holy Land**
5. Hinckley, Journal, Sept. 20, 1972; John A. Tvedtnes, "A Visit with President Lee," *New Era,* Apr. 1973, [6]–[7]; Gordon B. Hinckley, "Holy Land Tour Thrills Pres. Lee, Elder Hinckley," *Church News,* Dec. 16, 1972, 12; David Galbraith to E. Q. Cannon Jr., Jan. 15, 1972, Switzerland Zurich Mission, President's Files, CHL; Taylor, "Contest and Controversy," 54–56.
6. Lee, Diary, Sept. 16–17 and 21–24, 1972; Hinckley, Journal, Sept. 20–22, 1972; Dew, *Go Forward with Faith,* 321; Goates, *Harold B. Lee,* 486–87.
7. Thompson, *Stand as a Witness,* 211; Kapp, Oral History Interview, 80; Kapp, Journal, Nov. 7, 1972. **Topic: Ardeth G. Kapp**
8. Kapp, Oral History Interview, 80; Thompson, *Stand as a Witness,* 204–11.
9. Kapp, Oral History Interview, 80–81; Thompson, *Stand as a Witness,* 211; Kapp, Journal, Nov. 7, 1972.
10. Kapp, Oral History Interview, 81; Thompson, *Stand as a Witness,* 43–46, 64–67, 70–71, 127–31, 153–57, 167–71; Karen Thomas Arnesen, "Ardeth Greene Kapp: A Prairie Girl, a Young Woman Still," *Ensign,* Sept. 1985, 35, 38; Kapp, *My Neighbor, My Sister, My Friend,* 122–23; Doctrine and Covenants 9:9.
11. Kapp, Oral History Interview, 81; Thompson, *Stand as a Witness,* 211; Funk, "Ruth, Come Walk with Me," 122; "2 Priesthood-Oriented MIAs," *Church News,* Nov. 11, 1972, 3, 8–9. **Topics: Young Men Organizations; Young Women Organizations**
12. Kapp, Oral History Interview, 81; Thompson, *Stand as a Witness,* 211–12.
13. Kapp, Oral History Interview, 81; Thompson, *Stand as a Witness,* 212–13; "Moving Days Are Near," *Church News,* Aug. 5, 1972, 4. **Topics: Church Callings; Church Headquarters**
14. Kapp, Oral History Interview, 81; Thompson, *Stand as a Witness,* 212; "2 Priesthood-Oriented MIAs," *Church News,* Nov. 11, 1972, 3, 8–9; Romney, "History of the Correlation of L.D.S. Church Auxiliaries," [J3]; First Presidency to Regional

Representatives of the Twelve and others, Nov. 9, 1972, First Presidency, Circular Letters, CHL.
15. "2 Priesthood-Oriented MIAs," *Church News,* Nov. 11, 1972, 3; *Mission MIA Manual,* 69, 74, 84; Stephen W. Gibson, "New Bishop's Youth Council," *Church News,* May 3, 1969, 4; Victor L. Brown, "The Aaronic Priesthood MIA," *Ensign,* July 1973, 83; Pulsipher, *Ruth Hardy Funk,* 137.
16. Peterson and Gaunt, *Keepers of the Flame,* 112; Pulsipher, *Ruth Hardy Funk,* 135.
17. Kapp, Oral History Interview, 85; Kapp, Journal, Nov. 24 and Dec. 9, 1972; 1 Nephi 3:7.
18. Martins, *Autobiography of Elder Helvécio Martins,* 56–58. **Topic: Priesthood and Temple Restriction**
19. Martins, *Autobiography of Elder Helvécio Martins,* 53–54, 56–57; Rio de Janeiro Brazil Stake, Manuscript History and Historical Reports, Dec. 31, 1972; Shields, "Rio de Janeiro's Journey to Become a Center of Strength for the LDS Church," 108; *Deseret News 1989–90 Church Almanac,* 227–33; Martins, Martins, and Martins, Oral History Interview, 11–12. **Topic: Wards and Stakes**
20. Martins, *Autobiography of Elder Helvécio Martins,* 54.
21. Martins, *Autobiography of Elder Helvécio Martins,* 46, 51–52; Martins and Martins, Oral History Interview, 11, 18–19.
22. Martins, *Autobiography of Elder Helvécio Martins,* 47–48.
23. Martins, *Autobiography of Elder Helvécio Martins,* 61.
24. Martins, Martins, and Martins, Oral History Interview, 1, 13, 15–16; Rio de Janeiro Brazil Stake, Manuscript History and Historical Reports, Dec. 31, 1972, and Feb. 22, 1975; Martins, *Autobiography of Elder Helvécio Martins,* 63–64; Marcus Martins to Jed Woodworth, Email, June 20, 2022, copy in editors' possession. **Topic: Patriarchal Blessings**
25. Spencer W. Kimball, Journal, Jan. 6–7, 1961; Mar. 28, 1961; Dec. 25, 1973; Mangal Dan Dipty and John Santosh Murala, "My Journey as a Pioneer from India," *Ensign,* July 2016, 66–69; Mack, *Autobiography of Olive Beth Kimball Mack,* 83; Kimball and Kimball, *Spencer W. Kimball,* 1–2.
26. Haycock, Personal History, 67–69; Spencer W. Kimball, Journal, Dec. 26, 1973; Goates, *Harold B. Lee,* 581. **Topics: Harold B. Lee; Spencer W. Kimball**
27. Haycock, Personal History, 68–69; Gerry Avant, "Camilla Kimball Feels Mantle of Responsibility," *Church News,* Jan. 6, 1979, 6; Spencer W. Kimball, Journal, Dec. 26, 1973; Goates, *Harold B. Lee,* 579.
28. Haycock, Personal History, 69, 71; Spencer W. Kimball, Journal, Dec. 26, 1973; Romney, Journal, Dec. 26–27, 1973; Kimball, *Lengthen Your Stride,* 5; Goates, *Harold B. Lee,* 576, 580.
29. Kimball, *Lengthen Your Stride,* 5; Haycock, Personal History, 69–70; Spencer W. Kimball, Journal, Dec. 26, 1973; Edward L. Kimball, Notes, Dec. 26, 1973, Edward L. Kimball Papers, CHL.

Chapter 16: Just This Day

1. Maeta Beck and Dennis Beck, Oral History Interview, 29–33, 47, 88, 123–24; Shumway and Shumway, *Blossoming,* 98; "BYU 'Lamanite Generation' a Big Hit on Florida Tour," *Church News,* Jan. 8, 1972, 4. **Topic: Broadcast Media**
2. Beck, Journal, Dec. 17, 1973; Maeta Beck and Dennis Beck, Oral History Interview, 74–76, 80–83, 93–94, 100–101; Shumway and Shumway, *Blossoming,* 99–100.
3. Beck, Journal, Dec. 17, 1973; Shumway and Shumway, *Blossoming,* 99–100; Maeta Beck and Dennis Beck, Oral History Interview, 124.
4. Maeta Beck and Dennis Beck, Oral History Interview, 45–46, 73–74, 101–5, 124; Beck, Journal, Oct. 28, 1974.

5. Maeta Beck and Dennis Beck, Oral History Interview, 39–45, 109–10, 125; Shumway and Shumway, *Blossoming,* 100. Quotation edited for readability; original source has "She told me that they spent a lot of time on their knees, praying for me that I would make the right choices."
6. Maeta Beck and Dennis Beck, Oral History Interview, 39–41, 44, 76, 124, 137–38.
7. Spafford, "My Feeling upon Being Released as President of Relief Society," [1]–[3]; Derr, Cannon, and Beecher, *Women of Covenant,* 307, 347. **Topic: Belle S. Spafford**
8. Tanner, Journal, May 6, 1971; "Willis Earl Spafford," *Deseret News and Salt Lake Telegram,* Jan. 28, 1963, A14; "Mary S. Kemp," *Salt Lake Tribune,* Mar. 30, 1964, 26; "Relief Society Leader Dies at 86," *Salt Lake Tribune,* Feb. 4, 1982, B3.
9. *Saints,* volume 3, chapter 32; Derr, Cannon, and Beecher, *Women of Covenant,* 305–46; Relief Society, General Board Minutes, volume 35, Jan. 6, 1965, 208; volume 36, Mar. 23 and Nov. 16, 1966, 45–46, 153; Hangen, "Guide to a Generation," 83; Spafford, Oral History Interview, 67–73.
10. Relief Society, General Board Minutes, volume 36, Mar. 23, 1966, 45; volume 37, May 22, 1968, 117; volume 39, Feb. 10, 1971, 151–52; Mar. 24, 1971, 181–82; volume 41, Apr. 4, 1973, 133–34; Marion G. Romney and Boyd K. Packer to the First Presidency and Council of the Twelve, Mar. 5, 1971; Relief Society General Presidency to Marion G. Romney and Boyd K. Packer, Mar. 31, 1971, in Relief Society, General Board Minutes, volume 39, Mar. 31, 1971, 192A–92B; "Statement of Financial Condition of Relief Society," Aug. 31, 1971, Relief Society, General Board Minutes, volume 39, 286; Derr, Cannon, and Beecher, *Women of Covenant,* 345; *Handbook of Instructions of the Relief Society,* 43–44. **Topic: Relief Society**
11. Spafford, "My Feeling upon Being Released as President of Relief Society," [3].
12. Derr, Cannon, and Beecher, *Women of Covenant,* 347–48; Spruill, *Divided We Stand,* 14–41; Hartmann, *From Margin to Mainstream,* 48–106; Bruley, "Origins of the Women's Liberation Movement in 1960s Britain," 67–78; "Educator Sees Rebuff to Equality Bill as 'Humiliating Mistake,'" *Salt Lake Tribune,* Apr. 22, 1973, B1. **Topic: Equal Rights Amendment**
13. Public Communications Department, General Authority Advisers Minutes, May 29 and July 16, 1974; Belle S. Spafford, "The American Woman's Movement," July 12, 1974, First Presidency, General Correspondence, CHL; "Happy Homemakers Still Abound in Liberated World," *Democrat and Chronicle* (Rochester, NY), Aug. 20, 1974, C5.
14. Spafford, "My Feeling upon Being Released as President of Relief Society," [3].
15. Johnson, "History of The Church of Jesus Christ of Latter-day Saints in Ghana," [2]–[3]; Joseph Johnson, Oral History Interview [1988], 20–21; Joseph Johnson, Oral History Interview [1998], 6; Joseph Johnson to First Presidency, Sept. 9, 1978, International Mission Files, CHL.
16. Johnson, "History of The Church of Jesus Christ of Latter-day Saints in Ghana," [3]; Joseph Johnson, Oral History Interview [1988], 26; Joseph Johnson, Oral History Interview [1998], 6.
17. Joseph Johnson, Oral History Interview [1988], 21; Joseph Johnson, Oral History Interview [1998], 6.
18. "Girls Fill Home with Music, Love," *Church News,* Nov. 23, 1974, 14; Bronson, Oral History Interview, 12–14, 45, 48–49, 53–54, 57–58, 66–69, 88–89, 101; Hwang, "Hwang Keun Ok," 293; Shirleen Meek Saunders, "Whang Keun-Ok: Caring for Korea's Children," *Ensign,* Oct. 1993, 48–49. **Topic: Family Home Evening**
19. "Girls Fill Home with Music, Love," *Church News,* Nov. 23, 1974, 14; Till, Till, and Munoa, Oral History Interview, 4, 31; Greg Hill, "Singing Elders Took Korea by Storm," *Church News,* Nov. 29, 2008, 6; Gunter, Oral History Interview, 5–6; "First Institute Building Under Way in Korea," *Church News,* Aug. 23, 1975, 14; Bronson, Oral History Interview, 50–51; Eugene Till to Stan Bronson, Oct. 15, 1975, Stanley Bronson, Tender Apples Collection, CHL; Hinckley, Journal, June 8, 1973. **Topic: South Korea**

20. Eugene Till to First Presidency, June 30, 1977, First Presidency, Mission Correspondence, 1964–2010, CHL; Choi, "History of The Church of Jesus Christ of Latter-day Saints in Korea," 196–97; Till, Till, and Munoa, Oral History Interview, 4–5.
21. Till, Till, and Munoa, Oral History Interview, 4–8, 29–31; Davenport, Oral History Interview, 1–2, 6, 7–11; Osmond and Romanowski, *Life Is Just What You Make It*, 127–29; Osmond and Osmond, Oral History Interview, 12–18, 26; see also Dunn, *Osmonds*, 190–96, 239–46.
22. Till, Till, and Munoa, Oral History Interview, 4–7, 29–30; Davenport, Oral History Interview, 1–2, 6, 7–11; Wilberg, Oral History Interview, 2; Gunter, Oral History Interview, 1–2, 4–5; Korea Seoul Mission, Historical Records, Sept. 13, 21–24, and 28, 1974, [7]–[8].
23. Till, Till, and Munoa, Oral History Interview, 7–10; Bronson, Oral History Interview, 67; Hwang, "Hwang Keun Ok," 293–94; Gunter, Oral History Interview, 7, 11, 13; Davenport, Oral History Interview, 6–12; Wilberg, Oral History Interview, 2, 5–7.
24. Till, Till, and Munoa, Oral History Interview, 7–8, 11–12, 18–19; Davenport, Oral History Interview, 8–12; Gunter, Oral History Interview, 6, 16–17.
25. Till, Till, and Munoa, Oral History Interview, 11; Greg Hill, "Singing Elders Took Korea by Storm," *Church News*, Nov. 29, 2008, 6; Eugene Till to First Presidency, June 30, 1977, First Presidency, Mission Correspondence, 1964–2010, CHL; Bronson, Oral History Interview, 13–14; Shirleen Meek Saunders, "Whang Keun-Ok: Caring for Korea's Children," *Ensign*, Oct. 1993, 48–49; Davenport, Oral History Interview, 8–9, 13; Gunter, Oral History Interview, 6. **Topic: Globalization**
26. Monson, Journal, Mar. 27, 1975; Robert Barker to Victor Wolf, Dec. 10, 1974; First Presidency to Henry Burkhardt, Apr. 21, 1971, First Presidency, Mission Correspondence, 1964–2010, CHL; Kuehne, *Henry Burkhardt*, 68–72, 78–79. **Topic: General Conference**
27. Robert Barker to Kent Brown, Mar. 7, 1972; Robert Barker to Steven Vitale, Nov. 1, 1972; Robert Barker to Chief of the Consular Section, Oct. 13, 1973; Robert Barker to Henry Burkhardt, Feb. 18, 1975, First Presidency, Mission Correspondence, 1964–2010, CHL; Monson, Journal, Mar. 27, 1975; Kuehne, *Henry Burkhardt*, 69–72.
28. Spencer W. Kimball, "Why Call Me Lord, Lord, and Do Not the Things Which I Say?," *Ensign*, May 1975, 4–7; Kimball and Kimball, *Spencer W. Kimball*, 416–20; J M. Heslop, "Stockholm: 'Burning Memory,'" *Church News*, Aug. 24, 1974, 3; J M. Heslop, "Area Conference in Brazil," *Church News*, Mar. 8, 1975, 3; Hunter, Journal, Jan. 9, 1975; Kapp, Journal, Oct. 19, 1974; J M. Heslop, "Missionary Effort—'Lengthen Our Stride,'" *Church News*, Oct. 19, 1974, 3, 10. **Topic: Spencer W. Kimball**
29. *Saints*, volume 3, chapter 39; Kuehne, *Henry Burkhardt*, chapter 5.
30. Burkhardt, Oral History Interview [1991], 21–22; Monson, Journal, Oct. 9, 1982; Burkhardt, Journal, July 17, 1975; Mehr, "Enduring Believers," 150; Kuehne, *Mormons as Citizens of a Communist State*, 104; First Presidency to Henry Burkhardt and Charles Broberg, Apr. 24, 1972, First Presidency, Mission Correspondence, 1964–2010, CHL. **Topics: Cold War; Czech Republic; Germany; Hungary; Poland; Slovakia**
31. Kuehne, *Henry Burkhardt*, 79–82.
32. Nguyen and Hughes, *When Faith Endures*, 1, 5–7. Quotation edited for accuracy; instead of "The," original source has the phonetic spelling "Tay."
33. Nguyen and Hughes, *When Faith Endures*, 5; Britsch, *From the East*, 429–31.
34. Kiernan, *Việt Nam*, 385–91, 395–451; Taylor, *History of the Vietnamese*, 446–47, 478–83, 536–619.
35. Nguyen and Hughes, *When Faith Endures*, 1, 6, 119; Britsch, *From the East*, 435–37.
36. Nguyen and Hughes, *When Faith Endures*, 1, 7, 11.
37. Nguyen and Hughes, *When Faith Endures*, 7, 14–17.
38. Nguyen and Hughes, *When Faith Endures*, 6, 10, 17–18, 127–28; "Saigon Branch Evacuation List," May 13, 1975, First Presidency, General Correspondence, CHL; Le, Oral History Interview, 1–3.

39. Nguyen and Hughes, *When Faith Endures*, 8, 128–33, 136–37; Nguyen, "Escape from Vietnam," 29.
40. "Saigon Branch Evacuation List," May 13, 1975, First Presidency, General Correspondence, CHL; Le, Oral History Interview, 3, 19, 31–32; Ferren Christensen, Address, Newport Beach California Stake, Stake Conference, May 4, 1975, [00:13:40]–[00:18:14], [00:31:03]–[00:31:42]; Jack E. Jarrard, "To Help Viet Refugees: Church Members Open Their Hearts," *Church News*, May 17, 1975, 4; Spencer W. Kimball, Journal, May 3, 1975.
41. Le, Oral History Interview, 2–3, 10, 16, 21, 27.
42. Le, Oral History Interview, 9–12; Jack E. Jarrard, "A New Home in America," *Church News*, May 31, 1975, 5; Jack E. Jarrard, "To Help Viet Refugees: Church Members Open Their Hearts," *Church News*, May 17, 1975, 4, 10; Ferren Christensen to Spencer W. Kimball, May 9, 1975, Welfare Services Department, Vietnamese Refugee Files, CHL.
43. Le, Oral History Interview, 3–5, 9–10, 16–19; Nguyen and Hughes, *When Faith Endures*, 236.
44. Le, Oral History Interview, 5–6, 10, 13–15, 23.
45. Le, Oral History Interview, 14, 22, 25–28, 39; Nguyen and Hughes, *When Faith Endures*, 151–52; "Saigon Branch Evacuation List," May 13, 1975, First Presidency, General Correspondence, CHL; Jack E. Jarrard, "Viet Mormons Arrive in U.S.," *Church News*, May 10, 1975, 3, 13.
46. Le, Oral History Interview, 23.

Chapter 17: No Going Back

1. Footage of events at BYU Founders Day, Oct. 10, 1975, 16 mm film, rolls 25–26, [00:12:02]–[00:15:40], Historical Department, Church in Action Footage Collection, CHL; Dorothy O. Rea, "Bells Toll Second Century at Y," *Deseret News*, Oct. 10, 1975, B1; Dan Croft, "BYU Bell Tower Dedicated as Part of Founder's Day," *Provo (UT) Daily Herald*, Oct. 10, 1975, 1; Lynne Hollstein, "Celebration Marks 100 Years at BYU," *Church News*, Oct. 18, 1975, 3; Wilkinson, Diary, Oct. 10, 1975.
2. "Church Divests Self of Hospitals," *Church News*, Sept. 14, 1974, 3; "Athletic Program Changed for Greater Participation," *Church News*, June 26, 1971, 10; "June Conferences to End, Pres. Kimball Tells Session," *Church News*, June 28, 1975, 3; Kapp, Journal, Sept. 7, 1974; June 4 and 13, 1975; *Deseret News 1976 Church Almanac*, A7–A8. **Topics: Church Growth; Globalization**
3. *Deseret News 1976 Church Almanac*, A9–A10; Kimball and Kimball, *Spencer W. Kimball*, 343–44; Spencer W. Kimball, Journal, Apr. 4, 1974; Spencer W. Kimball, Address, Regional Representatives Seminar, Apr. 4, 1974, 11–15, Quorum of the Twelve Apostles, Regional Representatives Seminar Addresses, CHL. **Topic: Growth of Missionary Work**
4. Hunter, Journal, Oct. 31, 1974; *Deseret News 1976 Church Almanac*, A5, A9; Spencer W. Kimball, "The Time to Labor Is Now," *Ensign*, Nov. 1975, 4; Doctrine and Covenants 107:38; "Quorum of the Twelve Items of Discussion," Dec. 14, 1977, 3, Gordon B. Hinckley, First Presidency and General Authority Correspondence, Auxiliaries, Miscellaneous, CHL. **Topics: Adjustments to Priesthood Organization; Quorums of the Seventy**
5. Brigham Young University, Board of Trustees Minutes, Oct. 9, 1975, 2–5; Karen J. Winkler, "Brigham Young University Challenges Parts of Bias Law," *Chronicle of Higher Education*, Oct. 28, 1975, 1, 10; Turley, *In the Hands of the Lord*, 140–42; Wilkinson, *Brigham Young University*, 4:4–27, 79–137, 245–75, 298–305; First Presidency to Neal A. Maxwell and Dallin H. Oaks, May 14, 1973, First Presidency, General Correspondence, CHL; Board of Education, Church Board of Education Meeting Minutes, Apr. 7, 1971, 7–8; Jan. 5, 1972, 9–10. **Topic: Church Universities**

6. Lynne Hollstein, "Celebration Marks 100 Years at BYU," *Church News,* Oct. 18, 1975, 3; Wilkinson, Diary, Oct. 10, 1975; Kimball, *Second Century Address,* 1–3, 9–11. Quotation edited for readability; "that there are yet" in original changed to "there are yet."
7. Joseph Johnson, Oral History Interview [1988], 38, 99; Joseph Johnson, Oral History Interview [1998], 7, 31–32; Joseph Johnson, Oral History Interview [2005], 6; Imbrah, Oral History Interview, 40–42; William Bangerter to Spencer W. Kimball, May 27, 1976, Spencer W. Kimball, Headquarters Correspondence and Subject Files, CHL; Cannon and Bateman, "Report of a Visit to Ghana and Nigeria," 8.
8. Joseph Johnson, Oral History Interview [1988], 38; Joseph Johnson, Oral History Interview [1998], 31; Joseph Johnson, Oral History Interview [2005], 6; Imbrah, Oral History Interview, 42. Quotation edited for readability; "will" added to original.
9. Joseph Johnson, Oral History Interview [1988], 38–40; Joseph Johnson, Oral History Interview [1998], 31.
10. Joseph Johnson, Oral History Interview [1988], 38–39.
11. Joseph Johnson, Oral History Interview [1988], 39; Joseph Johnson, Oral History Interview [1998], 7, 31.
12. Joseph Johnson, Oral History Interview [1988], 40–41, 99–101; Joseph Johnson, Oral History Interview [1998], 31; Joseph Johnson, Oral History Interview [2005], 7.
13. Joseph Johnson, Oral History Interview [1998], 7. Quotation edited for readability; "take" in original changed to "takes."
14. Joseph Johnson, Oral History Interview [2005], 7–8.
15. Anthony Obinna to Spencer W. Kimball, Aug. 3, 1976, First Presidency, General Correspondence, CHL.
16. Anthony Obinna to Spencer W. Kimball, Aug. 3, 1976, First Presidency, General Correspondence, CHL; LaMar Williams to Anthony Obinna, June 11, 1974, Missionary Department, Africa and India Correspondence, CHL.
17. Kalu Oku and others to Lorry Rytting and Gloria Rytting, June 14, 1975; Lorry Rytting to William Bangerter, Aug. 4, 1975, Edwin Q. Cannon Collection, CHL; Lorry Rytting to "Friends and Brothers in Christ," Aug. 15, 1975, Ted and Janath Cannon Mission Papers, CHL; Lorry Rytting to Carlos E. Asay, Aug. 10, 1982, International Mission Files, CHL.
18. Anthony Obinna to Spencer W. Kimball, Aug. 3, 1976, First Presidency, General Correspondence, CHL.
19. William Bangerter to Anthony Obinna, Sept. 24, 1976, International Mission Files, CHL; "Mission Organized to Aid 'Unattached,'" *Church News,* Dec. 16, 1972, 4, 6; "International Mission Continues to Reach Out," *Ensign,* July 1976, 77.
20. Anthony Obinna, Oral History Interview, 24. Quotation edited for readability; "they were" in original changed to "are you."
21. Anthony Obinna, Oral History Interview, 22–24; Anthony Obinna to William Bangerter, Oct. 9, 1976, Edwin Q. Cannon Correspondence, CHL.
22. Anthony Obinna to William Bangerter, Jan. 25, 1977, International Mission Files, CHL.
23. Louisiana Baton Rouge Mission, Manuscript History and Historical Reports, Dec. 31, 1976, [71]; Warren, Oral History Interview, 3; Embry, *Black Saints in a White Church,* 54. Quotation edited for readability; "was" in original changed to "is."
24. Louisiana Baton Rouge Mission, Manuscript History and Historical Reports, Dec. 31, 1976, [71]; Warren, Oral History Interview, 3–4; Roger W. Carpenter, "13 of Convert's Relatives Join Church," *Church News,* Feb. 17, 1979, 13.
25. Warren, Oral History Interview, 5, 10–11.
26. Warren, Oral History Interview, 5; *Missionary Handbook,* 34–35; McKay, Diary, Feb. 26, 1964.
27. Warren, Oral History Interview, 5–6.
28. Warren, Oral History Interview, 6, 15.
29. Nguyen and Hughes, *When Faith Endures,* 158–60, 163, 184, 190. Quotation edited for readability; original source has "LIEN AND FAMILY FINE WITH CHURCH."
30. Nguyen and Hughes, *When Faith Endures,* 33–35, 53, 58–67, 154–62, 171, 174, 180–81, 189–90; Vo, *Bamboo Gulag,* 1–2, 53–92.

31. Nguyen and Hughes, *When Faith Endures*, 160–62, 165–73, 177; Vo, *Bamboo Gulag*, 62–63, 72, 77, 117–26.
32. Nguyen and Hughes, *When Faith Endures*, 162, 168–69, 174–75; Vo, *Bamboo Gulag*, 143–46, 151–56.
33. Nguyen and Hughes, *When Faith Endures*, 162, 176–79.
34. Nguyen and Hughes, *When Faith Endures*, 189. Quotation edited for readability; "would" in original changed to "will."
35. Nguyen and Hughes, *When Faith Endures*, 190–91.
36. Nguyen and Hughes, *When Faith Endures*, 193–94.

Chapter 18: All the Blessings of the Gospel

1. Martins, *Autobiography of Elder Helvécio Martins*, 59, 64–65; Spencer W. Kimball, Journal, Mar. 9, 1977; Romney, Journal, Mar. 9, 1977; Dell Van Orden, "Sao Paulo Temple Cornerstone Laid by President Romney," *Church News*, Mar. 19, 1977, 3, 8–9.
2. Martins, *Autobiography of Elder Helvécio Martins*, 47, 59–60. **Topic: Public Relations**
3. Martins, *Autobiography of Elder Helvécio Martins*, 64; Dell Van Orden, "Sao Paulo Temple Cornerstone Laid by President Romney," *Church News*, Mar. 19, 1977, 3; Dell Van Orden, Cornerstone Ceremony, Mar. 9, 1977, Photograph, in *Church News*, Mar. 19, 1977, 1; Faust, Oral History Interview, 15, 18–19.
4. Alan Blodgett to James E. Faust, Aug. 14, 1975, First Presidency, General Correspondence, CHL; Faust, Oral History Interview, 13–14; William Bangerter to Spencer W. Kimball, Nov. 16, 1977; First Presidency to James E. Faust, July 9, 1975, First Presidency, General Correspondence, CHL; Martins, Oral History Interview, 22. **Topic: South Africa**
5. Martins, *Autobiography of Elder Helvécio Martins*, 64; Martins, Oral History Interview, 23; Martins and Martins, Oral History Interview, 28–29; Martins, Martins, and Martins, Oral History Interview, 42.
6. Martins, *Autobiography of Elder Helvécio Martins*, 65–66; Martins and Martins, Oral History Interview, 28; Helvécio Martins, Interview, *Friend*, Jan. 1992, 7; Jack E. Jarrard, "Church Growth Is 'Solid' in So. America," *Church News*, Jan. 22, 1977, 4.
7. Martins, *Autobiography of Elder Helvécio Martins*, 66.
8. Kuehne, *Henry Burkhardt*, 80–82; Burkhardt, Journal, Oct. 27, 1977; German Democratic Republic Dresden Mission, Historical Record, Aug. 16 and 24, 1977; Henry Burkhardt to An alle Distrikt und Gemeindepräsidenten in der Mission, Aug. 17, 1977, in German Democratic Republic Dresden Mission, Historical Record, CHL; Burkhardt, Oral History Interview [1991], 15.
9. Kuehne, *Henry Burkhardt*, 82–83; Burkhardt, Journal, Oct. 27, 1977; German Democratic Republic Dresden Mission, Historical Record, Aug. 16 and 24, 1977; Burkhardt, Oral History Interview [1991], 15–16; Kennedy, Journal, Aug. 13–25, 1977; LaVarr G. Webb, "Pres. Kimball Ends Tour of 7 Countries," *Church News*, Sept. 3, 1977, 3.
10. Burkhardt, Oral History Interview [1991], 15; Benson, Journal, Apr. 12, 1972; Ezra Taft Benson to Harold B. Lee and N. Eldon Tanner, Apr. 11, 1962 [1972], in Benson, Journal, Apr. 19, 1972; Kuehne, *Henry Burkhardt*, 70; Lee, Diary, Apr. 8–9, 1972.
11. Burkhardt, Oral History Interview [1991], 15; Kuehne, *Henry Burkhardt*, 82; Articles of Faith 1:12; Kennedy, Journal, Aug. 24, 1977.
12. Burkhardt, Oral History Interview [1991], 15; Kuehne, *Henry Burkhardt*, 82–83.
13. Kuehne, *Henry Burkhardt*, 83, 89–90; Burkhardt, Oral History Interview [1991], 9, 12; Kennedy, Journal, July 20 and Aug. 28, 1978; see also Ortlieb and Ortlieb, "Political Isolation," 203–4.
14. Peterson, Journal, May 8–12, 1978; Burkhardt, "Wie kam es zum Bau des Freiberger [Freiberg] Tempels?," 2; Burkhardt, Oral History Interview [1991], 9. **Topic: Temple Endowment**

15. Burkhardt, Oral History Interview [1991], 9; Kuehne, *Henry Burkhardt,* 89–90; Burkhardt, "Wie kam es zum Bau des Freiberger [Freiberg] Tempels?," 3.
16. Burkhardt, Oral History Interview [1991], 6–7, 9, 15–17; Monson, Journal, Aug. 25, 1978; Peterson, Journal, May 8–12, 1978; Burkhardt, "Wie kam es zum Bau des Freiberger [Freiberg] Tempels?," 3–4; Kuehne, *Henry Burkhardt,* 90. Quotation edited for clarity; "there" in original changed to "here."
17. Burkhardt, "Wie kam es zum Bau des Freiberger [Freiberg] Tempels?," 3; Kuehne, *Henry Burkhardt,* 79–81, 90; Burkhardt, Oral History Interview [1991], 9–10.
18. "Women Garnered Massive Share of Headlines in 1976," *Hartford (CT) Courant,* Jan. 1, 1977, 8; Spruill, *Divided We Stand,* 1–3, 140–88; Young, "Mormon Church, LDS Women, and the Defeat of the Equal Rights Amendment," 632–35; Public Communications Department, General Authority Advisers Minutes, Feb. 1, 1977; Apr. 19, 1977; May 3 and 31, 1977; Oct. 25, 1977; "First Presidency Opposes ERA," *Church News,* Oct. 30, 1976, 2. **Topic: Equal Rights Amendment**
19. Smith, "Rights of Women," 1–9; Smith, "ERA—A Family Concern," 1–25; Boyd K. Packer, "The Equal Rights Amendment," *Ensign,* Mar. 1977, 6–9; "First Presidency Opposes ERA," *Church News,* Oct. 30, 1976, 2; "A Mormon Tells Why She Opposes ERA," *Washington (DC) Star,* May 11, 1976, A1, A6.
20. "Official Statement on Abortion," *Church News,* June 5, 1976, 3; Dell Van Orden, "Cornerstone Laid by President Romney," *Church News,* Mar. 19, 1977, 9; Kapp, Journal, Nov. 22, 1977. The Church also condemned incest and later added it and severe fetal defects to the list of possible exceptions. (First Presidency to All Stake Presidents, Jan. 15, 1976; "1991 Supplement to the 1989 General Handbook of Instructions," 1, in First Presidency to General Authorities and others, Oct. 1, 1991, First Presidency, Circular Letters, CHL.)
21. "First Presidency Opposes ERA," *Church News,* Oct. 30, 1976, 2; "A Mormon Tells Why She Opposes ERA," *Washington (DC) Star,* May 11, 1976, A1, A6; Smith, "Rights of Women," 5–7, 9; Smith, "ERA—A Family Concern," 24.
22. "IWY-Parley Involvement Urged," *Church News,* June 18, 1977, 5; Spencer W. Kimball, "The Foundations of Righteousness," *Ensign,* Nov. 1977, 6; Bradley, *Pedestals and Podiums,* 175–76; First Presidency to All Stake, Mission, and District Presidents in the United States, Apr. 9, 1976, First Presidency, Circular Letters, CHL; Pulsipher, *Ruth Hardy Funk,* 170–73; Funk, Interview, [6].
23. Colton, "My Personal Rubicon," 101–2; Public Communications Department, General Authority Advisers Minutes, Oct. 25, 1977; Spruill, *Divided We Stand,* 1–3.
24. Public Communications Department, General Authority Advisers Minutes, Oct. 25, 1977.
25. Colton, "My Personal Rubicon," 101–2. Quotation edited for readability; "I should explain" in original changed to "you should explain."
26. Colton, "My Personal Rubicon," 102; Colton, Memoir Excerpt, no date; Roderick, *For Time and All Eternity,* 232–33.
27. Colton, "My Personal Rubicon," 102; Doctrine and Covenants 100:5.
28. Colton, "My Personal Rubicon," 101–3; Public Communications Department, General Authority Advisers Minutes, Nov. 1, 1977; Eleanor Ricks Colton, "A Mormon Woman Looks at the ERA," *Washington Post,* Nov. 21, 1977, A19; "Trouble at Women's Meet: Abzug," *Daily Herald* (Arlington Heights, IL), Oct. 27, 1977, section 1, 9; Spruill, *Divided We Stand,* 117–25, 208.
29. Colton, "My Personal Rubicon," 103; Eleanor Ricks Colton, "A Mormon Woman Looks at the ERA," *Washington Post,* Nov. 21, 1977, A19, emphasis in original. Quotation edited for readability; original source has "if I'm not for ERA."
30. Le, Oral History Interview, 31, 56, 58–59; Nguyen and Hughes, *When Faith Endures,* 219.
31. Victor Brown to Spencer W. Kimball, Sept. 25, 1975, Spencer W. Kimball, Headquarters Correspondence and Subject Files, CHL; "Viet Refugee Processing Is Completed," *Church News,* Oct. 18, 1975, 12; Le, Oral History Interview, 36, 42, 46; Obituary for Philip Flammer, *Salt Lake Tribune,* Aug. 22, 1999, C11.
32. Le, Oral History Interview, 29, 48–49.

33. Le, Oral History Interview, 46–49.
34. Le, Oral History Interview, 45, 51–52, 55.
35. Le, Oral History Interview, 51–53.
36. Le, Oral History Interview, 45, 52–54; Nguyen and Hughes, *When Faith Endures*, 195–98, 203–13.
37. Le, Oral History Interview, 45, 53–54, 56, 59, 62–63.
38. Le, Oral History Interview, 57, 59–62.
39. Nguyen and Hughes, *When Faith Endures*, 220.
40. Gibbons, *Spencer W. Kimball*, 292–93, 295; Kimball, *Lengthen Your Stride*, 216–18; Kimball, Interview, 2, 5; Mauss, *All Abraham's Children*, 235; Romney, Interview, June 12, 1978; Perry, *L. Tom Perry*, 79–80. **Topic: Priesthood and Temple Restriction**
41. Kimball, *Lengthen Your Stride*, 216–17; Kimball, Interview, 4; Gibbons, *Spencer W. Kimball*, 292; Doctrine and Covenants 65:2; Daniel 2:31–45; Moses 7:62; "'News' Interviews Prophet," *Church News*, Jan. 6, 1979, 4; Dell Van Orden, "Door to China May Be Opening," *Church News*, Apr. 7, 1979, 3.
42. Kimball, *Lengthen Your Stride*, 216–19; Kimball, Interview, 4; Talmage, *House of the Lord*, 192–94; Spencer W. Kimball, Address, South African Mission, Oct. 23, 1978, South Africa Johannesburg Mission, Conference Recordings, CHL.
43. Romney, Journal, Mar. 9, 1978; Gibbons and McConkie, Interview, [3]; Hunter, Journal, June 1, 1978.
44. Hunter, Journal, Mar. 14 and June 1, 1978; Kimball, "Spencer W. Kimball and the Revelation on Priesthood," 46, 49; Benson, Journal, June 9, 1978; McConkie, "Receipt of the Revelation Offering the Priesthood to Worthy Men of All Races and Colors," [2]; Gibbons, *Spencer W. Kimball*, 293–95.
45. Kimball, Interview, 1–2; Kimball, *Lengthen Your Stride*, 218; Kimball, "Spencer W. Kimball and the Revelation on Priesthood," 46, 49–50, 54; Gibbons, *Spencer W. Kimball*, 294.
46. Kimball, *Lengthen Your Stride*, 217, 220–21; "'News' Interviews Prophet," *Church News*, Jan. 6, 1979, 4.
47. McConkie, "Receipt of the Revelation Offering the Priesthood to Worthy Men of All Races and Colors," [4]–[5]; Kimball, *Lengthen Your Stride*, 221; Hunter, Journal, June 1, 1978; Tanner, Journal, June 9, 1978.
48. Kimball, "Spencer W. Kimball and the Revelation on Priesthood," 56–58; Perry, *L. Tom Perry*, 80; Monson, Journal, June 1, 1978; McConkie, *Sermons and Writings of Bruce R. McConkie*, 159; McConkie, "Receipt of the Revelation Offering the Priesthood to Worthy Men of All Races and Colors," [5]; Tate, *David B. Haight*, 280.
49. Kimball, "Spencer W. Kimball and the Revelation on Priesthood," 56–59; McConkie, "Receipt of the Revelation Offering the Priesthood to Worthy Men of All Races and Colors," [5]–[7]; Benson, Journal, June 9, 1978; Ashton, Journal, June 1, 1978.
50. Perry, *L. Tom Perry*, 80; Kimball, "Spencer W. Kimball and the Revelation on Priesthood," 56–59; Perry, Journal, June [1], 1978; Romney, Journal, June 1, 1978.
51. Gordon B. Hinckley, "Priesthood Restoration," *Ensign*, Oct. 1988, 70. **Topic: Gordon B. Hinckley**
52. Benson, Journal, June 9, 1978. **Topic: Ezra Taft Benson**
53. Ashton, Journal, June 1, 1978.
54. McConkie, "New Revelation on Priesthood," 17–21.
55. Tanner, Journal, June 9, 1978.
56. Gray, Oral History Interview, 157–58.
57. Gray, Oral History Interview, 158–59.
58. "LDS Church Extends Priesthood to All Worthy Male Members," *Deseret News*, June 9, 1978, A1; Doctrine and Covenants, Official Declaration 2.
59. Gray, Oral History Interview, 159–60; Wolsey, "Funny Thing Happened to Me on the Road to the Millennium," 213–14.
60. Gray, Oral History Interview, 160; Wolsey, "Funny Thing Happened to Me on the Road to the Millennium," 214; Darius Gray to Edward Kimball, Email, June 16, 2000, 2–3, Edward L. Kimball Papers, CHL.

Chapter 19: United as a Family

1. Acquah and Acquah, Oral History Interview [2018], 16; E. Dale LeBaron, "Steadfast African Pioneer," *Ensign*, Dec. 1999, 49.
2. Acquah and Acquah, Oral History Interview [2018], 16; Joseph Johnson, Oral History Interview [1988], 22–23, 43–45. Quotation edited for readability; original source has "she came to me and said that very soon the missionaries would come, she said she had seen white men coming to our church, that they embraced us and joined us in worship."
3. E. Dale LeBaron, "Steadfast African Pioneer," *Ensign*, Dec. 1999, 49; Joseph Johnson, Oral History Interview [1988], 22–23; Kissi, *Walking in the Sand*, 28.
4. Johnson, Radio, images available at CHL; Joseph Johnson, Oral History Interview [1988], 43; E. Dale LeBaron, "Steadfast African Pioneer," *Ensign*, Dec. 1999, 49; Kissi, *Walking in the Sand*, 27–28; "Race and the Priesthood," Gospel Topics Essays, ChurchofJesusChrist.org/study/manual/gospel-topics-essays. **Topic: Ghana**
5. Kapp, Journal, June 9 and 12, 1978; "LDS Soon to Repudiate a Portion of Their Pearl of Great Price?," *Salt Lake Tribune*, July 23, 1978, A16; Spencer W. Kimball, Journal, June 11, 1978; Public Communications Department, General Authority Advisers Minutes, June 21, 1978; "Priesthood News Evokes Joy," *Church News*, June 17, 1978, 3–5; William Bangerter to Spencer W. Kimball, June 12, 1978, Spencer W. Kimball, Headquarters Correspondence and Subject Files, CHL; Kennedy, Journal, June 9, 1978. Quotation edited for readability; original source repeats "how thankful, how thankful."
6. Pulsipher, *Ruth Hardy Funk*, 174–75; Kapp, Journal, May 17, 1978; First Presidency to Ruth Funk, June 19, 1978, First Presidency, General Correspondence, CHL.
7. Kapp, Journal, June 18, 1978. **Topic: Ardeth G. Kapp**
8. Pulsipher, *Ruth Hardy Funk*, 174–76; Kapp, Oral History Interview, 91–96; Smith, Oral History Interview, 184–85.
9. Kapp, Oral History Interview, 96; J M. Heslop, "Priesthood to Direct Youth of the Church," *Church News*, June 29, 1974, 3; Romney, Journal, Apr. 25–26, 1974; May 30–31, 1974; June 6 and 23, 1974; Spencer W. Kimball, Journal, June 23, 1974; Kapp, Journal, June 5, 1974.
10. Kapp, Journal, Feb. 15, 1975; Nov. 22, 1975; Feb. 3, 1976; Apr. 8, 1976; June 13, 16, 19, and 25, 1976; Oct. 9, 1976; Nov. 27, 1976; Dec. 26, 1976; Jan. 23, 1977; Feb. 21, 1977; Dec. 26, 1977; Kapp, Oral History Interview, 91–92, 98–99, 106, 129, 154–55; Smith, Oral History Interview, 185–87; Funk, Interview, [4]; Pulsipher, *Ruth Hardy Funk*, 163.
11. Kapp, Oral History Interview, 128–29, 144–47; "Behold Thy Handmaiden," *Church News*, June 22, 1974, 8–9; "Love in Homes Stressed at June Conference Close," *Deseret News*, June 25, 1973, A7; "Excerpts from Talks Given at the 1973 Priesthood MIA June Conference," *New Era*, Nov. 1973, 9; "Young Women Possess Great Potential for Good," *Church News*, July 5, 1975, 4.
12. Kapp, Journal, Jan. 3, 1977; Mar. 30, 1977; Mar. 7, 1978; Young Women, General Board Minutes, Apr. 13, 1977, and Jan. 11, 1978; *My Personal Progress*, 4–11; Kapp, Oral History Interview, 146; Spencer W. Kimball, "The Angels May Quote from It," *New Era*, Oct. 1975, 4–5; Spencer W. Kimball, "We Need a Listening Ear," *Ensign*, Nov. 1979, 5.
13. Ardeth Greene Kapp, *Miracles in Pinafores and Bluejeans* (Salt Lake City: Deseret Book, 1977); Kapp, Journal, Mar. 30, 1977; Apr. 3, 1977; July 29, 1977; Kapp, Oral History Interview, 180–82. **Topic: Young Women Organizations**
14. Kapp, Journal, June 28, 1978; Black, "Monument to Women Memorial Garden," 189–211; Diane Cole, "LDS President Stresses Special Role of Women," *Salt Lake Tribune*, Sept. 17, 1978, B1; First Presidency to Stake Presidents and others, Apr. 30, 1976, First Presidency, Circular Letters, CHL; Gerry Avant, "Nauvoo Park Honors Women," *Church News*, July 8, 1978, 3.
15. First Presidency to Dean Larsen, June 21, 1978; Dean Larsen to First Presidency, June 27, 1978, First Presidency, General Correspondence, CHL; Kapp, Journal, July 12 and Aug. 1, 1978; Kapp, Oral History Interview, 110.

16. Kapp, Journal, July 16, 1978.
17. Kimball, "Uttermost Parts of the Earth," 4–5; Hunter, Journal, Sept. 29, 1978; "Statistical Report 1976," *Ensign,* May 1977, 18; "Statistical Report 1977," *Ensign,* May 1978, 17.
18. Spencer W. Kimball, "Hold Fast to the Iron Rod," *Ensign,* Nov. 1978, 4; "Mission Training Shifts to Provo," *Church News,* Sept. 9, 1978, 10; Golden Buchmiller, "Church Growth Measured for 5-Year Period," *Church News,* Jan. 6, 1979, 5; "Missionary Training Center Statistics," 1–6; Cowan, *Every Man Shall Hear,* 1:57, 105; "Sign Language in Spanish," *Church News,* July 8, 1978; Missionary Department, Annual Report, 1977, 38, First Presidency, General Correspondence, CHL.
19. Missionary Department, Annual Report, 1977, 38, First Presidency, General Correspondence, CHL; Kennedy, Journal, May 24, 1976; Feb. 1, 1977; May 30, 1977; Nov. 9, 1977; Dec. 23, 1977; Kimball, "Uttermost Parts of the Earth," 8; Gene R. Cook to John Hardy, May 14, 1974; First Presidency to David Kennedy, May 24, 1974; David Kennedy, Report, in Francis Gibbons to Ezra Taft Benson, Sept. 16, 1974, First Presidency, General Correspondence, CHL. **Topics: Church Growth; Globalization; Hungary; India; Poland; Portugal; Romania**
20. Kimball, "Uttermost Parts of the Earth," 3–11. Quotation edited for readability; "the Ivory Coast" and "the Sudan" in original changed to "Ivory Coast" and "Sudan."
21. N. Eldon Tanner, "Revelation on Priesthood Accepted, Church Officers Sustained," *Ensign,* Nov. 1978, 16; Faust, Journal, Sept. 30, 1978. **Topic: Common Consent**
22. Cannon and Cannon, *Together,* 161–62; Romney, Journal, Oct. 3, 1978; Kennedy, Journal, Oct. 3, 1978; Mabey and Allred, *Brother to Brother,* 17–18.
23. Martins, Martins, and Martins, Oral History Interview, 20–21.
24. Martins, *Autobiography of Elder Helvécio Martins,* 69–70; Marcus Martins to Jed Woodworth, email, Aug. 3, 2022, copy in editors' possession; Martins, Martins, and Martins, Oral History Interview, 21–22, 39, 43. **Topic: Sealing**
25. Martins, *Autobiography of Elder Helvécio Martins,* 70, 72–73; Martins, Martins, and Martins, Oral History Interview, 23–26, 30, 32–33; Martins, "Thirty Years after the 'Long-Promised Day,'" 80; Golden A. Buchmiller, "3 Black Members Called on Missions," *Church News,* Sept. 16, 1978, 5.
26. Cardall, "Glimpses of Prophets," 42; Dell Van Orden, "Sao Paulo Temple Dedicated," *Church News,* Nov. 4, 1978, 3; Martins, Martins, and Martins, Oral History Interview, 38; Martins, Journal, Nov. 2, 1978; Martins, *Autobiography of Elder Helvécio Martins,* 73. **Topic: Brazil**
27. Martins, *Autobiography of Elder Helvécio Martins,* 78–79; Martins, Martins, and Martins, Oral History Interview, 43–44; Martins, Oral History Interview, 23–24; Martins, Journal, Nov. 6, 1978.
28. Warren, Oral History Interview, 7; Baunchand, Oral History Interview, 2–4. Quotation edited for readability; original source has "She said she didn't want to pile too much on us at once."
29. Warren, Oral History Interview, 14–15; Baunchand, Oral History Interview, 3.
30. Beaulieu, Address, Jan. 16, 1982, 5; "Beaulieu, Freda Lucretia Magee," Biographical Entry, Century of Black Mormons website, exhibits.lib.utah.edu/s/century-of-black-mormons.
31. Warren, Oral History Interview, 9, 15.
32. Baunchand, Oral History Interview, 4; Baunchand and Baunchand, Oral History Interview, [00:33:00]–[00:34:10]; Warren, Oral History Interview, 7.
33. *Uniform System for Teaching Families,* C1–C39.
34. Baunchand, Oral History Interview, 4; Roger W. Carpenter, "13 of Convert's Relatives Join Church," *Church News,* Feb. 17, 1979, 13.
35. Warren, Oral History Interview, 7; Baunchand, Oral History Interview, 4; *Uniform System for Teaching Families,* H1, I1, J1.
36. Roger W. Carpenter, "13 of Convert's Relatives Join Church," *Church News,* Feb. 17, 1979, 13; Baker Ward, Manuscript History and Historical Reports, Jan. 21, 1979.
37. Warren, Oral History Interview, 7.

38. Mabey and Allred, *Brother to Brother,* 29–34; Mabey, Journal, Nov. 18, 1978.
39. Anthony Obinna, Oral History Interview, 8; Mabey, Journal, Nov. 18, 1978; Rendell Mabey, Footage of Mission to Nigeria, Nov. 1978, [00:01:45]–[00:01:51], [00:04:40], Rendell N. Mabey, Africa Mission Movies Collection, CHL. Quotation edited for readability; original source has "They asked me whether I am Anthony Obinna."
40. Mabey and Allred, *Brother to Brother,* 34–36; Mabey, Journal, Nov. 18, 1978.
41. Mabey and Allred, *Brother to Brother,* 36–37; Mabey, Journal, Nov. 18, 1978.
42. Mabey and Allred, *Brother to Brother,* 42–43; Mabey, Journal, Nov. 21, 1978; Cannon and Cannon, *Together,* 171.
43. Mabey and Allred, *Brother to Brother,* 46–47; Mabey, Journal, Nov. 21, 1978; Cannon and Cannon, *Together,* 171.
44. Mabey, Journal, Nov. 21, 1978; Mabey and Allred, *Brother to Brother,* 50; Imo State District, Aboh Branch Baptisms and Confirmations, Nov. 21, 1978, International Mission Files, CHL.

Chapter 20: Marvelous and Wonderful Way

1. Wilkinson, Interview, 2–3; Spencer W. Kimball, Journal, Feb. 9, 1979; Apr. 20, 1979; May 6, 1979; June 11 and 23, 1979; Aug. 23, 1979.
2. Wilkinson, Interview, 2; Spencer W. Kimball, Journal, Sept. 6–7, 1979; Camilla Kimball, Journal, Sept. 6 and Oct. 13, 1979. **Topic: Spencer W. Kimball**
3. Howard W. Hunter, "Jerusalem Center," Oct. 1983, [1]–[2], Budget Office, Jerusalem Center Records, CHL; Dell Van Orden, "Orson Hyde Garden Is on Vantage Seat of Biblical History," *Church News,* Nov. 3, 1979, 3; Galbraith, "Orson Hyde Memorial Garden Project," 7–9; Galbraith, Oral History Interview, 34–35; *Saints,* volume 1, chapter 36; Orson Hyde, "Interesting News from Alexandria and Jerusalem," *Millennial Star,* Jan. 1842, 133–34. **Topic: Dedication of the Holy Land**
4. Dell Van Orden, "Orson Hyde Garden Is on Vantage Seat of Biblical History," *Church News,* Nov. 3, 1979, 3; Galbraith, "Orson Hyde Memorial Garden Project," 7–9; Galbraith, Oral History Interview, 34–35; Kollek, "Jerusalem," 713; Hunter, Journal, Oct. 19 and 21, 1975; Nov. 19, 1975; May 21, 1976; Mar. 3, 1977; Apr. 7, 1977; Sept. 7, 1977; Oct. 20 and 22, 1978; July 31, 1979. **Topic: Howard W. Hunter**
5. George Albert Smith, in "Gospel of Eternal Father Being Preached to World; Truth Proclaimed in Spirit of Love and Helpfulness," *Deseret News,* Aug. 20, 1921, section 4, 7; George Albert Smith, in *One Hundred Sixteenth Semi-annual Conference,* 168; First Presidency, Statement, Feb. 15, 1978, First Presidency, Circular Letters, CHL; see also James A. Toronto, "A Latter-day Saint Perspective on Muhammad," *Ensign,* Aug. 2000, 53. **Topic: First Presidency**
6. Hunter, Journal, Oct. 24, 1979; Camilla Kimball, Journal, Oct. 23–24, 1979; Galbraith, "Orson Hyde Memorial Garden Project," 9, 15; Galbraith, Oral History Interview, 50; Spencer W. Kimball, in Orson Hyde Memorial Garden Dedication Service, 18.
7. Galbraith, "Orson Hyde Memorial Garden Project," 16; Hunter, Journal, Oct. 24, 1979; Baldridge, *Grafting In,* 51–52; Tanner, Journal, Oct. 24, 1979; Teddy Kollek, in Orson Hyde Memorial Garden Dedication Service, 3–4; Abraham Rabinovich, "Mormons Dedicate Park on Mount of Olives," *Jerusalem Post,* Oct. 25, 1979, 3.
8. Spencer W. Kimball, in Orson Hyde Memorial Garden Dedication Service, 18–22; Galbraith, "Orson Hyde Memorial Garden Project," 18–20.
9. Hunter, Journal, Oct. 24, 1979; "Campus Is Land of Bible," *Church News,* Nov. 3, 1979, 7; Galbraith, "Orson Hyde Memorial Garden Project," 21. **Topic: Interreligious Relations**
10. Galbraith, Oral History Interview, 54–55; Hunter, Journal, May 23, 1978; Feb. 8, 1979; Apr. 6, 1979; Aug. 3, 1979; Oct. 24, 1979; Camilla Kimball, Journal, Oct. 24, 1979; Howard W. Hunter to First Presidency, Jan. 6, 1976, First Presidency, General

Correspondence, CHL; "Jerusalem Center for Near Eastern Studies of the Brigham Young University, USA," in Brent Harker to Richard Lindsay, Aug. 2, 1985, Brigham Young University, Jerusalem Center File, CHL; Galbraith, "Lead-Up to the Dedication of the Jerusalem Center," 51–52.

11. Camilla Kimball, Journal, Nov. 16–17, 1979; Edward Kimball, Journal, Nov. 16–17, 1979; "Pres. Kimball Has Surgery," *Deseret News*, Nov. 17, 1979, A1–A2.

12. Allred, Oral History Interview [Aug. 2022], 1–2; Allred, Oral History Interview [2014], 1–3, 8, 27; First Presidency to Stake Presidents and others in the Central America Area, Aug. 10, 1979, First Presidency, Circular Letters, CHL; Peterson, Journal, Mar. 7, 1979, and May 19–22, 1980; Ezra Taft Benson, in *One Hundred Forty-Ninth Annual Conference*, 121; Jeff Allred, "Central America Area: 1980 Year End Report," Presiding Bishopric, International Offices Files, CHL.

13. Allred, Oral History Interview [Aug. 2022], 1, 6–7; Allred, Oral History Interview [Sept. 2022], 37; Allred and Allred, Email Interview [Apr. 2023]; Allred and Allred, Email Interview [May 2023].

14. Missionary Department, Full-Time Mission Monthly Progress Reports, Jan. 1963; "2nd Area Conference Set in Mexico City," *Church News*, Mar. 25, 1972, 3; Allred, Oral History Interview [Aug. 2022], 1–2; Allred, Oral History Interview [Feb. 2012], 11–12; Allred and Allred, Email Interview [Apr. 2023].

15. *Deseret News 1987 Church Almanac*, 173, 182–85, 187, 189, 203; Missionary Department, Annual Reports, 1979, 10, 12; Allred and Allred, Email Interview [Apr. 2023]. **Topics: Church Growth; Costa Rica; El Salvador; Honduras; Panama**

16. O'Donnal, *Pioneer in Guatemala*, 147–50; Allred, Oral History Interview [Aug. 2022], 3, 13; Allred and Allred, Email Interview [Apr. 2023]; O'Donnal and O'Donnal, Oral History Interview, 99, 103–4.

17. Missionary Department, Annual Reports, 1979, 22; Missionary Executive Committee to Council of the Twelve, June 14, 1977, First Presidency, General Correspondence, CHL; Carr, "History of Translation and Distribution," 222–34; O'Donnal, *Pioneer in Guatemala*, 147–50, 387; O'Donnal and O'Donnal, Oral History Interview, 63; Ronald K. Esplin, "A Church for All Lands—Guatemala," *Church News*, Jan. 13, 1979, 16.

18. Davis, Oral History Interview, 3–5; "New Manuals Are Available," *Church News*, June 10, 1978, 11; "New Books for LDS Readers," *Church News*, Dec. 9, 1978, 14; Allred, Oral History Interview [Aug. 2022], 15. **Topics: Guatemala; Sunday School**

19. Allred, Oral History Interview [Aug. 2022], 1, 13–15; Allred and Allred, Oral History Interview, 4; Allred and Allred, Email Interview [Apr. 2023]; Allred and Allred, Email Interview [May 2023]; *General Handbook of Instructions* [1976], 21–24; William B. Smart, "Sabbath Day," in Ludlow, *Encyclopedia of Mormonism*, 3:1242; O'Donnal and O'Donnal, Oral History Interview, 96–97, 103–4.

20. Allred and Allred, Email Interview [Apr. 2023]; O'Donnal and O'Donnal, Oral History Interview, 92–96, 112–13; O'Donnal, *Pioneer in Guatemala*, 241–71; "Converts Fill 10 New Chapels," *Church News*, June 23, 1979, 3–4; Presiding Bishopric International Office, Meetinghouse Sizing Charts, in Richard G. Scott, Mexico-Central America Files, CHL. **Topics: Building Program; Sacrament Meetings**

21. Allred, Oral History Interview [Aug. 2022], 3–4; First Presidency to All General Authorities and others, Feb. 1, 1980, First Presidency, Circular Letters, CHL; Hunter, Journal, Apr. 26, 1979; June 12, 1979; Nov. 18, 1979; Jan. 16–17 and 31, 1980; Presidency of the First Quorum of the Seventy, Memorandum, Nov. 14, 1979; Presidency of the First Quorum of the Seventy, Memorandum, Jan. 15, 1980; Gordon B. Hinckley, Miscellaneous Stake and Mission Correspondence, CHL; "Church Consolidates Meeting Schedules," *Ensign*, Mar. 1980, 73.

22. Allred, Oral History Interview [Aug. 2022], 14–15; Allred and Allred, Email Interview [May 2023]; "Panel on Consolidated Schedule at the Regional Representatives Seminar," Apr. 4, 1980, 3–4, 6–7, Quorum of the Twelve Apostles, Regional Representatives Seminar Addresses, CHL; William B. Smart, "Sabbath Day," in Ludlow, *Encyclopedia of Mormonism*, 3:1242.

23. Hinckley, Journal, Apr. 5–6, 1980; Dew, *Go Forward with Faith,* 367–68. **Topics: General Conference; Founding Meeting of the Church of Christ**
24. Francis M. Gibbons, "Statistical Report 1979," *Ensign,* May 1980, 20; John L. Hart, "Seven New Temples to Be Erected," *Church News,* Apr. 5, 1980, 3; "Temple to Be Built in Tokyo," *Ensign,* Oct. 1975, 86–87; "Plans Announced for Temple in Mexico," *Ensign,* May 1976, 138; "Mexico City Temple Visited by 120,000," *Church News,* Dec. 4, 1983, 3. **Topic: Temple Building**
25. Hunter, Journal, Dec. 7, 1979; Turner, "Church in Business," 52–53, 55; "Presiding Bishopric International Offices 1980 Year End Report," 1; Presidency of the First Quorum of the Seventy, "Presentation on Cost Reduction," Jan. 16, 1981, Presiding Bishopric, Committee for Reducing Financial Demands on Church Members Files, CHL; James B. Allen and Richard O. Cowan, "History of the Church," in Ludlow, *Encyclopedia of Mormonism,* 2:644; Perry, Brown, and Blease, *If the Walls Had Ears,* 213; "1979 Year End Report: Argentina-Paraguay-Uruguay Area," 5, Presiding Bishopric, International Offices Files, CHL. **Topics: Church Finances; Church Growth**
26. Haws, *Mormon Image in the American Mind,* 99–125; Gordon B. Hinckley to Ezra Taft Benson, Jan. 2, 1979, Gordon B. Hinckley, Miscellaneous Stake and Mission Correspondence, CHL; *Deseret News 1982 Church Almanac,* 218.
27. Hinckley, Journal, Jan. 15, 22, 24, and 26–28, 1980; Feb. 1 and 8, 1980; *The Church and the Proposed Equal Rights Amendment: A Moral Issue* ([Salt Lake City]: *Ensign* Magazine, 1980); William R. Bradford to Ezra Taft Benson, Feb. 20, 1980, Spencer W. Kimball, Headquarters Correspondence and Subject Files, CHL; Tullis, "Some Observations from Latin America," 67–70. **Topics: Equal Rights Amendment; Political Neutrality**
28. Hinckley, Journal, Feb. 7, 1980; Dew, *Go Forward with Faith,* 369. Quotation edited for clarity; "it" in original source changed to "the Church."
29. Hinckley, Journal, May 13, 1976; Sept. 20, 1978; Jan. 10 and 12, 1979; Apr. 6, 1980; Public Communications Department, General Authority Advisers Minutes, Jan. 11 and Feb. 1, 1977; Dew, *Go Forward with Faith,* 367–68. **Topics: Broadcast Media; Church Historic Sites**
30. Hinckley, Journal, Apr. 5–6, 1980; Dew, *Go Forward with Faith,* 366; Kimball, "No Unhallowed Hand Can Stop the Work."
31. Hinckley, Journal, Jan. 24 and Feb. 14, 1980; "Seven Church Leaders Get 'Emeritus' Status," *Church News,* Oct. 7, 1978, 5. **Topics: First Presidency; Quorums of the Seventy**
32. Hinckley, Journal, Apr. 6, 1980; Spencer W. Kimball, "Introduction to the Proclamation," *Ensign,* May 1980, 51; "Proclamation," *Ensign,* May 1980, 52–53.
33. Allred, Oral History Interview [Aug. 2022], 3–4, 14–15; *General Instructions for Stake Presidencies and Bishoprics,* 3–4, 6–7; Primary Association, General Board Minutes, Sept. 20, 1979; Jan. 24, 1980; May 27, 1980; Primary Association, Annual History Reports, 1980–88, 1–3; *Primary Handbook,* 32–33. Quotation edited for readability; "the new primary program" in original changed to "the new program."
34. Allred, Oral History Interview [Aug. 2022], 4, 17; Allred, Oral History Interview [Sept. 2022], 34. **Topic: Primary**
35. Allred, Oral History Interview [Aug. 2022], 15–16, 18; Allred, Oral History Interview [2014], 27; William R. Bradford to Ezra Taft Benson, Feb. 20, 1980, Spencer W. Kimball, Headquarters Correspondence and Subject Files, CHL; National Foreign Assessment Center, *Guatemala,* iii–v; Jack Davis to the Director and Deputy Director of Central Intelligence, Memorandum, Mar. 24, 1980, 2, General CIA Records, Freedom of Information Act Electronic Reading Room.
36. Allred, Oral History Interview [Aug. 2022], 5; Justice and Justice, Oral History Interview, [00:39:20]–[00:40:18].
37. Allred and Allred, Email Interview [May 2023]; Allred, Oral History Interview [Aug. 2022], 13, 16–19; Allred, Oral History Interview [2014], 27–28; Allred, Oral History Interview [Feb. 2012], 17.

38. Mehr, "Enduring Believers," 152; Kovářová, Oral History Interview, [6]; Campora, Oral History Interview [2020], 4, 8, 30–32; Campora, *Saint behind Enemy Lines*, 40–43, 52–53; Campora, "Fruits of Faithfulness," 141; *Saints*, volume 3, chapter 35.
39. Kovářová, Oral History Interview, [1]–[2], [6]–[7]; Campora, "Fruits of Faithfulness," 141–42; Campora, *Saint behind Enemy Lines*, 53–55; Vojkůvka, Statement, Oct. 3, 1990.
40. Campora, *Saint behind Enemy Lines*, 58–67; Campora, Oral History Interview [2020], 28–29; John A. Widtsoe, *Priesthood and Church Government: A Handbook and Study Course for the Quorums of the Melchizedek Priesthood of The Church of Jesus Christ of Latter-day Saints* (Salt Lake City: Deseret Book, 1939).
41. Vojkůvka, Oral History Interview, [00:06:49]–[00:10:12]; Ed Strobel, "Statistics of the Czechoslovakian Mission," July 22, 1989, 1, Europe Area, Files relating to Church Activities in Eastern Europe, CHL; Mehr, "Enduring Believers," 144–52; Vojkůvka, Statement, Oct. 3, 1990; Johann Wondra, "Meeting with President Jiri Snederfler," Aug. 31–Sept. 1, 1985, Europe Area, Eastern Europe Files, CHL. **Topic: Czechoslovakia**
42. Campora, "Fruits of Faithfulness," 141–42; Campora, *Saint behind Enemy Lines*, 69–71; 2 Nephi 2:25.
43. Campora, "Fruits of Faithfulness," 142, 144; Campora, *Saint behind Enemy Lines*, 70–74; Kovářová, Oral History Interview, [12]. Quotations edited for readability; "his disciple" in original changed to "Christ's disciple," and "I am" in original changed to "am I."

CHAPTER 21: A SEED OF LOVE

1. Mavimbela and Harper, "Mother of Soweto," 36–37, 61–62, 69–71; Mavimbela, Oral History Interview [1988], 32–33, 38–39; Mavimbela, "I Speak from My Heart," 68–69; McCombs and McCombs, Oral History Interview, 7–9; Clark and Worger, *South Africa*, 49–51; Barber, *South Africa in the Twentieth Century*, 140–43, 172–73, 211–14; Brown, *Road to Soweto*, 179–87; Johnson, *Soweto Speaks*, 9; Landis, "Apartheid Legislation," 46, 48. **Topics: Racial Segregation; South Africa**
2. Mavimbela and Harper, "Mother of Soweto," 43–44, 51–55; Mavimbela, Oral History Interview [1995], 15–17; Mavimbela, Oral History Interview [1988], 27–31, 39.
3. Mavimbela and Harper, "Mother of Soweto," 84–86; Mavimbela, Oral History Interview [1988], 33–35, 39–40; McCombs and McCombs, Oral History Interview, 5–7, 16–17; Mavimbela, Oral History Interview [1995], 18–19. **Topic: Baptism for the Dead**
4. Mavimbela and Harper, "Mother of Soweto," 88–89; Mavimbela, Oral History Interview [1988], 47–48, 61; Turley and Cannon, "Faithful Band," 13–37; Wood, *Personal History*, 265–67; Walshe, "Christianity and the Anti-apartheid Struggle," 385–92.
5. Mavimbela and Harper, "Mother of Soweto," 54–56, 89; Mavimbela, Oral History Interview [1988], 39–40. Quotation edited for readability; "had" in original changed to "have," and "could" in original changed to "can."
6. Burkhardt, "Wie kam es zum Bau des Freiberger [Freiberg] Tempels?," 3–4; Burkhardt, Oral History Interview [1991], 9–10; Kuehne, *Henry Burkhardt*, 89–91; Monson, Journal, Feb. 10, 1979.
7. Burkhardt, "Wie kam es zum Bau des Freiberger [Freiberg] Tempels?," 3–7; Burkhardt, Oral History Interview [1991], 10–11; Kuehne, *Henry Burkhardt*, 91–92; Bangerter, Journal, June 28, 1985.
8. Burkhardt, Oral History Interview [1991], 10–11; Burkhardt, "Wie kam es zum Bau des Freiberger [Freiberg] Tempels?," 7–8. Translated quotation edited for readability; original source has "in fact not that wrong."
9. Kuehne, *Henry Burkhardt*, 92–93; Kuehne, "Freiberg Temple," 125–27; Burkhardt, "Wie kam es zum Bau des Freiberger [Freiberg] Tempels?," 9–11; Burkhardt, Oral History Interview [1991], 11. **Topic: Germany**

10. Kuehne, *Henry Burkhardt,* 94; Burkhardt, "Wie kam es zum Bau des Freiberger [Freiberg] Tempels?," 9–10; Kuehne, *Mormons as Citizens of a Communist State,* 281; Apel, Oral History Interview, 1; Leonhardt, "Geschichte des Freiberg-DDR-Tempels," 43–45; Burkhardt, Oral History Interview [1991], 11; Kuehne, "Freiberg Temple," 115–16.
11. Monson, Journal, Feb. 27–28, 1982.
12. Monson, Journal, Feb. 28, 1982; Kuehne, *Mormons as Citizens of a Communist State,* 281; Burkhardt, "Wie kam es zum Bau des Freiberger [Freiberg] Tempels?," 10; Henry Burkhardt to Thomas S. Monson, Nov. 5, 1981, in Burkhardt, "Wie kam es zum Bau des Freiberger [Freiberg] Tempels?," [20]–[21]; Burkhardt, Oral History Interview [1991], 12; Kuehne, *Henry Burkhardt,* 93–94. Quotation edited for clarity; "Is that really" in original changed to "Is this really."
13. Monson, Journal, Feb. 28 and Sept. 1, 1982; Kuehne, *Mormons as Citizens of a Communist State,* 281–83; Burkhardt, "Wie kam es zum Bau des Freiberger [Freiberg] Tempels?," 10–11; see also Leonhardt, "Geschichte des Freiberg-DDR-Tempels," 46a. **Topic: Thomas S. Monson**
14. Robert Taylor to Howard W. Hunter, Memorandum, Apr. 1, 1982, Howard W. Hunter, Jerusalem Center Files, CHL; Galbraith, "Lead-Up to the Dedication of the Jerusalem Center," 54; Galbraith, "Miracles Open the Door"; Galbraith, Oral History Interview, 87, 150–52.
15. Galbraith, Oral History Interview, 166; Robert Taylor, "The Jerusalem Center: Organizational Structure," 1987, 1–4, Budget Office, Jerusalem Center Records, CHL.
16. Taylor, "Contest and Controversy," 62–64; Peterson, *Abraham Divided,* 343–45; Galbraith, Oral History Interview, 147–50; Kaminker, "Building Restrictions in East Jerusalem," 9; Robert Taylor to Howard W. Hunter, Memorandum, Apr. 1, 1982, Howard W. Hunter, Jerusalem Center Files, CHL.
17. Galbraith, Oral History Interview, 56, 85, 148–50, 166–67; Teddy Kollek to Delos Ellsworth, Dec. 18, 1983, Howard W. Hunter, Jerusalem Center Files, CHL; Galbraith, "Miracles Open the Door."
18. Galbraith, Oral History Interview, 87, 150–54, 167; Galbraith, "Lead-Up to the Dedication of the Jerusalem Center," 54; Galbraith, "Miracles Open the Door"; Robert Taylor to Howard W. Hunter, Memorandum, Apr. 1, 1982, Howard W. Hunter, Jerusalem Center Files, CHL; Berrett and Van Dyke, *Holy Lands,* 389.
19. Holcman, "Olga Campora Kovářová"; Kovářová, Oral History Interview, [11].
20. Campora, *Saint behind Enemy Lines,* 74–75.
21. Campora, *Saint behind Enemy Lines,* 75–77; Holcman, Scrapbook, 17.
22. Mehr, "Enduring Believers," 150–52; Ed Strobel, "Statistics of the Czechoslovakian Mission," July 22, 1989, 1, Europe Area, Files relating to Church Activities in Eastern Europe, CHL; Campora, *Saint behind Enemy Lines,* 77–78. **Topic: Czechoslovakia**
23. Campora, *Saint behind Enemy Lines,* 85–87; Kovářová, Oral History Interview, [11]–[12].
24. Alan Dawson and Marjorie E. Woods, "Spiritual Moment as S. African Temple Begins," *Church News,* Dec. 11, 1982, 5; Mavimbela and Harper, "Mother of Soweto," 95; Hal Knight, "Black Branches Thrive in South Africa," *Church News,* Nov. 28, 1981, 6; Marvin J. Ashton to First Presidency, Dec. 2, 1982, First Presidency, Temple Correspondence, CHL.
25. Alan Dawson and Marjorie E. Woods, "Spiritual Moment as S. African Temple Begins," *Church News,* Dec. 11, 1982, 5; "Transcript and Translation," 1, 11, 14–16; Mavimbela and Harper, "Mother of Soweto," 95–96.
26. Johannesburg 2nd Branch, Annual Historical Reports, 1982, [4]; Mavimbela and Harper, "Mother of Soweto," 92–94; Hal Knight, "Black Branches Thrive in South Africa," *Church News,* Nov. 28, 1981, 6.
27. "Learning to Listen"; Johannesburg 2nd Branch, Annual Historical Reports, 1981, [5]; 1982, [2]; Kwa Mashu Branch, Annual Historical Reports, 1980, [1]–[2]; Mavimbela and Harper, "Mother of Soweto," 91–92.

Chapter 22: More Like Our Lord and Master

1. Kapp, Journal, Apr. 9, 1984; Gordon B. Hinckley, "The Sustaining of Church Officers," *Ensign,* May 1984, 5; Kapp and Rasmus, Oral History Interview, 33. **Topics: Gordon B. Hinckley; Russell M. Nelson; Ardeth G. Kapp; Common Consent**
2. Kapp, Journal, Aug. 7, 1984; Kapp and Rasmus, Oral History Interview, ii, 32, 57; "First Presidency Calls Young Women Counselors," *Church News,* May 20, 1984, 7. **Topic: Fasting**
3. Kapp, Journal, Aug. 7, 1984, and Jan. 8, 1985; Kapp and Rasmus, Oral History Interview, 42, 44–45, 52–58, 65, 227–28; Kapp, "Young Women Presentation to PEC," 1–6.
4. Kapp, Journal, Aug. 7, 1984; Kapp and Rasmus, Oral History Interview, 52–54, 56–60; Carolyn Rasmus, "Events of Significance—1984," [1], Young Women, Carolyn J. Rasmus Office Papers, CHL.
5. Carolyn Rasmus to Jed Woodworth, Email, May 31, 2023, copy in editors' possession; Kapp and Rasmus, Oral History Interview, 45, 48–50, 52–54, 59–65; Thompson, *Stand as a Witness,* 267–73; Kapp, "Young Women Presentation to PEC," 2.
6. Priesthood Executive Council, Minutes and Records, Oct. 9, 1985; Kapp, Journal, Apr. 5, 1979; Oct. 9, 1984; Nov. 12, 1984; Jan. 8, 1985; Spencer W. Kimball, Address, Seminar for Regional Representatives, Oct. 5, 1979, Quorum of the Twelve Apostles, Regional Representatives Seminar Addresses, CHL; Monson, Journal, Mar. 5, 1982; Kapp and Rasmus, Oral History Interview, 65–68. The other executive councils were the Missionary Executive Council and the Temple and Genealogy Executive Council. **Topic: Correlation**
7. Kapp, Journal, Jan. 6, 1985.
8. Kapp and Rasmus, Oral History Interview, 65; Priesthood Executive Council, Minutes and Records, Feb. 20, 1985; Rasmus, Journal, Feb. 20, 1985; Kapp, "Young Women Presentation to PEC," 1–13.
9. Priesthood Executive Council, Minutes and Records, Feb. 20, 1985; Kapp, "Young Women Presentation to PEC," 1–9.
10. Kapp, "Young Women Presentation to PEC," 9–11; Rasmus, Journal, Feb. 20, 1985; Kapp, Journal, Apr. 9, 1984; Kapp and Rasmus, Oral History Interview, 67; Priesthood Executive Council, Minutes and Records, Feb. 20, 1985. **Topic: Young Women Organizations**
11. Gordon B. Hinckley, Carmen G. O'Donnal, in Guatemala City Temple, Dedication Services, 6, 115–16; *Saints,* volume 3, chapter 33; *Deseret News 1985 Church Almanac,* 254; Missionary Department, Annual Reports, 1979, 12. **Topic: Guatemala**
12. First Presidency to John O'Donnal, Aug. 2, 1984, First Presidency, Temple Correspondence, CHL; *Deseret News 1985 Church Almanac,* 12, 254–55; Isabel Santana, Oral History Interview [Feb. 2, 2022], 24, 27–28, 34–35; Isabel Santana, Oral History Interview [Apr. 19, 2022], 20; John L. Hart, "'We Are Here to Stay,' Say Mexican Members," *Church News,* May 5, 1985, 5. **Topic: Mexico**
13. Dell Van Orden, "Sao Paulo Temple Dedicated," *Church News,* Nov. 4, 1978, 3; Jerry Cahill, "Orientation Center Is in Sao Paulo," *Church News,* Oct. 21, 1978, 8; *Deseret News 1987 Church Almanac,* 172–99, 201–2, 256; John L. Hart, "Skills Gained in Military, Business and Ministry Prepared Him for New Calling," *Church News,* June 16, 1985, 4; Jason Swensen, "Church in Brazil Realizing Its Prophesied Potential," *Church News,* Feb. 11, 2012, 3; Gordon B. Hinckley, "The Sustaining of Church Officers," and Helio da Rocha Camargo, "He Is in Charge," *Ensign,* May 1985, 5, 85. **Topic: Brazil**
14. Allred, Oral History Interview [Sept. 2022], 8; Allred, Oral History Interview [2014], 33–34; Harold B. Lee to First Presidency and Quorum of the Twelve, Nov. 7, 1959, First Presidency, Mission Correspondence, 1964–2010, CHL; *Deseret News 1985 Church Almanac,* 255; *Deseret News 1991–1992 Church Almanac,* 200–218; John L. Hart, "Temple Dedicated in an Oasis of Calm," *Church News,* Sept. 25, 1983, 3. **Topic: Chile**
15. Martin P. Houseman, "Chile: 'The Field Is White,'" *Church News,* May 8, 1965, 8–9; Craig Hill, "Chile's 50th Stake—a Milestone Capping 32 Years of Growth," *Church News,* Nov. 12, 1988, 11; John L. Hart, "Temple Dedicated in an Oasis of

Calm," *Church News*, Sept. 25, 1983, 3; Carlos Cifuentes, in Santiago Chile Temple, Dedication Services, 39–40; Carlos Cifuentes and Elsa Cifuentes, Sept. 1983, Photograph, Dedicacion Templo de Santiago, CHL.

16. "Groundbreaking for 4th Temple in South America," *Church News*, May 1, 1983, 4; Beatriz Felisa Campi entry, Argentine Mission, Baptisms and Confirmations, 1942, 6, in Argentina (Country), part 3, Record of Members Collection, CHL; Campi, Diary, Sept. 23 and 30, 1984; Oct. 7 and 14, 1984; Annual Report of the Argentine Mission, 1942, Presiding Bishopric, Financial, Statistical, and Historical Reports of Wards, Stakes, and Missions, CHL; *Deseret News 1985 Church Almanac*, 255; *Saints*, volume 3, chapter 16; Curbelo, *History of the Mormons in Argentina*, 38, 182–83. **Topics: Argentina; Church Growth**

17. Gordon B. Hinckley to W. Grant Bangerter, Oct. 12, 1984, First Presidency, Temple Correspondence, CHL; "Midpoint in Groundbreakings," *Church News*, Sept. 18, 1982, 5; "New Temples Planned in 3 Countries," *Church News*, Apr. 3, 1982, 4; *Saints*, volume 2, chapter 44; volume 3, chapter 8. **Topics: Colombia; Peru; Ecuador; Temple Building**

18. Campora, *Saint behind Enemy Lines*, 88–90; Kovářová, Oral History Interview, [12]–[13]; Vojkůvka, Statement, Oct. 3, 1990.

19. Campora, *Saint behind Enemy Lines*, 90–95; Kovářová, Oral History Interview, [13]–[14]; Campora, Oral History Interview [2020], 28.

20. Campora, *Saint behind Enemy Lines*, 8–9, 96–114, 129–34.

21. Gordon B. Hinckley, Thomas S. Monson, Henry Burkhardt, in Freiberg Germany Temple, Dedication Services, 15, 17–19, 35; Gordon B. Hinckley, Memorandum, July 5, 1984, Gordon B. Hinckley, Temple Files, CHL; Burkhardt, Journal, July 24, 1984, and Feb. 18, 1985; *Saints*, volume 3, chapter 39; "Temple to Be Built in German Democratic Republic," *Church News*, Oct. 9, 1982, 2; "Freiberg Germany Temple District," 1–2, Temple Department, Temple District Maps, CHL. **Topics: Germany; Cold War**

22. Kuehne, "Freiberg Temple," 95–97, 129; Boone and Cowan, "Freiberg Germany Temple," 156–60; "Europe's 2nd Temple Begun in Freiberg," *Church News*, May 15, 1983, 5.

23. Kuehne, *Henry Burkhardt*, 97–98; Boone and Cowan, "Freiberg Germany Temple," 159–62; Henry Burkhardt, in Freiberg Germany Temple, Dedication Services, 35; Hinckley, Journal, June 28, 1985.

24. Henry Burkhardt, Inge Burkhardt, in Freiberg Germany Temple, Dedication Services, 36–38. **Topic: Temple Dedications and Dedicatory Prayers**

25. Haim Shapiro, "Prayers Said against Mormon Study Centre," *Jerusalem Post*, July 19, 1985, 2; "Ultra-Orthodox Jews Hold Pray-In to Protest Mormon Center in Israel," *Los Angeles Times*, July 19, 1985, 5; Arthur Max, "Rabbis Want Construction of Mormon Center Halted," *Salt Lake Tribune*, July 18, 1985, A6; Taylor, "Contest and Controversy," 122–23; Ogden, Journal, July 19, 1985; Galbraith, Oral History Interview, 167.

26. Peterson, *Abraham Divided*, 345; Faust, Journal, Aug. 14, 1984; Oct. 1 and 10, 1984; Jan. 3 and 31, 1985.

27. Taylor, "Contest and Controversy," 70–71, 125–85; Moshe Porush to Teddy Kollek, May 30, 1984; Jeffrey R. Holland to Gordon B. Hinckley, Howard W. Hunter, and James E. Faust, Mar. 22, 1985; Meir Kahane to Spencer W. Kimball, July 15, 1985, Gordon B. Hinckley, Church Educational System Files, CHL; Yosef Goell, "When the Saints Come Marching In," *Jerusalem Post Magazine*, June 7, 1985, 6–7; Hunter, Journal, July 30, 1985; see also Scott, "Reflections on Howard W. Hunter in Jerusalem," 14.

28. Hinckley, Journal, May 21 and July 18, 1985; Hunter, Journal, Mar. 9, 13, 23, and 27, 1984; Apr. 2, 1984; May 9, 1984; Feb. 8, 1985; Mar. 27, 1985; July 17 and 19, 1985; Faust, Journal, Mar. 28, 1985; June 7 and 12, 1985; July 19, 1985; Haim Shapiro, "Prayers Said against Mormon Study Centre," *Jerusalem Post*, July 19, 1985, 2; Taylor, "Contest and Controversy," 130–31; Benson, Journal, Apr. 26, 1983.

29. "Minutes of a Meeting with Rabbi Menachem Porush (MK) and Party—19 July 1985," 1–2, Gordon B. Hinckley, Church Educational System Files, CHL; Hunter, Journal, July 19, 1985; Faust, Journal, July 19, 1985; Taylor, "Contest and Controversy," 132. Quotation edited for clarity; original source includes a parenthetical: "Rabbis from all over Israel gathered together to give expression (by sitting on the floor)."
30. "Minutes of a Meeting with Rabbi Menachem Porush (MK) and Party—19 July 1985," 3, Gordon B. Hinckley, Church Educational System Files, CHL; Teddy Kollek to David Galbraith, Mar. 23, 1977, Gordon B. Hinckley, Church Educational System Files, CHL; "Fear of Bogeys," *Jerusalem Post,* July 21, 1985, 8; Haim Shapiro, "Mormon: Proselytizers Will Go Home," *Jerusalem Post,* Aug. 7, 1985, 3; Galbraith, Ogden, and Skinner, *Jerusalem,* 457.
31. "Minutes of a Meeting with Rabbi Menachem Porush (MK) and Party—19 July 1985," 4–5, Gordon B. Hinckley, Church Educational System Files, CHL; see also Hunter, Journal, July 19, 1985; Faust, Journal, July 19, 1985; and Taylor, "Contest and Controversy," 132–37.
32. Hunter, Journal, July 20 and 29–31, 1985; Aug. 1, 1985; Ogden, Journal, July 20, 1985; Hinckley, Journal, July 29 and 31, 1985; Faust, Journal, July 29–31, 1985; Taylor, "Contest and Controversy," 127–29, 137–38; Jeffrey R. Holland, Letter of Undertaking, Aug. 1, 1985, Gordon B. Hinckley, Church Educational System Files, CHL.
33. Mavimbela and Harper, "Mother of Soweto," 92–93.
34. *Relief Society Handbook,* 4; *Latter-day Saint Woman, Part A,* chapters 21–26; *Latter-day Saint Woman, Part B,* chapters 21–25; Mavimbela, Oral History Interview [1995], 24; Mavimbela, Oral History Interview [1988], 53–54.
35. Mavimbela and Harper, "Mother of Soweto," 93; Mavimbela, Oral History Interview [1995], 24–25. **Topic: Relief Society**
36. Mavimbela and Harper, "Mother of Soweto," 95–96; Maurice Bateman, Letter, Oct. 7, 1984, Maurice and Arlene Bateman Letters, CHL; Patrick Laurence, "SA Miners Waver on Strike after New Offer," *Guardian* (UK edition), Sept. 18, 1984, 7; Patrick Laurence, "'Six Killed' after Police Are Called to SA Mine," *Guardian* (UK edition), Sept. 19, 1984, 6. **Topic: Angel Moroni**
37. Mavimbela and Harper, "Mother of Soweto," 48, 57–59, 96; Mavimbela, Oral History Interview [1988], 94; Bateman and Bateman, "To Julia Mavimbela," [1].
38. Mavimbela and Harper, "Mother of Soweto," 86, 95–96; Mavimbela, Oral History Interview [1995], 13–14, 20; Mavimbela, Oral History Interview [1988], 63–64; Julia Mavimbela, "My Own Endowment," Sept. 14, 1985, Julia N. Mavimbela Papers, CHL; Julia Nompi Ngubeni Mavimbela, Report of Living Endowment, Sept. 14, 1985, Temple Records for the Living, 1955–91, microfilm 1,262,454, FSL. **Topics: Temple Endowment; Sealing**
39. Julia Mavimbela, "My Own Endowment," Sept. 14, 1985, Julia N. Mavimbela Papers, CHL.

Chapter 23: Every Effort

1. Kapp, Journal, Nov. 6, 1985; Kimball, *Lengthen Your Stride,* chapter 38.
2. Kapp, Journal, Feb. 20 and Nov. 6, 1985; Kapp and Rasmus, Oral History Interview, 67–68, 76–77; *New Era,* Young Women Special Issue, Nov. 1985, copy at CHL. **Topic: Church Periodicals**
3. Kapp and Rasmus, Oral History Interview, 77; Russell M. Nelson to Daniel Ludlow, June 25, 1985, Young Women Files, CHL; Kapp, Journal, June 6, 1985; Priesthood Executive Council, Minutes, June 12, 1985; Young Women, General Board Minutes, Aug. 21 and Oct. 9, 1985.
4. *Young Women General Fireside,* [1], in Kapp, Journal, Nov. 1985; "Pres. Kimball Dies at 90 after Many Years of Love and Service," *Church News,* Nov. 10, 1985, 3; "First

Young Women's Fireside," [00:00:36]–[00:01:05], [00:02:04]–[00:02:45]; Gerry Avant, "Young Women Are Challenged: 'Stand for Truth, Righteousness,'" *Church News*, Nov. 17, 1985, 10.
5. "First Young Women's Fireside," [00:03:11]–[00:06:35], [00:09:01]–[00:19:35]; Gerry Avant, "Young Women Are Challenged: 'Stand for Truth, Righteousness,'" *Church News*, Nov. 17, 1985, 10, 12; Gerry Avant, "New Hymnbook Rolls Off Presses," *Church News*, Aug. 11, 1985, 3; Davidson, *Our Latter-day Hymns*, 261. **Topic: Hymns**
6. Russell M. Nelson, "Daughters of Zion," Nov. 10, 1985, 3–4, Russell M. Nelson Addresses, CHL; "First Young Women's Fireside," [00:15:21]–[00:15:23], [00:18:45]–[00:19:00].
7. "First Young Women's Fireside," [00:19:35]–[00:36:19]; Kapp and Rasmus, Oral History Interview, 175, 180; Francis Gibbons to J. Thomas Fyans, Memorandum, Oct. 4, 1985, First Presidency, Committees, Departments, and Organizations Correspondence, CHL.
8. "First Young Women's Fireside," [00:22:10]–[00:23:12]; Gerry Avant, "Young Women Are Challenged: 'Stand for Truth, Righteousness,'" *Church News*, Nov. 17, 1985, 12.
9. Gerry Avant, "Young Women Are Challenged: 'Stand for Truth, Righteousness,'" *Church News*, Nov. 17, 1985, 10, 12; "First Young Women's Fireside," [00:36:19]–[01:29:26]; Mosiah 18:9; "Carry On," *Hymns*, no. 255.
10. Kapp, Journal, Nov. 10, 1985, emphasis in original; Kapp and Rasmus, Oral History Interview, 180. **Topic: Young Women Organizations**
11. Hinckley, Journal, Nov. 10–11, 1985; O. Wallace Kasteler, "Pres. Ezra Taft Benson Outlines Changes in the Church Leadership," Photograph, in *Deseret News*, Nov. 11, 1985, A5; Hunter, Journal, Nov. 10, 1985.
12. Benson, Journal, Nov. 5–6, 1985; Ezra Taft Benson, "Spencer W. Kimball: A Star of the First Magnitude," *Ensign*, Dec. 1985, 33–34.
13. Ezra Taft Benson, "Spencer W. Kimball: A Star of the First Magnitude," *Ensign*, Dec. 1985, 34; "Pres. Kimball Dies at 90 after Many Years of Love and Service," *Church News*, Nov. 10, 1985, 3, 7; Tullis, "Some Observations from Latin America," 65; Missionary Department, Annual Reports, 1985, 6; *Deseret News 1997–98 Church Almanac*, 290–91, 312–15, 319–20, 336–37, 366–67, 370–72, 380–81, 403–4; Spencer W. Kimball, Address, Seminar for Regional Representatives, Oct. 5, 1979, 1; Ezra Taft Benson, Address, Regional Representative Seminar, Apr. 2, 1982, 1, Quorum of the Twelve Apostles, Regional Representatives Seminar Addresses, CHL. **Topics: Church Growth; Adjustments to Priesthood Organization; Quorums of the Seventy; Bolivia; Colombia; Nicaragua; Paraguay; Puerto Rico; Venezuela**
14. Ezra Taft Benson, "Spencer W. Kimball: A Star of the First Magnitude," *Ensign*, Dec. 1985, 34; "Pres. Kimball Dies at 90 after Many Years of Love and Service," *Church News*, Nov. 10, 1985, 3; Kimball, "Events and Changes," 524, 526; Missionary Department, Annual Reports, 1985, 7; Monson, Journal, Aug. 29, 1979; Lavina Fielding Anderson, "Church Publishes First LDS Edition of the Bible," *Ensign*, Oct. 1979, 9–17; Kimball, *Lengthen Your Stride*, 101–3; Turley and Slaughter, *How We Got the Doctrine and Covenants*, 111–14. **Topics: Spencer W. Kimball; Priesthood and Temple Restriction; Doctrine and Covenants; Joseph Smith Translation of the Bible**
15. Hunter, Journal, Sept. 1, 1982; Hinckley, Journal, Nov. 28, 1983; Charles Didier, Angel Abrea, and Hartman Rector Jr. to M. Russell Ballard, Mar. 2, 1989, Missionary Executive Council, Meeting Materials, CHL; Grover, "Mormons in Latin America," 523–24; Dew, *Insights from a Prophet's Life*, 174; Mehr, *Mormon Missionaries Enter Eastern Europe*, 155–70; Van Orden, *Building Zion*, 247, 267–307.
16. Turley, *Victims*, chapters 2–8; "Document Deals and Murder: A Hofmann Chronology," *Salt Lake Tribune*, Aug. 1, 1987, A6; Haws, *Mormon Image in the American Mind*, 141–45; Ian Ball, "Mormon Row behind Salt Lake Bombings," *Daily Telegraph* (London), Oct. 19, 1985, 7; Hinckley, Journal, Oct. 18 and 21, 1985. **Topic: Hofmann Forgeries**
17. Vern Anderson, "Weight of Office Has Tempered Benson Views," *Daily Herald* (Provo, UT), Nov. 10, 1985, 70; Haws, "LDS Church Presidency Years, 1985–1994," 208–9;

Spencer W. Kimball, "A Report of My Stewardship," *Ensign*, May 1981, 5. **Topics: Ezra Taft Benson; Political Neutrality**

18. Navarro, Oral History Interview [Apr. 2023], 7–11, 24, 56; Navarro, Oral History Interview [2015], 1; Nazca Peru District, Annual Historical Reports, 1985; *Basic Unit Program*, 1–9; Spencer W. Kimball, "Ministering to the Needs of Members," *Ensign*, Nov. 1980, 46; Livingstone, "Establishing the Church Simply," 127–28, 133–43.
19. Navarro, Oral History Interview [Apr. 2023], 2–7, 10–11, 13, 21, 25; Nazca Peru District, Annual Historical Reports, 1985.
20. John L. Hart, "Prophecy Fulfilled for Peru Members," and John L. Hart, "Long Wait Over for Argentine LDS," *Church News*, Jan. 26, 1986, 3, 7; Lima Peru Temple, Annual Historical Reports, 1987; *Deseret News 1987 Church Almanac*, 276, 283, 311; Gordon B. Hinckley, in Lima Peru Temple, Dedication Services, 28; Navarro, Oral History Interview [Apr. 2023], 19–20, 44–46. **Topics: Peru; Argentina; Ecuador**
21. Navarro, Oral History Interview [Apr. 2023], 11–12, 33–34, 53–55; *Seek Learning Even by Study and by Faith*, 1; Griffiths, "Globalization of Latter-day Saint Education," 208–48; *By Study and Also by Faith*, 234, 241–45, 250–56, 263–67; Annual Historical Report, Peru, 1985, Church Educational System, Area Historical Reports, CHL.
22. Navarro, Oral History Interview [Apr. 2023], 11–12, 24–25, 33–34, 37–39; Carla Brimhall, "Films Urge Youths—Stay 'Free to Choose,'" *Church News*, Sept. 7, 1986, 8; "1 Nefi 3:7," *Dominio de las escrituras*; Administrative Council Meeting, Minutes, Jan. 16, 1985, Church Educational System, Executive Planning Minutes, CHL. **Topic: Seminaries and Institutes**
23. Moreno, Oral History Interview, [7]; Moreno, Interview, [1]–[2], [9]. **Topic: Mexico**
24. Moreno, Interview, [2]; Young Women General Presidency to "Young Woman and Your Parents," July 21, 1986, Young Women Files, CHL; "300,000 Young Women Send Balloon Messages of Hope Worldwide," *Ensign*, Nov. 1986, 102; Gerry Avant, "Balloons Bear Messages of Love, Hope and Peace," *Church News*, Oct. 19, 1986, 8–10; see also *Rising Generation*, 1–22.
25. Moreno, Oral History Interview, [15], [18]; Moreno, Interview, [2], [7], [9].
26. Moreno, Oral History Interview, [15], [18]; Moreno, Interview, [2]–[3]; Consuelo Moreno to Ardeth Kapp, Sept. 10, 1986, Maria del Consuelo Wong Moreno Papers, CHL; Gerry Avant, "Messages Sent by 'Rising Generation,'" *Church News*, Oct. 19, 1986, 10.
27. Benson, Journal, Aug. 2–3, 1986; Gerry Avant, "Prophet Retraces Paths of Church History," *Church News*, Aug. 10, 1986, 7–8; Argetsinger, "Hill Cumorah Pageant," 58–69; "Hill Cumorah Pageant," *Springville (NY) Journal*, Aug. 14, 1986, 14.
28. Ezra Taft Benson, "The Book of Mormon Is the Word of God," Aug. 3, 1986, 1, 3, Ezra Taft Benson Addresses, CHL; Gerry Avant, "Prophet Retraces Paths of Church History," *Church News*, Aug. 10, 1986, 7–8; Mason, "Ezra Taft Benson," 66–67; Reynolds, "Coming Forth of the Book of Mormon," 9–30.
29. Benson, Journal, Sept. 30, 1921; Nov. 18 and 20, 1921; Oct. 25, 1922; Dew, *Ezra Taft Benson*, 49, 55; Reynolds, "Coming Forth of the Book of Mormon," 30–31.
30. Hunter, Journal, Mar. 6, 1986; Dew, *Ezra Taft Benson*, 492; Shepherd and Shepherd, *Kingdom Transformed*, 76, 78, 101; Bowman, *Mormon People*, 231–32; Carmack, "Images of Christ in Latter-day Saint Visual Culture," 66.
31. Missionary Executive Council, Minutes, Sept. 1 and Oct. 6, 1982; John L. Hart, "Subtitle Testifies of Jesus Christ," *Church News*, Oct. 16, 1982, 3; Shipps, *Sojourner*, 102–4, 353–54; Haws, *Mormon Image in the American Mind*, 99–102, 108–25; Turner, *Mormon Jesus*, 44–46.
32. Dew, *Ezra Taft Benson*, 492–96; Reynolds, "Coming Forth of the Book of Mormon," 31. President Benson gave a talk called "The Book of Mormon Is the Word of God" in at least ten public settings during his first year as Church president. (Benson, Addresses, Jan. 5 and 26, 1986; Feb. 16, 1986; Mar. 2, 1986; Apr. 4, 1986; May 11 and 25, 1986; Aug. 3, 1986; Oct. 12, 1986; Nov. 2, 1986.)
33. Ezra Taft Benson, "Cleansing the Inner Vessel," *Ensign*, May 1986, 5–6.

34. Ezra Taft Benson, "The Book of Mormon—Keystone of Our Religion," *Ensign,* Nov. 1986, 4–7; see also Woodruff, Journal, Nov. 28, 1841. **Topic: Ezra Taft Benson**
35. Kapp, Journal, Oct. 17, 1986; Gerry Avant, "Balloons Bear Messages of Love, Hope and Peace," *Church News,* Oct. 19, 1986, 8.
36. Moreno, Interview, [2]–[4], [7], [9]; Ardeth Kapp to Consuelo Moreno, Oct. 14, 1986, Maria del Consuelo Wong Moreno Papers, CHL.
37. Ardeth Kapp to Consuelo Moreno, Oct. 14, 1986, Maria del Consuelo Wong Moreno Papers, CHL; Moreno, Interview, [4], [6].
38. Moreno, Interview, [2]–[5], [7], [9]; Moreno, Oral History Interview, [15]–[16], [19]–[20]; *Young Women Values,* 6; *Los valores de las mujeres jovenes,* 6.
39. Moreno, Interview, [4]–[5]; "Young Women: New Beginnings," 1. **Topic: Young Women Organizations**

CHAPTER 24: OUR SEARCH FOR TRUTH

1. Galbraith, Oral History Interview, 86, 102–3, 105–6; David Galbraith to Jeffrey R. Holland, Memorandum, Mar. 8, 1987, Howard W. Hunter, Jerusalem Center Files, CHL; Ogden, Journal, Mar. 8, 1987; Galbraith, Ogden, and Skinner, *Jerusalem,* 455.
2. David Galbraith to Jeffrey R. Holland, Memorandum, Mar. 8, 1987, Howard W. Hunter, Jerusalem Center Files, CHL; Casper, "Opposition," 13, note 3; Galbraith, Oral History Interview, 102–4, 107, 132, 168; Taylor, "Contest and Controversy," 237.
3. Haim Shapiro, "BYU Centre to Invite Israel Officials," *Jerusalem Post,* Aug. 8, 1985, 3; Haim Shapiro, "Mormon: Proselytizers Will Go Home," *Jerusalem Post,* Aug. 7, 1985, 3; Taylor, "Contest and Controversy," 138–48, 162–64, 222–28, 237; Casper, "Opposition," 78, 109–10, 149; Galbraith, Oral History Interview, 102, 168.
4. Taylor, "Contest and Controversy," 186–228; Peterson, *Abraham Divided,* 346–47; Galbraith, "Lead-Up to the Dedication of the Jerusalem Center," 56–57; Galbraith, Ogden, and Skinner, *Jerusalem,* 466; David Galbraith, "Call for a Dialogue," *Jerusalem Post,* Oct. 4, 1985, 7.
5. Galbraith, Oral History Interview, 101–2, 168; Ogden, Journal, Mar. 4, 1987.
6. David Galbraith to Jeffrey R. Holland, Memorandum, Mar. 8, 1987, Howard W. Hunter, Jerusalem Center Files, CHL; Galbraith, Oral History Interview, 106, 169.
7. Dew, *Insights from a Prophet's Life,* 174–75; Mehr, "Missionary Couples in Communist Europe," 182–92; Stewart, "LDS Church in Eastern Europe, Russia, and Central Asia," 562; Browning, *Russia and the Restored Gospel,* 13–16; Tobler, "Before the Wall Fell," 21–22, 26; Mehr, "Enduring Believers," 140–54. **Topic: Russell M. Nelson**
8. Patterson, *Restless Giant,* 213–17; Gaddis, *Cold War,* 229–36; Beverly Campbell to Richard Lindsay, Russell M. Nelson, and Robert L. Backman, Oct. 29, 1986; Russell M. Nelson, Memorandum, Nov. 18, 1986; Russell M. Nelson to First Presidency, Dec. 19, 1986, Russell M. Nelson, Area Files, CHL; "Skepticism Greets Soviet Hint of Religious Freedom," *Washington Post,* Nov. 1, 1986; Dew, *Insights from a Prophet's Life,* 176. **Topic: Russia**
9. Russell M. Nelson to Konstantin Kharchev, Apr. 30, 1987, Russell M. Nelson, Area Files, CHL; Russell M. Nelson and Hans B. Ringger, "Report of Trip to Moscow, Russia, USSR," June 9–12, 1987, 1, Beverly B. Campbell Papers, CHL; Dew, *Insights from a Prophet's Life,* 176–78; Condie, *Russell M. Nelson,* 268–69, emphasis in original.
10. Beverly Campbell to Richard Lindsay, Russell M. Nelson, and Robert L. Backman, Oct. 29, 1986, Russell M. Nelson, Area Files, CHL; Russell M. Nelson and Hans B. Ringger, "Report of Trip to Moscow, Russia, USSR," June 9–12, 1987, 1–7, Beverly B. Campbell Papers, CHL.
11. Condie, *Russell M. Nelson,* 269; Dew, *Insights from a Prophet's Life,* 177–78.
12. Nelson, "Personal Perspective and Prayer," 1–4; Russell M. Nelson and Hans B. Ringger, "Report of Trip to Moscow, Russia, USSR," June 9–12, 1987, 7, Beverly B.

Campbell Papers, CHL; Condie, *Russell M. Nelson,* 269; Matthew 28:19–20; Mark 16:15.
13. "Document Deals and Murder: A Hofmann Chronology," *Salt Lake Tribune,* Aug. 1, 1987, A6; Robert A. Jones, "The White Salamander Murders, Part II," *Los Angeles Times Magazine,* Apr. 5, 1987, 46; Turley, *Victims,* 114–45, 303–6.
14. Jeffrey R. Holland to BYU Board of Trustees, Mar. 19, 1986; Neal A. Maxwell and Dallin H. Oaks, "Report on BYU Religious Studies Center," Dec. 17, 1986, Dallin H. Oaks, Executive Council and Committee Files, CHL; Ricks, "Narrative Call Pattern in the Prophetic Commission of Enoch," 97–105; "Progress Report: Restoration of Major Doctrines through the Prophet Joseph Smith," 4.
15. "F.A.R.M.S. Work in Process," Mar. 26, 1986; Religious Studies Center Board Meeting, Minutes, June 8, 1987, Dallin H. Oaks, Executive Council and Committee Files, CHL; "Time Vindicates the Prophet," 1; Midgley, "Hugh Winder Nibley," xv–lxxxvii; Board of Education, Church Board of Education Meeting Minutes, Feb. 4, 1987. **Topic: Church History and Record Keeping**
16. Dallin H. Oaks, "Recent Events Involving Church History and Forged Documents," Aug. 6, 1987, Gordon B. Hinckley, Subject Files, CHL; "Forgeries Prove Lies, Innuendoes Were Groundless," *Church News,* Aug. 15, 1987, 3–4.
17. Brigham Young University, *Church History and Recent Forgeries: A Symposium,* Aug. 6, 1987, Gordon B. Hinckley, Subject Files, CHL; Mike Carter, "Plea Bargain Ends 26 Felony Counts," *Salt Lake Tribune,* Jan. 24, 1987, A1, A8; Stephen Hunt, "Board Tells Hofmann He'll Spend Life in Prison," *Salt Lake Tribune,* Jan. 30, 1988, B1–B2; Turley, *Victims,* 311–16, 334–36.
18. Dallin H. Oaks, "Recent Events Involving Church History and Forged Documents," Aug. 6, 1987, Gordon B. Hinckley, Subject Files, CHL; Dallin H. Oaks, "Recent Events Involving Church History and Forged Documents," *Ensign,* Oct. 1987, 63–69; Turley, *Victims,* 342. **Topic: Hofmann Forgeries**
19. Doctrine and Covenants 10:37; see also, for example, *Saints,* volume 1, chapters 35, 38, and 39; volume 2, chapters 20, 22, and 35.
20. Dallin H. Oaks, "Recent Events Involving Church History and Forged Documents," Aug. 6, 1987, 10–11, Gordon B. Hinckley, Subject Files, CHL; see also Dallin H. Oaks, "Recent Events Involving Church History and Forged Documents," *Ensign,* Oct. 1987, 69.
21. Ferguson, West Africa Trip Journal, Apr. 30, 1988.
22. Ferguson, Oral History Interview [Apr. 2022], 1.
23. Sorenson, "Mass Media and Discourse on Famine in the Horn of Africa," 223–25; First Presidency to General Authorities and others in the United States and Canada, Jan. 11, 1985, First Presidency, Circular Letters, CHL; Gerry Avant, "Fast Benefits Famine Victims," *Church News,* Feb. 3, 1985, 12; Gordon B. Hinckley, "The Victory over Death," *Ensign,* May 1985, 53–54; Pace, *Safe Journey,* 21–27; LeBaron, "Ethiopia," 342–43. **Topic: Fasting**
24. Pace, Oral History Interview, 3; Pace, *Safe Journey,* 24–27; Black and Walker, *Anxiously Engaged,* 180–87; Ferguson, Oral History Interview [1992–93], [1]–[2], [9], [17]–[18]; Ferguson, Oral History Interview [Apr. 2022], 2, 9–10; Ferguson, Oral History Interview [June 2022], 9–10.
25. Ferguson, Oral History Interview [June 2022], 9–10; Ferguson, Oral History Interview [1992–93], [17]–[18]; Ferguson, Oral History Interview [2013], [00:09:42]–[00:10:55]; Ferguson, Oral History Interview [Apr. 2022], 5–7; Welfare Services Executive Committee, Minutes, Nov. 14 and Dec. 12, 1985; First Presidency to Area Presidencies in the United States, Nov. 15, 1985, First Presidency, Circular Letters, CHL.
26. John K. Carmack and Keith B. McMullin to General Welfare Services Executive Committee, May 23, 1986; Latin America Health Fair, circa Jan. 1988; Freight Costs for Shipping Donated Medical Equipment to Budapest, Hungary, Humanitarian Service Proposal Review Summary, circa Oct. 1987; Self-Help Development Activities in Rural Bolivia, Humanitarian Service Proposal Review Summary, circa Oct. 1987, Welfare Services Executive Committee, Minutes, CHL; Welfare Services Executive Committee,

Minutes, Oct. 8, 1987, and Feb. 11, 1988; Isaac C. Ferguson to James Perry, Email, Apr. 26, 2023, Isaac Ferguson, Oral History Interview [2022], CHL. **Topic: Welfare Programs**

27. Ferguson, West Africa Trip Journal, May 1–5, 1988; Isaac C. Ferguson, "Freely Given," *Ensign,* Aug. 1988, 12; Ferguson, Oral History Interview [June 2022], 4; Isaac C. Ferguson to James Perry, Email, Feb. 24, 2023, Isaac Ferguson, Oral History Interview [2022], CHL.
28. Ferguson, West Africa Trip Journal, May 6–7 and 10–11, 1988; *Deseret News 1989–90 Church Almanac,* 86; "Abomosu Farm History," 1–7, Ghana Accra Mission District Report, CHL.
29. Ferguson, West Africa Trip Journal, May 11 and 18, 1988; "Abomosu Farm History," 5–8, Ghana Accra Mission District Report, CHL; Isaac C. Ferguson to Shawn Ferguson, May 12, 1988, Isaac Ferguson, Oral History Interview [2022], CHL; see also Petramalo and Petramalo, Oral History Interview, 29–30; and Petramalo, Mission Journal, Jan. 23 and 30, 1989; May 4–5, 1989.
30. Ferguson, West Africa Trip Journal, May 18, 1988. **Topic: Ghana**
31. Navarro, Oral History Interview [Apr. 2023], 8, 18, 21–22, 47–48, 55–58; Spencer W. Kimball, "When the World Will Be Converted," *Ensign,* Oct. 1974, 8–10; Navarro, Oral History Interview [2015], 2. Quotation edited for readability; "the mission" in English translation of original changed to "a mission."
32. Embry, "Without Purse or Scrip," 77–93; Jensen, "Without Purse or Scrip?," 3–14; Quorum of the Twelve Apostles, Missionary Executive Committee Minutes, Mar. 4 and 25, 1975; Apr. 1, 1975; May 20, 1975; June 10 and 13, 1975; First Presidency to Stake Presidents and others, Oct. 15, 1975; First Presidency to General Authorities and others, Dec. 1, 1988, First Presidency, Circular Letters, CHL; Gordon B. Hinckley, Address, Leadership Meeting, Apr. 4, 1986, 12–14, Quorum of the Twelve Apostles, Regional Representatives Seminar Addresses, CHL; "Exploratory Study of Returned Missionaries in Peru and Ecuador," Aug. 1987, Missionary Executive Council, Meeting Materials, CHL.
33. Missionary Executive Council to the Council of the Twelve, June 17, 1986, Missionary Executive Council, Meeting Materials, CHL; Missionary Executive Council, Minutes, Feb. 25, 1987; Navarro, Oral History Interview [Apr. 2023], 58.
34. Navarro, Oral History Interview [Apr. 2023], 51–52, 55–56; Navarro, Oral History Interview [2015], 3; Navarro, Email Interview.
35. Monson, Journal, Apr. 2, 1989; *Official Report of the One Hundred Fifty-Ninth Annual General Conference,* 102; Ezra Taft Benson, "To the Children of the Church," *Ensign,* May 1989, 81; Benson, *Come, Listen to a Prophet's Voice,* 1–61.
36. Primary Association, Annual History Reports, 1987, 50; 1988, 52; "Book of Mormon Emphasis for 1988," 1; Primary Association, General Board Minutes, Oct. 15, 1987, and Jan. 7, 1988; Ezra Taft Benson, "To the Children of the Church," *Ensign,* May 1989, 81; Moroni 10:30, 32.
37. Dew, *Ezra Taft Benson,* 15–20; Ezra Taft Benson, "To the Children of the Church," *Ensign,* May 1989, 82; Ezra Taft Benson, "After All We Can Do," Dec. 9, 1982, 3, Ezra Taft Benson Addresses, CHL.
38. Ezra Taft Benson, "After All We Can Do," Dec. 9, 1982, 3–4; Ezra Taft Benson, "After All We Can Do," Dec. 12, 1982, 3–4, Ezra Taft Benson Addresses, CHL; Ezra Taft Benson, "Feed My Sheep," Apr. 3, 1987, 2–3, Quorum of the Twelve Apostles, Regional Representatives Seminar Addresses, CHL; Kellene Ricks, "'The Power of Music' Found in New Songbook," *Church News,* May 20, 1989, 3, 5; *Children's Songbook,* 306–7, 309–11; *Sing with Me,* topical index. **Topics: Primary; Hymns**
39. Ezra Taft Benson, "To the Children of the Church," *Ensign,* May 1989, 82; Ezra Taft Benson, "Beware of Pride," *Ensign,* May 1989, 4–7; Gordon B. Hinckley, "Behold Your Little Ones," *Ensign,* Nov. 1978, 18–20; Gordon B. Hinckley, "To Please Our Heavenly Father," *Ensign,* May 1985, 50; Boyd K. Packer, "Little Children," *Ensign,* Nov. 1986, 16–18; *Child Abuse: Helps for Ecclesiastical Leaders* (Salt Lake City: The Church of Jesus Christ of Latter-day Saints, 1985).

40. *Official Report of the One Hundred Fifty-Ninth Annual General Conference*, 105–6; 159th Annual Conference, Sunday Afternoon Session, [01:49:00]–[01:49:57]. **Topic: Ezra Taft Benson**

CHAPTER 25: FOR THE GOSPEL'S SAKE

1. Alice Johnson Haney, "Mission Interrupted by the 'Freeze,'" *Liahona*, Dec. 2015, Africa West Area local pages, A4; Haney, Oral History Interview, [7]–[8].
2. Alice Johnson Haney, "Mission Interrupted by the 'Freeze,'" *Liahona*, Dec. 2015, Africa West Area local pages, A3–A4; Haney, Oral History Interview, [6]–[8]; Mabey, Journal, Oct. 3 and Dec. 8–10, 1978; Mabey and Allred, *Brother to Brother*, 64; Johnson, "History of The Church of Jesus Christ of Latter-day Saints in Ghana," [3]–[4]; Joseph Johnson, Oral History Interview [1998], 10; "Ghana Expels Missionaries, Bans Church," *Church News*, June 24, 1989, 12.
3. Alice Johnson Haney, "Mission Interrupted by the 'Freeze,'" *Liahona*, Dec. 2015, Africa West Area local pages, A4; Haney, Oral History Interview, [8]; "Ghana Expels Missionaries, Bans Church," *Church News*, June 24, 1989, 12; Kissi, *Walking in the Sand*, 202–3; Neal A. Maxwell to First Presidency and the Quorum of the Twelve Apostles, Memorandum, June 22, 1989, First Presidency, Mission Correspondence, 1964–2010, CHL; "Ghana Bans 2 Churches' Outposts," *Arizona Republic* (Phoenix), June 16, 1989, State edition, C7.
4. Haney, Oral History Interview, [8]; Alice Johnson Haney, "Mission Interrupted by the 'Freeze,'" *Liahona*, Dec. 2015, Africa West Area local pages, A4; Petramalo, Mission Journal, June 14, 1989. Quotation edited for readability; original source has "we have to show, we have to report, the mission home in Accra."
5. Alice Johnson Haney, "Mission Interrupted by the 'Freeze,'" *Liahona*, Dec. 2015, Africa West Area local pages, A3–A4; "Ghana Expels Missionaries, Bans Church," *Church News*, June 24, 1989, 12; Haney, Oral History Interview, [3], [5]; Robert L. Backman to Missionary Executive Council, June 14, 1989, Missionary Executive Council, Meeting Materials, CHL.
6. Alice Johnson Haney, "Mission Interrupted by the 'Freeze,'" *Liahona*, Dec. 2015, Africa West Area local pages, A4; Haney, Oral History Interview, [8]; Gunnell and Gunnell, Oral History Interview, 14; Petramalo, Mission Journal, June 14–15, 1989; Neal A. Maxwell to First Presidency and the Quorum of the Twelve Apostles, Memorandum, June 22, 1989, First Presidency, Mission Correspondence, 1964–2010, CHL.
7. Alice Johnson Haney, "Mission Interrupted by the 'Freeze,'" *Liahona*, Dec. 2015, Africa West Area local pages, A3–A4; Haney, Oral History Interview, [8]–[9], [11]; Kissi, *Walking in the Sand*, 202, 207.
8. Acquah, "The 'Freeze' and Three Days in Police Cells," [1]; Haws, "The Freeze and the Thaw," 27–30; "Ghana Expels Missionaries, Bans Church," *Church News*, June 24, 1989, 12; [Africa] Area Presidency to Neal A. Maxwell, June 11, 1990, Gordon B. Hinckley, Area Files, CHL; Kissi, *Walking in the Sand*, 199–200. **Topic: Ghana**
9. Acquah, "The 'Freeze' and Three Days in Police Cells," [1]–[2]; Acquah and Acquah, Oral History Interview [1999], 1–14.
10. Acquah, "The 'Freeze' and Three Days in Police Cells," [3]–[5]; Acquah and Acquah, Oral History Interview [1999], 28–29; Ampiah, Oral History Interview, 18–19. Quotation edited for readability; original source has "The officer . . . asked me to remove my shoes and give him my wrist watch."
11. Acquah, "The 'Freeze' and Three Days in Police Cells," [5]; Acquah and Acquah, Oral History Interview [1999], 29. Quotation edited for readability; original source has "He then said we were free to go."

Notes to pages 422–430

12. Campora, *Saint behind Enemy Lines,* 158–59; Kovářová, Oral History Interview, [27]; Oslzlý, "On Stage with the Velvet Revolution," 97–105.
13. Campora, *Saint behind Enemy Lines,* 152, 160; Fink, *Cold War,* 236–43; Krejčí and Machonin, *Czechoslovakia,* 209–11. **Topics: Cold War; Czechoslovakia**
14. Campora, *Saint behind Enemy Lines,* 155; Europe Area Presidency to Russell M. Nelson, Aug. 9, 1988; Russell M. Nelson to Miroslav Houštecký, Dec. 14, 1989; Russell M. Nelson, Area Files, CHL; Campora, Oral History Interview [2023], 1, 4–10; Temple Originated Records, Freiberg Temple, 1985–91, image 554, microfilm 1,233,716, FSL.
15. Campora, *Saint behind Enemy Lines,* 150–51, 159–60; Kovářová, Oral History Interview, [27].
16. Bradley, *Czechoslovakia's Velvet Revolution,* 80, 123; "200,000 March in Prague," *New York Times,* Nov. 21, 1989, A1, A9; Campora, *Saint behind Enemy Lines,* 160–63.
17. Bradley, *Czechoslovakia's Velvet Revolution,* 106–17; Campora, *Saint behind Enemy Lines,* 163, 167; Campora, Oral History Interview [2021], 54–55.
18. *Final Report of the Fact-Finding Commission,* 118–233; Espi, "Manila Philippines Temple during the Coup," [1]; Britsch, *From the East,* 318–73; *Deseret News 1991–1992 Church Almanac,* 156–57, 222, 233, 236–42; Philippines Area, Annual Historical Reports, 1989, [8]–[9]. **Topics: Philippines; Church Growth**
19. Espi, "Manila Philippines Temple, Coup d'Etat," [1]–[3]; Espi, "Manila Philippines Temple during the Coup," [1]–[2]; Hawkes, "Experience of Henry T. Solis," [1]; *Final Report of the Fact-Finding Commission,* 221–27; Dallin H. Oaks, "Miracles," *Ensign,* June 2001, 14; Dallin H. Oaks, Memorandum, Dec. 21, 1989, Gordon B. Hinckley, Area Files, CHL.
20. Espi, "Manila Philippines Temple, Coup d'Etat," [3]–[4]; *Final Report of the Fact-Finding Commission,* 228.
21. Espi, "Manila Philippines Temple, Coup d'Etat," [4]–[5]; Floyd H. Hogan, "History of the December 1989 Coup d'Etat in the Philippines as It Affected the Manila Philippines Temple," 3–4, in Dallin H. Oaks, Memorandum, Dec. 21, 1989, Gordon B. Hinckley, Area Files, CHL.
22. Navarro, Oral History Interview [May 10, 2022], 1–4; Navarro, Oral History Interview [2015], 3–4; *Directory of General Authorities and Officers, 1989,* [58].
23. Navarro, Oral History Interview [May 10, 2022], 4; Stern, "Beyond Enigma," 1–5; Switzer, "Sendero Luminoso and Peruvian Counterinsurgency," 53–57; Americas Watch, *Peru under Fire,* 1–5. **Topic: Peru**
24. Navarro, Oral History Interview [May 10, 2022], 4; Chuquimango, Oral History Interview, 1.
25. *Significant Incidents of Political Violence against Americans: 1988,* 4, 11–12, 15; *Significant Incidents of Political Violence against Americans: 1989,* 4, 6–8, 10–11, 13, 15–16; *Significant Incidents of Political Violence against Americans: 1990,* 3–5, 7–8; *Deseret News 1991–1992 Church Almanac,* 90–91, 155–56; Jim Robbins, "Mormons Face Latin Attacks," *Boston Globe,* Jan. 6, 1990, 3; Millett, "Aftermath of Intervention," 1–6, 12–14; "Anti-LDS Acts Rise in S. America," *Salt Lake Tribune,* Jan. 7, 1990, B1.
26. Richard T. Bretzing to M. Russell Ballard, Nov. 15, 1989; Robert L. Backman to Missionary Executive Council, Memorandum, Jan. 2, 1990; Charles Didier, Hartman Rector Jr., and F. Melvin Hammond to M. Russell Ballard, Feb. 6, 1990, Missionary Executive Council, Meeting Materials, CHL; Navarro, Oral History Interview [May 10, 2022], 4–7; Chuquimango, Oral History Interview, 6–7; Navarro, Oral History Interview [2015], 4.
27. Navarro, Oral History Interview [May 10, 2022], 5, 7, 14; Chuquimango, Oral History Interview, 7; Navarro, Oral History Interview [May 20, 2022], 1; Navarro, Oral History Interview [2015], 5. **Topic: Healing**

Chapter 26: I Want to Serve

1. Navarro, Oral History Interview [May 10, 2022], 2, 6–7, 9, 12; Navarro, Oral History Interview [Aug. 2022], 1–4; Chuquimango, Oral History Interview, 7.
2. Navarro, Email Interview; Navarro, Oral History Interview [May 10, 2022], 9–10; Navarro, Oral History Interview [Aug. 2022], 5–6.
3. Palomino, Oral History Interview, 1–2, 4; Navarro, Oral History Interview [May 10, 2022], 11. Quotation edited for readability; "wanted" in English translation of original changed to "want," and two instances of "was" changed to "is."
4. Navarro, Oral History Interview [May 10, 2022], 7, 10–11; Navarro, Oral History Interview [Aug. 2022], 6–8; Navarro, Email Interview; Navarro, Oral History Interview [May 20, 2022], 1–3; Palomino, Oral History Interview, 4, 6.
5. Gray, Oral History Interview, 225–26, 228, 287, 292; Allen, Embry, and Mehr, *Hearts Turned to the Fathers,* 295, 297–98; Taylor, Oral History Interview, [16], [21], [35]; R. Scott Lloyd, "Golden Anniversary of Microfilming," *Church News,* Dec. 3, 1988, 8; "'Remarkable Growth' in Church Will Increase Interest, Tourism in Utah," *Church News,* Feb. 4, 1989, 10. **Topic: Family History and Genealogy**
6. Gray, Oral History Interview, 226, 287; Josiah, "Providing for the Future," 2, 5, 7–9; Osthaus, *Freedmen, Philanthropy, and Fraud,* 1–3, 8–9, 95–96, 201–8; Fleming, *Freedmen's Savings Bank,* 129–30. **Topic: Slavery and Abolition**
7. Bob Mims, "Ex-slave Files a Prize for History Buffs," *Salt Lake Tribune,* Feb. 21, 2001, A1, A8; Bob Mims, "Rich Lode of Black History Opens," *Salt Lake Tribune,* Feb. 27, 2001, B1; Rose and Eichholz, *Black Genesis,* 22–23, 39, 49; Blockson, *Black Genealogy,* 2–5, 40–41, 44–45; Gray, "Tracing Ancestors"; Gray, Oral History Interview, 227.
8. Gray, Oral History Interview, 226–27, 287; Jason Swensen, "Freedman's Bank," *Church News,* Mar. 3, 2001, 3.
9. Gray, Oral History Interview, 226–27, 287–88; Allen, Embry, and Mehr, *Hearts Turned to the Fathers,* 272–73, 280–82, 312–17; Gray, Interview [Oct. 2022], [13]; Nelson, *Elijah Abel Freedman's Bank Project,* [4]–[5]; "Operating Statistics: Family History Department," Dec. 14, 1990, 19–20b, Family and Church History Department, Annual Reports, CHL; Jason Swensen, "Freedman's Bank," *Church News,* Mar. 3, 2001, 3.
10. Haney, Oral History Interview, [9]–[10], [12]–[13]; Alice Johnson Haney, "Mission Interrupted by the 'Freeze,'" *Liahona,* Dec. 2015, Africa West Area local pages, A4–A5.
11. Kissi, *Walking in the Sand,* 200–203, 207. **Topic: Ghana**
12. Haney, Oral History Interview, [8], [11]–[14]; Alice Haney to Brenda Homer, Email, Feb. 22, 2024, Alice Haney, Oral History Interview, CHL; Alice Johnson Haney, "Mission Interrupted by the 'Freeze,'" *Liahona,* Dec. 2015, Africa West Area local pages, A4.
13. Kissi, *Walking in the Sand,* 204–32, 239; Bruce Olsen to Eric Otoo, June 23, 1989, First Presidency, Mission Correspondence, 1964–2010, CHL; Stokes, Oral History Interview, 16–21; Haws, "The Freeze and the Thaw," 35–37. **Topic: Priesthood and Temple Restriction**
14. Kissi, *Walking in the Sand,* 200, 205; Bonnet, Oral History Interview [2017], 2, 4–7; Robert Sackley, "Historical Report," 1–2, in Africa Area, Annual Historical Reports, 1990; Bonnet, Journal, Dec. 10, 1990; see also Georges Bonnet to Richard Lindsay, Memorandum, Nov. 24, 1990, Georges Bonnet, Oral History Interview [2023], CHL.
15. Haney, Oral History Interview, [14]–[16]; *Directory of General Authorities and Officers, 1991,* 44; James E. Faust to First Presidency and Council of the Twelve, Memorandum, Dec. 19, 1990, Gordon B. Hinckley, Area Files, CHL; Kissi, *Walking in the Sand,* 238–39.
16. Africa Area, Annual Historical Reports, 1991, [4]; Faust, Journal, Apr. 20, 1991; Gunnell and Gunnell, Oral History Interview, 6, 14–15.
17. Haney, Oral History Interview, [17]–[18]; Alice Johnson Haney, "Mission Interrupted by the 'Freeze,'" *Liahona,* Dec. 2015, Africa West Area local pages, A5.

18. Kissi, Oral History Interview, 34–35; Haws, "The Freeze and the Thaw," 39; Gunnell and Gunnell, Oral History Interview, 15; Haney, Oral History Interview, [17]–[18].
19. Navarro, Oral History Interview [Aug. 2022], 8–10, 12; Navarro, Oral History Interview [May 10, 2022], 15; Navarro, Oral History Interview [May 20, 2022], 8; Navarro, Email Interview. Quotation edited for readability; English translation of original has "son, always remember the prayer."
20. Navarro, Oral History Interview [Jan. 2023], 2; Navarro, Oral History Interview [Aug. 2022], 10–12; Navarro, Oral History Interview [May 20, 2022], 7; Nunez, Oral History Interview, [00:01:54]–[00:04:03], [00:04:29]–[00:04:42], [00:16:20]–[00:16:54], [00:29:45]–[00:29:57]. **Topic: High Council**
21. Navarro, Oral History Interview [Aug. 2022], 10, 12; Navarro, Oral History Interview [May 10, 2022], 14; Navarro, Oral History Interview [May 20, 2022], 8; Cook, Oral History Interview, 5–17, 27–35. **Topic: Peru**
22. Hinckley, Journal, Apr. 22, 1991; Gordon B. Hinckley, "Struggle for Peace," Jan. 27, 1991, Gordon B. Hinckley Addresses, CHL; *Deseret News 1991–1992 Church Almanac,* 84; Missionary Department, Annual Reports, 1991, 7–8; see also Chou and Chou, *Voice of the Saints in Mongolia,* 1–27. **Topics: Gordon B. Hinckley; India; Malaysia; Singapore**
23. Howard W. Hunter to Merlin Lybbert, Nov. 7, 1990, Quorum of the Twelve Apostles, Circular Letters, CHL; Woodger, "Hong Kong Temple," 57–58; Hook, "From Repossession to Retrocession," 1–29; Hinckley, Journal, Oct. 22, 1986; Feb. 11, 1992; May 6, 1992; July 26, 1992. **Topic: Hong Kong**
24. Hinckley, Journal, Apr. 22, 1991, and Dec. 6, 1994; Gordon B. Hinckley, in Hong Kong Temple, Dedication Services, 8, 67; Nicholas D. Kristof, "Hong Kong Symbol Looks Away," *New York Times,* Jan. 7, 1991, D1; Britsch, *From the East,* 295.
25. Condie, *Russell M. Nelson,* 285–86; Gerry Avant, "Choir Leaves Trail of Joyful Tears," *Church News,* July 6, 1991, 3, 8–9; Jay M. Todd, "An Encore of the Spirit," *Ensign,* Oct. 1991, 32–35, 44. **Topics: Russell M. Nelson; Tabernacle Choir; Hungary**
26. Dew, *Insights from a Prophet's Life,* 174; Hans B. Ringger, Spencer J. Condie, and Albert Choules Jr. to Russell M. Nelson, Oct. 31, 1989; L. Tom Perry to Priesthood Executive Council, Oct. 1, 1991, Missionary Executive Council, Meeting Materials, CHL; Gaddis, *Cold War,* 237–57; Kuehne, *Mormons as Citizens of a Communist State,* 346–54; Nelson, Oral History Interview, 1; Jay M. Todd, "An Encore of the Spirit," *Ensign,* Oct. 1991, 33. **Topics: Bulgaria; Croatia; Poland; Romania; Slovenia**
27. Gerry Avant, "Singers Are Celebrities in Hungary's Capital City," *Church News,* June 22, 1991, 4; Dell Van Orden, "Church Granted Legal Recognition in Hungary," *Church News,* July 2, 1988, 13; Russell M. Nelson, Hans B. Ringger, and Spencer J. Condie, "Report Trip to Hungary," Apr. 19–22, 1987, Russell M. Nelson, Area Files, CHL; Jay M. Todd, "Church Growth in Tour Areas," *Ensign,* Oct. 1991, 37.
28. Condie, *Russell M. Nelson,* 286–87; Jay M. Todd, "Tour Milestones," *Ensign,* Oct. 1991, 44–46, 48; Browning, *Russia and the Restored Gospel,* 20–48; Gaddis, *Cold War,* 237–57. **Topics: Estonia; Russia**
29. Jepson, Journal, June 23–24 and 29, 1991; Condie, *Russell M. Nelson,* 287; Nelson, "Lord Uses the Unlikely"; Dew, *Insights from a Prophet's Life,* 191, 194–96, 204.
30. Browning, *Russia and the Restored Gospel,* 38–39, 44, 87, 137–38; "Registration of Leningrad Branch Approved," *Church News,* Sept. 29, 1990, 3; Russell M. Nelson to First Presidency and Quorum of the Twelve, Memorandum, Nov. 2, 1990, Russell M. Nelson, Area Files, CHL; Dew, *Insights from a Prophet's Life,* 181, 194–95.
31. Joan Browning to Family, June 30, 1991, Gary L. Browning Papers, CHL; Jerold D. Ottley, Oral History, 1991, 19–20, Jerold D. Ottley, Mormon Tabernacle Choir History, CHL; Bardsley, Journal, June 24, 1991; Russell M. Nelson to Pierce Campbell and Beverly Campbell, July 9, 1991, Beverly B. Campbell Papers, CHL.
32. "Announcement of Official Recognition of The Church of Jesus Christ of Latter-day Saints in the Russian Soviet Socialist Republic," June 24, 1991, Mormon Tabernacle Choir, Chronological Files, CHL; Dew, *Insights from a Prophet's Life,* 180–81;

"Certificate of Registration of the Charter of a Religious Association for The Church of Jesus Christ of Latter-day Saints," May 28, 1991, in Liudmila S. Terebenina, "History of the Church in the USSR and in Russia," 38. Quotation edited for accuracy; "Russian Republic" in original changed to "Russian Soviet Federative Socialist Republic."

33. Dew, *Insights from a Prophet's Life,* 181; Gerry Avant and Matthew Brown, "Church Is Recognized by Russian Republic," *Church News,* June 29, 1991, 3; Browning, Oral History Interview, 1–2; Browning, *Russia and the Restored Gospel,* 151.
34. Joan Browning to Family, June 30, 1991, Gary L. Browning Papers, CHL; Dew, *Insights from a Prophet's Life,* 197–98; Nelson and Oaks, Oral History Interview, 8; Nelson, "Lord Uses the Unlikely"; Hinckley, Journal, May 30, 1991.

Chapter 27: The Hand of Friendship

1. Wan, Oral History Interview [July 2022], [1]–[3]; Wan, Oral History Interview [2001], 1; Wan, *Heavens Are Higher,* 73; Asia Area Presidency to Neal A. Maxwell, June 19, 1992, Russell M. Nelson, Area Files, CHL; Carmack, Oral History Interview, 45–46; Hinckley, Journal, July 25, 1992. **Topics: Gordon B. Hinckley; Hong Kong**
2. Wan, Oral History Interview [July 2022], [2], [7]; Wan, *Heavens Are Higher,* 4; Wan, Oral History Interview [2001], 1–4, 6, 9; Wan and Wan, Oral History Interview, [3]; China Hong Kong Mission, Manuscript History and Historical Reports, Nov. 16, 1957; Xi, "History of Mormon-Chinese Relations," 63–74.
3. Wan, Oral History Interview [July 2022], [3], [7]; Wan, Oral History Interview [2001], 9–10; Wan and Wan, Oral History Interview, [2]–[3].
4. Wan, Oral History Interview [July 2022], [3]; Wan, Oral History Interview [2001], 10–11; Hinckley, Journal, July 26, 1992; Carmack, Journal, July 26, 1992; Asia Area Presidency to Neal A. Maxwell, June 19, 1992, Russell M. Nelson, Area Files, CHL.
5. Wan, Oral History Interview [2001], 10–11; Wan, Oral History Interview [July 2022], [3]; Wan, *Heavens Are Higher,* 73.
6. Wan, Oral History Interview [July 2022], [3], [14]; Wan and Wan, Oral History Interview, [5], [38], [42]–[43]; Carmack, Oral History Interview, 46; Wan, Journal, July 26, 1992; Carmack, Journal, July 26, 1992.
7. Hinckley, Journal, July 25–27, 1992; Wan, Oral History Interview [2001], 10–11; Gordon B. Hinckley, in Hong Kong Temple, Dedication Services, 8, 67; Wan, Oral History Interview [July 2022], [3]; Wan and Wan, Oral History Interview, [38].
8. Wan, Oral History Interview [July 2022], [3]; Wan, Oral History Interview [2001], 11; Ng and Chin, *History in Hong Kong,* 91; Wan and Wan, Oral History Interview, [43]; Hinckley, Journal, July 26, 1992; Gordon B. Hinckley, in Hong Kong Temple, Dedication Services, 8, 67. Quotation edited for readability; "of from seven to ten stories" in original changed to "of seven to ten stories."
9. Wan and Wan, Oral History Interview, [43]–[44]; Wan, Oral History Interview [July 2022], [3]; Gordon B. Hinckley, in Hong Kong Temple, Dedication Services, 8, 67; Hinckley, Journal, July 26–27, 1992; Wan, Oral History Interview [2001], 11.
10. Wan, *Hong Kong Kom Tong Hall,* 154; Wan, Oral History Interview [July 2022], [3]–[4].
11. Willy Binene, Oral History Interview [2019]; Willy Binene, Oral History Interview [2017]; Lewis and Lewis, "President Sabwe Binene's Story," [1]; *Directory of General Authorities and Officers, 1993,* 74.
12. Morrison, *Dawning of a Brighter Day,* chapter 8; "Church Growth Pervasive, Steady," *Church News,* June 4, 1994, 4; Missionary Department, Annual Reports, 1991, 3–4; "Status of Nations—Africa," 1–3, in Robert L. Backman to Missionary Executive Council, Memorandum, June 15, 1992, Missionary Executive Council, Meeting Materials, CHL; Plewe, *Mapping Mormonism,* 232–33.

13. "Zaire's People—Thirsty for Gospel," *Church News,* July 18, 1987, 3; *Deseret News 1991–1992 Church Almanac,* 174; LeBaron, "Interim Report to Africa Area Presidency," 3. **Topic: Democratic Republic of the Congo**
14. Willy Binene, Oral History Interview [2019]; Willy Binene, Oral History Interview [2017]; Lewis and Lewis, "President Sabwe Binene's Story," [1].
15. Willy Binene, Oral History Interview [2017]; Willy Binene, Oral History Interview [2019]; Lewis and Lewis, "President Sabwe Binene's Story," [1]. Quotation edited for readability; "asked why he was delaying" in original changed to "Why are you delaying."
16. Willy Binene, Oral History Interview [2017]; Willy Binene, Oral History Interview [2019]; Lewis and Lewis, "President Sabwe Binene's Story," [1]; Jeffrey Bradshaw to Jed Woodworth, Email, Mar. 5, 2023, copy in editors' possession; Kimball, *Le miracle du pardon,* 45–47.
17. Lewis and Lewis, "President Sabwe Binene's Story," [1]; Willy Binene, Oral History Interview [2019]; Willy Binene, Oral History Interview [2017].
18. Kenneth B. Noble, "Tens of Thousands Flee Ethnic Violence in Zaire," *New York Times,* Mar. 21, 1993, 3; Scott Peterson, "Thousands Are Displaced by Zaire's Ethnic Violence," *Christian Science Monitor,* May 6, 1993, 7; Lewis and Lewis, "President Sabwe Binene's Story," [1]; Vinckel, "Violence and Everyday Interactions between Katangese and Kasaians," 78–83; Willy Binene, Oral History Interview [July 2020].
19. Vinckel, "Violence and Everyday Interactions between Katangese and Kasaians," 79; Scott Peterson, "Thousands Are Displaced by Zaire's Ethnic Violence," *Christian Science Monitor,* May 6, 1993, 7; Willy Binene, Oral History Interview [May 20, 2020], [6]; Hussein, "Testimonies from Zaire," 28; Willy Binene, Oral History Interview [July 2020].
20. Scott Peterson, "Thousands Are Displaced by Zaire's Ethnic Violence," *Christian Science Monitor,* May 6, 1993, 7; Willy Binene, Oral History Interview [May 20, 2020], [6], [8]–[9]; Willy Binene, Oral History Interview [July 2020]; Lewis and Lewis, "President Sabwe Binene's Story," [1]; Binene, Interview [July 7, 2020], [1].
21. Scott Peterson, "Thousands Are Displaced by Zaire's Ethnic Violence," *Christian Science Monitor,* May 6, 1993, 7; Binene, Interview [July 7, 2020], [1]; Willy Binene, Oral History Interview [2019]; Willy Binene, Oral History Interview [May 20, 2020], [6]; Willy Binene, Oral History Interview [July 2020]; Welfare Services Executive Committee, Minutes, May 13, 1993.
22. Willy Binene, Oral History Interview [May 20, 2020], [6], [8]–[10], [12]; Binene, Interview [July 7, 2020], [1]–[2]; Jeffrey Bradshaw to Jed Woodworth, Email, Mar. 5, 2023, copy in editors' possession; Lewis and Lewis, "President Sabwe Binene's Story," [2].
23. Curbelo, *Historia de los Santos,* 185; Allred, Oral History Interview [Sept. 2022], 12–14, 18, 32; Allred, Oral History Interview [Jan. 2021], 1–3; "Reunión de la presidencia de la Misión Paraguay Asunción, I.J.S.U.D.," Aug. 10, 1993, Paraguay Asunción Mission, Mission Presidency Minutes, CHL; Clayton, "Harvest of Faith in Abundancia," 119–21.

Topic: Paraguay

24. Allred, Oral History Interview [Jan. 2021], 1–6; Allred and Allred, Oral History Interview, 25–26; Allred, Oral History Interview [Feb. 2012], 18–19; *Deseret News 1993–1994 Church Almanac,* 401–2; Curbelo, *Historia de los Santos,* 155, 183; Church Historical Department, "History of the Mission Paraguay-Asuncion 1992," in Paraguay Asunción Mission, Annual Historical Reports, CHL; "Total de bautismos 1991," in Chilean Mission, Baptism Statistics and Directories, CHL; Missionary Department Statistical Report, June 1992, 3; July 1992, 3, South America South Area, Mission Files, CHL.
25. Clayton, "Harvest of Faith in Abundancia," 117–19; Allred, Oral History Interview [Sept. 2022], 11–15; Curbelo, *Historia de los Santos,* 185–95; Nestor Curbelo, "Paraguay: Chulupi Colony, Mistolar, Thrives Deep in Interior," *Church News,* June 2, 1990, 8–9, 12; "Paraguayan Indians: Branch Thrives in Jungle," *Church News,* Nov. 27, 1983, 4, 14; Allred, Oral History Interview [Jan. 2021], 7.

26. First Presidency to General Authorities and others, Apr. 16, 1991, First Presidency, Circular Letters, CHL; Hinckley, Journal, Nov. 15, 1989; *General Handbook of Instructions* [1989], section 9, 2. **Topic: Church Finances**
27. Allred, Oral History Interview [Sept. 2022], 13–16; Allred, Oral History Interview [Jan. 2021], 7; Allred and Allred, Oral History Interview, 25–26; Ted E. Brewerton, "Mistolar: Spiritual Oasis," *Tambuli*, Sept. 1990, 11; "Water Piped into Aymara Village," *Church News*, Feb. 13, 1982, 11. **Topic: Welfare Programs**
28. Allred, Oral History Interview [Sept. 2022], 12; Silvia H. Allred, "Steadfast and Immovable," *Ensign* or *Liahona*, Nov. 2010, 117–18; Curbelo, *Historia de los Santos*, 195–97; Nestor Curbelo, "Paraguay: Chulupi Colony, Mistolar, Thrives Deep in Interior," *Church News*, June 2, 1990, 8–9, 12. **Topic: Sealing**
29. "Pres. Benson Dies at Age 94," *Church News*, June 4, 1994, 3–4; Howard W. Hunter, "A Strong and Mighty Man," *Ensign*, July 1994, 42; Ezra Taft Benson, "Beware of Pride," *Ensign*, May 1989, 4–7; Haws, "LDS Church Presidency Years, 1985–1994," 224–27.
30. "Special Bulletin," Mar. 1993, in Priesthood Executive Council, Minutes, CHL; Rather, "Welfare Compendium," 229–32; Welfare Services Executive Committee, Minutes, May 12, 1994; M. Russell Ballard to Missionary Executive Council, Jan. 30, 1985; Howard W. Hunter to All General Authorities and Mission Presidents, Apr. 15, 1986, Missionary Executive Council, Meeting Materials, CHL.
31. Haws, "LDS Church Presidency Years, 1985–1994," 214–15; "Church Growth Pervasive, Steady," "Heed Book of Mormon, Prophet Urged," "Prophet's Counsel Powerful, Timeless," and "Sermons Showed Love for People," *Church News*, June 4, 1994, 4, 6–7, 12; Hinckley, Journal, Aug. 29, 1989; Jan. 1, 1990; Dec. 20, 1991; Aug. 4, 1992; Nov. 8, 1992; Mar. 24, 1993; Mar. 31, 1994; Monson, Journal, Nov. 3, 1997; "Europe—Summary of Nations as of December 1993," Missionary Executive Council, Meeting Materials, CHL; Mehr, *Mormon Missionaries Enter Eastern Europe*, 203–42. **Topics: Ezra Taft Benson; First Presidency; Quorum of the Twelve**
32. Hunter, Journal, May 23, 1994; Peggy Fletcher Stack, "LDS Hail Hunter as President," *Salt Lake Tribune*, June 7, 1994, A1, A4; Hinckley, Journal, June 26, 1994; Dew, *Go Forward with Faith*, 497; "Valiant Servant of the Lord," *Church News*, June 11, 1994, 4, 14.
33. Hunter, Journal, June 5–6, 1994; "Pres. Hunter Is Ordained Prophet," *Church News*, June 11, 1994, 3. **Topics: Howard W. Hunter; Succession of Church Leadership**
34. Hunter, Journal, June 26, 1994; Hinckley, Journal, June 26, 1994; Dell Van Orden, "A Time to Remember, Honor, Respect," and "Sunstone Is Unveiled at Temple Site," *Church News*, July 2, 1994, 3, 7. **Topics: Nauvoo (Commerce), Illinois; Deaths of Joseph and Hyrum Smith**
35. Jim Yoggerst, "Nauvoo and Its Temple," *Waterloo (IL) Republic-Times*, Nov. 21, 1990, 8; "Sunstone Is Unveiled at Temple Site," *Church News*, July 2, 1994, 7. **Topic: Nauvoo Temple**
36. Hunter, Journal, June 26, 1994; Hinckley, Journal, June 26, 1994; "150th Milestone a Time of Reflection," *Church News*, July 2, 1994, 10; *Deseret News 1997–98 Church Almanac*, 298, 308, 322, 361–62, 393–94; Plewe, *Mapping Mormonism*, 232–33; Missionary Department, Annual Reports, 1993, vi, 3–9, 30; "Five New Temples Add 'Great Momentum,'" *Church News*, Apr. 15, 1984, 6; "New Temples Planned in 3 Countries," *Church News*, Apr. 3, 1982, 4.
37. Hunter, Journal, June 26, 1994; Hinckley, Journal, June 26, 1994; "We Celebrate Their Memory by Magnifying Message of Master," *Church News*, July 2, 1994, 6, 10.

Chapter 28: The Lord's Path

1. Hunter, Journal, Dec. 15, 1994; Scott, Journal, Jan. 14, 1995; Hinckley, Journal, Jan. 8 and 15, 1995; Feb. 1, 9, and 14–15, 1995; Mar. 3, 1995; Monson, Journal, Mar. 3, 1995; Gibbons, *Howard W. Hunter*, 165; Dew, *Go Forward with Faith*, 504–5.

2. "President Hunter Is Eulogized," *Church News*, Mar. 11, 1995, 4.
3. "Milestones in Pres. Hunter's Life," and "Nine Busy Months for 14th President," *Church News*, Mar. 11, 1995, 8, 18; Hinckley, Journal, Aug. 11, 1994; Africa Area, Annual Historical Reports, 1994, 4.
4. Faust, Journal, Nov. 1, 1994; Gerry Avant, "He Wanted to Visit the Holy Land 'Just One More Time,'" *Church News*, Mar. 11, 1995, 9. **Topic: Howard W. Hunter**
5. Hinckley, Journal, Mar. 9, 1995. **Topics: Gordon B. Hinckley; Salt Lake Temple**
6. Gray, Oral History Interview, 227–28, 232–33, 290–96; Nelson, *Elijah Abel Freedman's Bank Project*, [4]–[5].
7. Allen, Embry, and Mehr, *Hearts Turned to the Fathers*, 289–311, 324–34; Nelson, *Elijah Abel Freedman's Bank Project*, [6], [8]. **Topic: Family History and Genealogy**
8. Gray, Oral History Interview, 231, 234–35, 290–91, 295–98; Nelson, *Elijah Abel Freedman's Bank Project*, [5]–[8], [10]; Gray, Interview [Oct. 2022], [14], [16]–[17].
9. Gray, Oral History Interview, 232, 236–37, 291, 296; Nelson, *Elijah Abel Freedman's Bank Project*, [12]–[13]; Taylor, Oral History Interview, [7]–[8].
10. Allen, Embry, and Mehr, *Hearts Turned to the Fathers*, 290; Nelson, *Elijah Abel Freedman's Bank Project*, [6], [8]; Gray, Oral History Interview, 229–30; Taylor, Oral History Interview, [21], [26]; Gray, Interview [Oct. 2022], [16]–[17]. **Topic: Sealing**
11. Gray, Oral History Interview, 229–30, 296–97; Gray, Interview [Oct. 2022], [16].
12. Hinckley, Journal, Apr. 5 and 13, 1995; June 8, 1995; Aug. 10 and 16, 1995; Sept. 14, 1995; Oct. 4 and 12, 1995; Nov. 15, 1995; Dec. 14, 1995; Jan. 11, 1996; Feb. 8, 1996; Mar. 14, 1996; "Ground Is Broken for Hong Kong Temple to Serve 18,400 Members in Mission, Four Stakes," *Church News*, Feb. 5, 1994, 3.
13. Missionary Department, Full-Time Mission Monthly Progress Reports, Jan. 1955; *Deseret News 1997–98 Church Almanac*, 345–47, 349–50, 375–77, 393–95, 404–5, 525; Harper, "First Decade of Mormonism in Mongolia," 19–46; Chou and Chou, *Voice of the Saints in Mongolia*, 59–77; "Church Recognized in Cambodia," *Ensign*, May 1994, 110; Gill, "The Church of Jesus Christ of Latter-day Saints in India," 75. **Topics: Japan; South Korea; Philippines; Cambodia; India**
14. Lu, Reminiscences, 1–2; Laury Livsey, "Well Schooled," *New Era*, Oct. 1995, 28–32. **Topics: Taiwan; Sacrament Meetings**
15. Urtnasangiin, Oral History Interview, 1–12; "The Church in Mongolia," Aug. 9, 1994, in Carmack, Journal, Aug. 31, 1994; Chou and Chou, *Voice of the Saints in Mongolia*, 63; Briana Stewart, "Mongolia," *LDS Living*, Nov.–Dec. 2012, 73; Don L. Searle, "Mongolia: Steppes of Faith," *Liahona* (U.S./Canada), Dec. 2007, 20–21. **Topic: Mongolia**
16. David Mitchell, "The Saints of Thailand," *Tambuli*, May 1993, 41–43; Joan Porter Ford and LaRene Porter Gaunt, "The Gospel Dawning in Thailand," *Ensign*, Sept. 1995, 54. **Topic: Thailand**
17. Cruz and Cruz, Oral History Interview, [5]–[7]; "The Young Man from the Precious Book" to Celia Cruz, Feb. 10, 1996, Celia Cruz, Oral History Interviews, CHL; Cruz, Oral History Interview [Oct. 2022], [1]–[2]; Cruz, Oral History Interview [Dec. 2022], [1].
18. Cruz, Oral History Interview [Oct. 2022], [2]; Cruz, Oral History Interview [Dec. 2022], [2]; *Deseret News 1997–98 Church Almanac*, 317, 380; Fraticelli, "Brief Chronological History of the Church of Jesus Christ of the Latter Day Saints in the Caribbean," 31, 241–60; *Deseret News 2012 Church Almanac*, 418, 425–26, 428, 467–68, 487–88, 491, 502, 549, 555, 596; "Pres. Winder Visits Guantanamo," *Church News*, May 30, 1964, 7; Missionary Department, Annual Reports, 1995, 18; "Temple to Be Built in the Caribbean," *Church News*, Dec. 4, 1993, 3–4. **Topics: Puerto Rico; Dominican Republic**
19. Cruz, Oral History Interview [Oct. 2022], [1]; Cruz, Oral History Interview [Dec. 2022], [2]–[3]; Cruz and Cruz, Oral History Interview, [7]; John L. Hart, "When I Pray about It, I Feel All Warm Inside," *Church News*, July 30, 1988, 5; "Personalized Copy Puts You on Mission," *Church News*, Aug. 21, 1982, 14; Ezra Taft Benson to Stake Presidents and others, May 11, 1979, Quorum of the Twelve Apostles, Circular Letters, CHL.
20. Missionary Department to General Authorities and Mission Presidents in the United States and Canada, July 18, 1994, Missionary Executive Council, Meeting Materials,

CHL; First Presidency to Church Officers and Members in the United States and Canada, Dec. 19, 1990, First Presidency, Circular Letters, CHL; "New General Fund Will Provide More Copies of Book of Mormon," *Church News,* Dec. 29, 1990, 3; see also First Presidency to General Authorities and others, Dec. 17, 1992; First Presidency to General Authorities, Dec. 20, 1993, First Presidency, Circular Letters, CHL.
21. Cruz, Oral History Interview [Dec. 2022], [2]–[3]; Cruz and Cruz, Oral History Interview, [1]–[8]; Cruz, Oral History Interview [Oct. 2022], [1].
22. Cruz, Oral History Interview [Oct. 2022], [1]–[2]; Cruz, Oral History Interview [2023], [1]–[2]; Cruz, Oral History Interview [Dec. 2022], [1], [3]; Cruz and Cruz, Oral History Interview, [7]–[8]; "Your Secret Friend" to Celia Cruz, [Aug. 1995], Celia Cruz, Oral History Interviews, CHL.
23. Lewis and Lewis, "President Sabwe Binene's Story," [2]; Willy Binene, Oral History Interview [2019]; Vinckel, "Violence and Everyday Interactions between Katangese and Kasaians," 78–79.
24. Willy Binene, Oral History Interview [Jan. 2023]; Willy Binene, Oral History Interview [May 20, 2020], [9]; Lewis and Lewis, "President Sabwe Binene's Story," [2].
25. Willy Binene, Oral History Interview [May 20, 2020], [8]–[11]; Lewis and Lewis, "President Sabwe Binene's Story," [2]; Willy Binene, Oral History Interview [2019]; Willy Binene, Oral History Interview [2017]; Willy Binene, Oral History Interview [Jan. 2023].
26. Willy Binene, Oral History Interview [Jan. 2023]; Willy Binene, Oral History Interview [May 20, 2020], [11]–[12]; Willy Binene, Oral History Interview [2019]; Willy Binene, Oral History Interview [2017]; "New Mission Presidents Assigned," *Church News,* Mar. 18, 1995, 9; *Directory of General Authorities and Officers, 1996,* 70.
27. Willy Binene, Oral History Interview [Jan. 2023]; Willy Binene, Oral History Interview [May 20, 2020], [11]; Willy Binene, Oral History Interview [2019]; Willy Binene, Oral History Interview [2017]. **Topics: Tithing; Democratic Republic of the Congo**
28. Cruz, Oral History Interview [Oct. 2022], [2]; "My Life Has Changed," *Church News,* Jan. 6, 1996, 16; "Your Secret Friend" to Celia Cruz, [Aug. 1995], Celia Cruz, Oral History Interviews, CHL. Quotation edited for clarity; instead of "dollars," the original has "pesos," which is used synonymously with dollars in Puerto Rico.
29. Cruz, Oral History Interview [2023], [2].
30. William O. Nelson, "Christ's Teachings Explained Clearly," "A Chronology of the Book of Mormon," "Book Is 'Record of God's Dealings,'" "Teaching Tool," and "My Life Has Changed," *Church News,* Jan. 6, 1996, 4–5, 8–10, 13–14, 16; Cruz, Oral History Interview [2023], [3]. **Topic: Sunday School**
31. "The Young Man from the Precious Book" to Celia Cruz, Feb. 10, 1996, Celia Cruz, Oral History Interviews, CHL.

Chapter 29: One Great Family

1. Maridan Sollesta to James Perry, Emails, Mar. 8, 2022; Aug. 15, 2022; Oct. 3, 2022; Maridan Sollesta and Eusebio Sollesta, Oral History Interviews, CHL.
2. John L. Hart, "Over Half LDS Now Outside U.S.," *Church News,* Mar. 2, 1996, 3; Sollesta, Autobiography, 5; Philippines Area, Annual Historical Reports, 1991, 2; 1995, 1; Sollesta and Sollesta, Oral History Interview [Mar. 2023], 2; "Church Membership Worldwide," and "Church Growth: Selected Countries," *Church News,* Mar. 2, 1996, 3, 6. **Topics: Church Growth; Philippines**
3. Cannon and Cowan, *Unto Every Nation,* ix–xxv; *Deseret News 1997–98 Church Almanac,* 22, 28, 35, 69, 73–74; Gordon B. Hinckley, "This Work Is Concerned with People," *Ensign,* May 1995, 51–52; "Japan: Church Chronology," Global Histories, ChurchofJesusChrist.org/study/history/global-histories. **Topics: Adjustments to Priesthood Organization; Quorums of the Seventy**

4. Maridan Sollesta to James Perry, Emails, Mar. 8, 2022; Oct. 3, 2022; Maridan Sollesta and Eusebio Sollesta, Oral History Interviews, CHL; *Directory of General Authorities and Officers, 1996,* 207, 241, 243, 248–49, 254, 258, 264, 286; Sollesta, Oral History Interview [Mar. 2, 2022], 17–18; Sollesta, Autobiography, 6.
5. Sollesta, Oral History Interview [Mar. 2, 2022], 17; Maridan Sollesta to James Perry, Emails, Mar. 8, 2022; Aug. 15, 2022; Oct. 3, 2022, Maridan Sollesta and Eusebio Sollesta, Oral History Interviews, CHL; Philippines Area, Annual Historical Reports, 1991, 9; Philippines Area Presidency to All Regional Representatives and others, Mar. 14, 1995, Philippines Area, Presidency Meeting Minutes, CHL.
6. Okazaki, Journal, Feb. 24, 1996; Okazaki, "Three Great Questions," 5.
7. Okazaki, Journal, Feb. 25, 1996; Sollesta, Oral History Interview [Mar. 9, 2022], 8.
8. Dew, *Go Forward with Faith,* 516; Gordon B. Hinckley, Interview with David Fuster, May 30, 1996, [4], Gordon B. Hinckley Addresses, CHL; "The Family: A Proclamation to the World."
9. Hinckley, Journal, May 30, 1996; Gerry Avant, "Tears Flow, Faith Grows as Filipinos Greet Prophet," *Church News,* June 8, 1996, 4, 7. Quotation edited for readability; "happier man or woman" in original changed to "a happier man or woman."
10. Contreras and Contreras, Oral History Interview [2022], 10–11; Contreras and Contreras, Oral History Interview [Oct. 23, 2020], 1; Contreras and Contreras, Oral History Interview [Jan. 2023], 31–32; Contreras and Contreras, Oral History Interview [Oct. 2, 2020], 8–9.
11. Missionary Department, Annual Reports, 1982, 4, 6; 1989, 40–42; 1995, 53–59; Aburto, Oral History Interview, 26–30. **Topics: Church Growth; Chile**
12. Romney, Journal, Aug. 19 and Dec. 31, 1970; Spencer W. Kimball, Journal, Sept. 4, 1971; "Action List for New Converts," 2; Hunter, Journal, Mar. 25, 1979; Sept. 4, 1986; Oct. 1, 1986. **Topics: Adjustments to Priesthood Organization; Quorums of the Seventy**
13. Aburto, Oral History Interview, 27–33; First Presidency to Regional Representatives and others, June 17, 1991, Marlin K. Jensen, General Conference Training Files, CHL; Research Information Division, "Study of Missionary Activities in Retention, Activation, and Community Service," Mar. 1994, Missionary Executive Council, Meeting Materials, CHL; Missionary Executive Council to Area Presidencies, Memorandum, Oct. 6, 1993, South America South Area, Mission Files, CHL; Contreras and Contreras, Oral History Interview [Oct. 2, 2020], 8–9; Contreras and Contreras, Oral History Interview [2022], 12.
14. Contreras and Contreras, Oral History Interview [2022], 12–14. **Topic: Wards and Stakes**
15. Gordon B. Hinckley, "The Sustaining of Church Officers," *Ensign,* Nov. 1992, 21; Jue Family, Oral History Interview [2023], 5–8, 22; Jue Family, Oral History Interview [2019], 61–69, 90; Heaton, Personal History, volume 2, 158.
16. Jue Family, Oral History Interview [2023], 2–4, 6, 31–32; Jue Family, Oral History Interview [2019], 61–62, 68, 71–72, 86.
17. "Guests Feel Peace at Open House in Hong Kong Temple," *Church News,* May 18, 1996, 3; Ng and Chin, *History in Hong Kong,* 105; Jue, Journal, May 23, 1996; Jue Family, Oral History Interview [2023], 11. **Topic: Hong Kong**
18. Jue, Journal, May 24–25, 1996; Jue Family, Oral History Interview [2019], 86, 89–90; Corine Jue Neumiller to Jed Woodworth, Email, Jan. 24, 2023, Jue Family, Oral History Interview [2023], CHL; Jue Family, Oral History Interview [2023], 13–14, 17; "Guests Feel Peace at Open House in Hong Kong Temple," *Church News,* May 18, 1996, 3; Hong Kong Temple, Media Information Packet, 8.
19. Jue, Journal, May 26, 1996; Nora Koot Jue, Testimony, May 26, 1996, Jue Family, Oral History Interview [2023], CHL.
20. Jue, Journal, May 27, 1996; Jue Family, Oral History Interview [2023], 20–21, 23, 26; Thomas S. Monson, Neal A. Maxwell, in Hong Kong Temple, Dedication Services, 59–63; Jue, Reminiscence, 2–4.

21. Gordon B. Hinckley, Thomas S. Monson, in Hong Kong Temple, Dedication Services, 14, 69; "Dedicatory Prayer: Hong Kong China Temple, 26 May 1996," Temples, ChurchofJesusChrist.org.
22. Jue Family, Oral History Interview [2023], 23, 26–27.
23. Jue, Journal, May 27, 1996; Jue Family, Oral History Interview [2019], 27–28, 91; Jue Family, Oral History Interview [2023], 17–18, 25. **Topic: Temple Dedications and Dedicatory Prayers**
24. Naniuzeyi, "State of the State in Congo-Zaire," 669–83; Newbury, "Continuing Process of Decolonization in the Congo," 131–41; Reyntjens, *Great African War,* chapters 4 and 5; Prunier, *Africa's World War,* chapters 4 and 5. **Topic: Democratic Republic of the Congo**
25. "Historical Record: Democratic Republic of Congo Mission," chapter 7, pages 7–9; *Deseret News 1999–2000 Church Almanac,* 309–10, 545; Africa Area, Annual Historical Reports, 1996, 27, 39; *History of The Church of Jesus Christ of Latter-day Saints in the Democratic Republic of the Congo,* 50–54.
26. Willy Binene, Oral History Interview [2017]; Lewis and Lewis, "President Sabwe Binene's Story," [2]; Binene, Interview [circa July 2020]; *Directory of General Authorities and Officers, 2001,* 395.
27. Willy Binene, Oral History Interview [2017]; Lewis and Lewis, "President Sabwe Binene's Story," [2]; Willy Binene, Oral History Interview [2019]; Willy Binene, Oral History Interview [Jan. 2023]; "Exit Interview with President and Sister Homer LeBaron," [2].
28. Willy Binene, Oral History Interview [2019]; Willy Binene, Oral History Interview [May 20, 2020], [12].
29. Willy Binene, Oral History Interview [May 20, 2020], [12]–[13]; Willy Binene, Oral History Interview [2019]; Binene, Interview [circa July 2020].
30. Willy Binene, Oral History Interview [May 20, 2020], [12]–[13]; Willy Binene, Oral History Interview [2017].
31. Willy Binene, Oral History Interview [May 20, 2020], [12]–[13]. Quotations edited for readability; "We asked if we could pray" in original changed to "Can we pray?," and "he said we were men of God" changed to "You are men of God." **Topic: Healing**
32. Hinckley, Journal, June 5, 1997; John L. Hart, "Bueno! Juarez Academy Centennial," *Church News,* June 14, 1997, 3–4; Gordon B. Hinckley, Address, Juárez Mexico Member Fireside, June 5, 1997, [4], Gordon B. Hinckley Addresses, CHL.
33. Hinckley, Journal, June 5, 1997; John L. Hart, "Bueno! Juarez Academy Centennial," *Church News,* June 14, 1997, 3; *Saints,* volume 2, chapters 33 and 35; volume 3, chapters 10 and 11. **Topics: Mexico; Colonies in Mexico; Church Academies**
34. John L. Hart, "Bueno! Juarez Academy Centennial," *Church News,* June 14, 1997, 4; Gordon B. Hinckley, Address, Juárez Mexico Member Fireside, June 5, 1997, [4], Gordon B. Hinckley Addresses, CHL; Hinckley, Journal, June 5, 1997.
35. Hinckley, Journal, June 6, 1997; John L. Hart, "Bueno! Juarez Academy Centennial," *Church News,* June 14, 1997, 3–4, 8.
36. Gordon B. Hinckley, in Monticello Utah Temple, Dedication Services, 23–24; Gordon B. Hinckley, in Colonia Juárez Chihuahua Mexico Temple, Dedication Services, 11–13.
37. Temple Department, Temple Sites Minutes, Apr. 29, 1997; Hinckley, Journal, Feb. 2, 1997.
38. "Excitement Grows, as Work on New Temple in Recife, Brazil, Progresses," *Church News,* Jan. 31, 1998, 3; Hawkins, *Temples of the New Millennium,* 204–7; "Details on New Assembly Building, Two More Temples Announced," *Ensign,* May 1997, 101; *Deseret News 1999–2000 Church Almanac,* 548; Craig Zwick, Claudio Costa, and Kent Jolley to Gordon B. Hinckley, May 6, 1998, First Presidency, Area Presidency Correspondence, CHL. **Topic: Brazil**
39. John L. Hart, "Strengthening New Members," *Church News,* Nov. 29, 1997, 8, 11; First Presidency to Members of The Church of Jesus Christ of Latter-day Saints, May 15,

1997, First Presidency, Circular Letters, CHL; Gordon B. Hinckley, Address, Potomac Virginia Regional Conference, Priesthood Leadership Meeting, Apr. 26, 1997, [2], Gordon B. Hinckley Addresses, CHL.

40. First Presidency to Members of The Church of Jesus Christ of Latter-day Saints, May 15, 1997, First Presidency, Circular Letters, CHL; Gordon B. Hinckley, "Some Thoughts on Temples, Retention of Converts, and Missionary Service," *Ensign,* Nov. 1997, 50–51.
41. Gordon B. Hinckley, in Monticello Utah Temple, Dedication Services, 23–24; Gordon B. Hinckley, in Anchorage Alaska Temple, Dedication Services, 18–19; Gordon B. Hinckley, in Colonia Juárez Chihuahua Mexico Temple, Dedication Services, 12–13.
42. Hinckley, Journal, Jan. 11 and 19, 1973; Apr. 19, 1973; Mar. 4, 1975; July 31, 1981; Aug. 20, 1981; Jan. 4, 1989; Mar. 6, 1999; Hawkins, *Temples of the New Millennium,* 36–37, 68–69, 98–99.
43. Dell Van Orden, "Inspiration Came for Smaller Temples on Trip to Mexico," *Church News,* Aug. 1, 1998, 3; Gordon B. Hinckley, in Colonia Juárez Chihuahua Mexico Temple, Dedication Services, 13; Gordon B. Hinckley, in Anchorage Alaska Temple, Dedication Services, 19. **Topics: Gordon B. Hinckley; Temple Building**

Chapter 30: Precious Blessings

1. Gordon B. Hinckley, "Some Thoughts on Temples, Retention of Converts, and Missionary Service," *Ensign,* Nov. 1997, 49–50.
2. Turley, Oral History Interview, [2], [4]; Brough, Oral History Interview, 12.
3. Turley, Oral History Interview, [3]–[4].
4. Allen, Embry, and Mehr, *Hearts Turned to the Fathers,* 324–26; Joseph Walker, "Digging Family Roots with Home Computers," *Church News,* Apr. 1, 1984, 3; *Member's Guide to Temple and Family History Work,* 8–9; *FamilySearch,* section C, glossary; Russell M. Nelson, "The Spirit of Elijah," *Ensign,* Nov. 1994, 85.
5. Turley, Oral History Interview, [4]–[6].
6. Turley, Oral History Interview, [4]–[5].
7. Turley, Oral History Interview, [5]–[7], [14]–[15]; Mehr, "Dawning of the Digital Age," 53–54; Sarah Jane Weaver, "Church Enters World Wide Web 'Carefully and Methodically,'" *Church News,* Mar. 1, 1997, 6; Family History Department, Executive Director's Meeting Minutes, Mar. 3, 1998. **Topic: Information Age**
8. Gordon B. Hinckley, "New Temples to Provide 'Crowning Blessings' of the Gospel," *Ensign,* May 1998, 88; Doctrine and Covenants 20:1.
9. Turley, Oral History Interview, [4]–[6], [14]. **Topics: Family History and Genealogy; Temple Building**
10. Contreras and Contreras, Oral History Interview [Oct. 2, 2020], 9; Contreras and Contreras, Oral History Interview [2022], 10–11, 14; Missionary Department Executive Directors to Missionary Executive Council, Memorandum, May 6, 1998, Missionary Executive Council, Meeting Materials, CHL; Felicindo Contreras, Bishop of El Manzano Ward, Mar. 29, 1998, Church Directory of Organizations and Leaders, ChurchofJesusChrist.org. **Topic: Chile**
11. Contreras and Contreras, Oral History Interview [Oct. 2, 2020], 9; Molina, Oral History Interview, 1–3; Contreras and Contreras, Oral History Interview [2022], 14–15; First Presidency to General Authorities and others, June 19, 1998, First Presidency, Circular Letters, CHL. **Topic: Patriarchal Blessings**
12. Contreras and Contreras, Oral History Interview [Oct. 2, 2020], 24; First Presidency to General Authorities and others, May 15, 1997; First Presidency to General Authorities and others, June 19, 1998, First Presidency, Circular Letters, CHL; Gordon B. Hinckley, "Converts and Young Men," *Ensign,* May 1997, 47–48; Moroni 6:4; Contreras and

Contreras, Oral History Interview [Oct. 16, 2020], 9; Contreras and Contreras, Oral History Interview [Dec. 2023], 2–3, 9. **Topic: Sunday School**

13. Contreras and Contreras, Oral History Interview [2022], 16–17, 21–22. **Topic: Wards and Stakes**
14. McKenna, Oral History Interview [June 1, 2023], 3–4; McKenna, Oral History Interview [June 29, 2023], 4–6; Wilcox, Oral History Interview, 25–27; Catherine Lanford, "Education Week Grows in Size, Popularity," *Daily Universe* (Provo, UT), Aug. 1997, Alumni edition, 4; Denise Palmer, "Youth Fill Many Roles in Education Week," *Daily Universe*, Aug. 19–22, 1997, Education Week edition, 5; Wilcox, "Taking the Dead out of Dedication," 120–31; Wilcox, "Filling Your Testimony Tank," 262–69.
15. Newton, *Southern Cross Saints,* 23–25, 195, 199; *Deseret News 1997–98 Church Almanac,* 285–86; *Deseret News 1999–2000 Church Almanac,* 272–74; McKenna, Oral History Interview [June 1, 2023], 5; Wilcox, Oral History Interview, 25; Scott, Journal, Aug. 24, 2000. **Topic: Australia**
16. McKenna, Oral History Interview [June 1, 2023], 4–5; Wilcox, Oral History Interview, 1–4, 24–26; Bytheway, "History of 'Especially for Youth,'" 1–6; Perry, Mary McKenna Interview Notes, 1; Carl Maurer to Jed Woodworth, Email, Feb. 27, 2024, Carl Maurer, Jed Woodworth, and Bradley R. Wilcox Emails, CHL.
17. McKenna, Oral History Interview [June 1, 2023], 6–9; McKenna, Oral History Interview [June 29, 2023], 6–8; Wilcox, Oral History Interview, 3; Perry, Mary McKenna Interview Notes, 2; Carl Maurer to Brad Wilcox, Email, Feb. 12, 2024, Carl Maurer, Jed Woodworth, and Bradley R. Wilcox Emails, CHL; *1st Queensland "Especially for Youth."*
18. Wilcox, Journal, Apr. 11, 1999; McKenna, Oral History Interview [June 1, 2023], 9–10; Wilcox, Oral History Interview, 4, 26–27.
19. McKenna, Oral History Interview [June 1, 2023], 9; Wilcox, Oral History Interview, 5–6; McKenna, Oral History Interview [June 29, 2023], 12–15; Wilcox, Journal, Apr. 11, 1999. **Topics: Young Men Organizations; Young Women Organizations**
20. Toro, Oral History Interview, 2–4; Juliet Toro, "Pre-interview Questionnaire," [circa Feb. 2023], 1, Juliet Toro, Oral History Interview, CHL; Juliet Toro to James Perry, Email, Nov. 6, 2023, Juliet Toro, Oral History Interview, CHL.
21. Meli U. Lesuma, "Members in Fiji 'Bask in Joy' after Temple Announcement," *Church News,* Dec. 26, 1998, 10; Alan Wakeley, "'Warm Spirit' Prevails in Fiji," *Church News,* May 22, 1999, 3; "Cares of the World 'Melt Away' in Temple," *Church News,* June 24, 2000, 4; *Deseret News 2001–2002 Church Almanac,* 322–23; Balenagasau, Oral History Interview, 16; Gordon B. Hinckley, "New Temples to Provide 'Crowning Blessings' of the Gospel," *Ensign,* May 1998, 87–88. **Topics: Fiji; Samoa; Tonga; Vanuatu; Kiribati**
22. Alan Wakeley, "'Warm Spirit' Prevails in Fiji," *Church News,* May 22, 1999, 3; Toro, Oral History Interview, 4; Jacob and Hansen, "Fiji Distance Learning Program," 110–21; Jacob, "Fiji Distance Learning Program," 67–74, 85, 113, 258; Wilkinson, *Brigham Young University,* 4:425; Board of Education, Church Board of Education Meeting Minutes, Feb. 23, 1994; Dec. 18, 1996; Apr. 23, 1997; Dec. 23, 1997. **Topics: Church Universities; Information Age**
23. Toro, Oral History Interview, 3–6; Juliet Toro, "Pre-interview Questionnaire," [circa Feb. 2023], 1, Juliet Toro, Oral History Interview, CHL; Jacob, "Fiji Distance Learning Program," 208, 278.
24. Balenagasau, Oral History Interview, 3, 6, 9; Toro, Oral History Interview, 8; Jacob and Hansen, "Fiji Distance Learning Program," 110, 114–15, 117.
25. Jacob and Hansen, "Fiji Distance Learning Program," 110–11, 118; Balenagasau, Oral History Interview, 4; Jacob, "Fiji Distance Learning Program," 105–11, 133–38, 270–73; Toro, Oral History Interview, 8–9.
26. Toro, Oral History Interview, 2; Balenagasau and Toro, Oral History Interview, 2; Juliet Toro, "Pre-interview Questionnaire," [circa Feb. 2023], 1, Juliet Toro, Oral History Interview, CHL; Juliet Toro to James Perry, Email, Nov. 6, 2023, Juliet Toro, Oral History Interview, CHL.

27. Temple and Family History Executive Council, Minutes, Apr. 15 and 29, 1998; May 13, 1998; June 3, 1998; Sept. 16, 1998; Family History Department, Executive Director's Meeting Minutes, Apr. 28 and Sept. 15, 1998; Turley, Oral History Interview, [6], [15]; Mehr, "Dawning of the Digital Age," 53.
28. Nikki Miller to Marilyn Foster, Memorandum, May 29, 1998, Family History Department, Executive Director's Meeting Minutes, CHL; Family History Department, Executive Director's Meeting Minutes, Sept. 8, 1998; Mehr, "Dawning of the Digital Age," 54; Turley, Oral History Interview, [6]; Temple and Family History Executive Council, Minutes, Sept. 9, 1998.
29. "Family History Web Site Launched," *Ensign*, Aug. 1999, 74–75; R. Scott Lloyd, "Today We Are Taking a Historic Step," *Church News*, May 29, 1999, 3, 8–9; Turley, Oral History Interview, [6]–[7].
30. Turley, Oral History Interview, [7]; Family History Department, Executive Director's Meeting Minutes, May 11, 1999; "Family History Web Site Launched," *Ensign*, Aug. 1999, 74–75; R. Scott Lloyd, "Today We Are Taking a Historic Step," *Church News*, May 29, 1999, 3, 8.
31. R. Scott Lloyd, "Today We Are Taking a Historic Step," *Church News*, May 29, 1999, 3, 8; Turley, Oral History Interview, [7].
32. "Summary of FamilySearch Internet Compliments," May 13, 1999, 1, 3, Family History Department, Executive Director's Meeting Minutes, CHL. Quotation modified for readability; "THANK YOU" in original standardized to "Thank you," and "making the available" changed to "making it available."
33. Turley, Oral History Interview, [7]; Richard E. Turley Jr., Interview by Katie Couric, *Today*, NBC, May 25, 1999.
34. Bob Mims, "LDS Web Site Undergoes Major Upgrades to Accommodate Millions of Family-History Buffs," *Salt Lake Tribune*, May 28, 1999, A1; Turley, Oral History Interview, [7]. **Topic: Family History and Genealogy**

Chapter 31: Mysterious Ways

1. Bonnet, Journal, Nov. 7, 1999; Hinckley, Journal, Oct. 26, 1999; Bonnet, Oral History Interview [2017], 12–13; Budget Office, Appropriations Committee Minutes, Oct. 26, 1999. **Topic: Ghana**
2. Bonnet, Oral History Interview [2017], 12–13; Bonnet, Journal, Apr. 28, 1995; May 11, 1995; Nov. 7, 1999; James E. Faust to Georges Bonnet and Carolyn Bonnet, May 7, 1991, in Bonnet, Journal, May 1991; James E. Faust to Georges Bonnet and Carolyn Bonnet, Oct. 30, 1991, in Bonnet, Journal, Nov. 1991; Grant Gunnell and Alice Gunnell to Georges Bonnet, July 2, 1992, in Bonnet, Journal, July 1992; Emelia Ahadjie to Georges Bonnet and Carolyn Bonnet, June 13, 1995, in Bonnet, Journal, June 1995; Steve Fidel, "A Temple to Be Built in Ghana," *Church News*, Feb. 21, 1998, 3.
3. Bonnet, Oral History Interview [2017], 12–13; Bonnet, Journal, Nov. 7, 1999; Champagnie, Holladay, and Holladay, Oral History Interview, 17–18; Steve Fidel, "A Temple to Be Built in Ghana," *Church News*, Feb. 21, 1998, 3; James Mason to Africa West Area Presidency and others, Mar. 4, 1999; James Mason to Jeffrey R. Holland, circa Apr. 1999, John K. Buah Papers, CHL; Rod Pulley to Keith Stepan, June 9, 1999, in Temple Department, Temple Sites Minutes, June 10, 1999.
4. Bonnet, Journal, Nov. 7, 1999; Bonnet, Oral History Interview [2017], 12–13; Budget Office, Appropriations Committee Minutes, Oct. 26, 1999.
5. Bonnet, Journal, Nov. 7 and Dec. 21, 1999; Bonnet, Oral History Interview [2017], 13–14; Bonnet, Oral History Interview [2023], [11]; *Deseret News 1991–1992 Church Almanac*, 328; *Deseret News 2001–2002 Church Almanac*, 332; Steve Fidel, "A Temple to Be Built in Ghana," *Church News*, Feb. 21, 1998, 3; Kissi, *Walking in the Sand*, 274–76, 289; Hinckley, Oral History Interview, 17–18.

6. Bonnet, Oral History Interview [2017], 14; Bonnet, Oral History Interview [2023], [11]–[15]; Bonnet, Notes, Nov. 1999; Pace, Official Journal, Oct. 23, 1999; Nov. 7–8 and 20–25, 1999; Africa West Area, Annual Historical Reports, 1999, 46–47; Bonnet, Journal, Dec. 21, 1999.
7. Balenagasau and Toro, Oral History Interview, 6–8; Jacob and Hansen, "Fiji Distance Learning Program," 123–24.
8. Jacob, "Fiji Distance Learning Program," 109–10, 262, 282–83; Balenagasau and Toro, Oral History Interview, 15–16.
9. Balenagasau and Toro, Oral History Interview, 10–11; Toro, Oral History Interview, 10; Balenagasau, Oral History Interview, 2, 16–17; Jacob, "Fiji Distance Learning Program," 130–31.
10. Balenagasau and Toro, Oral History Interview, 6–7, 22; Toro, Oral History Interview, 6, 10.
11. Jacob, "Fiji Distance Learning Program," 130–32, 158–59, 265; Toro, Oral History Interview, 10, 12; Balenagasau and Toro, Oral History Interview, 17.
12. Jacob, "Fiji Distance Learning Program," 208, 334.
13. "The Living Christ: The Testimony of the Apostles"; First Presidency to General Authorities and others, Dec. 10, 1999, First Presidency, Circular Letters, CHL.
14. "Special Witnesses of Christ," [00:00:19]–[00:02:56]; Gordon B. Hinckley, in "Special Witnesses of Christ," *Ensign,* Apr. 2001, 4; Mark 15:39.
15. "Special Witnesses of Christ"; Neal A. Maxwell, Henry B. Eyring, James E. Faust, Gordon B. Hinckley, in "Special Witnesses of Christ," *Ensign,* Apr. 2001, 6, 11, 18, 21; Matthew 10:29. **Topic: Quorum of the Twelve**
16. Fraenkel, "Clash of Dynasties and Rise of Demagogues," 295–308; "Fiji Rebels Release 10 of 50 Captive Officials," *New York Times,* May 21, 2000, 13.
17. Toro, Oral History Interview, 15–16; Lesuma, Oral History Interview, 6; Barbie Dutter and Benedict Brogan, "Fiji under Martial Law after President Resigns," *Daily Telegraph* (London), May 30, 2000, 1–2.
18. " 'Fortress of Faith' Prompts Brotherhood and Tears," *Church News,* June 24, 2000, 3–4; Balenagasau, Oral History Interview, 14.
19. Rohan Sullivan, "Martial Law Imposed in Fiji," *Philadelphia Inquirer,* May 30, 2000, A4; Nixon and Nixon, "Our Mission to Suva, Fiji," 38–39; Roy Gene Bauer, "Fiji Suva Mission History, July 1999 through 2001," 6, Fiji Suva Mission, Annual Historical Reports, CHL; Bauer and Bauer, Oral History Interview, [00:21:04]–[00:21:57]; Barbie Dutter, "Fiji Peace Force Restores Calm at Home," *Daily Telegraph* (London), May 30, 2000, 15.
20. Toro, Oral History Interview, 15; "Four Temples Dedicated in One Overseas Tour," and " 'Fortress of Faith' Prompts Brotherhood and Tears," *Church News,* June 24, 2000, 3–4; Hinckley, Journal, June 18, 2000.
21. Gordon B. Hinckley, in Suva Fiji Temple, Dedication Services, 11; Romney and Cowan, *Colonia Juárez Temple,* 158–59; *Deseret News 2003 Church Almanac,* 474; *Deseret News 2001–2002 Church Almanac,* 332. **Topics: Fiji; Temple Dedications and Dedicatory Prayers**
22. "Cares of the World 'Melt Away' in Temple," *Church News,* June 24, 2000, 4; Toro, Oral History Interview, 16.
23. Bonnet, Journal, Apr. 9, 2000; June 25, 2000; Aug. 10, 2000; Bonnet, Oral History Interview [2017], 15–17, 21; Presiding Bishopric to General Authorities and others, May 22, 2000, Historical Department, Circular Letters, CHL.
24. Bonnet, Oral History Interview [2017], 21–22; Bonnet, Journal, Sept. 3 and 17, 2000; F. Michael Watson to Presiding Bishopric, Memorandum, Mar. 14, 2000, First Presidency, Presiding Bishopric Correspondence, CHL; Earl C. Tingey to Missionary Executive Council, Memorandum, Sept. 1, 2000, Missionary Executive Council, Meeting Materials, CHL. Quotation edited for readability; original source has "There's too many problems."
25. Bonnet, Journal, Sept. 29, 2000; Nov. 13 and 26, 2000; Georges Bonnet, "Africa West Area—Stewardship Report, October 2000," [2], in Bonnet, Journal, Oct. 2000; Bonnet, Oral History Interview [2023], [73]–[81]; Bonnet, Oral History Interview [2017], 23.

26. Bonnet, Journal, Dec. 9, 2000; Bonnet, Oral History Interview [2017], 23–25; Bonnet, Oral History Interview [2023], [29]–[35]; Pace, Official Journal, Dec. 5, 2000.

Chapter 32: Our Strength Is Our Faith

1. Romney and Cowan, *Colonia Juárez Temple*, 158–60, 173; Temple Department, Annual Reports, 2000, 1, 10; David E. Sorensen to First Presidency, Apr. 25, 2001, Temple Department, Annual Reports, 2000; Gordon B. Hinckley, "New Temples to Provide 'Crowning Blessings' of the Gospel," *Ensign*, May 1998, 88; Temple Department, Temple Sites Minutes, Dec. 9, 1999. **Topic: Temple Building**
2. *Deseret News 1991–1992 Church Almanac*, 243; *Deseret News 1997–98 Church Almanac*, 530; Plewe, *Mapping Mormonism*, 132–33; Cowan, *Church in the Twentieth Century*, 223; *Proclaiming the Gospel: 2000 Annual Report*, 27; Gordon B. Hinckley, "This Great Millennial Year," *Ensign*, Nov. 2000, 67–68; Temple Department, Annual Reports, 2000, 4. **Topic: Temple Endowment**
3. Hinckley, Journal, Feb. 6, 1995; Apr. 6, 1996; Apr. 16, 1997; July 24, 1997; Sept. 17, 1999; Gordon B. Hinckley, "This Great Millennial Year," *Ensign*, Nov. 2000, 68–69. **Topic: General Conference**
4. F. Michael Watson to Jeffrey R. Holland, Nov. 7, 1996; F. Michael Watson to M. Russell Ballard, Aug. 10, 2000; F. Michael Watson to Dallin H. Oaks, Nov. 2, 2000, First Presidency, Committees, Departments, and Organizations Correspondence, CHL; Sheila Sanchez, "LDS Church's Official Web Site Up and Running," *Daily Herald* (Provo, UT), Feb. 15, 1997, A4; Sarah Jane Weaver, "Church Enters World Wide Web 'Carefully and Methodically,'" *Church News*, Mar. 1, 1997, 6; The Church of Jesus Christ of Latter-day Saints (website), www.lds.org, capture [11:40:23], Apr. 12, 1997, archived at Wayback Machine, web.archive.org. **Topic: Information Age**
5. Gordon B. Hinckley, Address, Jordan Utah South Regional Conference, Priesthood Leadership Meeting, Mar. 1, 1997, Gordon B. Hinckley Addresses, CHL; *Church Handbook of Instructions, Book 1* [1998], 95–96, 157–58; Boyd K. Packer to General Authorities and others, Dec. 1, 1997, Priesthood Executive Council, Minutes, CHL; *Preventing and Responding to Spouse Abuse; Responding to Abuse*.
6. Boyd K. Packer to General Authorities and others, Jan. 13, 1998; Apr. 15, 1998, Quorum of the Twelve Apostles, Circular Letters, CHL; First Presidency to General Authorities and others, June 19, 1998, First Presidency, Circular Letters, CHL; "Members: Key to Missionary Success," *Church News*, Feb. 27, 1999, 3, 12.
7. Aggregated Area Report, Oct. 16, 2000, 1, Missionary Executive Council, Meeting Materials, CHL; Gordon B. Hinckley, Address, General Authority Training, Mar. 30, 2000; Gordon B. Hinckley, Address, General/Area Authority Training, Oct. 3, 2000, Gordon B. Hinckley Addresses, CHL; Missionary Department, Missionary Report, 2000, 1, 19, Missionary Executive Council, Meeting Materials, CHL.
8. Gordon B. Hinckley, "Your Greatest Challenge, Mother," Sept. 23, 2000; Gordon B. Hinckley, Press Conference, June 21, 2000, Gordon B. Hinckley Addresses, CHL; Hinckley, Journal, May 10–11, 2000, and Aug. 7, 2001; Rachel Sterzer Gibson, "An Approach to Educating Disciples," *Church News*, Aug. 21, 2021, 13–14. **Topic: Church Universities**
9. Hinckley, Journal, June 2, 1999; Nov. 26, 2000; Dec. 6, 2000; Monson, Journal, Feb. 11, 1999; Sept. 1, 1999; Feb. 25, 2000; June 28, 2000; Oct. 12 and 27, 2000; Dec. 6, 2000; Gordon B. Hinckley, Interview by Paul Cobb, Nov. 28, 2000, Gordon B. Hinckley Addresses, CHL; Gordon B. Hinckley, "The Perpetual Education Fund," *Ensign*, May 2001, 51–53.
10. Gordon B. Hinckley, "A Prophet's Counsel and Prayer for Youth," Nov. 12, 2000, Gordon B. Hinckley Addresses, CHL.
11. Hinckley, Journal, Dec. 31, 2000. **Topic: Gordon B. Hinckley**

12. Jason Swensen, "Freedman's Bank," *Church News,* Mar. 3, 2001, 3; Bob Mims, "Rich Lode of Black History Opens," *Salt Lake Tribune,* Feb. 27, 2001, B1, B3; "Introductory Remarks for Elder Christofferson: Freedman's Bank Announcement," circa Feb. 26, 2001, [1]–[2], Church History Department Reports, CHL; Gray, Oral History Interview, 228, 238–40, 299; Henry B. Eyring, "Freedman's Bank Records Announcement," circa Feb. 26, 2001, 1–2, Church History Department Reports, CHL; Gray, Interview [Oct. 2022], [13]; Mae Gentry, "Blacks Gain Cyberlink to Ancestry," *Atlanta Constitution,* Feb. 27, 2001, A1, A15.
13. Gray, Oral History Interview, 239; Temple and Family History Executive Council, Minutes, Aug. 30, 2000; Henry B. Eyring, "Freedman's Bank Records Announcement," circa Feb. 26, 2001, 2, Church History Department Reports, CHL.
14. Gray, Oral History Interview, 237, 239.
15. Nelson, *Elijah Abel Freedman's Bank Project,* [6], [8]–[9]; Monte Brough to Ernest Michel and Herbert Kronish, Apr. 11, 1995, in Monte Brough to Wilford Kirton Jr., Apr. 19, 1995; F. Michael Watson to Temple and Family History Executive Council, Apr. 27, 1995; Monte Brough to Russell M. Nelson, Memorandum, May 5, 1995, Temple and Family History Executive Council, Meeting Materials, CHL; "Names Submitted for Temple Ordinances," 1; First Presidency to All Members of the Church, June 16, 1995, First Presidency, Circular Letters, CHL. **Topic: Baptism for the Dead**
16. Nelson, *Elijah Abel Freedman's Bank Project,* [13]; John L. Hart, "Freedman's Bank Project Left an Impact on Inmates," *Church News,* Mar. 24, 2001, 5.
17. Gray, Oral History Interview, 238–39, 300.
18. Jason Swensen, "Freedman's Bank," and "Bank Records Open Picture to the Past, Re-connect Families," *Church News,* Mar. 3, 2001, 3–4; "Freedman's Bank Records Release: Summary of Report," May 5, 2001, [1], in "Freedman's Bank Records"; Area Summaries, in "Freedman's Bank Records."
19. Gray, Oral History Interview, 240–41; "Bank Records Open Picture to the Past, Re-connect Families," *Church News,* Mar. 3, 2001, 4.
20. Jason Swensen, "Freedman's Bank," *Church News,* Mar. 3, 2001, 3. **Topic: Family History and Genealogy**
21. Contreras and Contreras, Oral History Interview [Oct. 16, 2020], 9–10; Contreras and Contreras, Oral History Interview [Apr. 2023], 3–5.
22. Griffiths, "Globalization of Latter-day Saint Education," 13, 116–25, 237–48; *By Study and Also by Faith,* 228–29, 234, 236–37, 255–56, 270, 285–87. **Topics: Church Academies; Seminaries and Institutes**
23. Board of Education, Church Board of Education Meeting Minutes, May 28, 1997; "Pilot Report and Recommendations"; Contreras and Contreras, Oral History Interview [Oct. 16, 2020], 9–10; Contreras and Contreras, Oral History Interview [Jan. 2023], 8; Contreras and Contreras, Oral History Interview [Apr. 2023], 5–8.
24. Cancino, Oral History Interview, 5–7; Contreras and Contreras, Oral History Interview [Apr. 2023], 5–8; Contreras and Contreras, Oral History Interview [Dec. 2023], 10–11.
25. Contreras and Contreras, Oral History Interview [Apr. 2023], 8–11; Cancino, Oral History Interview, 6.
26. Sollesta and Sollesta, Oral History Interview [Apr. 2023], 2–7; Sollesta, Oral History Interview [Mar. 2, 2022], 21–22; Sollesta and Sollesta, Oral History Interview [Mar. 2023], 1–2; "New Stake Presidencies," *Church News,* Apr. 19, 1997, 13; Sollesta and Sollesta, Email Interview. Quotation edited for readability; "think it very wisely" in original changed to "think it over very wisely," and "live in one roof" changed to "live under one roof."
27. Sollesta and Sollesta, Oral History Interview [Apr. 2023], 2–7; Boyle, "War on Terror," 191–209.
28. Gordon B. Hinckley, "Living in the Fulness of Times," *Ensign,* Nov. 2001, 6.
29. Hinckley, Journal, June 16, 1995; Jan. 13, 1998; May 29, 2001; Haws, "Why the 'Mormon Olympics' Didn't Happen," 365–87; Shipps, "Mormonism and the Olympic Games," 134–39. **Topic: Public Relations**

746

30. Dallin H. Oaks, "Sharing the Gospel," *Ensign*, Nov. 2001, 9; Charles Didier to Missionary Executive Council, Jan. 3, 2002, in Missionary Executive Council, Minutes, Jan. 9, 2002; Shipps, "Mormonism and the Olympic Games," 136; Hinckley, Journal, Feb. 2, 2001; R. Scott Lloyd, "A Musical Celebration of Light, Life," *Church News*, Jan. 26, 2002, 6; Celia R. Baker, "'Light of the World' a Bit Confusing but Splashy," *Salt Lake Tribune*, Feb. 7, 2002, B3. **Topic: Church Headquarters**
31. Hinckley, Journal, June 29, 1999; May 29, 2001; Feb. 7 and 11, 2002; Haws, "Why the 'Mormon Olympics' Didn't Happen," 365–87; Shaun D. Stahle, "Thousands Enlist as Volunteers," *Church News*, Feb. 2, 2002, 5; Barbara Jean Jones, "Church Joins Salt Lake City in Welcoming the World," *Ensign*, Apr. 2002, 75–76; Peggy Fletcher Stack, "News Media Put LDS at Center Stage," *Salt Lake Tribune*, Feb. 28, 2002, A6; Sarah Jane Weaver, "Olympics Earn Friends and Respect for Church," *Church News*, Mar. 2, 2002, 3. **Topic: Tabernacle Choir**
32. Hinckley, Journal, Feb. 24, 2002; Brown, *Life of a Pioneer*, 122.

Chapter 33: What Is This Church?

1. Hinckley, Journal, Apr. 28, 2002; Hawkins, *Temples of the New Millennium*, 222–23; Jason Swensen, "Patience Rewarded in Monterrey," *Church News*, May 11, 2002, 3. **Topics: Temple Building; Mexico**
2. Hinckley, Journal, Mar. 6–7, 1999; Romney and Cowan, *Colonia Juárez Temple*, 130, 155–56; "Colonia Juárez Chihuahua México Temple," Newsroom, no date, newsroom.ChurchofJesusChrist.org; "Temple Dimensions," Temples of The Church of Jesus Christ of Latter-day Saints, churchofjesuschristtemples.org.
3. Marilena Kretly Pretel Busto, "Grandma's Baptism," *Ensign*, Oct. 2009, 74. **Topics: Baptism for the Dead; Sealing; Temple Endowment; Portugal**
4. Judy C. Olsen, "Bolivia: A Bounty of Blessings," *Liahona* (U.S./Canada), Aug. 2000, 37, 42. **Topic: Bolivia**
5. Hawkins, *Temples of the New Millennium*, 178–79; Greg Hill, "Fukuoka: Japan's Southern Center," *Church News*, Nov. 4, 2000, 8–10; Yamashita, Interview, 33; Kazuhiko Yamashita to James Perry, Email, Dec. 19, 2023, Kazuhiko Yamashita, Interviews, CHL. **Topic: Japan**
6. Don L. Searle, "One Million in Mexico," *Ensign*, July 2004, 35–36.
7. "Anne C. Pingree," *Church News*, June 1, 2002, 11; Parkin, "History of the Relief Society," section 1, 4–5, 18–19; Pingree, Hughes, and Parkin, Oral History Interview, [00:07:42]–[00:08:27].
8. Gordon B. Hinckley, "Ambitious to Do Good," *Ensign*, Mar. 1992, 6; "Anne C. Pingree," *Liahona* (U.S./Canada), July 2002, 125; George C. Pingree and Anne C. Pingree to Nelson Dibble, Oct. 14, 1996; Elaine L. Jack, "The Effects of the Gospel Literacy Effort," Sept. 28, 1995, 1–2, Relief Society, Sesquicentennial Files and Gospel Literacy Program, CHL; *Gospel Literacy Guidelines for Priesthood and Relief Society Leaders*, [1]; Sheridan R. Sheffield, "Aim of Gospel Literacy Effort: Enrich Lives," *Church News*, Jan. 30, 1993, 3. **Topics: Relief Society; Globalization**
9. Parkin, "History of the Relief Society," section 1, 18–19; George C. Pingree and Anne C. Pingree to Nelson Dibble, Oct. 14, 1996, Relief Society, Sesquicentennial Files and Gospel Literacy Program, CHL; Anne C. Pingree to MarJean Wilcox, Sept. 9, 1996; Sept. 29, 1996; Anne C. Pingree to Family, Nov. 18, 1996, Anne C. Pingree, Kathleen H. Hughes, and Bonnie D. Parkin, Oral History Interview, CHL. **Topic: Nigeria**
10. Parkin, "History of the Relief Society," section 1, 18–19; Pingree, Journal, June 11, 2003; Hughes, Oral History Interview, [01:05:20]–[01:07:55]; Ann L. Cannaday and others, "Illiteracy," Apr. 12, 1993, 1, Relief Society, Sesquicentennial Files and Gospel Literacy Program, CHL; "Literacy and Church Activity: A Study of Adult Members of

The Church of Jesus Christ of Latter-day Saints in the United States," Apr. 1997, 1–10, Relief Society, Sesquicentennial Files and Gospel Literacy Program, CHL.
11. Parkin, "History of the Relief Society," section 1, 18–19; Hughes, Oral History Interview, [01:05:20]–[01:07:55]; Pingree, Hughes, and Parkin, Oral History Interview, [00:03:22]–[00:04:20], [00:23:17]–[00:23:43].
12. Parkin, "History of the Relief Society," section 1, 18–19; section 2, 27; Pingree, Journal, June 1 and 11, 2003; Pingree, Hughes, and Parkin, Oral History Interview, [00:29:20]–[00:31:10]; Relief Society, General Board Minutes, volume 66, June 18, 2003, 83; Nov. 6 and 13, 2003, 118, 121; Hughes, Oral History Interview, [01:04:22]–[01:05:10].
13. Sollesta and Sollesta, Oral History Interview [Apr. 2023], 3–5.
14. Sollesta, Autobiography, 2; Sollesta and Sollesta, Oral History Interview [Mar. 2023], 2, 5, 8; Sollesta and Sollesta, Email Interview; Maridan Sollesta to James Perry, Email, Oct. 3, 2023, Maridan Sollesta and Eusebio Sollesta, Oral History Interviews, CHL; Philippines Area, Annual Historical Reports, 2003, 3; Turley, *In the Hands of the Lord,* 263–65, 269–70; "Elder Oaks and Elder Holland to Serve among Local Saints," *Liahona* (U.S./Canada), July 2002, 126.
15. Turley, *In the Hands of the Lord,* 265; Philippines Area, Presidency Meeting Minutes, Aug. 28, 2002; Oct. 23, 2002; Nov. 13 and 27, 2002; Dec. 4 and 6, 2002; Jan. 15 and 22, 2003; Feb. 12 and 26, 2003; "Report to the First Presidency," in Dallin H. Oaks, Angel Abrea, and Richard Maynes to the First Presidency, May 27, 2003, Philippines Area, Annual Historical Reports, CHL; Dallin H. Oaks, "Establishing Gospel Culture," Jan. 25, 2003, First Presidency, Area Presidency Correspondence, CHL.
16. Sollesta and Sollesta, Oral History Interview [Mar. 2023], 11.
17. "Report to the First Presidency," in Dallin H. Oaks, Angel Abrea, and Richard Maynes to the First Presidency, May 27, 2003, Philippines Area, Annual Historical Reports, CHL; Sollesta and Sollesta, Oral History Interview [Mar. 2023], 14; Sollesta and Sollesta, Email Interview.
18. Sollesta and Sollesta, Oral History Interview [Mar. 2023], 14, 16–17.
19. Sollesta and Sollesta, Oral History Interview [Apr. 2023], 7–8; Dallin H. Oaks, "Establishing Gospel Culture," Jan. 25, 2003, First Presidency, Area Presidency Correspondence, CHL. **Topic: Philippines**
20. "Sydney Australia Greenwich Stake," 52, 59; Blake McKeown, Oral History Interview [May 2023], [6]–[8]; Jackson and Jackson, Oral History Interview, [4], [8]–[9]; Wade McKeown, Oral History Interview, [1], [5].
21. McKenna, Oral History Interview [June 1, 2023], 9, 11; Kenneth Johnson, Oral History Interview, 18; Perry, Mary McKenna Interview Notes, 3; Riwai-Couch, "Historical Information about 'Especially for Youth' in the Pacific Area," 3; "New Zealand Conference Attended by 425 Youth," *Church News,* Feb. 8, 2003, 15; Blake McKeown, Oral History Interview [May 2023], [6].
22. Blake McKeown, Oral History Interview [May 2023], [6]–[7], [9]; Wade McKeown, Oral History Interview, [2]; *Deseret Morning News 2004 Church Almanac,* 265. **Topic: Australia**
23. Wade McKeown, Oral History Interview, [2]–[4]; Jackson and Jackson, Oral History Interview, [4]–[7], [9]; "Sydney Australia Greenwich Stake," 52; Blake McKeown, Oral History Interview [May 2023], [7].
24. Blake McKeown, Oral History Interview [May 2023], [1]–[3], [9], [11]–[12]; *Church Handbook of Instructions, Book 2,* 182. **Topic: Young Men Organizations**
25. Blake McKeown, Oral History Interview [May 2023], [7]–[9]; Blake McKeown, Oral History Interview [Aug. 2023], [6]; McKeown and McKeown, Oral History Interview, [3], [8]–[9]; "Sydney Australia Greenwich Stake," 52; Jackson and Jackson, Oral History Interview, [7], [10].
26. Gerry Avant, "Bright Day for Youth in Ghana," *Church News,* Jan. 17, 2004, 8–9; Bonnet, Oral History Interview [2017], 39–40; Kissi, *Walking in the Sand,* 296–97; Priesthood Executive Council, Minutes, Sept. 17, 2003; Hinckley, Journal, Aug. 8 and 14, 2003; Gordon B. Hinckley, Address, Columbia, SC, Priesthood Leadership

Meeting, Nov. 20, 2004, [4], Gordon B. Hinckley Addresses, CHL; Maurine Jensen Proctor, "A Day of Celebration," *Meridian Magazine,* Jan. 13, 2004, in Africa West Area, Annual Historical Reports, 2004.
27. Bonnet, Oral History Interview [2017], 40; Gordon B. Hinckley, Alice Gunnell, Grant Gunnell, Russell M. Nelson, Emmanuel A. Kissi, Georges Bonnet, in Accra Ghana Temple, Dedication Services, 1–9, 36; Kissi, *Walking in the Sand,* 307–12; Thomas S. Monson, "The Sustaining of Church Officers," *Ensign,* May 2002, 21; Joseph Johnson, Oral History Interview [2005], 25–27.
28. Gordon B. Hinckley, in Accra Ghana Temple, Dedication Services, 11–14.
29. Bonnet, Journal, Jan. 11, 2004; Gordon B. Hinckley, Georges Bonnet, in Accra Ghana Temple, Dedication Services, 33, 36–37. **Topics: Temple Dedications and Dedicatory Prayers; Ghana**
30. Gerry Avant, "Ghana President Visited by Pres. Hinckley," *Church News,* Jan. 17, 2004, 7; Bonnet, Oral History Interview [2017], 41–42; Sarah Jane Weaver, "Ghana President Welcomed in Salt Lake City," *Church News,* Sept. 21, 2002, 2.
31. Fallentine, Recollections, 1; "The Family: A Proclamation to the World."
32. Gordon B. Hinckley, "Stand Strong against the Wiles of the World," *Ensign,* Nov. 1995, 100–102; Petersen and Scott, "Proclamation on the Family," 210, 216–21; Amy K. Stewart, "A Proclamation to the World," *Daily Herald* (Provo, UT), Dec. 30, 2000, A11; Angela Fallentine, Oral History Interview [Feb. 2023], 17–18.
33. Fallentine, Recollections, 1–3.

Chapter 34: Strength for Any Situation

1. "Chile Area Training"; Pingree, "Chile Area Auxiliary Leadership Training," 1, 5–6; "Welfare," 1–26; "Bienestar," 1–25. **Topic: Chile**
2. Carl B. Pratt to Anne C. Pingree, Email, Aug. 26, 2004, Relief Society, Anne C. Pingree Relief Society General Presidency Papers, CHL; "Relief Society Challenges in Chile," [1]; Pratt, "Area Presidency Focus," [1].
3. "Incomings from Chile Training"; Pingree, "Chile Area Auxiliary Leadership Training," 1, 6; "Relief Society Challenges in Chile," [1]; Pratt, "Area Presidency Focus," [1].
4. "Chile Area Training"; Pingree, "Chile Area Auxiliary Leadership Training," 2–4; Jeffrey R. Holland to First Presidency, Dec. 13, 2002, First Presidency, Area Presidency Correspondence, CHL; Chile Area, Annual Historical Reports, 2004, 1; Turley, *In the Hands of the Lord,* 263–77; Holland, Oral History Interview, 11.
5. Jeffrey R. Holland to First Presidency, Dec. 13, 2002; Aug. 21, 2003; May 11, 2004, First Presidency, Area Presidency Correspondence, CHL; Pingree, "Chile Area Auxiliary Leadership Training," 2–4; Chile Area, Annual Historical Reports, 2003, 5, appendix II; Chile Area, Annual Historical Reports, 2004, 1, 7.
6. "General Leadership Meeting," 3–5. Quotation edited for readability; "example of First Presidency & Twelve" in original changed to "example of the First Presidency and the Twelve."
7. "General Leadership Meeting," 5; Pingree, "Chile Area Auxiliary Leadership Training," 5–6; "Welfare," 19–23; Anne Pingree, Notes, Oct. 2004, [7], Relief Society of The Church of Jesus Christ of Latter-day Saints, Scrapbooks, Special Collections, J. Willard Marriott Library, University of Utah, Salt Lake City. **Topics: Bishop; Relief Society; Wards and Stakes; Welfare Programs**
8. Pingree, "Chile Area Auxiliary Leadership Training," 6–7.
9. Kilbert, Oral History Interview [Jan. 2023], 8; Bonham, Oral History Interview, 2–3; Missionary Executive Council, Minutes, Sept. 17, 2003, and June 1, 2004; "Mission President's Resource for Implementing '*Preach My Gospel,*'" Aug. 24, 2004, 3, 5, Missionary Executive Council, Meeting Materials, CHL; M. Russell Ballard, "Preach My Gospel," June 22, 2004; David Edwards to Edward Brandt and Max Molgard, June 17,

2004, Missionary Department, Seminar for New Mission Presidents Meeting Materials, CHL; White, "History of *Preach My Gospel,*" 129–31.

10. Kilbert, Oral History Interview [Jan. 2023], 2–3, 9; Allwyn Arokia Raj Kilbert, "Moved by My First *Liahona,*" *Liahona* (U.S./Canada), Oct. 2002, 1; Kilbert, Email Interview [Oct. 4, 2023].
11. India Bengaluru Mission, "Church in India," 1–2; Britsch, *From the East,* 8–30, 462, 506–36; Gill, "The Church of Jesus Christ of Latter-day Saints in India," 75; *Deseret Morning News 2006 Church Almanac,* 371. **Topic: India**
12. Kilbert, Oral History Interview [Jan. 2023], 10–11; Bonham, Oral History Interview, 4; India Bengaluru Mission, "Church in India," 1, 3; Rutherford, "Shifting Focus to Global Mormonism," 81; Stewart and Martinich, *Reaching the Nations,* 2:907.
13. Kilbert, Oral History Interview [Jan. 2023], 10–11; *Preach My Gospel,* vii–xi, 1–11, 29–30, 31–32; White, "History of *Preach My Gospel,*" 128–58; *Uniform System for Teaching Investigators; Uniform System for Teaching the Gospel.*
14. "Mission President's Resource for Implementing '*Preach My Gospel,*'" Aug. 24, 2004, 1–5, Missionary Executive Council, Meeting Materials, CHL; *Preach My Gospel,* 137–54; Kilbert, Oral History Interview [Jan. 2023], 8; Kilbert, Notebook, [Aug. 25], 2004; Allwyn Kilbert to Family, Aug. 26, 2004, Allwyn Arokiaraj Kilbert, Oral History Interviews, CHL. Quotation edited for readability; "which" in original changed to "that."
15. Kilbert, Oral History Interview [Jan. 2023], 6–8; Kilbert, Oral History Interview [May 2023], 2; Allwyn Kilbert to James Perry, Email, Feb. 17, 2023, Allwyn Arokiaraj Kilbert, Oral History Interviews, CHL; Bonham, Oral History Interview, 3.
16. Kilbert, Oral History Interview [Jan. 2023], 6–7, 10, 15; Kilbert, Oral History Interview [Feb. 2023], 1–4; Kilbert, Oral History Interview [May 2023], 4, 7; Nelaballe, Oral History Interview, 5–7, 10; Kilbert, Email Interview [Oct. 4, 2023]. **Topic: Growth of Missionary Work**
17. Wan, Oral History Interview [July 2022], [19]; Wan, Oral History Interview [Oct. 2022], [9], [12]–[13]; *Directory of General Authorities and Officers, 2005,* 3; Sarah Jane Weaver, "Proposing Projects to Villages of Tsunami Survivors," *Church News,* Mar. 19, 2005, 8.
18. Nick Cumming-Bruce and Campbell Robertson, "Most Powerful Quake in 40 Years Triggers Death and Destruction," *New York Times,* Dec. 26, 2004, nytimes.com. **Topics: Malaysia; Thailand**
19. Wan, Oral History Interview [July 2022], [19]–[20]; Wan, Oral History Interview [Oct. 2022], [9]–[10], [14], [19]; *Deseret Morning News 2006 Church Almanac,* 449; Garry Flake to James Perry, Email, Nov. 8, 2023, CHL; Jason Swensen, "Tsunami Disaster: More Than 100,000 Dead," *Church News,* Jan. 1, 2005, 2; Nick Cumming-Bruce and Campbell Robertson, "Most Powerful Quake in 40 Years Triggers Death and Destruction," *New York Times,* Dec. 26, 2004, nytimes.com.
20. Rather, *Supporting the Rescue,* 40; Welfare Services Department, Fact Sheets, 2002; "An Eyewitness to Tragedy," in Presiding Bishopric, Welfare Executive Committee Meeting Materials, Feb. 24, 2005; Jason Swensen, "Tsunami Disaster: More Than 100,000 Dead," *Church News,* Jan. 1, 2005, 2, 15; Wan, Oral History Interview [July 2022], [20]; Garry Flake to James Perry, Email, Nov. 8, 2023, CHL; Wan, Oral History Interview [Oct. 2022], [9]–[10], [19].
21. Wan, Oral History Interview [July 2022], [20]–[21]; Flake, "Tsunami (Southeast Asia)"; Jason Swensen, "Tsunami Disaster: More Than 100,000 Dead," *Church News,* Jan. 1, 2005, 15; "An Eyewitness to Tragedy," in Presiding Bishopric, Welfare Executive Committee Meeting Materials, Feb. 24, 2005; Wan, Oral History Interview [July 2022], [20]–[21].
22. Nick Cumming-Bruce and Campbell Robertson, "Most Powerful Quake in 40 Years Triggers Death and Destruction," *New York Times,* Dec. 26, 2004, nytimes.com; Amy Waldman, "Thousands Die as Quake-Spawned Waves Crash onto Coastlines across Southern Asia," *New York Times,* Dec. 27, 2004, A11.
23. Kilbert, Oral History Interview [Jan. 2023], 11–12; Nelaballe, Oral History Interview, 15.

24. Kilbert, Oral History Interview [Jan. 2023], 12; Dan Caldwell and Ethel Caldwell to Family and Friends, Email, Dec. 26, 2004, Daniel W. Caldwell, Mission Photographs and Emails, CHL.
25. Kilbert, Oral History Interview [Jan. 2023], 12; Kilbert, Oral History Interview [May 2023], 11; Nelaballe, Oral History Interview, 15–17; Kumar, "Incentives and Expectations," 135; Justin Huggler, "The Struggle for Survival in a Town of Orphans," *Independent* (London), Jan. 5, 2005, 7.
26. Kilbert, Oral History Interview [Jan. 2023], 12–13; Nelaballe, Oral History Interview, 16; Dan Caldwell to Brent Bonham, Email, Dec. 27, 2004, Daniel W. Caldwell, Mission Photographs and Emails, CHL; Jason Swensen, "Tsunami Disaster: More Than 100,000 Dead," *Church News*, Jan. 1, 2005, 2, 15.
27. Kilbert, Oral History Interview [Jan. 2023], 12–13; Nelaballe, Oral History Interview, 16, 19–20; Kilbert, Oral History Interview [Feb. 2023], 8–9; Kilbert, Oral History Interview [May 2023], 8, 10. **Topic: Welfare Programs**
28. Emma Hernandez to James Perry, Email, Sept. 18, 2023, Emma Acosta Hernandez and Hector David Hernandez, Oral History Interviews, CHL; Hernandez and Hernandez, Oral History Interview [2023], [13], [15]–[16]; Hernandez and Hernandez, Oral History Interview [2019], [4], [10]; Hernandez and Hernandez, Oral History Interview [2022], [2], [4], [10], [19]–[22], [27]; Gordon B. Hinckley, "Stay on the High Road," *Ensign* or *Liahona*, May 2004, 113.
29. Hernandez and Hernandez, Oral History Interview [2023], [3], [13], [20]; Hernandez and Hernandez, Oral History Interview [2022], [21]; Hernandez and Hernandez, Oral History Interview [2019], [9]; *Eternal Marriage*, 188–97.
30. Hernandez and Hernandez, Oral History Interview [2019], [9], [13]; Hernandez and Hernandez, Oral History Interview [2023], [12]–[14], [16]–[17], [20]; Hernandez and Hernandez, Oral History Interview [2022], [13]. **Topics: Honduras; Guatemala**
31. Hernandez and Hernandez, Oral History Interview [2023], [12]–[14], [17]–[19]; Hernandez and Hernandez, Oral History Interview [2019], [9]–[10].
32. Hernandez and Hernandez, Oral History Interview [2023], [4], [9]–[11], [21]–[22]; Hernandez and Hernandez, Oral History Interview [2022], [10]–[11], [14]–[15]; Hernandez and Hernandez, Oral History Interview [2019], [10].
33. Hernandez and Hernandez, Oral History Interview [2022], [5], [29]; F. Michael Watson to Presiding Bishopric, Memorandum, Dec. 4, 2001, First Presidency, Presiding Bishopric Correspondence, CHL; Rather, *Supporting the Rescue*, 52–54; "Employment Resource Services," 8–9; Emma Acosta [Hernandez] to James Perry, Email, May 24, 2023, Emma Acosta Hernandez and Hector David Hernandez, Oral History Interviews, CHL; Gordon B. Hinckley, "The Perpetual Education Fund," *Ensign*, May 2001, 51–53; Hernandez and Hernandez, Oral History Interview [2023], [11].
34. Hernandez and Hernandez, Oral History Interview [2023], [2], [21], [24]; Hernandez and Hernandez, Oral History Interview [2019], [10]; Hernandez and Hernandez, Oral History Interview [2022], [16]–[17]; Matthew 14:22–32.
35. Fallentine, Recollections, 2–3; Angela Fallentine, Oral History Interview [Feb. 2023], 1–2, 15–17; Angela Fallentine, Oral History Interview [Sept. 2023], 2–5, 15.
36. Fallentine, Recollections, 3–5; Angela Fallentine to James Perry, Email, Feb. 14, 2024, Angela Fallentine and John Fallentine, Oral History Interviews, CHL.
37. Fallentine, Recollections, 5; Angela Fallentine, Oral History Interview [Feb. 2023], 15–16; Angela Fallentine, Oral History Interview [Sept. 2023], 18–19. **Topic: Interreligious Relations**

CHAPTER 35: HAND IN HAND

1. Lewis and Lewis, "President Sabwe Binene's Story," [2]–[3]; Willy Binene, Oral History Interview [May 22, 2020], [1]–[3]; Willy Binene, Oral History Interview [May 20, 2020], [9]; Willy Binene, Oral History Interview [2017].

2. Chris Fee and Eve Fee, comps., "Africa Southeast Area History for 2006," 2, in Africa Southeast Area, Annual Historical Reports, CHL; *Directory of Organizations and Leaders, 2007,* 5; Willy Binene, Oral History Interview [May 22, 2020], [3]–[4]; Willy Binene, Oral History Interview [2017]; Willy Binene, Oral History Interview [2019].
3. *Deseret Morning News 2006 Church Almanac,* 160; *Deseret Morning News 2007 Church Almanac,* 339–40, 366, 384, 389, 394, 396, 420, 453, 489. **Topics: Church Growth; Democratic Republic of the Congo; Republic of the Congo; Liberia; South Africa; Zimbabwe**
4. Mary Richards, "Restored Gospel's Place in Ivory Coast and Africa," *Church News,* July 30, 2022, 21. **Topic: Côte d'Ivoire**
5. Ituma, Oral History Interview, [00:01:10]–[00:03:25], [00:44:43]–[00:49:10], [00:52:55]–[00:55:22], [01:05:15]–[01:05:32], [01:09:05]–[01:13:19]. **Topic: Nigeria**
6. Sitati, Oral History Interview, [00:00:22]–[00:00:49]; Jason Swensen, "Full Joy Found in Principles of the Gospel," *Church News,* May 23, 2009, 11; Gladys N. Sitati, "Resolving Conflicts Using Gospel Principles," in Reeder and Holbrook, *At the Pulpit,* 332–33; E. Dale LeBaron, "Pioneers in East Africa," *Ensign,* Oct. 1994, 22–23; Gerald Jensen and Carolyn Jensen, "First Stake in Kenya Created," *Church News,* Sept. 29, 2001, 5; Thomas S. Monson, "The Sustaining of Church Officers," *Ensign* or *Liahona,* May 2004, 24–25; Clark and Clark, Oral History Interview, 61. **Topic: Kenya**
7. Julie Dockstader Heaps, "Serving in Africa," *Church News,* May 31, 2003, 7. **Topic: Sealing**
8. Blake McKeown, Oral History Interview [May 2023], [13]–[14].
9. Blake McKeown, Oral History Interview [May 2023], [10]–[11], [14]–[15], [25]; Lowell M. Snow, "Scouting," in Ludlow, *Encyclopedia of Mormonism,* 3:1275–77; "Aaronic Priesthood Achievement and Scouting (Outside the United States)," June 3, 1999, [1]–[4], Dallin H. Oaks, Executive Council and Committee Files, CHL; *Church Handbook of Instructions, Book 2,* 186–88; Scott McKeown to James Perry, Email, Oct. 11, 2023, Scott McKeown and Kara McKeown, Oral History Interview, CHL; *Bondi Rescue,* season 2, episode 1, [00:03:53]–[00:04:39]; *Bondi Rescue,* season 2, episode 5, [00:10:54]–[00:11:53]. **Topic: Young Men Organizations**
10. Blake McKeown, Oral History Interview [May 2023], [17]; Blake McKeown to James Perry, Email, Feb. 23, 2024, Blake McKeown, Oral History Interviews, CHL; *Bondi Rescue,* season 2, episode 1, [00:08:39]–[00:10:07]; *Bondi Rescue,* season 2, episode 2, [00:00:26]–[00:03:30]; *Bondi Rescue,* season 2, episode 3, [00:09:44]–[00:10:41], [00:11:45]–[00:12:32]; *Bondi Rescue,* season 2, episode 5, [00:00:15]–[00:00:24], [00:12:51]–[00:15:11].
11. Blake McKeown, Oral History Interview [May 2023], [15]–[18], [20]; Blake McKeown to James Perry, Email, Feb. 23, 2024, Blake McKeown, Oral History Interviews, CHL.
12. *Bondi Rescue,* season 2, episode 7, [00:00:13]–[00:00:24], [00:05:13]–[00:10:46]; Blake McKeown, Oral History Interview [May 2023], [26]–[28].
13. *Bondi Rescue,* season 2, episode 7, [00:10:46]–[00:24:15]; Blake McKeown, Oral History Interview [May 2023], [28]–[29]; Blake McKeown, Oral History Interview [Aug. 2023], [18]–[19].
14. Thomas S. Monson, "The Sustaining of Church Officers," *Ensign* or *Liahona,* May 2007, 6; Allred, Oral History Interview [Mar. 2012], 24–27; Silvia Allred to James Perry, Email, Feb. 15, 2023, Silvia Allred, Oral History Interviews, CHL.
15. Gordon B. Hinckley, "The Sustaining of Church Officers," *Ensign* or *Liahona,* Nov. 2007, 4; Relief Society General Presidency and Executive Director of the Priesthood Department, Meeting Minutes, June 5, 2007, in Relief Society, General Presidency Meeting Minutes, CHL; Beck, Oral History Interview [2012], 118–19; Allred, Oral History Interview [Mar. 2012], 26–27, 29; Beck, Relief Society General Presidency Executive Summary, [18], [49]; Relief Society, General Presidency Meeting Minutes, May 27 and June 12, 2009; Relief Society, General Board Minutes, volume 39, Dec. 9, 1970, 108; Relief Society, Research Files on History of the Relief Society, CHL.

Notes to pages 587–595

16. Beck, Oral History Interview [2012], 119; Allred, Oral History Interview [Mar. 2012], 29; Beck, Relief Society General Presidency Executive Summary, [18], [49]; Relief Society, General Presidency Meeting Minutes, May 27 and June 12, 2009; Relief Society, General Board Minutes, volume 61, Apr. 8, 1993, 24; Mar. 17, 1994, 95; volume 63, Mar. 17, 1999, 95; volume 65, June 13 and Sept. 4, 2002, 4, 16–17; volume 66, Jan. 22, 2003, 43; Derr, Cannon, and Beecher, *Women of Covenant*, vii, 544.
17. Meeting with Boyd K. Packer and Julie B. Beck, June 19, 2007, Relief Society, General Presidency Meeting Minutes, CHL; Allred, Oral History Interview [Mar. 2012], 28–29; Allred, Oral History Interview [2014], 64.
18. Allred, Oral History Interview [Mar. 2012], 29–30; Beck, Oral History Interview [2012], 119; Beck, Relief Society General Presidency Executive Summary, [18].
19. Beck, Oral History Interview [2012], 83, 88–89; Allred, Oral History Interview [Mar. 2012], 30–31; Beck, Relief Society General Presidency Executive Summary, [23].
20. Derr and others, *First Fifty Years*, 22–26; Beck, Oral History Interview [2012], 85–86, 88–91; Allred, Oral History Interview [Mar. 2012], 30; *Handbook 2*, 63–74.
21. Allred, Oral History Interview [Mar. 2012], 28–37; Allred, Oral History Interview [2023], 1–6, 13–15; Beck, Relief Society General Presidency Executive Summary, [36]. **Topic: Relief Society**
22. Mouhsen, Oral History Interview [Mar. 2023], [1], [7], [14]–[15]; Mouhsen and Mouhsen, Oral History Interview, [10]–[11], [14], [18], [27]–[28]; Campi, Diary, Feb. 16, 2005; Mouhsen, Interview, [1].
23. Mouhsen, Oral History Interview [May 2023], [13]; Mouhsen, Oral History Interview [Mar. 2023], [13]–[14]; Mouhsen and Mouhsen, Oral History Interview, [11]–[12]; Mouhsen, Interview, [1].
24. Mouhsen, Oral History Interview [Mar. 2023], [13]–[14], [16]–[17]; Mouhsen and Mouhsen, Oral History Interview, [8], [12]–[13], [15], [17]–[19], [21]; Mouhsen, Interview, [2].
25. Mouhsen, Oral History Interview [Mar. 2023], [13], [16]–[17]; Mouhsen and Mouhsen, Oral History Interview, [21]–[22].
26. Alexander B. Morrison, "Myths about Mental Illness," *Ensign*, Oct. 2005, 31–35; Sean E. Brotherson, "When Your Child Is Depressed," *Ensign*, Aug. 2004, 52–57; Mary Bramwell, "Living by the Scriptures," *Church News*, Mar. 24, 2001, 2; *Deseret Morning News 2004 Church Almanac*, 139; Livingstone, "Historical Highlights of LDS Family Services," 290; "LDS Social Services Re-named LDS Family Services," *Church News*, Nov. 27, 1999, 6. **Topics: Social Services; Welfare Programs**
27. "International Welfare Operations Strategy," 1; "LDS Family Services International Strategy," 2; "LDS Family Services Worldwide Strategy," 1; Chile Area Presidency to Presiding Bishopric, Dec. 22, 2005, Presiding Bishopric, Welfare Executive Committee Meeting Materials, CHL; "Tsunami Response Update"; Sarah Jane Weaver, "Tsunami Support Turns to Mental Health," *Church News*, May 14, 2005, 6.
28. Mouhsen and Mouhsen, Oral History Interview, [12]–[20], [32]; Mouhsen, Oral History Interview [Mar. 2023], [14]–[15], [17]–[18]; Mouhsen, Oral History Interview [May 2023], [19]–[21]; "The Family: A Proclamation to the World."
29. Mouhsen, Oral History Interview [Mar. 2023], [17]–[20]; Mouhsen, Interview, [2]; Mouhsen and Mouhsen, Oral History Interview, [16]–[17]. **Topic: Healing**
30. Hernandez and Hernandez, Oral History Interview [2022], [23], [26]–[27].
31. Hernandez and Hernandez, Oral History Interview [2019], [11]; Hernandez and Hernandez, Oral History Interview [2022], [2], [4], [22]–[23], [30].
32. Hernandez and Hernandez, Oral History Interview [2022], [4], [23], [29].
33. Hernandez and Hernandez, Oral History Interview [2022], [4]–[5], [23]–[25], [28], [32]–[33].
34. "I Want a Loan," Self-Reliance Services, ChurchofJesusChrist.org; Hernandez and Hernandez, Oral History Interview [2022], [4], [34].
35. Hernandez and Hernandez, Oral History Interview [2022], [24]–[25], [30]–[31].
36. Hinckley, Journal, Jan. 11–13, 2004; Apr. 6, 2004; Nov. 21, 2004; Apr. 29, 2005; Dec. 16, 2005; Apr. 29, 2007; Jan. 12, 2008; Gordon B. Hinckley, "Concluding Remarks," *Ensign*

or *Liahona,* May 2004, 103–4; Carrie Moore and Tom Hatch, "Marjorie Hinckley Dies," *Deseret News,* Apr. 7, 2004, deseret.com.

37. Hinckley, Journal, Apr. 6, 2004; May 14, 2005; Mar. 18, 2006; Gordon B. Hinckley, "Concluding Remarks," *Ensign* or *Liahona,* May 2004, 104.
38. Hinckley, Journal, Jan. 22–24, 2006; Nov. 26, 2007; Jan. 12, 2008; Hinckley, "Wishes regarding Death and Burial," [1]–[2]; John L. Hart, "President Hinckley Ends Mortal Journey," *Church News,* Feb. 2, 2008, 3.
39. Hinckley, "Wishes regarding Death and Burial," [1].
40. Hinckley, "Wishes regarding Death and Burial," [1]; *Church Handbook of Instructions, Book 1,* [2006], 68; "My Redeemer Lives," *Hymns,* no. 135; Davidson, *Our Latter-day Hymns,* 161. **Topic: Gordon B. Hinckley**

Chapter 36: Press Forward

1. Monson, Journal, Jan. 27, 2008.
2. Julie Dockstader Heaps, "In Remembrance," *Church News,* Feb. 9, 2008, 9; Monson, Journal, Feb. 2–3, 2008; Thomas S. Monson, "God Be with You Till We Meet Again," *Ensign,* supplement, Mar. 2008, 29–30.
3. "Milestones in the Presidency of Gordon B. Hinckley," *Ensign,* supplement, Mar. 2008, 13; John L. Hart, "President Hinckley Ends Mortal Journey," *Church News,* Feb. 2, 2008, 3; Hinckley, Journal, Aug. 22 and 28, 2002; Jan. 3–4 and 11, 2003; June 19, 2005; Aug. 21, 2005; Sept. 11, 2005; Nov. 5, 2005; Sept. 23, 2007; "Priesthood Leaders Gather for Satellite Broadcast," *Church News,* Jan. 18, 2003, 3; *Worldwide Leadership Training Meeting: The Priesthood and the Auxiliaries of the Relief Society, Young Women, and Primary, January 10, 2004* (Salt Lake City: The Church of Jesus Christ of Latter-day Saints, 2004); Monson, Journal, Jan. 28, 2004; Mar. 13, 2004; Apr. 24, 2004; Apr. 30, 2005; Mar. 5, 2006. **Topic: Broadcast Media**
4. John L. Hart, "President Hinckley Ends Mortal Journey," *Church News,* Feb. 2, 2008, 3; Robert Freeman, "Nauvoo Temple Milestones, 1840–1850," *Ensign,* July 2002, 12–13; Carrie A. Moore, "Nauvoo Temple Dedication Spurs Torrent of Tears, Joy," *Deseret News,* June 29, 2002, deseret.com; *Saints,* volume 2, chapter 2. **Topics: Nauvoo Temple; Temple Building**
5. Baker and Baker, "Pioneers of Cameroon," 111–12. **Topic: Cameroon**
6. Hinckley, Journal, June 12, 1997; July 1, 1997; Aug. 21, 1997; Hinckley, "Why These Temples?," 18.
7. Dew, *Go Forward with Faith,* 78–79; Hinckley, Journal, Apr. 24, 2003; Scott, Journal, Jan. 31, 2003; Kaufmann, Goujon, and Skirbekk, "End of Secularization in Europe?," 74–79; F. Michael Watson to L. Tom Perry and Area Committee, Memorandum, May 29, 2003, Johann Wondra Family Papers, CHL; Europe Area, Meeting Minutes, Aug. 13, 2003; "Centers for Young Adults: Europe Area Locations." **Topic: Single Adults**
8. Sarah Jane Weaver, "Church Enters World Wide Web 'Carefully and Methodically,'" *Church News,* Mar. 1, 1997, 6; Bowman, *Mormon People,* 245–46; Haws, *Mormon Image in the American Mind,* 158–60, 166–67; Gordon B. Hinckley, *Standing for Something: Ten Neglected Virtues That Will Heal Our Hearts and Homes* (New York: Times Books, 2000); Gordon B. Hinckley, *Way to Be!: Nine Ways to Be Happy and Make Something of Your Life* (New York: Simon and Schuster, 2002); R. Scott Lloyd, "New Era Dawns in LDS Publishing," *Church News,* Mar. 1, 2008, 6. **Topics: Public Relations; Church History and Record Keeping**
9. Monson, Journal, June 15, 2005, and Jan. 29, 2008; "Perpetual Education Fund: Key Indicators," [1]–[3], [5]; Perpetual Education Fund, Board of Directors Meeting Minutes, Oct. 24, 2007. **Topic: Gordon B. Hinckley**
10. Monson, Journal, Feb. 3, 2008. **Topic: Thomas S. Monson**

11. "Temple List," Temples, ChurchofJesusChrist.org; Burton, Oral History Interview, [1]; "Nauvoo Master Plan," [1]; "Project Update," [1]–[11]; "City Creek Center," [1]–[24].
12. Striner, *Hard Times,* 187–93; Fligstein and Goldstein, "Roots of the Great Recession," chapter 2; Dominguez, "International Dimensions of the Great Recession and the Weak Recovery," 119–21.
13. Monson, Journal, Mar. 4, 2009.
14. Burton, Oral History Interview, [2]–[3], [10]. **Topics: Church Finances; First Presidency**
15. Blake McKeown, Oral History Interview [May 2023], [29]–[30].
16. Blake McKeown, Oral History Interview [May 2023], [21]; McKeown and McKeown, Oral History Interview, [17]–[19].
17. Blake McKeown, Oral History Interview [May 2023], [6]–[7], [9]–[10], [12], [21], [30]; Trent Toone, "How FSY Conferences Developed Internationally," *Church News,* Mar. 15, 2020, 21; Hafen, Oral History Interview, 5.
18. M. Russell Ballard, "The Greatest Generation of Missionaries," *Ensign* or *Liahona,* Nov. 2002, 47–48; Charles Didier to Missionary Executive Council, Memorandum, Apr. 12, 2002, Missionary Executive Council, Meeting Materials, CHL; Priesthood Executive Council, Minutes, June 11, 2003; "From Bondi to Baguio," *New Era,* Nov. 2008, 46; *Directory of Organizations and Leaders, 2008,* 35–40. **Topic: Growth of Missionary Work**
19. *Bondi Rescue,* season 3, episode 12, [00:15:43]–[00:16:47], [00:18:10]–[00:20:20], [00:20:52]–[00:21:37], [00:21:55]–[00:22:52]; Blake McKeown, Oral History Interview [May 2023], [23].
20. Blake McKeown, Oral History Interview [May 2023], [21].
21. Willy Binene, Oral History Interview [May 20, 2020], [9], [16]; Willy Binene, Oral History Interview [2017]; Binene and Binene, Oral History Interview [June 2023]; Willy Binene, Oral History Interview [2019]; Lewis and Lewis, "President Sabwe Binene's Story," [3].
22. Sarah Jane Weaver, "Clean Water: An Answer to Villagers' Prayers," *Church News,* May 3, 2008, 4–5; Howard Collett, "A Prayer for Clean Water," *Church News,* Sept. 11, 2010, 7–10; Willy Binene, Oral History Interview [May 22, 2020], [7]–[9]; Africa Southeast Area, Annual Historical Reports, 2010, 20, 40; Binene and Binene, Oral History Interview [June 2023]; General Welfare Committee, Minutes, Dec. 5, 2007, Welfare Services Department, David Frischnecht's Executive Committee Minutes, CHL; "Water Reaches 'End of the Row' in Congolese Villages," Newsroom, Nov. 23, 2009, newsroom.ChurchofJesusChrist.org.
23. Harold C. Brown to Thomas S. Monson, Oct. 25, 1996, Presiding Bishopric, Meeting Materials, CHL; Presiding Bishopric, Minutes, Jan. 29–30, 1997; Rather, *Supporting the Rescue,* 61; "Mormons in Africa: Church Humanitarian Initiatives Give Life," Newsroom, Feb. 21, 2011, newsroom.ChurchofJesusChrist.org; General Welfare Committee, Minutes, June 6, 2007, Welfare Services Department, David Frischnecht's Executive Committee Minutes, CHL; General Welfare Committee, Minutes, Mar. 5, 2008, Presiding Bishopric, Welfare Executive Committee Meeting Materials, CHL.
24. Sarah Jane Weaver, "Clean Water: An Answer to Villagers' Prayers," *Church News,* May 3, 2008, 4–5; Howard Collett, "A Prayer for Clean Water," *Church News,* Sept. 11, 2010, 8–10; Willy Binene, Oral History Interview [May 22, 2020], [8]; Binene and Binene, Oral History Interview [June 2023]. **Topic: Democratic Republic of the Congo**
25. Binene and Binene, Oral History Interview [June 2023]; Willy Binene, Oral History Interview [Dec. 2023]; *Dotés d'en haut: Séminaire de préparation au temple* (Salt Lake City: The Church of Jesus Christ of Latter-day Saints, 2003).
26. Binene and Binene, Oral History Interview [June 2023]; Lilly Binene, Oral History Interview [Apr. 2023]. **Topics: Temple Endowment; Sealing**
27. Fallentine, Recollections, 6–7; Angela Fallentine, Oral History Interview [Feb. 2023], 2–4; Angela Fallentine, Oral History Interview [Jan. 2023], 2–4.

28. "Pageant Reflects Heritage," *Church News,* Oct. 2, 2004, 14; *Deseret News 2010 Church Almanac,* 540–42; Missionary Department, Full-Time Mission Monthly Progress Reports, Apr. 1958. **Topic: New Zealand**
29. Angela Fallentine, Oral History Interview [Feb. 2023], 2–4, 8–9; Angela Fallentine, Oral History Interview [Sept. 2023], 25–27; John Fallentine, Oral History Interview, 2–3; Fallentine and Fallentine, Email Interview, 1.
30. Fallentine, Recollections, 6–8; Angela Fallentine, Oral History Interview [Jan. 2023], 5–7; Angela Fallentine, Oral History Interview [Feb. 2023], 5, 7, 10, 13; Fallentine and Fallentine, Email Interview, 3.
31. Gerry Avant, "Joining Celebration at Catholic Cathedral," *Church News,* Aug. 15, 2009, 3; Thomas S. Monson, "A Civic Service of Thanksgiving: Cathedral of the Madeleine Centennial Celebration," Aug. 9, 2009, 1–4, Thomas S. Monson Addresses, CHL; Glen Warchol, "Good Samaritans Feed Area's Hungry," *Salt Lake Tribune,* Dec. 10, 2000, B1–B2; Carrie A. Moore, "Madeleine Milestone," *Deseret News,* Aug. 10, 2009, A1, A5; R. Scott Lloyd, "With 'Catholic Friends' Reaching Out to the Distressed," *Church News,* Oct. 16, 2004, 3, 10. **Topic: Interreligious Relations**
32. Hout, Levanon, and Cumberworth, "Job Loss and Unemployment," 63, 70, 72–78; Burton, Oral History Interview, [3], [8]; First Presidency to General Authorities and others, May 16, 2008; First Presidency to General Authorities, Mission and MTC Presidents, Feb. 6, 2009, First Presidency, Circular Letters, CHL; Leadership Council, Minutes, Sept. 3, 2008.
33. Burton, Oral History Interview, [4]; General Welfare Committee, Minutes, Mar. 4, 2009, Presiding Bishopric, Welfare Executive Committee Meeting Materials, CHL; Swinton, *To the Rescue,* 141–43; Monson, Journal, Dec. 9, 1995; Jan. 25, 2006; Mar. 9 and 30, 2008; June 29, 2008; Dec. 24, 2008; Feb. 8, 2009; Apr. 19, 2009; June 21, 2009; "President Thomas S. Monson: Prophet and Friend," *Ensign,* supplement, Feb. 2018, 8; Thomas S. Monson, "What Have I Done for Someone Today?," *Ensign* or *Liahona,* Nov. 2009, 87. **Topic: Thomas S. Monson**
34. Sarah Jane Weaver, "Provident Living: A Self-Reliance Link," *Church News,* Jan. 25, 2003, 8–9; "Provident Living Web Site," 1–2; General Welfare Committee, Minutes, Dec. 3, 2008, and Mar. 4, 2009, Presiding Bishopric, Welfare Executive Committee Meeting Materials, CHL; Sarah Jane Weaver, "Self-Reliance Highlighted in DVD, Pamphlet," *Church News,* May 2, 2009, 5; First Presidency to General Authorities and others, Jan. 16, 2009, First Presidency, Circular Letters, CHL; *Basic Principles of Welfare and Self-Reliance,* 2–3, 5, 13.
35. Spencer W. Kimball, "A Report of My Stewardship," *Ensign,* May 1981, 5; "Welfare Handbook," 1; Presiding Bishopric, Secretary to the Presiding Bishopric Meeting Notes, Oct. 2, 2007; Brook Hales to Dallin H. Oaks, Memorandum, Sept. 14, 2009, First Presidency, Committees, Departments, and Organizations Correspondence, CHL; Scott Taylor, "Caring for Needy Has Been Longtime Emphasis for LDS," *Deseret News,* Dec. 12, 2009, B1, B8.
36. Thomas S. Monson, "What Have I Done for Someone Today?," *Ensign* or *Liahona,* Nov. 2009, 86. **Topic: Welfare Programs**

Chapter 37: Answers Will Come

1. Villavicencio and Villavicencio, Oral History Interview [May 2023], 2–3, 8; Villavicencio, Oral History Interview, 1–3; *Deseret News 2010 Church Almanac,* 474–75. **Topic: Ecuador**
2. Villavicencio, Oral History Interview, 1–5; Villavicencio and Villavicencio, Email Interview [Aug. 2023]; Presiding Bishopric to General Authorities and others, June 11, 2004, Quorum of the Twelve Apostles, Written Communications Collection,

CHL; Joshua J. Perkey, "Hungry for the Word in Ecuador," *Ensign,* Feb. 2012, 47, 51; Villavicencio, Email Interview.
3. Villavicencio, Email Interview; Joshua J. Perkey, "Hungry for the Word in Ecuador," *Ensign,* Feb. 2012, 46–47; Villavicencio, Oral History Interview, 4–7.
4. Villavicencio, Oral History Interview, 6–7, 9–10; Villavicencio and Villavicencio, Oral History Interview [May 2023], 2–3.
5. Villavicencio, Oral History Interview, 5–7, 10; *Handbook 1,* 90, 93.
6. Fallentine, Recollections, 7–8; Fallentine and Fallentine, Email Interview, 3; Angela Fallentine, Oral History Interview [Jan. 2023], 5. Quotations edited for readability; "have always been" in original changed to "she has always been," and "learn from it and answers will come" changed to "learn from it, answers will come."
7. Fallentine, Recollections, 6–7; Angela Fallentine, Oral History Interview [Jan. 2023], 7; Angela Fallentine, Oral History Interview [Feb. 2023], 7, 13; Angela Fallentine to James Perry, Email, Nov. 6, 2023, Angela Fallentine and John Fallentine, Oral History Interviews, CHL. **Topic: Social Services**
8. Fallentine, Recollections, 8–9; Angela Fallentine, Oral History Interview [Feb. 2023], 5–7; Fallentine and Fallentine, Email Interview, 3; "The Family: A Proclamation to the World."
9. Angela Fallentine, Oral History Interview [Feb. 2023], 8–11; Angela Fallentine, Oral History Interview [Jan. 2023], 3–5; Fallentine and Fallentine, Email Interview, 1–2; Angela Fallentine, Oral History Interview [Sept. 2023], 22–25; Angela Fallentine to James Perry, Email, Nov. 6, 2023, Angela Fallentine and John Fallentine, Oral History Interviews, CHL.
10. "The Family: A Proclamation to the World"; Fallentine, Recollections, 8–11; Angela Fallentine, Oral History Interview [Feb. 2023], 11; Sheri L. Dew, "Are We Not All Mothers?," *Ensign,* Nov. 2001, 96–98. Quotation edited for readability; two instances of "did" in original changed to "do," and "were" changed to "are."
11. Villavicencio and Villavicencio, Oral History Interview [May 2023], 2.
12. Villavicencio and Villavicencio, Email Interview [July 2023]; Villavicencio, Oral History Interview, 10–11, 19; Sloan, Oral History Interview, 19–20, 23; Villavicencio and Villavicencio, Email Interview [Aug. 2023].
13. Villavicencio, Oral History Interview, 11, 17; Villavicencio and Villavicencio, Email Interview [July 2023]; Villavicencio and Villavicencio, Email Interview [Aug. 2023]. **Topic: Wards and Stakes**
14. Villavicencio, Oral History Interview, 21–24; Villavicencio and Villavicencio, Oral History Interview [May 2023], 20, 36.
15. Villavicencio and Villavicencio, Oral History Interview [May 2023], 3–4, 30–31; Villavicencio and Villavicencio, Oral History Interview [July 2023], 1; "Training for Clerks," *Church News,* Feb. 11, 2006, 10; "Policies and Guidelines for Computers Used by Clerks for Church Record Keeping," in Priesthood Executive Council, Minutes, Aug. 18, 2009; Sloan, Oral History Interview, 29.
16. Villavicencio, Oral History Interview, 23–24; Villavicencio and Villavicencio, Oral History Interview [May 2023], 2, 5, 36; Thomas S. Monson, "Welcome to Conference," *Ensign* or *Liahona,* Nov. 2009, 4; First Presidency to General Authorities and others, Aug. 20, 2009, First Presidency, Circular Letters, CHL; Villavicencio and Villavicencio, Email Interview [July 2023]; Villavicencio and Villavicencio, Email Interview [Aug. 2023]; Priesthood Executive Council, Minutes, Jan. 14, 2009. **Topics: Broadcast Media; Information Age**
17. Villavicencio and Villavicencio, Email Interview [July 2023]; Villavicencio and Villavicencio, Oral History Interview [May 2023], 5–6; Villavicencio and Villavicencio, Email Interview [Aug. 2023]. **Topic: General Conference**
18. *Deseret News 2011 Church Almanac,* 163, 184, 475–77; Hinckley, Journal, Sept. 16–17, 2000; Mortensen, *Witnessing the Hand of the Lord in the Dominican Republic,* 275. **Topic: Dominican Republic**

19. Rappleye and Rappleye, Oral History Interview, 6, 8, 11–15; Bodden, Oral History Interview, 2–4; William B. Smart, "2 Families Bring Gospel to a Nation," *Church News,* July 11, 1981, 12; Mortensen, *Witnessing the Hand of the Lord in the Dominican Republic,* 23–36, 41–43.
20. *Saints,* volume 2, chapter 10; Edwin O. Haroldsen, "Jamaica Branch Sees Chain of Baptisms," *Church News,* Aug. 28, 1976, 14; Wanda Kenton Smith, "Jamaica: Lush Isle of Friendly People," *Church News,* Jan. 29, 1984, 14; Nugent and Nugent, Oral History Interview, 7–9, 11–13, 18; Nugent, Oral History Interview, 4–6, 13–14. **Topic: Jamaica**
21. Millett, "History of The Church of Jesus Christ of Latter-day Saints in the Caribbean," 136–38; "Barbados," Global Histories, ChurchofJesusChrist.org/study/history/global-histories. **Topic: Barbados**
22. Alexandre Mourra, Testimony, Mar. 1981, CHL; Millett, "History of The Church of Jesus Christ of Latter-day Saints in the Caribbean," 125–31; "Merchant Seeking Truth Opened Way for Church," *Church News,* May 3, 2003, 10. **Topic: Haiti**
23. LaRene Porter Gaunt, "Bringing Hope to Haiti," *Ensign,* June 2000, 39; *Deseret News 2011 Church Almanac,* 12, 501–2; Erikson and others, "Political Forces and Actors," 67–74; Bailey, *Humanitarian Crises,* 5; Haiti Port-au-Prince Mission, Annual Historical Reports, 2010, [1].
24. Jennifer Samuels, "Family Reunited in Miami after Trauma in Haiti," *Church News,* Jan. 30, 2010, 6; Neil L. Andersen, "What Thinks Christ of Me?," *Ensign* or *Liahona,* May 2012, 113–14.
25. *Deseret News 2011 Church Almanac,* 12; Lauren Allen, "Members in Haiti Moving Forward, Firm in the Gospel," and "Church Aid," *Ensign* or *Liahona,* May 2010, 138–39; "Haiti Report," 4. **Topic: Welfare Programs**
26. Jennifer Samuels, "Family Reunited in Miami after Trauma in Haiti," *Church News,* Jan. 30, 2010, 6.
27. Howard Collett, "A Prayer for Clean Water," *Church News,* Sept. 11, 2010, 7, 10.
28. Willy Binene, Oral History Interview [May 22, 2020], [7]–[9]; Howard Collett, "A Prayer for Clean Water," *Church News,* Sept. 11, 2010, 7, 9; Binene and Binene, Oral History Interview [June 2023].
29. Binene and Binene, Oral History Interview [June 2023]; Sarah Jane Weaver, "Clean Water: An Answer to Villagers' Prayers," *Church News,* May 3, 2008, 4–5; Howard Collett, "A Prayer for Clean Water," *Church News,* Sept. 11, 2010, 8–10.
30. Willy Binene, Oral History Interview [May 22, 2020], [8]; Howard Collett, "A Prayer for Clean Water," *Church News,* Sept. 11, 2010, 10; Farrell and Barlow, "Celebration of Clean Water in Luputa"; Binene and Binene, Oral History Interview [June 2023].
31. Africa Southeast Area, Annual Historical Reports, 2010, 40–41; Farrell and Barlow, "Celebration of Clean Water in Luputa"; Willy Binene, Oral History Interview [Dec. 2023]; Binene and Binene, Oral History Interview [June 2023]. Quotation edited for readability; "had performed" in original changed to "performed." **Topic: Democratic Republic of the Congo**

CHAPTER 38: REAL AND IMMEASURABLE

1. Perkey, Oral History Interview, [00:00:54]–[00:06:48], [00:13:07]–[00:13:55]; Villavicencio and Villavicencio, Email Interview [July 2023]; Joshua Perkey to Marco Villavicencio, Email, Feb. 7, 2011, Marco Villavicencio and Claudia Villavicencio, Oral History Interviews, CHL; Villavicencio and Villavicencio, Oral History Interview [May 2023], 21–28. **Topics: Church Periodicals; Globalization; Ecuador**
2. Joshua J. Perkey, "Hungry for the Word in Ecuador," *Ensign,* Feb. 2012, 46–51; Villavicencio, Oral History Interview, 17.
3. Joshua Perkey to Marco Villavicencio, Email, Feb. 7, 2011, Marco Villavicencio and Claudia Villavicencio, Oral History Interviews, CHL; Perkey, Oral History Interview,

[00:07:10]–[00:07:50]; R. Scott Lloyd, "'One in a Million' Feature Spotlights Primary Children," *Church News,* Feb. 12, 2011, 14; "Danil," and "Giordayne," One in a Million, ChurchofJesusChrist.org/media/video; Villavicencio and Villavicencio, Email Interview [July 2023]; Villavicencio and Villavicencio, Oral History Interview [May 2023], 2, 8, 21–28.
4. Villavicencio and Villavicencio, Email Interview [July 2023]; "Sair," One in a Million, ChurchofJesusChrist.org/media/video. **Topic: Primary**
5. Hernandez and Hernandez, Oral History Interview [2023], [21]–[29], [34]–[41]; Hernandez and Hernandez, Oral History Interview [2022], [5], [7]–[11], [15], [23]–[25], [33], [37]–[38]; Emma Hernandez to James Perry, Emails, Oct. 11, 2023; Mar. 14, 2024, Emma Acosta Hernandez and Hector David Hernandez, Oral History Interviews, CHL.
6. Hernandez and Hernandez, Oral History Interview [2023], [35], [39]–[41]. **Topic: Sealing**
7. Hernandez and Hernandez, Oral History Interview [2023], [25], [27], [29], [32]–[33]; Hernandez and Hernandez, Oral History Interview [2022], [5], [11], [17], [19], [24]–[26], [30]–[31], [33], [36]; Emma Hernandez to James Perry, Emails, Sept. 12, 2023; Oct. 11, 2023; Mar. 12, 2024, Emma Acosta Hernandez and Hector David Hernandez, Oral History Interviews, CHL.
8. Hernandez and Hernandez, Oral History Interview [2023], [25]–[27], [29]–[33]; Hernandez Family at Emma Hernandez's University Graduation, Mar. 4, 2011, Photograph; Emma Hernandez to James Perry, Email, Sept. 12, 2023, Emma Acosta Hernandez and Hector David Hernandez, Oral History Interviews, CHL.
9. Thomas S. Monson, "It's Conference Once Again," and Brook P. Hales, "Statistical Report, 2010," *Ensign* or *Liahona,* May 2011, 4, 6, 29; Monson, Journal, Jan. 31, 2011; Feb. 1, 2011; Mar. 2 and 16, 2011.
10. Haws, *Mormon Image in the American Mind,* 172–75, 195–99, 207–38; Shipps, *Sojourner,* 98–123; Walter Kirn, "The Mormon Moment," *Newsweek,* June 5, 2011, newsweek.com. **Topic: Public Relations**
11. Haws, *Mormon Image in the American Mind,* 237–38; Thomas S. Monson, "Priesthood Power," *Ensign* or *Liahona,* May 2011, 66; Monson, Journal, Feb. 16, 1999; Mar. 30, 1999; Oct. 8, 1999; May 31, 2006.
12. NeJaime, "Before Marriage," 87–172; Russell M. Nelson, "Elder Russell M. Nelson: The Family: The Hope for the Future of Nations," *Church News,* Aug. 12, 2009, thechurchnews.com; First Presidency to General Authorities and others, June 20, 2008, in "California and Same-Sex Marriage," Newsroom, June 30, 2008; "Church Readies Members on Proposition 8," Newsroom, Oct. 8, 2008, newsroom.ChurchofJesusChrist.org; Young, "Mormons and Same-Sex Marriage," 159–60.
13. Young, "Mormons and Same-Sex Marriage," 161–62; "Catholic Bishop Decries Religious Bigotry against Mormons," Newsroom, Nov. 7, 2008, newsroom.ChurchofJesusChrist.org.
14. Young, "Mormons and Same-Sex Marriage," 164–66; "Church Issues Statement on Proposition 8 Protest," Newsroom, Nov. 7, 2008, newsroom.ChurchofJesusChrist.org; Scott Taylor, "Mormon Church Supports Salt Lake City's Protections for Gay Rights," *Deseret News,* Nov. 10, 2009, deseret.com; "Church Responds to HRC Petition: Statement on Same-Sex Attraction," Newsroom, Oct. 12, 2010, newsroom.ChurchofJesusChrist.org.
15. *God Loveth His Children,* 1; "New Pamphlet: 'God Loveth His Children,'" *Church News,* Aug. 4, 2007, 5; Doug Andersen and others to Michael Otterson, Jan. 25, 2010; "Gays and Mormons," Feb. 22, 2010; Doug Andersen to Michael Otterson, Mar. 10, 2010; Paul Pieper to Michael Otterson, Apr. 12, 2011; "Mormon Issues: Sexual Orientation and Identity," webpage mockup, Mar. 8, 2012; Dallin H. Oaks, "Helping Leaders, Families, and Individuals Deal with Same-Gender Attraction," Mar. 30, 2012, Public Affairs Department, Michael Otterson Files, CHL.
16. "Disciples of Christ Love All People," "True to Beliefs," and "I Never Stopped Going to Church," video transcripts, Love One Another: A Discussion on Same-Sex Attraction, Mormons and Gays (website), capture [21:20:06], Sept. 14, 2016, archived at Wayback Machine, web.archive.org.
17. Thomas S. Monson, "At Parting," *Ensign* or *Liahona,* May 2011, 114.

18. "Directors' Council Discussion on Branding," May 8, 2009, Public Affairs Department, Michael Otterson Files, CHL; "Driving Core Messages for the Church," Jan. 12, 2010, in Michael Otterson to Quorum of the Twelve, Memorandum, Jan. 13, 2010; Church Messaging Presentation, July 2010, Public Affairs Department, Michael Otterson Files, CHL.
19. Allred, Journal, Aug. 17, 2011; Chris Morales, "New Temple for El Salvador," *Church News*, Nov. 24, 2007, 3; Allred and Allred, Oral History Interview, 7; Allred, Oral History Interview [June 2021], 10; First Presidency to Silvia Allred, Feb. 24, 2011, Relief Society, Silvia Allred Files, CHL.
20. Beck, Relief Society General Presidency Executive Summary, [6]–[10], [18]–[20], [29]–[32]; Priesthood Executive Council, Minutes and Records, Feb. 9, 2011; Priesthood Executive Council to First Presidency, Memorandum, Mar. 9, 2011, Priesthood Executive Council, Minutes and Records, CHL; Priesthood Department to General Authorities and others, Oct. 5, 2011, Historical Department, Circular Letters, CHL.
21. Beck, Relief Society General Presidency Executive Summary, [45]–[48]; Allred, Oral History Interview [2023], 13–15.
22. "Relief Society History Book Proposal," May 19, 2009, Relief Society, General Presidency Meeting Minutes, CHL; Priesthood Executive Council, Minutes, May 20, 2009; Priesthood Executive Council, Minutes and Records, Jan. 12, 2011; Mar. 22, 2011; Apr. 6, 2011; Beck, Relief Society General Presidency Executive Summary, [41]–[44], [49]–[54]; Sarah Jane Weaver, "Witness of Divine Roles," *Church News*, Sept. 10, 2011, 3; *Daughters in My Kingdom*, xi–xiv. **Topic: Relief Society**
23. Allred, Oral History Interview [Mar. 2012], 41–42; Allred, Oral History Interview [June 2021], 10–12; Allred, Oral History Interview [2023], 17–18. **Topic: El Salvador**
24. Silvia Allred, Address, San Salvador El Salvador Temple Dedication, Aug. 21, 2011, 1–2, Relief Society, General Presidency Meeting Minutes, CHL; Allred, Oral History Interview [June 2021], 10–13; Allred, Oral History Interview [2023], 18; Jason Swensen, "El Salvador Temple: A Symbol of Peace and Hope," *Church News*, Aug. 27, 2011, 6.
25. Allred, Oral History Interview [June 2021], 13; First Presidency to General Authorities and others, Jan. 28, 2011, First Presidency, Circular Letters, CHL; Silvia Allred, Address, San Salvador El Salvador Temple Dedication, Aug. 21, 2011, 1, 4, Relief Society, General Presidency Meeting Minutes, CHL. **Topic: Temple Dedications and Dedicatory Prayers**
26. Willy Binene, Oral History Interview [Dec. 2023]; Binene and Binene, Oral History Interview [June 2023]; First Presidency to General Authorities and others, Aug. 18, 2011, First Presidency, Circular Letters, CHL.
27. "Growth of Church in Remote Central Africa Is Remarkable," *Church News*, July 23, 2011, 10; "Membership by Branch in the Luputa Democratic Republic of the Congo District for Years 2006–2012," copy in editors' possession; Willy Binene, Oral History Interview [Dec. 2023]; Willy Binene and Church Leaders with Newly Called Missionaries, [June 26, 2011], Photograph, Luputa Democratic Republic of the Congo Stake Photographs, CHL.
28. Monson, Journal, Sept. 30–Oct. 1, 2011; Thomas S. Monson, "As We Meet Again," *Ensign* or *Liahona*, Nov. 2011, 4; "Growth of Church in Remote Central Africa Is Remarkable," *Church News*, July 23, 2011, 10; Binene and Binene, Oral History Interview [June 2023].
29. Thomas S. Monson, "As We Meet Again," *Ensign* or *Liahona*, Nov. 2011, 5; Cowan and Bray, *Provo's Two Temples*, 148–71, 176–79, 185. A copy of a painting of Christ's Second Coming survived the fire. (Ryan Morgenegg, "Fire Devastates Historic Provo Tabernacle," *Church News*, Dec. 25, 2010, 2.)
30. Thomas S. Monson, "As We Meet Again," *Ensign* or *Liahona*, Nov. 2011, 5; Binene and Binene, Oral History Interview [June 2023]. **Topics: Democratic Republic of the Congo; Temple Building**

CHAPTER 39: EVER AT THE HELM

1. "Message from President Thomas S. Monson," *Church News,* Feb. 3, 2013, 3, 9.
2. Thomas S. Monson, "To the Rescue," *Ensign,* May 2001, 48–50; "Message from President Thomas S. Monson," *Church News,* Feb. 3, 2013, 3, 9; Thomas S. Monson, "To the Rescue," Apr. 2, 2009, 1–10, Thomas S. Monson Addresses, CHL; Swinton, *To the Rescue,* 525; "President Thomas S. Monson: Prophet and Friend," *Ensign,* supplement, Feb. 2018, 12–13; Tad Walch, "President Thomas S. Monson, 16th Prophet of the LDS Church, Dies after a Lifetime Spent Going 'to the Rescue,'" *Deseret News,* Jan. 3, 2018, deseret.com.
3. "Message from President Thomas S. Monson," *Church News,* Feb. 3, 2013, 3, 9; Matthew 25:40. **Topic: Thomas S. Monson**
4. "Message from President Thomas S. Monson," *Church News,* Feb. 3, 2013, 3; Thomas S. Monson, "Welcome to Conference," *Ensign* or *Liahona,* Nov. 2012, 4–5; Scott Taylor, "Revisiting 'the Surge': 10 Years since Missionary Age Change," *Church News,* Oct. 1, 2022, 6; Priesthood Executive Council, Minutes and Records, Apr. 13, 2011. **Topic: Growth of Missionary Work**
5. "Message from President Thomas S. Monson," *Church News,* Feb. 3, 2013, 3, 9.
6. Willy Binene, Oral History Interview [Dec. 2023]; Lilly Binene, Oral History Interview [Dec. 2023]; Willy Binene, Oral History Interview [2019]; Willy Binene, Oral History Interview [2017]; "New Mission Presidents," *Church News,* June 4, 2017, 13. **Topic: Côte d'Ivoire**
7. Marianne Holman Prescott, "Construction Begins for a New Temple in Africa," *Church News,* Feb. 21, 2016, 3, 13; Rachel Sterzer, "We Found Great Faith," *Church News,* Mar. 13, 2016, 5, 13; Willy Binene, Oral History Interview [Dec. 2023]; Andersen, "Live Younger, Think Older."
8. Willy Binene, Oral History Interview [2017]; Willy Binene, Oral History Interview [Dec. 2023]; Lilly Binene, Oral History Interview [Dec. 2023]; Lilly Binene, Oral History Interview [2019]; Willy Binene, Oral History Interview [2019]. **Topic: Democratic Republic of the Congo**
9. Willy Binene, Oral History Interview [2019]; Willy Binene, Oral History Interview [Dec. 2023]; Lilly Binene, Oral History Interview [Dec. 2023].
10. Rachel Sterzer, "Update on President Monson," *Church News,* May 28, 2017, 2; Monson, Journal, Apr. 6, 2017; Aug. 24 and 31, 2017; Sept. 30, 2017; Oct. 1, 2017; Peggy Fletcher Stack and David Noyce, "Mormon Church President Thomas S. Monson—Known for Private Visits to the Needy and Public Declarations of Faith—Dies at Age 90," *Salt Lake Tribune,* Jan. 3, 2018, sltrib.com; Dieter F. Uchtdorf, "A Prophet for Our Time," *Ensign,* supplement, Feb. 2018, 26.
11. Ryan Morgenegg, "Sharing General Conference," *Church News,* Mar. 25, 2012, 4; "President Thomas S. Monson: Prophet and Friend," *Ensign,* supplement, Feb. 2018, 17; "Church Leaders on Social Media," *Church News,* June 23, 2013, 2; Philip M. Volmar, "Church Mobile Apps 'Flooding the Earth' with Good Media," *Church News,* Feb. 25, 2012, 7.
12. "President Thomas S. Monson: Prophet and Friend," *Ensign,* supplement, Feb. 2018, 16–17; Sarah Jane Weaver, "We Are Trying to Help People Who Are Suffering," *Church News,* Nov. 11, 2012, 8–9; Rachel Sterzer, "I Was a Stranger," *Church News,* Apr. 2, 2017, 6; Rather, "Welfare Compendium," 251.
13. Sarah Jane Weaver, "BYU–Pathway Worldwide," *Church News,* Feb. 12, 2017, 3; Marianne Holman Prescott, "The Chance I Didn't Think I Was Going to Have," *Church News,* Oct. 21, 2018, 7–9; Howard M. Collett, "Pathway Provides Opportunity for a Brighter Future," *Church News,* Apr. 28, 2013, 6, 10, 13. **Topic: Church Universities**

14. Peggy Fletcher Stack and David Noyce, "Mormon Church President Thomas S. Monson—Known for Private Visits to the Needy and Public Declarations of Faith—Dies at Age 90," *Salt Lake Tribune,* Jan. 3, 2018, sltrib.com; Tad Walch, "President Thomas S. Monson, 16th Prophet of the LDS Church, Dies after a Lifetime Spent Going 'to the Rescue,'" *Deseret News,* Jan. 3, 2018, deseret.com. **Topic: Thomas S. Monson**
15. "Message from the First Presidency," 1–4, in Camille West, "New First Presidency Speaks to Members Worldwide," *Church News,* Jan. 16, 2018, ChurchofJesusChrist.org. **Topic: Russell M. Nelson**
16. Russell M. Nelson, "Introductory Remarks," D. Todd Christofferson, "The Elders Quorum," Russell M. Nelson, "Ministering," Jeffrey R. Holland, "Be with and Strengthen Them," and Jean B. Bingham, "Ministering as the Savior Does," *Ensign* or *Liahona,* May 2018, 54, 57, 100–101, 104; John 13:34–35. **Topic: Adjustments to Priesthood Organization**
17. Tad Walch, "First Stop: London—President Nelson Begins Global Ministry Tour," *Church News,* Apr. 15, 2018, 3; Sarah Jane Weaver, "President Nelson's Fast-Paced Effort to Reach the World," *Church News,* Jan. 2, 2021, 8; "President Nelson Concludes Global Ministry Tour in Hawaii," Newsroom, Apr. 23, 2018, newsroom.ChurchofJesusChrist.org. **Topic: Globalization**
18. Russell M. Nelson, "Opening Remarks," and Quentin L. Cook, "Deep and Lasting Conversion to Heavenly Father and the Lord Jesus Christ," *Ensign* or *Liahona,* Nov. 2018, 7–11; Sarah Jane Weaver, "'A New Balance' to Fortify Families," *Church News,* Oct. 14, 2018, 5–6.
19. Russell M. Nelson, "The Correct Name of the Church," *Ensign* or *Liahona,* Nov. 2018, 87–89, emphasis in original. **Topic: Name of the Church**
20. Jason Swensen, "Historic Changes for Children and Youth," *Church News,* May 13, 2018, 3, 16; "Church Expands Global Youth Conference Program," Newsroom, updated Sept. 12, 2019, newsroom.ChurchofJesusChrist.org.
21. Sarah Jane Weaver, "First Presidency Releases New General Handbook for Church Leaders, Members," *Church News,* Feb. 19, 2020, ChurchofJesusChrist.org.
22. Scott Taylor, "A Call for Civility, a Plan to Partner," *Church News,* May 20, 2018, 3; Sarah Jane Weaver, "The Church's Unique Partnership with NAACP," *Church News,* July 28, 2019, 3–5; Russell M. Nelson, "President Nelson Remarks at Worldwide Priesthood Celebration," Newsroom, circa June 1, 2018; "President Nelson Shares Social Post about Racism and Calls for Respect for Human Dignity," Newsroom, June 1, 2020, newsroom.ChurchofJesusChrist.org; Russell M. Nelson, "Let God Prevail," *Ensign* or *Liahona,* Nov. 2020, 94.
23. McBaine and Wayment, "Representation of Women in Today's Church," 107–17; Russell M. Nelson, "Helping Women of the Church Feel More Valued," Mar. 28, 2013, 1, Russell M. Nelson Addresses, CHL; Russell M. Nelson, "A Plea to My Sisters," *Ensign* or *Liahona,* Nov. 2015, 97; Dallin H. Oaks, "The Keys and Authority of the Priesthood," *Ensign* or *Liahona,* May 2014, 51; Sarah Jane Weaver, "Women Leaders to Serve on Church's General Councils," *Church News,* Aug. 23, 2015, 3; First Presidency to General Authorities and others, Oct. 2, 2019, First Presidency, Circular Letters, CHL; Sarah Jane Weaver, "Women, Youth, Children Can Serve as Witnesses," *Church News,* Oct. 6, 2019, 3–4. **Topics: Church Callings; Adjustments to Temple Work**
24. First Presidency to General Authorities and others, June 29, 2015, First Presidency, Circular Letters, CHL; Dallin H. Oaks, "Going Forward with Religious Freedom and Nondiscrimination," Newsroom, Nov. 12, 2021, newsroom.ChurchofJesusChrist.org; see also Russell M. Nelson, "The Love and Laws of God," Newsroom, Sept. 17, 2019, newsroom.ChurchofJesusChrist.org.
25. "Same-Sex Attraction: Kindness, Inclusion, and Respect for All of God's Children," Same-Sex Attraction, ChurchofJesusChrist.org; Ballard, "Questions and Answers."

26. "Message from the First Presidency," 3, in Camille West, "New First Presidency Speaks to Members Worldwide," Church News, Jan. 16, 2018, ChurchofJesusChrist.org; Nelson and Nelson, "Hope of Israel"; Russell M. Nelson, "Let Us All Press On," *Ensign* or *Liahona*, May 2018, 119; Russell M. Nelson, "Becoming Exemplary Latter-day Saints," *Ensign* or *Liahona*, Nov. 2018, 114; Russell M. Nelson, "Closing Remarks," *Ensign* or *Liahona*, May 2019, 112; Russell M. Nelson, "Spiritual Treasures," *Ensign* or *Liahona*, Nov. 2019, 79. **Topics: Gathering of Israel; Temple Building; Russell M. Nelson; India; Papua New Guinea; Hungary**
27. "Rome Italy Temple Is Dedicated," Newsroom, Mar. 10, 2019, newsroom.ChurchofJesusChrist.org; Sarah Jane Weaver, "Events in Rome Are a 'Hinge Point' for the World," "President Nelson, Pope Francis Meet," and "The Story behind Iconic Photographs," *Church News*, Mar. 17, 2019, 3, 9, 16. **Topic: Italy**
28. Russell M. Nelson, "Closing Remarks," *Ensign* or *Liahona*, Nov. 2019, 122.
29. Lindsey, Oral History Interview [Oct. 5, 2023], 7–9, 13, 22; "Thousands Attend Latin American Cultural Celebration Held at Conference Center," Newsroom, Nov. 2, 2019, newsroom.ChurchofJesusChrist.org.
30. Lindsey, Oral History Interview [Oct. 5, 2023], 1–9. Quotation edited for readability; "minister you" in original changed to "minister to you."
31. Lindsey, Oral History Interview [Oct. 5, 2023], 8–9; Laudy Kaouk, "How the Priesthood Blesses Youth," *Ensign* or *Liahona*, May 2020, 56–57; 1 Nephi 3:7.
32. "WHO Director-General's Statement on IHR Emergency Committee on Novel Coronavirus (2019-nCoV)," World Health Organization, Jan. 30, 2020, who.int; "CDC Museum COVID-19 Timeline," Centers for Disease Control and Prevention, last reviewed Mar. 15, 2023, cdc.gov.
33. "CDC Museum COVID-19 Timeline," Centers for Disease Control and Prevention, last reviewed Mar. 15, 2023, cdc.gov; Jason Swensen, "Prophet Asks China 'How Can We Help?,'" *Church News*, Feb. 2, 2020, 3; Sydney Walker, "Coronavirus Update," *Church News*, Mar. 1, 2020, 24; Evans, "The Church of Jesus Christ of Latter-day Saints' Response to the 2019–20 Coronavirus Pandemic," 787.
34. "CDC Museum COVID-19 Timeline," Centers for Disease Control and Prevention, last reviewed Mar. 15, 2023, cdc.gov; *Saints*, volume 3, chapter 13; "COVID-19 Prompts Temporary Adjustments," *Church News*, Mar. 22, 2020, 5; Sarah Jane Weaver, "COVID-19 Concerns Spark Three Major Changes," *Church News*, Mar. 15, 2020, 3–4; Evans, "The Church of Jesus Christ of Latter-day Saints' Response to the 2019–20 Coronavirus Pandemic," 784–86. **Topics: Influenza Pandemic of 1918; Sacrament Meetings**
35. Tad Walch, "'I Remain Optimistic for the Future': President Nelson Offers Video Message of Hope during COVID-19 Pandemic," *Deseret News*, Mar. 14, 2020, deseret.com.
36. Lindsey, Oral History Interview [Oct. 31, 2023], 1; Scott Taylor, "'Lasting Effects' from General Conference," *Church News*, Apr. 12, 2020, 3. **Topic: Church Headquarters**
37. Russell M. Nelson, "Opening Message," *Ensign* or *Liahona*, May 2020, 6, emphasis in original; Evans, "The Church of Jesus Christ of Latter-day Saints' Response to the 2019–20 Coronavirus Pandemic," 784–88; "Saturday Morning Session," Apr. 2020 General Conference, [00:01:03]–[00:01:10], ChurchofJesusChrist.org; Russell M. Nelson, "Closing Remarks," *Ensign* or *Liahona*, Nov. 2019, 122. **Topic: General Conference**
38. Lindsey, Oral History Interview [Oct. 5, 2023], 10–11, 14, 19, 24; Russell M. Nelson, "Closing Remarks," *Ensign* or *Liahona*, Nov. 2019, 122; Laudy Kaouk, "How the Priesthood Blesses Youth," *Ensign* or *Liahona*, May 2020, 56–57. **Topic: Joseph Smith Jr.**
39. Gerrit W. Gong, "Hosanna and Hallelujah—The Living Jesus Christ: The Heart of Restoration and Easter," *Ensign* or *Liahona*, May 2020, 52–55; Lindsey, Oral History Interview [Oct. 31, 2023], 1–2; Lindsey, Oral History Interview [Oct. 5, 2023], 16–17; Laudy Kaouk, "How the Priesthood Blesses Youth," *Ensign* or *Liahona*, May 2020, 56.

40. Lindsey, Oral History Interview [Oct. 5, 2023], 12–13, 16–17, 21.
41. Laudy Kaouk, "How the Priesthood Blesses Youth," *Ensign* or *Liahona*, May 2020, 56–57.
42. Enzo Petelo, "How the Priesthood Blesses Youth," *Ensign* or *Liahona*, May 2020, 58–59; Lindsey, Oral History Interview [Oct. 5, 2023], 17–19.
43. Russell M. Nelson, "Hear Him," *Ensign* or *Liahona*, May 2020, 88–90; Joseph Smith—History 1:17. **Topic: Joseph Smith's First Vision Accounts**
44. Russell M. Nelson, "Hear Him," *Ensign* or *Liahona*, May 2020, 90–92.
45. Russell M. Nelson, "Hosanna Shout," *Ensign* or *Liahona*, May 2020, 92; Sydney Walker, "Hosanna Shout: Way to Express Gratitude," *Church News*, Apr. 12, 2020, 6–7. **Topic: Kirtland Temple**

SOURCES CITED

This list serves as a comprehensive guide to all sources cited in the fourth volume of *Saints: The Story of the Church of Jesus Christ in the Latter Days*. In entries for manuscript sources, dates identify when the manuscript was created, which is not necessarily the time period the manuscript covers. Many sources are available digitally, and links are found in the electronic version of the book, available at saints.ChurchofJesusChrist.org and in the Gospel Library.

Citation of a source does not imply that it is endorsed by the Church. For more information about the types of sources used in *Saints*, see "Note on Sources."

The sources for the epigraphs found in the book are as follows:

Volume epigraph: Joseph Smith, "Church History," Mar. 1, 1842, in *JSP*, H1:499–500
Part 1 epigraph: Hélio da Rocha Camargo, "Meu testemunho," *Liahona* (São Paulo, Brazil), Mar. 1959, 76
Part 2 epigraph: Joseph Johnson, Oral History Interview [1998], 7 (quotation edited for readability; "take" in original changed to "takes")
Part 3 epigraph: Campora, *Saint behind Enemy Lines*, 147
Part 4 epigraph: Allred, Oral History Interview [Mar. 2012], 42

The following abbreviations are used in notes and in this list of sources cited:

BYU: L. Tom Perry Special Collections, Harold B. Lee Library, Brigham Young University, Provo, Utah
CHL: Church History Library, The Church of Jesus Christ of Latter-day Saints, Salt Lake City
FSL: FamilySearch Library, The Church of Jesus Christ of Latter-day Saints, Salt Lake City

159th Annual Conference, Sunday Afternoon Session. The Church of Jesus Christ of Latter-day Saints. Broadcast on Apr. 2, 1989. Video, [02:01:33]. General Conference Digital Video, 1949–2020. CHL.
"1967 Membership Population Report: The Church of Jesus Christ of Latter-day Saints," 1967. Typescript. David O. McKay Papers, 1901–70. CHL.
1st Queensland "Especially for Youth": Joy in the Journey. Brisbane: Brisbane Australia Stake, circa 1999. Copy in Melanie Riwai-Couch, "Historical Information about 'Especially for Youth' in the Pacific Area," Aug. 25, 2023. Matthew Cowley Pacific Church History Centre, Hamilton, New Zealand.
Abner, John. Italian Mission Reminiscences, 2013. CHL.
Aburto, Eduardo Ayala. Oral History Interview by Gordon Irving, July 12, 2005. CHL.
Accra Ghana Temple. Dedication Services, Jan. 11, 2004. CHL.
Acquah, William E. Daniel. "The 'Freeze' and Three Days in Police Cells," no date. Typescript. James Nyankah, "Ghana Freeze" Reminiscences, 1989. CHL.
Acquah, William E. Daniel, and Charlotte Andoh-Kesson Acquah. Oral History Interview by Dallin Morrow and Angela Hallstrom, June 19, 2018. CHL.
———. Oral History Interview by Matthew K. Heiss, Oct. 16, 1999. CHL.
"Action List for New Converts." *Bulletin*, no. 23 (May 1982): 2. Newsletter published by Corporation of the President of The Church of Jesus Christ of Latter-day Saints. Copy at CHL.
Adult Correlation Committee. Minutes, June 1965–Oct. 1970. Typescript. Deseret Sunday School Union Files, 1950–71. CHL.
———. "A Review of Present and Proposed Programs for the Adults of the Church," Apr. and Sept. 1965. Photocopy of typescript. CHL.
Africa Area. Annual Historical Reports, 1990–98. Africa Southeast Area, Annual Historical Reports, 1990–2007, 2009–21. CHL.
Africa Southeast Area. Annual Historical Reports, 1990–2007, 2009–21. CHL.
Africa West Area. Annual Historical Reports, 1998–2018. CHL.

Albrecht, Joachim, Kurt Nikol, and Marianne Nikol. "Book Burning." In *Behind the Iron Curtain: Recollections of Latter-day Saints in East Germany, 1945–1989,* compiled and translated by Garold N. Davis and Norma S. Davis, 150–73. Provo, UT: BYU Studies, 1996.

Allen, James B. LaMar Williams Interview Notes, July 6 and 11, 1988. James B. Allen Papers, circa 1950–99. BYU.

———. "The Rise and Decline of the LDS Indian Student Placement Program, 1947–1996." In *Mormons, Scripture, and the Ancient World: Studies in Honor of John L. Sorenson,* edited by Davis Bitton, 85–119. Provo, UT: Foundation for Ancient Research and Mormon Studies, 1998.

———. "The Significance of Joseph Smith's 'First Vision' in Mormon Thought." *Dialogue: A Journal of Mormon Thought* 1, no. 3 (Fall 1966): 29–46.

———. "Would-Be Saints: West Africa before the 1978 Priesthood Revelation." *Journal of Mormon History* 17, no. 1 (1991): 207–47.

Allen, James B., and Leonard J. Arrington. "Mormon Origins in New York: An Introductory Analysis." *BYU Studies* 9, no. 3 (Spring 1969): 241–74.

Allen, James B., Jessie L. Embry, and Kahlile B. Mehr. *Hearts Turned to the Fathers: A History of the Genealogical Society of Utah, 1894–1994.* Provo, UT: BYU Studies, 1995.

Allen, James B., and Glen M. Leonard. *The Story of the Latter-day Saints.* 2nd ed. Salt Lake City: Deseret Book, 1992.

Allred, Silvia H. Journal Excerpts, 1985, 2011. CHL.

———. Oral History Interview by Katherine Kitterman and Elizabeth Maki, Feb. 13, 2014. CHL.

———. Oral History Interviews by James Perry, Sheridan Sylvester, David Bolingbroke, and/or Lisa Christensen, 2021–23. Silvia H. Allred and Jeff Allred, Oral History Interviews, 2021–23. CHL. English translation of Spanish oral history interviews in possession of editors.

———. Oral History Interviews by Justin R. Bray, 2012. CHL.

Allred, Silvia H., and Jeff Allred. Email Interviews by David Bolingbroke, 2023. Silvia H. Allred and Jeff Allred, Oral History Interviews, 2021–23. CHL.

———. Oral History Interview by David Bolingbroke and James Perry, Nov. 2, 2022. Silvia H. Allred and Jeff Allred, Oral History Interviews, 2021–23. CHL. English translation in possession of editors.

Americas Watch. *Peru under Fire: Human Rights since the Return to Democracy.* New Haven, CT: Yale University Press, 1992.

Ampiah, Kwamina Ato. Oral History Interview by Matthew K. Heiss, Robert McCullough, and Laura Christensen, May 5, 2019. CHL.

Anchorage Alaska Temple. Dedication Services, Jan. 9–10, 1999. CHL.

Andersen, Neil L. "Live Younger, Think Older." Commencement speech given at Brigham Young University–Hawaii, Laie, HI, Oct. 31, 2016. https://speeches.byuh.edu/commencement/live-younger-think-older.

Anderson, Joseph. *Prophets I Have Known.* Salt Lake City: Deseret Book, 1973.

Antorcha de Chiquihuite: Centro Escolar Benemerito de las Americas, 1969–1970. Mexico City: El Centro Escolar Benemérito de las Americas, [1970].

Apel, Frank H. Oral History Interview by Matthew K. Heiss, Oct. 15, 1991. CHL. English translation in possession of editors.

Argentina Buenos Aires North Mission. Manuscript History and Historical Reports, Aug. 1935–Dec. 1974. CHL.

Argetsinger, Gerald S. "The Hill Cumorah Pageant: A Historical Perspective." *Journal of Book of Mormon Studies* 13, nos. 1–2 (2004): 58–69, 171.

Arrington, Leonard J. *Adventures of a Church Historian.* Urbana: University of Illinois Press, 1998.

Arsenault, Raymond. *Freedom Riders: 1961 and the Struggle for Racial Justice.* New York: Oxford University Press, 2006.

The Articles of Faith of The Church of Jesus Christ of Latter-day Saints. See *Pearl of Great Price.*

Ashton, Marvin J. Journal, Nov. 1977–May 1982, Jan. 1983. CHL.

Sources Cited

Astle, Randy. "Mormons and Cinema." In *Cinema, Television, Theater, Music, and Fashion*, edited by J. Michael Hunter, 1–44. Vol. 1 of *Mormons and Popular Culture: The Global Influence of an American Phenomenon*. Santa Barbara, CA: Praeger, 2013.

"The Awakening": A Sound-Filmstrip Presentation of the General Board of Relief Society. [Salt Lake City]: The Church of Jesus Christ of Latter-day Saints, 1964. Filmstrip script. CHL.

Backman, Milton V., Jr. "Awakenings in the Burned-Over District: New Light on the Historical Setting of the First Vision." *BYU Studies* 9, no. 3 (Spring 1969): 301–20.

———. *Joseph Smith's First Vision: The First Vision in Its Historical Context*. Salt Lake City: Bookcraft, 1971.

Bailey, Garrick, and Roberta Glenn Bailey. *A History of the Navajos: The Reservation Years*. Santa Fe, NM: School of American Research Press, 1986.

Bailey, Sarah. *Humanitarian Crises, Emergency Preparedness and Response: The Role of Business and the Private Sector; a Strategy and Options Analysis of Haiti*. London: Overseas Development Institute, 2014.

Baker, Dan, and Edith Baker, comps. and eds. "Pioneers of Cameroon," Aug. 2009. Typescript. Copy at CHL.

Baker Ward, Union Stake. Manuscript History and Historical Reports, 1890–1983. CHL.

Baldridge, Steven W. *Grafting In: A History of the Latter-day Saints in the Holy Land*. Jerusalem: Jerusalem Branch, The Church of Jesus Christ of Latter-day Saints, 1989.

Balenagasau, Sera. Oral History Interview by James Perry and Scott A. Hales, Feb. 15, 2023. CHL. Transcript in possession of editors.

Balenagasau, Sera, and Juliet Toro. Oral History Interview by James Perry and Scott A. Hales, Feb. 28, 2023. CHL. Transcript in possession of editors.

Ballard, M. Russell. "Questions and Answers." Devotional given at Brigham Young University, Provo, UT, Nov. 14, 2017. https://speeches.byu.edu/talks/m-russell-ballard/questions-and-answers/.

Bangerter, William Grant. Diaries, 1958–63, 1965. Microfilm. CHL.

———. Journals, 1941, 1958–63, 1974–2005. William Grant Bangerter Papers, 1939–2002. Microfilm. CHL.

———. Oral History Interviews by Gordon Irving, 1974, 1976–77. CHL.

———. Papers, 1951–2010. CHL.

———. Reminiscences, May–June 1995. Typescript. CHL.

Barber, James. *South Africa in the Twentieth Century: A Political History—In Search of a Nation State*. Oxford: Blackwell, 1999.

Bardsley, Stephen J. Journal Excerpt, July 1, 1991. Typescript. CHL.

Barney, Kevin L. "The Facsimiles and Semitic Adaptation of Existing Sources." In *Astronomy, Papyrus, and Covenant*, compiled and edited by John Gee and Brian M. Hauglid, 107–30. Provo, UT: Foundation for Ancient Research and Mormon Studies, Brigham Young University, 2005.

Basic Principles of Welfare and Self-Reliance. Salt Lake City: The Church of Jesus Christ of Latter-day Saints, 2009.

Basic Unit Program: What It Is and How to Use It to Establish the Church. Salt Lake City: The Church of Jesus Christ of Latter-day Saints, 1982.

Bateman, Maurice, and Arlene Bateman. "To Julia Mavimbela," July 18, 2000. Typescript. CHL.

Bauer, Roy G., and Michele Parr Bauer. Oral History Interview by Ken Adkins, Dec. 4, 2020. CHL.

Baunchand, Betty Jean Wright. Oral History Interview by Alan Cherry, June 10, 1987. BYU.

Baunchand, Severia, and Betty Jean Wright Baunchand. Oral History Interview by R. Bruce Gordon, Oct. 28, 2015. CHL.

Beaulieu, Freda Magee. Address, New Orleans Louisiana Stake Conference, Jan. 16, 1982. CHL.

Beck, Julie B. Oral History Interviews by Gordon Irving and Justin R. Bray, 2012. CHL.

———. Relief Society General Presidency Executive Summary, 2013. CHL.

Beck, Maeta Holiday. Journal Excerpts, 1973–74. CHL.
———. Scrapbook. CHL.
Beck, Maeta Holiday, and Dennis Beck. Oral History Interviews by Jed Woodworth and Tesia Tsai, 2021–22. CHL. Transcript in possession of editors.
Beck, Wayne M., and Evelyn M. Beck. Oral History Interviews by Gordon Irving, 1974. CHL.
Benson, Ezra Taft. Addresses, 1943–89. CHL.
———. *Come, Listen to a Prophet's Voice*. Salt Lake City: Deseret Book, 1990.
———. Journal, 1921–27, 1938–39, 1943–88. CHL.
Bentley, Joseph T. *Life and Family of Joseph T. Bentley: An Autobiography*. Provo, UT: By the author, 1982.
Bergera, Gary James. "'This Time of Crisis': The Race-Based Anti-BYU Athletic Protests of 1968–1971." *Utah Historical Quarterly* 81, no. 3 (Summer 2013): 204–29.
"Bericht über die Genealogische Arbeitswoche in Dresden," June 9–14, 1969. Typescript. German Democratic Republic Dresden Mission, Historical Record, 1969–83. CHL.
Berlo, Janet Catherine. "Navajo Cosmoscapes—Up, Down, *Within*." *American Art* 25, no. 1 (Spring 2011): 10–13.
Berrett, LaMar C., and Blair G. Van Dyke. *Holy Lands: A History of the Latter-day Saints in the Near East*. American Fork, UT: Covenant Communications, 2005.
Beverley Branch, England North Mission. Manuscript History and Historical Reports, 1850–1982. CHL.
Bible. See *Holy Bible*.
Bidamon, Lewis, Emma Smith Bidamon, and Joseph Smith III. Certificate of Sale to Abel Combs, May 26, 1856. CHL.
"Bienestar," circa Oct. 2004. Typescript. Relief Society, Anne C. Pingree Relief Society General Presidency Papers, 1992–2008. CHL.
Binene, Lilly. Oral History Interview by Benjamin Wood, Dec. 12, 2023. Willy Binene and Lilly Binene, Oral History Interviews, 2023. CHL. English translation in possession of editors.
———. Oral History Interview by Jeffrey Bradshaw, Apr. 4, 2023. CHL. English translation in possession of editors.
———. Oral History Interview by Norbert Ounleu, Dec. 23, 2019. CHL. English translation in possession of editors.
Binene, Willy. Interviews by [John Lewis and Ann Lewis], July 2020. CHL. English translation in possession of editors.
———. Oral History Interview by Edouard Ngindu, Apr. 3, 2017. CHL. English translation in possession of editors.
———. Oral History Interview by John Lewis and Ann Lewis, July 7, 2020. CHL. English translation in possession of editors.
———. Oral History Interview by Norbert Ounleu, Dec. 23, 2019. CHL. English translation in possession of editors.
———. Oral History Interviews by Benjamin Wood, 2023. Willy Binene and Lilly Binene, Oral History Interviews, 2023. CHL. English translation in possession of editors.
———. Oral History Interviews by John Lewis and Ann Lewis, May 2020. CHL.
Binene, Willy, and Lilly Binene. Oral History Interview by Benjamin Wood, June 13, 2023. Willy Binene and Lilly Binene, Oral History Interviews, 2023. CHL. English translation in possession of editors.
Black, Newell Spencer, and Venna Wright Parkinson Black. *The Life Stories of Newell Spencer Black and Venna Wright Parkinson as Written by Themselves*. Publication place unidentified: By the authors, MemoryMixer, no date. Copy in possession of editors.
Black, Susan Easton. "Monument to Women Memorial Garden." In *An Eye of Faith: Essays Written in Honor of Richard O. Cowan*, edited by Kenneth L. Alford and Richard E. Bennett, 189–211. Provo, UT: Religious Studies Center, Brigham Young University; Salt Lake City: Deseret Book, 2015.
Black, Susan Easton, and Joseph Walker. *Anxiously Engaged: A Biography of M. Russell Ballard*. Salt Lake City: Deseret Book, 2021.

Sources Cited

Blockson, Charles L. *Black Genealogy.* With Ron Fry. Englewood Cliffs, NJ: Prentice-Hall, 1977.
Blumell, Bruce D. "Priesthood Correlation, 1960–1974," circa 1975. Typescript. CHL.
Board of Education. Church Board of Education Meeting Minutes, 1888–2006. CHL.
Bodden, Rodolfo. Oral History Interview by Clinton D. Christensen, Sept. 27, 2005. CHL.
Bondi Rescue. Season 2. Aired Feb. 5–Apr. 9, 2007, on Network 10 in Australia.
———. Season 3. Aired Feb. 5–May 6, 2008, on Network 10 in Australia.
Bonham, Brent. Oral History Interview by James Perry, Feb. 1, 2023. CHL. Transcript in possession of editors.
Bonnet, Georges A. Journals, 1980–2014. Georges A. Bonnet Papers, 1980–2016. CHL.
———. Notes, Nov. 1999. Georges A. Bonnet Papers, 1980–2016. CHL.
———. Oral History Interview by Matthew K. Heiss, Feb. 22, 2017. CHL.
———. Oral History Interview by Scott A. Hales, June 27, 2023. CHL. Transcript in possession of editors.
The Book of Abraham. See *Pearl of Great Price.*
The Book of Mormon: Another Testament of Jesus Christ. Salt Lake City: The Church of Jesus Christ of Latter-day Saints, 2013.
"Book of Mormon Emphasis for 1988." *Bulletin,* no. 6 (1987): 1. Newsletter published by Corporation of the President of The Church of Jesus Christ of Latter-day Saints. Copy at CHL.
The Book of Moses. See *Pearl of Great Price.*
Boone, David F., and Richard O. Cowan. "The Freiberg Germany Temple: A Latter-day Miracle." In *Regional Studies in Latter-day Saint Church History: Europe,* edited by Donald Q. Cannon and Brent L. Top, 147–67. Provo, UT: Department of Church History and Doctrine, Brigham Young University, 2003.
Boot, Max. *Invisible Armies: An Epic History of Guerrilla Warfare from Ancient Times to the Present.* New York: Liveright, 2013.
Bowman, Matthew. *The Mormon People: The Making of an American Faith.* New York: Random House, 2012.
———. "Zion: The Progressive Roots of Mormon Correlation." In *Directions for Mormon Studies in the Twenty-First Century,* edited by Patrick Q. Mason, 15–34. Salt Lake City: University of Utah Press, 2016.
Boyer, Selvoy J. Oral History Interview by Gordon Irving, 1978. CHL.
Boyle, Michael J. "The War on Terror in American Grand Strategy." *International Affairs* 84, no. 2 (Mar. 2008): 191–209.
Bradley, John F. N. *Czechoslovakia's Velvet Revolution: A Political Analysis.* Boulder, CO: East European Monographs, 1992.
Bradley, Martha Sonntag. *Pedestals and Podiums: Utah Women, Religious Authority, and Equal Rights.* Salt Lake City: Signature Books, 2005.
Branch, Taylor. *Parting the Waters: America in the King Years, 1954–63.* New York: Simon and Schuster, 1988.
Brazilian Mission. *Congresso da Associação da Primária.* São Paulo, Brazil, 1962–[65]. Copy at CHL. English translation of portions in possession of editors.
Brazil São Paulo North Mission. Manuscript History and Historical Reports, 1927–77. CHL.
Brazil South Area. Statistical Reports, 1935–98. CHL.
"A Brief History of the Church Education in Japan and Okinawa," no date. Typescript. Church Educational System, Division Histories, 1946–74. CHL.
Brigham Young University. Board of Trustees Executive Committee Minutes. Brigham Young University, Meeting Minutes, 1875–1974. BYU.
———. Board of Trustees Minutes. Brigham Young University, Board of Trustees Records, 1875–1985. BYU.
———. Jerusalem Center File, 1985. CHL.
British Mission. Manuscript History and Historical Reports, 1841–1971. CHL.
Britsch, R. Lanier. "Charles ('Chuck') J. Woodworth: Fighting for Salvation." In *Tongan Saints: Legacy of Faith,* translated and edited by Eric B. Shumway, 173–77. Laie, HI: Institute for Polynesian Studies, 1991.

———. *From the East: The History of the Latter-day Saints in Asia, 1851–1996*. Salt Lake City: Deseret Book, 1998.

———. *Unto the Islands of the Sea: A History of the Latter-day Saints in the Pacific*. Salt Lake City: Deseret Book, 1986.

Bronson, Stanley Warren. Oral History Interviews by Lisa Christensen, 2022. CHL.

———. The Tender Apples Collection, circa 1967–2000. CHL.

Brough, Monte J. Oral History Interview by Jay Burrup, Aug. 11, 1998. CHL.

Brown, Hugh B. *An Abundant Life: The Memoirs of Hugh B. Brown*. Edited by Edwin B. Firmage. Salt Lake City: Signature Books, 1988.

Brown, James S. *Life of a Pioneer: Being the Autobiography of James S. Brown*. Salt Lake City: George Q. Cannon and Sons, 1900.

Brown, Julian. *The Road to Soweto: Resistance and the Uprising of 16 June 1976*. Woodbridge, England: James Currey, 2016.

Browning, Gary L. Oral History Interview by Gerry Pond, June 1991. Mormon Tabernacle Choir, Chronological Files, 1883–2004. CHL.

———. Papers, 1988–93. Microfilm. CHL.

———. *Russia and the Restored Gospel*. Salt Lake City: Deseret Book, 1997.

Bruley, Sue. "'It Didn't Just Come Out of Nowhere Did It?': The Origins of the Women's Liberation Movement in 1960s Britain." *Oral History* 45, no. 1 (Spring 2017): 67–78.

Buah, John K. Papers, 1983–2005, 2014. CHL.

Budget Office. Appropriations Committee Minutes and Supporting Documents, 1983–2000. CHL.

———. Jerusalem Center Records, 1979–91. CHL.

Burkhardt, Johannes Henry. Journals, 1950–2007. J. Henry Burkhardt Collection, 1950–2007. Photocopy. CHL.

———. Oral History Interview by Matthew K. Heiss, Oct. 24, 1991. English translation by Sylvia Ghosh. CHL.

———. Oral History Interview by Phillip Lear and Doreen Lear, Feb. 14, 2018. CHL.

———. "Wie kam es zum Bau des Freiberger [Freiberg] Tempels?," Oct. 1985. Photocopy of typescript. CHL.

Burton, H. David. Oral History Interview by Jed Woodworth, July 18, 2023. CHL. Transcript in possession of editors.

Busche, F. Enzio. "The Church in Germany, Switzerland, and Austria." In *Mormonism: A Faith for All Cultures*, edited by F. LaMond Tullis, 48–51. Provo, UT: Brigham Young University Press, 1978.

Bushman, Richard L. "The First Vision Story Revived." *Dialogue: A Journal of Mormon Thought* 4, no. 1 (Spring 1969): 82–93.

Bushman, Richard L., and Claudia L. Bushman. Papers, 1946–2012. BYU.

By Study and Also by Faith: One Hundred Years of Seminaries and Institutes of Religion. Salt Lake City: The Church of Jesus Christ of Latter-day Saints, 2015.

Bytheway, John G. "A History of 'Especially for Youth'—1976–1986." Master's thesis, Brigham Young University, 2003.

Caldwell, Daniel W. Mission Photographs and Emails, circa 2004–5. CHL.

Camargo, Fernando, Paulo Camargo, Márcia Camargo, Josué Camargo, and Milton Camargo. Oral History Interview by Scott A. Hales, Apr. 27, 2021. CHL. English translation in possession of editors.

Camargo, Hélio da Rocha. Oral History Interview by Frederick G. Williams, Sept. 9, 1975. CHL. English translation of portions in possession of editors.

———. Reminiscences, 2007. Digital copy. CHL. English translation of portions in possession of editors.

Cameron, Steven B. Mission Journal, July 1958–Jan. 1961. CHL.

Campbell, Beverly B. Papers, 1960–2013. CHL.

Campi de Mouhsen, Beatríz Felisa. Diaries, 1946–2017. CHL.

Campora, Olga Kovářová. "Fruits of Faithfulness: The Saints of Czechoslovakia." In *Women Steadfast in Christ: Talks Selected from the 1991 Women's Conference Co-sponsored by*

Brigham Young University and the Relief Society, edited by Dawn Hall Anderson and Marie Cornwall, 134–47. Salt Lake City: Deseret Book, 1992.
———. Oral History Interviews by James Perry, Dallin Morrow, and/or Jed Woodworth, 2020–23. CHL. Transcript in possession of editors.
———. *Saint behind Enemy Lines.* Salt Lake City: Deseret Book, 1997.
Cancino Castillo, Maria de las Nieves. Oral History Interview by David Bolingbroke and James Perry, Feb. 1, 2023. CHL. English translation in possession of editors.
Cannon, Donald Q., and Richard O. Cowan. *Unto Every Nation: Gospel Light Reaches Every Land.* Salt Lake City: Deseret Book, 2003.
Cannon, Edwin Q., Jr. Collection, 1965–80. CHL.
———. Correspondence, 1972–80. CHL.
———. Papers, 1963–86. CHL.
Cannon, Edwin Q., Jr., and Merrill J. Bateman. "Report of a Visit to Ghana and Nigeria," 1978. Typescript. International Mission Files, 1950–92. CHL.
Cannon, Janath Russell, and Edwin Q. Cannon Jr. *Together: A Love Story.* Salt Lake City: Elayne L. Hess, 1999.
Cardall, Duane. "Glimpses of Prophets: An Eyewitness Account," circa 2020. Typescript. Duane Cardall, Research Files, circa 1972–2000. CHL.
Cardon, Louis B. "The First World War and the Great Depression, 1914–39." In *Truth Will Prevail: The Rise of The Church of Jesus Christ of Latter-day Saints in the British Isles, 1837–1987,* edited by V. Ben Bloxham, James R. Moss, and Larry C. Porter, 335–60. Salt Lake City: The Church of Jesus Christ of Latter-day Saints, 1987.
———. "War and Recovery, 1939–1950." In *Truth Will Prevail: The Rise of The Church of Jesus Christ of Latter-day Saints in the British Isles, 1837–1987,* edited by V. Ben Bloxham, James R. Moss, and Larry C. Porter, 361–93. Salt Lake City: The Church of Jesus Christ of Latter-day Saints, 1987.
Carey, Elaine. *Plaza of Sacrifices: Gender, Power, and Terror in 1968 Mexico.* Albuquerque: University of New Mexico Press, 2005.
Carmack, John K. Journal, Aug. 1983–May 2003. Microfilm. CHL.
———. Oral History Interviews by Ronald Barney, 1997. CHL.
Carmack, Noel A. "Images of Christ in Latter-day Saint Visual Culture, 1900–1999." *BYU Studies* 39, no. 3 (2000): 18–76.
Carr, John E. "'For in That Day . . .': A History of Translation and Distribution, 1965–1980," circa 1980. Typescript. CHL.
Casper, Alan R. "Opposition to the Construction of the Brigham Young University Jerusalem Center." Master's thesis, Brigham Young University, 2003.
"Centers for Young Adults: Europe Area Locations," July 31, 2008. Map. Johann Wondra Family Papers, 1955–2013. CHL.
Century of Black Mormons. University of Utah, Salt Lake City. Accessed Mar. 23, 2023. https://exhibits.lib.utah.edu/s/century-of-black-mormons.
Champagnie, Carl A., Lynne Holladay, and Darlene Holladay. Oral History Interview by Matthew K. Heiss and Steven R. Sorensen, Oct. 18, 1999. CHL.
Children's Songbook of The Church of Jesus Christ of Latter-day Saints. Salt Lake City: The Church of Jesus Christ of Latter-day Saints, 1989.
Chilean Mission. Baptism Statistics and Directories, 1989–91. CHL.
Chile Area. Annual Historical Reports, 1996, 2000–2012. CHL.
"Chile Area Training," circa Oct. 2004. Typescript. Bonnie D. Parkin Collection, 2002–7. CHL.
China Hong Kong Mission. Manuscript History and Historical Reports, 1955–71. CHL.
———. Publications, 1956–73. CHL.
Chinese Mission. Manuscript History and Historical Reports, 1949–53. CHL.
Chipman, Colleen Sorensen, and David E. Richardson. Oral History Interview by Ronald A. Young, Nov. 3, 2009. CHL.
Choi, Dong Sull. "A History of The Church of Jesus Christ of Latter-day Saints in Korea, 1950–1985." PhD diss., Brigham Young University, 1990.

Chou, Po Nien (Felipe), and Petra Chou. *Voice of the Saints in Mongolia.* Provo, UT: Religious Studies Center, Brigham Young University; Salt Lake City: Deseret Book, 2022.
———. *Voice of the Saints in Taiwan.* Provo, UT: Religious Studies Center, Brigham Young University; Salt Lake City: Deseret Book, 2017.
Christensen, J. Dale. Mission Journal, 1961–63. CHL.
Chuquimango Matos, Julián Guillermo. Oral History Interview by Orlando Handa Vargas, May 21, 2022. CHL. English translation in possession of editors.
Church Board of Education. Advisory/Executive Committee Minutes, 1928–89. CHL.
Church Educational System. Area Historical Reports, 1967–2008. CHL.
———. Executive Planning Minutes, 1980–86, 2003–4. CHL.
———. Harvey L. Taylor Administrative Files, 1965–70. CHL.
Church Handbook of Instructions. Book 1, Stake Presidencies and Bishoprics. Salt Lake City: The Church of Jesus Christ of Latter-day Saints, 1998.
Church Handbook of Instructions. Book 1, Stake Presidencies and Bishoprics. Salt Lake City: The Church of Jesus Christ of Latter-day Saints, 2006.
Church Handbook of Instructions. Book 2, Priesthood and Auxiliary Leaders. Salt Lake City: The Church of Jesus Christ of Latter-day Saints, 1998.
Church History Department. Reports, 1986–2007. CHL.
"City Creek Center," Mar. 21, 2008. Slide presentation. Presiding Bishopric, First Presidency Meeting Materials, 1985–2013. CHL.
Clark, Nancy L., and William H. Worger. *South Africa: The Rise and Fall of Apartheid.* 2nd ed. Harlow, England: Pearson, 2011.
Clark, Paul K., and Gretchen K. Clark. Oral History Interviews by Matthew K. Heiss, 1998. CHL.
Clayton, Kathy K. "Harvest of Faith in Abundancia." *Religious Educator* 6, no. 2 (2005): 117–28.
Collection of Materials pertaining to the Song "I Am a Child of God," circa 1957–77. CHL.
Collette, Emmy, comp. *Hermine Weber.* Idaho Falls, ID: By the author, 1983. Copy at CHL.
Colonia Juárez Chihuahua Mexico Temple. Dedication Services, Mar. 6–7, 1999. CHL.
Colonia Suiza Branch. General Minutes, 1959–70. 2 vols. CHL.
Colton, Eleanor Ricks. Memoir Excerpt, no date. Copy in possession of editors.
———. "My Personal Rubicon." *Dialogue: A Journal of Mormon Thought* 14, no. 4 (Winter 1981): 101–8.
"Comparative Report." *L. D. S. Newsheet* 1, no. 10 (June 3, 1956): 1–3. Newsletter published by the Niue District of the Tongan Mission of The Church of Jesus Christ of Latter-day Saints. In Niue District Publications, 1955–61. CHL.
Condie, Spencer J. *Russell M. Nelson: Father, Surgeon, Apostle.* Salt Lake City: Deseret Book, 2003.
"The Construction Program." *El Chasqui* (Mar. 1962): 8. Newsletter published by the Argentine Mission of The Church of Jesus Christ of Latter-day Saints. In Argentine Mission Newsletters, 1962–64. CHL.
Contreras, Felicindo, and Veronica Ines Pacheco Urra Contreras. Oral History Interviews by James Perry, Rob Swanson, David Bolingbroke, and/or Lisa Christensen, 2020–23. CHL. English translation in possession of editors.
Cook, Gene R. Oral History Interview by Gordon Irving, Nov. 13, 2007. CHL.
Cornwall, J. Spencer. *A Century of Singing: The Salt Lake Mormon Tabernacle Choir.* Salt Lake City: Deseret Book, 1958.
Correspondence regarding the Establishment of LDS Church in Ghana, 1967–72, 2004. CHL.
Cowan, Richard O. *The Church in the Twentieth Century.* Salt Lake City: Bookcraft, 1985.
———. *Every Man Shall Hear the Gospel in His Own Language.* 2 vols. Provo, UT: Missionary Training Center, 2001.
———. *The Los Angeles Temple: A Beacon on a Hill.* Provo, UT: Religious Studies Center, Brigham Young University; Salt Lake City: Deseret Book, 2018.
———. "A Tale of Two Temples." In *Regional Studies in Latter-day Saint Church History: The British Isles,* edited by Cynthia Doxey, Robert C. Freeman, Richard Neitzel Holzapfel,

Sources Cited

and Dennis A. Wright, 219–35. Provo, UT: Religious Studies Center, Brigham Young University, 2007.

Cowan, Richard O., and Justin R. Bray. *Provo's Two Temples*. Provo, UT: Religious Studies Center, Brigham Young University; Salt Lake City: Deseret Book, 2015.

Crossley, J. Dennis. Mission Journals, 1958–61. Southern Far East Mission Collection, 1958–95. CHL.

Cruz, Celia Ayala de. Oral History Interviews, 2022–23. CHL. English translation in possession of editors.

Cruz Martinez, Juan A., and Celia Ayala de Cruz. Oral History Interview by Wade Jewkes and Connie Jewkes, Feb. 28, 2015. CHL. English translation in possession of editors.

Cummings, David W. *Mighty Missionary of the Pacific: The Building Program of The Church of Jesus Christ of Latter-day Saints—Its History, Scope and Significance*. Salt Lake City: Bookcraft, 1961.

Curbelo, Néstor. *Historia de los Santos de los Últimos Días en Paraguay: Relatos de Pioneros*. Publication place unidentified: By the author, 2003.

———. *The History of the Mormons in Argentina*. Translated by Erin B. Jennings. Salt Lake City: Greg Kofford Books, 2009.

Curriculum Department. Priesthood Correlation Executive Committee Meeting Minutes, 1961–72. 3 vols. Typescript. CHL.

Curtis, Jim. *Rock Eras: Interpretations of Music and Society, 1954–1984*. Bowling Green, OH: Bowling Green State University Popular Press, 1987.

Cuthbert, Derek A. *The Second Century: Latter-day Saints in Great Britain, Volume I, 1937–1987*. Cambridge: Cambridge University Press, 1987.

Cutler, Virginia Farrer. Oral History Interview by Reed Clegg, May 17, 1986. CHL.

———. Oral History Interviews by Chere H. Romney, 1981, 1983. In Chere H. Romney, "Virginia Farrer Cutler: An Oral History of Her Remarkable Accomplishments," master's thesis, Brigham Young University, 1983.

Dalton, Lela J. Autobiography, 1999. CHL.

"Danil." One in a Million. Media Library. The Church of Jesus Christ of Latter-day Saints. Video, [00:01:34]. Accessed Mar. 22, 2024. https://www.ChurchofJesusChrist.org/media/collection/one-in-a-million.

Daughters in My Kingdom: The History and Work of Relief Society. Salt Lake City: The Church of Jesus Christ of Latter-day Saints, 2011.

Davenport, Randall W. Oral History Interview by Lisa Christensen, May 19, 2022. CHL. Transcript in possession of editors.

Davidson, Karen Lynn. *Our Latter-day Hymns: The Stories and the Messages*. Salt Lake City: Deseret Book, 1988.

Davis, Ebbie. Oral History Interview by James Perry, Apr. 13, 2022. CHL. Transcript in possession of editors.

Davis, Jack. Memorandum to the Director and Deputy Director of Central Intelligence, Mar. 24, 1980. General CIA Records. Freedom of Information Act Electronic Reading Room. https://www.cia.gov/readingroom/document/cia-rdp83b01027r000300080023-5.

"A Day I'll Never Forget." *Reaper* 4, no. 30 (May 14, 1966): [1]–[2]. Newsletter published by the Swiss Mission of The Church of Jesus Christ of Latter-day Saints. In Swiss Mission Newsletters, 1964–66. CHL.

Dedicacion Templo de Santiago, Sept. 1983. CHL.

"Dedicatory Prayer: Hong Kong China Temple, 26 May 1996." Temples. The Church of Jesus Christ of Latter-day Saints. https://www.ChurchofJesusChrist.org/temples/details/hong-kong-china-temple/prayer/1996-05-26.

Dennis, Mike. *The Rise and Fall of the German Democratic Republic, 1945–1990*. Harlow, England: Longman, 2000.

Denton Ward, Fort Worth Stake. Relief Society Minutes and Records, 1962–73. Microfilm. CHL.

de Oliveira, Saul M. Oral History Interview by Frederick G. Williams, Sept. 8, 1975. CHL. English translation of portions in possession of editors.

de Queiroz, Walter Guedes. Oral History Interview by J. Roberto Viveiros and Michael N. Landon, Nov. 18, 2011. CHL.
———. Oral History Interview by Mark L. Grover, Apr. 16, 1982. Mark L. Grover, Oral History Interviews with Latter-day Saints in Brazil. BYU.
Derr, Jill Mulvay. "A Period of Transition: Unified Social Services, 1969–73." In "A History of Social Services in The Church of Jesus Christ of Latter-day Saints, 1916–1984," Nov. 3, 1988, 1–56. Photocopy of typescript. Copy at CHL.
Derr, Jill Mulvay, Janath Russell Cannon, and Maureen Ursenbach Beecher. *Women of Covenant: The Story of Relief Society*. Salt Lake City: Deseret Book, 1992.
Derr, Jill Mulvay, Carol Cornwall Madsen, Kate Holbrook, and Matthew J. Grow, eds. *The First Fifty Years of Relief Society: Key Documents in Latter-day Saint Women's History*. Salt Lake City: Church Historian's Press, 2016.
Deseret Morning News 2004 Church Almanac. Salt Lake City: Deseret Morning News, 2004.
Deseret Morning News 2006 Church Almanac. Salt Lake City: Deseret Morning News, 2005.
Deseret Morning News 2007 Church Almanac. Salt Lake City: Deseret Morning News, 2006.
Deseret News 1976 Church Almanac. Salt Lake City: Deseret News, 1976.
Deseret News 1982 Church Almanac. Salt Lake City: Deseret News, 1981.
Deseret News 1985 Church Almanac. Salt Lake City: Deseret News, 1985.
Deseret News 1987 Church Almanac. Salt Lake City: Deseret News, 1987.
Deseret News 1989–1990 Church Almanac. Salt Lake City: Deseret News, 1989.
Deseret News 1991–1992 Church Almanac. Salt Lake City: Deseret News, 1990.
Deseret News 1993–1994 Church Almanac. Salt Lake City: Deseret News, 1992.
Deseret News 1997–98 Church Almanac. Salt Lake City: Deseret News, 1996.
Deseret News 1999–2000 Church Almanac. Salt Lake City: Deseret News, 1998.
Deseret News 2001–2002 Church Almanac. Salt Lake City: Deseret News, 2000.
Deseret News 2003 Church Almanac. Salt Lake City: Deseret News, 2002.
Deseret News 2010 Church Almanac. Salt Lake City: Deseret News, 2010.
Deseret News 2011 Church Almanac. Salt Lake City: Deseret News, 2011.
Deseret News 2012 Church Almanac. Salt Lake City: Deseret News, 2012.
Dew, Sheri L. *Ezra Taft Benson: A Biography*. Salt Lake City: Deseret Book, 1987.
———. *Go Forward with Faith: The Biography of Gordon B. Hinckley*. Salt Lake City: Deseret Book, 1996.
———. *Insights from a Prophet's Life: Russell M. Nelson*. Salt Lake City: Deseret Book, 2019.
Directory of General Authorities and Officers, 1989: The Church of Jesus Christ of Latter-day Saints. Salt Lake City: The Church of Jesus Christ of Latter-day Saints, 1988.
Directory of General Authorities and Officers, 1991: The Church of Jesus Christ of Latter-day Saints. Salt Lake City: The Church of Jesus Christ of Latter-day Saints, 1991.
Directory of General Authorities and Officers, 1993: The Church of Jesus Christ of Latter-day Saints. Salt Lake City: The Church of Jesus Christ of Latter-day Saints, 1993.
Directory of General Authorities and Officers, 1996: The Church of Jesus Christ of Latter-day Saints. Salt Lake City: The Church of Jesus Christ of Latter-day Saints, 1996.
Directory of General Authorities and Officers, 2001: The Church of Jesus Christ of Latter-day Saints. Salt Lake City: The Church of Jesus Christ of Latter-day Saints, 2000.
Directory of General Authorities and Officers, 2005: The Church of Jesus Christ of Latter-day Saints. Salt Lake City: The Church of Jesus Christ of Latter-day Saints, 2004.
Directory of Organizations and Leaders, 2007. Salt Lake City: The Church of Jesus Christ of Latter-day Saints, 2006.
Directory of Organizations and Leaders, 2008. Salt Lake City: The Church of Jesus Christ of Latter-day Saints, [2007].
"District News." *L. D. S. Newsletter* 1, no. 14 (Oct. 6, 1956): 1–3. Newsletter published by the Niue District of the Tongan Mission of The Church of Jesus Christ of Latter-day Saints. In Niue District Publications, 1955–61. CHL.
The Doctrine and Covenants of The Church of Jesus Christ of Latter-day Saints: Containing Revelations Given to Joseph Smith, the Prophet, with Some Additions by His Successors

Sources Cited

in the Presidency of the Church. Salt Lake City: The Church of Jesus Christ of Latter-day Saints, 2013.

Dominguez, Kathryn M. E. "International Dimensions of the Great Recession and the Weak Recovery." In *Confronting Policy Challenges of the Great Recession: Lessons for Macroeconomic Policy,* edited by Eskander Alvi, 107–24. Kalamazoo, MI: W. E. Upjohn Institute for Employment Research, 2017.

Dominio de las escrituras. Bogotá, Colombia: The Church of Jesus Christ of Latter-day Saints, [1983?]. Copy of flash cards at CHL.

Dresden District, Germany Dresden Mission. Quarterly Reports, 1956–82. CHL.

Dunbabin, J. P. D. *The Cold War: The Great Powers and Their Allies.* 2nd ed. The Postwar World. Harlow, England: Pearson Longman, 2008.

Dunn, Paul H. *The Osmonds: The Official Story of the Osmond Family.* Salt Lake City: Bookcraft, 1975.

Dunning, Geoffrey, and Suzette Dunning. "Conversion Story at Beverley," no date. Digital copy. Suzette T. and Geoffrey Dunning Papers, 2021–22. CHL.

Dunning, Suzette Towse. Email Interviews by James Perry, 2021. Suzette T. and Geoffrey Dunning Papers, 2021–22. CHL.

———. Excerpts from Letters and Journals, Oct. 21, 2021. Digital copy. Suzette T. and Geoffrey Dunning Papers, 2021–22. CHL.

———. Oral History Interview by Freda Entwistle, Aug. 18, 2018. CHL.

———. "Suzette Towse Dunning—My Life and Legacy," no date. Digital copy. Suzette T. and Geoffrey Dunning Papers, 2021–22. CHL.

Dunning, Suzette Towse, and Geoffrey Dunning. Email Interview by James Perry, Sept. 12, 2021. Suzette T. and Geoffrey Dunning Papers, 2021–22. CHL.

Durham, G. Homer. *N. Eldon Tanner: His Life and Service.* Salt Lake City: Deseret Book, 1982.

Eichengreen, Barry. *The European Economy since 1945: Coordinated Capitalism and Beyond.* The Princeton Economic History of the Western World. Princeton, NJ: Princeton University Press, 2007.

Eighty-Seventh Semi-annual Conference of The Church of Jesus Christ of Latter-day Saints. Held in the Tabernacle and Assembly Hall, Salt Lake City, Utah, October 6th, 7th and 8th, 1916, with a Full Report of the Discourses. Salt Lake City: Deseret News, 1916.

Eleven Year Report of the President (1950–51 to 1960–61) of Brigham Young University and Eight Year Report of the Administrator (1953–54 to 1960–61) of Other Areas of the Unified Church School System. [Provo, UT?], [1961?].

Embry, Jessie L. *Black Saints in a White Church: Contemporary African American Mormons.* Salt Lake City: Signature Books, 1994.

———. "Without Purse or Scrip." *Dialogue: A Journal of Mormon Thought* 29, no. 3 (1996): 77–93.

Embry, Jessie L., and John H. Brambaugh. "Preaching through Playing: Sports and Recreation in Missionary Work, 1911–64." *Journal of Mormon History* 35, no. 4 (Fall 2009): 53–84.

"Employment Resource Services," circa June 10, 2005. Slide presentation. Presiding Bishopric, Welfare Executive Committee Meeting Materials, 2000–2010. CHL.

Erikson, Dan, Emma Grant, Franka Braun, Gillette Hall, Katherine Bain, Mark Mattner, Stephanie Kuttner, and Willy Egset. "Political Forces and Actors." In *Social Resilience and State Fragility in Haiti,* edited by World Bank, 67–74. Washington, DC: World Bank, 2007.

Espi, Dignardino F. "Manila Philippines Temple, Coup d'Etat, December 2–4, 1989," no date. John M. Madsen, Area Files, 1992–2005. CHL.

———. "Manila Philippines Temple during the Coup of Dec. 2 and 3, 1989," circa 1989. Philippines Area, Annual Historical Reports, 1989, 1991, 1993–96, 2002–7, 2010–21. CHL.

Eternal Marriage: Student Manual. Salt Lake City: The Church of Jesus Christ of Latter-day Saints, 2003.

European Mission. Historical Reports, 1960–65. CHL.

Europe Area. Eastern Europe Files, 1985–86. CHL.

———. Files relating to Church Activities in Eastern Europe, 1985–89. CHL.

———. Meeting Minutes, 1995–2007. CHL.

Evans, Matthew T. "The Church of Jesus Christ of Latter-day Saints' Response to the 2019–20 Coronavirus Pandemic." In *The Palgrave Handbook of Global Mormonism,* edited by R. Gordon Shepherd, A. Gary Shepherd, and Ryan T. Cragun, 783–816. Cham, Switzerland: Palgrave Macmillan, 2020.

Ewudzie, James. Oral History Interview by Clinton D. Christensen, Aug. 23, 2010. CHL.

"Exit Interview with President and Sister Homer LeBaron: Recently Released from Presiding over the Zaire Mission," Jan. 11, 1994. Typescript. Richard P. Lindsay, Africa Area Files, 1990–94. CHL.

Fallentine, Angela Peterson. Oral History Interviews by James Perry or Lisa Christensen, 2023. Angela Peterson Fallentine and John Fallentine, Oral History Interviews, 2023. CHL. Transcript in possession of editors.

———. Recollections, Jan. 3, 2023. CHL.

Fallentine, Angela Peterson, and John Fallentine. Email Interview by Lisa Christensen, Sept. 11, 2023. Angela Peterson Fallentine and John Fallentine, Oral History Interviews, 2023. CHL.

Fallentine, John. Oral History Interview by Lisa Christensen, Sept. 15, 2023. Angela Peterson Fallentine and John Fallentine, Oral History Interviews, 2023. CHL. Transcript in possession of editors.

Falola, Toyin, and Matthew M. Heaton. *A History of Nigeria.* Cambridge: Cambridge University Press, 2008.

Family and Church History Department. Annual Reports, 1952–70, 1990, 1999–2007. CHL.

"The Family: A Proclamation to the World," Sept. 23, 1995. The Church of Jesus Christ of Latter-Day Saints. https://www.ChurchofJesusChrist.org/study/scriptures/the-family-a-proclamation-to-the-world/the-family-a-proclamation-to-the-world.

Family History Department. Executive Director's Meeting Minutes, 1993–2008. CHL.

Family Home Evening Manual: Part of the Priesthood Program of Teaching and Living the Gospel in the Home. Salt Lake City: Council of the Twelve Apostles of The Church of Jesus Christ of Latter-day Saints, [1965].

FamilySearch: TempleReady Reference Guide. Salt Lake City: The Church of Jesus Christ of Latter-day Saints, 1995.

Farrell, Lincoln, and Marilyn Barlow. "The Celebration of Clean Water in Luputa," Jan. 8, 2011. *The Barlows in Uganda* (blog). https://barlowsinuganda.blogspot.com/2011/01/celebration-of-clean-water-in-luputa.html.

Faust, James E. Journal, 1978–2007. CHL.

———. Oral History Interviews by Gordon Irving, 1977–78. Photocopy of typescript. CHL.

Feinga, Adele F. "Labor Missions in Tonga and Hawai'i." In *Pioneers in the Pacific: Memory, History, and Cultural Identity among the Latter-day Saints,* edited by Grant Underwood, 45–56. Provo, UT: Religious Studies Center, Brigham Young University, 2005.

Ferguson, Isaac Clyde. Oral History Interview by Loy Keate Despain and Emily McLaws Despain, Feb. 12, 2013. Loy K. Despain, Humanitarian Services Collection, 1970–2017. CHL.

———. Oral History Interviews by James Perry, Apr. 25 and June 29, 2022. CHL. Transcript in possession of editors.

———. Oral History Interviews by Matthew K. Heiss, 1992–93. CHL.

———. West Africa Trip Journal, Apr. 29–May 19, 1988. Typescript. Isaac Ferguson, Oral History Interviews, Apr. 25 and June 29, 2022. CHL.

Fetzer, Percy K. Mission President Journal, Oct. 1959–Mar. 1963. Percy K. and Thelma W. Fetzer Papers, 1926–81. CHL.

———. Papers, circa 1959–69. CHL.

Fifty-First Annual Conference of the Primary Association. [Salt Lake City]: [The Church of Jesus Christ of Latter-day Saints], 1957. In Collection of Materials pertaining to the Song "I Am a Child of God," circa 1957–77. CHL.

Fiji Suva Mission. Annual Historical Reports, 1978–95, 1997–2009, 2011–21. CHL.

Sources Cited

Final Report of the Fact-Finding Commission (Pursuant to R.A. No. 6832). Manila, Philippines: Bookmark, 1990.
Fink, Carole K. *Cold War: An International History.* Boulder, CO: Westview, 2014.
The First Mexico and Central America Area General Conference of The Church of Jesus Christ of Latter-day Saints, Held in Mexico City, Mexico, August 25, 26, 27, 1972, with Report of Discourses. Salt Lake City: The Church of Jesus Christ of Latter-day Saints, 1973.
First Presidency. Area Presidency Correspondence, 1984–2016. CHL.
———. Circular Letters, 1855–2013. CHL.
———. Committees, Departments, and Organizations Correspondence, 1980–94, 1998–2017. CHL.
———. General Administration Files, 1921–72. CHL.
———. General Administration Files, 1923, 1932, 1937–67. CHL.
———. General Correspondence, 1970–2006. CHL.
———. General Correspondence Files, 1940–59. CHL.
———. Letterpress Copybooks, 1877–1949. CHL.
———. Miscellaneous Correspondence, 1915–39. CHL.
———. Mission Correspondence, 1946–69. CHL.
———. Mission Correspondence, 1950–59. CHL.
———. Mission Correspondence, 1964–2010. CHL.
———. Presiding Bishopric Correspondence, 1980–84, 1986–2007. CHL.
———. Temple Correspondence, 1964–94. CHL.
"The First Young Women's Fireside: Stand for Truth and Righteousness (1985)." The Church of Jesus Christ of Latter-day Saints. Broadcast on Nov. 10, 1985. YouTube video, [01:33:33]. https://youtu.be/B451SzXC7fo?si=kBtp6TK0_dXeHo5G. Copy also available in Young Women Fireside, 1985–87. CHL.
Fisher, Glen G. Report, Sept. 16, 1960. CHL.
Flake, Garry. Email to James Perry, Nov. 8, 2023. CHL.
———. "The Tsunami (Southeast Asia)," no date. Typescript. CHL.
Fleming, Walter L. *The Freedmen's Savings Bank: A Chapter in the Economic History of the Negro Race.* Westport, CT: Negro Universities Press, 1970. First published in 1927 by University of North Carolina Press (Chapel Hill).
Fletcher, David George. Oral History Interview by Stephen C. Young, July 24, 1987. CHL.
Fligstein, Neil, and Adam Goldstein. "The Roots of the Great Recession." In *The Great Recession,* edited by David B. Grusky, Bruce Western, and Christopher Wimer, 21–55. New York: Russell Sage Foundation, 2011.
For the Strength of Youth: LDS Standards. Salt Lake City: The Church of Jesus Christ of Latter-day Saints, 1965.
Fraenkel, Jon. "The Clash of Dynasties and Rise of Demagogues; Fiji's Tauri Vakaukauwa of May 2000." *Journal of Pacific History* 35, no. 3 (Dec. 2000): 295–308.
Fraticelli, Nivea Rebecca. "Brief Chronological History of the Church of Jesus Christ of the Latter Day Saints in the Caribbean, 1945–2000," circa 2015. Typescript. Becky Fraticelli, Local Histories, 1945–2000. CHL.
"Freedman's Bank Records: Media Coverage, Feb. 26, 2001," [2001]. Typescript. CHL.
Freiberg Germany Temple. Dedication Services, June 28–30, 1985. CHL.
Fritz, Albert. Oral History Interviews by Leslie G. Kelen, 1983, 1984. Interviews with African Americans in Utah, 1982–88. Special Collections, J. Willard Marriott Library, University of Utah, Salt Lake City.
Funk, Ruth Hardy. Interview by Andrew Kimball, Nov. 27, 1979. Andrew Eyring Kimball, Spencer W. Kimball Biography Research Files, 1924–80. CHL.
———. Oral History Interviews by Gordon Irving, 1979. CHL.
———. "Ruth, Come Walk with Me." In *He Changed My Life,* edited by L. Brent Goates, 118–26. Salt Lake City: Bookcraft, 1988.
Gaddis, John Lewis. *The Cold War: A New History.* New York: Penguin, 2005.
Galbraith, David B. "The Lead-Up to the Dedication of the Jerusalem Center." *BYU Studies Quarterly* 59, no. 4 (2020): 49–60.

———. "Miracles Open the Door to Build on the Mount of Olives," no date. Typescript. David B. Galbraith, Oral History Interviews, 2021–22. CHL.

———. Oral History Interviews by Amber Taylor, 2021–22. CHL. Transcript in possession of editors.

———. "The Orson Hyde Memorial Garden Project: A Forerunner, 1972–1979," no date. Typescript. David B. Galbraith, Oral History Interviews, 2021–22. CHL.

Galbraith, David B., D. Kelly Ogden, and Andrew C. Skinner. *Jerusalem: The Eternal City.* Salt Lake City: Deseret Book, 1996.

Garrett, Matthew. *Making Lamanites: Mormons, Native Americans, and the Indian Student Placement Program, 1947–2000.* Salt Lake City: University of Utah Press, 2016.

Garrow, David J. *Protest at Selma: Martin Luther King, Jr., and the Voting Rights Act of 1965.* New Haven, CT: Yale University Press, 1978.

Gee, John. "'A Stranger in a Strange Land': Hugh Nibley as an Egyptologist." In *Hugh Nibley Observed,* edited by Jeffrey M. Bradshaw, Shirley S. Ricks, and Stephen T. Whitlock, 497–522. Orem, UT: Interpreter Foundation; Salt Lake City: Eborn Books, 2021.

General Handbook of Instructions. Salt Lake City: The Church of Jesus Christ of Latter-day Saints, 1976.

General Handbook of Instructions. Salt Lake City: The Church of Jesus Christ of Latter-day Saints, 1989.

General Handbook: Serving in The Church of Jesus Christ of Latter-day Saints, December 2020. Salt Lake City: The Church of Jesus Christ of Latter-day Saints, 2020.

General Instructions for Stake Presidencies and Bishoprics: Consolidated Schedule of Sunday Meetings. [Salt Lake City]: The Church of Jesus Christ of Latter-day Saints, [1980].

"General Leadership Meeting: Chile Relief Society Training," Oct. 14–23, 2004. Typescript. Relief Society, Anne C. Pingree Relief Society General Presidency Papers, 1992–2008. CHL.

Genesis Group. First Meeting, Oct. 19, 1971. Audiocassette. CHL.

German Democratic Republic Dresden Mission. Historical Record, 1969–83. Typescript. CHL.

Germany Hamburg Mission. Manuscript History and Historical Reports, 1937–77. 12 vols. CHL.

Germany North Mission. President's Files, 1959–73. CHL.

Gesangbuch: Kirche Jesu Christi der Heiligen der Letzten Tage. Frankfurt, Germany: Der Kirche Jesu Christi der Heiligen der Letzten Tage Europäische Mission, 1964.

"Geschichte der Dresdener Mission," 1969. Typescript. German Democratic Republic Dresden Mission, Historical Record, 1969–83. CHL.

Ghana Accra Mission District. Report, no date. Miles H. and Stella Cunningham Papers, 1984–91. CHL.

Gibbons, Francis M. *Howard W. Hunter: Man of Thought and Independence, Prophet of God.* Salt Lake City: Deseret Book, 2011.

———. *Spencer W. Kimball: Resolute Disciple, Prophet of God.* Salt Lake City: Deseret Book, 1995.

Gibbons, Francis M., and Bruce R. McConkie. Interview by Edward L. Kimball, May 12, 1982. Spencer W. Kimball Papers. CHL.

Gill, Gurcharan S. "The Church of Jesus Christ of Latter-day Saints in India." In *"For Ye Are All One in Christ Jesus": The Global Church in a World of Ethnic Diversity, Proceedings of the Sixth Annual Conference of the International Society,* 75–76. Provo, UT: David M. Kennedy Center for International Studies, Brigham Young University, 1995.

"Giordayne." One in a Million. Media Library. The Church of Jesus Christ of Latter-day Saints. Video, [00:02:22]. Accessed Mar. 22, 2024. https://www.ChurchofJesusChrist.org/media/collection/one-in-a-million.

Giurintano, Antonino. Interview by James Toronto, May 2001. CHL.

Givens, Terryl. *The Pearl of Greatest Price: Mormonism's Most Controversial Scripture.* With Brian M. Hauglid. New York: Oxford University Press, 2019.

Goates, L. Brent. *Harold B. Lee: Prophet and Seer.* Salt Lake City: Bookcraft, 1985.

Godfrey, Donald G., Val E. Limburg, and Heber G. Wolsey. "KSL, Salt Lake City: 'At the Crossroads of the West.'" In *Television in America: Local Station History from Across the*

Nation, edited by Michael D. Murray and Donald G. Godfrey, 338–52. Ames: Iowa State University Press, 1997.

Godfrey, Matthew C. "Kenneth W. Godfrey." In *Conversations with Mormon Historians,* edited by Alexander L. Baugh and Reid L. Neilson, 233–76. Provo, UT: Religious Studies Center, Brigham Young University; Salt Lake City: Deseret Book, 2015.

God Loveth His Children. Salt Lake City: The Church of Jesus Christ of Latter-day Saints, 2007.

Goodman, Michael A. "Correlation: The Early Years." In *A Firm Foundation: Church Organization and Administration,* edited by David J. Whittaker and Arnold K. Garr, 319–38. Provo, UT: Religious Studies Center, Brigham Young University; Salt Lake City: Deseret Book, 2011.

Goodman, Robert Maurice. *Niue of Polynesia: Savage Island's First Latter-day Saint Missionaries.* Powhatan, VA: By the author, 2002.

Görlitz Branch, Germany Dresden Mission. General Minutes, 1934–55, 1965–75. CHL.

Gospel Literacy Guidelines for Priesthood and Relief Society Leaders. Salt Lake City: The Church of Jesus Christ of Latter-day Saints, 1993.

"Gospel Topics Essays." The Church of Jesus Christ of Latter-day Saints. Accessed Apr. 10, 2024. https://www.ChurchofJesusChrist.org/study/manual/gospel-topics-essays.

Gould, Michael. *The Struggle for Modern Nigeria: The Biafran War, 1967–1970.* New York: I. B. Tauris, 2012.

Gray, Darius A. Interviews by Jed Woodworth or Lisa Christensen and Scott A. Hales, 2022. CHL.

———. Oral History Interviews by Jed Woodworth and Angela Hallstrom, 2017–19. CHL.

———. "Tracing Ancestors: Mormon Church Publishes Post-Civil War Database." Interview by Leon Harris. *Early Edition,* CNN, Feb. 27, 2001. http://www.cnn.com/TRANSCRIPTS/0102/27/ee.13.html.

Griffiths, Casey Paul. "The Globalization of Latter-day Saint Education." PhD diss., Brigham Young University, 2012.

Grover, Mark L. *A Land of Promise and Prophecy: Elder A. Theodore Tuttle in South America, 1960–1965.* Provo, UT: Religious Studies Center, Brigham Young University, 2008.

———. "Mormonism in Brazil: Religion and Dependency in Latin America." PhD diss., Indiana University, 1985.

———. "The Mormon Priesthood Revelation and the São Paulo, Brazil Temple." *Dialogue: A Journal of Mormon Thought* 23, no. 1 (Spring 1990): 39–53.

———. "Mormons in Latin America." In *The Oxford Handbook of Mormonism,* edited by Terryl L. Givens and Philip L. Barlow, 515–28. New York: Oxford University Press, 2015.

Guatemala City Temple. Dedication Services, Dec. 14–16, 1984. CHL.

Guide for Primary Stake Boards. [Salt Lake City]: General Board of Primary Association, 1962.

Gunnell, Grant, and Alice Petersen Gunnell. Oral History Interview by Matthew K. Heiss, Sept. 22, 1993. CHL.

Gunter, Ernest L. Oral History Interview by Lisa Christensen, May 20, 2022. CHL.

Hafen, Bruce C. Oral History Interview by Blake Miller, Aug. 10, 2007. CHL.

Haiti Port-au-Prince Mission. Annual Historical Reports, 1984–89, 1992–94, 1996–97, 2000–2003, 2009–14, 2017–22. CHL.

"Haiti Report," circa June 2, 2010. Slide presentation. Presiding Bishopric, Welfare Executive Committee Meeting Materials, 2000–2010. CHL.

Hall, Bruce W. "And the Last Shall Be First: The Church of Jesus Christ of Latter-day Saints in the Former East Germany." *Journal of Church and State* 42, no. 3 (Summer 2000): 485–505.

Handbook 1: Stake Presidents and Bishops, 2010. Salt Lake City: The Church of Jesus Christ of Latter-day Saints, 2010.

Handbook 2: Administering the Church, 2010. Salt Lake City: The Church of Jesus Christ of Latter-day Saints, 2010.

Handbook of Instructions of the Relief Society of The Church of Jesus Christ of Latter-day Saints. Salt Lake City: General Board of Relief Society, 1968.

Haney, Alice Johnson. Oral History Interview by James Perry and Scott A. Hales, May 20, 2022. CHL. Transcript in possession of editors.

Hangen, Tona J. "Guide to a Generation: Belle Spafford's Latter-day Saint Leadership." In *New Scholarship on Latter-day Saint Women in the Twentieth Century: Selections from the Women's History Initiative Seminars, 2003–2004,* edited by Carol Cornwall Madsen and Cherry B. Silver, 81–97. Provo, UT: Joseph Fielding Smith Institute for Latter-day Saint History, 2005.

Hanks, Marion D. Recollections, Dec. 2004. Marion D. Hanks Collection, 1873, 1904–2018. CHL.

Hardy, Warren Brent. "W. Brent Hardy Personal History." 4 vols. In W. Brent Hardy, Autobiography, circa 2011. CHL.

Harline, Craig. *Sunday: A History of the First Day from Babylonia to the Super Bowl.* New Haven, CT: Yale University Press, 2011.

Harper, Steven C. *First Vision: Memory and Mormon Origins.* New York: Oxford University Press, 2019.

———. "'Nothing Less Than Miraculous': The First Decade of Mormonism in Mongolia." *BYU Studies* 42, no. 1 (Jan. 2003): 19–49.

Harris, Matthew L., and Madison S. Harris. "The Last State to Honor MLK: Utah and the Quest for Racial Justice." *Utah Historical Quarterly* 88, no. 1 (Winter 2020): 5–23.

Hartley, William G. "From Men to Boys: LDS Aaronic Priesthood Offices, 1829–1996." *Journal of Mormon History* 22, no. 1 (1996): 80–136.

Hartlyn, Jonathan, and Arturo Valenzuela. "Democracy in Latin America since 1930." In *Latin America since 1930: Economy, Society and Politics, Part 2, Politics and Society,* edited by Leslie Bethell, 99–162. Vol. 6 of *The Cambridge History of Latin America.* Cambridge: Cambridge University Press, 1994.

Hartmann, Susan M. *From Margin to Mainstream: American Women and Politics since 1960.* New York: Alfred A. Knopf, 1989.

Harvey, Brian. *Europe's Space Programme: To Ariane and Beyond.* Chichester, England: Praxis, 2003.

Hatch, Gayle Collette, comp. *Alois and Hermine: A Cziep Family History, 1893–2005.* Durham, NC: By the compiler, 2005. Copy at CHL.

Hawkes, Lorraine. "Experience of Henry T. Solis at the Manila Philippines Temple, Dec. 1989," no date. Typescript. Henry Tiongson Solis, Oral History Interview, June 10, 2021. CHL.

Hawkins, Chad S. *Temples of the New Millennium: Facts, Stories, and Miracles from the First 150 Temples.* Salt Lake City: Deseret Book, 2016.

Hawkins, John T. Oral History Interview by June Jones, Aug. 18, 2018. CHL.

Haws, J. B. "The Freeze and the Thaw: The LDS Church and the State of Ghana of the 1980s." In *The Worldwide Church: Mormonism as a Global Religion,* edited by Michael A. Goodman and Mauro Properzi, 21–46. Provo, UT: Religious Studies Center, Brigham Young University; Salt Lake City: Deseret Book, 2016.

———. "LDS Church Presidency Years, 1985–1994." In *Thunder from the Right: Ezra Taft Benson in Mormonism and Politics,* edited by Matthew L. Harris, 208–38. Chicago: University of Illinois Press, 2019.

———. *The Mormon Image in the American Mind: Fifty Years of Public Perception.* New York: Oxford University Press, 2013.

———. "Why the 'Mormon Olympics' Didn't Happen." In *An Eye of Faith: Essays Written in Honor of Richard O. Cowan,* edited by Kenneth L. Alford and Richard E. Bennett, 365–87. Provo, UT: Religious Studies Center, Brigham Young University; Salt Lake City: Deseret Book, 2015.

Haycock, David Arthur. Personal History, 1975–76. CHL.

Heaton, Herald Grant. Oral History Interview by Brian Reeves and Melvin Thatcher, June 14, 2001 [Interview 3]. CHL.

———. Personal History, 1993–2001. 2 vols. CHL.

Sources Cited

Heaton, Herald Grant, and Luana C. Heaton, comps. *A Documentary History of the Chinese Mission, 1949–53; Southern Far East Mission, 1955–59*. Salt Lake City: By the compilers, 1999.
Hernandez, Emma Acosta, and Hector David Hernandez. Oral History Interviews by David Bolingbroke, James Perry, and/or Tesia Tsai, 2022–23. CHL. English translation in possession of editors.
Hernandez, Hector David, and Emma Acosta Hernandez. Oral History Interview by Clate W. Mask Jr. and Carol Mask, Mar. 24, 2019. CHL. English translation in possession of editors.
Hicks, Michael. "Mormons and the Music Industry." In *Cinema, Television, Theater, Music, and Fashion*, 183–99. Vol. 1 of *Mormons and Popular Culture: The Global Influence of an American Phenomenon*, edited by J. Michael Hunter. Santa Barbara, CA: Praeger, 2013.
Hillam, Harold G. Missionary Journal, 1954–57. Microfilm. CHL.
———. Oral History Interviews by Gordon Irving, 2005. CHL.
Hilton, Christopher. *The Wall: The People's Story*. Stroud, England: Sutton, 2001.
Hilton, John, III. "The LDS Church in Taiwan: The First Three Years." *Mormon Historical Studies* 17, no. 1 (2016): 37–83.
Hinckley, Gordon B. Addresses, 1947, 1958–2008. CHL.
———. Area Files, 1986–2002. CHL.
———. Church Educational System Files, 1984–88. CHL.
———. Files, circa 1935–70. CHL.
———. Files, circa 1971–77. Typescript. CHL.
———. First Presidency and General Authority Correspondence, Auxiliaries, Miscellaneous, 1976–80. Typescript. CHL.
———. Journals, 1946–2008. Typescript. CHL.
———. Miscellaneous Stake and Mission Correspondence, 1970–79. Typescript. CHL.
———. Subject Files, circa 1980–85. Typescript. CHL.
———. Temple Files, circa 1961–90. Typescript. CHL.
———. "Why These Temples?" *Temples of The Church of Jesus Christ of Latter-day Saints*, 14–19. Salt Lake City: The Church of Jesus Christ of Latter-day Saints, Curriculum Department, 1999.
———. "Wishes regarding Death and Burial," Jan. 15, 2008. Typescript. Gordon B. Hinckley, Journals, 1946–2008. CHL.
Hinckley, Richard G. Oral History Interview by Matthew K. Heiss, Aug. 8, 1998. CHL.
Historical Department. Church in Action Footage Collection, circa 1970–85. CHL.
———. Circular Letters, 1855–2023. CHL.
"Historical Record: Democratic Republic of Congo Mission," circa 2005. Typescript. Zaire Kinshasa Mission History, circa 2005. CHL.
History of The Church of Jesus Christ of Latter-day Saints in the Democratic Republic of the Congo. Johannesburg: The Church of Jesus Christ of Latter-day Saints, 2019.
Holbrook, Stephen. Oral History Interview by Kathryn French, Oct. 17, 2006. Oral History of Utah Peace Activists Project. Utah Valley University, Orem, UT.
Holcman, Jaromír. "Olga Campora Kovářová," no date. Typescript. Jaromír Holcman Papers. CHL.
———. Scrapbook. Jaromír Holcman Papers. CHL.
Holland, Jeffrey R. Oral History Interviews by Gordon Irving, 2004. CHL.
Holt, Marilyn Irvin. *Cold War Kids: Politics and Childhood in Postwar America, 1945–1960*. Lawrence: University Press of Kansas, 2014.
The Holy Bible, Containing the Old and New Testaments Translated Out of the Original Tongues: And with the Former Translations Diligently Compared and Revised, by His Majesty's Special Command. Authorized King James Version with Explanatory Notes and Cross References to the Standard Works of The Church of Jesus Christ of Latter-day Saints. Salt Lake City: The Church of Jesus Christ of Latter-day Saints, 2013.
Holzapfel, Richard Neitzel, and James S. Lambert. "Photographs of the First Mexico and Central America Area Conference, 1972." *BYU Studies* 41, no. 4 (2002): 65–73.

"A Home of Our Own: The Story of the Relief Society Building." Church History Department. The Church of Jesus Christ of Latter-day Saints. Accessed Dec. 18, 2023. https://history.ChurchofJesusChrist.org/exhibit/relief-society-building.

Home Teaching: Priesthood Correlation Program, The Church of Jesus Christ of Latter-day Saints. Salt Lake City: Corporation of the President of The Church of Jesus Christ of Latter-day Saints, 1963.

Honey, Michael K. *To the Promised Land: Martin Luther King and the Fight for Economic Justice.* New York: W. W. Norton, 2018.

Hong Kong Temple. Dedication Services, May 26–27, 1996. CHL.

———. Media Information Packet, 1995–96. CHL.

Hook, Brian. "From Repossession to Retrocession: British Policy towards Hong Kong, 1945–1997." In *Political Order and Power Transition in Hong Kong,* edited by Li Pang-kwong, 1–29. Sha Tin, Hong Kong: Chinese University Press, 1997.

Hout, Michael, Asaf Levanon, and Erin Cumberworth. "Job Loss and Unemployment." In *The Great Recession,* edited by David B. Grusky, Bruce Western, and Christopher Wimer, 59–81. New York: Russell Sage Foundation, 2011.

Hubbard, George U. *When the Saints Came Marching In: A History of The Church of Jesus Christ of Latter-day Saints in Denton, Texas, 1958–2008.* Denton, TX: Tattersall, 2009.

Hughes, Kathleen H. Oral History Interview by Jeanne H. Fetzer, Nov. 11, 2019. CHL.

Hunter, Howard W. Jerusalem Center Files, 1979–92. CHL.

———. Journal, 1918, 1927–29, 1958–94. Typescript. CHL.

Hurlbut, D. Dmitri. "The LDS Church and the Problem of Race: Mormonism in Nigeria, 1946–1978." *International Journal of African Historical Studies* 51, no. 1 (2018): 1–16.

Hussein, Amby, trans. "Testimonies from Zaire." *Focus on Gender* 2, no. 1 (Feb. 1994): 26–29.

Hwang, Keun Ok. "Hwang Keun Ok." In *The Korean Saints: Personal Stories of Trial and Triumph, 1950–1980,* edited by Spencer J. Palmer and Shirley H. Palmer, 291–94. Provo, UT: Religious Education, Brigham Young University, 1995.

Hyatt, Wesley. *Emmy Award Winning Nighttime Television Shows, 1948–2004.* Jefferson, NC: McFarland, 2006.

Hymns of The Church of Jesus Christ of Latter-day Saints. Salt Lake City: The Church of Jesus Christ of Latter-day Saints, 1985.

Imbrah, William Fifi. Oral History Interview by Matthew K. Heiss and Sunday Oyedeji, Mar. 20, 2011. CHL.

"Incomings from Chile Training," circa Oct. 2004. Typescript. Relief Society, Anne C. Pingree Relief Society General Presidency Papers, 1992–2008. CHL.

India Bengaluru Mission. "The Church in India," 2003. Typescript. CHL.

International Mission Files, 1950–92. CHL.

"International Welfare Operations Strategy," circa Feb. 24, 2005. Slide presentation. Presiding Bishopric, Welfare Executive Committee Meeting Materials, 2000–2010. CHL.

"Italian Zone." *Reaper* 3, no. 20 (Feb. 20, 1965): [1]. Newsletter published by the Swiss Mission of The Church of Jesus Christ of Latter-day Saints. In Swiss Mission Newsletters, 1964–66. CHL.

Ituma, Abigail O. Oral History Interview by Kwame Ampaw, Sept. 28, 2019. CHL.

"I Want a Loan." Self-Reliance Services. The Church of Jesus Christ of Latter-day Saints. Accessed Mar. 9, 2024. https://www.ChurchofJesusChrist.org/self-reliance/pef-perpetual-education-fund/i-want-a-loan.

Jackson, Kirk, and Jane Jackson. Oral History Interview by James Perry, July 5, 2023. CHL. Transcript in possession of editors.

Jackson, Richard W. *Places of Worship: 150 Years of Latter-day Saint Architecture.* Provo, UT: Religious Studies Center, Brigham Young University, 2003.

Jackson, Thomas F. *From Civil Rights to Human Rights: Martin Luther King, Jr., and the Struggle for Economic Justice.* Philadelphia: University of Pennsylvania Press, 2007.

Jacob, W. James. "Fiji Distance Learning Program: Issues and Potential for Developing Countries." Master's thesis, Brigham Young University, 2001.

Jacob, W. James, and David J. Hansen. "Fiji Distance Learning Program: Issues and Potential for Developing Countries." *Journal of the Utah Academy of Sciences, Arts, and Letters* 77 (2000): 110–25.

Jensen, Marlin K. General Conference Training Files, 1995–2012. CHL.

Jensen, Richard L. "Without Purse or Scrip?: Financing Latter-day Saint Missionary Work in Europe in the Nineteenth Century." *Journal of Mormon History* 12 (1985): 3–14.

Jepson, Karen Ann. Journal Entries from Tabernacle Choir European Tour, 1991. Typescript. Mormon Tabernacle Choir, Historic Tour to Europe and USSR, June 8–29, 1991. CHL.

Jessee, Dean C. "The Early Accounts of Joseph Smith's First Vision." *BYU Studies* 9, no. 3 (Spring 1969): 275–94.

Johannesburg 2nd Branch, Johannesburg South Africa Stake. Annual Historical Reports, 1981–83. CHL.

Johnson, Brigham T. Oral History Interview by Laura Christensen, June 20, 2019. CHL.

Johnson, Jill. *Soweto Speaks*. London: Wildwood House, 1979.

Johnson, Joseph William Billy. "The History of The Church of Jesus Christ of Latter-day Saints in Ghana," circa 1985. Photocopy of typescript. CHL.

———. Oral History Interview by Clinton D. Christensen, Nov. 3, 2005. CHL.

———. Oral History Interview by E. Dale LeBaron, May 23, 1988. E. Dale LeBaron, Oral History Project on Africa. BYU.

———. Oral History Interview by Steven R. Sorensen, Sept. 17, 1998. CHL.

———. Radio. Church History Museum, The Church of Jesus Christ of Latter-day Saints, Salt Lake City. Images available at CHL.

———. "We Felt the Spirit of the Pioneers." In *All Are Alike unto God,* edited by E. Dale LeBaron, 13–23. Salt Lake City: Bookcraft, 1990.

Johnson, Kenneth. Oral History Interview by Jeff L. Anderson, Sept. 30, 2005, CHL.

Jones, Marvin R. Diary, Oct.–Nov. 1961. CHL.

Joseph Smith—History. See *Pearl of Great Price.*

Josephson, Marba C. *History of the YWMIA*. Salt Lake City: Young Women's Mutual Improvement Association, The Church of Jesus Christ of Latter-day Saints, 1955.

Josiah, Barbara P. "Providing for the Future: The World of the African American Depositors of Washington, DC's Freedmen's Savings Bank, 1865–74." *Journal of African American History* 89, no. 1 (Winter 2004): 1–16.

JSP, H1 / Davidson, Karen Lynn, David J. Whittaker, Mark Ashurst-McGee, and Richard L. Jensen, eds. *Histories, Volume 1: Joseph Smith Histories, 1832–1844.* Vol. 1 of the Histories series of *The Joseph Smith Papers,* edited by Dean C. Jessee, Ronald K. Esplin, and Richard Lyman Bushman. Salt Lake City: Church Historian's Press, 2012.

JSP, R4 / Jensen, Robin Scott, and Brian M. Hauglid, eds. *Revelations and Translations, Volume 4: Book of Abraham and Related Manuscripts.* Facsimile edition. Vol. 4 of the Revelations and Translations series of *The Joseph Smith Papers,* edited by Ronald K. Esplin, Matthew J. Grow, Matthew C. Godfrey, and R. Eric Smith. Salt Lake City: Church Historian's Press, 2018.

Jue, Lorine. Journal Excerpts, 1996. Jue Family, Oral History Interview, 2023. CHL.

Jue, Nora S. Koot. Mission Reminiscences, circa 1999. Nora S. Koot Jue, Reminiscence, circa 1995. CHL.

———. Reminiscence, circa 1995. Compiled by Arthur Jue, Corine Jue Neumiller, Daniel Jue, and Lorine Jue Turnbull. CHL.

Jue Family (Arthur Jue, Corine Jue Neumiller, Daniel Jue, and Lorine Jue Turnbull). Oral History Interview by Angela Hallstrom and Clinton D. Christensen, July 15, 2019. CHL.

———. Oral History Interview by Jed Woodworth and Scott A. Hales, Jan. 23, 2023. CHL. Transcript in possession of editors.

Justice, O. Lynn, and Bonita H. Justice. Oral History Interviews by Clate W. Mask Jr., 2019. CHL.

Kaminker, Sarah. "For Arabs Only: Building Restrictions in East Jerusalem." *Journal of Palestine Studies* 26, no. 4 (Summer 1997): 5–16.

Kapp, Ardeth Greene. Journals, 1948–2020. Ardeth G. Kapp Papers, 1969–2007. CHL.

———. *My Neighbor, My Sister, My Friend*. Salt Lake City: Deseret Book, 1990.
———. Oral History Interviews by Gordon Irving, 1978–79. CHL.
———. "Young Women Presentation to PEC," Feb. 20, 1985. Typescript. Young Women Files, 1984–90. CHL.
Kapp, Ardeth Greene, and Carolyn J. Rasmus. Oral History Interviews by Gordon Irving, 1992. CHL.
Kaufmann, Eric, Anne Goujon, and Vegard Skirbekk. "The End of Secularization in Europe?: A Socio-demographic Perspective." *Sociology of Religion* 73, no. 1 (Spring 2012): 69–91.
Kennedy, David M. Journal, Dec. 1974–Feb. 1990. Typescript. CHL.
Kiernan, Ben. *Việt Nam: A History from Earliest Times to the Present*. New York: Oxford University Press, 2017.
Kilbert, Allwyn Arokiaraj. Email Interview by James Perry, Oct. 4, 2023. Allwyn Arokiaraj Kilbert, Oral History Interviews, 2023. CHL.
———. Notebook Excerpts, 2004. Allwyn Arokiaraj Kilbert, Oral History Interviews, 2023. CHL.
———. Oral History Interviews by James Perry, 2023. CHL. Transcript in possession of editors.
Kimball, Camilla Eyring. *Autobiography of Camilla Eyring Kimball*. Publication place unidentified: By the author, 1975.
———. Journals, 1929–86. Camilla Eyring Kimball Papers, 1924–87. CHL.
———. Oral History Interview by Jessie Embry, 1977. Photocopy of typescript. CHL.
Kimball, Edward L. "Events and Changes during the Administration of Spencer W. Kimball." In *A Firm Foundation: Church Organization and Administration,* edited by David J. Whittaker and Arnold K. Garr, 521–32. Provo, UT: Religious Studies Center, Brigham Young University; Salt Lake City: Deseret Book, 2011.
———. Journal Excerpts, Nov. 16–17, 1979. CHL.
———. *Lengthen Your Stride: The Presidency of Spencer W. Kimball*. Salt Lake City: Deseret Book, 2005.
———. Papers, 1956–2007. CHL.
———. "Spencer W. Kimball and the Revelation on Priesthood." *BYU Studies* 47, no. 2 (2008): 4–78.
Kimball, Edward L., and Andrew E. Kimball Jr. *Spencer W. Kimball: Twelfth President of The Church of Jesus Christ of Latter-day Saints*. Salt Lake City: Bookcraft, 1977.
Kimball, Spencer W. Headquarters Correspondence and Subject Files, 1974–85. CHL.
———. Interview by Edward L. Kimball, June 21, 1978. Spencer W. Kimball Papers. CHL.
———. Journals, 1905–81. CHL.
———. *Le miracle du pardon*. Salt Lake City: Bookcraft, 1969.
———. *The Miracle of Forgiveness*. Salt Lake City: Bookcraft, 1969.
———. "No Unhallowed Hand Can Stop the Work." The Church of Jesus Christ of Latter-day Saints. Broadcast on Apr. 5, 1980. Video, [00:16:47]. https://www.ChurchofJesusChrist.org/study/general-conference/1980/04/no-unhallowed-hand-can-stop-the-work.
———. *Second Century Address and Dedication of Carillon Tower and Bells*. Provo, UT: Brigham Young University, 1975.
———. "The Uttermost Parts of the Earth," Sept. 29, 1978. Typescript. O. Leslie and Dorothy C. Stone Family Papers, 1916–85. CHL.
Kissi, Emmanuel Abu. Oral History Interviews by Matthew K. Heiss, 1999, 2002. CHL.
———. *Walking in the Sand: A History of The Church of Jesus Christ of Latter-day Saints in Ghana*. Edited by Matthew K. Heiss. Studies in Latter-day Saint History. Provo, UT: Brigham Young University Press, 2004.
Kogan, Nathaniel Smith. "The Mormon Pavilion: Mainstreaming the Saints at the New York World's Fair, 1964–65." *Journal of Mormon History* 35, no. 4 (Fall 2009): 1–52.
Kollek, Teddy. "Jerusalem." *Foreign Affairs* 55, no. 4 (July 1977): 701–16.
Korea Seoul Mission. Historical Records, 1960–2017. CHL.
Kovářová, Olga Miroslava. Oral History Interview by Matthew K. Heiss, Aug. 8, 1991. CHL.
Krejčí, Jaroslav, and Pavel Machonin. *Czechoslovakia, 1918–92: A Laboratory for Social Change*. New York: St. Martin, 1996.

Sources Cited

Kriza, Elisa. "Anti-communism, Communism, and Anti-interventionism in Narratives Surrounding the Student Massacre on Tlatelolco Square (Mexico, 1968)." *Bulletin of Latin American Research* 38, no. 1 (2019): 82–96.

Kuehne, Raymond. "The Freiberg Temple: An Unexpected Legacy of a Communist State and a Faithful People." *Dialogue: A Journal of Mormon Thought* 37, no. 2 (Summer 2004): 95–131.

———. *Henry Burkhardt and LDS Realpolitik in Communist East Germany*. Salt Lake City: University of Utah Press, 2011.

———. *Mormons as Citizens of a Communist State: A Documentary History of The Church of Jesus Christ of Latter-day Saints in East Germany, 1945–1990*. Salt Lake City: University of Utah Press, 2010.

Kumar, Nakul. "Incentives and Expectations: Community Resiliency and Recovery in Tamil Nadu after the Indian Ocean Tsunami." *Independent Review* 22, no. 1 (Summer 2017): 135–51.

Kwa Mashu Branch, South Africa Johannesburg Mission. Annual Historical Reports, 1980–83. CHL.

Landis, Elizabeth S. "Apartheid Legislation." *Africa Today* 4, no. 6 (Nov.–Dec. 1957): 45–48.

Large, David Clay. *Berlin*. New York: Basic Books, 2000.

The Latter-day Saint Woman: Basic Manual for Women, Part A. Rev. ed. Salt Lake City: The Church of Jesus Christ of Latter-day Saints, 1981.

The Latter-day Saint Woman: Basic Manual for Women, Part B. Salt Lake City: The Church of Jesus Christ of Latter-day Saints, 1979.

"LDS Family Services International Strategy," circa Aug. 25, 2005. Slide presentation. Presiding Bishopric, Welfare Executive Committee Meeting Materials, 2000–2010. CHL.

"LDS Family Services Worldwide Strategy," circa Oct. 26, 2006. Slide presentation. Presiding Bishopric, Welfare Executive Committee Meeting Materials, 2000–2010. CHL.

Le, Lien My. Oral History Interviews by Tesia Tsai, 2021. CHL. Transcript in possession of editors.

Leadership Council. Minutes, 1985–2013. Presiding Bishopric, First Presidency Meeting Materials, 1985–2013. CHL.

"Learning to Listen." Church History. The Church of Jesus Christ of Latter-day Saints. Video, [00:07:43]. Accessed Jan. 23, 2024. https://history.ChurchofJesusChrist.org/content/pioneers-in-every-land/learning-to-listen.

LeBaron, E. Dale. "Ethiopia." In *Encyclopedia of Latter-day Saint History*, edited by Arnold K. Garr, Donald Q. Cannon, and Richard O. Cowan. Salt Lake City: Deseret Book, 2000.

LeBaron, Homer M. "Interim Report to Africa Area Presidency on Brief Historical Background, Status and Recommendations for Zaire Kinshasa Mission," Aug. 30, 1993. Typescript. Zaire Kinshasa Mission, Interim Report to Africa Area Presidency, Aug. 30, 1993. CHL.

Lee, Benjamin D., ed. *Ruffin Bridgeforth*. [Cedar City, UT?]: By the editor, 2017. Copy at CHL.

Lee, Harold B. Diary, 1941–73. CHL.

———. *Ye Are the Light of the World*. Salt Lake City: Deseret Book, 1974.

Leonhardt, Karlheinz F. "Die Geschichte des Freiberg-DDR-Tempels: Von seinen Anfängen im Denken der Kirchenführer bis zum Beginn der Tempelarbeit." Vol. 1, "Geschichte des Freiberg-Tempels," 1985. Typescript. Freiberg Germany Temple, Scrapbook Histories, 1985–2001. CHL.

Lesuma, Meli. Oral History Interview by James Perry, Feb. 23, 2023. CHL. Transcript in possession of editors.

Lewis, Ann, and John Lewis. "My Desire to Serve a Full-Time Mission: President Sabwe Binene's Story," Apr. 22, 2020. Typescript. CHL.

Lewis, Colin M. *Argentina: A Short History*. Oxford: Oneworld, 2002.

Lima Peru Temple. Annual Historical Reports, 1985–2004. CHL.

———. Dedication Services, Jan. 10–12, 1986. CHL.

Lindsey, Laudy Kaouk. Oral History Interviews by Lisa Christensen, 2023. CHL. Transcript in possession of editors.

"Listening Post." *Salt Lake City Tab* 3, no. 8 (Oct. 2, 1949): 1, 3–4. Newsletter published by the Mormon Tabernacle Choir of The Church of Jesus Christ of Latter-day Saints. In Mormon Tabernacle Choir, Chronological Files, 1883–2004. CHL.

"The Living Christ: The Testimony of the Apostles," Jan. 1, 2000. The Church of Jesus Christ of Latter-day Saints. https://www.ChurchofJesusChrist.org/study/scriptures/the-living-christ-the-testimony-of-the-apostles/the-living-christ-the-testimony-of-the-apostles.

Livingstone, John P. "Establishing the Church Simply." *BYU Studies* 39, no. 4 (2000): 127–60.

———. "Historical Highlights of LDS Family Services." In *Salt Lake City: The Place Which God Prepared*, edited by Scott C. Esplin and Kenneth L. Alford, 285–303. Regional Studies in Latter-day Saint Church History. Provo, UT: Religious Studies Center, Brigham Young University; Salt Lake City: Deseret Book, 2011.

"Local Sister Called to Be a Missionary." *Southern Far East Bulletin* 11, no. 6 (June 1957): [18]. Newsletter published by the Southern Far East Mission of The Church of Jesus Christ of Latter-day Saints. In China Hong Kong Mission Publications, 1956–73. CHL.

Los valores de las mujeres jovenes: una guia para los lideres de las mujeres jovenes. Salt Lake City: The Church of Jesus Christ of Latter-day Saints, 1986.

Louisiana Baton Rouge Mission. Manuscript History and Historical Reports, 1930–76. CHL.

Lovell, Peggy A. "Development and the Persistence of Racial Inequality in Brazil: 1950–1991." *Journal of Developing Areas* 33, no. 3 (Spring 1999): 395–418.

Lozano Herrera, Agrícol. Oral History Interviews by Gordon Irving, 1975, 1977. CHL. English translation of portions in possession of editors.

Lu, Anne. Reminiscences, Jan. 24, 2024. Typescript. CHL.

Ludlow, Daniel H. "A Brief List of Some Church History Events Concerned with Correlation Development," [1974?]. Typescript. CHL.

———, ed. *Encyclopedia of Mormonism*. 4 vols. New York: Macmillan, 1992.

Luputa Democratic Republic of the Congo Stake. Photographs, 2011. Digital copy. CHL.

Lythgoe, Dennis Leo. "The Changing Image of Mormonism in Periodical Literature." PhD diss., University of Utah, 1969.

Lytle, Mark Hamilton. *America's Uncivil Wars: The Sixties Era from Elvis to the Fall of Richard Nixon*. New York: Oxford University Press, 2006.

Mabey, Rendell N. Africa Mission Movies Collection, 1978–79. CHL.

———. "The Amazing Swiss Mission." *Reaper* 3, no. 49 (Sept. 18, 1965): [1]. Newsletter published by the Swiss Mission of The Church of Jesus Christ of Latter-day Saints. In Swiss Mission Newsletters, 1964–66. CHL.

———. Journals, 1965–91. CHL.

———. "A Sicilian Baptism." *Reaper* 4, no. 7 (Dec. 4, 1965): [1]–[2]. Newsletter published by the Swiss Mission of The Church of Jesus Christ of Latter-day Saints. In Swiss Mission Newsletters, 1964–66. CHL.

Mabey, Rendell N., and Gordon T. Allred. *Brother to Brother: The Story of the Latter-day Saint Missionaries Who Took the Gospel to Black Africa*. Salt Lake City: Bookcraft, 1984.

Macey, Waldo L. Biographical Sketch, circa 1990. CHL.

Mack, Olive Beth Kimball. *Autobiography of Olive Beth Kimball Mack*. Publication place and publisher unidentified, [2009].

Macke, Lois Woodworth. "Oral History of Lois Maurine Lambert Woodworth Macke," 1993. Typescript. Charles J. Woodworth Papers, 1948–2009. CHL.

Madsen, Truman G. Correspondence, 1967–68. CHL.

———. "Guest Editor's Prologue." *BYU Studies* 9, no. 3 (Spring 1969): 235–40.

Mahoney, F. John. "The Merthyr Tydfil Chapel." United Kingdom and Ireland Church History. The Church of Jesus Christ of Latter-day Saints. Accessed Nov. 10, 2021. https://uk.ChurchofJesusChrist.org/merthyr-tydfil-chapel.

Martins, Helvécio. *The Autobiography of Elder Helvécio Martins*. With Mark Grover. Salt Lake City: Aspen Books, 1994.

Martins, Helvécio, and Rudá Martins. Oral History Interview by Mark Grover, Apr. 18, 1982. In Mark L. Grover, Oral History Interviews with Latter-day Saints in Brazil, 1975–84. BYU.

Sources Cited

Martins, Marcus H. Journal, 1978–80. Photocopy. CHL.

———. "Thirty Years after the 'Long-Promised Day': Reflections and Expectations." *BYU Studies* 47, no. 2 (2008): 79–85.

Martins, Marcus H., Mirian B. Martins, and Rudá Martins. Oral History Interview by Dallin Morrow and Angela Hallstrom, July 8, 2019. CHL.

Martins, Rudá. Oral History Interview by Mark Grover, [2018]. Copy of English translation by Michael N. Landon in possession of editors.

Mason, Patrick Q. "Ezra Taft Benson and Modern (Book of) Mormon Conservatism." In *Out of Obscurity: Mormonism since 1945*, edited by Patrick Q. Mason and John G. Turner, 63–80. New York: Oxford University Press, 2016.

———. "The Prohibition of Interracial Marriage in Utah, 1888–1963." *Utah Historical Quarterly* 76, no. 2 (Spring 2008): 108–31.

Massidda, Luca. "The Cold War, a Cool Medium, and the Postmodern Death of World Expos." In *World's Fairs in the Cold War: Science, Technology, and the Culture of Progress*, edited by Arthur P. Molella and Scott Gabriel Knowles, 183–93. Pittsburgh: University of Pittsburgh Press, 2019.

Maurer, Carl, Jed Woodworth, and Bradley R. Wilcox. Emails, Jan.–Feb. 2024. CHL.

Maurice and Arlene Bateman Letters, 1984–87. CHL.

Mauss, Armand L. *All Abraham's Children: Changing Mormon Conceptions of Race and Lineage*. Urbana: University of Illinois Press, 2003.

Mavimbela, Julia. "I Speak from My Heart: The Story of a Black South African Woman." In *Women of Wisdom and Knowledge: Talks Selected from the BYU Women's Conferences*, edited by Marie Cornwall and Susan Howe, 61–72. Salt Lake City: Deseret Book, 1990.

———. Oral History Interview by Dale LeBaron, July 22, 1988. E. Dale LeBaron, Oral History Project on Africa. BYU.

———. Oral History Interview by Francine Bennion and Matthew K. Heiss, Aug. 28, 1995. CHL.

———. Papers, 1943–2011. CHL.

Mavimbela, Julia, and Laura Harper. "'Mother of Soweto': Julia Mavimbela, Apartheid Peace-Maker and Latter-day Saint," Feb. 2010. Typescript. Julia Mavimbela Collection, 1958–2001. CHL.

McBaine, Neylan, and Thomas A. Wayment. "Discussing Difficult Topics: The Representation of Women in Today's Church." *Religious Educator* 17, no. 2 (2016): 106–17.

McCombs, David, and Elizabeth Manning McCombs. Oral History Interview by Jed Woodworth, June 24, 2023. CHL. Transcript in possession of editors.

McConkie, Bruce R. "The New Revelation on Priesthood," 1981. Typescript. Spencer W. Kimball Papers. CHL.

———. "The Receipt of the Revelation Offering the Priesthood to Worthy Men of All Races and Colors," June 30, 1978. Typescript. Spencer W. Kimball Papers. CHL.

McConkie, Mark L. *Sermons and Writings of Bruce R. McConkie*. Salt Lake City: Bookcraft, 1989.

McDonald, Ronald H. "The Struggle for Normalcy in Uruguay." *Current History* 81, no. 472 (Feb. 1982): 69–73, 85–86.

McDougall, Walter A. "Technocracy and Statecraft in the Space Age—Toward the History of a Saltation." *American Historical Review* 87, no. 4 (Oct. 1982): 1010–40.

McKay, David O. Diary, 1932, 1936–70. David O. McKay Papers, 1901–70. CHL.

———. Papers, 1901–70. CHL.

———. Scrapbooks, 1906–70. CHL.

———. *Statements on Communism and the Constitution of the United States*. [Salt Lake City]: Deseret Book, 1964.

McKenna, Mary. Oral History Interviews by James Perry, 2023. CHL. Transcript in possession of editors.

McKeown, Blake. Oral History Interviews by James Perry, 2023. CHL. Transcript in possession of editors.

McKeown, Scott, and Kara McKeown. Oral History Interview by James Perry, Aug. 21, 2023. CHL. Transcript in possession of editors.

McKeown, Wade. Oral History Interview by James Perry, Aug. 2, 2023. CHL. Transcript in possession of editors.
McMurrin, Sterling M. "A Note on the 1963 Civil Rights Statement." *Dialogue: A Journal of Mormon Thought* 12, no. 2 (Summer 1979): 60–63.
McMurrin, Sterling M., and L. Jackson Newell. *Matters of Conscience: Conversations with Sterling M. McMurrin on Philosophy, Education, and Religion.* Salt Lake City: Signature Books, 1996.
Mecham, Lucian M., Jr. Oral History Interview by Gordon Irving, Apr. 9, 1974. CHL.
Mehr, Kahlile B. "Dawning of the Digital Age: The Family History Department, 1995–2011." Unpublished manuscript, last modified Feb. 21, 2014. PDF file. Copy at CHL.
———. "Enduring Believers: Czechoslovakia and the LDS Church, 1884–1990." *Journal of Mormon History* 18, no. 2 (Fall 1992): 111–54.
———. "Missionary Couples in Communist Europe." *Journal of Mormon History* 29, no. 1 (Spring 2003): 179–99.
———. *Mormon Missionaries Enter Eastern Europe.* Provo, UT: Brigham Young University Press; Salt Lake City: Deseret Book, 2002.
Meier, August, and Elliott Rudwick. *CORE: A Study in the Civil Rights Movement, 1942–1968.* New York: Oxford University Press, 1973.
A Member's Guide to Temple and Family History Work: Ordinances and Covenants. Salt Lake City: The Church of Jesus Christ of Latter-day Saints, 1993.
Merrill, Timothy G., and Brian Q. Cannon. "Ox in the Mire?: The Legal and Cultural War over Utah's Sunday Closing Laws." *Journal of Mormon History* 38, no. 4 (Fall 2012): 164–94.
Metcalf, R. Warren. "'Which Side of the Line?': American Indian Students and Programs at Brigham Young University, 1960–1983." In *Essays on American Indian and Mormon History,* edited by P. Jane Hafen and Brenden W. Rensink, 225–45. Salt Lake City: University of Utah Press, 2019.
Midgley, Louis, comp. "Hugh Winder Nibley: Bibliography and Register." In *By Study and Also by Faith,* edited by John M. Lundquist and Stephen D. Ricks, xv–lxxxvii. Vol. 1. Salt Lake City: Deseret Book; Provo, UT: Foundation for Ancient Research and Mormon Studies, 1990.
Miller, Stephen. *The Peculiar Life of Sundays.* Cambridge, MA: Harvard University Press, 2008.
Millett, Richard L. "The Aftermath of Intervention: Panama 1990." *Journal of Interamerican Studies and World Affairs* 32, no. 1 (Spring 1990): 1–15.
———. "Think of Your Brethren Like unto Yourselves: The Beginning of a Marvelous Work and a Wonder in the Caribbean. A History of The Church of Jesus Christ of Latter-day Saints in the Caribbean, 1977 to 1980," 1992. Photocopy of typescript. CHL.
Mintz, Steven, and Susan Kellogg. *Domestic Revolutions: A Social History of American Family Life.* New York: Free Press, 1988.
Missionary Department. Africa and India Correspondence, 1960–74. CHL.
———. Annual Reports, 1977–2021. CHL.
———. Executive Secretary General Files, 1940–62. CHL.
———. Full-Time Mission Monthly Progress Reports, 1953–2019. CHL.
———. Missionary Registers, 1860–1959. CHL.
———. Seminar for Mission Leaders, 1961. CHL.
———. Seminar for New Mission Presidents Meeting Materials, 1972–73, 1976–77, 1981–82, 1985, 1993, 1997–98, 2000–2007. CHL.
Missionary Executive Council. Meeting Materials, 1982–2004. CHL.
———. Minutes. Missionary Executive Council, Meeting Materials, 1982–2004. CHL.
Missionary Handbook. Salt Lake City: The Church of Jesus Christ of Latter-day Saints, 1973.
"Missionary Training Center Statistics for Arrivals, Transfers, Releases and Completed Training, January 1, 1978 to December 31, 1978," 1978. Typescript. Language Training Mission, Historical Files, 1966–81. CHL.

Sources Cited

Mission MIA Manual: For Missions outside of the United States and Canada. Salt Lake City: General Boards of the Mutual Improvement Association of The Church of Jesus Christ of Latter-day Saints, 1961.

Moffat, Riley M., Fred E. Woods, and Brent R. Anderson. *Saints of Tonga: A Century of Island Faith.* Provo, UT: Religious Studies Center, Brigham Young University; Salt Lake City: Deseret Book, 2020.

Molina, Juan. Oral History Interview by David Bolingbroke and James Perry, Jan. 5, 2023. CHL. English translation in possession of editors.

Monson, Thomas S. Addresses, 1953–2017. CHL.

———. *Faith Rewarded: A Personal Account of Prophetic Promises to the East German Saints.* Salt Lake City: Deseret Book, 1996.

———. Journals, 1963–2017. Typescript. CHL.

Monticello Utah Temple. Dedication Services, July 26–27, 1998. CHL.

Moreno, Maria del Consuelo Wong. Interviews by David Bolingbroke, 2023. Typescript. Maria del Consuelo Wong Moreno, Oral History Interviews, 2023. CHL. English translation in possession of editors.

———. Oral History Interview by David Bolingbroke, Apr. 13, 2023. Maria del Consuelo Wong Moreno, Oral History Interview, 2023. CHL. English translation in possession of editors.

———. Papers. CHL.

Morgan, Barbara E. "Benemérito de las Américas: The Beginning of a Unique Church School in Mexico." *BYU Studies Quarterly* 52, no. 4 (2013): 89–116.

———. "A Century of LDS Church Schools in Mexico Influenced by Lamanite Identity." In *The Worldwide Church: Mormonism as a Global Religion,* edited by Michael A. Goodman and Mauro Properzi, 355–78. Provo, UT: Religious Studies Center, Brigham Young University; Salt Lake City: Deseret Book, 2016.

———. "The Impact of Centro Escolar Benemérito de las Americas, a Church School in Mexico." *Religious Educator* 15, no. 1 (2014): 144–67.

Mormon Tabernacle Choir. Chronological Files, 1883–2004. CHL.

———. Fan Mail, 1939–99. CHL.

Morrison, Alexander B. *The Dawning of a Brighter Day: The Church in Black Africa.* Salt Lake City: Deseret Book, 1990.

Mortensen, Kevin L., comp. *Witnessing the Hand of the Lord in the Dominican Republic* [. . .]. Centerville, UT: DR History Project, 2008.

Mortensen, Ronald S. Mission Journals, 1955–58. Typescript. Ronald S. Mortensen, Mission Papers, 1955–58, circa 2011, 2021–22. CHL.

———. "Serving in Paradise: Niue Island District, Tongan Mission, 1955–1958," no date. Typescript. Ronald S. Mortensen, Mission Papers, 1955–58, circa 2011, 2021–22. CHL.

Moss, James R. "The Great Awakening." In *Truth Will Prevail: The Rise of The Church of Jesus Christ of Latter-day Saints in the British Isles, 1837–1987,* edited by V. Ben Bloxham, James R. Moss, and Larry C. Porter, 394–423. Salt Lake City: The Church of Jesus Christ of Latter-day Saints, 1987.

Mouhsen, Silvina. Interview by David Bolingbroke, Sept. 18, 2023. Silvina Mouhsen and David Mouhsen, Oral History Interviews, 2023. CHL. English translation in possession of editors.

———. Oral History Interviews by David Bolingbroke, 2023. Silvina Mouhsen and David Mouhsen, Oral History Interviews, 2023. CHL. English translation in possession of editors.

Mouhsen, Silvina, and David Mouhsen. Oral History Interview by David Bolingbroke, Apr. 24, 2023. Silvina Mouhsen and David Mouhsen, Oral History Interviews, 2023. CHL. English translation in possession of editors.

Mourra, Alexandre A. Testimony, Mar. 1981. Typescript. CHL.

Moyle, Henry D. Papers, 1900–1964. CHL.

Mueller, Max Perry. "The Pageantry of Protest in Temple Square." In *Out of Obscurity: Mormonism since 1945,* edited by Patrick Q. Mason and John G. Turner, 123–43. New York: Oxford University Press, 2016.

Muhlestein, Kerry. "Papyri and Presumptions: A Careful Examination of the Eyewitness Accounts Associated with the Joseph Smith Papyri." *Journal of Mormon History* 42, no. 4 (Oct. 2016): 31–50.

Mullin, Robert Bruce. *A Short World History of Christianity.* Rev. ed. Louisville, KY: Westminster John Knox, 2014.

Muti, Mosese L. Book of Remembrance, no date. Digital copy. Hosea Family Papers, 1945–98. CHL. English translation of portions in possession of editors.

———. "Mosese Lui Muti: 'Faithful . . . over Many Things.'" In *Tongan Saints: Legacy of Faith,* translated and edited by Eric B. Shumway, 167–72. Laie, HI: Institute for Polynesian Studies, 1991.

———. Oral History Interview by R. Lanier Britsch, Jan. 15, 1974. Historical Department, Uncompleted Oral Histories, 1960, 1972–80. CHL.

Muti, Paula F. Interview Notes by Jed Woodworth, Jan. 30, 2012, and Dec. 3, 2021. Digital copy of typescript. CHL.

Muti, Paula F., and Sisi K. Muti. *Mosese L. Muti: A Man of Service, 1911–1993.* Bountiful, UT: Paula Muti, 2016. Copy at CHL.

My Personal Progress. Salt Lake City: The Church of Jesus Christ of Latter-day Saints, 1977.

"Names Submitted for Temple Ordinances." *Bulletin,* no. 1 (1995): 1–3. Newsletter published by The Church of Jesus Christ of Latter-day Saints. Copy at CHL.

Naniuzeyi, Mabiengwa Emmanuel. "The State of the State in Congo-Zaire: A Survey of the Mobutu Regime." *Journal of Black Studies* 29, no. 5 (May 1999): 669–83.

National Foreign Assessment Center. *Guatemala: The Climate for Insurgency, An Intelligence Assessment.* Feb. 1981. General CIA Records. Freedom of Information Act Electronic Reading Room. https://www.cia.gov/readingroom/document/cia-rdp03t02547r000100210001-8.

"Nauvoo Master Plan," Feb. 22, 2008. Typescript. Presiding Bishopric, First Presidency Meeting Materials, 1985–2013. CHL.

Navarro Alvarez, Victor Manuel. Email Interview by Alexander A. Nunez, May 2, 2023. Victor Manuel Navarro Alvarez, Oral History Interviews, 2022–23. CHL. English translation in possession of editors.

———. Oral History Interview by Alexander A. Nunez, Nov. 3, 2015. CHL. English translation in possession of editors.

———. Oral History Interviews by David Bolingbroke and Alexander A. Nunez, 2022–23. CHL. English translation in possession of editors.

Nazca Peru District, Peru Lima South Mission. Annual Historical Reports, 1985–86, 1990–2006, 2008, 2010–17, 2019–21. CHL.

Neilson, Reid L., and Scott D. Marianno. "True and Faithful: Joseph Fielding Smith as Mormon Historian and Theologian." *BYU Studies Quarterly* 57, no. 1 (2018): 6–64.

NeJaime, Douglas. "Before Marriage: The Unexplored History of Nonmarital Recognition and Its Relationship to Marriage." *California Law Review* 102, no. 1 (Feb. 2014): 87–172.

Nelaballe, Revanth. Oral History Interview by James Perry, Mar. 29, 2023. CHL. Transcript in possession of editors.

Nelson, Blaine. *The Elijah Abel Freedman's Bank Project,* edited by Noel Enniss. [Utah], 2004.

Nelson, Russell M. Addresses, 1965–2022. CHL.

———. Area Files, 1985–97. CHL.

———. *From Heart to Heart.* [Salt Lake City]: Quality Press, 1979.

———. "The Lord Uses the Unlikely to Accomplish the Impossible." Devotional given at Brigham Young University–Idaho, Rexburg, ID, Jan. 27, 2015. https://www.byui.edu/devotionals/elder-russell-m-nelson.

———. Oral History Interview by Jay M. Todd, May 29, 1991. *Ensign,* Tabernacle Choir Interviews, 1991. CHL.

———. "A Personal Perspective and Prayer," June 12, 1987. Typescript. Beverly B. Campbell Papers, 1960–2013. CHL.

Nelson, Russell M., and Wendy Watson Nelson. "Hope of Israel." Worldwide Youth Devotional, Salt Lake City, June 3, 2018. The Church of Jesus Christ of Latter-day Saints. https://www.ChurchofJesusChrist.org/study/broadcasts/worldwide-devotional-for-young-adults/2018/06/hope-of-israel.

Nelson, Russell M., and Dallin H. Oaks. Oral History Interview by Gerry Pond and Gerry Avant, July 3, 1991. Mormon Tabernacle Choir, Chronological Files, 1883–2004. CHL.

Netter, Frank H. *The CIBA Collection of Medical Illustrations.* Vol. 5, *A Compilation of Paintings on the Normal and Pathologic Anatomy and Physiology, Embryology, and Diseases of the Heart,* edited by Frederick F. Yonkman. New York: CIBA Pharmaceutical Company, 1969.

Newbury, David. "The Continuing Process of Decolonization in the Congo: Fifty Years Later." *African Studies Review* 55, no. 1 (Apr. 2012): 131–41.

Newport Beach California Stake. Stake Conference, May 4, 1975. Audio recording. CHL.

Newton, Marjorie. *Southern Cross Saints: The Mormons in Australia.* Mormons in the Pacific Series, edited by R. Lanier Britsch. Laie, HI: Institute for Polynesian Studies, 1991.

———. *Tiki and Temple: The Mormon Mission in New Zealand, 1854–1958.* Salt Lake City: Greg Kofford Books, 2012.

The New Zealand Official Year-Book, 1951–52. Vol. 57. Wellington, New Zealand: R. E. Owen, 1952.

New Zealand Temple. Dedication Services, 1958. CHL.

Ng, Shee-Nan, and Ching-Man Chin. *The Church of Jesus Christ of Latter-day Saints: History in Hong Kong, 1949–1997.* Translated by Anita Chin. [Hong Kong]: Hong Kong Family History Department, 1997.

Nguyen, The Van. "Escape from Vietnam: An Interview with Nguyen Van The." Interview by William Bradshaw and Marjorie Bradshaw. *Dialogue: A Journal of Mormon Thought* 13, no. 1 (Spring 1980): 23–39.

Nguyen, The Van, and David Lynn Hughes. *When Faith Endures: One Man's Courage in the Midst of War.* American Fork, UT: Covenant Communications, 2004.

Nibley, Hugh. *An Approach to the Book of Abraham.* Edited by John Gee. The Collected Works of Hugh Nibley 18. Salt Lake City: Deseret Book; Provo, UT: Foundation for Ancient Research and Mormon Studies, Neal A. Maxwell Institute for Religious Scholarship, Brigham Young University, 2009.

———. *An Approach to the Book of Mormon.* Salt Lake City: The Council of the Twelve Apostles of The Church of Jesus Christ of Latter-day Saints, 1957.

———. "As Things Stand at the Moment." *BYU Studies* 9, no. 1 (1969): 69–102.

———. *Lehi in the Desert and the World of the Jaredites.* Salt Lake City: Bookcraft, 1952.

———. *The Message of the Joseph Smith Papyri: An Egyptian Endowment.* Salt Lake City: Deseret Book, 1975.

———. "Phase One." *Dialogue: A Journal of Mormon Thought* 3, no. 2 (Summer 1968): 99–105.

———. *Since Cumorah: The Book of Mormon in the Modern World.* Salt Lake City: Deseret Book, 1967.

Niue District, Tongan Mission. General Minutes, 1952–65. 4 vols. CHL.

Nixon, Bert W., and Shirley B. Nixon. "Our Mission to Suva, Fiji, 1999–2001," circa 2001. Typescript. CHL.

North British Mission. Manuscript History and Historical Reports, 1960–72. CHL.

North German Mission. Auxiliary Training Meeting Minutes, 1961–69. CHL. English translation by Sylvia Ghosh in possession of editors.

Nugent, Victor. Oral History Interview by Clinton D. Christensen, Jan. 28, 2003. CHL.

Nugent, Victor, and Verna Nugent. Oral History Interview by Lavar D. Skousen and Jeanine Skousen, June 26, 2012. CHL.

Nunez, Alexander. Oral History Interview by James Perry and David Bolingbroke, May 17, 2022. CHL.

Nwachukwu, Anthonia, and Chubudi Nwachukwu. Oral History Interview by Matthew K. Heiss, Oct. 28, 1999. CHL.
Oakes, Phyllis R. "Gifts My Mother Gave Me: Life Sketch of Naomi W. Randall," circa 2013. Typescript. Phyllis R. Oakes, Naomi Randall Biographical Sketch, circa 2013. CHL.
Oaks, Dallin H. Executive Council and Committee Files, 1984–96. CHL.
Obinna, Anthony U. Autobiography, no date. Typescript. Edwin Q. Cannon Papers, 1963–86. CHL.
———. Oral History Interview by E. Dale LeBaron, June 4, 1988. E. Dale LeBaron, Oral History Project on Africa. BYU.
Obinna, Fidelia. Oral History Interview by E. Dale LeBaron, June 4, 1988. E. Dale LeBaron, Oral History Project on Africa. BYU.
Obinna, Francis I. Oral History Interview by Matthew K. Heiss, Nov. 9, 2005 CHL.
Obinna, Raymond I., Elizabeth O. Obinna, Charles Obinna, and Francis I. Obinna. Oral History Interview by Clinton D. Christensen, Nov. 9, 2005. CHL.
Obinna, Stella. Oral History Interview by E. Dale LeBaron, June 4, 1988. E. Dale LeBaron, Oral History Project on Africa. BYU.
Odd, Gilbert. *Encyclopedia of Boxing*. New York: Crescent Books, 1983.
O'Dea, Thomas F. *The Mormons*. Chicago: University of Chicago Press, 1957.
O'Donnal, John Forres. *Pioneer in Guatemala: The Personal History of John Forres O'Donnal*. Yorba Linda, CA: Shumway Family History Services, 1997.
O'Donnal, John Forres, and Carmen G. O'Donnal. Oral History Interviews by Gordon Irving, 1979. CHL.
Official Report of the One Hundred Fifty-Ninth Annual General Conference of The Church of Jesus Christ of Latter-day Saints. Held in the Tabernacle, Salt Lake City, Utah, April 1 and 2, 1989. Salt Lake City: The Church of Jesus Christ of Latter-day Saints, 1989.
Ogden, D. Kelly. Journal, May 1977–Dec. 1991. Typescript. CHL.
Okazaki, Chieko N. Journals, 1989–2007. Chieko N. Okazaki Papers, circa 1980–2010. CHL.
———. "Three Great Questions," Feb. 23, 1996. Typescript. Chieko N. Okazaki Papers, circa 1980–2010. CHL.
———. *What a Friend We Have in Jesus*. Salt Lake City: Deseret Book, 2008.
Oliva, Giuseppa. Papers, 1965–66. CHL.
Oliva, Maria. Family Papers, circa 1920–2021. CHL.
One-Hundred and First Semi-annual Conference of The Church of Jesus Christ of Latter-day Saints. Held in the Tabernacle, Salt Lake City, Utah, October 3, 4, 5, 1930, with a Full Report of All the Discourses. Salt Lake City: The Church of Jesus Christ of Latter-day Saints, 1930.
One Hundred Eighteenth Annual Conference of The Church of Jesus Christ of Latter-day Saints. Held in the Tabernacle, Salt Lake City, Utah, April 4, 5 and 6, 1948, with Report of Discourses. Salt Lake City: The Church of Jesus Christ of Latter-day Saints, 1948.
One Hundred Fortieth Semi-annual Conference of The Church of Jesus Christ of Latter-day Saints. Held in the Tabernacle, Salt Lake City, Utah, October 2, 3, 4, 1970, with Report of Discourses. Salt Lake City: The Church of Jesus Christ of Latter-day Saints, 1970.
One Hundred Forty-Ninth Annual Conference of The Church of Jesus Christ of Latter-day Saints. Held in the Tabernacle, Salt Lake City, Utah, March 31, April 1, 1979, with Report of Discourses. Salt Lake City: The Church of Jesus Christ of Latter-day Saints, 1979.
One Hundred Fourth Semi-annual Conference of The Church of Jesus Christ of Latter-day Saints. Held in the Tabernacle, Salt Lake City, Utah, October 6, 7, 8, 1933, with Report of Discourses. Salt Lake City: The Church of Jesus Christ of Latter-day Saints, 1933.
One Hundred Nineteenth Annual Conference of The Church of Jesus Christ of Latter-day Saints. Held in the Tabernacle, Salt Lake City, Utah, April 3, 4 and 6, 1949, with Report of Discourses. Salt Lake City: The Church of Jesus Christ of Latter-day Saints, 1949.
One Hundred Sixteenth Semi-annual Conference of The Church of Jesus Christ of Latter-day Saints. Held in the Tabernacle, Salt Lake City, Utah, October 5, 6 and 7, 1945, with Report of Discourses. Salt Lake City: The Church of Jesus Christ of Latter-day Saints, 1945.

Sources Cited

One Hundredth Annual Conference of The Church of Jesus Christ of Latter-day Saints. Held in the Tabernacle, Salt Lake City, Utah, April 6, 7, 8, 9, 1930, with a Full Report of All the Discourses. Salt Lake City: The Church of Jesus Christ of Latter-day Saints, 1930.

One Hundred Thirty-First Annual Conference of The Church of Jesus Christ of Latter-day Saints. Held in the Tabernacle, Salt Lake City, Utah, April 6, 8, and 9, 1961, with Report of Discourses. Salt Lake City: The Church of Jesus Christ of Latter-day Saints, 1961.

One Hundred Thirty-First Semi-annual Conference of The Church of Jesus Christ of Latter-day Saints. Held in the Tabernacle, Salt Lake City, Utah, September 29, 30, and October 1, 1961, with Report of Discourses. Salt Lake City: The Church of Jesus Christ of Latter-day Saints, 1961.

One Hundred Thirty-Fourth Semi-annual Conference of The Church of Jesus Christ of Latter-day Saints. Held in the Tabernacle, Salt Lake City, Utah, October 2, 3, 4, 1964, with Report of Discourses. Salt Lake City: The Church of Jesus Christ of Latter-day Saints, 1964.

One Hundred Thirty-Seventh Annual Conference of The Church of Jesus Christ of Latter-day Saints. Held in the Tabernacle, Salt Lake City, Utah, April 6, 8, 9, 1967, with Report of Discourses. Salt Lake City: The Church of Jesus Christ of Latter-day Saints, 1967.

One Hundred Thirty-Seventh Semi-annual Conference of The Church of Jesus Christ of Latter-day Saints. Held in the Tabernacle, Salt Lake City, Utah, September 29, 30, October 1, 1967, with Report of Discourses. Salt Lake City: The Church of Jesus Christ of Latter-day Saints, 1967.

One Hundred Thirty-Sixth Annual Conference of The Church of Jesus Christ of Latter-day Saints. Held in the Tabernacle, Salt Lake City, Utah, April 6, 9, 10, 1966, with Report of Discourses. Salt Lake City: The Church of Jesus Christ of Latter-day Saints, 1966.

One Hundred Thirty-Third Annual Conference of The Church of Jesus Christ of Latter-day Saints. Held in the Tabernacle, Salt Lake City, Utah, April 5, 6, 7, 1963, with Report of Discourses. Salt Lake City: The Church of Jesus Christ of Latter-day Saints, 1963.

One Hundred Thirty-Third Semi-annual Conference of The Church of Jesus Christ of Latter-day Saints. Held in the Tabernacle, Salt Lake City, Utah, October 4, 5, 6, 1963, with Report of Discourses. Salt Lake City: The Church of Jesus Christ of Latter-day Saints, 1963.

One Hundred Twentieth Annual Conference of The Church of Jesus Christ of Latter-day Saints. Held in the Tabernacle, Salt Lake City, Utah, April 6, 8, and 9, 1950, with Report of Discourses. Salt Lake City: The Church of Jesus Christ of Latter-day Saints, 1950.

One Hundred Twenty-Fifth Semi-annual Conference of The Church of Jesus Christ of Latter-day Saints. Held in the Tabernacle, Salt Lake City, Utah, October 1, 2 and 3, 1954, with Report of Discourses. Salt Lake City: The Church of Jesus Christ of Latter-day Saints, 1954.

One Hundred Twenty-Ninth Annual Conference of The Church of Jesus Christ of Latter-day Saints. Held in the Tabernacle, Salt Lake City, Utah, April 4, 5 and 6, 1959, with Report of Discourses. Salt Lake City: The Church of Jesus Christ of Latter-day Saints, 1959.

One Hundred Twenty-Seventh Annual Conference of The Church of Jesus Christ of Latter-day Saints. Held in the Tabernacle, Salt Lake City, Utah, April 5, 6, and 7, 1957, with Report of Discourses. Salt Lake City: The Church of Jesus Christ of Latter-day Saints, 1957.

One Hundred Twenty-Sixth Semi-annual Conference of The Church of Jesus Christ of Latter-day Saints. Held in the Tabernacle, Salt Lake City, Utah, September 30, and October 1 and 2, 1955, with Report of Discourses. Salt Lake City: The Church of Jesus Christ of Latter-day Saints, 1955.

One Hundred Twenty-Third Semi-annual Conference of The Church of Jesus Christ of Latter-day Saints. Held in the Tabernacle, Salt Lake City, Utah, October 3, 4 and 5, 1952, with Report of Discourses. Salt Lake City: The Church of Jesus Christ of Latter-day Saints, 1952.

Orr, Eugene. "Eugene Orr's Life History," no date. Typescript. Eugene Orr Papers, 1968–2018. CHL.

———. Interview by Jed Woodworth, May 25, 2022. Typescript. Copy in possession of editors.

———. Oral History Interview by Clint Christensen, Dan Baker, and Edith Baker, June 3, 2013. CHL.

Orson Hyde Memorial Garden Dedication Service, Oct. 24, 1979. CHL.

Ortlieb, Erich, and Marianne Zwirner Ortlieb. "Political Isolation." In *Behind the Iron Curtain: Recollections of Latter-day Saints in East Germany, 1945–1989*, compiled and translated by Garold N. Davis and Norma S. Davis, 196–206. Provo, UT: BYU Studies, 1996.

Osborne, Virgus C. "An Appraisal of the Education Program for Native Americans at Brigham Young University 1966–1974, with Curricular Recommendations." PhD diss., University of Utah, 1975.

Oslzlý, Petr. "On Stage with the Velvet Revolution." *TDR* 34, no. 3 (Autumn 1990): 97–108.

Osmond, Alan, and Suzanne Osmond. Oral History Interview by Scott A. Hales and Jed Woodworth, Nov. 21, 2022. CHL. Transcript in possession of editors.

Osmond, Donny, and Patricia Romanowski. *Life Is Just What You Make It: My Story So Far*. New York: Hyperion, 1999.

Osmond, Jay. Oral History Interview by Scott A. Hales and Jed Woodworth, Nov. 28, 2022. CHL. Transcript in possession of editors.

———. *Stages: An Autobiography*. With Kandilyn Osmond and Terri Shoemaker. San Clemente, CA: Sourced Media Books, 2010.

Osmond, Merrill, and Janice Barrett Graham. *Let the Reason Be Love: A Song of Faith*. Pleasant Grove, UT: Tidal Wave Books, 2003.

Osmond, Olive. Journal. Osmond Family Papers. BYU.

Osmond, Virl. *The Untold Story of Olive Osmond*. Pleasant Grove, UT: Knowledge Unlimited, 2009.

Osthaus, Carl R. *Freedmen, Philanthropy, and Fraud: A History of the Freedman's Savings Bank*. Urbana: University of Illinois Press, 1976.

Ottley, Jerold D. Mormon Tabernacle Choir History (1990s), 2009–15. CHL.

Owens, David R. "Future Prophets, the Berlin Wall and Missionaries," Mar. 1, 2020. Typescript. CHL.

Pace, Glenn L. Official Journal, 1985–92, 1997–2001. Typescript. CHL.

———. Oral History Interview by Steven R. Sorensen, Sept. 15, 1998. CHL.

———. *Safe Journey: An African Adventure*. Salt Lake City: Deseret Book, 2003.

Palmer, Spencer J. *The Church Encounters Asia*. Salt Lake City: Deseret Book, 1970.

———. *Mormons in West Africa: New Terrain for the Sesquicentennial Church*. Provo, UT: Brigham Young University, 1979.

Palomino, Luis. Oral History Interview by David Bolingbroke and James Perry, May 18, 2022. CHL. Transcript in possession of editors.

Paraguay Asunción Mission. Annual Historical Reports, 1978–80, 1992–95, 2001–6, 2009, 2013–21. CHL.

———. Mission Presidency Minutes, Jan. 1992–June 1996. CHL.

Parkin, Bonnie D. "History of the Relief Society: The Bonnie Parkin Administration, 2002–2007," 2012. Typescript. CHL.

Patterson, James T. *Grand Expectations: The United States, 1945–1974*. The Oxford History of the United States. New York: Oxford University Press, 1996.

———. *Restless Giant: The United States from Watergate to Bush v. Gore*. The Oxford History of the United States. New York: Oxford University Press, 2005.

Paul, Christopher, Colin P. Clarke, Beth Grill, and Molly Dunigan. *Paths to Victory: Detailed Insurgency Case Studies*. Santa Monica, CA: RAND, 2013.

The Pearl of Great Price: A Selection from the Revelations, Translations, and Narrations of Joseph Smith, First Prophet, Seer, and Revelator to The Church of Jesus Christ of Latter-day Saints. Salt Lake City: The Church of Jesus Christ of Latter-day Saints, 2013.

Perkey, Joshua J. Oral History Interview by James Perry and David Bolingbroke, May 24, 2023. CHL.

Perpetual Education Fund. Board of Directors Meeting Minutes, 2001–14. CHL.

"The Perpetual Education Fund: Key Indicators," Jan. 23, 2008. Slide presentation. Perpetual Education Fund, Board of Director Meeting Minutes, 2001–14. CHL.

Perry, James. Mary McKenna Interview Notes, Feb. 16, 2024. Typescript. CHL.

Perry, James, Sylvia Brown, and Frank Blease. "If the Walls Had Ears, and the Floor Could Talk: A History of The Church of Jesus Christ of Latter-day Saints' Meeting Places in the

British Isles (1837–1965)." Unpublished manuscript, 2023. PDF file. Copy in James Perry Collection, 1957–2023. CHL.

Perry, L. Tom. Journals and Daybooks, 1973–2014. CHL.

Perry, Lee Tom. *L. Tom Perry: An Uncommon Life.* Vol. 2, *Years of Hastening the Work of Salvation.* Salt Lake City: Deseret Book, 2019.

Petersen, Boyd J., and David W. Scott. "The Art of Scripture and Scripture as Art: The Proclamation on the Family and the Expanding Canon." In *The Expanded Canon: Perspectives on Mormonism and Sacred Texts,* edited by Blair G. Van Dyke, Brian D. Birch, and Boyd J. Petersen, 208–26. Salt Lake City: Greg Kofford Books, 2018.

Peterson, Daniel C. *Abraham Divided: An LDS Perspective on the Middle East.* Salt Lake City: Aspen Books, 1992.

Peterson, Gerald Joseph. "History of Mormon Exhibits in World Expositions." Master's thesis, Brigham Young University, 1974.

Peterson, Glen. "Crisis and Opportunity: The Work of Aid Refugee Chinese Intellectuals (ARCI) in Hong Kong and Beyond." In *Hong Kong in the Cold War,* edited by Priscilla Roberts and John M. Carroll, 141–59. Hong Kong: Hong Kong University Press, 2016.

Peterson, H. Burke. Journal, 1972–2001. Microfilm. CHL.

Peterson, H. Donl. *The Story of the Book of Abraham: Mummies, Manuscripts, and Mormonism.* Salt Lake City: Deseret Book, 1995.

Peterson, Janet, and LaRene Gaunt. *Elect Ladies.* Salt Lake City: Deseret Book, 1990.

———. *Keepers of the Flame.* Salt Lake City: Deseret Book, 1993.

Peterson, Paul H. "An Historical Analysis of the Word of Wisdom." Master's thesis, Brigham Young University, 1972.

Petramalo, Gilbert, and Gretchen Petramalo. Oral History Interview by Matthew K. Heiss, Oct. 2, 1992. CHL.

Petramalo, Gretchen. Mission Journal, 1988–89. CHL.

Philippines Area. Annual Historical Reports, 1989, 1991, 1993–96, 2002–7, 2010–21. CHL.

———. Presidency Meeting Minutes, 1987–89, 1990, 1994–96, 2000–2005. CHL.

Photographs of Artifacts Donated to the Relief Society Building Fund, circa 1960. CHL.

Pierce, Lucy Black. Oral History Interview by Jed Woodworth and Tesia Tsai, Oct. 4, 2021. CHL. Transcript in possession of editors.

"Pilot Report and Recommendations," Apr. 26, 2000. Slide presentation. Church Educational System, Administrator's Files, 1977–2001. CHL.

Pingree, Anne C. "Chile Area Auxiliary Leadership Training," circa Oct. 2004. Typescript. Relief Society of The Church of Jesus Christ of Latter-day Saints, Scrapbooks, 1990–2007. Special Collections, J. Willard Marriott Library, University of Utah, Salt Lake City.

———. Journal Excerpts, June 1 and 11, 2003. CHL.

Pingree, Anne C., Kathleen H. Hughes, and Bonnie D. Parkin. Oral History Interview by Scott A. Hales, Sept. 20, 2023. CHL.

Plewe, Brandon S., ed. *Mapping Mormonism: An Atlas of Latter-day Saint History.* Provo, UT: Brigham Young University Press, 2012.

Poll, Richard D. *Working the Divine Miracle: The Life of Apostle Henry D. Moyle.* Edited by Stan Larson. Salt Lake City: Signature Books, 1999.

Powaski, Ronald E. *The Cold War: The United States and the Soviet Union, 1917–1991.* New York: Oxford University Press, 1998.

Pratt, Carl B. "Area Presidency Focus," circa Oct. 2004. Typescript. Relief Society, Anne C. Pingree Relief Society General Presidency Papers, 1992–2008. CHL.

"Preach My Gospel": A Guide to Missionary Service. Salt Lake City: The Church of Jesus Christ of Latter-day Saints, 2004.

Presiding Bishopric. Committee for Reducing Financial Demands on Church Members Files, Nov. 1980–June 1981. CHL.

———. Financial, Statistical, and Historical Reports of Wards, Stakes, and Missions, 1884–1955. CHL.

———. International Offices Files, 1979–85. CHL.

———. Meeting Materials, 1985–2003. CHL.

———. Minutes, 1985–2003. Presiding Bishopric, Meeting Materials, 1985–2003. CHL.
———. Secretary to the Presiding Bishopric Meeting Notes, 1999–2016. CHL.
———. Welfare Executive Committee Meeting Materials, 2000–2010. CHL.
Preventing and Responding to Spouse Abuse: Helps for Members. Salt Lake City: The Church of Jesus Christ of Latter-day Saints, 1997.
Price, Relva R. "History of the Church of Jesus Christ of Latter Day Saints on Niue Island," May 1973. Mimeograph of typescript. CHL.
Priesthood Committee. Meeting Minutes, 1944–63. CHL.
Priesthood Department. Melchizedek Priesthood General Committee Minutes, 1973–87. CHL.
Priesthood Executive Council. Minutes, 1982–2006, 2008–10. CHL.
———. Minutes and Records, 1982–85, 2012–15. Priesthood and Family Executive Council, Minutes and Records, 1982–85, 2012–18. CHL.
Primary Association. Annual History: Reports, 1980–94. Photocopy of typescript. CHL.
———. General Board Minutes, 1889–1994, 2005–14. CHL.
———. Primary Children's Hospital Files, 1911, 1925–75. CHL.
Primary Handbook. Salt Lake City: The Church of Jesus Christ of Latter-day Saints, 1978.
Proclaiming the Gospel: 2000 Annual Report. [Salt Lake City], [2001]. Missionary Executive Council, Meeting Materials, 1982–2004. CHL.
"Programa Dinamismo (edificar homens e capelas)," no date. Typescript. Copy at CHL.
"Progress Report: Restoration of Major Doctrines through the Prophet Joseph Smith." *Religious Studies Center Newsletter,* no. 3 (June 1987): 4–5. Newsletter published by Religious Studies Center, Brigham Young University, Provo, UT. Copy in Dallin H. Oaks, Executive Council and Committee Files, 1984–96. CHL.
"Project Update," Feb. 8, 2008. Slide presentation. Presiding Bishopric, First Presidency Meeting Materials, 1985–2013. CHL.
"Provident Living Web Site," Jan. 26, 2006. Slide presentation. Presiding Bishopric, Welfare Executive Committee Meeting Materials, 2000–2010. CHL.
Prucha, Francis Paul. *The Great Father: The United States Government and the American Indians.* 2 vols. Lincoln: University of Nebraska Press, 1984.
Prunier, Gérard. *Africa's World War: Congo, the Rwandan Genocide, and the Making of a Continental Catastrophe.* New York: Oxford University Press, 2009.
Public Affairs Department. Michael Otterson Files, circa 2001–16. CHL.
Public Communications Department. General Authority Advisers Meeting Minutes, July 1972–Apr. 1984. Typescript. CHL.
Pulsipher, Nancy Ruth Funk. *Ruth Hardy Funk: A Journey of Joy and Gratitude.* Salt Lake City: Marcus C. Funk Family History Association, 2000.
Pykles, Benjamin C. *Excavating Nauvoo: The Mormons and the Rise of Historical Archaeology in America.* Critical Studies in the History of Anthropology. Lincoln: University of Nebraska Press, 2010.
Quinn, D. Michael. *The Mormon Hierarchy: Wealth and Corporate Power.* Salt Lake City: Signature Books, 2017.
Quorum of the Twelve Apostles. Circular Letters, 1914, 1923–2012, 2020. CHL.
———. Missionary Committee Minutes. Quorum of the Twelve Apostles, Missionary Committee/Missionary Executive Committee Meeting Materials, 1953–77. CHL.
———. Missionary Executive Committee Minutes. Quorum of the Twelve Apostles, Missionary Committee/Missionary Executive Committee Meeting Materials, 1953–77. CHL.
———. Regional Representatives Seminar Addresses, 1967–91. CHL.
———. Written Communications Collection, 1944, 1946, 1960–2016. CHL.
Randall, Naomi. "'I Am a Child of God'—a Heavenly Truth in Words and Music," no date. Typescript. Copy in possession of editors.
———. Interview, 1989. Video. Copy in possession of editors.
———. Interview, Nov. 3, 1976. Collection of Materials pertaining to the Song "I Am a Child of God," circa 1957–77. CHL.
Rappleye, John, and Nancy Rappleye. Oral History Interview by James Perry, Aug. 31, 2020. CHL.

Sources Cited

Rasmus, Carolyn J. Journal, 1984–93. Young Women, Carolyn J. Rasmus Office Papers, 1984–93. CHL.

Rasmussen, Matthew Lyman. *Mormonism and the Making of a British Zion.* Salt Lake City: University of Utah Press, 2016.

Rather, Susan Clayton. *Supporting the Rescue of All That Is Finest: A Management History of Welfare Services, 1995–2004.* [Salt Lake City: Welfare Services Department], 2005.

———, ed. "Welfare Compendium, 2014." Typescript. Welfare Services Department, Welfare Compendium, 2014. CHL.

Record of Members Collection, 1836–1970. CHL.

Reed, Christopher Robert. *The Chicago NAACP and the Rise of Black Professional Leadership, 1910–1966.* Bloomington: Indiana University Press, 1997.

Reeder, Jennifer. "'To Do Something Extraordinary': Mormon Women and the Creation of a Usable Past." PhD diss., George Mason University, 2013.

Reeder, Jennifer, and Kate Holbrook, eds. *At the Pulpit: 185 Years of Discourses by Latter-day Saint Women.* Salt Lake City: Church Historian's Press, 2017.

Reid, Michael. *Brazil: The Troubled Rise of a Global Power.* New Haven, CT: Yale University Press, 2014.

Reiser, A. Hamer. Diary, Sept. 2–15, 1958. Copy in David O. McKay Papers, 1901–70. CHL.

Relief Society. Anne C. Pingree Relief Society General Presidency Papers, 1992–2008. CHL.

———. Belle S. Spafford Files, 1933–77. CHL.

———. General Board Minutes, 1842–2007. CHL.

———. General Presidency Meeting Minutes, Jan. 2007–May 2012. CHL.

———. Magazine Department, 1942–73. CHL.

———. Research Files on History of the Relief Society, circa 1993–97. CHL.

———. Sesquicentennial Files and Gospel Literacy Program, 1987–2001. CHL.

———. Silvia Allred Files, 1997–2012. CHL.

Relief Society Building. Files, 1945–60, 1982. CHL.

———. Fund Files, 1946–56. CHL.

———. Inventory, circa 1956. CHL.

"Relief Society Challenges in Chile," circa Oct. 2004. Typescript. Relief Society, Anne C. Pingree Relief Society General Presidency Papers, 1992–2008. CHL.

Relief Society Handbook. Salt Lake City: The Church of Jesus Christ of Latter-day Saints, 1983.

Relief Society of The Church of Jesus Christ of Latter-day Saints. Scrapbooks, 1990–2007. Special Collections, J. Willard Marriott Library, University of Utah, Salt Lake City.

Responding to Abuse: Helps for Ecclesiastical Leaders. Salt Lake City: The Church of Jesus Christ of Latter-day Saints, 1995.

Retail Food Prices by Cities, October 15, 1947. Prepared by the U.S. Department of Labor, Bureau of Labor Statistics. Washington, DC, 1947.

Reynolds, Noel B. "The Coming Forth of the Book of Mormon in the Twentieth Century." *BYU Studies* 38, no. 2 (1999): 6–47.

Reyntjens, Filip. *The Great African War: Congo and Regional Geopolitics, 1996–2006.* New York: Cambridge University Press, 2009.

Richards, LeGrand. *A Marvelous Work and a Wonder.* Salt Lake City: Deseret Book, 1950.

Ricks, Stephen D. "The Narrative Call Pattern in the Prophetic Commission of Enoch (Moses 6)." *BYU Studies* 26, no. 4 (Fall 1986): 97–105.

Rinne, Anna-Liisa. *Kristuksen Kirkko Suomessa.* Publication place and publisher unidentified, 1986.

Rio de Janeiro Brazil Stake. Manuscript History and Historical Reports, 1972. CHL.

The Rising Generation. Salt Lake City: Deseret Book, 1987.

Riwai-Couch, Melanie. "Historical Information about 'Especially for Youth' in the Pacific Area," Aug. 25, 2023. Matthew Cowley Pacific Church History Centre, Hamilton, New Zealand.

Roby, Jini. Oral History Interview by Lisa Christensen, May 3, 2022. CHL.

Rochon, Delia. *Come and See.* Provo, UT: Y Mountain, 2020.

———. Interviews by James Perry, David Bolingbroke, Lisa Christensen, and/or Scott A. Hales, 2021. CHL. Transcript in possession of editors.

Roderick, Lee. *For Time and All Eternity: The Sterling and Ellie Colton Story.* Los Angeles: Probitas, 2017.

Rodriguez, Derin Head. *From Every Nation.* Salt Lake City: Deseret Book, 1990.

Romney, Antone K. "History of the Correlation of L.D.S. Church Auxiliaries," Aug. 1961. Typescript. CHL.

Romney, Marion G. Interview by Edward L. Kimball, June 12, 1978. Edward L. Kimball Papers, 1956–2007. CHL.

———. Journal, 1941–86. Typescript. CHL.

Romney, Virginia Hatch, and Richard O. Cowan. *The Colonia Juárez Temple: A Prophet's Inspiration.* Provo, UT: Religious Studies Center, Brigham Young University, 2009.

Rose, James M., and Alice Eichholz. *Black Genesis: A Resource Book for African-American Genealogy.* 2nd ed. Baltimore: Genealogical Publishing, 2003.

Rupp, Monty. Journal Excerpt, July 17, 1971. Copy in possession of editors.

Rutherford, Taunalyn. "Shifting Focus to Global Mormonism." In *The Worldwide Church: Mormonism as a Global Religion,* edited by Michael A. Goodman and Mauro Properzi, 71–94. Provo, UT: Religious Studies Center, Brigham Young University; Salt Lake City: Deseret Book, 2016.

Saettler, Paul. *A History of Instructional Technology.* New York: McGraw-Hill, 1968.

Saints: The Story of the Church of Jesus Christ in the Latter Days. Vol. 1, The Standard of Truth, 1815–1846. Salt Lake City: The Church of Jesus Christ of Latter-day Saints, 2018.

Saints: The Story of the Church of Jesus Christ in the Latter Days. Vol. 2, No Unhallowed Hand, 1846–1893. Salt Lake City: The Church of Jesus Christ of Latter-day Saints, 2020.

Saints: The Story of the Church of Jesus Christ in the Latter Days. Vol. 3, Boldly, Nobly, and Independent, 1893–1955. Salt Lake City: The Church of Jesus Christ of Latter-day Saints, 2022.

"Sair." One in a Million. Media Library. The Church of Jesus Christ of Latter-day Saints. Video, [00:01:45]. Accessed Mar. 22, 2024. https://www.ChurchofJesusChrist.org/media/collection/one-in-a-million.

Santana Guirado, Hilda. Oral History Interview by David Bolingbroke and James Perry, Dec. 15, 2021. CHL. English translation in possession of editors.

Santana Guirado de Machuca, Isabel. Oral History Interviews by David Bolingbroke, 2022. CHL. English translation in possession of editors.

Santana Guirado de Machuca, Isabel, and Juan Antonio Machuca Cañas. Oral History Interview by David Bolingbroke and Tesia Tsai, Jan. 19, 2022. Isabel Santana, Oral History Interviews, 2022. CHL. English translation in possession of editors.

Santiago Chile Temple. Dedication Services, Sept. 15–17, 1983. CHL.

Saunders, Chris. "1968 and Apartheid: Race and Politics in South Africa." In *The Third World in the Global 1960s,* edited by Samantha Christiansen and Zachary A. Scarlett, 133–41. Protest, Culture and Society 8. New York: Berghahn Books, 2013.

Scharffs, Gilbert W. *Mormonism in Germany: A History of The Church of Jesus Christ of Latter-day Saints in Germany between 1840 and 1970.* Salt Lake City: Deseret Book, 1970.

Scott, Mark. "Reflections on Howard W. Hunter in Jerusalem: An Interview with Teddy Kollek." *BYU Studies* 34, no. 4 (1994–95): 6–15.

Scott, Richard G. Journal, 1948, 1957, 1965–2013. Richard G. Scott, Electronic Files, 1964–2015. Digital Copy. CHL.

———. Mexico-Central America Files, circa 1978–81. CHL.

"Seek Learning Even by Study and by Faith": Report for 1971 from Commissioner of Education of The Church of Jesus Christ of Latter-day Saints. Salt Lake City: The Church of Jesus Christ of Latter-day Saints, 1971.

Sharp, J. Vernon. Autobiography, circa 1987. CHL.

Sheffer, Edith. *Burned Bridge: How East and West Germans Made the Iron Curtain.* New York: Oxford University Press, 2011.

Shepherd, Gordon, and Gary Shepherd. *A Kingdom Transformed: Themes in the Development of Mormonism.* Salt Lake City: University of Utah Press, 1984.

Sources Cited

Shields, Garret S. "'A Fine Field': Rio de Janeiro's Journey to Become a Center of Strength for the LDS Church." Master's thesis, Brigham Young University, 2016.
Shipps, Jan. *Sojourner in the Promised Land: Forty Years among the Mormons*. Urbana: University of Illinois Press, 2000.
———. "Spinning Gold: Mormonism and the Olympic Games." *Dialogue: A Journal of Mormon Thought* 36, no. 1 (Spring 2003): 133–49.
Shumway, Dale L., and Margene Shumway, eds. *The Blossoming: Dramatic Accounts of the Lives of Native Americans in the Foster Care Program of The Church of Jesus Christ of Latter-day Saints*. Publication place and publisher unidentified, circa 2002.
Significant Incidents of Political Violence against Americans: 1988. Prepared by the Bureau of Diplomatic Security, United States Department of State. Washington, DC, 1989.
Significant Incidents of Political Violence against Americans: 1989. Prepared by the Bureau of Diplomatic Security, United States Department of State. Washington, DC, 1990.
Significant Incidents of Political Violence against Americans: 1990. Prepared by the Bureau of Diplomatic Security, United States Department of State. Washington, DC, 1991.
Simoncini, Luca. "La storia dei primi pionieri del ramo di Palermo: Tratto dai racconti dei protagonist," no date. Typescript. Copy in possession of editors.
Simoncini, Umberto. Oral History Interview by Matthew McBride and James Perry, June 10, 2021. Copy in possession of editors.
Sing with Me: Songs for Children. Salt Lake City: The Church of Jesus Christ of Latter-day Saints, 1976.
Sitati, Gladys. Oral History Interview by Kate Holbrook, May 5, 2016. CHL.
Sloan, Julia. "Carnivalizing the Cold War: Mexico, the Mexican Revolution, and the Events of 1968." *European Journal of American Studies* 4, no. 1 (Spring 2009), https://journals.openedition.org/ejas/7547.
Sloan, Tim. Oral History Interview by James Perry and David Bolingbroke, Apr. 19, 2023. CHL. Transcript in possession of editors.
Smith, Barbara B. "ERA—a Family Concern," June 4, 1977. Typescript. Gordon B. Hinckley, Special Affairs Committee Files, 1976–79. CHL.
———. "The Rights of Women," Jan. 15, 1977. Typescript. Gordon B. Hinckley, Special Affairs Committee Files, 1976–79. CHL.
Smith, Hortense H. Child. Oral History Interviews by Gordon Irving, 1978–80. CHL.
Smith, Joseph F., Anthon H. Lund, and Charles W. Penrose. *To the Presidents of Stakes, Bishops and Parents in Zion*. [Salt Lake City]: [The Church of Jesus Christ of Latter-day Saints], 1915.
Smith, Joseph Fielding. Journals. Joseph Fielding Smith Papers, 1893–1973. CHL.
Smith, S. Percy. *Niue: The Island and Its People*. With contributions by Pulekula. Suva, Fiji: Institute of Pacific Studies and the Niue Extension Centre of the University of the South Pacific, 1983.
Solari, Victor Gerardo. Oral History Interview by James Perry and David Bolingbroke, Dec. 8, 2021. CHL.
Sollesta, Maridan. Autobiography. CHL.
———. Oral History Interviews by James Perry, 2022. Maridan Sollesta and Eusebio Sollesta, Oral History Interviews, 2022–23. CHL. Transcript in possession of editors.
Sollesta, Maridan, and Eusebio Sollesta. Email Interview by James Perry, Sept. 21, 2023. Maridan Sollesta and Eusebio Sollesta, Oral History Interviews, 2022–23. CHL. Transcript in possession of editors.
———. Oral History Interviews by David Bolingbroke, 2023. Maridan Sollesta and Eusebio Sollesta, Oral History Interviews, 2022–23. CHL. Transcript in possession of editors.
Sorensen, Asael Taylor. "Asael Taylor Sorensen, Sr.: A Personal History," 2001. Microfilm. CHL.
Sorenson, John. "Mass Media and Discourse on Famine in the Horn of Africa." *Discourse and Society* 2, no. 2 (1991): 223–42.
South Africa Johannesburg Mission. Conference Recordings, 1978. 2 audiocassettes. CHL.
South America South Area. Mission Files, 1986–2007. CHL.
Southern Far East Asian Mission Reports. China Hong Kong Mission, Manuscript History and Historical Reports, 1955–71. CHL.

Spafford, Belle S. Interviews, circa 1980. 12 audiocassettes. CHL.
———. Letters, 1937–80. BYU.
———. "My Feeling upon Being Released as President of Relief Society," no date. Typescript. Belle S. Spafford, Scrapbook. CHL.
———. Oral History Interviews by Jill Mulvay Derr, 1975–76. CHL.
Spafford, Marion I. Papers, 1933–89. CHL.
Spät, Walter. Oral History Interview by Frederick G. Williams, Sept. 7, 1975. CHL. English translation of portions in possession of editors.
"Special Witnesses of Christ." The Church of Jesus Christ of Latter-day Saints. Broadcast on Apr. 1, 2000. Video, [01:05:06]. https://www.ChurchofJesusChrist.org/media/video/2000-01-0000-special-witnesses-of-christ.
Spruill, Marjorie J. *Divided We Stand: The Battle over Women's Rights and Family Values That Polarized American Politics.* New York: Bloomsbury, 2017.
Stalker, Nancy K. *Japan: History and Culture from Classical to Cool.* Oakland: University of California Press, 2018.
Steininger, Rolf. *Germany and the Middle East: From Kaiser Wilhelm II to Angela Merkel.* New York: Berghahn Books, 2019.
Stern, Steve J. "Beyond Enigma: An Agenda for Interpreting Shining Path and Peru, 1980–1995." In *Shining and Other Paths: War and Society in Peru, 1980–1995,* edited by Steve J. Stern, 1–8. Durham, NC: Duke University Press, 1998.
Stevenson, Russell. "To Recognize One's Face in That of a Foreigner: The Latter-day Saint Experience in West Africa." In *The Palgrave Handbook of Global Mormonism,* edited by R. Gordon Shepherd, A. Gary Shepherd, and Ryan T. Cragun, 585–605. Cham, Switzerland: Palgrave Macmillan, 2020.
Stewart, David G., Jr. "The LDS Church in Eastern Europe, Russia, and Central Asia." In *The Palgrave Handbook of Global Mormonism,* edited by R. Gordon Shepherd, A. Gary Shepherd, and Ryan T. Cragun, 559–83. Cham, Switzerland: Palgrave Macmillan, 2020.
Stewart, David G., Jr., and Matthew Martinich. *Reaching the Nations: International LDS Church Growth Almanac.* 2 vols. Henderson, NV: Cumorah Foundation, 2013.
Stewart, Ora Pate. *Tender Apples.* Salt Lake City: Deseret Book, 1965.
Stokes, Catherine M. Oral History Interview by Matthew K. Heiss, Nov. 11, 2009. CHL.
Stout, Hosea. Diary, 1844–61. In *On the Mormon Frontier: The Diary of Hosea Stout, 1844–1861,* edited by Juanita Brooks. Salt Lake City: University of Utah Press, 1982.
Striner, Richard. *Hard Times: Economic Depressions in America.* The American Ways Series. Lanham, MD: Rowman and Littlefield, 2018.
Strong, Arthur H. Autobiography Excerpt, circa 1970–80. CHL.
Suri, Jeremi. *Power and Protest: Global Revolution and the Rise of Detente.* Cambridge, MA: Harvard University Press, 2003.
Suva Fiji Temple. Dedication Services, June 18, 2000. CHL.
Suzette T. and Geoffrey Dunning Papers, 2021–22. CHL.
Swinton, Heidi S. *To the Rescue: The Biography of Thomas S. Monson.* Salt Lake City: Deseret Book, 2010.
Switzer, Russell W. "Sendero Luminoso and Peruvian Counterinsurgency." Master's thesis, Louisiana State University and Agricultural and Mechanical College, 2007.
Switzerland Zurich Mission. President's Files, 1946–74. CHL.
"Sydney Australia Greenwich Stake, February 1995–February 2004: A Historical Record," [2004]. Typescript. CHL.
"Taiwan Firsts." *Southern Far East Bulletin* 3, no. 6 (June 1958): [20]. Newsletter published by the Southern Far East Mission of The Church of Jesus Christ of Latter-day Saints. In China Hong Kong, Mission Publications, 1956–73. CHL.
Talmage, James E. *The House of the Lord: A Study of Holy Sanctuaries Ancient and Modern, including Forty-Six Plates Illustrative of Modern Temples.* Salt Lake City: Deseret News, 1912.
Tanner, N. Eldon. Journals, 1936–82. Typescript. N. Eldon Tanner, Journals, Calendar Books, and Appointment Books, 1936–82. CHL.
Tate, Lucile C. *David B. Haight: The Life Story of a Disciple.* Salt Lake City: Bookcraft, 1987.

Sources Cited

Taylor, Amber. "Contest and Controversy in the Creation of the Brigham Young University Jerusalem Center." PhD diss., Brandeis University, 2019.

Taylor, Frederick. *The Berlin Wall: A World Divided, 1961–1989*. New York: HarperCollins, 2006.

Taylor, Harvey L. *The Story of L.D.S. Church Schools*. 2 vols. [Salt Lake City?], 1971. Copy at CHL.

Taylor, K. W. *A History of the Vietnamese*. Cambridge: Cambridge University Press, 2013.

Taylor, Marie. Oral History Interview by Lisa Christensen, Dec. 19, 2022. CHL. Transcript in possession of editors.

Ted and Janath Cannon Mission Papers, circa 1978–81. CHL.

Temple and Family History Executive Council. Meeting Materials, 1983–2013, 2015–18. CHL.

———. Minutes, 1983–2013, 2015–18. Temple and Family History Executive Council, Meeting Materials, 1983–2013, 2015–18. CHL.

Temple Department. Annual Reports, 1982–2009. CHL.

———. Temple District Maps, 1988–96. CHL.

———. Temple Sites Minutes, 1997–99. CHL.

"Temple Dimensions." Temples of The Church of Jesus Christ of Latter-day Saints. Accessed Mar. 9, 2024. https://churchofjesuschristtemples.org/statistics/dimensions/.

"Temple List." Temples. The Church of Jesus Christ of Latter-day Saints. Accessed Mar. 11, 2024. https://www.ChurchofJesusChrist.org/temples/list.

Temple Records for the Living, 1955–91. FSL.

Terebenina, Liudmila S. "History of the Church in the USSR and in Russia," 1989–94. Typescript. CHL.

Thompson, Anita. *Stand as a Witness: The Biography of Ardeth Greene Kapp*. Salt Lake City: Deseret Book, 2005.

Thomsen, Russel J. "The History of the Sabbath in Mormonism." Master's thesis, Loma Linda University, 1968.

Till, Eugene, Diane Till, and Philip L. Munoa. Oral History Interview by Lisa Christensen, May 4, 2022. CHL. Transcript in possession of editors.

"'Time Vindicates the Prophet'—Nibley Volume 3 Focuses on Mormonism and Early Christianity." *Insights: An Ancient Window* 7, no. 1 (Spring 1987): 1. Newsletter published by the Foundation for Ancient Research and Mormon Studies, Provo, UT. Available at Book of Mormon Central: A Division of Scripture Central. https://archive.bookofmormoncentral.org/content/insights-vol-7-no-1-spring-1987.

Tobler, Douglas F. "Before the Wall Fell: Mormons in the German Democratic Republic, 1945–89." *Dialogue: A Journal of Mormon Thought* 25, no. 4 (Winter 1992): 11–30.

———. "The Church in Europe: Challenges of the Second Century, Introduction." In *Mormonism: A Faith for All Cultures,* edited by F. LaMond Tullis, 37–44. Provo, UT: Brigham Young University Press, 1978.

Toro, Juliet. Oral History Interview by James Perry, Feb. 20, 2023. CHL. Transcript in possession of editors.

Toronto, James A., Eric R Dursteler, and Michael W. Homer. *Mormons in the Piazza: History of the Latter-day Saints in Italy*. Provo, UT: Religious Studies Center, Brigham Young University; Salt Lake City: Deseret Book, 2017.

Trachtenberg, Marc. *A Constructed Peace: The Making of the European Settlement, 1945–1963*. Princeton, NJ: Princeton University Press, 1999.

"Transcript and Translation of Ground-Breaking Ceremony for Johannesburg South Africa Temple Held at 7, Jubulee Road, Parktown, on November 27, 1982." Typescript. Johannesburg South Africa Temple History. Clive D. Nicholls, Collection on the History of the Church in South Africa, circa 1982–2008. CHL.

"Tsunami Response Update: Completed Projects," May 2005. Slide presentation. Presiding Bishopric, Welfare Executive Committee Meeting Materials, 2000–2010. CHL.

Tullis, F. LaMond. "Church Development Issues among Latin Americans: Introduction." In *Mormonism: A Faith for All Cultures,* edited by F. LaMond Tullis, 85–105. Provo, UT: Brigham Young University Press, 1978.

———. "The Church Moves outside the United States: Some Observations from Latin America." *Dialogue: A Journal of Mormon Thought* 13, no. 1 (Spring 1980): 63–73.
Turley, Richard E., Jr. *In the Hands of the Lord: The Life of Dallin H. Oaks*. Salt Lake City: Deseret Book, 2021.
———. Oral History Interview by Jed Woodworth, Feb. 25, 2022. CHL. Transcript in possession of editors.
———. *Victims: The LDS Church and the Mark Hofmann Case*. Urbana: University of Illinois Press, 1992.
Turley, Richard E., Jr., and Jeffrey G. Cannon. "A Faithful Band: Moses Mahlangu and the First Soweto Saints." *BYU Studies Quarterly* 55, no. 1 (2016): 9–38.
Turley, Richard E., Jr., and William W. Slaughter. *How We Got the Doctrine and Covenants*. Salt Lake City: Deseret Book, 2012.
Turner, John G. *The Mormon Jesus: A Biography*. Cambridge, MA: Belknap Press of Harvard University Press, 2016.
Turner, Judd. "The Church in Business." *This People* 10 (Summer 1989): 50–53, 55.
Tuttle, A. Theodore. Files, circa 1950–70. CHL.
The Uniform System for Teaching Families. Salt Lake City: The Church of Jesus Christ of Latter-day Saints, 1973.
A Uniform System for Teaching Investigators. Salt Lake City: The Church of Jesus Christ of Latter-day Saints, 1961.
Uniform System for Teaching the Gospel: Instructions for the Discussions. Salt Lake City: The Church of Jesus Christ of Latter-day Saints, 1986.
University of Utah Annual Commencement, 1974: June Eighth, Special Events Center. [Salt Lake City]: [University of Utah, 1974].
Urtnasan, Soyolmaa. Oral History Interview by Michael N. Landon, Sept. 12, 2001. CHL.
Van Orden, Bruce A. *Building Zion: The Latter-day Saints in Europe*. Salt Lake City: Deseret Book, 1996.
Villavicencio, Marco. Email Interview by David Bolingbroke, July 24, 2023. Marco Villavicencio and Claudia Villavicencio, Oral History Interviews, 2023. CHL. English translation in possession of editors.
———. Oral History Interview by David Bolingbroke, Mar. 22, 2023. Marco Villavicencio and Claudia Villavicencio, Oral History Interviews, 2023. CHL. English translation in possession of editors.
Villavicencio, Marco, and Claudia Villavicencio. Email Interviews by David Bolingbroke, 2023. Marco Villavicencio and Claudia Villavicencio, Oral History Interviews, 2023. CHL. English translation in possession of editors.
———. Oral History Interviews by David Bolingbroke, 2023. Marco Villavicencio and Claudia Villavicencio, Oral History Interviews, 2023. CHL. English translation in possession of editors.
Vinckel, Sandrine. "Violence and Everyday Interactions between Katangese and Kasaians: Memory and Elections in Two Katanga Cities." *Africa: Journal of the International African Institute* 85, no. 1 (Feb. 2015): 78–102.
Vo, Nghia M. *The Bamboo Gulag: Political Imprisonment in Communist Vietnam*. Jefferson, NC: McFarland, 2004.
Vojkůvka, Gad M. Oral History Interview by George M. Herrmann and Launa H. Herrmann, Oct. 13, 2010. CHL.
Vojkůvka, Otakar Karel. Statement, Oct. 3, 1990. CHL.
Wagner, Alberto Kenyon, and Leona Farnsworth Romney de Wagner. *Historia del Centro Escolar Benemérito de las Américas, 1963–1975*. Santa Anita, México: Centro Escolar Benemérito de las Américas, 1977.
Walshe, Peter. "Christianity and the Anti-apartheid Struggle: The Prophetic Voice within Divided Churches." In *Christianity in South Africa: A Political, Social and Cultural History*, edited by Richard Elphick and Rodney Davenport, 383–99. Oxford: James Currey, 1997.
Walters, Wesley P. "New Light on Mormon Origins from the Palmyra Revival." *Dialogue: A Journal of Mormon Thought* 4, no. 1 (Spring 1969): 59–81.

Wan, Kathleen. Journal Excerpt, July 26, 1992. CHL.
Wan, Stanley. *The Heavens Are Higher Than the Earth*. [Hong Kong]: China Hong Kong Mission, 2000. Copy at CHL.
———. *Hong Kong Kom Tong Hall: My Old Home*. Hong Kong, 2008.
———. Oral History Interview by Brian Reeves, Oct. 26, 2001. CHL.
———. Oral History Interviews by James Perry or Tesia Tsai, 2022. Stanley Wan and Kathleen Wan, Oral History Interviews, 2022. CHL. Transcript in possession of editors.
Wan, Stanley, and Kathleen Wan. Oral History Interview by Tesia Tsai, Sept. 16, 2022. Stanley Wan and Kathleen Wan, Oral History Interviews, 2022. CHL. Transcript in possession of editors.
Warren, Katherine. Oral History Interview by Alan Cherry, June 12, 1987. BYU.
"Welfare," circa Oct. 2004. Typescript. Relief Society, Anne C. Pingree Relief Society General Presidency Papers, 1992–2008. CHL.
"Welfare Handbook," Mar. 26, 2009. Slide presentation. Presiding Bishopric, First Presidency Meeting Materials, 1985–2013. CHL.
Welfare Services Department. David Frischknecht's Executive Committee Minutes, 2005–19. CHL.
———. Fact Sheets, 1997–2006. CHL.
———. Vietnamese Refugee Files, 1975. CHL.
Welfare Services Executive Committee. Minutes, 1973–2007. Typescript. CHL.
Whitaker, Wetzel O. *Looking Back: An Autobiography*. Publication place unidentified: By the author, circa 1978.
———. *Pioneering with Film: A History of the Church and Brigham Young University Films*. Provo, UT: Brigham Young University, [1982?].
White, Benjamin Hyrum. "The History of *Preach My Gospel*." *Religious Educator* 14, no. 1 (2013): 128–58.
White, Richard. *The Roots of Dependency: Subsistence, Environment, and Social Change among the Choctaws, Pawnees, and Navajos*. Lincoln: University of Nebraska Press, 1983.
Wilberg, Mack J. Oral History Interview by Lisa Christensen, May 12, 2022. CHL.
Wilcox, Brad. "Filling Your Testimony Tank." In *Serving with Strength throughout the World: Favorite Talks from Especially for Youth*, 262–69. Salt Lake City: Deseret Book, 1994.
———. Journal Excerpts, Apr. 1999. Brad Wilcox, Oral History Interviews, 2023. CHL.
———. Oral History Interviews by James Perry, 2023. CHL. Transcript in possession of editors.
———. "Taking the Dead out of Dedication." In *High Fives and High Hopes: Favorite Talks Especially for Youth*, 120–31. Salt Lake City: Deseret Book, 1990.
Wilke, Manfred. *The Path to the Berlin Wall: Critical Stages in the History of Divided Germany*. Translated by Sophie Perl. Berlin: Berghahn Books, 2014.
Wilkinson, Ernest L., ed. *Brigham Young University: The First One Hundred Years*. Vol. 4. Provo, UT: Brigham Young University Press, 1976.
———. Diary. Ernest L. Wilkinson Papers, 1917–78. BYU.
Wilkinson, Ernest L., Jr. Interview by Edward L. Kimball, Nov. 20, 1979. Edward L. Kimball Papers, 1956–2007. CHL.
Williams, LaMar S. Journal, Dec. 1960–Nov. 1965. Typescript. CHL.
———. Papers, 1959–62. CHL.
Williams, LaMar S., and Nyal B. Williams. Oral History Interviews by Gordon Irving, 1981. Photocopy of typescript. CHL.
Wilson, John A. "A Summary Report." *Dialogue: A Journal of Mormon Thought* 3, no. 2 (Summer 1968): 67–85.
Wolsey, Heber G. "A Funny Thing Happened to Me on the Road to the Millennium," after 1987. Typescript. BYU.
Wondra, Johann. Family Papers, 1955–2013. CHL.
Wood, Lorna C. *For the Love of Family: The Personal History of Lowell Dale Wood and Lorna Cox Wood*. Publication place unidentified: By the author, 2007.
Woodger, Mary Jane. "The Hong Kong Temple: A Temple for Every Corner of the World." *Mormon Historical Studies* 21, no. 1 (Spring 2020): 57–90.

———. "The Restoration of the Perpetual Covenant to Hallow the Sabbath Day." In *Foundations of the Restoration: Fulfillment of the Covenant Purposes,* edited by Craig James Ostler, Michael Hubbard MacKay, and Barbara Morgan Gardner, 289–310. Provo, UT: Religious Studies Center, Brigham Young University; Salt Lake City: Deseret Book, 2016.
Woodruff, Wilford. Journals and Papers, 1828–98. CHL.
Woodworth, Charles J. Autobiography, 2010. Charles J. Woodworth Papers, 1948–2009. CHL.
———. "District News." *L. D. S. Newssheet* 1, no. 10 (June 3, 1956): 1–3. Newsletter published by the Niue District of the Tongan Mission of The Church of Jesus Christ of Latter-day Saints. In Niue District Publications, 1955–61. CHL.
———. Mission Journal, 1955–58. Charles J. Woodworth Papers, 1948–2009. CHL.
———. Oral History Interviews by Jed Woodworth, 2008–9. Charles J. Woodworth Papers, 1948–2009. CHL.
———. Papers, 1948–2009. CHL. English translation of portions of letters in possession of editors.
Xi, Feng. "A History of Mormon-Chinese Relations: 1849–1993." PhD diss., Brigham Young University, 1994.
Xue, Charlie Q. L., Hong Jing, and Ka Chuen Hui. "Technology over Public Space: A Study of Roofed Space in the Osaka, Hannover, and Shanghai Expos." *Journal of Architectural and Planning Research* 30, no. 2 (Summer 2013): 108–26.
Yamashita, Kazuhiko. Interviews by Lisa Christensen, Scott A. Hales, and/or Jed Woodworth, 2022. CHL. Transcript in possession of editors.
Young, George Cannon. Oral History Interview by Paul L. Anderson, Dec. 1973. CHL.
Young, Neil J. "'The ERA Is a Moral Issue': The Mormon Church, LDS Women, and the Defeat of the Equal Rights Amendment." *American Quarterly* 59, no. 3 (2007): 623–44.
———. "Mormons and Same-Sex Marriage: From ERA to Prop 8." In *Out of Obscurity: Mormonism since 1945,* edited by Patrick Q. Mason and John G. Turner, 144–69. New York: Oxford University Press, 2016.
Young Women. Carolyn J. Rasmus Office Papers, 1984–93. CHL.
———. Files, 1984–90. CHL.
———. General Board Minutes, 1891–1992, 1997–2008. CHL.
"Young Women: New Beginnings." *Bulletin,* no. 33 (Dec. 1986): 1–2. Newsletter published by Corporation of the President of The Church of Jesus Christ of Latter-day Saints. Copy at CHL.
Young Women Values: A Guide for Leaders of Young Women. Salt Lake City: The Church of Jesus Christ of Latter-day Saints, 1986.
Zimelis, Andris. "Let the Games Begin: Politics of Olympic Games in Mexico and South Korea." *India Quarterly* 67, no. 3 (Sept. 2011): 263–78.
Zwirner, Wolfgang, and Karin Zwirner. "Church or School?" In *Behind the Iron Curtain: Recollections of Latter-day Saints in East Germany, 1945–1989,* compiled and translated by Garold N. Davis and Norma S. Davis, 207–33. Provo, UT: BYU Studies, 1996.

ACKNOWLEDGMENTS

Hundreds of people have contributed to this new history of the Church, and we are grateful to each one of them. We are indebted to the generations of Latter-day Saints who meticulously collected and preserved the records on which this book is based. We thank especially the many living Saints who shared their stories with us and whose names appear in the book.

Special thanks to David Golding, Taunalyn Ford, James Goldberg, David Grua, Melissa Wei-Tsing Inouye, Robin Jensen, Jessica Nelson, Jennifer Reeder, Ryan Saltzgiver, Jonathan Stapley, and Amber Taylor for creating the Church History Topics and Global Histories articles that supplement *Saints*. Thanks also to Hannah Johnson Lenning and John Heath for assisting with the images that accompany the digital version of this book. The digitization of sources was led by Audrey Spainhower Dunshee, Trevor Wylie, Scott Marianno, and Natalie Johnson Pearmain and completed by staff of the Church History Department's Access Services team.

Dozens of staff members, missionaries, and volunteers in the Church History Department contributed directly or indirectly to this book. In particular, we thank the following for their research contributions or for offering feedback on draft material: Jeff Anderson, Jay Burrup, Clint Christensen, Christine Cox, Wayne Crosby, Emily Marie Crumpton, Christian Fingerle, Matthew Heiss, James Miller, Alexander Nunez, Norbert Ounleu, Melanie Riwai-Couch, Javier Romero, Jeremy Talmage, Tyson Thorpe, Soyolmaa Urtnasan, and Todd Welker in the Archives and Area Support Division; Ben Godfrey in the Audience Needs Division; Doris R. Dant, Brett Dowdle, David Grua, Melissa Wei-Tsing Inouye, Robin Jensen, Jonathan Stapley, Sheridan Sylvester, and Amber Taylor in the Publications Division; Jenny Lund, Chad Orton, Benjamin Pykles, Ryan Saltzgiver, Ryan W. Smith, and Emily Utt in the Historic Sites Division; and Justin Bray, Keith Erekson, Matthew Godfrey, and Brandon Metcalf in the Research and Outreach Division. We thank Catherine Reese Newton, Laura Rawlins, Kathryn Burnside, McKinsey Kemeny, Hannah Johnson Lenning, Keaton Reed, Kate Staker, Stephanie Steed, Sam Lambert, Ashley Skinner, and Jessica Lawrence for editorial contributions; Brenda Homer, Benjamin Whisenant, and Sharley McCorristin for assistance with intellectual property and permissions; and Sylvia Coates for indexing the volume.

Many expert readers reviewed chapters or parts of chapters. These include William Acquah, Ralph Addy, James B. Allen, Jeffry Allred, Silvia Allred, Michelle Wright Amos, Olivia Barlow, Betty Jean Baunchand, Severia Baunchand, Dennis Beck, Maeta Holiday Beck, Riley Berones, Lilly Binene, Willy Binene, Brent Bonham, Georges A. Bonnet, Matthew Bowman, Jeffrey M. Bradshaw, Marilyn Rolapp Brinton, R. Lanier Britsch, Stanley Warren Bronson, Tracy Y. Browning, Tobias Burkhardt, H. David Burton, Milton Camargo, Olga Kovářová Campora, Joe Chelladurai, Michael Colemere, Felicindo Contreras, Veronica Contreras, Ahmad S. Corbitt, Virginia Hinckley Pearce Cowley, Michelle D. Craig, Celia Ayala de Cruz, J. Anette Dennis, Jill Mulvay Derr, Ann Monson Dibb, Geoffrey Dunning, Suzette Towse Dunning, Allen Erekson, Sharon Eubank, Angela Peterson Fallentine, Ike Ferguson, Garry Flake, David Galbraith, Matthew Garrett, Sariah Goury, Darius Gray, Casey Griffiths, Angela

Hallstrom, Alice Johnson Haney, Laura Harper, Steven C. Harper, J. B. Haws, Emma Hernandez, Hector David Hernandez, Greg Hill, Laura Paulsen Howe, James Jacob, Daniel K Judd, Arthur Jue, Daniel Jue, Ardeth Greene Kapp, Allwyn Kilbert, Farina King, Raymond Kuehne, Le My Lien, Emily Limb, Laudy Kaouk Lindsey, Anne Lu, Steven J. Lund, Ken Macey, Juan Machuca, Louise Paulsen Manning, Marcus Martins, Patrick Mason, Carl Maurer, William Maycock, Neylan McBaine, David McCombs, Elizabeth Manning McCombs, Mary McKenna, Blake McKeown, Kara McKeown, Scott McKeown, Wade McKeown, Khumbulani Mdletshe, Kahlile Mehr, Tarienne Mitchell, Consuelo Wong Moreno, Ronald Mortensen, Silvina Mouhsen, Paula Muti, Manuel Navarro, Corine Jue Neumiller, Eugene Orr, Bonnie L. Oscarson, Alan Osmond, Jay Osmond, Michael Otterson, Bonnie D. Parkin, Eryn Phillips, Anne C. Pingree, Carolyn Rasmus, Delia Rochon, Isabel Santana, Manfred Schütze, LuAnn Snow, Franck Yohann Sokora, Maridan Sollesta, Seb Sollesta, Marie Taylor, Nguyen Van The, Ruth Todd, Juliet Toro, Richard E. Turley Jr., Lorine Jue Turnbull, Laurel Thatcher Ulrich, Claudia Villavicencio, Marco Villavicencio, Gád Vojkůvka, Kathleen Wan, Stanley Wan, Annaliese White, Bradley R. Wilcox, Steve Williams, and Kazuhiko Yamashita. We thank Casey Olson, Brian Garner, Benjamin Peterson, and Matt Lund of the Correlation Department's Evaluation Division as well as their review committee members. We also thank Derek Roughton, Renee Furgeson, and Jeffrey Mahas for assistance with oral histories; and Jeffrey R. Bradshaw, Judith Romo, Sherida Marshall, and Bonnie Linck for assistance with translation of research materials.

John Heath, Debra Abercrombie, and Matt Rasmussen contributed to publicity and outreach. Brooke Jurges provided administrative expertise, and Jo Lyn Curtis and Cindy Pond offered additional support.

Many members of the Publishing Services Department assisted in the publication process, including Cathy Cooper, Katie Parker, Patric Gerber, Ivan Gavarret, Preston Shewell, Andrea Bird, Bret Morris, Benson Y. Parkinson, Michael Wright, and Travis Stevens. Other contributors include Alan Paulsen, Paul VanDerHoeven, David Morris, Michelle Karrick, and Dragonfly Editorial. Translators carefully prepared the entire text in thirteen languages. Jen Ward coordinated printing of the books by the Materials Management Department.

We especially thank Elders Marlin K. Jensen, Steven E. Snow, and LeGrand R. Curtis Jr., emeritus General Authority Seventies who each served as Church Historian and Recorder and who believed in the *Saints* project and did much to foster it. We thank Elder Kyle S. McKay, present Church Historian and Recorder, for his guiding hand on the project.

INDEX

Aaronic Priesthood. *See* priesthood
Aba Nigeria Temple, 598–99
abortion, 299
Abrea, Angel, 481
Accra Ghana Temple
    building permit for, 516–17, 526–29
    dedication (2004) of, 556–59
    Georges A. Bonnet asked to find barriers to progress, 515–18
    Gordon B. Hinckley announces, 516–17
Acosta, Emma, 574–77, 592–95, 634–36
Acquah, Charlotte, 419
Acquah, William, 418–22, 437
Addy, Isaac, 437, 516, 527–29
ADIR (humanitarian organization), 606–7, 629
adoption, 617
Afghanistan, 570
Africa
    Church growth over a thirty-year period, 581–83
    obstacles to missionary work in 1950s, 8
    See also specific countries
Africare, 409–10
Agu, Charles, 88–91, 125, 136
AIDS epidemic statement (1988), 459
Aki, Sai Lang, 5
All-Church Coordinating Council
    on challenge of writing correlated lessons, 124
    creation and purpose of, 78–79, 111
    priesthood executive committees and ward councils created by, 123
    See also Correlation Committee
Allen, James, 181
Allred, Jeff
    attending San Salvador Temple dedication, 641–44
    challenges of moving to Guatemala, 25, 336–35
    moving to Costa Rica, 342–44
    serving as mission leader in Paraguay, 456–59
    serving as MTC president in Dominican Republic, 586
Allred, Silvia H.
    attending San Salvador Temple dedication, 642–44
    challenges of moving to Guatemala, 337–38
    Primary and new Church schedule concerns of, 342
    relocating to Church's temporal affairs office in Costa Rica, 342–44
    service in Relief Society general presidency, 586–87, 641–42
    serving as mission leader in Paraguay, 456–59

    on sharing vision of Relief Society with sisters, 587–89
Amado, Carlos H., 481
'Amasio, 'Atonio, 12–13
American Samoa, 151
Amparo, Eddie, 624
Amparo, Mercedes, 624
Ampiah, Ato, 419–22
Ampiah, Elizabeth, 419–22
Andersen, Kathy, 651
Andersen, Neil L., 650–51
Anderson, Joseph, 187
Andoh-Kesson, Charlotte, 219
Andoh-Kesson, Jacob, 218–19
Andoh-Kesson, Lily, 219–19
apartheid (South Africa), 348–49
Apel, Frank, 354
the Apostasy, 80
area general conferences, 238–43
Argentina
    Buenos Aires Temple in, 458
    continued growth of Church in, 55, 113, 370
    Quilmes meetinghouse in, 112
    Spencer W. Kimball's tour (1959) of, 55
Argentine Mission, 55, 113
Arlene (Zuni girl), 254
Arrington, Leonard, 181
article of faith, twelfth, 296
Ashton, Marvin J., 307, 360
Asia. *See specific countries*
"As Zion's Youth in Latter Days" (hymn), 383
Atiya, Aziz, 149–50, 162
Atkerson, Ervin, 69
Atonement of Jesus Christ
    Ezra Taft Benson's message on, 414
    Georges A. Bonnet testifying of power of, 526
    Preach My Gospel passage on, 567
    See also Jesus Christ
Auditorio Nacional (Mexico City), 238–42
Australia
    Bondi Rescue (reality television show) in, 583–84, 604–5
    Time for Youth (TFY) held in, 554–56, 603
Austria, 25, 445
The Awakening (Relief Society filmstrip), 110
Ayala, Eduardo, 481
Ayaviri, Antonio, 547
Ayaviri, Gloria, 547

Backman, Milton, 180, 182
Balenagasau, Sera, 518–19

Ballard, Melvin J., 370
Ballard, M. Russell, 408, 461–62, 658
Bangerter, Grant, 104–6, 133, 284–85
Bankhead, Lucile, 199, 214
baptism
    infant, 15–17
    placing greater emphasis on conversion before, 532
    priesthood authority and, 11
    requirements for, 60, 323
    requiring husband's permission for, 288
    women serving as witnesses during, 657
    See also converts
Barbados, 625
Bauer, Roy, 524
Baunchand, Betty, 321–23
Baunchand, Severia, 322–23
Beaulieu, Freda, 287, 321–22
Beck, Dennis, 257–59
Beck, Julie B.
    Relief Society history presented to, 586–87
    on sharing vision of Relief Society with sisters, 587–89
    sustained as Relief Society general president, 586
Beck, Wayne, 104–5, 131, 139–40
Bednar, David A., 533
Benemérito de las Américas school (Mexico), 150, 152–53, 168–71, 239, 241
Benson, Ezra Taft
    addressing the press on his new presidency, 385, 387–88
    applauding presentation for future of Young Women, 367
    asking the Saints to read the Book of Mormon, 394–96
    on Book of Mormon as keystone in witness of Jesus Christ, 395–96
    death and legacy of, 459–60
    at Hill Cumorah, 393–94
    ordained as president of Church (1985), 385
    on receiving confirmation to lift priesthood restriction, 307
    response to Church registration in Russia, 447
    singing to children, 415
    Thomas S. Monson reads conference message (1989) of, 413–15
Berlin Wall, 75–76, 171
Beverley Branch (United Kingdom), 93–96, 120
Bidamon, Lewis, 150
Binene, Lilly, 580, 605, 607–8, 650–52
Binene, Willy Sabwe
    called as branch missionary in DRC, 491–93
    called to serve in Côte d'Ivoire Abidjan Mission, 650
    career aspirations of, 453

on completion of water pipeline, 627–30
    delivering tithing of Luputa Saints to district president, 475–77
    desire to serve mission, 453–54
    local violence forcing family to flee, 455–56, 474–77
    serving as Luputa District president, 580–81, 605–6
Bingham, Jean B., 654
Black, Larry, 166
Black, Lucy, 166, 190, 259
Black, Spencer, 166, 236, 238, 258–59
Black, Venna, 189–92, 236–38, 258–59
Black Saints
    Elders Hinckley, Monson, and Packer's discussion on priesthood issue with, 207–8
    Freedman's Bank genealogy project's value to, 433–36, 466–69, 534–37
    Genesis Group organized for, 213–15, 435
    Helvécio Martins's question to missionaries about, 231
    holding priesthood in early days of Church, 205
    Martinses' devotion to Church despite priesthood restriction, 251–53
    reactions to revelation on receiving priesthood and temple blessings, 308–12, 318–23
    Salt Lake City's community of, 199–200
    Spencer W. Kimball asked about priesthood and, 56
    struggle with priesthood restriction, 205–8
    See also priesthood and temple restriction
Bodden, Noemí, 624
Bodden, Rodolfo, 624
Bolivia, 103, 386, 389, 409, 428
Bolshoi Theater (Moscow), 446
Bondi Rescue (Australian reality television show), 583–84
Bonham, Brent, 565, 567–68, 573
Bonham, Robin, 565, 567–68
Bonnet, Georges A., 437–38, 515–18, 526–29, 556–59
Book of Abraham (Pearl of Great Price), 149–50, 162, 180
Book of Mormon
    "Another Testament of Jesus Christ" subtitle, 395
    and conversion in Caribbean, 624–25
    conversion results from stolen copy of, 472–74, 477–79
    edition with maps, footnotes, and cross-references (1981), 386
    Ezra Taft Benson asking that Saints read, 394–96
    giving promise that all commandments may be accomplished, 250
    Hélio da Rocha Camargo's study of, 26

Index

Hugh Nibley's evidence on authenticity of, 162, 180–81
Hugh Nibley's scholarship in support of, 405
Katherine Warren's belief in, 286–87
as keystone in witness of Jesus Christ, 395–96
Korean translation published in 1967, 157
Luputa Branch missionaries threatened with burning of, 492
missionaries teaching about, 457–58
nine films to supplement Sunday School lessons, 478
Olga Kovářová family's love for, 373
presented to Queen Elizabeth II by Olive Osmond, 233–35
purchased by Yamashita brothers, 195
read in Ghana's unofficial congregations, 220
scripture mastery, 390
translated into Indigenous languages, 336
translated into Vietnamese, 270
Washington DC Temple Visitors' Center display of, 578
at world's fair in Japan, 210
See also Church publications
Boston Massachusetts Temple, 530
Bountiful Utah Temple, 608
Bowser, Suzanne, 639–40
Bradford, Reed, 84
Brazil
  Black Saints restricted from holding priesthood in, 8, 27, 56
  Church publications central editorial office established in, 132–33, 143
  Cristo Redentor statue in, 53
  fewer racial divides than in U.S., 27
  fifth stake organized in, 251
  growth of Church in, 494
  new stake in São Paulo, 139–40, 143–46
  number of Saints (1950s) in, 26
  revelation on all worthy men holding priesthood comes to, 318–21
  São Paulo Second Ward in, 145–46, 368
  Spencer W. Kimball's tour (1959) of, 55, 92
Brazilian Mission, 103–6, 139–40
BRD. *See* Federal Republic of Germany (BRD)
Bridgeforth, Helena, 200
Bridgeforth, Ruffin, 200, 205–8, 213–15
Brigham Young University
  Ardeth Kapp's work as faculty at, 247
  "The Family: A Proclamation to the World" course given at, 560
  Fiji LDS Technical College distance learning program, 509–10, 518–20
  Founders Day (1975), 277, 280–81
  J. Reuben Clark Law School founded at, 280
  Maeta Holiday in Lamanite Generation at, 257

Religious Studies Center of, 405
scholarship fund for Nigerian students, 125
Spencer W. Kimball on upholding Church standards at, 280–81
student population and honor code of, 279–80
University of Wyoming controversy with, 200–202
See also BYU–Pathway Worldwide program
Brigham Young University–Hawaii, 279
Brigham Young University–Idaho
  BYU–Pathway Worldwide program piloted at, 653
  converting Ricks College into, 532–33
  See also Ricks College (Idaho)
Brigham Young University Jerusalem Center
  approval of site for, 355–57
  David Galbraith's work to establish, 355–57
  efforts to generate goodwill toward, 400
  opened to eighty students (1987), 399–401
  Orthodox Jews protesting against (1985), 376–78, 400
  Spencer W. Kimball's desire to build, 334, 355–56
  See also Jerusalem
Brimah, Hetty, 416–18
British Broadcasting Corporation (BBC), 312
British Mission, 50, 70, 72
Brno Branch (Czechoslovakia), 357
Bronson, Stan, 157–59, 177
Brough, Lanette, 450
Brough, Monte J., 450–51
Brown, Hugh B.
  informing Harold B. Lee of Henry D. Moyle's death, 98
  reservations about correlation plan, 97
  role in civil rights statement issued by Church, 101–2
  as third counselor in First Presidency, 85
Brown, Victor L., 131–32
Budapest Opera House (Hungary), 443–44
Buenos Aires Argentina Temple, 458
building program. *See* Church building program
Bulgaria, 444
Burkhardt, Henry
  arrested by GDR police, 42–46
  attending Freiberg Temple dedication (1985), 373–75
  attending Görlitz district conference (1968), 171–73
  called as president of Dresden Mission, 182–84
  called as president of Freiberg Temple, 373
  concerns over Berlin Wall, 75–76, 171
  concerns over East German Saints (1960s), 64–67
  on continued work of God, 76

discussion with GDR officials on building
  temple in GDR, 297–98
frustration dealing with GDR government, 172–73
invited to attend general conference, 267–70
positive interaction with government informant,
  295–96
role in selecting temple site in Freiberg (GDR),
  352–55
sealed to wife in Swiss Temple, 373
Spencer W. Kimball's advice on GDR to,
  269–70, 298
Burkhardt, Inge, 44, 172, 182, 267–69, 354, 373, 375
Burkhardt, Tobias, 172
Burton, H. David, 516–17
Burton, Linda K., 555
Bushman, Richard, 159–60
Busto, Marilena Kretly Pretel, 546–47
Butler Stake Relief Society (Salt Lake City), 110
BYU. *See* Brigham Young University
BYU–Pathway Worldwide program, 653
BYU Studies (journal), 180–82, 405

California marriage proposition (2008), 638–39
Call, Roger, 11–12
Camargo, Hélio da Rocha
  brings son for priesthood blessing, 56
  called to serve as São Paulo Second Ward
    bishop, 145–46
  comparing function of branch to race car, 133
  conversion process and baptism of, 26–28, 31–33
  doubts about infant baptism, 15–17
  hired to manage Church publications in Brazil,
    132–33
  introduction to gospel, 10–12
  mission leadership responsibilities of, 103–6
  opening Church's Brazilian central editorial
    office, 143
  serving in Brazilian Mission presidency, 103
  sustained as First Quorum of the Seventy
    member, 369
  witnesses organization of new São Paulo
    Stake, 144
Camargo, Josué, 16
Camargo, Milton, 56
Camargo, Nair
  desire for additional study of gospel, 32
  family of, 12
  Spencer W. Kimball's blessing given to son
    of, 56
  supporting husband on infant baptism issue,
    16–17
  visiting Utah and entering Salt Lake Temple,
    132–33
  working in Primary, 105

Cambodia, 470
Cameroon, 598–99
Campbell, Beverly, 446
Campi, Betty, 370
Canada, 188, 247, 408, 560
Cannon, Edwin, 318, 324
Cannon, George I., 425–26
Cannon, Janath, 318
Cape Coast (Ghana), 438
Caribbean, 624–27
"Carry On" (hymn), 384
Carthage jail (Illinois), 462
Cathedral of the Madeleine (Salt Lake City), 610–11
Central Europe, 401
Centro Escolar Benemérito de las Américas
  (Mexico), 150, 152–53, 168–71, 368
Charles, Ezzard, 40
Chavez, Bertha, 546
Chenche, Lourdes, 632
Chennai, India, 571–73
children
  Ezra Taft Benson seeking to comfort, 415
  "One in a Million" video series with, 632–34
  See also Primary
Chile
  concerns about retaining recent converts in,
    485–86
  growth of Church in, 55
  Jeffrey R. Holland called as president of area,
    551, 563–64
  low rate of youth attending institute in, 538
  missionaries entering (1950s), 55
  Santiago Temple in, 369, 485, 502
  welfare training in, 562–65
Christensen, Jess L., 578
Christofferson, D. Todd, 512
Christus statue (Thorvaldsen), 193, 522, 578
Chukwurah, Christopher N., 550
Chukwurah, Florence, 550
Chuquimango, Guillermo, 427–30
Church Administration Building, 25
Church building program
  David O. McKay's expansion of, 68–70
  Denton, Texas, Saints apply for meetinghouse
    to, 68
  expansion in South America (1959) of, 54
  to serve local Saints, 15
  See also labor missionaries; meetinghouses
Church Educational System
  adapting institutes to operate as part of, 537–40
  BYU–Pathway Worldwide program, 653
  Centro Escolar Benemérito de las Américas
    school (Mexico), 150, 152–53, 168–71
  closing Church schools, 537–38
  early-morning seminary (Peru), 389–90

Juárez Academy (Mexico), 493
Perpetual Education Fund (PEF) program of, 533, 576, 594–94, 600, 634–36, 653
Church Handbook of Instructions, 562, 588–89, 596, 641
Church Historical Department, 222
Church History Library, 601
Church humanitarian projects
Ezra Taft Benson's expansion of, 459
fast to raise funds for Ethiopia famine (1985), 408
Haiti earthquake (2010), 626–27
under Howard W. Hunter's authority, 464
Indian Ocean tsunami disaster (2004), 568–73
Isaac "Ike" Ferguson sent to check on, 407–10
Latter-day Saint Charities, 606–7
to pipe clean water into Luputa (DRC), 606–7, 627–30
providing disaster relief around world, 570
reforestation project in Niger, 409
Thomas S. Monson on partnering with Catholics on, 610–13
See also Church Welfare Services; people in need
Church schools
Centro Escolar Benemérito de las Américas (Mexico), 150, 152–53, 168–71, 239, 241
in Mexico, 152
moving toward institutes and seminaries instead, 537–38
operating in South Pacific and Chile, 151
See also Brigham Young University; institutes and seminaries
Church sports teams, 73–74, 86, 121–22
Church standards
David O. McKay on happiness by living, 155
law of chastity, 312
LGBTQ issues and, 638–40
Spencer W. Kimball on BYU upholding, 280–81
Thomas S. Monson's concerns over drift away from, 638
Word of Wisdom, 27, 58–60, 225
Church Welfare Services
Basic Principles of Welfare and Self-Reliance (publication), 612
as "fourth leg of stool" of Church mission, 612–13
improving ward-level cooperation on, 562–65
inspired of God, 612
partnering with relief agencies, 408–9
providing counseling with trained therapists, 591
See also Church humanitarian projects; people in need
Cifuentes, Carlos, 369–70
Cifuentes, Elsa, 369
civil rights, 100–103. *See also* racial divides
Clark, J. Reuben, 7–9, 24, 85
Clegg, Dezzie, 58–59

Clegg, Naomi, 419
Clegg, Reed, 419
Cochabamba Bolivia Temple, 547
Colombia, 185, 570
Colonia Juárez, Mexico, 493
Colonia Juárez Chihuahua Mexico Temple, 545–46
Colonia Suiza Branch (Uruguay), 119
Colton, Ellie, 299–301
Columbian Exposition (1893), 111
"Come, Come, Ye Saints" (hymn), 272
Come, Follow Me, 656
Conference Center, 531, 543, 636
Confucius, 332
Cong Ton Nu Tuong-Vy, 270
Contreras, Felicindo, 484–86, 502–5, 537
Contreras, Veronica, 484–86, 502, 537–40
converts
concerns about retaining recent, 485–86
David O. McKay on focusing on fellowshipping, 86, 121–22
Gordon B. Hinckley's admonition on fellowshipping, 631
See also baptism
Cordon, Bonnie H., 660
Correlation Committee
Harold B. Lee's leadership of, 86, 88, 96–99, 111
plan presented to First Presidency and Quorum of the Twelve by, 96–97
Ruth Funk's appointment and contributions to, 84–85, 122–25
Thomas S. Monson's appointment to, 85
See also All-Church Coordinating Council
correlation programs
Belle Spafford's support of Relief Society, 109–11, 124–25, 198
components of, 96–97
curriculum to be organized by age group, 79
David O. McKay on benefits of, 156–57
General Handbook of Instructions published as part of, 241
Harold B. Lee speaking on new, 77–79, 97
Harold B. Lee's proposed changes under, 86, 88
home teaching and family home evening, 123–24
inspiration leading to, 79
presented to First Presidency and Quorum of the Twelve, 96–97
proposed expansion over missionary program, 86–88
reservations by Henry D. Moyle to proposed, 97–98
to unify (1961) Church curriculum, 77–79
See also Church publications
Costa Rica, 55
Côte d'Ivoire, 581, 650–52

811

Cottle, Archie, 34
Couric, Katie, 513
COVID-19 pandemic, 661–63
Crank, Evelyn, 165–66, 191–92, 259
Croatia, 444
Cruz, Celia Ayala de, 472–74, 477–79
cultural differences
   at Benemérito de las Américas school (Mexico), 153, 169
   Brazil and U.S. racial divides, 27
   developing a "gospel culture" to overcome, 552
   Gold and Green Ball (Hong Kong) example of, 52–53
   language as barrier to Church attendance in Philippines, 482
   Southern Far East Mission challenges related to, 38, 52–53
Cumorah's Southern Messenger (South African mission magazine), 197
curriculum correlation. *See* correlation program
Cutler, Virginia, 174
Czechoslovakia
   baptism and confirmation of Olga Kovářová in, 357–60
   Brno Branch in, 357
   government forces missionaries (1950) to leave, 346
   new government established (1989) in, 424
   official recognition of Church (1991) in, 444
   Otakar Vojkůvka sharing gospel in, 344–47
   protests and general strike called (1989) in, 422–24
   Russell M. Nelson working to have Church officially recognized by, 423
   Tabernacle Choir tour (1991) through, 445
Cziep, Hermine, 25

Daddy Big Boots: Stan Bronson and the Song Jook Won Girls (album), 159
Daughters in My Kingdom: The History and Work of Relief Society, 642
Davenport, Randy, 265–67
Democratic Republic of the Congo (DRC)
   announcement of new temple in, 647
   Church-funded project to pipe clean water into Luputa in, 606–7, 627–30
   Church growth in, 581
   Kinshasa Mission and Kinshasa Stake, 490
   Luputa Branch, 491–93, 644–47, 651–52
   Luputa District, 580–81, 605–6
   Zaire government collapse and renaming, 490
   See also Zaire
Denton, Texas, Saints in, 68–69
de Queiroz, Walter Guedes, 143

Derricott, Leitha, 200
Der Stern (Church's German-language magazine), 45
Deseret News (newspaper), 88, 100, 308–9
Didier, Charles A., 431
Dipty, Mangal Dan, 254
Doctrine and Covenants
   comforting Olive Osmond, 235
   edition with maps, footnotes, and cross-references (1981), 386
   Hélio da Rocha Camargo's study of, 26
   on "lifting up your voices unto this people," 300
   publishing revelation extending priesthood and temple blessings, 386
   on Quorum of the Twelve and Seventy, 279
   sections 137 and 138 included in new edition of, 386
Dominican Republic, 624
Dresden Mission (GDR), 182–84
Dunning, Geoff, 94, 96, 120–22
Dyer, Alvin R., 65–66

Eastern Europe, 401
East German Saints
   Berlin Wall's impact on, 75–76, 171
   continued faith of, 76
   denied visas to attend Swiss Temple, 173, 297–98
   increased number by 1968, 184
   leaving GDR, 65
   restrictions placed on (1950s–1960s) by GDR, 44, 65–67, 183
   Spencer W. Kimball's talk to, 296
   Thomas S. Monson's promise of gospel blessings to, 173
   See also German Democratic Republic (GDR)
Ecuador, 598, 615–16, 620–23
Ekong, Honesty John, 61–63, 80–81
Ekpenyong, Atim, 125
El Coca, Ecuador, Saints in
   Marco Villavicencio helping to organize, 615–16, 620–23
   Marco Villavicencio made president of Orellana Branch, 621–22
   missionaries coming to teach, 620
   "One in a Million" video series featuring, 632–34
   watching conference live, 623
Elijah Able "family file," 468
Elizabeth II (queen of Great Britain), 233–35
El Salvador
   Church humanitarian work in, 570
   missionaries entering (1940s), 55
   San Salvador Temple dedication in, 641–44
Encyclopedia of Mormonism, 405

Index

Endowed from on High (manual), 607
endure to the end, 323
Ensign (Church magazine), 197
Equal Rights Amendment, U.S. (1972), 261, 298–301, 339
Especially for Youth (EFY), 505–8, 554
Espi, Dignardino, 420–27
Estonia, 445
Ethiopian famine humanitarian fast (1985), 408
Europe
    outreach centers for young adult singles in, 599
    Russell M. Nelson assigned to open up central, 401
    See also specific countries
"Every Member a Missionary," 70, 86
Ewudzie, James, 220–21
Expo '70 (Japan), 192–95, 210
Eyring, Henry B., 520, 522, 535, 600

Fakahoa, Langi, 20
Fallentine, Angela Peterson, 559–61, 577–79, 608–10, 617–20
Fallentine, John, 608–10, 617
families
    Binene family sealed in temple, 605, 607–8
    change to Sunday meeting schedules to help, 655–56
    counseling Filipino Saints against taking job and leaving, 553–54
    Emma Hernandez sealed to, 634–35
    focusing reactivation efforts on, 552–54
    Gordon B. Hinckley testifying about importance of, 578
    Katherine Warren sharing gospel with, 321–23
    Martins family sealed in temple, 320–21
    of Olga Kovářová sealed in temple, 423
    Sitati family sealed in temple, 583
    See also temples
"The Family: A Proclamation to the World"
    Angela Peterson Fallentine's efforts to understand, 559, 561, 618–19
    description and contents of, 483–84
    Middle Eastern official introduced to, 578–79, 620
    video of Gordon B. Hinckley testifying on families, 578
Family History Department
    authorized to create searchable family history database, 511–14
    Personal Ancestral File (PAF) developed by, 500
    Rick Turley managing director of, 499–502
    simpler way of submitting names for temple work, 501
    TempleReady program developed by, 467–68, 500

    working to streamline submitting names for temple, 501
Family History Library
    Freedman's Bank records in, 433–36, 466–69, 534–37
    TempleReady program, 467
    Utah State Prison family history center, 435–36, 466–69
family home evening, 123–24
FamilySearch.org, 511–14, 535
Faust, James E., 295, 466, 496
Federal Republic of Germany (BRD), 43, 65, 444. *See also* German Democratic Republic (GDR); Germany
Felix, Barbara, 114
Felix, John, 114
Felix Family, 114, 215
Ferguson, Isaac ("Ike"), 407–10
Ferrante, Girolamo, 141–42
Ferrante, Salvatore, 140–42
Fetzer, Emil, 374–75
Fetzer, Percy K., 76
Fiji
    Gordon B. Hinckley announces new temple in, 509
    government coup (2000) in, 523
    Juliet and Iliesa Toro investigate Church in, 508–11
    LDS Technical College distance learning program in, 509–10, 518–20
    Saints awaiting construction of a temple in, 509
    Suva Temple in, 523–25
Finland, 445
First Presidency
    AIDS epidemic statement (1988) issued by, 459
    announcing lifting of priesthood restriction, 308–9, 625
    approve creation of São Paulo Stake (Brazil), 140
    calling on Saints to keep Sabbath holy, 108
    concerns over Nigerian Saints and priesthood restriction, 134–35
    David O. McKay's changes in counselors of, 85
    fasting and praying for Spencer W. Kimball's successful surgery, 228
    featured in *Special Witnesses of Christ* (Church film), 521–22
    "The Living Christ: The Testimony of the Apostles" declaration of, 520–21, 531
    missionary work traditionally directed by, 87–88
    priesthood correlation plan presented to, 96–97
    Priesthood Executive Council policy recommendations to, 365–67
    reviewing status of projects with Presiding Bishopric, 602

813

sends Isaac "Ike" Ferguson to check on
   humanitarian projects, 407–10
 on threefold mission of Church, 388
 Truman Madsen's request for First Vision
   research funds from, 162–63
First Quorum of the Seventy
 Doctrine and Covenants on Quorum of the
   Twelve being helped by, 279
 establishment of, 386
 members from outside United States, 481
 new policy on members of receiving emeritus
   status, 340
First Vision
 BYU Studies publishing research on, 180–82
 historical evidence supporting truth of, 179–82
 Katherine Warren's belief in, 286
 refuting scholarly attacks on, 159–63
 See also Smith, Joseph
Fischer, Mrs., 295–96
Fisher, Glen, 71
Flake, Garry, 570–71
Flammer, Mildred, 302
Flammer, Philip, 302
Fleming, Frances, 199
Fleming, Monroe, 199
Flores, Walter, 458
forgiveness, 349–50, 352
For the Strength of Youth (pamphlet), 155
For the Strength of Youth (FSY) conferences, 656
Foundation for Ancient Research and Mormon
 Studies, 405
Founders Day, BYU (1975), 277, 280–81
Francesca, Vincenzo di, 128–29
Freedman's Bank genealogy project
 description and start of, 433–36
 presentation reporting on outcomes of, 534–37
 TempleReady used to clear names for temple
   ordinances from, 468
 Utah State Prison family history center working
   on, 435–36, 466–69
Freiberg Temple (GDR), 373–75, 423
French Guiana, 625
Friend (Church magazine), 197
Fritz, Albert, 101–3
Fukuoka Japan Temple, 547
Funk, Marcus, 83
Funk, Ruth
 asked to serve on Correlation Committee,
   83–85, 122–30
 called as general president of Young Women,
   249
 "My Personal Progress" program under, 314
 on new curriculum for women, 124–25
Fyans, Thomas, 92

Galbraith, David, 244, 246, 334, 355–57, 399–401
Garcia, Virgilio, 480
Garden Tomb (Jerusalem), 245
Garmendia, Leonor Esther, 169
General Handbook of Instructions, 241
General Handbook: Serving in The Church of
 Jesus Christ of Latter-day Saints, 656–57
Genesis Group, 213–15, 435
German Democratic Republic (GDR)
 Berlin Wall constructed by, 75–76, 171
 division of West Germany and, 43
 Freiberg Temple built in, 373–75, 423
 Görlitz district conference (1968) held in, 171–73
 Henry Burkhardt arrested by police of, 42–46
 new Dresden Mission organized in, 182–84
 release of all missionaries (1960) in, 66
 restrictions placed on Church (1950s–1960s) in,
   44, 65–67, 183
 reunited with West Germany, 444
 Spencer W. Kimball's talk to Dresden Saints
   in, 296
 Thomas S. Monson's visit to, 354–55
 See also Federal Republic of Germany (BRD);
   Germany
Germany
 reunification of, 444
 Tabernacle Choir tour (1991) through, 445
 See also Federal Republic of Germany (BRD);
   German Democratic Republic (GDR)
Ghana
 Accra Ghana District in, 436
 Africare consulting on Church welfare farm in
   Abomosu, 409–10
 Billy Johnson's commitment to gospel in,
   174–77, 218–21
 Billy Johnson's response to criticism of Church
   in, 262–64
 Church growth after lifting priesthood restriction
   in, 438–39, 517, 581
 condition of Saints during freeze of Church
   activities in, 436–37
 Gordon B. Hinckley and Saints attending cultural
   event in, 556–57
 government freeze of all Church activities
   (1989) in, 416–22
 growth of Cape Coast congregations (1972) in,
   218–21
 James Ewudzie's dream that missionaries would
   come to, 221
 lifting of government freeze in, 437
 Saints arrested for preaching in Cape Coast,
   220–21, 437
 support for Church (2002) by president of,
   558–59

Index

unofficial congregations organized in, 173, 281–83
Ghana Accra Mission, 409, 438
Gibbons, Francis, 246
Giurintano, Antonino, 127–30, 140–41
Godhead, 11, 80
Gold and Green Ball (Hong Kong, 1959), 51–53
Gong, Gerrit W., 664
"Good Samaritan" program (Cathedral of the Madeleine), 610
Görlitz district conference, GDR (1968), 171–73
gospel culture, 552
Gospel Essentials Sunday School class, 504
Gospel Library app, 653
Gospel Literacy Effort, 549–50
Gospel Principles (Church Sunday School manual), 336
Grade, Lew, 233–34
Granda, Ana, 390
Grant, Heber J., 9
Gray, Darius
    appointed first counselor of Genesis Group, 214
    bearing testimony during Genesis Group meeting, 215
    on being a Black member of Church, 201–2
    discussions of priesthood restriction, 205–8, 213
    and Freedman's Bank genealogy project, 433–36, 466–69, 534–37
    helping with BYU race-related controversy, 200–202
    introduction and conversion to gospel, 114–17, 198
    response to lifting of priesthood restriction, 308–10
Gray, Elsie, 115
Great Britain. *See* United Kingdom
Green, Matt, 584
Grenada, 625
Guadeloupe, 625
Guam, 6
Guatemala
    Book of Mormon translated into Indigenous languages of, 336
    Church growth in, 335–38
    Churchwide meeting schedule helping Saints in, 337–38
    Gordon B. Hinckley dedicates temple in, 367
    Guatemala City Temple, 367–68, 574–75, 593, 634–35
    Jeff and Silvia Allred move their family to, 334–35
    missionaries entering (1940s), 55
Guatemala City Temple in, 367–68, 574–75, 593, 634–35
Gunnell, Grant, 438

Haight, David B., 306
Haiti, 625–27
Hale, Arta, 30
Hamilton New Zealand Temple
    built to serve local Saints, 15
    dedication of, 47–48
    Fallentines working as ordinance workers in, 609
    fifty years since dedication of, 609
    financial challenge of traveling to, 36
    labor missionaries helping to build, 46, 48
    Muti family's trip to, 36–37, 39–42, 46–48
    See also New Zealand
Han In Sang, 481
Hanks, Marion D., 154
Harris, Elaine, 586–87
Hawaii Temple, 15, 448
Haycock, Arthur, 187, 206–7, 254–55
Heaton, Grant, 5, 38, 58, 488
Heaton, Luana, 5, 37
Hebrew University of Jerusalem, 356
Hernandez, Emma. *See* Acosta, Emma
Hernandez, Hector David, 574–75, 592–95, 634–36
Hillam, Harold, 32
Hill Cumorah Pageant, 394
Hinckley, Gordon B.
    as additional counselor in First Presidency, 363
    on anniversary of martyrdom of Joseph and Hyrum Smith, 461–62
    attending Suva Fiji Temple dedication, 524–25
    on benefits and negatives of internet, 532
    blessing given to Harold B. Lee by, 246
    broadcasting general conference (1980) from Whitmer farm, 338–41
    on challenges of early and modern Church, 462
    Church growth during life of, 530–31
    closing remarks at Young Women's satellite broadcast (1985), 384–85
    conducting first Genesis Group meeting (1971), 214–15
    counseling Saints following September 11 attacks, 542–43
    death and legacy of, 597–600
    dedicating South Vietnam for gospel (1967), 155
    desire to provide education and career training to youth, 532–33
    discussions of priesthood restriction, 207–8, 213
    encouraging young women to get education, 574
    on family proclamation, 483–84
    on fellowshipping converts, 631
    and Ghana Temple, 515–16
    and Hong Kong Temple, 442–43, 448–52, 469–70
    learns of Howard W. Hunter's death, 463–64
    mandating simpler way of submitting names for temple work, 501
    and Mark Hofmann's deceptions, 406

815

new, simplified temple design, 494–96, 499, 502
ordained as First Presidency counselor (1985), 385
on organizing Genesis Group for Black Saints, 213–15
Perpetual Education Fund (PEF) innovation of, 533, 576, 594–94, 600, 634–36, 653
planning for his own funeral service, 595–96
on receiving confirmation to lift priesthood restriction, 307
reflecting on his life, 534
reflecting on new responsibilities as Church president, 465–66
on sharing gospel during Olympic Games (2002), 544
six B's, 533
speaking to Saints living in Colonia Juárez, Mexico, 493
temple building during administration of, 545–48
testifying in front of *Christus* statute, 522
traveling to Europe and Israel (1972) with Harold B. Lee, 244–46
Hinckley, Marjorie, 244–46, 463–64, 525, 595
Hofmann, Mark, 387, 405–7
Hogan, Floyd, 425
Holcman, Jaromír, 357–60
Holcman, Maria, 358
Holiday, Maeta
arriving at home of Black family, 166–67
being loved by and loving Black family, 191–92
courtship and sealing to Dennis Beck, 257–59
entering Indian Student Placement Program, 189–90
entering local high school and seminary, 190–91
leaving BYU to work at KSL, 257
leaving Indian Student Placement Program after graduation, 235–38
life on Navajo reservation, 163–66, 237
traveling to join placement program family, 163–64, 166
Holland, Jeffrey R.
called as president of Chile Area, 551, 563–64
good impression during Jerusalem trip, 400
Howard W. Hunter's wish to visit Jerusalem with, 464
Jerusalem Center report to, 401
urging embrace of "heartfelt discipleship," 655
Holland, Patricia, 363–64
Holy Child Teacher Training College (Takoradi, Ghana), 436
home evening, 123–24
home teaching, 123–24
Honduras, 55
Honecker, Erich, 296–97

Hong Kong
Gold and Green Ball held in Tai Po area of, 52–53
return of Church to, 3–6
transfer to People's Republic of China, 442–43
Hong Kong Temple
announcement and dedication of, 487–89
dedicatory prayer of, 489
progress of construction of, 469–70
search for site of, 442–43, 448–50
site of, 451–52
The House of the Lord (Talmage), 607
Hughes, Kathleen, 552
humanitarian projects. *See* Church humanitarian projects
Hungary, 443–44
Hunter, Howard W.
asked to research priesthood and temple restriction, 305
character of, 460
death, funeral, and legacy of, 463–65
encouraging temple attendance, 461
ordination as Church president (1994), 460–61
speaking in Nauvoo, Illinois, on history of Church, 461–62
work on Orson Hyde Memorial Garden, 332–33
Hunter, Inis, 463
Hurley, Dorothy, 274
Hwang Keun Ok
forced to resign her position at orphanage, 157–59, 179
helping to improve government opinion about Church, 265–67
as local Relief Society president, 264
Tender Apples Foundation run by, 264
working with Songjuk Orphanage girls, 177–79
Hyde, Orson, 244, 333

"I Am a Child of God" (Primary song), 28–31, 326, 415, 557, 626, 633
Ibarra, Enrique, 431
Ica Stake (Peru), 440–41
idolatry, condemnation of, 454
Iloilo North Stake (Philippines), 552–54
Improvement Era (Church magazine), 162, 197
India
Chennai First Branch in, 572
Church growth in, 470, 566
India Bangalore Mission in, 565–68
missionaries first arrive in 1850s, 566
tsunami disaster in, 568–73
India Bangalore Mission, 565–68
Indian Student Placement Program
different experiences with, 236

Index

founding and description of, 164–65
Kimball family's participation in, 254
Maeta Holiday's participation in, 165–67, 235–38
See also Native Americans
Indonesia, 568–71
infant baptism, 15–17
infertility
Angela Fallentine's struggle with, 609–10, 617–20
Ardeth Kapp navigating, 248, 617
institutes and seminaries
benefits to students, 538–40
Manuel Navarro attending in Peru, 389–90
scripture mastery program, 390
shift from Church schools to, 537–38
Veronica Contreras serving in Chile, 538–40
See also Church schools
Institut Supérieur Technique et Commerciale (Lubumbashi, Zaire), 453
Instructor (Church magazine), 197
International Red Cross, 274, 303
internet, 532
Isaacson, Thorpe B., 134
Israel
Gordon B. Hinckley and Harold B. Lee's visit to, 244–46
Orson Hyde Memorial Garden dedicated by Spencer W. Kimball, 332–34
Orson Hyde's prayer on Mount of Olives (1841), 244–45
Orthodox Jews protesting against Saints in, 376–78
Spencer W. Kimball's desire to build Church campus in Jerusalem, 334, 355–56
working to establish Jerusalem Center in, 355–57
See also Jerusalem
Italy
Giuseppa Oliva moving back to, 112–14
Giuseppa Oliva sharing gospel in, 127–30, 140–42
lack of missionaries in Sicily, 128
Palermo Branch organized in, 142
Rome Temple in, 659
Swiss Mission overseeing (1965), 128
Waldensian Protestant converts emigrating to Utah (1860s), 127
Ituma, Abigail, 581–82
Ivory Coast Abidjan Mission, 581
"I Walk by Faith" (Janice Kapp Perry), 384

Jack, Elaine L., 480, 549
Jacob, James, 511
Jamaica, 624–25, 632
James, Jane Manning, 199

Japan
Church growth since 1955 in, 470
Expo '70 in, 192–95, 210
Fukuoka Temple built in, 547
growth of Church post–World War II in, 209
Jensen, Joan. *See* Lee, Joan (Jensen)
Jerusalem
Gordon B. Hinckley and Harold B. Lee's visit (1972) to, 244–46
Hebrew University in, 356
Orson Hyde's prayer on Mount of Olives (1841) in, 244–45
Orthodox Jews protesting against Saints (1985) in, 376–78
See also Brigham Young University Jerusalem Center; Israel
Jerusalem Center. *See* Brigham Young University Jerusalem Center
Jessee, Dean, 182
Jesus Christ
Ezra Taft Benson's message on, 414
Gordon B. Hinckley reflecting on price paid by, 465
"The Living Christ: The Testimony of the Apostles" declaration on, 520–21, 531
missionary lesson on accepting as Redeemer, 323
Primary's "Come unto Christ" theme (1988) on, 413–14
reflecting on His sacrifice as we attend temples, 599
Resurrection of, 585–88
Russell M. Nelson on Restoration of gospel of Jesus Christ proclamation, 665–66
San Salvador Temple painting of, 642–43
Special Witnesses of Christ (Church film) on, 521–22
Thomas S. Monson on following example of, 640, 650
See also Atonement of Jesus Christ
Johannesburg South Africa Temple, 360, 380–81, 490, 583, 605, 607–8
Johnson, Alice
released as missionary following government ban, 417–18
returning to Ghana Mission, 438–39
serving as missionary in Ghana, 416
studying to become a teacher in Ghana, 436
Johnson, Betty, 60
Johnson, Brigham, 219
Johnson, Joseph William Billy
American Protestant churches solicit, 281–83
arrested and then preaching to police, 220–21
dreams and visions experienced by, 175
engaging in religious discussions with James Ewudzie, 220–21

growth of unofficial congregations (1972) run by, 218–21, 281–83
introduction to gospel, 174–75
James Ewudzie's dream of missionaries in Ghana told to, 221
learning that priesthood restriction was lifted, 311–12
opposition experienced by, 175–77
responding to criticism of Church, 262–64
serving as missionary after Ghana freeze, 417–18, 437
Johnson, Matilda, 175–77, 218, 416–18
Jones, Dale, 106, 108
Jones, Marvin, 80
Jordan River Utah Temple, 469
Joseph Smith Memorial Building, 543
Joseph Smith Papers Project, 600
J. Reuben Clark Law School, 280
Juárez Academy (Mexico), 493
Jue, Lorine, 488
Jue, Nora Koot. *See* Koot, Nora Siu Yuen
Jue, Raymond, 487–89
Julian, Remigio, 425

Kaouk, Laudy, 659–65
Kapp, Ardeth
  accepts new calling as Laurel adviser, 315
  called as second counselor of Young Women, 246–50
  correspondence with Consuelo Wong Moreno, 392–93, 397
  loss of Spencer W. Kimball felt by, 382
  Miracles in Pinafores and Bluejeans by, 314–15
  navigating infertility, 248, 617
  preparing for first-ever Young Women satellite broadcast, 382–85
  preparing to submit ideas for future of Young Women, 365–67
  released from presidency of Young Women, 313, 315
  speaking at Rising Generation celebration, 396
  sustained as Young Women general president, 363
Kazadi, Daniel, 607
Kennedy, David, 316
Kenya, 581–83
Kharchev, Konstantin, 402–3
Kikuchi, Yoshihiko, 481
Kilbert, Allwyn, 565–68, 571–73
Kimball, Camilla, 53–58, 223, 253, 277–78
Kimball, Heber C., 50
Kimball, Spencer W.
  address and advice to GDR Saints, 269–70, 296, 298
  asked about priesthood restriction, 56
  assigned to minister to Indigenous peoples, 54
  attending Founders Day at BYU (1975), 277–78, 280–81
  attending São Paulo Temple cornerstone ceremony, 293–95
  becoming acting president of Quorum of the Twelve, 211, 240
  broadcasting general conference (1980) from Whitmer farm, 338–41
  calling for more missionaries to serve, 278–79
  Church growth under leadership of, 385–86
  continuing Church service despite health issues, 185–86, 222–24
  counsel while addressing annual conference (1975), 268
  death of, 382
  death of Harold B. Lee as shock to, 253–56
  decision-making through councils under, 365
  dedicating Orson Hyde Memorial Garden in Jerusalem, 332–34
  desire to build Jerusalem Center in Israel, 334, 355–56
  discussing his health with Presidents Lee and Tanner and Russell M. Nelson, 222–24
  fasting and blessing by Quorum of the Twelve for, 186–87, 228
  Harold B. Lee's blessing on health concerns of, 189
  Hélio and Nair Camargo sealed by, 133
  Indian Student Placement Program (1954) founded under guidance of, 164
  inviting all members to keep a journal, 314
  The Miracle of Forgiveness by, 454
  miracle of restored voice experienced by, 55
  praying and fasting over priesthood and temple restriction, 304–6
  priesthood blessings requested from (1959), 56
  recommendations following South American tour, 57–58
  revelation on ending priesthood and temple restriction, 306, 625
  Russell M. Nelson's successful surgery on, 211–12, 223, 227–28
  São Paulo Stake (Brazil) organized by, 143–46
  South American missions toured (1959) by, 53–58, 92
  speaking to new West African missionaries, 318
  speaking to regional representatives on Church growth, 315–18
  thinking about his own mortality, 212–13
  two surgeries (1979), 331
Kim Ho Jik, 157
King, Martin Luther, Jr., 101
Kinshasa DRC Temple, 647

Index

Kinshasa Mission (DRC), 490
Kirtland Temple, 666
Kiribati, 509
Kissi, Emmanuel, 436–37, 557–58
Kollek, Teddy, 244–45, 333–33, 356
Koot, Nora Siu Yuen
    attending Hong Kong Temple dedication, 487–89
    called as Southern Far East Mission missionary, 37–39
    dream about a temple, 39
    Gold and Green Ball attended by, 51–53
    meeting old friend at mission reunion, 489–90
    "send Church back" message received by, 3–6
    serving in Taiwan (1959), 58–61
    working as Oakland Temple ordinance worker, 487
Korea Mission, 4
Kosovo, 570
Kovář, Zdeněk, 372–73
Kovářová, Danuška, 372–73
Kovářová, Olga
    baptism and confirmation of, 357–60
    challenge of living in an atheistic society, 370–71
    interest in yoga and purpose in life, 344–45
    introduced to gospel by Otakar Vojkůvka, 345–47
    longing for government to recognize Church, 423–24
    sharing gospel with her parents, 372–73
    teaching and sharing gospel with yoga students, 371–72
KSL-TV (Salt Lake City news station), 199–200
Kufuor, John, 558–59

labor missionaries
    age requirements for young women, 94
    Mutis called as, 12–15, 19–20, 34–36
    New Zealand Temple built by, 46, 48
    Tongan Mission call for new chapels built by, 12–15
    See also Church building program; meetinghouses; missionaries
Ladd, Don, 299
Lamanite Generation (BYU), 257
Larsen, Dean L., 367
Latin America
    Book of Mormon portions translated into Indigenous languages of, 336
    Church growth (1960s) in, 103
    Church growth (1980s) in, 335–38, 367–70, 389
    Church growth under Spencer W. Kimball's leadership, 385–86
    concerns over nationalist groups threatening Saints in, 387
    local Saints put in leadership positions, 92
    Luz de las Naciones (cultural celebration), 660
    missionaries serving throughout (1950s), 55
    Spencer W. Kimball's recommendations for change in, 57–58
    Spencer W. Kimball's tour (1959) of, 53–58, 92
Latter-day Saint Charities, 606–7
Lave, Kitione ("Tongan Torpedo"), 40–42
law of chastity, 323
Layne, Rex, 40
LDS Business College (Salt Lake City), 279
LDS Family Services, 591
LDS.org, 531, 641
Leadership Training Library resources, 641
Lee, Fern, 97
Lee, Harold B.
    blessing given by Gordon B. Hinckley to, 246
    called as First Presidency counselor, 189
    calling Ardeth Kapp as president of Young Women, 246–50
    Correlation Committee leadership of, 86, 88, 96–99, 111
    death of, 254–56
    death threats and police escort of, 243
    marriage to Joan Jensen, 97–98
    on new program to unify Church curriculum (1961), 77–79, 97
    Nora Koot's message for, 3–6
    on power of "I Am a Child of God," 31
    prayer on behalf of Spencer W. Kimball, 186
    proposed correlation program expand to oversee missionary work, 86, 88
    Ruth Funk's meeting on curriculum alignment with, 84
    set apart as president of Church, 240
    speaking at Henry D. Moyle's funeral, 99
    Spencer W. Kimball discussing his health with, 222–24
    statement on priesthood restriction being lifted, 304
    strain over correlation with Henry D. Moyle, 97–98
    sustained during Mexico City area general conference (1972), 243
    tells the Osmond brothers to choose the right, 225–26
    traveling to Europe and Israel (1972) with Gordon B. Hinckley, 244–46
Lee, Joan (Jensen), 97–98, 244–46, 255
Lee Nai Ken, 38
Leffler, Ed, 232–35
Le My Lien. *See* Lien, My Le
Leningrad Branch (Soviet Union), 445

819

LGBTQ community, 638–40, 658
A Liahona (Church's Portuguese-language magazine), 143
Liahona College (Tonga), 13, 36–37
Liahona magazine, 616
Liberia, 581
Lien, My Le
  escaping Vietnam with her children, 272–76
  making a home for family in U.S., 302–3
  promised that husband will be preserved, 275–76
  sending word to imprisoned husband, 291
  working to bring husband to U.S. from Vietnam, 301, 303–4
Light of the World pageant (Conference Center), 543
Lim, Augusto A., 481–82
Lima Peru Temple, 389
Liu, Kuan-ling ("Anne"), 470–71
"The Living Christ: The Testimony of the Apostles" declaration, 520–21, 531
London England Temple, 49–51
London Stake (1960), 70
Los Angeles California Temple, 9, 487
Luputa (DRC)
  celebration of completed water pipeline in, 629–30
  Church-funded project to pipe clean water into, 606–7, 627–30
  Luputa District in, 475–77, 580–81, 605–6
Luputa Branch (DRC)
  Binene family moving from, 651–52
  celebrating announcement of new temple in Kinshasa, 647
  organization and growth of, 491–93
  watching Church conference broadcast (2022) in, 644–47
Luz de las Naciones (Latin American cultural celebration), 660
Lyman, Amy Brown, 260

Mabey, Rachel, 318, 324
Mabey, Rendell, 128–29, 140–42, 318, 324–27
Macey, Walt, 106–9
Machuca, Isabel Santana. *See* Santana, Isabel
Machuca, Juan, 217–18, 238–42, 368
Madagascar, 581
Madsen, Arch, 199
Madsen, Louise, 109
Madsen, Truman, 159–63, 179–82
Malaysia, 568–71
Manchester England Stake (1960), 70
Manila Philippines Temple, 424–27, 471–72, 481
Man's Search for Happiness (film), 111, 194, 624–25
Marriott, J. Willard, 188

Martinique, 625
Martins, Helvécio
  attending São Paulo Temple cornerstone ceremony, 293–95
  called as general authority, 481
  challenges of Church membership, 251–53
  conversion of, 229–32
  encouraged by Spencer W. Kimball, 295
  receiving Aaronic and Melchizedek Priesthoods, 319
  receiving endowment and being sealed to family, 320–21
Martins, Marcus, 229, 232, 253, 320–21
Martins, Marisa, 229, 320–21
Martins, Rudá Tourinho de Assis, 229–32, 251–53, 294, 318–21
A Marvelous Work and a Wonder (Richards), 18, 26
Mary Magdalene, 245
Mauritius, 453
Mavimbela, John, 384
Mavimbela, Julia, 348–52, 361–62, 379–81
Maxwell, Neal A., 488, 521–22
Maycock, William, 580
McConkie, Bruce R., 251, 305, 307
McIntire, Thomas, 230–31
McKay, David O.
  approving statement on civil rights (1956), 102
  attending dedication of Merthyr Tydfil meetinghouse (Wales), 95
  on benefits of correlation programs, 156–57
  contemplating obstacles to Church growth, 7–9
  death, funeral, and legacy of, 187–88
  "Every Member a Missionary" approach of, 70, 86
  expanding building program, 68–70
  focus on member retention, 86, 121–22
  general conference (October 1967) message on future of Church by, 156–57
  introducing program to unify Church curriculum (1961), 77–79
  journal entry on his life and world strife (1967), 153–55
  London Temple dedication by, 49–51
  on mission of Church, 51
  moved by faith and generosity of Saints, 67–70
  New Zealand Temple dedication by, 47–48
  reflecting on Church growth opportunities, 49–50
  seeking guidance on priesthood restriction, 71
  speaking at Los Angeles Temple dedication, 9
  statement on priesthood restriction being lifted, 304
  on Swiss Temple dedication, 6–7
  on teaching children the gospel, 31
McKay, Emma Ray, 6
McKay, Robert, 156
McKenna, Mary, 505–8, 554

Index

McKeown, Blake, 554–56, 583–86, 602–5
McKeown, Wade, 554–56, 603
McMullin, Keith B., 516–17
McMurrin, Sterling, 101
meetinghouses
    benefits for ward members, 504–5
    Beverley chapel (Great Britain), 94
    building new (1960s), 68–70
    Church covering costs of building and maintaining, 458
    David O. McKay authorizing new Tongan, 13
    Denton, Texas, 68–69
    difficulties in providing Saints with, 8
    Merthyr Tydfil (Wales), 95
    Mosese Muti's work building new, 34–36
    South American expansion in 1959 of, 54
    of unofficial congregation in Ghana, 219
    See also Church building program; labor missionaries
Meha, Stuart, 47
Melchizedek Priesthood. *See* priesthood
Member and Leader Services (computer program), 622
Mensah, Frank, 174–75
mental health, 589–92
Mercau de Aquino, María, 547
Merthyr Tydfil meetinghouse (Wales), 95
Mesa Arizona Temple, 218, 546, 643
Metropolitan Museum of Art (New York City), 149–50, 162, 180
Mexico
    area general conference held in Auditorio Nacional (1972) in, 238–42
    Benemérito de las Américas school in, 150, 152–53, 168–71
    Gordon B. Hinckley speaking to Colonia Juárez Saints in, 493
    growth of Church in, 151
    Mexico City Temple in, 368, 391–92
    Monterrey Temple in, 545, 548
    temple building in (1999–2002), 545–46
    university student protests and Tlatelolco massacre (1968) in, 170
Mexico City Temple, 368, 391–92
Millennial Star (UK mission magazine), 197
ministering, 655
The Miracle of Forgiveness (Kimball), 454
Miracles in Pinafores and Bluejeans (Kapp), 314–15
missionaries
    Blake McKeown announces mission call on Australian TV show, 604–5
    concerns over nationalist groups opposing, 387
    David O. McKay invites every Saint to be a, 70
    expelled from Ghana by government (1989), 416–18
    GDR restrictions on, 44–44, 64–65
    increasing numbers of applications, 649
    introducing Hélio da Rocha Camargo to gospel, 10–12
    Missionary Training Center (Provo, Utah) to train, 316
    New Horizon (missionary musical group) in South Korea, 265–67
    release of all East German (1960), 66
    requirements for serving as, 603
    serving in South America (1950s), 55
    Spencer W. Kimball on need for Church growth through, 278–79, 315–18
    unique obstacles in Africa, 8
    working with local Saints, 57
    Yamashita Kazuhiko's visits with, 208–11
    See also labor missionaries
Missionary Training Center (Provo, Utah), 316
missionary work
    building meetinghouses, 12–15
    "Every Member a Missionary" approach to, 70, 86
    focus on retention, 121–22
    Henry D. Moyle's responsibilities related to, 86–87
    Preach My Gospel (missionary guide) for, 565–68
    priesthood restriction as challenge in Nigeria, 71, 89–91
    proposed Correlation Committee responsibility over, 86–88
    seven lessons for, 27
    Spencer W. Kimball's emphasis on, 386
    sports activities used as part of, 73–74, 86
    Thomas S. Monson oversees expansion of, 653
    The Uniform System for Teaching Families (missionary discussions), 322–23
    as way to come to rescue of others, 649
    See also specific missions
Mobutu Sese Seko, 490
Mongolia, 470–71
Monson, Frances, 354
Monson, Thomas S.
    appointed to Correlation Committee, 85
    called as first counselor to Gordon B. Hinckley, 466
    calling Henry B. Eyring and Dieter F. Uchtdorf as his counselors, 600
    on challenge of producing correlated lessons, 124
    concerns over drift from Church standards, 638
    construction projects taken over by new presidency of, 601
    death and legacy of, 652–54
    discussions of priesthood restriction, 207–8, 213

facing economic crisis (2008) impact on Church, 601–2
gives blessing to Gordon B. Hinckley prior to his death, 597
on home teaching and family home evening correlation, 123–24
on joint efforts with Roman Catholics to help people in need, 610–13
on need for service, 611–12
offering comfort to Inis Hunter, 463
"One in a Million" video with Primary children, 632
ordained as First Presidency counselor (1985), 385
promising GDR Saints gospel blessings, 173
reading conference message (1989) of Ezra Taft Benson, 413–15
receiving a letter from a "lost Latter-day Saint," 648–49
reflecting on his presidency's five-year anniversary, 648–50
speaking about Gordon B. Hinckley, 597, 600
speaking at Freiberg Temple dedication service, 373
speaking at Görlitz district conference (1968), 171–73
thanking Saints for their faith and devotion, 637
urging Saints to follow Jesus Christ, 640
visiting GDR to check on Saints, 354–55
Monterrey Mexico Temple, 545, 548
Monument to Women Memorial Garden (Nauvoo, Illinois), 315
Moreno, Consuelo Wong, 391–93, 397–98
Mouhsen, David, 589, 591–92
Mouhsen, Nicolás, 590
Mouhsen, Silvina, 589–92
Mount of Olives (Jerusalem), 244–45, 355–56, 399
Mount Scopus (Jerusalem), 355–56, 399
Mourra, Alexandre, 625
Moyle, Henry D., 85–87, 97–99
Mozambique, 570
Muhammad, 332
Mukadi, Simon, 454
Muti, Mosese
    asked to serve labor mission, 12–15, 19–20
    Chuck Woodworth's funding of temple trip for, 36–37, 39–42
    fasting to feed other missionaries, 36
    George Albert Smith's promise to, 15, 47
    visit to New Zealand Temple by, 46–48
    working to build new meetinghouse and mission home, 34–36
Muti, Paula, 39
Muti, Salavia
    accepts mission call, 13–14, 19

Chuck Woodworth's funding of temple trip for, 36–37, 39–42
letter to Chuck Woodworth from, 40
missionary work, 20–22, 35–36
visit to New Zealand Temple by, 46–48
Mutual Improvement Associations (MIA)
    Gold and Green Ball held by, 51–53
    new program to unify curriculum (1961) of, 77–79
    sports teams of, 73–74, 86
    and Suzie Towse's conversion, 72–75
    See also Young Men organizations; Young Women organizations
"My Personal Progress" (Young Women program)
    establishment of, 314
    focus on improving (1984), 364
    New Beginnings event recognizing, 398
"My Redeemer Lives" (hymn), 596

NAACP (National Association for the Advancement of Colored People), 100–103, 657
Naime, John, 625
Naime, June, 625
Nairobi Kenya Stake, 582
Namibia, 453
National Press Club (Washington, DC), 512
Native Americans, 163–67. *See also* Indian Student Placement Program
Nauvoo Illinois Temple, 522, 598, 601
Navarro, Manuel
    called to Peru Lima North Mission, 410–13
    choosing to live gospel, 388–90
    injured by car bomb, 427–30
    moving to Ica Stake while attending university, 440–42
    recovery from car bomb and return to mission, 431–32
    released from mission, 439–40
    teaching and baptizing Luis Palomino, 432–33
    working to overcome challenges of eye injury, 440–42
    working to save money for mission, 411–12
"The Need for a Living Prophet" (missionary lesson), 27
Nelaballe, Revanth, 572–73
Nelson, Dantzel, 444
Nelson, Russell M.
    accompanying Tabernacle Choir on Eastern European tour (1991), 443–47
    addressing Saints during COVID-19 pandemic, 662–62
    announcing change to Sunday meeting schedules, 655–56

Index

approving *New Era* issue on seven values for Young Women, 382
assigned to oversee Church affairs in Europe and Africa, 401–2
attending Accra Ghana Temple dedication, 556–58
called as apostle, 363
conducting FamilySearch.org launch event, 512
on correct name of Church, 656
on covenants, 654
on future of Church, 659
global ministry tours with wife Wendy, 655
introducing ministering, 654–55
meeting with Konstantin Kharchev of Soviet Union, 402–4
ordained and set apart as Church president, 654
Restoration of gospel of Jesus Christ proclamation announced by, 665–66
speaking at Young Women's satellite broadcast (1985), 383
successful surgery on Spencer W. Kimball, 211–12, 222–24, 227–28
thankful for Church's registration in Soviet Union, 446–47
working with NAACP to promote racial harmony, 657
working to get Czechoslovak government to officially recognize Church, 423
Nelson, Wendy, 655
New Beginnings event (Young Women), 398
New Era (Church magazine), 197, 383
New Horizon (missionary musical group), 265–67
New York Times, 7
New Zealand
    Auckland Stake (1958) organized in, 57
    encouraged to hold Time for Youth (TFY) in, 554
    Fallentines move to North Island of, 608–10
    See also Hamilton New Zealand Temple
Nghia, Tran Van, 273
Nguyen, Huy, 302
Nguyen, Linh, 302
Nguyen, Vu, 302
Nguyen Van The. *See* The, Nguyen Van
Nibley, Hugh, 162, 180–81, 405
Nicaragua, 386
Nigeria
    Aba Temple dedicated in, 598–99
    Abigail Ituma working to reactivate sisters in, 581–82
    Anthony Obinna's letter to president of Church from, 202, 204
    BYU scholarship fund for students from, 125
    Church decision to not send missionaries (1976) to, 284–85
    Church growth in, 581
    Church representatives sent to observe faith in, 71–72
    civil war (1967) in, 155, 202
    difficulties of LaMar Williams obtaining visa to, 125–27
    faith and testimony (1961) of people of, 80–82
    First Presidency's consideration of missionaries in, 70–71
    Honesty John Ekong's request for Church materials in, 61–63
    LaMar Williams recalled by First Presidency from, 127, 134–35
    LaMar Williams's role in bringing gospel to, 61–63, 70–71, 79–82
    letters requesting missionaries from, 70
    local worship group granted government recognition in, 126
    military coup (1966) in, 135–36
    missionaries come (1978) to, 324–27
    priesthood restriction as challenge to missionary work in, 71, 89–91, 134–35
Nigerian Outlook (newspaper), 89–91
Niger reforestation project, 409
Niue, 19–22, 34–36
Niv, Amnon, 355
Nivaclé people (Paraguay), 456, 458–59
North British Mission, 70
Northeast British Mission, 95–96
North German Mission, 43–43
Nugent, Verna, 624–25
Nugent, Victor, 624–25
Nuku'alofa Tonga Temple, 509
Nunez, Alexander, 440

Oakland California Temple, 487
Oaks, Dallin H.
    in Armenia overseeing humanitarian aid (1991), 445
    BYU's honor code under, 279–80
    called as apostle, 363
    called as president of Philippines Area, 551–52, 563
    counseling Filipino Saints against leaving families for work, 553–54
    on developing a "gospel culture," 552
    meeting with Russell M. Nelson during Tabernacle Choir tour, 445–47
    speaking about Mark Hofmann's deceptions, 405–7

thankful for Church's registration in Soviet Union, 446–47
Obinna, Anthony Uzodimma
asking Grant Bangerter to send Church to Nigeria, 285
baptized after waiting for many years, 325–26
dream about Salt Lake Temple, 202–3, 324
meeting with American missionaries in Nigeria, 324–25
ordained to Aaronic Priesthood, 326–27
receiving a letter from LaMar Williams, 204
writing letters to president of Church, 202, 204, 284–86
Obinna, Fidelia, 202–3, 285, 326–27
Obot, Dick, 90, 125–26
O'Donnal, Carmen, 367–68
O'Donnal, John, 368
Ogden Utah Temple, 222
Okazaki, Chieko, 194, 480–83
Okazaki, Ed, 194
Oliva, Giuseppa, 112–14, 127–30, 140–42
Oliva, Maria, 130
Oliva, Renato, 112–13
Olympic Games (2002), 543–44, 637
"One in a Million" video series, 632–34
Orellana Branch (El Coca, Ecuador), 621–22
Orr, Eugene, 199–200, 205–8, 213–14
Orr, Leitha (Derricott), 200
Orson Hyde Memorial Garden (Jerusalem), 332–34
Oscarson, Bonnie L., 657
Osmond, Alan, 224–27
Osmond, Donny, 224–27
Osmond, George, 224–25, 233–34
Osmond, Jay, 224–27
Osmond, Jimmy, 226
Osmond, Marie, 226, 233
Osmond, Merrill, 224–27
Osmond, Olive, 224–27, 233–35
Osmond, Tom, 224
Osmond, Virl, 224
Osmond, Wayne, 224–27
Osmond brothers (pop group), 224–27, 233–35, 265
Ounleu, Norbert, 581
Ounleu, Valerie, 581
outreach centers (Europe), 599
Owens, David, 76

Pace, Glenn L., 517–18
Packer, Boyd K.
asked to research priesthood and temple restriction, 305
dedicating meetinghouses in Guatemala, 336
discussions of priesthood restriction, 207–8, 213

presenting new Relief Society presidency with Relief Society history, 586–87, 642
Thomas S. Monson ordained and set apart by, 600
Palermo Branch (Italy), 142
Palomino, Luis, 432–33
Panama, 55
Papua New Guinea, 658
papyrus fragments (Book of Abraham), 149–50, 162, 180
Paraguay, 55, 456–59
Parkin, Bonnie D., 549–50, 587
Parmley, LaVern W., 28
patriarchal blessings, 503
Paul, Apostle, 421
Pearl of Great Price
Book of Abraham in, 149–50, 162, 180–81
edition with maps, footnotes, and cross-references (1981), 386
First Vision account by Joseph Smith in, 160
Hélio da Rocha Camargo's study of, 26
Hugh Nibley's scholarship in support of, 405
Laudy Kaouk's study of, 663
Pellegrini, Miryam, 137
people in need
partnering with Catholics to help, 610–11
Thomas S. Monson on serving, 611–12
welfare as "fourth leg of stool" of Church mission, 612–13
See also Church humanitarian projects; Church Welfare Services
People's Republic of China, 442–43
Perkey, Joshua, 631–33
Perpetual Education Fund (PEF), 533, 576, 594–94, 600, 634–36, 653
Perpetual Emigrating Fund, 533
Perry, Janice Kapp, 383–84
Personal Ancestral File (PAF), 500
Personal Progress. See "My Personal Progress" (Young Women program)
Peru
Ica Stake in, 440–41
Lima Temple dedicated in, 389
missionaries entering (1950s), 55
Missionary Training Center in, 427
San Carlos Branch in Nazca, 388
seminary in, 389–90
Shining Path violence in, 427–29
Peru Lima North Mission, 412–13, 427–30, 439–40
Petelo, Enzo, 665
Peterson, Angela (Fallentine), 559–61, 577–79, 608–10, 617–20
Peterson, H. Burke, 297
Petramalo, Gilbert, 418
Pettit, Mildred, 28–30

Index

Philip, Prince (Great Britain), 233–34
Philippines
    barriers to Church attendance in, 481–82
    Chieko Okazaki speaks to sisters in, 480–83
    Church growth and population in, 425, 470, 481
    Dallin H. Oaks serving as president of Philippines Area, 551–52, 563
    efforts to reactivate families in, 552–54
    Gordon B. Hinckley gives interview in, 483–84
    Manila Temple in, 424–27
    two hundred Thai Saints flying to Manila Temple, 471–72
Philippines Baguio Mission, 604
Phithakphong, Kriangkrai, 472
Phithakphong, Mukdahan, 472
Pingree, Anne C., 548–51, 562–65
Pi Yi-shu, Madam, 58–59
The Plan (Osmond brothers album), 265
plan of salvation
    how the family proclamation teaches, 592
    Resurrection as part of, 585–88
    Russell M. Nelson on women as full partners in, 657
Plato, 332
Po Fiafia (Night of Fun), Niuean Relief Society, 21
Poland, 444–45
pornography, 532
Porter, John, 68–69
Porter, Margaret, 68
Portugal, 316, 546
Pratt, Carl B., 562–63
Preach My Gospel (missionary guide), 565–68
Presiding Bishopric, 602, 612
priesthood
    Anthony Obinna ordained to Aaronic Priesthood, 326–27
    authority to baptize, 11
    Church organizations under authority of, 97
    correlation plan presented to First Presidency, 96–97
    First Presidency statement on all worthy men to hold, 317–18
    Harold B. Lee speaking on correlation under, 77–79, 97
    as key to Church growth in Brazil, 26, 318–21
    men in South America not being regularly advanced in, 56
    Russell M. Nelson on women fulfilling their callings using authority of, 657
    Young Men's Mutual Improvement Association renamed Aaronic Priesthood, 313
    Young Women and Young Men restructured under leadership of, 248–49
priesthood and temple restriction
    apostles receive revelation to end, 306–7
    Billy Johnson learns of revelation ending, 311–12
    BYU race-related controversy over, 200–202
    as challenge to missionary work in Brazil, 8, 27, 56
    as challenge to missionary work in Ghana, 262–63, 437
    as challenge to missionary work in Nigeria, 71, 89–91, 134–35
    Darius Gray learns of revelation ending, 308–10
    David O. McKay seeking guidance on, 71
    Doctrine and Covenants edition including revelation ending, 386
    Elders Hinckley, Monson, and Packer's discussion with Black Saints on, 207–8
    First Presidency announcement on ending, 308–9
    Helvécio Martins's question to missionaries about, 231
    Spencer W. Kimball's questions, prayers, and fasting over, 56, 304–6
    struggle of Black Saints with, 116–17, 205–8
    See also Black Saints; temples
priesthood executive committees, 123
Priesthood Executive Council, 365–67, 383
priesthood quorums
    First Quorum of the Seventy, 279, 340, 386, 481
    high priests to attend meetings with elders, 655
    new program to unify curriculum (1961) of, 77–79
    Second Quorum of the Seventy, 481
Primary
    "A Child's Plea" program (1957), 28–31
    "Come unto Christ" theme (1988) of, 413–14
    Delia Rochon called to teach in Uruguayan branch, 92–93
    Delia Rochon fundraising for Primary Children's Hospital, 118–20
    end of annual conferences (1974) of, 278
    Nair Camargo's work in Brazilian Mission, 105
    new program to unify curriculum (1961) of, 77–79
    "One in a Million" video series with children from, 632–34
    requested to submit lessons for correlation approval, 111
    "sharing time" activities in, 342
    See also children
Primary Children's Hospital (Salt Lake City), 118–20
Provo Utah Temple, 222
Puerto Rico, 386, 473
"The Purpose of Mortality" (missionary lesson), 27

Queiroz, Walter Guedes de, 143
Quilmes meetinghouse (Argentina), 112

Quorum of the Seventy. *See* First Quorum of the Seventy; Second Quorum of the Seventy
Quorum of the Twelve Apostles
 approval of simple floor plan for temple essentials, 496
 approving creation of São Paulo Stake (Brazil), 140
 asked to fast and pray over priesthood restriction, 305–6
 commissioned to go out into world to teach, 404
 Doctrine and Covenants instructing Seventy to help, 279
 fasting and blessing on behalf of Spencer W. Kimball by, 186, 228
 featured in *Special Witnesses of Christ* (Church film), 521–22
 "The Living Christ: The Testimony of the Apostles" declaration of, 520–21, 531
 priesthood correlation plan presented to, 96–97
 Priesthood Executive Council policy recommendations to, 365–67
 regional representatives called (1967) to assist, 156
 Russell M. Nelson ordained and set apart as Church president by, 654
 Spencer W. Kimball becomes acting president of, 211, 240
 to supervise program to unify curriculum (1961), 78
 on threefold mission of Church, 388

racial divides
 BYU–University of Wyoming controversy, 200–202
 comparing Brazil and U.S., 27
 David O. McKay's concern over strife of, 155
 Russell M. Nelson's work with NAACP to overcome, 657
 South African apartheid, 348–50
 See also civil rights
Ramos, Felipe, 425
Randall, Naomi, 28–31
Rappleye, John, 624
Rappleye, Nancy, 624
Rasmus, Carolyn, 364
Rawlings, Jerry, 437, 516, 521, 526–29, 558
reforestation project (Niger), 409
refugees, aiding, 570, 610
regional representatives, 156
Relief Society
 The Awakening (filmstrip), 110
 Belle Spafford's leadership of, 22–26, 109–12, 259–62, 586

Boyd K. Packer presenting Relief Society history to presidency of, 586–87, 642
 changes to encourage enrollment in, 260
 Church Handbook of Instructions revised, 588–89, 641
 correlation plans for, 109–11, 124–25, 198
 Daughters in My Kingdom: The History and Work of Relief Society published by, 642
 efforts to implement correlation program (1964) into, 109–12
 end of annual conferences (1974) of, 278
 Gospel Literacy Effort program of, 549–50
 leadership training videos available through, 641
 need for sisters to understand history of, 587, 642
 new program to unify curriculum (1961) of, 77–79
 organized in Niue, 20–22
 organized in Taiwan, 60
 "Relief Society Day" (New York World's Fair, 1964), 111–12
 sharing with sisters the vision of, 587–89
 strengthening visiting teaching goal of, 641
 three purposes of, 588
 See also women
Relief Society Building (1956), 22–26
"Relief Society Day" (New York World's Fair, 1964), 111–12
Relief Society Magazine, 24, 109, 197
Relief Society Social Services Department, 591
Republic of the Congo, 581
the Resurrection, 585–88
Reznik, David, 356
Richards, LeGrand, 18, 26
Richards, Stephen L, 7–9, 85
Richards, Steve, 230–31
Richardson, David, 11–12
Ricks College (Idaho), 279, 396, 532–33. *See also* Brigham Young University–Idaho
Ringger, Hans B., 402–4
Rising Generation event (Young Women), 392–93, 396–97
Robbins, Burtis, 43–45
Rochon, Delia
 desire to pay tithing, 91–93
 as new Primary president, 118
 prompted to leave home, 136–37
 standing up for her testimony, 138–39
 vintenes fundraising for Primary Children's Hospital, 118–20
Rodríguez, Norma, 548
Rodríguez, Román, 548
Rolapp, Marilyn, 300–301
Roman Catholics, 610–13
Romania, 444
Rome Italy Temple, 659

Index

Romney, George W., 188
Romney, Marion C., 84, 98–99, 240, 255
Romney, Mitt, 637–38
Russia, 445–47. *See also* Soviet Union
Rutskoi, Alexander, 446–47
Rwanda, 464, 490
Rytting, Lorry, 284

Sabbath, 106–9
Saigon Branch (Vietnam), 270–73
Saintelus, Gancci, 626–27
Saintelus, Olghen, 626–27
Saintelus, Soline, 626
Saint Lucia, 625
Saint Vincent, 625
Salt Lake Olympic Committee, 544
Salt Lake Tabernacle, 531
Salt Lake Temple
    Anthony Obinna's dream about, 202–3, 324
    Henry B. Eyring testifying on steps of, 522
    prophets seeking inspiration in, 304, 465–66
    replica at World's Fair, 111
    sealings in, 98, 133, 258, 449
same-sex marriage, 638–40
Samoa, 25, 110, 187, 509
San Carlos Branch (Nazca, Peru), 388
San Salvador El Salvador Temple, 641–44
Santana, Hilda, 152–53, 168
Santana, Isabel
    attending area general conference (Mexico City, 1972), 238–42
    attending Mexico City Temple, 368
    experiences at Benemérito de las Américas school, 150, 152–53, 169–71, 241
    feeling part of Church, 242
    friendship and eventual sealing to Juan Machuca, 217–18
    making decisions about future career, 215–17
Santiago Chile Temple, 369, 485, 502
São Paulo, Brazil
    Brazilian central editorial office set up in, 143
    São Paulo Second Ward in, 145–46, 368
    Spencer W. Kimball visits, 56
    stake organized in, 139–40, 143–46
São Paulo Brazil Temple
    announcement of, 268
    cornerstone ceremony, 293–95
    dedication of, 320
    Martins family sealed in, 320–21
São Paulo Second Ward (Brazil), 145–46, 368
Schmeil, Paul, 624
schools. *See* Church schools
Scouting, 583, 656
Second Quorum of the Seventy, 481

seminaries. *See* institutes and seminaries
September 11, 2001, 542–44
Seventy. *See* First Quorum of the Seventy; Second Quorum of the Seventy
sexual abuse, 532
Sharp, Marianne, 23, 109
Shining Path terrorist group (Peru), 427–29
Sierra Leone, 570
Silva, Walmir, 253
Simonsen, Velma, 23
Singapore, 442, 566
Singapore Mission, 566
Sint Maarten, 625
Sitati, Gladys, 582–83
Sitati, Joseph, 582–83
Six B's broadcast (Gordon B. Hinckley), 533
Sloan, Timothy, 616, 621
Slovenia, 444
Smith, Barbara B., 261, 298
Smith, Eldred G., 133
Smith, Emma, 150
Smith, George Albert, 15, 47, 54, 187
Smith, Harold, 489–90
Smith, Hyrum, 188, 461
Smith, Jessie, 107–8
Smith, Joseph
    Howard W. Hunter speaking on martyrdom of, 461–62
    scholarship on, 159–63, 180, 405
    warned about telling wicked from righteous, 407
    See also First Vision
Smith, Joseph, III, 150
Smith, Joseph Fielding
    area general conferences under direction of, 238, 240
    assigning Church leaders to discuss priesthood restriction, 207–8, 213
    called as counselor to David O. McKay, 134
    death and legacy of, 239–40
    encouraging Saints to set aside evening for family, 123
    on keeping Sabbath holy, 107–9
    prophecy on temples across earth, 370
    proposing Genesis Group for Black Saints, 213–15
    reminding Osmond brothers to share gospel, 225
    sustained as new president of Church, 188–89
Šnederfler, Jiří, 358
Socrates, 332
Solari, Victor (Uruguayan branch president), 92–93, 137
Sollesta, Maridan Nava, 480–83, 541–41, 551, 637
Sollesta, Seb, 480–81, 540–42, 551–54

827

Songjuk Orphanage (Seoul, South Korea), 157–59, 177–79
Sorensen, Asael, 10–11, 26–27, 31, 133
Sorensen, Ida, 31
South Africa
    apartheid policy of racial segregation, 348–49
    Black and white members worshipping together in, 351–52
    Church growth in, 581
    Johannesburg Stake in, 361–62
    Johannesburg Temple in, 360, 380–81, 490, 583, 605, 607–8
South America. *See specific countries*
Southern Far East Mission, 6–8, 37–39, 51–53
South Korea
    Church growth since 1955 in, 157, 470
    improving government opinion about Church, 265–67
    New Horizon (missionary musical group) in, 265–67
    Songjuk Orphanage in, 157–59
    Tender Apples Foundation in, 264
    Tender Apples (musical group) in, 264, 266–67
South Vietnam, 154–55
Soviet Union
    central and eastern Europe under influence of, 401
    Church leaders meeting with representatives of, 402–4
    Cold War between U.S. and, 43
    collapse of, 460
    growing government tolerance toward Church in, 445–46
    official registration of Church in, 446–47
    political and social changes (1991) in, 445
    Russell M. Nelson's visit (1987) to, 445
    Tabernacle Choir tour (1991) through, 445
Spafford, Belle
    celebrating new Relief Society building, 22–26
    on correlation plan for Relief Society, 109–11, 124–25, 198
    leadership during transition of Relief Society (1969–1970), 195–98
    position on Equal Rights Amendment (1972), 261
    reflecting on tenure as Relief Society president, 259–62
    on "Relief Society Day" (New York World's Fair, 1964), 111–12
Spain, 546
Spät, Walter, 145
Special Witnesses of Christ (Church film), 521–22
"The Spirit of God" (hymn), 489
sports activities and missionary work, 73–74, 86, 121–22

Sri Lanka, 568–71
Stone, Fred, 12–14
Stone, Sylvia, 12
Strong, Arthur, 113–14
Sunday School
    change to meeting schedules, 655–56
    Come, Follow Me curriculum for, 656
    end of annual conferences (1974) of, 278
Suva Fiji Temple, 523–25
Swanson, Riley, 69
Swiss Mission, 128
Swiss Temple, 6–7, 173, 297–98, 373

Tabernacle Choir
    Budapest Opera House performance (1991) by, 443–44
    Eastern European tour (1991) of, 443–47
    international popularity of, 7
    at Moscow's Bolshoi Theater, 446
    singing at 2002 Olympics, 544
    singing during general conferences, 623
Taipei First Girls High School (Taiwan), 470
Taiwan
    Anne Liu's faith in gospel in, 470–71
    Church growth since 1955 in, 470
    Church humanitarian work in, 570
    growth of Church in, 58, 60
    Nora Siu Yuen Koot's missionary work (1959) in, 58–61
Takoradi Branch (Ghana), 438
Talmage, James E., 607
Tanner, N. Eldon
    advising focus on Mount Scopus for Jerusalem Center, 356
    arranging for papyrus fragments' return to Church, 162
    called as First Presidency counselor, 189
    dedicating new buildings at Benemérito school (Mexico), 168
    First Presidency statement on all worthy men to hold priesthood read by, 317–18
    on issuing Church statement on civil rights (1956), 102
    on receiving confirmation to lift priesthood restriction, 307
    recommending fast on behalf of Spencer W. Kimball, 186
    speaking at Mexico City's area general conference (1972), 241
    Spencer W. Kimball discussing his health with, 222–24
    visiting Nigeria prior to opening mission there, 88–89
Tanner, Sara, 88

Index

Tate, Lucile, 586–87
Tavella, Jeanine, 476–77
Tavella, Roberto, 476–77
Taylor, Margery ("Marie")
    attending report on Freedman's Bank project, 534–37
    role in Freedman's Bank genealogy project, 433–36, 466–69
temple design, simplified, 495–96, 499, 525, 545–48
TempleReady program, 467–68
temples
    Anthony Obinna's dream about, 202–3
    being built to serve local Saints, 15
    built and planned for throughout Latin America (1980s), 367–70, 389
    David O. McKay on dedication of Swiss Temple, 6–7
    dedicated by David O. McKay, 188
    developing simpler way of submitting names for, 501
    doubling in number under Gordon B. Hinckley, 598–99
    Elijah Able "family file," 468
    Gordon B. Hinckley's desire to bring blessings to more Saints, 494–96
    Howard W. Hunter encouraging attendance in, 461
    importance to keeping on "covenant path," 658
    increase during life of Gordon B. Hinckley, 530
    increase in Polynesian islands, 513
    Jordan River Temple sealings from Freedman's Bank records, 469
    reflecting on Jesus Christ in, 599
    Russell M. Nelson's announcement of new, 658–59
    Spencer W. Kimball's emphasis on, 386
    TempleReady program, 467–68, 500
    Thomas S. Monson on making accessible to all members, 650
    women serving as witnesses in sealings, 657
    See also families; priesthood and temple restriction; *specific temples*
Tender Apples (musical group in South Korea), 264, 266–67
Tender Apples Foundation (South Korea), 264
Tenorio, Horacio A., 481
Thailand, 470–72, 568–71
The, Nguyen Van
    efforts to save Saigon Branch members by, 270, 273
    placed in North Vietnamese "reeducation" course, 289–92
    prophetic promise to wife that he would be preserved, 275–76
    released from camp and joins family in U.S., 301, 303–4
Thompson, Barbara, 586–89
Thorn, Grant, 95–96
Thorvaldsen, Bertel, 193
Thurman, Elaine, 51–52
Till, Eugene, 264–65, 267
Time for Youth (TFY), Australia, 554–56, 603
Times and Seasons (Church newspaper in 1840s), 160
tithing
    Delia Rochon's desire to pay, 91–93
    faith of Luputa, Zaire, Saints in paying, 474–77
    missionary lesson on, 323
    required for baptism, 60
Tlatelolco massacre, Mexico City (1968), 170
Today show (morning television program), 513
Tokyo Japan Temple, 279
Tonga, 12–15
Tongan Mission, 12–15
Toro, Iliesa, 508–11, 519–20, 525
Toro, Juliet, 508–11, 518–20, 523, 525
To the Rescue (painting), 649
Tourinho de Assis, Rudá (Martins), 229–32, 251–53
Towse, Suzie, 72–75, 93–96, 120–22
Tran Van Nghia, 273
Tseung Kwan O (Hong Kong), 449–50
tsunami disaster (2004), 568–71
Tuong-Vy, Cong Ton Nu, 270
Turkey, 570
Turley, Maurine, 363–64, 384
Turley, Richard, 499–502, 511–14
Tuttle, A. Theodore, 275

Uchtdorf, Dieter F., 600, 651
Udo, Oscar, 125
Udo-Ete, Matthew, 81–81
Uganda, 453
Ukraine, 632
The Uniform System for Teaching Families (missionary discussions), 322–23
United Kingdom
    Beverley Branch chapel built in, 93–96, 120
    British Mission, 50, 70, 72
    North British Mission, 70
    Northeast British Mission, 95–96
    Osmond brothers' visit to, 232–35
United States (U.S.)
    Cold War between Soviet Union and, 43
    perceived association of Church with, 8
    racial divisions in, 27
University of Ghana, 174
University of Wyoming–BYU controversy, 200–202
Urtnasan, Soyolmaa, 471
Uruguay, 55, 138–39

Uruguayan Mission, 92
Utah State Prison family history center, 435–36, 466–69

Vanuatu, 509
Van Wagenen, Glen, 165
Venezuela, 570
Vietnam, 270–73, 470
Vietnam War, 155, 195, 270–73
Villavicencio, Claudia, 614–16, 621, 623, 631–34
Villavicencio, Marco, 614–16, 620–23, 631–33
Villavicencio, Sair, 614, 616, 632–34
Viñas, Francisco J., 563
visiting teaching
  efforts to strengthen, 641
  ministering to replace, 655
Vojkůvka, Gád, 344–45, 358
Vojkůvka, Otakar
  attending Olga Kovářová's baptism, 358
  encouraging Olga Kovářová to teach yoga, 371
  holding sacrament meetings at his home, 357
  introducing Olga Kovářová to gospel, 345–47
  overjoyed at freedom to worship, 424
  sealed to family in Freiberg Temple, 423
  sharing gospel with yoga students, 372
Vojkůvková, Terezie, 344

Wagner, Kenyon, 171
Wales, 95
Walters, Wesley, 160–61, 163, 179–82
Wan, Ka Wah Ng ("Kathleen"), 449–52
Wan, Tak Chung ("Stanley"), 448–52, 469–71
ward councils, 123
Warren, Katherine
  grateful for blessing to attend temple, 322
  journey to baptism, 286–89
  sharing gospel with family, 321–23
Washington DC Temple, 577–78
Washington Post (newspaper), 301
Welfare. *See* Church Welfare Services
West Germany. *See* Federal Republic of Germany (BRD)
West Indies Mission, 625
Whitmer farm (Fayette, New York), 338–41
Widtsoe, John A., 345
Wilberg, Mack, 265–67
Wilkinson, Ernest L., 200, 279
Williams, LaMar
  answering Anthony Obinna's letter, 204
  called as missionary to Nigeria, 88–90
  Church's Missionary Department position of, 61
  concern for Nigerian friends following military coup (1966), 135–36
  contacted about sending missionaries to Nigeria, 61–63
  difficulties of obtaining visa to Nigeria, 125–27
  meeting with First Presidency on Nigeria, 134–35
  recalled from Nigeria by First Presidency, 127, 134–35
  requesting Church open mission in Nigeria, 70–71, 79–82
  sends missionaries to Katherine Warren's home, 287–89
  visit to Nigeria by, 79–82
Winter Olympic Games (2002), 543–44, 637
Wixom, Rosemary M., 657
Wolsey, Heber, 200–202, 309–10
women
  changes in Church practice related to, 657
  Church policy on abortion and, 299
  Equal Rights Amendment (1972) potential impact on, 261, 298–301
  Gordon B. Hinckley encouraging education for, 574
  Monument to Women Memorial Garden (Nauvoo, Illinois) honoring, 315
  sitting on key general administrative counsels and serving as witnesses, 657
  See also Relief Society
Woodworth, Chuck, 20–20, 35–37, 39–42
Word of Wisdom
  description of principle of, 59
  missionaries serving in Taiwan keeping, 58–59
  missionary lesson on, 27, 323
  Osmond brothers' obedience of, 225
  required for baptism, 60
World Health Organization, 661
World's Fair, New York City (1964), 194

Yamashita, Kazuhiko, 192–95, 208–11, 547–48
Yamashita, Masahito, 195
Yegros, Julio, 458–59
Yegros, Margarita, 458–59
Ye Shall Have My Words (LDS manual), 550
Young, Brigham, 544
Young, Dwan J., 413–14
Young, Greg, 625
Young Men organizations
  Blake McKeown's positive experience with, 555
  Church sports teams for, 73–74, 86, 121–22
  Gold and Green Ball held by, 51–53
  new program to unify curriculum (1961) of, 77–79
  requested to submit lessons for correlation approval, 111

Index

restructured to be under general priesthood leaders, 248–49
Scouting adopted as part of, 583
sports activities of, 73–74, 86
Young Men's Mutual Improvement Association renamed Aaronic Priesthood, 313
See also Mutual Improvement Associations (MIA); youth
young single adult outreach centers (Europe), 599
Young Women organizations
  annual conference (1962) held by, 83
  Ardeth Kapp called as second counselor of, 246–50
  Ardeth Kapp sustained as general president of, 363
  Church sports teams for, 73–74, 86, 121–22
  communication issues faced by, 134
  end of annual conferences (1974) of, 278
  first-ever satellite broadcast, 382–85
  focus on improving Personal Progress program, 364
  general presidency released (1978), 313
  Gold and Green Ball held by, 51–53
  "My Personal Progress" program (1977) of, 314
  New Beginnings annual event of, 398
  new program to unify curriculum (1961) of, 77–79
  presenting Priesthood Executive Council with future of, 365–67
  requested to submit lessons for correlation approval, 111
  requiring sufficient resources and support, 367
  restructured to be under general priesthood leaders, 248–49
  Rising Generation event of, 392–93, 396–97
  "Stand for Truth and Righteousness" motto of, 384
  and Suzie Towse's conversion, 72–75
  values of, developing, 364–65, 367, 382–85
  Young Women's Mutual Improvement Association renamed Young Women, 313
  See also Mutual Improvement Associations (MIA); women; youth
youth
  David O. McKay's concerns over, 121–22, 155
  efforts to reactivate in Philippines, 552–54
  Especially for Youth (EFY) events for, 505–8, 554
  Felicindo Contreras's concerns over inactive, 502–5
  For the Strength of Youth (pamphlet), 155
  For the Strength of Youth (FSY) conferences for, 656
  Gordon B. Hinckley's broadcast on the six B's, 533
  Gordon B. Hinckley's efforts to provide education and career training to, 532–33
  Russell M. Nelson instituting new programs for, 656
  Time for Youth (TFY), Australia, 554–56, 603
Youth Correlation Committee, 247
Yuvaraj (convert in India), 568

Zaire
  government collapse (1997) in, 490
  Katangan majority's violence toward Kasaians in, 455–56
  missionaries arriving in 1986, 453
  Zaire Kinshasa Mission in, 476–77
  See also Democratic Republic of the Congo (DRC)
Zimbabwe, 581

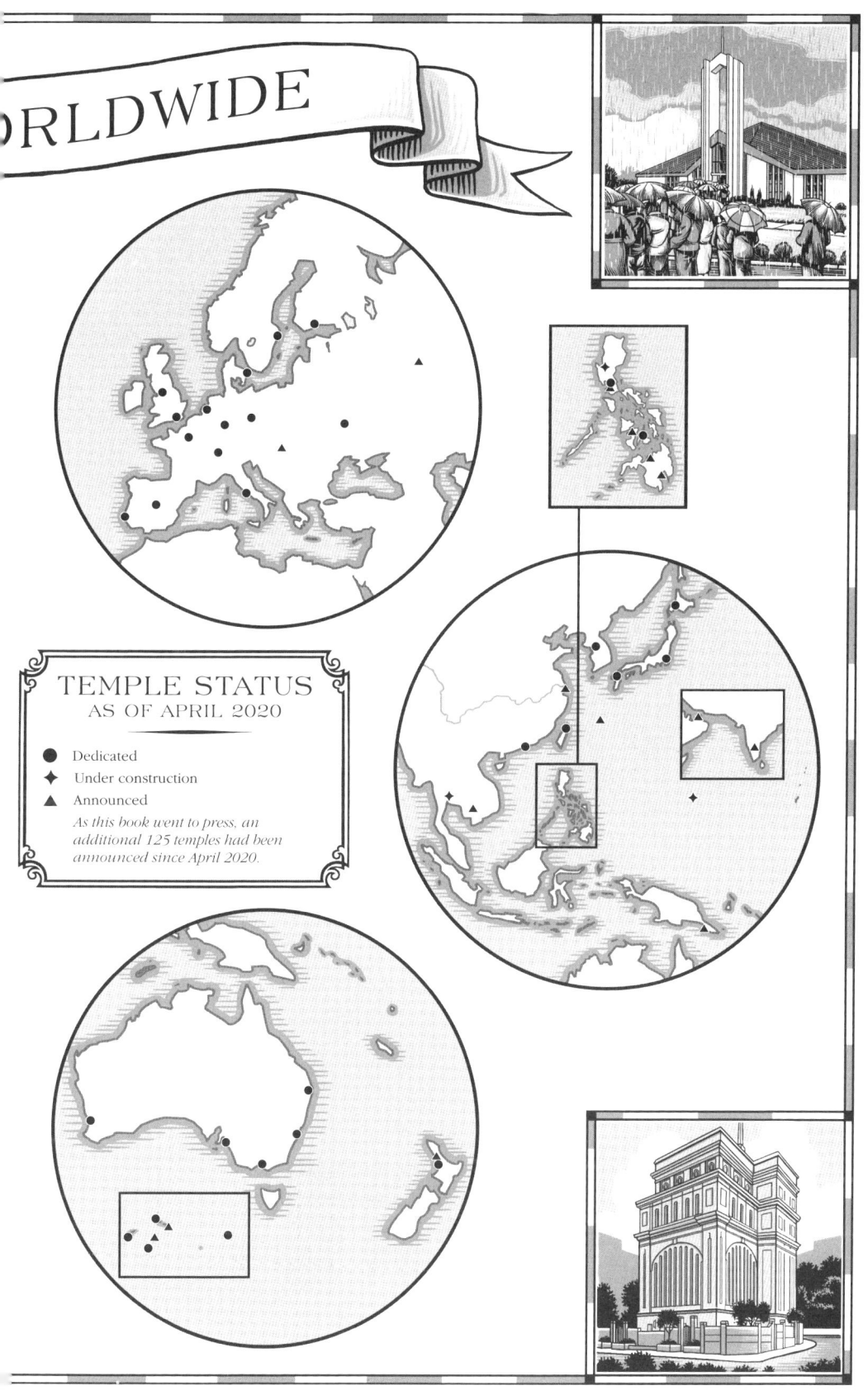

PRINTED IN HONG KONG